African American Religions, 1500–2000

This book provides a narrative historical, postcolonial account of African American religions. It examines the intersection of Black religion and colonialism over several centuries to explain the relationship between empire and democratic freedom. Rather than treating freedom and its others (colonialism, slavery, and racism) as opposites, Sylvester A. Johnson interprets multiple periods of Black religious history to discern how Atlantic empires (particularly that of the United States) simultaneously enabled the emergence of particular forms of religious experience and freedom movements as well as disturbing patterns of violent domination. Johnson explains theories of matter and spirit that shaped early indigenous religious movements in Africa, Black political religion responding to the American racial state, the creation of Liberia, and FBI repression of Black religious movements in the twentieth century. By combining religious studies methods with analysis of empire, Johnson explains the seeming contradictions that have shaped Black religions over several centuries.

Sylvester A. Johnson is Associate Professor of African American Studies and Religious Studies at Northwestern University. He is a founding coeditor of the *Journal of Africana Religions*, the only English-language peer-reviewed journal devoted to publishing research on religions in Africa and throughout the Black diaspora.

African American Religions, 1500–2000

Colonialism, Democracy, and Freedom

SYLVESTER A. JOHNSON

Northwestern University

CAMBRIDGE
UNIVERSITY PRESS

CAMBRIDGE
UNIVERSITY PRESS

32 Avenue of the Americas, New York NY 10013-2473, USA

Cambridge University Press is part of the University of Cambridge.

It furthers the University's mission by disseminating knowledge in the pursuit of education, learning and research at the highest international levels of excellence.

www.cambridge.org
Information on this title: www.cambridge.org/9780521157001

© Sylvester A. Johnson 2015

First published 2015

A catalogue record for this publication is available from the British Library

Library of Congress Cataloguing in Publication data
Johnson, Sylvester A., 1972– author.
African American religions, 1500–2000 : colonialism, democracy, and freedom / Sylvester A. Johnson, Northwestern University.
pages   cm
Includes bibliographical references and index.
ISBN 978-0-521-19853-0 (hardback) – ISBN 978-0-521-15700-1 (pbk.)
1. African Americans – Religion – History.   2. United States – Church history.   I. Title.
BL625.2.J64   2015
200.89´96073–dc23   2015009567

ISBN 978-0-521-19853-0 Hardback
ISBN 978-0-521-15700-1 Paperback

Contents

List of Figures		*page* vii
Acknowledgments		ix
Introduction		1

PART ONE

1	Black Atlantic Religion and Afro-European Commerce	13
	Afro-European Commercialism: Contact, Exchange, and Religion	14
	Elmina Castle and Afro-European Commerce	20
	Religion and Transnationalism in Cape Coast	33
2	On Religious Matters	56
	Empire and the Problem of Matter	59
	Dueling Revelations and Atlantic Exchanges	67
	Corporatism, New Rationalities, and the Commodity Fetish	91
3	Colonial Governance and Religious Subjectivity	107
	Empire, the Company-State, and Rationalities of Freedom	107
	Black Religion, Christian Freedom, and Racial Slavery	128
	Colonialism, Temporalities, and Christian Subjectivity	145

PART TWO

4	Stateless Bodies, African Missions, and the Black Christian Settler Colony	159
	White Revolution and Internal Colonialism	160
	From Internal Colony to Settler Colony	167
	Free Africans and the Black Settler Colony	177

5   Black Political Theology, White Redemption, and Soldiers
     for Empire '   209
     Abolitionism and African American Political Theology   210
     Reconstruction, White Redemption, and Black Settler Colonialism 235
     Internal Colonialism and Overseas Imperialism   246

                          PART THREE

6   Garveyism, Anticolonialism, and State Repression of
     Black Religions   273
     The UNIA and Black Diaspora   274
     Black Ethnic Religions and Anticolonial Theology   294
     The Intelligence State and Black Religious Subversion   312

7   Fundamentalism, Counterintelligence, and the
     "Negro Rebellion"   325
     Orthodoxy and the Cold War   326
     Counterintelligence and the Civil Rights Movement   346
     Anticolonialism and Black Cultural Revolution   362

8   Black Religion, the Security State, and the
     Racialization of Islam   377
     African American Islam, Federal Repression, and US Empire   377
     Racializing Islam   384
     American Islam, Democracy, and Counterintelligence   395

Conclusion: Black Religion, Freedom, and Colonialism   401

Selected Bibliography   407
Index   419

Figures

1.1 The West and West–Central regions of Africa became known as the "land of Guinea" following the rise of Afro-European commercialism in the 1400s. The phrase became interchangeable with "Black Africa." This map is an early illustration of the region by the Dutch cartographer Jan Jansson (1588–1664). *page 15*

1.2 Prospect of Cape Corse, or Coast Castle. This illustration of Cape Coast Castle appeared in John Green's *New General Collection of Voyages and Travels; Consisting of the Most Esteemed Relations, Which Have Been Hitherto Published in Any Language; Comprehending Everything Remarkable in Its Kind, in Europe, Asia, Africa, and America* (1745–1747). 34

2.1 This seventeenth-century map of West Central Africa, created by the Dutch cartographer Jan Jansson (1588–1664), shows the Kongo Kingdom and the Angola Kingdom as they were situated just decades before Dona Beatriz was born. Note that the north is oriented toward the left end of the map. 71

4.1 Map of the West Coast of Africa from Sierra Leone to Cape Palmas, including the colony of Liberia. This map of West Africa is based on Jehudi Ashmun's surveys for the American Colonization Society. The inset on the upper right shows the ACS's plans for the settler town of Monrovia. 204

Acknowledgments

One of the rewards of writing a book is the profound debt of gratitude that accrues during the process. I will begin by thanking Eric Crahan, under whose editorship this project began. Eric saw the potential of this book from the very start. Thanks for your vision, Eric. I also hold tremendous gratitude for Debbie Gershenowitz, who guided this project to completion. Dana Bricken was especially helpful in directing me through the preparation and production process.

My colleagues in the Department of Religious Studies at Indiana University–Bloomington kindly devoted one of our faculty colloquia to this book project at an early stage and provided generative feedback and encouragement. The College of Arts and Sciences at IU also provided me a generous research leave that was essential to enabling this project's conceptualization and early research. Aaron Stalnaker, David Haberman, "Bert" Harrill, Candy Gunther Brown, Kevin Jaques, David Brakke, Steven Weitzman, Constance Furey, Richard Miller, Sarah Imhoff, Michael Ing, Shaul Magid, Patrick Michelson, Richard Nance, Stephen Selka, Lisa Sideris, and Rebecca Manring were not just conversation partners but also gracious colleagues whose support of my intellectual work has inspired much gratitude. The faculty in the Department of African American and African Diaspora Studies at IU also helped to nurture this project, inviting me to present some of the early research at a brown-bag discussion. Valerie Grim, Iris Rosa, Frederick McElroy, and Micol Seigel are among those who posed productive questions and offered helpful suggestions as this project began.

My move to Northwestern University provided a continuing community of intellectual support. The faculty members in the Department of African American Studies have helped me to sharpen my intellectual grasp of fairly difficult concepts and have suggested resources that have proved invaluable to my work. In fact, the book would have taken a different shape were it not for the rich feedback, constructive challenges, and unselfish support from Sherwin Bryant, Richard Iton, Darlene Clark Hine, Nitasha Sharma, Martha Biondi, Celeste-Watkins Hayes, Michelle Wright, Alex Weheliye, Mary Pattillo, Dwight McBride, Tracy Vaughn, and Sandra Richards. Barnor Hesse has been especially helpful in challenging me to engage with a more deliberate account of race, and our numerous conversations have been richly rewarding. The Department of Religious Studies has also generated a stimulating atmosphere through faculty and graduate student colloquia, spurring my understanding of many important themes that have benefited this study. Robert Orsi has been especially generous in pointing me to essential reading and providing feedback about the problems of materiality in religion. My colleagues in the "Pacific Century" reading group – Nitasha Sharma, Simeon Man, Kathleen Belew, Jinah Kim, Beth Lew-Williams, Camilla Fojas, and Daniel Immerwahr – provided wonderfully astute feedback on Chapter 4 of the book. The Weinberg College of Arts and Sciences also kindly arranged a research leave early after my arrival that allowed me to devote uninterrupted time to finishing this book manuscript. No less important has been the feedback I have received from graduate students in doctoral seminars in African American Studies and Religious Studies. The vigorous discussions of freedom, empire, and religion in these exchanges remained present with me as I worked through various sections of the book.

I have reached out to many trusted colleagues who have proved immensely resourceful. Edward E. Curtis IV, with whom I coedit the *Journal of Africana Religions*, has been faithfully encouraging and deserves special credit for planting the seeds of this book. Edward invited me to contribute to a volume he was editing several years ago, and that collaboration marked the beginnings of this book project. Dianne Stewart has been an intellectual partner for many years and provided helpful suggestions for making this a better book. The Young Scholars of American Religion program, run by the Center for the Study of Religion and American Culture at Indiana University–Purdue University in Indianapolis, was a special catalyst in helping me to concretize key aspects of this project. Equally important has been the network of colleagues from that group who have remained essential interlocutors. Tracy Leavelle, especially, has inspired me to engage more directly with the formation of the United States as an empire. The collaborators in the

"Religion and US Empire" working group have also been generous and gracious in suggesting resources to prod my thinking about the book project.

Among the countless others who contributed to this book's completion is Mina Chung of the University of Manitoba, who allowed us to stay in her home in Winnipeg, Manitoba, during a research leave. It was an intensely rewarding experience of productivity and respite. Jeffrey Wheatley's astute research skills and attention to detail were essential to preparing the manuscript for production. His reliability is exceeded only by his brilliance. And Jeremy Rehwaldt embodies an unrelenting standard of excellence and meticulous attention to the intellectual and mechanical aspects of writing. His assistance with the book was immensely valuable.

Along the way, I have benefited from multiple opportunities to present sections of the project to various audiences. I am especially grateful to the faculty and students of Hanover College, Drake University, Stanford University, Princeton University, and the University of Chicago Divinity School. John Corrigan, Amanda Porterfield, and the American religions PhD students at Florida State University were especially kind to devote one of their colloquium meetings to discussing Chapter 3. The feedback and constructive challenges I received in these venues have continued to inform my thinking.

I continue to be enriched by the mentorship and intellectual shaping of James H. Cone, who supervised my graduate training with intellectual generosity and superb attention, and Ronald Liburd, whose profound guidance and endlessly stimulating intellection sparked and nurtured my undergraduate study of the humanities. Stephen Angell was also a kind mentor in my undergraduate years and continues to be a supportive intellectual presence.

My family has been a special source of encouragement and support. In countless way, my parents Jean and S.L. Johnson inspired my confidence, gifted me with joyfulness, and repeatedly affirmed my ambitions. Neither lived to see this book come to fruition, but with every breath I remember how I am infused with and shaped by them. My sisters frequently checked in to ask how the manuscript was progressing and express their affirmation. Our older daughter Ayanna grew into a young woman during the writing of this book. Her generous spirit and loving affirmations have reminded me of how rewarding it is to be a parent. Our younger daughter Rainah was born the same year the project started. I will always smile as I remember the many weeks she spent dancing around me and giving me hugs while I was on leave completing the final chapters. Finally, my wife Heather Nicholson has been a true partner in life. It was Heather who invited my father to live with us when his health began to fail. As a result, in the last year of his life my father filled our home with lasting memories of warmth, laughter, and love. Beyond that, I have talked through literally every section of the book manuscript with Heather, and she has listened with unfailing affirmation, critical interest, and enthusiastic challenge. Her intellectual brilliance has informed this work in many ways, especially through her feedback on multiple chapter drafts. This proved essential to my formulating a clearer conception of the book. Most of all, Heather's fearless, steadfast love and friendship have encouraged me to inhabit my ideas unabashedly and to feel supported in the most profound way. Heather, you will always command my deepest thanks.

Introduction

This book is a study of Black religion and its intersection with empire. It starts where Albert J. Raboteau began his classic, watershed study of African American slave religions – with the rise of Afro-European commercialism in West Africa in 1441. When Raboteau composed his history of Black religions in the 1970s, the terms "Black Atlantic" and "Atlantic world" were not in currency. Yet, the history of scholarship has vindicated Raboteau's periodization and the geographical purview of his narrative frame. He realized that the study of African American religions could not be contained by the time and space of the United States of America. As Charles H. Long has demonstrated in his scholarship, moreover, what is conveniently termed "African American religion" is always already constitutive of a diasporic formation of peoples within and beyond Africa whose subjectivity is rooted in racial Blackness. Long has repeatedly emphasized that the study of African American religion must be conceived through engaging with the Atlantic world instead of being constrained and controlled by the idea of the United States. The specific historical formations that have constituted African American religion have been derived through transnational networks and global linkages of trade, politics, and religious exchanges. The same holds true for White American religion. Scholars of White American religion have usually begun their narratives across the Atlantic – typically starting with Europe during the 1400s. Although their focus has usually veiled the significance of Africa, they have nevertheless found it necessary to tell their story as an Atlantic account – Sidney Ahlstrom's "European prologue" is a case in point.[1]

---

[1] Albert J. Raboteau, *Slave Religion: The "Invisible Institution" in the Antebellum South* (New York: Oxford University Press, 1978). Charles H. Long, *Significations: Signs,*

To speak of the Atlantic world is to speak of Atlantic empires, although not in a reductive sense. Given the long history of studying African American religions through their relationship to slavery, it is now time for a study of Black religion that explains the deep ties to the architecture of empire – by which I mean the political order of governing through the colonial relation of power. I examine Black religion and colonialism in multiple Atlantic geographies, including the Kongo Kingdom, Liberia, and the United States. The phenomenon of US colonialism, however, is the most pivotal for this book. This study conceptualizes colonialism as the political order that dominating polities administer over subjugated peoples. Colonialism encompasses military, economic, political, and psychological modes of subordinating a population. This form of political order structures occupation or foreign control of one people by another. Most concisely, colonialism is the constitutive work of imperial polities. It is what makes empire socially real and efficacious. Most importantly for this study, colonialism is the essential matrix of racialization. It is what makes race. Not every instance of colonialism results in racialization. But the colonial form of power is essential to racial formation. This means race is politics or, more precisely, biopolitics. If there was any silver lining to Michel Foucault's refusal to engage with Europe's external colonies, it was his lack of interest in phenotype when attempting to account for the emergence of the racial state. He rightly perceived that racism was a state practice achieved through "internal colonialism" by producing exclusive forms of political community.[2]

Colonialism, furthermore, is formed not through a spatial differential but rather through a *power* differential. It is constituted by politics, not physical distance. This means we must dispense with the "saltwater fallacy" that claims colonialism happens only overseas or in distant lands. This book engages with both internal and external modes of colonialism. With more than 300 reservations currently within the geopolitical boundaries of the contiguous United States,

Symbols, and Images in the Interpretation of Religion (Aurora, CO: Davies Group, 1999). Charles H. Long, "What Is Africa to Me?: Reflection, Discernment, and Anticipation," *Journal of Africana Religions* 1, no. 1 (January 2013): 91–108. Sidney E. Ahlstrom, *A Religious History of the American People* (New Haven, CT: Yale University Press, 1972).

[2] See Alyosha Goldstein's introduction to his edited *Formations of United States Colonialism* (Durham: Duke University Press, 2014), 8–9. Alejandro Colás, *Empire* (Malden, MA: Polity Press, 2007). Michel Foucault, *Society Must Be Defended: Lectures at the Collège de France, 1975-76*, ed. Mauro Bertani and Alessandro Fontana, trans. David Macey (New York: Picador, 2003), 103. Bernard Porter, *Empire and Superempire: Britain, America and the World* (New Haven: Yale University Press, 2006).

one might expect that Western scholars would have produced far more engagement with internal colonialism. Instead, outside of indigenous studies or ethnic studies scholarship, studies of empire that account for indigeneity remain the exception rather than the rule. And yet, internal colonialism is one of the key theoretical frameworks that has been richly informed by colonized people themselves. The scholarship on internal colonialism and, more recently, internal neo-colonialism has particularly demonstrated the importance of attending to "the colonized" as human populations and not merely "territory" or "regions" under "foreign" control.[3]

Internal colonialism is especially important for interpreting the history of African American religions. One of the unique factors of African American religion is the difficulty of discerning and appreciating the colonial status of African American religious actors. Frankly, African Americans have been studied as victims of slavery and not as people who have been colonized. The reasons for this are profoundly historical as well as ideological. To examine the colonial status of African Americans requires one to call into question the fundamental paradigm of the United States as a noble, democratic, freedom-loving society. This conflicts with the liberal integrationist paradigm through which African Americans are viewed as always having been members of the United States. More precisely, this analysis requires an intellectual study of the West that makes visible the ties that bind freedom and democracy to colonialism. As this book demonstrates, the political experiment of the United States in democratic freedom (this includes the African American quest for freedom) has been anchored in and enabled by colonialism. This is a deeply complicated subject, but its explication lies at the heart of this book. African American religions have functioned in most scholarly studies and in the US political imaginary as a symbol of the American promise, as a type of sentimental proof that the West – especially the United States – most fully embodies what

---

[3] Robert L. Allen, "Reassessing the Internal (Neo) Colonialism Theory," *The Black Scholar* 35 (Spring 2005): 2–11. Roderick Bush, "The Internal Colony Hybrid: Reformulating, Structure, Culture, and Agency," in *Hybrid Identities: Theoretical and Empirical Examinations*, ed. Keri E. Iyall Smith and Patricia Leavy (Chicago: Haymarket Books, 2009). Albert Memmi, *The Colonizer and the Colonized* (New York: Orion Press, 1965). Charles Pinderhughes, "21st Century Chains: The Continuing Relevance of Internal Colonialism Theory," PhD diss., Boston College, 2009. Michael Hechter, *Internal Colonialism: The Celtic Fringe in British National Development, 1536–1966* (Berkeley: University of California Press, 1975). Alexander Etkind, *Internal Colonization: Russia's Imperial Experience* (Malden, MA: Polity Press, 2011).

Francis Fukuyama has so poignantly called the "end of history," the most sublime form of political order.[4] As I have studied the intersection of Black religion and empire, however, I have become convinced that no thoughtful human being can understand the linkages of colonialism, democracy, and freedom I have sought to make visible in this account and still perceive African American religions in harmony with the triumphalist strains of the American myth. It is because of *colonialism* (even more so than slavery per se) that African American religions have so frequently and continually taken form under the sign of freedom. As Orlando Patterson has argued so compellingly, the *myth of freedom* that swells the hearts of billions with pride and loyalty must give way under the lens of intellectual study to the reality of the *institution of freedom* (I mean this in the way that scholars understand slavery to be an institution). These are the terms at stake in this study of Black religion.[5]

There can be little legitimate debate over whether the United States of America is the world's greatest emblem of democratic freedom. The fact that the United States enjoys this singular status has long been recognized. The United States, after all, emerged as the world's first constitutional democracy. France might be credited with elevating freedom as the supreme political value, and republican democracy as the highest political order during the eighteenth century. It was the United States, however, that first actualized the vision of republican democracy. The French author Alexis de Tocqueville devoted several years to composing his two-volume *Democracy in America* precisely because he grasped the vast implications of the United States as an unparalleled political experiment in republican, democratic freedom.

The United States is also a powerful empire. Unlike its status as the greatest emblem of freedom, however, the imperial status of the United States has cycled through widespread acknowledgment and denial for most of its history as a sovereign state. Particularly since the US military response to 9/11, literally hundreds of monographs and thousands of articles have examined its formation as an empire of global proportions. At the same time, the arguments against assigning this imperial status to the United States have also been vigorous in recent years. With few exceptions, moreover, studies of the United States as an empire have typically been unconcerned with religion. And the scholarship examining

---

[4] Francis Fukuyama, *The End of History and the Last Man* (New York: Free Press, 2006).
[5] Orlando Patterson, *Freedom in the Making of Western Culture* (New York: Basic Books, 1991).

American religion have in turn only occasionally devoted significant attention to empire.[6]

Even a cursory examination of Atlantic colonialism, however, quickly reveals that religion has been a central element of colonial formations. The political authorization for establishing Western colonial rule in the Mediterranean lands, throughout Africa, and in the Americas resided with papal power. Christendom itself was an imperial formation that mirrored and opposed massive Islamicate polities such as the Ottoman Empire. The Reconquista, moreover, which defined the fundamental context for the so-called age of discovery, was largely conceived and executed as the defense of Christian imperium against Muslims. Scholars of religion are of course familiar with the role of Christianity as a *political* entity in the viceroyalty of New Spain and in the British colonies of North America. The role of missionary religion, furthermore, is inseparable from the efforts to expand secular Western rule over indigenous polities throughout North America and in Asia and Africa. Finally, although the so-called secularization thesis of twentieth-century scholarship seemed to promise that religion had ceased to be relevant to Western politics, that claim now rings patently hollow given the ascent of the Religious Right and the focus of the US security state on Islamism.

Atlantic slavery was at the center of the Atlantic empires through which emerged White settler states, finance capitalism, and liberal democracies. The vaunted ideals of freedom and democracy that resonated throughout the Atlantic world were espoused and institutionalized by Europeans devoted to racism, slavery, and imperial conquest. The relationship between freedom and its others has to be *explained* instead of being dismissed as mere hypocrisy or contradiction. This singular imperative guides the entire study before the reader. And it is why I argue, for instance, that settler colonialism became a strategy of utmost significance for African Americans who sought to forge freedom from racial rule and enslavement under a White racial state. This is certainly counterintuitive and disturbing, but it is only one of several connections to which we should resist blinding ourselves. As the narrative of this book unfolds, the relationship among colonialism, democracy, and freedom emerges with irony, intrigue, and perhaps even terror.

The book accounts for the linkage of colonialism, democracy, and freedom by proffering a particular *story* of African American religions.

---

[6] Paul Kramer, "Power and Connection: Imperial Histories of the United States in the World," *American Historical Review* 116 (December 2011): 1348–91.

There are many stories that deserve to be told in the process of interpreting the history of religion and its intersection with political orders. This is one of them. The entire book is driven by narrative. To a considerable degree, this narrative structure works to explain concepts and produce analytical claims. There are real limits, however, to the ability of narrative to explicate theoretical problems. For this reason, the narrative material is synthesized throughout with more explicitly theoretical discussion of major concepts and themes. I have aimed to do this in a way that provides serious engagement with the actual nature of colonialism, democracy, and freedom. I have sought to avoid merely bandying about these terms and have aspired instead to *account* for them as socially real and historically derived concepts and institutions. This structure – synthesizing narrative with theory – presents a special challenge. The narrative accretions are essential to the larger analytical demonstrations of the book, which means that some arguments (e.g., that race is politics, not phenotypic meanings) simply take time to demonstrate and do not elapse over the course of a few pages. The entire book composes an extended argument, and each section works to demonstrate conclusions that I personally have found deeply disturbing and even difficult to accept (which is not the same as "difficult to believe").

Throughout this book, I explain the connections among freedom, democracy, and colonialism by interpreting the data about Black religion at points of intersection with empire (i.e., the political order of colonial governance). Put differently, this is not a general survey of African American religions. Rather, it is a study of how Black religion (and Atlantic religion, more broadly) has been caught up with empire, where the latter is both problematic and generative. I make no pretensions of telling the "whole story" of Black religion or providing a "full account" of the subject. It has always been my impression that such is an impossible, fictive quest. Instead, this book selectively spans several centuries and engages with multiple geographies (particularly West and West Central Africa and North America) to demonstrate how African American religions have been deeply enmeshed within the interstices of colonialism (particularly that of the United States) and that this colonialism (again, especially that of an American empire) is the matrix for the venerable freedom and democracy to which both colonizers and the colonized alike are intensively devoted.

This book unfolds over three major parts. Part 1 comprises three chapters and spans the creation of networks of religion and empire in West Central Africa during the 1400s to the formations of race, religion, and colonial governance in North America as late as the 1700s, before the formal creation of the United States as a racial state. I locate the foundation of Atlantic networks of power and social institutions in the commercial relations that African states established with European polities (beginning with Portuguese merchants of Lisbon). For this reason, commercialism and corporatism feature prominently throughout Part 1. Chapter 1 examines this commercialism as a central context for religious exchange in the Kongo Empire and in the city-states of Elmina and Cape Coast. Chapter 2 elucidates the central role of materiality (the philosophy of matter – understanding the nature of things as things) in formations of Atlantic religion and in the intellectual paradigms that shaped the study of religion as a colonial enterprise. Chapter 3 focuses on the role of early corporations in forming democratic freedom as a settler-colonial form of Christian governance. I examine Black religious subjectivity through its connection to empire by interpreting racial slavery as a critical element of colonialism. I also argue that religion among enslaved Africans was a quest for specific liberties (in the case of New Spain's Blacks) and an effort to become visible to religious ideas about time and history (in the case of Blacks under British colonialism). The Christian experience of Africans in New Spain, particularly, demonstrates the exceeding complexity of Christian domination because the Christian Inquisition there enabled enslaved Blacks to disrupt slavery's totalizing demands.

In Part 2, I examine Black settler colonialism as a central paradigm of political theology and self-determination among African-descended peoples in the United States. Chapter 4, the first of two chapters in Part 2, begins by interpreting how free Blacks experienced the United States as a White Christian settler state. I explain why the American Revolutionary War, as a White settler rebellion, induced lasting consequences that both crystallized the racial rule of Whites over free and enslaved Africans and intensified the imperative for Black settler colonies. I then explain the creation of Liberia as a Black Christian settler state. I demonstrate that Liberia emerged through a richly ironic conflagration of competing interests (particularly those of Whites seeking to preserve White-only citizenship in the United States and free Africans devoted to self-determination). More importantly, I argue that democratic freedom became a reality for African American settlers because, as with the US settler state, Americo-Liberian democracy was a colonial project of racial governance, and Christianity was absolutely central to that enterprise. Chapter 5 examines Black political theology from the 1850s to the 1890s to demonstrate how African American religion continued to be shaped by the imperatives of Black self-governance and, increasingly, the imperial ambitions of US militarism in the decades following the Civil War. In this fifth chapter, I argue that the failure of Reconstruction, as an effort to create a multiracial democracy, underscored for African Americans the specific nature of the United States as a White racial state. I also argue that US militarism became a pivotal factor that created Black loyalty to the political aims of a White republic. On a larger scale, Part 2 demonstrates how Black religion was distinctly and overwhelmingly shaped by the problem of colonialism.

Part 3 of the book devotes central attention to the interface between Black anticolonial religious movements and US counterintelligence. I demonstrate how the national security paradigm (repressing internal enemies of the state) functioned as a central element of United States empire during the twentieth century, both responding to and shaping the history of Black anticolonial religion. Chapter 6 opens this final section by attending to the diasporic themes and theological force of the Garvey movement as realized through the Universal Negro Improvement Association (UNIA)'s global activism and institutional presence. Among the lasting consequences of this movement was the creation of Black ethnic religions. Because of their political theology, Black ethnic religions such as the Moorish Science Temple of America and the Nation of Islam were targeted for pervasive, perduring repression by the Federal Bureau of Investigation (FBI). In Chapter 7, I explain how the FBI's counterintelligence measures produced lasting changes in the architecture of state racism by wedding practices of national security to a philosophy of military engagement with domestic enemies. To this end, the United States formally associated its exercise of external colonialism to internal colonialism as federal agents repressed Black liberation activism, which they perceived as one of myriad global efforts countering Western colonialism. Throughout the Cold War years, moreover, Christian nationalism became an increasingly influential element of US politics, specifically as officials and laypersons of the United States articulated that their nation was a Western, "Christian America" in a fundamental, civilizational struggle against "godless" communism. I argue that the US empire managed and rendered this clash of civilizations as a racial conflict that, by the century's end, was easily legible as a struggle of a Western, Christian society against religious, civilizational others. By the last decade of the twentieth century, in fact, African American religions comprised conflicting elements such as an expansive Christian nationalism, a strident rejoinder to the cultural imperialism of the United States among African-derived religions (such as Oyotunji African Village), and a keen critique of the US racial state (as reflected in the Nation of Islam).

In the concluding chapter, I explain the ways that colonialism, democracy, and freedom have been mutually constituting and deeply interwoven in a continuing pattern of racial governance. I point to the current racialization of Islam and explain how it has been so deeply shaped by the longer history of the FBI repressing African American Muslims.

I undertake this study of religion as a worthwhile enterprise in its own right *and* as an opportunity to examine a set of larger questions about the nature of freedom, not as some mythological concept imagined as virtuous and celestial in origin but as a worldly, social institution of profoundly anthropological provenance. Scholars who have no specific interest in African American religions and who instead are chiefly concerned with other religious actors in the Americas and throughout the Atlantic world should find the book to be of great relevance. This is because it is very much a study of Atlantic empires and the West. By extension, it is my hope that scholars who have no professional interest in studying religion per se but whose research concerns democracy, race, government, or political theory will find much to engage (and argue) with in this book.

PART ONE

I

Black Atlantic Religion
and Afro-European Commerce

The merchants and political elites of West Central Africa began to establish commercial trade relations with Lisbon (the Portuguese) in the mid-fifteenth century and, in subsequent decades, with other European metropoles. In so doing, they were setting in motion a series of market formations, trade networks, and commoditizing processes that would prove profoundly generative and transformative for Black religion. This commercialism was pivotal because it established the intersection of Atlantic religion and empire, and it features centrally in the first section of this chapter.

Of central importance are the means and motivations of African and European merchants who participated in imperial practices of commerce. Their reasons essentially derived from the fact that the colonial relations of transoceanic empire were highly generative of the commercial aims to which these business agents aspired. Colonialism, in other words, uniquely enabled the expansion of old trade networks in Africa and the creation of new ones connecting to Europe, and this guaranteed an unprecedented scale of lucrative opportunities for trade throughout Atlantic geographies. Trade and profit thus were inextricable from the architecture of Atlantic empire.

The rise of Afro-European commerce consequently instigated new religious formations within the social, political, and economic structures of colonialism. This requires attention not so much to the so-called marketplace of religion but to the *market* (i.e., the commercial practices of commodities exchange) as a central factor in constituting new formations of Black religion. The public career of the African Anglican priest Philip Quaque is a telling example of this development because his religious experiences emerged within the larger context of commercial interests. So, after accounting for the nature and scale of commercialism, this chapter culminates in an account of Quaque's career to explain major transformations of Black Atlantic religion at the point of intersection with empire.

Afro-European Commercialism: Contact, Exchange, and Religion

More than four decades after the first Africans were purchased as slaves by Portuguese merchants in 1441, the Portuguese imperial sailor Diogo Cão ventured into the interior region of Central Africa, sailing his ship from the Atlantic into the wide riverways that led to the highlands bordering the Kongo State. It was the year 1483, and the crew accompanying Diogo Cão was slowly working their ship along the coastline of Soyo, a major province of the Kongo State. Local officials in Soyo greeted the visitors warmly. For many years the neighboring regions had circulated colorful rumors of lucrative trading arrangements with Portuguese merchants; Diogo's hosts eagerly anticipated establishing similar trade relations to their own benefit. The nobility of the Soyo province sent Diogo Cão's men to the imperial capital city of Mbanza Kongo, populated by about 40,000 people. When they arrived, Nzinga a Nkuwu, the Kongolese monarch whose subjects numbered more than two million, received them with pomp and hospitality. The king was so pleased that he arranged for the visitors to stay indefinitely so that the two peoples could learn of each other's language and culture. Realizing after many days that his men's return was uncertain, Cão took with him several members of the royal court from Soyo and returned to Lisbon. Two years would pass before he and his royal guests would return to West Central Africa (see Figure 1.1). In the meantime, they sought to ingratiate themselves to each other, staking their hopes on the potential wealth that might ensue from establishing entirely new trade markets.[1]

---

[1] Linda M. Heywood and John K. Thornton, *Central Africans, Atlantic Creoles, and the Foundation of the Americas, 1585–1660* (New York: Cambridge University Press, 2007), 60–61. Peter Mark, *"Portuguese" Style and Luso-African Identity: Precolonial Senegambia, Sixteenth–Nineteenth Centuries* (Bloomington: Indiana University Press, 2002), 13–32. Malyn D. D. Newitt, ed., *A History of Portuguese Overseas Expansion, 1400–1668* (New York: Routledge, 2004), 3–17. Harvey M. Feinberg, *Africans and Europeans in West Africa* (Philadelphia: American Philosophical Society, 1989), 25–37. Filipa Ribeiro da Silva, *Dutch and Portuguese in Western Africa: Empires, Merchants, and the Atlantic System, 1580–1674* (Leiden, the Netherlands: Brill, 2011), 17–32.

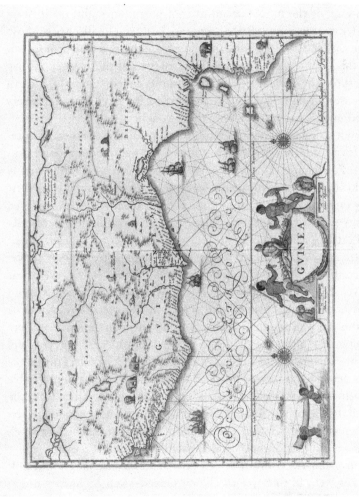

FIGURE I.I. The West and West-Central regions of Africa became known as the "land of Guinea" following the rise of Afro-European commercialism in the 1400s. The phrase became interchangeable with "Black Africa." This map is an early illustration of the region by the Dutch cartographer Jan Jansson (1588–1664). *Source*: The Melville J. Herskovits Library of African Studies and Government and Geographic Information and Data Services at Northwestern University.

So began one of the most distinctive and momentous cultural and commercial exchanges between the powerful Kongo empire and the younger, nascent Portuguese empire. The emergence of Afro-European commerce is frequently imagined as an enterprise of Europeans coercing unwilling Africans into a slave trade. For myriad reasons, however, African states could not be forced into transacting business with these newly arrived strangers. One of the most important transportation highways in West Central Africa – the Congo River – mounted difficult challenges to those unfamiliar with it. Powerful African militaries, equipped with armory tailored for the local terrain, guarded the territories of the most expansive states. So, throughout what European venturers called "Guinea," African militias possessed light, agile ships engineered for navigating the rivers that passed inland, each carrying up to 100 soldiers.[2]

This is not to suggest specific European states had no interest in dominating African polities. Indeed, they did. Over many decades and centuries, the Portuguese, Dutch, English, and French would repeatedly attempt through military means to force Africans to comply with their monopoly imperatives for trading. Until the nineteenth century, however, this strategy would fail repeatedly. West African naval fleets successfully defeated Portuguese invaders in the 1440s along the coast. Through their military strength, West Africans forced the Portuguese to abide by peaceful trade relations. The Portuguese discovered, moreover, that there was a well-developed commercial economy in West Africa that they could simply participate in, so this peaceful approach was even more profitable and thus more rewarding than one established through militarism. There were exceptional instances of violence from Europeans, but peaceful trade became the norm and violence the exception.[3] As a rule, Portuguese merchants depended on the protections, civility, and interest in profitable business ventures that African polities extended to them. Thus, from the 1400s until the 1800s, the West and Central African states encountered by the commercialists of Western Christendom rivaled and defied Europe's technological, military, and political capacities to dominate them.[4]

Afro-European trade brought not only material exchanges but cultural ones as well. In this arena, religion played a central and enduring

---

[2] Heywood and Thornton, *Central Africans*, 52–55. Loso Kiteti Boya, *D.R. Congo* (Bloomington, IN: Xlibris Corporation, 2010), 41.

[3] John K. Thornton, *Africa and Africans in the Making of the Atlantic World, 1400–1800,* 2nd ed. (New York: Cambridge University Press, 1998), 36–40.

[4] Walter Rodney, *A History of the Upper Guinea Coast, 1545–1800* (New York: Monthly Review Press, 1982), 16–18.

role. When the royal court of the Kongo Kingdom decided to adopt Christianity, it did so out of its own motivations for wealth and prestige and not under any compulsion of Europe colonialism. The Kongo Kingdom's dealings with Lisbon were in every sense an affair between mutually sovereign states. The African kingdom's imperial status was rooted in its thirteenth-century rise to power over the smaller, surrounding polities. Two local monarchs had formed an alliance and had built a new capital city in Mbanza Kongo, situated on a mountain that overlooked the populations they eventually forced into subjugation. The conquered polities provided a ready source of soldiers for war, productive agricultural markets, and tributary wealth. By the time of the Portuguese arrival, the Kongo Kingdom was a vast empire with an elaborate judicial system whose supreme judge was the monarch. It generated regular revenues from the taxation of approximately 350,000 people who viewed themselves as belonging to the Kongo, and it operated an efficiently centralized cult that honored the political rulers and linked the veneration of ancestors with a system of devotion to territorial gods.[5]

From the first days of his meeting with the Portuguese merchants, Nzinga a Nkuwu wasted little time implementing his newly conceived plan to formalize relations with Portugal and further expand his own political power by designating Christianity as the official state religion. He selected numerous representatives from the royal court and from the elite families of the Kongo and sent them to Lisbon to learn the language, to absorb its culture, and to study Christianity. Within a few years, on their return, these Kongolese ambassadors of culture coordinated the construction of European-styled churches and schools for the local elites. They taught Portuguese. And they experimented with the agricultural practices of Portugal, to the extent that these methods were fruitful in the Kongo climate. Most important, however, was the decision of Nzinga a Nkuwu himself to be baptized in May 1491. To mark the transition, he adopted the name of the Portuguese monarch, João I. One month later, the Kongolese queen performed the same ritual, adopting the name of the Portuguese queen, Eleanor.[6]

At that time Nzinga Mvemba, the governor of a local Kongo province, aligned himself formally with this Christianization paradigm that was sweeping Kongolese nobility. Mvemba, christened Afonso I, assumed the throne following the death of Nzinga a Nkuwu (João I) in 1506. Whereas

[5] Heywood and Thornton, *Central Africans*, 52–55, 59–61.
[6] Boya, *D.R. Congo*, 29. Heywood and Thornton, *Central Africans*, 61.

King João I was reserved in his turn to Christianity, Afonso I proved to be far more aggressive. One of his first actions on taking office was to destroy the sacred house of the gods that sat on the royal grounds, where the bodies of the royal deceased were interred. The structure was integral to the state-sanctioned system of cultic veneration. In its place he built a Christian church. His goal was to create an elite Christian society throughout the kingdom. To this end, Afonso I commissioned priests to travel throughout the land to baptize converts and instruct local peoples in the doctrines and liturgical practices of Catholic Christianity. By 1516 he had established a school system that served 1,000 students of the polity's wealthy, elite families. Afonso I himself devoted long periods to studying Portuguese law and scrutinizing Christian theology. Like his predecessor, he housed the invited Portuguese guests and the Kongolese emissaries who had studied in Portugal with other members of the royal court, creating ease of access to the men who engaged him in hours of discussion as he challenged them with his questions about law and religion.[7]

There can be little doubt that Afonso I was keen to the idea of fortifying his political authority by placing his stamp on the steadily expanding Kongolese church. As part of this effort, he sent his son Henrique to Rome to study Christian theology. The determined Prince Henrique proved himself an exceptionally talented student. His mastery of the Christian theological tradition eventually compelled Pope Leo X to ordain Henrique to the bishopric in 1518. This marked a momentous achievement for the young Kongolese scholar, and it assured Lisbon of important influence in the royal court of the Kongo Kingdom. Afonso I, for his part, was assured that the next generation of political rulers would continue his efforts to create a Christianized elite. In this way, Kongolese religion entered a pivotal phase of transformation that continued to manifest the old political concerns of state officials while undergirding a new class of cosmopolites in urban centers. This was just one reason why the Kongo State's expansion of diplomacy with Lisbon and Western Christendom cannot be conceived as a European colonial imposition.[8]

---

[7] John K. Thornton, "Firearms, Diplomacy, and Conquest in Angola: Cooperation and Alliance in West Central Africa, 1491–1671," in *Empires and Indigenes: Intercultural Alliance, Imperial Expansion, and Warfare in the Early Modern World*, ed. Wayne E. Lee (New York: New York University Press, 2011), 172–75. Ch Didier Gondola, *The History of Congo* (Westport, CT: Greenwood Press, 2002), 29–32. Heywood and Thornton, *Central Africans*, 59–63. Jason Young, *Rituals of Resistance: African Atlantic Religion in Kongo and the Lowcountry South in the Era of Slavery* (Baton Rouge: Louisiana State University, 2007).

[8] Gondola, *History of the Congo*, 31. Elizabeth W. Kiddy, *Blacks of the Rosary: Memory and History in Minas Gerais, Brazil* (University Park: Pennsylvania State Press, 2007), 28–30.

At the same time, however, Christianity would never transcend the philosophical and practical imperatives of empire. The Portuguese were in Africa, after all, because they wanted to control new lands and greater resources. Christianity in the western Mediterranean had for centuries been forged in the crucible of Christian guerrilla warfare against Muslim empires. In the mid-1400s, while the Kongo Kingdom was still in the relatively friendly phase of its commercial alliance with Portugal, Muslim political rule continued to extend into Iberia in the form of the Emirate of Granada, which Ibn Al-Ahmar had established in 1228. Within a decade of its founding, however, Granada would become a tributary state under vassalage to Castile. Until 1492 this state would thrive under the Nasrid dynasty by linking Iberian Christendom to the lucrative trade in gold and slaves taken from the lands of Africa south of the Sahara. The hounds of Christian conquest would remain unsated over the centuries, however. Frequent skirmishes between Muslims and Christians (rebels against rulers on either side) culminated in a full-scale war by the 1480s. Isabella I of Castile and Ferdinand II of Aragon united to make war against Granada in a decade-long struggle for domination that equally implied political and religious assertions of supremacy. In 1492 Muhammad XII, the last monarch of Granada, finally surrendered to the Catholic rulers. This culminating Iberian Christian victory over Islam, known as the Reconquista, did not end the Christian thirst for war, however. Rather, it created a professional class of militarists and mercenaries for hire who sought and found abundant opportunities for military employment in Morocco to fight against Muslims there. This was the background to the Christian expansionism that shaped the Kongo Kingdom's foray into diplomatic relations and commercial exchange with Christendom.[9]

By the time of his death in 1542, Afonso I's dream of creating a thoroughly Christianized society throughout the Kongo empire was largely unrealized. The growth of Christianity was expansive but not intensive. That is, it was certainly easy enough to find Christian priests in many regions where Kongolese upper-class families dwelled. They took great pride in acquiring a Christian education steeped in literate culture, attended mass regularly, and studied the teachings of the new faith. Throughout the provincial capitals of the Kongo State, moreover, Christian schools operated to ensure that elite Kongolese families could access an

[9] Kenneth Meyer Setton, *A History of the Crusades: The Fourteenth and Fifteenth Centuries* (Madison: University of Wisconsin Press, 1975), 450–55. Lawrence McCrank, "Cities," in *Medieval Iberia: An Encyclopedia*, ed. E. Michael Gerli and Samuel G. Armistead, 234–37 (New York: Routledge, 2003).

education in Christian literacy. Even some rural families had undergone the central rite of baptism. But the vast majority of Kongolese were poor and rural. They held no truck with the elite desire to adopt the trappings of Portuguese culture. It was not that they were philosophically opposed to communing with the deities of the Christian merchants and priests who had become a regular part of the urban scene in the kingdom. They were keen to adopt these into the community of divine beings they venerated. Rather, Afonso I's aggressive program to Christianize the kingdom entailed desecrating the sacred grove and sending numerous missionaries to compete with the local, traditional priests who were already firmly established figures of authority. Those state-sanctioned Christian priests, for this reason, were viewed as imposters. Their disputes were politically charged. Although Afonso I did not establish a totalizing Christianity, he did successfully seed Catholicism in Central Africa. As the decades of roiling change continued ahead, an authentically Kongolese Christianity would thrive, anchored as much in the grammatology and traditions of indigenous revealed religion of early fifteenth-century Kongo as in the formal, high-church doctrines and ritual formations of Lisbon.[10]

Elmina Castle and Afro-European Commerce

The intersection of religion and Atlantic empire was deeply shaped by the activity and institutions of Afro-European business partnerships. The relationships among merchants and the creation of new trade networks (and expansion of preexisting ones) were integral to the developments of religious change and colonial formations of governance. What was the nature of religion and commerce among the peoples ~~~~~~~~ Africa during the trans-Atlantic slave trade? The ans~~~~ question comes to light in the careers of two cities a~ Coast Castle (see Figure 1.2) and the Elmina Castle

From the late 1400s until the nineteenth century ~ a total of nine European states would operate fort~ coastal region of West Africa. These were virtually always possessed by private corporate entities, bringing together the military, colonial, and commercial tactics that constituted the distinctive capacities of European companies. The sole exception to this ownership pattern was the Elmina

---

[10] John K. Thornton, "The Development of an African Catholic Church in the Kingdom of Kongo, 1491–1750," *Journal of African History* 25, no. 2 (January 1984): 147–67. Gondola, *History of Congo*, 29–32.

fort. Unlike the others, it was owned and directly controlled by a monarch, the Portuguese crown.[11]

Elmina, a corruption of the Portuguese *a mina*, meaning "the mine," was originally established under the name "São Jorges da Mina" (St. George of the Mine). It was the earliest European castle-fort to be erected in West Africa. In 1482 the Portuguese ruler João II commissioned an expedition to locate a suitable site for a fortified trading house. Diogo da Azambuja was the commanding officer in charge. His expedition of 600 men – a combination of 100 carpenters and masons and the rest soldiers – sailed to the Gold Coast laden with bricks, timber, stone, lime, and enough tools to erect a towering structure from start to finish. After surveying the coastline of present-day Ghana, Azambuja recognized that the site's extensive rocky structure could be quarried for building stone, and its strategic location ensured ease of defense and ready access to large ships that could find safe harbor in the site's calm waters.[12]

Elmina represented first and foremost the exercise of brutality to ensure profits. But like the fort at Cape Coast, it would generate complicated and ironic relations through the contacts and exchanges among African merchants, European militarists, corporate officials, White settlers, and the interracial families who played a pivotal role in the towns that thrived in the vicinity of the fortified castles. The residents surrounding the castle would be drawn by the bustle of economic activities that Africans were establishing with these peculiar traders from afar. Because Elmina was the first fort established by Europeans in Africa, it also represented in the minds of European and West African peoples the breaching of a new horizon, the irruption of a strange and novel commercial alliance fraught with slavery, war, death, profit, and adventure.

Until the fifteenth century, sailing prowess in the Mediterranean lands had been the domain of Muslim navigators. Because Muslims controlled Mediterranean naval routes, moreover, European Christians were limited to the more costly and slower land-based trade routes in the region. The Portuguese king Henry IV set out to change that by soliciting the most daring sailors to venture farther south into the Atlantic in hopes of establishing an all-sea route to the East or perhaps to new markets with other peoples beyond the Sahara Desert. In 1441 they finally succeeded by sailing more than 1,400 miles from the familiar harbors of disembarkation

---

[11] A. W. Lawrence, *Trade Castles and Forts of West Africa* (London: Jonathan Cape, 1963), 25–26.

[12] Ibid., 104–5.

in Portugal, first reaching the uninhabited Atlantic islands of West Africa and subsequently the mainland itself. Within just a few years, the first trading house had been built on an offshore island. But the West African mainland would create vast allure and lucrative trading opportunities beyond anything European sailors had previously imagined.[13]

The origins of Elmina predated even Diogo Cão's foray into Central Africa. When farmers on the West African coast first encountered European sailors wandering the region in the 1440s, they were astounded and bewildered. These seemingly exotic men with pale skin and odd clothing babbled in an incomprehensible tongue. But the farmers could easily tell that these strangers were excited by the indigo-dyed shirts worn by the farmers; indigo was in great demand throughout Europe. The gold and ivory jewelry the farmers wore, moreover, made the sailors wild with delirium. The farmers themselves were also eager to trade with the Portuguese. Steel implements, for instance, could be had for a small bit of gold. Local people who had been enslaved were also traded in these initial exchanges. These captive people were taken back to Portugal. On their return to Lisbon, the Portuguese sailors produced abundant evidence of the riches to be had in gold, ivory, indigo, and human chattel by trading with West African merchants beyond the Sahara. This quickly led to a trade in African slaves numbering several hundred per year. Elite Portuguese families gladly employed them as household workers.[14]

After exploring the Senegal and Gambia Rivers, the Portuguese established trade with peoples farther south, living in present-day Liberia. They began calling the region the "Grain Coast" because of the pepper grains local farmers cultivated there. Until the sea route to the East Indies was established and subsequently reduced the price of Indian spices, this West African grain trade was vibrant and critical to European markets. Farther south, the Portuguese bought and traded for more ivory. And they remained astounded by the ease with which local West Africans wore gold, as if it were a mere common trinket.[15]

There were other specific conditions of natural mineral wealth, native flora, and economic exigencies that shaped the nature of trade relations African merchants would establish with Europeans. For instance, in

[13] Ibid., 30–32.

[14] William D. Phillips, *Slavery from Roman Times to the Early Transatlantic Trade* (Minneapolis: University of Minnesota Press, 1985), 141–46. Lawrence, *Trade Castles and Forts*, 30–32.

[15] Mary Kingsley, *West African Studies* (London: Richard Clay and Sons, 1889), 615–30. Lawrence, *Trade Castles and Forts*, 33, 34.

addition to gold, iron was the other mineral to be had in abundance in West Africa. But in this same region cotton could not be grown. Furthermore, goats and sheep of the region had short hair, which was not suitable for weaving into textiles. This provided Europeans with the ability to trade textiles for gold and ivory. Because other metals besides gold and iron were not plentiful, Europeans also imported cooking pots and basins made of brass. Brass soon became so popular with African merchants that the Portuguese began to manufacture monstrously sized bracelets of solid brass or copper just for such trade. The Portuguese also resold items acquired through trade with North African merchants, such as cloth, and with merchants of India, such as hatchets, knives, beads, and wine.[16]

In this early period, no other commodity came close to being as valuable as gold in either the marketplace of commodities exchange or the imagination of European adventurers motivated by greed and dreams of extravagant wealth. By 1557 African merchants were purchasing an eighty-ounce brass bracelet for a single ounce of gold. Gold was so highly prized by Europeans that African merchants easily acquired a massive quantity of other goods for a small amount of the metal, often in the form of just a few ornaments or pieces of jewelry. This created an ironic dilemma for African merchants, who could travel from the interior to the coast with a single ivory tusk or a box of gold and then return from trading with far too much to carry by themselves. Because these loads had to be carried by people (the tsetse fly killed beasts of burden), the merchants would typically purchase slaves in addition to their goods to carry merchandise back to the interior. As it happened, African merchants were typically buying these slaves from the Portuguese, paying twice the price for which these slaves could be had in Portugal. This meant that the Portuguese could purchase African slaves at the coast from African slave traders and sell them to other African merchants without ever leaving the coast. Of course, they still had to satisfy the demand for slaves in Portugal.[17]

Given these conditions, it was obvious to African merchants and to European traders that a permanent, capacious trading station would simplify matters by making it unnecessary for Portuguese ships to wait on the coast for weeks or months to unload their wares or to accumulate a

---

[16] Phillips, *Slavery from Roman Times to the Early Transatlantic Trade*, 141–46. Kingsley, *West African Studies*, 615–30. Lawrence, *Trade Castles and Forts*, 33, 34.

[17] Lawrence, *Trade Castles and Forts*, 32–34. Phillips, *Slavery from Roman Times to the Early Transatlantic Trade*, 141–46. Kingsley, *West African Studies*, 615–30.

sufficient quantity of material goods or enslaved women, men, and children. Moreover, the Portuguese quickly determined that their newfound profitable trade with merchants in West Africa was a magnet for piracy and rival aggression from other Europeans such as the British, Dutch, and French. Thus was born the idea for the trading castle-fort. The Elmina fort was completed in 1482. Like the other castle-forts that would appear along the West African coast many years later, its thriving and bountiful trade was rooted in African slavery. The fort was emblematic of the tangled web of relations that characterized Afro-European commerce. The castle-fort was the central node in a network of financiers, ports, company-states, polities of Africa and Europe, militias, gold, and slaves. Eventually both the fort and the town came to be known as Elmina.[18]

For roughly the next 150 years, the Portuguese monarch directly controlled the fort in a futile effort to enforce a monopoly on trade with a number of African polities, while the latter reserved the right to pursue a free-market approach with any number of European trade partners. The Portuguese aimed to dominate by undercutting rivals such as Britain, the Netherlands, and Spain. Theirs was a context of Atlantic empire, and Elmina was fundamental to that strategy. By the early 1600s, however, the Dutch had developed a fierce devotion to toppling Portuguese dominance in West African trade. In 1637 they effected a major coup by winning control of the fort from Portugal. For the next 245 years, the Dutch benefited immensely through controlling this most important castle-fort.[19]

In hindsight, the metonymic association between castle-forts and human trafficking seems a virtually ineluctable outgrowth of Afro-European commerce. But things did not begin this way. The fort was a novel institution in Atlantic relations that undergirded the fundamental mechanisms of international commerce. Given the dominance of gold as the prized object of merchants' desires, however, few could have predicted at the time of its emergence in the 1440s that the Atlantic system of human trafficking would rapidly become the most profitable element in international commerce. So integral were the forts to the trade in slaves that they would become known as "slave castles," a title earned by their capacity to hold in basement dungeons hundreds of abducted people awaiting

---

[18] Saidiya V. Hartman, *Lose Your Mother: A Journey Along the Atlantic Slave Route* (New York: Farrar, Straus and Giroux, 2007), 55. Theresa A. Singleton, "The Slave Trade Remembered on the Former Gold and Slave Coasts," in *From Slavery to Emancipation in the Atlantic World*, ed. Sylvia R. Frey and Betty Wood (London: Frank Cass, 1999), 151.

[19] Singleton, "The Slave Trade Remembered on the Former Gold and Slave Coasts," 151.

transport by ship. In the upper floors of these castles dwelled White company officials, one or more clerics, soldiers, and special guests – all attended by enslaved Africans. In this way, the castle-fort was an unnerving architectural metaphor for the terror of modernity, whose literal and symbolic foundations of Black chattel supported wealth and civility.

The fort eventually became a corporate office of the Dutch West India Company (WIC). In 1621 the Netherlands created this company to alleviate competition among the various Dutch merchants seeking to fully exploit international markets. Up until that time, Asian markets had been the more dominant focal point for international commerce. But there was no question that, by the seventeenth century, trafficking in captured Africans, the acquisition of African gold and ivory, and the colonization of the Americas made for an Atlantic revolution in commerce. Early corporations, such as the English East India Company, formed in 1600, and the Dutch WIC, were central to a spate of innovations and new rationalities in exercising political power and conceiving the nature of value. These companies were paradigmatic in and of themselves because they were novel institutions of social power and because they invested in and shaped materialities – that is, theories of matter – that were resulting from the explicitly colonial contacts created through Afro-European commercial relations.[20]

There was of course far more to the business of Afro-European commerce than finance, corporatism, and exchange. There was also brutality. When West and Central African states established trade relations with Portuguese and, subsequently, other European merchants, they were unleashing one of the most consequential commercial enterprises in human history: the global network of trafficking in Africans who had been abducted from their homes and families, or along with their kin, and forced into a life of abject domination and regimes of labor that created existential misery and early demise. This unprecedented volume of trade culminated in the deaths of between 50 and 100 million Africans and the removal of up to 14 million peoples from Africa. These enslaved populations were dispersed throughout the Americas, the Indian and

---

[20] Stephen R. Bown, *Merchant Kings: When Companies Ruled the World, 1600–1900* (London: Conway, 2010). John Keay, *The Honourable Company: A History of the English East India Company* (New York: Macmillan, 1994). K. N. Chaudhuri, *Emergence of International Business 1200–1800*, Vol. 4, *English East India Company* (New York: Routledge, 2000). Niels Steensgaard, "The Dutch East India Company as an Institutional Innovation," in *Trade in the Pre-Modern Era, 1400–1700*, ed. Douglas A. Irwin (Cheltenham, UK: Edward Elgar Publishing, 1996), 443–65.

Pacific geographies of Asia, the Caribbean, and Europe. For this reason, European commercialism in sub-Saharan Africa is frequently imagined as a chiefly exploitative system by which Europeans economically and politically dominated mostly hapless African victims. The historical record could hardly be more contrary to this impression, however. It is certainly true that European merchants (the Portuguese, singularly) initiated these trading relations; this much is evident by virtue of the simple fact that the Portuguese first landed on the shores of the Atlantic islands and subsequently of continental West Africa proper, rather than African venturers wandering into the ports of Lisbon. The resulting commerce, however, was in every sense mutually enjoined and maintained by Africans and Europeans alike.

Understanding why this was so clarifies the relationship between religion and Afro-European commercialism. The globalization of West Africa's gold trade was in and of itself a watershed event that, like an earthquake, quickly transformed the very ground beneath the feet of merchants in Africa and Asia's European cape. In its own right, the gold trade produced a rapid acceleration in wealth acquisition. By creating African markets for European goods and vice versa, the trade intensified the rate and scale of exchange across economic, cultural (including religious), and geographical domains. As the initial jewel in the crown of Afro-European market consumption, the gold trade also reconfigured, on a tectonic scale, the economic and geographical center of commerce in West Central Africa. Whereas West Africa's coastal cities had been on the periphery of trade networks that faced toward central Africa, they were now at the heart of exchange. But this was not all. The gold trade's exposure to international markets led to the globalization of Africa's slave trade, the consequences of which far exceeded anything imaginable to those historical actors of the 1400s who actually set in motion what scholars now regard as Atlantic world history.

Beyond all this, capitalism, as a central domain of Atlantic societies, was the greatest factor in changing the face of commercialism in Africa, especially Africa's already thriving slave trade. The aggressive and innovative corporatism of the Dutch was matched by the architecture of wealth that defined West Central African economies. This wealth structure was paradigmatically rooted in the possession of slaves. As a result, what is often viewed by casual twenty-first-century observers as a puzzlement (why would some Africans willingly sell other Africans into European slavery?) was, in historical and economic terms, an unfortunately rational and (by its internal logic) compelling phenomenon. The preexisting slave trade in West Africa grew explosively to generate unprecedented opportunities for wealth creation among Africans and Europeans. As with any economic revolution, it was not merely the trade in the chief 'commodity' itself – abducted human beings – that created economic opportunities. It was also the rapid emergence of secondary and tertiary businesses and markets – shipbuilding, insurance, banking, militarism (and its attendant plunder), the sex trade, the expansion of empires (such as the Kongo State, Dahomey, Portugal, and Britain) and their administration, the creation of new markets for luxury goods (such as rum, West African textiles, European beads, and ivory), weapons sales, and linguistic and translation services.[21]

By the seventeenth century it became abundantly clear to European polities that the future of empire and economic gain lay with African trade. As a result, Sweden, Denmark, France, Britain, the Netherlands, and the Brandenburger dynasty were vying for participation and domination in trade along West Africa. All operated forts – a total of forty-three. From piracy on the seas (such as that of the British against Spanish galleons) to proxy wars in West Africa to "New World" rivalries such as that between New Spain and the British colonies in North America, the stakes of conquest and dominance among Europe's Atlantic empires were manifested across multiple geographies and involved a range of actors and theaters. Commercialism – more specifically, control over trade monopolies and trade routes – was at the center of this imperial competition. The Netherlands had long fastened its gaze on the strategic importance of the so-called Guinea region of West Africa. This region of Africa, in particular, captured the imagination of Europeans because of its heightened association with gold, slaves, and lucre.[22]

By the late 1600s, the Dutch and the British were enjoying their status as the two chief slave-trading polities of Europe, a status resulting from their success in cultivating the most generous trade concessions from the African polities of the Gold Coast. The Dutch West India Company operated fifteen forts throughout the region and selected Elmina as its headquarters. The British, by comparison, operated nine forts, placing their headquarters at Cape Coast, just a few miles east of Elmina. The Fante Kingdom controlled Cape Coast. Elmina, on the other hand,

[21] Thornton, *Africa and Africans*, 78–89. Thornton, "Firearms, Diplomacy, and Conquest in Angola," 172–75.

[22] Phillips, *Slavery from Roman Times to the Early Transatlantic Trade*, 141–46. Bayo Holsey, *Routes of Remembrance: Refashioning the Slave Trade in Ghana* (Chicago: University of Chicago Press, 2008), 30.

was one of the prized city-states controlled by the Asante. Both of these Akan-speaking polities shared a matrilineal system of social structure, kinship, and inheritance. And their religious systems were also quite similar. For the European polities, most important was that the Asante and Fante were willing to grant concessions for land use so that European forts could be built.[23]

Long before establishing trade relations with Portugal, the Asante were involved in a regional slave trade, purchasing captives from the Hausa, Mossi, and Wangara nations to the north. Muslim merchants were central to the numerous trade networks that crossed through Central and West Africa. These merchants, for instance, had long-established routes by which they purchased gold and kola nuts from the Asante. From there, they traveled toward Timbuktu and then east across the Sahara Desert, where they exchanged those commodities for other products at a handsome profit. The Asante gold mines, meanwhile, afforded West African merchants a valuable resource to trade for commodities such as salt, copper, fabrics, and livestock from northern regions. The Asante also used gold to purchase slaves. The Portuguese entry into the gold trade, for this reason, did not *introduce* a system of trade. Rather, it added to and shifted an elaborate, preexisting network of markets and intensified the overall activity and value of these markets.[24]

The Portuguese foray into West Africa involved two layers of trade in human chattel: trade with the Asante and the shipping of slaves to the Atlantic sea island of São Tomé and the Lisbon metropole. The Portuguese began purchasing slaves from the coast of Benin in the 1470s, and by the first decade of the 1500s they were purchasing more than 500 slaves per year from this region. These captive men, women, and children were taken to the fort at Elmina, where some were immediately enslaved for their labor (this included providing sexual service to the White men who worked there). Most, however, were traded to the Asante for gold. By 1520 the number of Africans who were being enslaved annually as part of the Portuguese trade had surged to more than 5,000. This increase was a result of multiple factors. There was, for instance, the growing demand for slaves by West African merchants, who used them as porters. In addition, the Kongo Kingdom was rapidly increasing the scale and scope of its trade

[23] Lawrence, *Trade Castles and Forts*, 32–34. Holsey, *Routes of Remembrance*, 31. Phillips, *Slavery from Roman Times to the Early Transatlantic Trade*, 141–46.

[24] Paul E. Lovejoy, *Transformations in Slavery: A History of Slavery in Africa*, 3rd ed. (New York: Cambridge University Press, 2011), 37–38. Bruce S. Hall, *A History of Race in Muslim West Africa, 1600–1960* (New York: Cambridge University Press, 2011).

with the Portuguese. Of special importance was the formerly uninhabited island of São Tomé. Portuguese entrepreneurs had fundamentally transformed the region into a vast array of sugarcane plantations, for which a steady supply of slaves was required. Lisbon even forcibly resettled convicts from Portugal to São Tomé to administer the forced labor of enslaved Africans. The region also enticed Jewish entrepreneurs who had fled to Portugal from Spain, eyeing the prospect of living free of persecution in new environs where all Europeans enjoyed extravagant privilege in stark contrast to African slaves. The project proved robustly profitable, and the island eventually surpassed the Portuguese archipelago of Madeira as the leading producer of sugar in the late sixteenth century. São Tomé also incorporated all of the brutality, morbidity, and racial tectonics of plantation power that would eventually feature throughout the Americas.[25] In 1532 more than 200 enslaved Africans found themselves bound aboard the Portuguese vessel *Santo Antonio* for transport from São Tomé to the royal factor in present-day Puerto Rico. The ominous voyage was among the earliest of its kind, sending Africans far across the Atlantic to work the plantations in the so-called New World. Just one year later approximately 500 Africans were forced from São Tomé to the Spanish Indies. By that time Elmina was receiving 500 slaves per year from São Tomé. And at least 200 were also being sent to Lisbon annually.[26]

For the next century the Portuguese enjoyed unsurpassed dominance in the slave trade among their European rivals, largely as a result of their control of Elmina and the special relations and concessions of the Asante. This abruptly ended in 1637, however, when the Dutch finally succeeded in a decisive struggle to commandeer the Elmina fort. For most of their history in Afro-European commerce, the Dutch had served as middlemen in the trade of slaves and agricultural commodities such as sugar, coffee, and tobacco. They supplied these products to both European markets and to those of the European colonies in the Americas. In addition to controlling Elmina, the Dutch also controlled other forts throughout West Africa. By gaining ownership of Elmina, however, they were finally positioned to acquire slaves and material commodities directly from African merchants in the heart of the Guinea coast.[27]

---

[25] Hall, *History of Race in Muslim West Africa*, 38. David Birmingham, *Trade and Empire in the Atlantic, 1400–1600* (New York: Routledge, 2000), 23–24.

[26] Deckle Edge, *The Golden Empire: Spain, Charles V, and the Creation of America* (New York: Random House, 2011), 156.

[27] John Ralph Willis, ed., introduction to *A New and Accurate Description of the Coast of Guinea*, by Willem Bosman (New York: Barnes and Noble, 1967), viii–ix.

The European contest of empires was, however, an ongoing struggle. Just as the Netherlands gained the upper hand through their control of the Elmina fort, the French and English renewed their determination to eliminate the Dutch as middlemen and thereby magnify their margins in the Atlantic trade networks. This meant competing with the Dutch for the prized trade concessions granted by both African polities and individual merchants. Numerous parameters, furthermore, complicated the potential for market advantages and leveraging mercantile power. One should bear in mind that Europeans appealed to African polities for the rights to operate forts on the lands controlled by Africans in exchange for rents paid to African officials. In addition to paying these rents, the particular European nations operating forts pledged military support to the host African nation (such as the British in alliance with the Fante at Cape Coast or the Portuguese in alliance with the Asante at Elmina) in their wars against other African polities. But these African polities went only so far in granting special consideration to Europeans. They imposed limits on land concessions for forts because they prudently recognized that European dominance was a threat they had to preempt, and they did so by routinely denying many of these requests. In addition, the monopolies that European states sought to establish with Africans were frequently thwarted by Africans themselves. This was especially so with individual African merchants, who recognized they could operate more profitably by exercising the prerogative to trade with multiple European commercial partners.[28]

In this context a Dutch youth by the name of Willem Bosman first took interest in Atlantic commercialism. Born in Utrecht, Netherlands, in 1672, the young Willem had grown up hearing amazing stories of travel, profit, and adventure among the Blacks of Africa. Like most Europeans of his era, he easily absorbed discussions about Africa as a land of mystery and barbarism, a place that provided – for adventuresome White men – the opportunity for exploration, power, sex, and liberties unrivaled by any that these same men might enjoy in Europe. During his fifteen years at Elmina, Bosman worked his way into one of the leading positions with the Dutch WIC as a chief merchant. By the end of his career, in fact, he had become the second most powerful Dutch official in the Gold Coast. Operating in the most important office of the company, Bosman exercised tremendous influence and functioned astutely to promote the company's interests and to optimize the Dutch standing in the

---

[28] Willis, introduction to *A New and Accurate Description of the Coast of Guinea*, 10–11.

enslavement of Black people and the exchange in gold, textiles, and other African commodities.[29]

The city-state of Elmina that Bosman experienced as a young man was a bustling site of internationalism and economic opportunity. By that time, the Portuguese had operated the Elmina fort for roughly 200 years and, as a consequence, had helped establish one of the coast's most creolized geographies. Through their mercantilism and skills as linguists or laborers, a small but significant class of elite Africans had arisen on the coattails of coastal capitalism. Moreover, because Elmina was the corporate headquarters of the Dutch WIC, the company concentrated a range of economic activities and exchange markets in Elmina that in turn attracted African traders from the hinterlands. The Elmina that Bosman experience, in consequence, featured an uncommon scale of ethnic diversity. Residents of the city, in addition, were rarely if ever enslaved as part of the trans-Atlantic trade that had arisen. To reinforce diplomatic relations with the Elminans, in fact, the Dutch had banned the enslavement of Africans within roughly thirty-five miles of the city-state. The Dutch company appointed up to a hundred European men to work at the fort during the 1700s. The women of Elmina regularly entered relationships with these European company men. Given the virtually complete absence of White women in Elmina, these White company men eagerly sought out African women as sexual partners. This happened through either keeping female slaves as concubines or entering relations of mutual consent with free Asante women. Like the vast majority of White men living in West Africa, Bosman established sexual relations with a woman of the Gold Coast and sired several children with her.[30]

By the end of the 1600s, after Bosman returned to the Netherlands, important political changes redefined fundamental conditions of the Afro-Dutch slave trade. Akwamu, a state that had provided a great number of slaves to the Gold Coast, succumbed to conquest by the neighboring Akim polity. Of even greater significance was the Asante conquest over the Denkyira State, which had been the primary sources of gold and slaves for Dutch merchants in the Gold Coast region. The demand for slaves had surged thanks to expanding European markets and particularly the rapid growth of plantations in Europe's colonial possessions in the Americas. To meet this demand, however, Akwamu and Denkyira had made recourse to more frequent and expansive raids on neighboring

[29] Thornton, *Africa and Africans*, 50–62. Lawrence, *Trade Castles and Forts*, 28–42.

[30] Willis, introduction to *A New and Accurate Description of the Coast of Guinea*, vii–xv. Feinberg, *Africans and Europeans in West Africa*, 88–92. Mark Meuwese, *Brothers in Arms, Partners in Trade* (London: Brill, 2011), 303–5.

polities, a cyclical process that severely destabilized and depopulated the region, threatening its ability to function effectively. In an effort to stem this problem and simultaneously to win dominance over the trade routes leading to coastal regions, the Asante and the Akim state waged strategic wars to defeat the slave-raiding powers.[31]

The contradictory complications and constraints of these economic relations and political imperatives only multiplied in the wake of the Asante conquest, however. After all, the Asante themselves were purchasing slaves from the Dutch, who in turn had been supplied by the Denkyira. This peculiar dynamic characterized the larger world of Afro-European commerce. The entire trade in slaves and gold with European business partners had become the principal reason for the unprecedented wealth creation that the Asante were enjoying. By defeating the Denkyira, they were weakening the Dutch supply chain and, in the short term, dampening the scale of their own business profits. The Asante position was helped, however, by the fact that they gained more immediate control over a greater number of trade routes.[32]

Amid such political turmoil, Bosman's role as a company official granted him historically invaluable access to life in this coastal city. He eventually composed twenty-two letters to an uncle in the Netherlands, wherein he explained the history and social nature of West Africa, particularly the Gold Coast. Few aspects of West African culture intrigued Bosman as much as did religion in the Elmina city-state. Like other European Christian writers, Bosman assumed the supremacy of his own religious tradition, and he easily derided what he called the "religion of the blacks" as something deriving from illusion. Central to what Bosman perceived is what local Blacks called *bossum* in the Akan language and the Portuguese referred to as "fetish." The Akan term seems to derive from *abo* (stones) and *som* (worship) and likely reflects the influence of European Christian ideology that vilified African indigenous religion as the worship of things *as things*.[33] Bosman contrasted the fetish with the

---

[31] Deborah Pellow, *Landlords and Lodgers: Socio-Spatial Organization in an Accra Community* (Chicago: University of Chicago Press, 2008), 22–23. Willis, introduction to *A New and Accurate Description of the Coast of Guinea*, xi.

[32] J. Pashington Obeng, *Asante Catholicism: Religious and Cultural Reproduction Among the Akan of Ghana* (Leiden, the Netherlands: Brill, 1996), 16.

[33] I am indebted to David Amponsah for bringing to my attention the etymological association between "bossum" and the derisive notion of worshipping stones. Amponsah emphasizes that this terminology is used even if deities reside in rivers or trees. The idea that Africans worshipped rocks (symbolizing inert matter), therefore, seems a distinct formation of the Christian ideology of animism.

belief in a creator deity. The former he claimed was an "idol" whereas the latter was the "true" god, one that Bosman identified with the deity of his own religion – Christianity. According to Bosman, Elminans had no cult devoted to the creator god. Instead, they devoted numerous cults to the fetishes. These varied from one household or family to another. It was customary to "make fetish," in the local parlance, which he compared to "making worship." But the fetish, or *bossum*, could also be an object of awe or adoration.[34]

Religion and Transnationalism in Cape Coast

Willem Bosman's ethnographic claims about Black religion would be echoed by others in Elmina. The Elmina fort, moreover, was not the only major slave castle in the region. Just a few miles away was another, Cape Coast Castle (see Figure 1.2). Like so many other forts that European merchants had raised along West Africa's coast, this one made for an imposing edifice. It was sandwiched between the Atlantic coastline and a plethora of small towns that sprouted up with the frenetic pace of commercial exchange among local peoples. Cape Coast Castle was emblematic of the irony and complicating logics common to slave forts. Like Elmina, it was in strictest terms a military installation that served chiefly to protect the vigorous and lucrative trade in African slaves. More specifically, it protected the interests of the White merchants or corporate officials who stood to gain the most from the enterprise of raiding and trading Black people for dispersion throughout the Americas. The castle was the permanent home of numerous agents – mostly Europeans – who carried on the administrative duties inherent to slave trading. But these same forts created the most intensified zones of contact and exchange among a multiethnic array of Africans and Europeans. Local African merchants seized on the opportunity to supply the castles with fresh produce, eggs, and other foods – and at a steep profit, as continually lamented by the European merchants. Within a few years of the castle's creation, numerous polyethnic settlements sprang forth – as with Elmina – resulting from migratory laborers and the frequent sexual unions between African women and European merchants, who were rarely accompanied by European women. The offspring of these unions were a visible sign of the extent to which the trans-Atlantic slave trade created complicated

---

[34] Bosman, *New and Accurate Description of the Coast of Guinea*, 148.

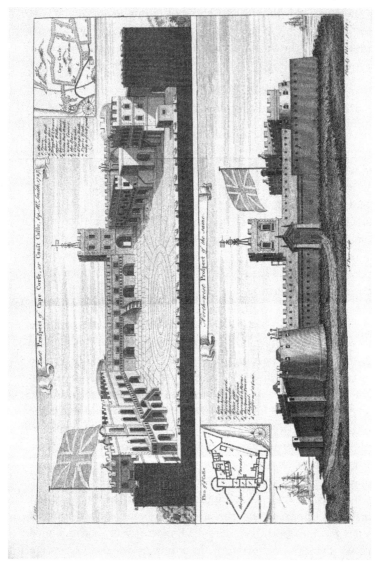

FIGURE 1.2. Prospect of Cape Corse, or Coast Castle. This illustration of Cape Coast Castle appeared in John Green's *New General Collection of Voyages and Travels; Consisting of the Most Esteemed Relations, Which Have Been Hitherto Published in Any Language; Comprehending Everything Remarkable in Its Kind, in Europe, Asia, Africa, and America* (1745–1747). *Source:* Rare Books Division, The New York Public Library, Astor, Lenox and Tilden Foundations.

relationships of exchange and interdependency. Cape Coast Castle, for this reason, was not viewed so much with resentment among the local Africans and multiracial settlements as with a gracious pragmatism, so long as peace reigned between the company men of the fort and African officials. Local political elites, after all, were ultimately concerned with their sovereignty and with ensuring the profitable status of trade with Europeans. So long as these two conditions were satisfied, they were content to embrace the invigorating changes occurring under their political jurisdiction.[35]

Outside these castle walls, in 1741, a child was born to a particular Fante family. His parents named him Quaque, which means "born on Wednesday." As a resident of Cape Coast, Quaque grew up taking for granted the international ethos of the town. Cape Coast, located in present-day Ghana, was first established by the Fetu people as a fishing village during the 1300s. Its original name was Ogua. At that time, the heart of regional trade was in West Central Africa, so this coastal village thrived on the margins of a larger region of African trade. The rise of Atlantic commerce between Europe and Africa, however, fundamentally altered the life of the town. None of the Fetu founders of the village could have predicted that in less than two centuries the Atlantic coast itself would become the center of African commerce and wealth. Nevertheless, they could not have been more strategic in establishing Ogua's location. Gold was plentiful in the region and attracted a host of European traders seeking wealth to fund personal and imperial ambitions. By the latter 1400s, political officials of coastal West Africa began to formalize trade relations with the Portuguese, and then with Swedish, Dutch, and British traders. Along the way Ogua grew to become a city-state, boasting a lively pace of economy activity as a result of trade in gold, ivory, and increasingly women, men, and children abducted for enslavement.[36]

Because of its strategic location on the coast, the Swedes desired to establish a fortified trading house in this bustling city-state. In 1652 they petitioned the Fetu king Badema and his advisor Acrosan and were

[35] Feinberg, *Africans and Europeans in West Africa*, 68–80. Meuwese, *Brothers in Arms, Partners in Trade*, 303–5.

[36] Ty M. Reese, "Philip Quaque: African Anglican Missionary on the Gold Coast" in *The Human Tradition in the Black Atlantic, 1500–2000*, ed. Beatriz G. Mamigonian and Karen Racine (Lanham, MD: Rowman and Littlefield, 2010), 39–40. Vincent Carretta and Ty M. Reese, eds., *The Life and Letters of Philip Quaque, the First African Anglican Missionary* (Athens: University of Georgia Press, 2010), 2–3.

granted permission to lease the land in exchange for monthly rent.[37] Thus, in 1655 the first European fortified structure, named Carolusborg, appeared in Cape Coast. So strategic was the fort that the Swedes quickly lost control over it. In fact, over the next decade no fewer than six different European polities possessed the fort, all vying for privileged access to the exchange of slaves and gold. As it happened, the British would seize lasting control. From 1664 to 1807 Cape Coast Castle served as the headquarters for the whole of British slaving.[38] But Europeans were not the only ones struggling to maintain a hold on such a strategic posture. By the 1700s the Fetu themselves would lose their political independence to the conquering Fante. These new rulers, like the Fetu, were a subgroup of the Akan people. But the Fante were an expanding imperial presence and were far more militarized, boasting armies of 25,000 to 50,000 troops by the early 1700s. They held extensive experience in dominating the European traders who continually arrived to seek monopoly rights of exchange with African merchant polities. The Fante had expelled the Portuguese from the coast to invite the Dutch and eventually the British, who were more pliable trade partners. By the eighteenth century European polities were accustomed to the military and diplomatic superiority the Fante wielded, and they worried that Fante control of an ever-expanding network of African commerce meant the terms of trade along the coast might hew to the interests of African polities. The Fante conquest of Cape Coast in the 1700s thus ensured they would continue to control Afro-European commerce in the greater region of the Gold Coast.[39]

Quaque understood not only that trading was the economic basis for his people but also that they were deeply connected to peoples and lands far distant from his hometown – merchants, militarists, and corporate officials who routinely arrived aboard the massive ships that quietly navigated the harbors of the cape, like silent monsters of brawn. By the eighteenth century the slave trade easily outsized the trade in gold and ivory, although these latter commodities continued to be an important source

---

[37] William St. Clair, *The Door of No Return: The History of Cape Coast Castle and the Atlantic Slave Trade* (New York: BlueBridge, 2007), 30–31.

[38] Ibid., 1–2.

[39] Ray A. Kea, "City-State Culture on the Gold Coast: Fante City-States in the Seventeenth and Eighteenth Centuries," in *A Comparative Study of Thirty City-State Cultures: An Investigation*, ed. Mogens Herman Hansen (Copenhagen: Kongelige Danske Videnskabernes Selskab, 2000), 528. Rebecca Shumway, *The Fante and the Transatlantic Slave Trade* (Rochester, NY: University of Rochester Press, 2011), 99. Lawrence, *Trade Castles and Forts*, 183.

of profit.[40] While he was yet a child, Quaque became familiar with the regular scene of scores of African captives being led through Cape Coast to the fortified castle, where they would await the behemoth ships that carried up to one-fifth of their Black human cargo to a watery grave – many would die en route – and the others to distant destinations in the Americas and the Caribbean. But Quaque did not necessarily have reason to identify with the horrific fate of these captives, at least not in a political sense. He was aware, however, that they were all "Blacks," to cite the term he employed as an adult to describe the varieties of native Africans, slave and free, in and about Cape Coast. Racial Blackness, in other words, was already an active and central formation of the Atlantic regimes of slavery, religion, empire, and commerce within which Quaque was firmly embedded. It is clear that the colonial architecture of race in Cape Coast and throughout West Central Africa superseded and overwhelmed the ethnic or national identities of myriad Africans. At the same time, nevertheless, it is also clear that the free or noncaptive Africans like Quaque stood to profit from the dynamic growth of the slave trade.[41]

The social structures and practices of political life in Cape Coast, as in Elmina, thoroughly reflected the imperatives and benefits that ensued from transnational capitalist commerce. Black merchants and African political elites could generate great profit by granting concessions to European merchants (such as the right to fish the waters and to build fortifications) and by selling human chattel. The trade in gold and, more importantly, slaves was catapulted to an entirely new level with the introduction of the slave forts. Cape Coast Castle employed a range of African slaves and local servants for daily operations. Their work revolved around more menial tasks such as cleaning, cooking, and maintaining the physical grounds. African servants, like White workers, were paid not with money but with commodities including alcohol and tobacco.[42]

In addition to these workers, an entirely different class of Africans was also employed by the company operating the castle to handle matters of diplomacy and security. In contrast to the slaves and servants who were engaged in daily operations, these positions were held by elite African politicians. In exchange for bimonthly wages, these Black political elites

---

[40] Caretta and Reese, *Life and Letters of Philip Quaque*, 3.

[41] St. Clair, *Door of No Return*, 30–31. Mary Priestley, introduction to "The Narrative of Philip Quaque," in *Africa Remembered: Narratives by West Africans from the Era of the Slave Trade*, ed. Philip D. Curtin et al. (Madison: University of Wisconsin Press, 1967), 99–108.

[42] Carretta and Reese, *Life and Letters of Philip Quaque*, 4–6.

employed by the castle drew on their alliances with African comilitarists to ensure that company fortifications were defended from enemy attacks (from both European enemies vying for commercial control and foreign African armies seeking to expand their dominance). Of equal importance was the diplomatic power exercised by African officials. As the ultimate aim of African and European merchants was optimizing profit, it was always preferable to avoid military hostilities by smoothing over tensions and forming alliances. And the African system of patronage was well suited for just this purpose. Through patronage, elites cultivated loyalty from those with less social power, creating a network of ties on which they could draw to advance a range of political, military, and economic interests. As in European cities, very few people in and about Cape Coast were wealthy; most labored intensively merely to survive. Thus, it made sense for them to trade political loyalty for material items of want and need from the hands of wealthy elites.[43]

There were, moreover, two classes of political elites in Cape Coast. On the one hand were those who held power because their families had inherited political status. On the other hand were those who gained power through wealth acquired as a result of their work with the company castle. The company wages afforded them the ability to create their own networks of patronage and thereby acquire political standing that easily rivaled the influence of traditional elites. Such is the enduring heritage of capitalism, creating a newly monied class and, in some ironic sense, equalizing access to political power by transcending the monopoly of descent or ancestry while also generating macro-level disparities in economic status. Birempon Cudjo, known to Cape Coast's European company men as Cudjoe Caboceer, was part of this newer class of Cape Coast's mercantile elites. Derived from the Portuguese *caboceiro* (captain), the term *caboceer* came into use by European merchants to refer to African elites in general, and by the mid-1700s it was more regularly associated with this new class of African mercantile elites.[44]

Cudjoe Caboceer was not just any caboceer. He was the governor of Cape Coast, the city-state's most powerful official. This was a testament to the potency of capital to refashion the architecture of social power in these regions of Africa. Given the immense wealth and power to be had by those Africans who could gain access to company employment, it is easy to understand why local officials promoted hearty business

[43] Ibid., 5–6.
[44] Ibid., 5–6.

relations with European corporations to encourage the growth of coastal slave castles. It is also clear why the Gold Coast hosted two of these – Cape Coast Castle and Elmina – within just seven miles of each other. Caboceer's power, moreover, sealed his status as a *penyin*, one of several leaders of the matriarchal kinship groups, the heads of which controlled the region's legal system and determined its official policies.[45]

At the intersection of Atlantic empire and commerce, of course, was religion. Among the European trading polities, Christian expansionism was an integral phenomenon of Atlantic colonialism. Religion was also an explicitly political affair. Since the 1500s the British Crown had prided itself on its break from Rome's papal authority, opting instead to nationalize the empire's established religion as the Church of England – that is, the Anglican Church. Among the most brazen acts of the British monarch James I, the official head of this national church, was his decision to sponsor an English translation of the Christian scriptures, a laborious process that was finally completed in 1611. This, in addition to the English Book of Common Prayer, served as a bold assertion of British rivalry against the Catholic empires of the Atlantic. But British colonists, an ocean away from the Anglican metropole, were at best floundering in their efforts to maintain institutional Christianity, given the dearth of priests and formal parishes in the colonies. It was primarily for this reason the Society for Promoting Christian Knowledge (SPCK) was founded in 1699. To further bolster Anglican perseverance, England's King William III issued a charter in 1701 to create the "Society for Propagating the Gospell [*sic*] in Foreign Parts" (SPG). This Anglican missionary society was devoted to formalizing Christian adherence among the British colonists in North America and the Caribbean. It also aimed to convert Native Americans to the Anglican tradition.[46] Both the SPCK and the SPG were in every sense products of European colonialism, since they were initially devised to maintain Christian fidelity among the White settler colonies in the Americas and the many European merchants stationed abroad in the Americas and in Africa. The concomitant interest in missionizing Africans and Native Americans expanded briskly, however.

The British kept in mind at least two factors on the subject of religious expansionism. First, the empire was a self-consciously Protestant one. In the prejudicial parlance of Reformed ideology, the "benighted heathens"

[45] John Mensah Sarbah, *Fanti Customary Laws: A Brief Introduction* (London: William Clowes and Sons, 1904), 12. Carretta and Reese, *Life and Letters of Philip Quaque*, 6.
[46] Brian Stanley, *Christian Missions and the Enlightenment* (Grand Rapids, MI: Eerdmans, 2001), 47.

in the Americas could be left to neither the spiritual darkness of paganism nor the "error" of Romanism. In their effort to control territories, the last thing the British monarchs desired was more Catholic converts, whether of Native American, African, or European provenance. Second, expanding Christendom was inextricably wed to global, commercial conquest. For centuries, Western Christians had enjoyed a tradition of missionary discourse that was steeped in the expansive grammatology of the Roman imperialism that had formed the seedbed of their religion. But the thousands of more recent encounters between European Christians and many nations of Native peoples throughout the Americas and Africa had completely altered the actual import of expansionist theology. The idea of spreading Christianity throughout the world, for the first time, now carried with it the prospect of massive economic prosperity through global networks and institutions. This globalization was at the root of the SPG's mission.[47]

Among the missionaries the SPG employed in North America was the cleric Thomas Thompson. Although these historical actors could not have guessed it, fate was about to bring Thompson together with the young Quaque and Cudjoe Caboceer. Thompson had served as a curate of Christ's College in Cambridge before entering the employ of the SPG. He began his first appointment in the New Jersey colony in 1745. Although White colonists were supposed to be the primary concern of his efforts, Thompson encountered a number of Africans enslaved in the New Jersey colony, and he succeeded in converting a few of them to his church. This whetted his appetite and prompted his interest in traveling to West Africa as a missionary. The eager cleric requested such and was not disappointed when in 1751 SPG officials arranged for him to serve as a chaplain at the Cape Coast Castle with an annual stipend of seventy pounds.[48]

Thompson arrived at Cape Coast on May 13, 1752, just two years after the English Company of Merchants Trading to Africa (CMTA) replaced the dissolved Royal African Company. As a matter of policy, chaplains had been appointed to the castle-forts to fulfill the basic mission of the SPG during the era of the Royal African Company. As a chartered entity under the Crown, the CMTA bore the same obligation to function as a base for Anglican missions to the Europeans inhabiting

---

[47] Lamin Sanneh, *Disciples of All Nations: Pillars of World Christianity* (New York: Oxford University Press, 2008), 108–12. Stanley, *Christian Missions and the Enlightenment*, 45–52.

[48] J. Kofi Agbeti, *West African Church History: Christian Missions and Church Foundations, 1482–1919* (Leiden, the Netherlands: Brill, 1986), 7.

the castle, the local population of Blacks, and the rapidly growing multiracial population of Cape Coast. Based on his limited success with enslaved Africans in North America, Thompson was certain of succeeding in spreading the gospel among the "heathen," particularly now that he had access to a greater population of Africans. Because of his supremacist assumptions, he arrogated an exclusive authority to Christianity and saw African religion as its antipode, which dulled his attention to the vibrancy and sophistication of the indigenous religion of Cape Coast. A small number of Cape Coast's mulattoes did entertain his entreaties. To his great surprise, however, the local people generally – particularly the Blacks – held not the slightest interest in Thompson's pontifications of the superiority of Christianity. Fortunately for Thompson, the small but growing number of African elites were keenly interested in education for their children, seeking like most of the world's elites an exclusive education to ensure their offspring's access to the most privileged echelons of power and wealth. Cudjoe Caboceer himself appealed to Thompson to arrange for his son Frederick Adoy to travel to England and obtain a formal British education. Thompson was soon persuaded that this was a far more promising strategy for conversion. He obliged, and Cudjoe's son successfully pursued this foreign study opportunity. Other African youths had preceded Frederick Adoy in studying abroad and returning as cultural ambassadors. Among them were two from the Gold Coast: Christian Protten, who studied in Denmark then returned in 1737 as a Moravian missionary, and Jacobus Eliza Capitein, whose skillful acquisition of Latin during his study in the Netherlands was put to use in what became his popular defense of the African slave trade. Capitein returned to serve as a chaplain at the Elmina Castle, just a few miles from Cape Coast.[49]

Caboceer, of course, had other plans for his son besides serving as a religious promoter. It was for secular reasons that he wished Frederick to possess an English education, meriting employ as a linguist or similar occupation with the Cape Coast company fort. But Thompson's aspiration of producing a cohort of native African Anglican missionaries was piqued, and he collaborated with Cudjoe Caboceer to locate other youths among Cudjoe's kin who might be trained as priests and then serve as missionaries upon returning to Cape Coast. And so it was that Quaque, at the tender threshold of his teenage years, met with the opportunity for travel to England. In Quaque the SPG hoped to find a

---

[49] Agbeti, *West African Church History*, 7–8.

sure means to institutionalize native evangelization and propagation of the Christian gospel. By immersing Quaque in British society at such a young age, the Anglican missionary society aimed to overwhelm his native orientations and reshape the lad as a Western Christian. His training thus was an investment they hoped would garner returns for years to come.[50] This strategy did not benefit only the church, however. Like Cudjoe Caboceer, Quaque's parents were aware of the social status and economic advantages such an education would afford. By entrusting Quaque to the care of strangers in a distant land, they all anticipated privileged opportunities and material and political gains for their son and the extended family.[51]

Quaque was one of three African youths for whom Thompson had arranged passage to England. The other two – Thomas Caboro and William Cudjoe – were also the kin of African elites. Sponsored by the SPG, they arrived together in England in 1754, eager with curiosity and keen to soak up all that they could learn. They were placed with the headmaster of the Islington Parish charity school, where they began their studies in earnest. In 1758, unfortunately, Thomas Caboro contracted tuberculosis and died. Quaque and William Cudjoe were sent to live with a Reverend John Moore, who had previously hosted two other young scholars from Cape Coast – John Aqua and George Sackee. In the ensuing period, William Cudjoe became mentally unstable and was hospitalized until his death a few years later. For the next several years, however – until 1765 – Quaque continued to study under the auspices of England's SPG.[52]

Quaque became fluent in written and spoken English, and he devoted himself fully to learning the history, liturgy, and theology of Anglican Christianity. Quaque's distance from his family was doubtless a burdensome experience. At the same time, the import of his selection to study abroad was not lost on him. The expenses and efforts exhausted to enable his training in the European metropole were a measured investment in Quaque's potential to promote the growth of Christianity in West Africa. Every aspect of his preparation, therefore, was steeped with the meanings and intentions of the Christian missionary purview. During his eleven-year stay in Britain, the young man came to admire the elaborate, historic traditions of Christianity. Over time, it ceased to

---

[50] Curtin, *Africa Remembered*, 99, 100. Agbeti, *West African Church History*, 7–9.
[51] Curtin, *Africa Remembered*, 99–100.
[52] Reese, "Philip Quaque (1741–1816)," 40. Curtin, *Africa Remembered*, 99–100.

be a tradition that he studied as an outsider. It became *his* tradition, one whose heritage he internalized as his own, whose rituals and theology in their particular Anglican manifestation constituted a familiar, existential home. SPG officials reported Quaque's academic progress as stellar. In Quaque's final years in England, the bishop of Exeter ordained him as a deacon. The apex of his Christian preparation, however, occurred when the bishop of London ordained him into the Anglican priesthood. With this ordination, the young Quaque became the first African to be admitted to this office within the Church of England. In a broader context, however, Quaque was repeating the vocational path charted by other Blacks from West Central Africa by pursuing Christian study and ordination in Europe. Like the Kongolese youths of the 1400s who studied in Lisbon and, closer to his own context, Protten and Capitein who studied in Protestant Europe, Quaque was refashioning himself into an intermediary between the imperial and commercial worlds of Europeans and those of Africans.[53]

Of course, Quaque developed not only as a religious scholar cultivating intellectual talent. He was also a virile, flesh-and-blood adult, and he grew as interested as any of his peers in courtship and establishing a family. When he met Catherine Blunt, a young English woman, the two developed a romantic relationship. Catherine was a member of the St. Andrew Church in Holborn. They cultivated a mutual fondness and were married on May 2, 1765, just months before Quaque's return to West Africa.[54]

In 1766 Quaque finally stepped foot on Cape Coast, accompanied by his new wife and a servant devoted to attending her. Quaque was now twenty-four years old. He had left as a child. He was returning as a married man to serve as the face of Christianity at the slave castle and in the surrounding region. His official title was "Missionary, School Master and Catechist to the Negroes on the Gold Coast." In this capacity Quaque earned an annual salary of sixty pounds. Following the custom of the time, his White wife received an annual allowance of thirteen pounds in compensation (payable in goods, not cash) for living in West Africa, away from the familiar comforts of British society. Even with such an enticing remuneration, the number of White women willing to venture abroad to risk a starkly new environment was meager, which is why most of the White male merchants who lived in West Africa quickly

---

[53] Reese, "Philip Quaque (1741–1816)," 40–41.
[54] Curtin, *Africa Remembered*, 98–99. Carretta and Reese, *Life and Letters of Philip Quaque*, 9.

sought sexual liaisons with African women and established informal families on that basis.[55]

Having returned to his native city-state, Quaque immediately set about the work he had been trained to perform. His most important contact among his kin was Cudjoe Caboceer, who had after all arranged for Quaque's travel. He assured Quaque that he would assemble a number of youths for whom Quaque might provide instruction. In fact, on his arrival Quaque was repeatedly visited by Cape Coast's Fante residents and those in the neighboring hinterland seeking information about when he would start a school for their children. Like Cudjoe Caboceer, they were interested in the secular benefits of English literacy because it portended access to company employment and company wages. This should have signaled to Quaque the significant disparity between the SPG's (and Quaque's own) missionary agenda of religious conversion and the Cape Coast residents' concern with immersing themselves in the dynamic opportunities of capitalism afforded by a growing slave trade and exchange in other commodities. But the zealous missionary saw only the opportunity to save begrimed souls from what he had been taught was the spiritual darkness of a benighted Africa. In February 1766, brimming with enthusiasm, Quaque reported to the London office of the SPG, "I shall be able with ease to draw all Men unto my Doctrine, and make the greatest part of them true Disciples of Christ Jesus."[56]

Determined to make good on his ambitious pronouncement, on Sunday, February 16, 1766, just eleven days after his return to Cape Coast, Quaque held his first religious service in his own private room at Cape Coast Castle. The castle was without a formal chapel, although Quaque might have used a public space but for the lack of formal priestly robes in which to appear. His mother and a small number of his other relatives attended the service. In addition to contacting several Fante elites in Cape Coast, Quaque also performed a burial during his first days as a missionary and chaplain. By the fall of 1766 he had baptized two infants, the offspring of the castle's White company employees. He also administered burial rites for several deceased individuals, most likely the White company soldiers whose deaths punctuated the first months of Quaque's residence at Cape Coast.[57]

---

[55] Feinberg, *Africans and Europeans in West Africa*, 68–80. Meuwese, *Brothers in Arms, Partners in Trade*, 298–311.

[56] Philip Quaque to the Reverend Doctor Daniel Burton, SPG Secretary, February 29, 1766, in *Life and Letters of Philip Quaque*, 36.

[57] Quaque to Burton, SPG Secretary, September 28, 1766, in *Life and Letters of Philip Quaque*, 43.

By that time, however, Quaque's strident confidence had already withered into a tepid pessimism. Announcing that all his initial hopes were "in vain," Quaque related to the SPG secretary Daniel Burton that he felt misled by Cudjoe Caboceer. Quaque had not at all understood the system of patronage that governed relations among the Fante. By assisting Quaque in establishing access to some of the youths of Cape Coast for instruction, Cudjoe expected payment in return. This was, after all, the larger point behind sending Fante youths like Quaque to study abroad – there was to be a collective material benefit to the larger kinship network. But in Quaque's eyes, Cudjoe was merely attempting to wrest away Quaque's hard-earned wages, of "getting from Me, if possible, the little Income I have from the [SPG] into his own Custody." Not only this, but also Cudjoe had resisted Quaque's quite forward and repeated entreaties to submit to Christian baptism. Quaque understood clearly how strategic such a victory would be, for then other Fante elders and their families would face considerable pressure to follow suit. But it was not for nothing that Cudjoe was a caboceer. The office required utmost diplomacy. He was skilled at resisting without adding the insult of explicit rejection, as Quaque related the leader's response: "Pray, Son don't You think I am too old to enter into Covenant with God?" Tactfully implying he was too aged and thus unworthy of such a rite, Cudjoe, like virtually every other Fante prospect Quaque aspired to convert, slipped around his missionary machinations with Teflon agility.[58]

Beyond this, it soon became apparent that Quaque would have to overcome other obstacles. After more than a decade in England, he had lost facility in his native language.[59] As a result, he actually required a translator to interact with his own kin and with all of the African residents of Cape Coast. Quaque also exhibited a deep revulsion toward the religious life of the Fante. Of course, this only better suited him to his official task, which was to persuade his kin to abandon their religious ways and replace them with Christianity. But so deeply racialized were his filters of religious identification that Quaque felt compelled to highlight any factors that differentiated his new religious self from his countrymen. Thus, he emphasized to his European superiors the radical discontinuities between Christianity as made meaningful through

---

[58] Ibid., 40, 42.
[59] It is curious that despite having shared the company of fellow Fante student William Cudjo for several years before the lad's hospitalization, Quaque did not maintain facility in his native tongue. On his return to Cape Coast, Cudjoe Caboceer's son Frederick Adoy served as a translator for Quaque.

his own grasp of that faith and what Quaque referred to as "heathen" religion.[60]

As a well-trained theologian and missionary of the Anglican faith, Quaque did not reserve his religious contempt for Fante religion alone or even African religion broadly. Quakers, Baptists, and Catholics alike were, in his view, treacherous enemies of true faith. While en route to Cape Coast from England, the ship on which Quaque sailed had stopped over briefly at Madeira, one of the Portuguese-settled archipelagos off the northwest coast of Africa. While there, the newly minted missionary visited a Catholic congregation on Christmas Eve to settle his curiosity about the Christmas Mass. He found nothing, he claimed, beyond their "Superstitious forms of Worship, Rites and Ceremonies," the whole thing but an "outward show of Magnificence and Grandieur [*sic*] and superb adornings therein." For the first and only time in his life, Quaque observed the counting of the rosary (prayer) beads, recitation of the Ave Maria (Hail Mary) prayer, and what he described as "the Saluting of a Dumb-Wax-Infant most gorgeously Deck'd." In condescending tones that must have pleased his SPG sponsors back in Britain, Quaque reported that the whole affair caused him to conclude that "the worship of God is here turned by these pretended Saints into Idolatry and the utmost Ridicule."[61]

In his denigration of Portuguese Catholicism, the eager Anglican chaplain was reinscribing a common Protestant representation of European Catholics by explaining their worship as idolatry. This invective discourse had first emerged among Reformation activists of the fifteenth century at the very time Afro-European business partnerships were bringing native African religion into contact with Western Christianity. As West Central Africans continued to encounter and increase trade relations with European Christians, the Western grammar of idolatry would become a highly routinized means of deriding native African religion. Within this discursive mix were Protestant ethnographers who delighted in impugning their White Catholic opponents for sharing with Black people a religion of idolatry.[62]

In the same year that he returned to Cape Coast, Quaque established a school in one of the rooms of the castle-fort to provide formal instruction

---

[60] Margaret Priestly, "Philip Quaque of Cape Coast," in *Africa Remembered*, 107–9.

[61] Quaque to Burton, SPG Secretary, February 29, 1766, in *Life and Letters of Philip Quaque*, 36–37.

[62] Gary F. Waller, *Walsingham and the English Imagination* (Burlington, VT: Ashgate, 2011), 41–43.

to mulatto youths. The curriculum comprised reading, writing, math, and theology. It was his dream to establish a more elaborate school housed in its own separate structure, but this was never to materialize for want of funding. Of equal challenge was the small number of pupils. Over the next few decades Quaque would never succeed in attracting a total of more than sixteen pupils; the actual number at any given time was usually far more meager, at times only one or two.[63]

The death of his wife, Catherine, in November 1766 dealt a major blow to the young priest. It also led to one of his rare acts of acquiescence to the local culture, as he thereafter married two local women, conforming to the dominant norm of polygamous marriage. In 1784, on what was to be his last trip to England, he accompanied his son, Samuel, whom he wanted to be educated in a Christian society. Quaque returned to Cape Coast the next year after entrusting his son to the care of SPG officials.[64]

In 1787 a Torridzonian Society was created at Cape Coast Castle to enhance relations between locals and company officials. This soon became a funding source for educating mulatto children. The program was short lived, however, because of internal company dynamics and because locals strongly opposed the deracinating influences of Westernization. In the face of mounting pressure from company officials and English missionaries, the Fante clearly preferred their indigenous religion and culture to the missionary religion being peddled to them. In fact, from the very start of his missionary enterprise, Quaque encountered not just difficulty but active resistance. When he traveled to the town center to deliver an announced sermon on the Christian religion, those who had promised him their attendance reneged, afterward reporting that they were fatigued from labor and could not travel. Even Quaque realized, however, that this was a veneer of politeness and that they were simply not interested in Christian conversion. He did, however, have some success entertaining an audience by performing Anglican hymns. The locals, he reported back to the SPG, were especially "vulnerable" to music and "expressed a great veneration towards it." It did not occur to him that his audience thought the same of him, as singing might have struck them as a peculiar means of winning over an audience. In the end, however, even this peculiar strategy of singing failed to yield converts.[65]

---

[63] Margaret Priestly, "Philip Quaque of Cape Coast," in *Africa Remembered*, 108–10.
[64] Priestly, "Philip Quaque of Cape Coast," in *Africa Remembered*, 108–9. Carretta and Reese, *Life and Letters of Philip Quaque*, 11.
[65] Priestly, "Philip Quaque," 110–11, 123–24.

Although he castigated Catholics as idolaters, derided Quakers and Baptists as steeped in theological error, and perpetually bemoaned the White residents of Cape Coast Castle for what he perceived as their brazen immorality and entrenched debauchery, Quaque directed his most intensive vitriol toward the indigenous religion of his own kin. The theological and cultic dimensions of religion among the people of Cape Coast were especially striking and confounding to Quaque. When he managed to win the audience of several Fante *penyins*, or elders, he read to them the text of a religious lesson and offered prayers. The next day the *penyins* sent word to him of their request for rum to satisfy the dynamic of exchange. They indicated, moreover, that he had made them Christians by reading and sharing with them Christian scriptures, an act for which they thanked him. He had shown to them "the way to Yangcumpon."[66] What Quaque transliterated as *Yangcumpon* is a reference to "Nana Nyankopon." As *Nana* is employed to refer to the head of a kinship network, this reference was to the chief deity, to whom the Fante attributed creation. Quaque, lacking facility in the Fante language, was ill equipped to comprehend the move these elders were making; they had comprehended his lofty, theological pontifications about an omnipotent, transcendent Christian deity superior to their so-called fetishes, and they had associated this with their own theological traditions about Nana Nyankopon, the Akan deity who was above all other deities – the high-god.[67]

Quaque returned to town the next Sunday only to find that the elders failed to show for his planned religious service. Cudjoe explained to him that the elders were busy sacrificing a sheep to "their chief God ... the Goddess Aminsor."[68] Throughout the early years of his work at Cape Coast, in fact, Quaque would have abundant opportunity to become acquainted with the theology and worship of Cape Coast Fante. He worked assiduously, with the help of the linguist Frederick Adoy (Cudjoe Caboceer's son, who had trained in London), to explain to the Fante elders the doctrines concerning the attributes of the Christian deity. And the Fante, for their part, were as skillful in rejoinder by explaining their obligation to honor the deities who inhabited the physical and spiritual

---

[66] Quaque to Burton, SPG Secretary, September 20–October 20, 1767, in *Life and Letters of Philip Quaque*, 54.

[67] Robert B. Fisher, *West African Religious Traditions: Focus on the Akan of Ghana* (Maryknoll, NY: Orbis, 1998), 120–22. Edward Geoffrey Parrinder, *West African Religion* (London: Epsworth Press, 1949), 16, 17.

[68] Quaque to Burton, SPG Secretary, September 20–October 20, 1767, in *Life and Letters of Philip Quaque*, 54.

realms of Cape Coast. So, they sacrificed to Aminsor to seek divine assistance in fighting an epidemic that struck the town in 1767. And they sacrificed to Taberah to ensure a bountiful supply of fish for food.

Like virtually every other Christian supremacist who encountered the indigenous religions of West Africa, however, Quaque failed to grasp the philosophy of matter and spirit that undergirded indigenous religion in West Africa. He described Aminsor as "a spacious thick Bush just by the Sea side, in which they say She visible inhabits, and is often seen by them. It has a narrow Rivulet before it, [which] projects into the Sea, wherein She purifies herself daily invisible."[69] Quaque described another Fante deity through a similar struggle with divine materiality: "As for Taberah, He is a prodigious high Rock, whereon the better part of the Castle stands, & the remaining Part [launches] out into the Sea. [A]nd they'll make You believe that this God of Stone is the only support of the Garrison, the Inhabitants therein, and the whole Towns People, so that this Custom of [sacrificing] was to procure Fish for them to eat ... because ... the moving Creatures in the Great Ocean are ... under their Command & Direction."[70]

It seemed obvious enough to Quaque that rocks or stones were not controlling the fish supply. He attributed that power to his own Christian deity. On this score, he eventually moved from merely pressuring Cape Coast's Cudjoe Caboceer to partake of baptism, to brazenly debating him in an attempt to prove that Fante theology was a diabolical delusion. At one point he confronted Cudjoe about why he continued to invest in what Quaque called "deceitful Dum-lying Fetishes." Eventually, he dared to directly challenge the religion of this Cape Coast ruler: "Why ... are You all so silly & so very deluded as to place [your] Confidence in [dumb] Stones & Bushes & many more, [which] no Body knows but yourselves." Cudjoe Caboceer smiled in response. Instead of answering such an ill-conceived question, in what was clearly an act of placation he invited Quaque to conduct a small religious service.[71]

The Fante, of course, were not worshipping stone or bushes. They were worshipping the gods, extraordinary beings they believed were responsible for creating the phenomenal world and its life forms, controlling disasters and auspicious events, and effecting wholeness and well-being. The Fante and other subgroups of the Akan, moreover, conceived of

[69] Ibid., 56.
[70] Ibid., 56.
[71] Quaque to Burton, [Letter 6, undated], 1767, in *Life and Letters of Philip Quaque*, 56.

divine efficacy and power as an ontology that transcended the domain
of deified personalism. In other words, a network of powerful energies
paradigmatically defined their view of the cosmos. The Akan understood
these in both personified and nonpersonified terms. The Yoruba, in a
parallel fashion, have employed the term *ashe* in precisely this way. It
appears that the root *nyama* operated in this fashion among the various
Akan peoples. As a result, indigenous West African theology involved a
bifold conception of the divine as an impersonal force for which ritual
was a technology of access and control and as a personified entity, a deity
or extraordinary being to whom humans could appeal for assistance and
from whom wrath or gracious beneficence might be received.[72]

This Akan theology of the divine placed considerable emphasis on sacramentalism, which concerns the capacity of *things* to bear divine efficacy – to exert the powerful energy of the gods or even become the abode
of divine energy in its personified or nonpersonified forms. So, when the
Fante elders told Quaque that the deity Aminsor dwelled in a bush by the
seaside, they were not claiming that the bush was a god. In theological
terms, rather, the bush was a sacred site because Aminsor was believed to
dwell there. The bush, thus, was a metonym for divine efficacy. The same
goes for the deity Taberah, whom the Fante associated with the rocky
structure on which the slave castle stood. Quaque mistook his informants to have worshipped the rock, a mere thing, instead of worshipping the divine. And for Quaque, this was the epitome of idolatry. His
caricature of Akan religion recalls precisely the anti-Catholic invectives
Quaque employed in his first report to the SPG. This strategy, in turn,
mirrors the iconoclastic controversies that marked the rivalry between
Eastern Orthodox Christians and their Latin adversaries in medieval
Christianity.[73]

Of major importance as well in the Akan theology of Cape Coast was
the general absence of a cult to a high god, to Nana Nyankopon, whom
at least a few of the Fante elders (*penyin*) associated with the Christian
deity of whom Quaque preached. With the exception of the religious
traditions of the Ashanti, who established a formal cult of the high deity
(comprising temples, priests, and altars), the indigenous religions of West
Africa were not concerned with directly venerating this high god, whom

---

[72] Parrinder, *West African Religion*, 15–20. Fisher, *West African Religious Traditions*,
120–22.
[73] Quaque to Burton, [September 20 to October 20] 1767, in *Life and Letters of Philip
Quaque*, 56.

they typically associated with the sky. Just as the sky was over all the earth, so also was the high god elevated in authority above all the phenomenal world. In cultic and theological terms, this was precisely the limitation of the high god – so far removed from the domain of everyday affairs and networks of power. The myriad demands of quotidian life – healing sickness, promoting social stability, and ensuring physical sustenance – compelled the Fante to engage with those deities who governed the world through limited domains of authority. These deities were concerned with very specific aspects of life and were thus closer to the affairs that directly concerned human needs and interests. Such ranged from the spirits that protected particular villages to those territorial and ancestral spirits that guarded individual homes. The practices of the Fante, in this regard, were not unlike those of European Christians, who venerated a range of saints on a daily basis.[74]

Perhaps the most consequential difference between Christianity and West Africa's indigenous religions was the principle of scarcity and exclusivism that animated Christian derision against the so-called religion of the Blacks. African indigenous religions easily incorporated new revelations from recently arrived gods and embraced their cults by operating on a principle of plurality and plenitude. To speak of the divine was to conceive of a divine *community*, as the economy of veneration was bountiful and multiple. There was more than enough devotion to go around. It did not occur to the Fante to persuade Quaque or any other Christian missionaries to abandon their biblical god. Devotion to one deity was by no means a threat to others. In fact, at the heart of this dominant West African theology was the maxim that the people's primary assurance of well-being depended on venerating many gods, not one. Nothing, however, could have been further from the dominant sensibilities of Christianity. The worship of any gods other than the Christian deity was arguably the most incriminating action in the Christian imagination. Its theological importance easily outweighed that of such horrendous acts as murder, pillaging, sexual violence, or genocide. In Christian grammar, it was an exceptional category – idolatry – and it constituted the most direct form of rebellion against the Christian deity. This, more than anything else, explains Quaque's failure to apprehend the religion he was futilely attempting to extirpate. Like that of his predecessor Thomas Thompson, Quaque's grasp of the religion of the Cape Coast peoples

---

[74] Fisher, *West African Religious Traditions*, 120–22. Parrinder, *West African Religion*, 16, 17.

rendered before him only a mass of incomprehensible madness, theological incoherence, and diabolical servitude. Thus, when met with empirical demonstrations of the efficacy of Fante religion, Quaque had easy recourse to the Christian strategy of diabolism. In his debates with and reproach of the Fante, he harangued against their "Fetishes, & false Gods and Goddesses" as "nothing but Conjurings & Witchcrafts made by the [sleight] of Hand & Art of Men to impose upon them." Any gain to be had from these manipulations, Quaque believed, was "thro' the Means of our Spiritual Enemy, the Devil."[75]

But the Christian gaze on Black religion in West Africa that derisively dismissed it as an evil delusion was met with a staunch skepticism by the Fante, who by Quaque's own admission perceived his pontification about Christian salvation and the mighty attributes of the Christian deity to be so many fanciful tales. He did win a few converts. The half dozen or so youths whom he instructed in the castle followed him on his travels into town to meet with the elders. These students were evidence for the townspeople that he had some following. He also performed several baptisms – usually of the White men who were castle employees. For the most part, however, the Fante easily resisted Quaque's preachments. Two years into his appointment at Cape Coast, the native Cape Coast priest was already reporting to the London SPG office that he was faring no better than his predecessor Thomas Thompson, largely because the Fante were "a very Stoborn [sic] & stiff-necked People, extreamly [sic] bigoted to their own Principals & Customs, which is the hardest Thing in Nature for the most sagacious Man [who] ever lived to root out of them."[76]

Of particular ire to Quaque was the use of alcohol as a social drink within the castle and among the native people of Cape Coast. The fact that company employees received wages in the form of rum and tobacco meant the local market of Cape Coast was flooded with these at a price easily accessible to the public. Just as in Europe, major gatherings mixed with alcohol became lively and normative venues for socializing. Quaque was outdone, however, to find that the few times he managed to attract a Fante audience to his religious meetings, they drank rum quite liberally afterward, turning his evangelism into what he perceived as a den of debauchery. For their part, the Fante individuals who attended were going to great lengths to assuage the frustrated fellow whose decade-plus

---

[75] Quaque to Burton, [September 20 to October 20] 1767, in *Life and Letters of Philip Quaque*, 60.

[76] Quaque to Burton, March 7, 1767, in *Life and Letters of Philip Quaque*, 47.

estrangement from Cape Coast had robbed him of facility in his native language and endowed him with a seemingly endless capacity for deriding and insulting the most basic aspects of Fante life, such as honoring the divine hosts who provided them with health and sustenance. In his correspondence to SPG officials, Quaque proclaimed his determination to send his children to England to "secure their tender Minds from receiving the bad Impressions of the County, the vile Customs and Practices and above all the Happiness of [losing] their Mother Tongue (to institute a better)." He not only derided the Fante language as inferior but also declared it "the only obstacle of Learning in these Parts."[77] Pragmatist that he was, though, Quaque was not above compromising on some of his sharp objections to alcohol. In an effort to encourage attendance at the Sunday religious services he advertised among the Fante, Quaque took to serving alcohol himself. Not even this, however, was enough to convince his listeners to convert and submit to baptism into the Anglican faith.[78]

There is no evidence that Quaque's kin ever returned the insults he doled out in his effort to persuade them they had doomed themselves to eternal damnation by following their own traditions and needed to convert. Indeed, throughout the roughly fifty years of his work as a company chaplain for the SPG, Quaque reported his continuing efforts to produce converts among the Fante and complained only of their polite lack of interest and never wanton hostility on their part. It is unclear, however, to what extent if any Frederick Adoy, his translator, may have edited or omitted Quaque's harangues of insult when communicating to his audience. What does emerge with overwhelming clarity is a portrait of a man living among multiple social worlds while belonging to none. He had no desire to identify closely with the Fante because he was a Christian. But those European Christians who operated the castle were nominally Christian in Quaque's estimation, given their love of alcohol and consequent drunkenness and given the unprincipled sexual relations the White men pursued with Fante and mulatto women. Moreover, the White company men made very clear to Quaque that they viewed him as their racial inferior. Although he was formally entitled to dine with them, he was in practice strictly forbidden from eating at the common table. This meant he was left to his own devices to trade for food and provide for himself through his rum and tobacco wages.[79]

---

[77] Quaque to William Morice, August 7, 1782, Cape Coast Castle, in *Life and Letters of Philip Quaque*, 156.

[78] Reese, "Philip Quaque (1741–1816)," 43.

[79] Carretta and Reese, *Life and Letters of Philip Quaque*, 12.

By the 1770s, roughly half a decade after his return to his homeland, Quaque had concluded similarly to his predecessor Thomas Thompson that attempting to convert the people of Cape Coast was a largely futile task. He began to focus on children. On Quaque's initial return from England, Cudjoe Caboceer had urged Quaque to focus on education, not religion, as English literacy and mathematical skill were the essential elements for qualifying oneself for company employment. Not surprisingly, this was precisely the route Quaque eventually settled for. Beginning in 1779, the White employees of Cape Coast Castle created what they called a Torridzonian Society, which supported twelve local youths (among whom were four offspring of White company employees) by providing clothing, education, and food. Over the remaining decades of his career as the Cape Coast Castle chaplain, the aging missionary remained content with instructing these children in basic literacy skills and Christian doctrine. Quaque was assisted in this by his son, Samuel, who had by then returned from England. By 1795, however, the school had ceased to function as a project of the short-lived society, partly because of waning interest by most of the youths. Quaque nevertheless continued to instruct three promising students of whose erudition he boasted to the SPG office in London.[80]

In his early career at Cape Coast, Quaque's correspondence was virtually silent on the subject of the tens of thousands of abductees he saw being forced into the slave trade. Several years before his death, however, Quaque was awakened to the abolitionist critique of racial slavery. That much is evident from his correspondence with the White New England abolitionist Samuel Hopkins in 1773. Joining a larger network of trans-Atlantic correspondence, Quaque described the trade as "horrid, Barbarious and Inhuman." He lamented both the devastation wreaked by the kidnapping of peoples for the trade and the resulting rise of a sex trade between Europeans on the West African coast and African women, whose families stood to gain materially from their employ as sexual partners of the White men. To judge strictly from the tone and content of his writings about slavery, however, one might never realize that Quaque penned his letters from within the slave castle itself. Not only did he work to service the spiritual needs of slave-trading officials, but even his salary was supported by the profits of the thriving commerce in Black chattel.[81]

---

[80] Reese, "Philip Quaque (1741–1816)," 45. Priestly, "Philip Quaque," 110–11.
[81] Quaque to Samuel Hopkins, May 19, 1773, in *Life and Letters of Philip Quaque*, 113.

Until his death in 1816, Quaque remained devoted to his life as a chaplain, where he lived literally one or two stories above the dungeon held hundreds of Africans at a time, bound and destined for racial slavery in the Americas. Their location in the basement of the castle was distressingly emblematic of their commoditized placement within the Atlantic economies of race, slavery, and commerce. Traumatized, broken, and destitute, they were the human underside of a brutally dehumanizing regime whose intersectionality underscored the astounding perversity of all that Cape Coast had come to represent – an alliance of capital, empire, and religion.

2

On Religious Matters

In 1625 the Portuguese merchant André Donelha was on business at the port of Gambia and serendipitously met with an enslaved acquaintance, Gaspar Vaz, a Mandinga youth. Donelha himself was born in the Cape Verde Islands of Portuguese parentage. He had become familiar with Vaz because the young man was bound under the employ of Donelha's White neighbor. Donelha later detailed an account of their meeting:

The black was a good tailor and button-maker. As soon as he knew that I was in the port he came to see me and paid a call on me with great enthusiasm. He embraced me, saying that he could not believe it was me he saw, and that God had brought me there so that he could do me some service. For this I gave him thanks, saying that I was very pleased to see him too, so that I could give him news of his master and mistress and acquaintances, but that I was distressed to see him dressed in a Mandinga smock, with amulets of his fetishes (gods) around his neck to which he replied: "Sir, I wear this dress because I am nephew of Sandeguil, lord of this town, whom the tangomaos[1] call duke, since he is the person who commands after the king. On the death of Sandeguil, my uncle, I will be inheritor of all his goods, and for this reason I dress in the clothes that your Honour sees, but I do not believe the Law of Mohammed, rather I abhor it. I believe in the Law

[1] The term *tangomaos* refers to Portuguese merchants who lived in coastal West Africa and who typically adopted the local culture and intermarried with the families of local Africans. They established themselves as a very influential class of middlemen, brokering transactions between Portuguese and African merchants. Among these *tangomaos* were many Jewish merchants who sought relief from the anti-Jewish politics of Europe by relocating to West Africa and becoming central actors in the transnational networks of the emerging slave trade. See William D. Phillips, *Slavery from Roman Times to the Early Transatlantic Trade* (Manchester: Manchester University Press, 1985). Peter Mark and José de Silva Horta, *The Forgotten Diaspora: Jewish Communities in West Africa and the Making of the Atlantic World* (New York: Cambridge University Press, 2011).

of Christ Jesus, and so that your Honour may know that what I say is true" – he took off his smock, beneath which he wore a doublet and shirt in our [European] fashion, and from around his neck drew out a rosary of Our Lady – "every day I commend myself to God and the Virgin Our Lady by means of this rosary. And if I do not die, but come to inherit the estate of my uncle, I will see to it that some slaves are sent to Santiago, and when I have found a ship to take me I will go to live in that island and die among Christians." It was no small advantage to me to meet him in the Gambia, because he was of service to me in everything, and what I bought was at the price current among the people themselves, very different from the price they charged the tangomaos. And he served me as interpreter and linguist.[2]

Gaspar Vaz's exchange with Donelha demonstrates multiple fascinating aspects of religion in Guinea Africa. It is evident that the presence of Catholicism throughout the region enabled networks of positive affiliation between Africans and Portuguese merchants. Vaz bestows generosity on Donelha precisely because they share a common religious affiliation. Donelha, obsessed with the specter of so-called fetish religion, gently castigates Vaz for continuing to wear his fetishes despite having converted to Christianity. Vaz, in the common fashion of African creoles, proves himself a capable cosmopolite who nimbly and tactfully navigates multiple, overlapping worlds of exchange and belonging. In one fell swoop, he disarms any suspicion of sincere devotion to fetish religion and performs his display of fetishism as a literal façade that pragmatically veils his deeper Christian devotion. He wears the fetishes, he claims, merely to assure his uncle that he is a worthy heir to his assets. But his heart is devoted to the Christian deity and the Virgin. Finally, he assures Donelha that he longs to die in a *Christian* land (i.e., one of the Cape Verde Islands with a majority Christian settler population).

Of course, there are other complicated signs that merit careful apprehension as well. Donelha means to render for his readers a renunciation of fetish religion. But as he relates his exchange with Vaz, it is clear that Vaz understands the fetishes that adorn his attire to represent Islam, "the Law of Mohammed." But for Donelha and numerous other European merchants writing about Black religion in West Central Africa, it was the fetish, not Islam, that perplexed them and commanded their intellectual attention. For roughly five centuries – from the 1400s to the twentieth century – the fetish operated at the heart of intellectuals' studies

---

[2] Andre Donelha, *Descrição da Serra Leoa e dos Rios de Guiné do Cabo Verde*, ed. and tr. P. E. H. Hair (Lisbon: Junta de Investigações Científicas do Ultramar, 1977), 149. Also see Mark, *"Portuguese" Style and Luso-African Identity*.

concerning the nature of religion and theories of human culture. It was the fetish in fact that generated distinctly Enlightenment notions of religion in Atlantic discourse. Within the first decades of Afro-European commercialism, what African and European interlocutors termed fetish religion had come to represent the quintessential religion of West Central Africa – what European writers of the era commonly called "the religion of the Blacks." The fetish became not only the established synecdoche for African indigenous religion but also the most potent intellectual category for the colonial enterprise of interpreting and studying religion comparatively. By the nineteenth century, even the young Friedrich Max Müller would embrace the claim that fetishism was the original form of religion and that it was the basis for the entire cultic and theological notions in the global history of religion. The more mature Müller, however, would eventually break sharply from this orthodoxy and thereby distinguish himself from his intellectual peers in the study of global human cultures.[3]

As a central element of religion in West Central Africa, however, the fetish was important not merely as a matrix of ideas. Rather, its fundamental significance lay with its constitution at the intersection of spirit and matter. As we have seen in Chapter 1, this issue was at the heart of Philip Quaque's puzzlement and derision of indigenous religion in Cape Coast. Fetish religion was nothing if not a materiality – a complex theory of matter, a rich assemblage of philosophical modes and social practices predicated on a certain apprehension of *things as things*, their nature, and their capacity to exist simultaneously as something more than inert objects of the material world.

How did peoples of the Atlantic world, wrestling with matters of explicitly religious concern, conceive of the material world? And how did matter as such become a religious matter of such domineering concern that it remained essential for contemporary interpreters of religion for roughly half a millennium? A response to these questions demands that we examine one of the novel problems that emerged precisely because of the contacts and exchanges that Africans experienced with Europeans and American Indians in the Atlantic geographies.

---

[3] Friedrich Max Müller, *Lectures on the Origin and Growth of Religion as Illustrated by the Religions of India* (London: Longmans, Green, and Co., 1878), 64–66. Müller was especially critical of Charles de Brosses and charged the latter with muddling discrete stages of religion by categorizing as a fetish a range of various cultic entities, from crafted objects to living animals to mountains and trees.

Empire and the Problem of Matter

It was chiefly in the lands of the Akan and Ewe nations (European merchants would refer to these as the Gold Coast and the Slave Coast, respectively) that the grammar of the fetish would develop during the fifteenth and sixteenth centuries.[4] This discourse of the fetish was generated from deeply rooted, powerful theories of matter that had taken shape over many centuries among the peoples of Western and Central Africa and that continually evolved. African merchants employed an understanding of matter corresponding to the fetish idea that elaborately attended social exchanges. The fetish, in other words, was a richly comprehensive theory of *matter* and *social power* undergirding a range of human activities, from the quotidian to the exquisitely ceremonial, from business transactions to acts of vengeance to ritual techniques affecting health and well-being.

The varieties of polities and societies (urban and rural) in West Africa, moreover, spoke of the fetish concept in ways that *both* mirrored and tersely departed from the materialities of European Christians. In conventional parlance, the African merchants interacting with European buyers might invite their partners to "make fetish." This was roughly equivalent to the Western Christian conception of "making religious worship." Or alternatively, to seal a business contract or any other multiparty agreement, it was common as a further confirmation to "make fetish," thereby obligating the parties to fulfill their vows of commitment under pain of sickness or death. As one Dutch corporate official based in West Africa observed in the early eighteenth century, this means of "making fetish" usually involved consuming an "oath-draught" or drink that had been spoken over by a "feticheer" (African priest) and reciting "an Imprecation, that the Fetiche [*sic*] may kill them if they do not perform the Contents of their Obligation." In this context, the fetish was identified as both the drink consumed and the power conveyed through ritual. This power, furthermore, was conceived as ontological and as bearing the capacity to guard fidelity to a vow and to inflict injury, disease, or death on any party violating the oath. Ritual of this nature attests to a code of ethics and a tactic of force designed to achieve obligatory fiduciary adherence, a necessary condition for functioning markets.[5]

---

[4] By the nineteenth century, however, Western theoretical claims about fetish religion was being shaped immensely by English and Dutch colonialism in southern Africa. See David Chidester, *Empire of Religion: Imperialism and Comparative Religion* (Chicago: University of Chicago Press, 2014).

[5] Bosman, *New and Accurate Description of the Coast of Guinea*, 146–51.

Further complicating the discourse of the fetish was the overwhelming tendency for European merchants to project the Christian ideology of idolatry on the religious practices of their African hosts and business partners and by extension the larger complex of West Central Africa. So, Europeans regularly described the material manufactures of West Africans as "idols" and "fetishes" interchangeably. African merchants and priests themselves further strengthened this convention by employing the term "fetish" to denote both these manufactures and also the Orisha and ancestors whom they venerated and with whom they sought to establish ritual communion.[6]

The larger context for the fetish idea, then, was not strictly commercial but was more comprehensive. It functioned as part of a grander social economy of exchange broadly conceived, establishing a mechanism of trust and obligation. So, for instance, treaties between Akan polities might be sealed by one of several elevated rituals that established obligatory bonds between parties. One of these rites, for instance, required smoking a pipe filled with a variety of material objects – soil, blood, human and nonhuman bones, feathers, hair, and so on. The oath taker, positioned opposite the pipe, would vow to the particular Orisha under pain of death to fulfill an obligation or vow and afterward walk around the pipe three times. Next, the priest would rub some of the material from the pipe onto the oath taker's body, then clip the nails from one hand and one foot of the individual and place those inside the pipe. These Africans often explained to European observers that the "fetish" (denoting either

---

[6] Ibid. Throughout this chapter, I employ the anglicized term *Orisha* and the phrase "Orisha-type" as a taxonomic concept for denoting the general category of indigenous religion in West–Central Africa. The term is based on the Yoruba word *òrìṣà*, denoting the extraordinary powerful beings who are the gods of the Yoruba pantheon. The *òrìṣà* of Yoruba religion emblematize the dynamic characteristics of power and ontology that African merchants presumed to be germane to the extraordinary beings with whom they sought communion. Most importantly, the *òrìṣà* comprise properties of spirit *and* matter, not one to the exclusion of the other. Readers should not interpret my use of *Orisha* as extolling or exceptionalizing Yoruba culture to the exclusion of other indigenous cultures, just as one should not necessarily equate describing African religion using the Latin-derived term *spirit* (from *spiritus*) with privileging Western European culture. The finer point here is that specific African concepts and terminology can legitimately have a broader application, as do European cultural concepts. This approach is inspired by Dianne Diakité's persuasive account of what she terms "classical African religion." See Dianne M. Stewart, *Three Eyes for the Journey: African Dimensions of the Jamaican Religious Experience* (New York: Oxford University Press, 2005), 8 and passim. Among the definitive studies of Yoruba religion informing this conceptualization is that by Jacob Olúpònà, *City of 201 Gods: Ilé-Ifè in Time, Space, and the Imagination* (Berkeley: University of California Press, 2011).

the Orisha or the essential, powerful matter or both) resided in the pipe, although this description of the object was clearly not meant reductively; the fetish was never conceived as confined to a particular locus.[7]

In the early 1500s the German author Valentim Fernandes, who spent the latter part of his adult career in Lisbon, recorded the experiences of several Portuguese merchants. Their accounts, rooted in extensive familiarity with West African culture, point to the legitimate role that material culture enjoyed at the center of the region's cultic life. Fernandes noted that the Wolof Kingdom, for instance, had been deeply influenced by the expansion of Islam. The materiality that defined the region's culture significantly shaped the practice and experience of Islam. The king, nobles, and lords of the Wolof, he notes, were Muslims. But Fernandes calls the majority of the Wolof "idolaters" (*ydolatras*), typical of the European Christian discourse applied to explicate religion in West Africa. Fernandes's informant was especially struck by the prolific sacred items that the itinerant Muslim preachers from the northern region of Morocco manufactured and sold to the local Wolof population.[8] Like the crucifixes that were so prolific among Christians, these sacred objects (often referred to as "amulets" by present-day scholars) were virtually always worn to ensure constant protection. Known as *bolsas*, they typically consisted of a leather pouch containing verses from the Qur'an, which might also be combined with feathers, hair, and other objects whose confluence in the pouch would stand as a potent analogue for the thick exchange that was occurring on multiple levels in Guinea Africa. So common was the leather pouch containing Arabic verses that the seventeenth-century Jesuit priest Manuel Álvares noted the Portuguese officially banned the sale of paper to their West African clients in an effort to stamp out this so-called idolatry. Thus, it is clear that these missionary preachers of Islam employed the pouches as a means of promoting Islamic conversion.[9]

---

[7] Bosman, *New and Accurate Description of the Coast of Guinea*, 146–51.

[8] In reference to these Muslim preachers, Fernandes employs both *bischerijs* and *bisserijs*. See Valentim Fernandes, *Description de la Côte Occidentale d'Afrique (Sénégal au Cap de Monte, Archipels) par Valentim Fernandes (1506–1510)*, ed. Théodore Monod et al. Centro de Estudos da Guiné Portuguesa, Memórias, no. 11 (Bissau: Centro de Estudos da Guiné Portuguesa, 1951), 4–8.

[9] Ibid., 8. Fernandes writes: "Estes bisserĳs fazẽ nomeas em mourisco e os lançã aos negros ao pescoço, e assy aos seus cauallos." Translation: "These priests make amulets written in Arabic, and they place them on the necks of the Blacks and also on those of their horses." Monod's edited version of Fernandes's work provides both the original Portuguese and a French translation. I have made use of both the Portuguese and French for producing this and subsequent translations into English.

This use of pouches was so common among peoples of the Mandinga nation that Portuguese writers employed the terms *feitiçaria* and *mandinga* interchangeably. Throughout the Lusophone Atlantic world, in fact, Africans (typically enslaved) were subject to prosecution by Inquisition authorities for using *bolsas de mandinga* ("mandinga pouches" or "fetish pouches"); such was the case for Luis de Lima, a slave of African descent born in Ouida. Luis was prosecuted and interrogated for manufacturing a sacred pouch that he sold to the Christian man who enslaved him. Portuguese Christians made frequent use of these sacred items. In Lisbon, in fact, African Muslims sold them to European Christian clients whose pluralist pragmatism led them to seek spiritual protection through the agency of these sacred objects. This was not first time European Christians had used such pouches. But the African presence in Portugal caused a rapid proliferation in the use of *bolsas* by the seventeenth century.[10]

André Donelha of Cape Verde, the Portuguese merchant who wrote of Gaspar Vaz, described the Manes of sixteenth-century Sierra Leone as being without faith (*fé*) and not belonging to any religious sect (*seita*).[11] It is evident that Donelha meant they did not belong to a recognizable

---

[10] James H. Sweet, *Recreating Africa: Culture, Kinship, and Religion in the African-Portuguese World, 1441–1770* (Chapel Hill: University of North Carolina Press, 2003). Roger Sansi-Roca, "The Fetish in the Lusophone Atlantic," in *Cultures of the Lusophone Atlantic*, ed. Roger Sansi-Roca et al. (New York: Palgrave, 2007), 24. James H. Sweet, "Slaves, Convicts, and Exiles: African Travellers in the Portuguese Atlantic World, 1720–1750," in *Bridging the Early Modern Atlantic: People, Products, and Practices on the Move*, ed. Caroline A. Williams (Farnham, Surrey, UK: Ashgate, 2009), 193–95.

[11] Donelha writes of the Manes, "Não têm seita nem fé." Donelha's language is likely shaped by the language of schism and Reformation that rocked the world of Western Christendom during his time. Religious factions proliferated throughout Europe. Donelha found nothing in West Africa that closely resembled this factional denominationalism. Moreover, although other English translators have rendered *fé* as religion, it is important to keep in mind that European Christians of the seventeenth century were only beginning to conceive of an anthropological (i.e., universal) category of religion in the sense familiar to present-day readers. For instance, the English cleric and bibliophile Samuel Purchas introduced this mode of interpreting non-European cultures to English readers in 1613 in his *Purchas His Pilgrimage*. Purchas was keenly aware of the novelty attending his use of the term *religion* to refer to a global phenomenon and to describe cultic behaviors that had previously been designated as idolatry or paganism by Christian, Jewish, and Muslim authors. For this reason, he went to great lengths to argue for what was at the time an eccentric use of the term. Purchas was a contemporary of Donelha. The point is that it is clear that Donelha encountered among the Manes what he perceived to be rituals of worship or veneration, which present-day readers would call "religion." Donelha called this "idolatry." See Anthony Vieyra Transtagano, *A Dictionary of the Portuguese and English Languages*, vol. 1 (London: J. Nourse, 1773), s.v. *religiam*, *sect*, and *seita*.

institution of Christian faith, for he clearly interpreted their use of sacred matter as worship and cultic behavior. In fact, this is precisely why he accused the Manes of idolatry, reporting that "they worship pots into which they put feathers which they then sprinkle with the blood of hens which they kill so that the feathers stick to the blood, and the pot is covered with feathers outside and in. They also fashion many idols of wood, in the form of men or monkeys or other animals."[12]

Donelha's explanation of the use of clay pots containing the blood and feathers of chickens demonstrates the vast disconnect between the materiality of certain Christian observers and that of practitioners of African indigenous religions. Donelha saw these pots as "mere things." But the Manes of whom he wrote, like other Africans of the region, took as the object of veneration the extraordinary beings and the divine power that lay at the heart of their theology of matter and spirit. When the Manes manufactured these cultic artifacts, they were consecrating matter to render it consonant with the spiritual power they believed undergirded all of life and to which they sought recourse on their own behalf. Donelha might have engaged religion among the Manes with greater comprehension. After all, the missionary was well versed in the European Christian rubric of sacramentalism, which accorded to *things* the ability to embody the power and reality of the spiritual or divine realm – thus the use of holy water; the Eucharistic elements; and the prolific use of altars, relics, and the like.

Donelha's description of what he calls "idols" is also striking.[13] He noted that the Manes called these objects *corfis*, from the Tamne *korfi*, meaning "spirit or spiritual power." They placed these *corfis* at strategic

---

[12] See André Donelha, *Descrição da Serra Leoa e dos Rios de Guiné do Cabo Verde*, cited in "Document 19: Relations Between the Coastal Peoples of Upper Guinea and the Cape Verde Islands," in *The Portuguese in West Africa, 1415–1670: A Documentary History*, ed. Maylin Newitt (New York: Cambridge University Press, 2010), 81–82. Of major importance in Donelha's account, as in those of other writers, is his distinction between worshipping "idols" and worshipping things (i.e., the clay pots). There are, in other words, three layers to this early Portuguese discourse about African cultic practices. First is the claim of idolatry – typically objects fashioned to resemble people or animals. Second is the claim that Africans worship things in distinction from idols. And third is the charge of witchcraft. In other words, inchoate are the diffusions of materiality that would become more explicit in the work of Charles de Brosses, as I discuss later in this chapter.

[13] Donelha writes: "Também fazem muitos ídalos" (meaning, "they also make many idols"). The manufacture of such objects is precisely the type of activity that Christian observers would seize upon to represent African religion as diabolical and particularly as witchcraft (*feitiçaria*).

locations – near villages or beside roads – to provide protection from danger or to bring auspicious results. The Portuguese merchant was especially struck by the sheer variety of uses to which the Manes applied *corfis*, including petitioning for good weather, ending famine, and ensuring military victory. Those disappointed by the failure of the *corfis* to effect good results, he explained, might "throw the idols down and beat them and make new ones," or they might "implore them, caressing them." The Manes also made offerings of food such as meat or rice to appeal to the *corfis*. This economy of exchange was a central aspect of theology in the Orisha religions of West Africa. Moreover, the manufacture of sacred objects was in no way an obstacle to their efficacy as sacred matter within the context of cultic ritual and behavior. But this theological subtlety was lost on Donelha. He easily concluded, instead, that the Manes, like the other peoples of Guinea Africa who followed their indigenous religions, were simple, intellectually obtuse, and thus so unsophisticated as to worship *things* instead of the Christian god whom Donelha presumed was the maker of all things.[14]

The use of a clay pot containing the blood and feathers of a chicken was also common in the sixteenth-century Wolof kingdom. Contemporary observers noted both this use of the clay pot as an altar for making prayers and the common use of a fetish worn about the neck by Wolof clients who purchased horses. It was not unusual, in fact, for these to be placed around the necks of horses, highly prized animals whose individual value easily exceeded that of a half dozen slaves.[15] The profitable trade in horses among the Wolof was also marked by another frequent ritual in which a Muslim cleric would write a blessing on a wooden slate and then wash the letters into a container of water that the horse was given to drink. The power of this blessing was literally incorporated into the body of the newly purchased animal. This helps to explain the expansive trend in West Africa of associating literacy (particularly of Muslim clerics and missionaries) with ritual power.[16]

[14] See Donelha, *Descrição da Serra Leoa e dos Rios de Guiné do Cabo Verde*, cited in Document 19, "Relations Between the Coastal Peoples of Upper Guinea and the Cape Verde Islands," in *Portuguese in West Africa, 1415–1670: A Documentary History*, ed. Maylin Newitt (New York: Cambridge University Press, 2010), 81–82.

[15] According to Valentim Fernandes, who wrote an early sixteenth-century description of West Africa, a single horse cost fourteen or more slaves. See his *Description de la Côte Occidentale d'Afrique*, 8, note a.

[16] Fernandes, O *Manuscrito de Valentim Fernandes*, cited in "Document 18: The Wolof Kingdom at the End of the Fifteenth Century," in *Portuguese in West Africa, 1415–1670*, 76–78.

The early sixteenth-century author Fernandes also provided a striking account of a "universal idol" – a widely venerated deity – that associated the serpent with divine power.

From Sierra Leone [going] towards the River of Palmas, among the Tempe people, there is a country called Hatschinel, where there is found a universal idol for all the country [*ydolo vniuersal de todas estas terras*] and that they call *tshyntrchin*, and which is found inside a village, in a forest, one-third of a mile from a village called Catell, which has sixty inhabitants. This idol is found in the middle of the forest; the trees that are located in its vicinity are cut; the biggest, under which it is found, is made into a shade so that [the idol] is always sheltered from the sun. This idol is a slab of sculpted wood that has a human appearance and the height of a man. It has a spear in hand and is dressed in shirts of a colored cloth coming from the inside, and it has a cap of red cloth on its head. It has some rings of gold in its nostrils and ears. On her head, she wears a cornaline [stone] of great size as jewelry, and some people come from very far to visit this idol and offer it goats and chickens for sacrifice. This idol has a priest or cleric, a position that is passed down within the same family. A most ancient lineage, it is he who is the priest. This lineage is called *tangomas*. The priest lives in the village. And when the pilgrims come to visit this ... great idol, they [come] to the village and they call the priest. And they give him their offerings: some goats, some chickens, or a little gold – 7 or 8 grains, more or less. And soon the priest with the offering goes to the idol and speaks to it as if it were a person. At the entrance of the forest, before entering it, the priest yells: "Who is there? I am about to enter." In understanding, the snakes recognize him and they know that he is not coming empty-handed, and they go toward the place from where the voice is coming to him up to the said idol. The priest informs him that a man – from whatever place or village – makes him an offering and asks him to relieve a sick person, a prisoner, or give him a blessing, or deliver him from evil (a curse), etc. And, in ending the prayer, he kills the goat or the chicken at the idol's feet, onto which he pours the blood. From the forest come the serpents that live in the forest of the blood of sacrifices. They are very big, sometimes they are up to ten feet in length and the girth or plumpness of two palms [in height], and they drink this blood.[17]

This account parallels numerous others that describe the veneration of extraordinary beings who were associated with serpents or who were believed to manifest materially as living, flesh-and-blood creatures. At the same time, the wooden sculpture of this widely revered shrine was also understood to be the locus of the spiritual entity to whom the priest addressed himself and to whom faithful clients made offerings in exchange for blessings, restoration of health, relief from captivity (a growing problem with the rapid expansion of the slave trade), and so on.

[17] See Fernandes, *Description de la Côte Occidentale*, 100–102.

Among the more vilifying portrayals of religion in the regions of Atlantic commerce is that of the Jesuit missionary Manuel Álvares, who wrote of religion in Cape Verde. Writing around 1615, Álvares opposed the formidable persistence of West African religion on this Atlantic archipelago that the Portuguese had settled during the 1400s. The Cape Verde Islands were officially Christian, a consequence of Portuguese settler colonialism. In reality, however, most of the people there were Africans, largely enslaved. The strategic value of the islands lay in their proximity to the West African coast, their tropical climate, and their arable soil. These were ideal conditions for the Portuguese to create a massive slave labor force that was an overture to the plantations that were to feature so centrally in the Americas. So, what was often called a Christian land (this was Gaspar Vaz's description of Santiago, the largest of the Cape Verde Islands) was in fact no less complex and polycultural than other Atlantic geographies.[18]

And this was precisely the problem for Álvares. In his desire to structure a purist society, he regarded West African religion as witchcraft (*maleficium*). Those Africans who employed medicines made from local flora, he claimed, were dangerous because they infused their victims with sensual desire, something he called *maleficium amatório* (love-craft). In contrast to this was *maleficium venefacio* (poison-craft) – poisoning victims to either kill them or make them severely ill. He listed infertility as yet another consequence of witchcraft. He saw African religion among the slaves of Cape Verde through the lens of diabolism, attributing the forms and agency of their religion to evil spirits – minions of Satan – who he claimed supplied knowledge of herbal properties to African practitioners. Álvares claimed that even the devil himself (in Christian myth, the powerful archenemy of the Christian high-god) personally appeared in the home of one Wolof woman who seemed to have controlled part of the sex trade in Cape Verde. The priests and missionaries of Cape Verde evidently enjoyed considerable autonomy and arranged for sexual relations with African women through the services of this woman, who recruited young girls into the trade. The woman, Álvares claimed, personally entertained the devil in her home at night and worshipped him by constructing an altar of a bowl of water surrounded by candles. In his zeal, Álvares even asserted that those entering into the sex trade under

---

[18] Manuel Álvares, *Etiópia Menor e Descrição Geográfica da Província da Serra Leoa*, ch. 24, excerpted in "Document 44: Maleficium and Its Forms," *Portuguese in West Africa, 1415–1670, 175–77*.

her tutelage were required to become servants of the devil, worshipping him as he appeared physically in the woman's home and paying reverence to him. On feast days, claimed the missionary, the "entire scum of the island" danced around the dish-and-candle altar. Using a style of discourse highly characteristic of the repressive propaganda that targeted suspected Christians in Europe, he claimed this revelry was followed by the young women having sex with the devil himself in the woman's home. For Álvares, diabolism explained the opulence of these women, who then wore fine clothes and enjoyed an enviable level of financial status (they were maintained by the European men who underwrote their employ). Such material excess, however, was merely the grounds for buttressing his claim that these African women had sold their souls to the devil. Sex, indeed, was at the core of the economic exchange operating in Afro-European commerce. And the actual historical events that Álvares grossly distorted (by rendering them as diabolical) in all likelihood included a process of sexual initiation that constituted traditional rites of passage.[19]

Dueling Revelations and Atlantic Exchanges

In this context, we can appreciate more fully the role of materiality in religious dynamics of the Kongo State. Few histories of religious change were as tumultuous, sudden, and socially disruptive as that of the Kongo State in the fifteenth and sixteenth centuries. Unlike any other region of West Central Africa, as we have seen, the Kongo State officially adopted Christianity as its imperial cult in the early 1500s, a development that immediately crystallized long-standing tensions between this new Christian religion and the region's established indigenous religion. And yet, the instantiation of Christianity in the Kongo State was achieved strictly through the internal agencies of Kongolese officials in response to Portuguese missionaries. In the typical style of precolonial African states, the Kongolese monarch (*Mani Kongo*) was both the head of state and the official religious authority. So, in addition to administering the business of the empire, the *Mani Kongo* also officiated over the cult of powerful beings, including ancestors. This meant serving as the most visible human actor negotiating between the worlds of the living and the ancestors, the living-dead.[20]

---

[19] Ibid.
[20] Gondola, *History of Congo*.

The *Mani Kongo* easily recognized the rich opportunity for establishing profitable trade with the visitors, learning of their Christianity and acquiring superior weapons technology to repress rebellions. Conversely, the Portuguese expedition hoped to expand the religious domain of the Portuguese empire. The problem was that the Portuguese had now met with a much older, more powerful empire that would not be dominated in any simple fashion. But they shared an interest in cultivating prosperity, and that was more than sufficient to ensure the mutuality of collaborative interests. In 1485 the Portuguese began to pursue Christian conversion more assertively. The *Mani Kongo* entreated European officials to supply architects, masons, agriculturalists, and other arbiters who might infuse the Kongo Kingdom with the styles and manufactures of European culture. To the delight of the Portuguese, the Kongolese monarch also requested holy water for baptism.[21]

Within a decade, in 1491, King João II of Portugal sent to Mbanza Kongo yet a third missionary caravan, comprising priests of the Franciscan and Dominican orders in addition to soldiers, as well as masons and carpenters, at the invitation of the *Mani Kongo* Nzinga a Nkuwu. In that same year, Nzinga a Nkuwu, along with a limited number of officials, was baptized into the Catholic Church. To signal his new affiliation with Lisbon, moreover, he adopted the name of the Portuguese monarch, João II. Just one month later, on June 4, 1491, the Kongolese queen did the same, adopting the name Eleanor in honor of the Portuguese queen. Joining her in baptism was Nzinga Mvemba, who governed the Nsundi province. It seems clear enough that the Kongolese royalty, whose native religion already emphasized fidelity to the deceased and consecration in exchange for assistance from the spiritual realm, saw this initiation into Christianity as yet another means of accessing the favor of powerful spirits. In fact, they were reluctant to allow too many other officials the privilege of initiation into the new cult, lest their special advantage be diluted.[22] For the next fifteen years Catholicism flourished as a legitimate religion of the state, buoyed by royal affiliation yet increasingly at odds with the traditional cult.[23]

---

[21] Wyatt MacGaffey, "Europeans on the Atlantic Coast of Africa," in Stuart B. Schwartz, *Implicit Understandings: Observing, Reporting, and Reflecting on the Encounters Between Europeans and other Peoples in the Early Modern Era* (New York: Cambridge University Press, 1994).

[22] Ibid.

[23] Gondola, *History of Congo.*

Conflict with indigenous religion steadily intensified. Whereas Nzinga a Nkuwu had operated in the pluralist style of Orisha-type religions, Afonso I vied for a European paradigm of established religion rooted in Christian identity and a principle of devotional scarcity. In strictly official terms, there was now no room for devotion to the ancestors and *minkisi* (the plural form of *nkisi*). In a manner not entirely unlike that of ancient Christianity's ascent to hegemonic status in fourth-century Rome, the new cult of Kongolese Catholicism ceased to be merely legitimate; it now became the only legal religion. All else was now illegitimate in the eyes of the state. Over the ensuing decades, in fact, state officials harried by European missionaries privileged attempts at Portuguese orthodoxy and sought to marginalize priests of indigenous religion.[24]

The indigenous religion of the Kongolese comprised theologies and ritual practices rooted in the power of *minkisi*. These were the powerful beings to whom the Kongolese devoted their prayers, sacrifice, and homage in return for divine protection, revelation, health, and general auspices. As one form of Orisha-style devotion, native Kongolese religion linked devotion to *minkisi* to the veneration of ancestors. These ancestors varied, of course, from one region to another and even from household to household. As in popular forms of European Christianity, the Kongolese attributed an array of capacities to the deceased, especially those holding great social power during their lifetimes. Individual Kongolese families sought guidance and protection from their living-dead, enacting a cosmology that likewise undergirded public, state-level rituals of religious observance and spiritual obligation. In other words, this indigenous religion had also been the official, established, imperial cult. For this reason, as Kongolese state officials become more aligned with Christianity's monotheistic ideology and its political economy of singularity, the resulting efforts to persecute and purge indigenous religion and local priests from their established positions of power generated bitter upheaval and religious violence.[25]

The Antonian Movement

The simultaneous conflicts and symbiosis between Kongolese indigenous religion and Kongolese Christianity were especially evident in the famous

---

[24] Ibid.

[25] Young, *Rituals of Resistance*. John K. Thornton, *The Kongolese Saint Anthony: Dona Beatriz Kimpa Vita and the Antonian Movement, 1684–1706* (New York: Cambridge University Press, 1998). Ras Michael Brown, *African-Atlantic Cultures and the South Carolina Lowcountry* (New York: Cambridge University Press, 2012).

Antonian movement of the early 1700s. This movement of religious renewal was led by the young, charismatic Dona Beatriz, who claimed to be possessed by Saint Anthony, Christianity's popular patron. From 1704 until her execution in 1706, Dona Beatriz and her supporters brought new life and energy to a preexisting movement that had been inspired by the elder woman Apollonia Mafuta. The movement aimed to reunify what had become a divided kingdom stricken with civil war. This political objective, according to both women, was a direct command from the Christian deity, and it involved challenges to existing state and ecclesiastical authority.[26]

Dona Beatriz was born in 1684 during the reign of the regional monarch Pedro IV in the eastern Kongo, near the towering Mount Kibangu (see Figure 2.1). Her entire life was marked by the kingdom's civil wars and ceaseless instability. Because Dona Beatriz's family was of royal lineage, they were among the more established and politically influential of the town's residents. They were not particularly wealthy, but the fact that they owned slaves (likely captives of war from distant lands) and employed clients to manage household chores indicates they were far better off than the town's poorest citizens. Even before her teenage years, Dona Beatriz had earned tremendous respect for being spiritually gifted and attuned to the world of extraordinary beings. Hence it was assumed that she would become an *nganga*, a professional Kongolese medium whose job was to communicate with the Orisha-type beings and powerful dead ancestors on behalf of the living.[27]

As a teenager, Dona Beatriz was initiated into the Kimpasi Society. This exclusive association was created by *banganga* (plural of *nganga*) when a community was suffering from anything of major importance. And the violence from seemingly unending civil wars, uncertain supply of material goods, frequent loss of family members in battle, and general social instability created difficult and painful challenges for everyone. The Kimpasi Society typically initiated new members on the verge of adolescence, which was the case with Dona Beatriz. During this process, Dona Beatriz was bound with cords along with the other initiates. After slipping into unconsciousness, the neophytes were revived but now under the influence of an *nkita*, a possessing spirit. Unlike in other forms of possession, the *nkita* did not overwhelm the *nganga* but began a permanent residence within the host, endowing the individual with exceptional

---

[26] Thornton, *Kongolese Saint Anthony*, 108, 109.
[27] Ibid., 7–19, 53–57.

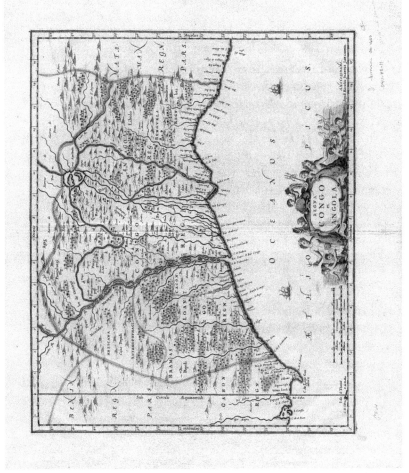

FIGURE 2.1. This seventeenth-century map of West Central Africa, created by the Dutch cartographer Jan Jansson (1588–1664), shows the Kongo Kingdom and the Angola Kingdom as they were situated just decades before Dona Beatriz was born. Note that the north is oriented toward the left end of the map. *Source*: The Melville J. Herskovits Library of African Studies and Government and Geographic Information and Data Services at Northwestern University.

abilities to communicate with other spirits. As established within indigenous religion, revelation (through divination, visions, and possession
speeches) was the means for delivering divine guidance and correction.
And the *banganga* were central to providing this service.

Unlike Christianity, Kongolese indigenous religion institutionalized
religious authority for both women and men; there was nothing remarkable about women becoming *banganga*. This fact produced ongoing
conflicts with the ecclesiastical priests. The strictly male priesthood of
Christianity regarded women as inherently and ontologically incapable
of embodying religious authority. This meant that ecclesiastical efforts to
repress indigenous religious dissidents in the Kongo (particularly as workers of diabolical spiritual power or witchcraft) resembled the gendered
nature of witchcraft repression in Europe and its settler colonies. Like
the Portuguese and Jesuit priests before them, the Kongo's Capuchin friars constantly represented themselves as impartial instruments of purely
righteous, divine authority who simply desired an authentic Christianity.
But this ineluctably meant excluding women from the newer Christian
notion of ritual and spiritual authority, a practice that stood in sharp contrast to the indigenous understanding of religion and gender.

For Dona Beatriz, working as an *nganga* signified no conflict with
the Kongo's established Christian cult. In contrast to European priests
and missionaries, most Kongolese Christians embraced the services of the
banganga as coherent with other Christian spiritual work. This should
not be taken to mean, however, that Kongolese Christianity was ecumenical or universalist in ideology. Far from it. The binary exclusivism
of Christianity was absorbed early in the history of the kingdom's imperial adoption of Catholicism. In Dona Beatriz's own day, for instance,
Kongolese Christians typically viewed Africans of the surrounding
nations as "heathens" because most of these others did not live under the
rule of a Christian state.[28]

But the dissension animated by the Christian–heathen binary also
governed relations within the Kongo Kingdom. European priests who
worked in the Kongo had always viewed the far more numerous, indigenous *banganga* and other nonecclesiastical spiritual experts as a threat
and complained that they encouraged the mixture of Christianity and
indigenous religion. The situation was further muddled by the fact that
Portuguese priests themselves had instigated a tradition of claiming
that indigenous Kongolese religion already contained divinely revealed

[28] Ibid., 17.

knowledge about the "true" Christian deity. This was a familiar practice among European missionaries in Africa, Asia, and the Americas. It enabled them to claim that any beneficent religious power experienced by prospective converts was the work the Christian deity. Significantly, this strategy validated indigenous religion at some level, and it necessarily encouraged what European priests condemned as religious impurity.[29]

For all its complexity as a distinctly African form of Catholicism, however. Kongolese state religion was still Christian, and as such it thrived on the ideology of monotheism, producing a vilifying alterity. This manifested most aggressively through the persecution of indigenous religion as "fetish religion" or "idolatry." The indigenous secular priests were in long-standing tension with the priests that Lisbon provided to the Kongo. The fact that Lisbon had been supplying priests to the Kongo soon became an explosive source of hostility between the two empires. After all, the Kongo Kingdom was no Portuguese vassal. It was a formidable hegemon, autonomous and more powerful than Lisbon. By the early 1600s, the two states reached a solution: Italy, viewed as a neutral party, would supply priests to the Kongo's provinces. And so it came to be that Italy's Capuchin order of friars, which had begun one century earlier as a splinter group of Franciscan monks, became the staple of European-trained priests in the Kongo Kingdom.[30]

The first of these Capuchin priests arrived in 1645. By the time Dona Beatriz became a professional spiritual expert, the Italian priests were a familiar, if widely dispersed, presence throughout the kingdom. By 1699 they had established a hospice at Kibangu, in the vicinity of Dona Beatriz's home. In return for the priests' political support of King Pedro, the regional monarch assured the Capuchins of protection and financial support and provided them differential treatment. These Capuchins, unfortunately, immediately set upon the local Kimpasi Society, claiming that the professional class of *banganga* were servants of Satan. The priests soon destroyed two Kimpasi Society houses, first vandalizing the structures and then setting them ablaze. Although many local residents defended the *banganga*, the priests knew they had the backing of the king, so they were openly strident in their offensive. The priests even went

[29] John Thornton, "The Development of an African Catholic Church in the Kingdom of Kongo, 1491–1750," *Journal of African History* 25, no. 2 (1984): 147–67.

[30] Richard Gray, *Black Christians and White Missionaries* (New Haven, CT: Yale University Press, 1990), 38–42. Thornton, "Development of an African Catholic Church in the Kingdom of Kongo, 1491–1750."

so far as to excommunicate all members of the Kimpasi Society. This had a traumatic impact on Dona Beatriz. It compelled the young ritual expert to abandon her work as an *nganga*. Instead, she began to regard the professional work of the *banganga* as a corrupt practice and retreated to a private life.[31]

The most consequential development for Dona Beatriz's professional career was instigated by a severe illness she experienced in August of 1704. Despite the spiritual and medicinal intervention of multiple experts, she teetered on the brink of death. At that point she saw Saint Anthony appear before her – dressed as a Capuchin monk – and enter her head. She was immediately healed. But she was also possessed by the saint. As with the *nkita* that had possessed Dona Beatriz on her initiation into the Kimpasi Society, this new possession was an indefinite one. And it propelled her to a level of unprecedented influence as a religious leader and public critic of the political disarray that plagued the kingdom.[32]

Dona Beatriz immediately began to challenge the conventional theology of Kongolese Christianity. The young prophetic leader openly castigated the European priests for claiming Christianity was an essentially European religion. She argued that it was authentically Kongolese. The Christian faith, she claimed, began with the Blacks of Kongo. In fact, she urged, Jesus himself was a Black Kongolese man who had been born in São Salvador (Mbanza Kongo), the historic Kongolese capital city. She explained that Europeans claimed he was a White person to hide the truth from the Kongolese. And whereas Kongolese Christians had prioritized veneration of Jesus and Mary ("the Virgin" who gave birth to the human-god Jesus), the newly possessed Dona Beatriz now preached that Saint Anthony, already the most popular in the Kongo, was "restorer of the Kingdom of Kongo," "the door to Heaven," and "above the Angels and the Virgin Mary." Saint Anthony, in fact, was "the second God." At the same time, Dona Beatriz promoted a theology of material religion that echoed the problematic claims of the Capuchins who a few years earlier had destroyed Kongolese Christian objects. In an effort to enforce Christian purity, she destroyed some divine statues that commonly adorned public and private sacred spaces – she derided these as idols – and even denounced the Christian paraphernalia derived from Europe. Her hostility to the materiality of Kongolese religion (whether

---

[31] Thornton, *Kongolese Saint Anthony*, 72–75.
[32] Young, *Rituals of Resistance*, 60–61.

Christian or more fully indigenous) resonated with broader trends in the elite conception of Western Christian orthodoxy.[33]

Above all, the intersection of politics and religion defined the movement and enthralled Dona Beatriz's followers. She preached that Saint Anthony, as an all-powerful celestial deity, desired reunification of the Kongo Empire and that King Pedro, the regional monarch, should immediately reoccupy the old capital city of São Salvador to assert a unifying rule over the old empire. But when she addressed the curious King Pedro, he refused to heed her message. As a political calculation, he figured, the timing was premature (other rival monarchs were equally aspiring). He did, however, protect Dona Beatriz from the locally stationed European priest Bernardo da Gallo. This friar was immediately antagonized by Dona Beatriz's critique of the Eurocentric theology of the White priests. In his view, the Kongolese had no claims to Christianity except through the lineage of Europeans, whom he viewed as the true arbiters of the faith. There were no Black saints. In fact, the friar claimed, Dona Beatriz was possessed by the devil himself, or at least by one of the demons, the minion spirits that served the devil.[34]

Although she was disappointed that King Pedro turned a deaf year and was shaken by Bernardo's denunciations, Dona Beatriz continued to build a following. In October of 1704 she traveled north to visit a rival monarch, King João II of Bula. He was even less tolerant of her message than was Pedro. By that time, however, Dona Beatriz was performing miracles of healing. She even claimed to heal infertility, a boast that resulted in a rapid increase of followers. Although the political elites of Kongo generally rejected the Antonian movement, it was steadily embraced by the average Kongolese. They were all devastated by war and were eager to see an end to the political instability that inspired a vicious cycle of war, death, disease, hunger, displacement, and despair. By November of 1704 Dona Beatriz had led a massive group of settlers to the old capital city on her own. They took up residency in São Salvador as a grassroots strategy of restoring the old imperial unity. Meanwhile, more followers from afar were attracted to the movement and continued to arrive. Apollonia Mafuta, widely revered for her authority, joined the resettlement as an avid supporter of Dona Beatriz. By early 1705 the city, although still in ruins, was busy and alive with throngs of new residents.

---

[33] Thornton, *Kongolese Saint Anthony*, 116–17.
[34] Young, *Rituals of Resistance*, 61, 62. Thornton, *Kongolese Saint Anthony*, 120–24.

Around this same time Dona Beatriz began sending out missionaries of the new movement to spread its message and accelerate its growth.[35]

In addition, she created a new version of the Salve Regina that became known as the Salve Antoniana. This creedal prayer institutionalized and reinforced the distinctive theology of the Antonians. The Salve Regina emphasized the primacy of the Virgin Mary as an intercessor and object of devotion. The Salve Antoniana, by contrast, emphasized that most Kongolese had yet to grasp the authentic meaning of the Salve, that the Christian high-god desired pure intention (sacramentalism and good works were not salvific), and that intercession – most notably that of Saint Anthony – was central and efficacious.[36]

When Antonians asserted that sacramentalism was not efficacious, they were declaring that even baptism failed to fulfill the Christian high-god's desire for pure intentions. As a result, thousands of Kongolese began to forgo the rite. The implications were deep and politically charged. Because only European priests (in this case, the Capuchins) were allowed to perform baptism and typically visited any given town or village no more than once per year, the Capuchins normally devoted most of their time in villages to administering this sacrament. In fact, it was not unusual for a single priest to baptize hundreds of people in a single day. The new Antonian theology, for this reason, seems to have elaborated on the Capuchin derision of Kongolese materiality to spiritualize religious efficacy in a way that actually undermined the institutional authority and relevance of European priests throughout the Kongo.[37]

This Antonian skepticism toward religious matter and ritual was by no means thoroughgoing, however. The very body of Dona Beatriz was treated as religiously powerful. Her followers considered themselves blessed by the mere act of sitting in her presence as she received her meals. The food crumbs that escaped her mouth – even the trickles of water that she cleverly released from her lips as she imbibed – were immediately grasped by the eager hands of her devotees who surrounded her in hopes of receiving a miracle from physical contact with this human host of Saint Anthony.

In the end, the Antonian movement was undermined by Dona Beatriz's jealous rivals – the regional kings themselves – through the very issues of materiality and embodiment that concerned Antonian theology. Dona

---

[35] Thornton, *Kongolese Saint Anthony*, 140–43.
[36] Ibid., 116–17.
[37] Thornton, "Development of an African Catholic Church," 165.

Beatriz had twice become pregnant after she developed an intimate relationship with a young man who became a steadfast follower and companion. She was able to abort the first two pregnancies, but the third time she carried the pregnancy to term and gave birth to a son, whom she named Antonio. Emulating the austerity of the European priests, Dona Beatriz had elevated chastity as the ideal form of piety within the movement, and she had purposely modeled for her devotees a life of sexual abstinence. This chastity, however, was itself a product of Christian patriarchy, which encoded sexuality and reproduction as manifestations of ontological distance from the Christian deity. It was just one ideological rationale for the exclusively male priesthood. In June 1706, when Kongolese state officials learned that Dona Beatriz had given birth to a child, they arrested her as part of a state campaign against the Antonian movement. With insistent prodding from the Capuchin priest Bernado de Gallo, the Kongolese state charged her with witchcraft and heresy. In a tragic turn, the once powerful religious leader now renounced what she viewed as a sinful fall into sexual temptation, and she futilely begged the mercy of the court. The prosecuting officials only took pleasure in her desperation, however, and quickly sentenced Dona Beatriz to death. The next month, in July 1706, Kongolese state officials executed the young woman, still in her early twenties, by publicly burning her alive.[38]

To her credit, Dona Beatriz had built her movement around a cause much larger than herself. So, not even her execution brought an immediate end to the Antonian struggle for reunification. Kongolese unity would be restored only after many more years of struggle. But by creating one of the earliest religious movements rooted in a specifically Black theology, Dona Beatriz created a permanent, indelible critique of Eurocentric Christianity in the region. Moreover, she helped to legitimize the self-conscious reform of Christianity along lines that made it more responsive to the political interests of Kongolese sovereignty vis-à-vis the stubborn efforts of European priests who presumed an exclusive right of European control over Kongolese religion. The Antonian movement also embodied a powerful challenge to the strictly patriarchal code of ecclesiastical authority. Christian priesthood was available only to men. But Kongolese *banganga* included women and men. And as both Dona Beatriz and Apollonia Mafuta demonstrated, indigenous religion

---

[38] Kongolese state officials initially condemned Dona Beatriz, her male companion (João Barro), and Apollonia Mafuta to death. But Apollonia Mafuta was allowed to live. Dona Beatriz and Barro were burned together. See Thornton, *Kongolese Saint Anthony*, 168–80.

institutionalized the religious authority of women, who continued to operate at the center of Kongolese religious life.[39]

European Christian Materialities

Few aspects of the fetish concept were more bewildering to European merchants than the radically material understanding of spiritual agency and social power in African indigenous religion. Their business travel in West Central Africa was devoted to scouting potential business partners or conducting trade in slaves, gold, and ivory. For this reason, early European observers of so-called fetish religion were typically merchants, and they played a disproportionate role in shaping the concept of the fetish, a fact that would be of no small consequence for the enterprise of representing and conceiving of Black religion in Guinea Africa. Put bluntly, White Christian merchants conceived of physical objects as merely material in the realm of commercial exchange. Unlike those Western Christians who participated in materialities that characterized popular religion in Europe, these merchants understood matter through the rationalities of capitalism and market commoditization, which stood in sharp contrast to theories of matter that shaped the theology of Orisha-type religion.

Of chief importance to understanding the fetish paradigm is the concept of extraordinary, Orisha-type powerful beings. These were individually attuned and governed specific dimensions of social concern. This plurality is what enabled the view that specific people could be loyal to specific Orisha (often problematically termed "fetishes") and be bound in such individual ways as to be guarded or protected. This is also what confounded those Europeans who wanted to apply the monotheistic idea to make sense of indigenous African theology. One must be careful, however, not to rarify African materialities into some obscure realm beyond any resonance with European Christian views of matter and power. After all, Protestant European authors repeatedly compared African "fetish" religion to Catholicism, Europe's most dominant form of Christianity. It was apparent to them that explicit parallels existed between the religion of the fetish and Western Christian materiality.

We have seen how African theories of matter operated to constitute theologies of indigenous religion. But what was the larger background of materiality for European observers? To speak of religious matters within the context of Western Christendom is to map a genealogy of materiality

---

[39] Ibid., 177–84.

at once similar to yet distinct from that of African materiality.[40] On the one hand, it is clear from the historical record that Western Christians regularly perceived matter itself as possessing organic qualities. Material objects were capable of behaving as – of in fact becoming – living creatures. This was especially true of Eucharistic objects such as wafers and altar cloths. But this view extended far beyond such specific objects to include virtually all matter. On the other hand, among the most prolific of European clerical writings from the period of emerging Afro-Portuguese commercialism is that genre devoted to condemning this mass phenomenon of "living objects" in Christian materiality. It is no exaggeration, in fact, to say that the battle for clerical control over religious matter was itself chief among the religious matters that consumed the intellectual elites of Christendom.[41]

For this reason, a few caveats are in order. First, we must distinguish between the actual religion of Christendom's masses and the ideology of Christian intellectual elites, whose religious pronouncements increasingly sought to constrain the expansive economy of Christian materiality in ways that enhanced their own power as arbiters of access to the extraordinary divine community that Christians conceptualized – angels, demons, saints, and gods. Second, instead of being cynical toward elites, we should recognize the gap between these two poles – Christianity as it was actually conceived and practiced by most of Christendom and the powerful elites who sought to control it – as the productive social force it was. The normative claims and boundaries of clerics, although in the minority, powerfully shaped the valence and experience of Christian materiality, and on this score, as I discuss later, immense, consequential differences existed between African materiality and that of Christianity. Third, any contemporary assessment of what experts have termed "medieval" Christianity must interpret with nuance the dominant trends of Christian materiality. Earlier histories of medieval Christianity have often interpreted the growth of Christian interiority – that is, the turn to privileging cognitive modes of Christian experience – as the declension of Christian materiality, as a retreat from focusing on things, on material

---

[40] There is of course no single "European materiality," just as there is no single "African materiality." There are, rather, paradigms and trends dominating among myriad varieties, and it is in reference to these that I employ the respective rubrics.

[41] Caroline Walker Bynum, *Christian Materiality: An Essay on Religion in Late Medieval Europe* (New York: Zone Books, 2011), 15–25. Charles Freeman, *Holy Bones, Holy Dust: How Relics Shaped the History of Medieval Europe* (New Haven: Yale University Press, 2011). Louise M. Bishop, *Words, Stones, & Herbs: The Healing Word in Medieval and Early Modern England* (Syracuse, NY: Syracuse University Press, 2007).

objects. But for all it was, mysticism was not the decline of materiality. In fact, the varieties of Christian interiority usually functioned to affirm the long-standing and enduring materiality of Christianity.[42]

As it happened, the rise of commerce between African and European states coincided with a pitched battle over the very nature of matter in Western Christendom. In the fifteenth-century world of Christian experience, humans were believed capable of becoming nonhuman animals (werewolves), living entities could come into being in the absence of organic progenitors (spontaneous generation), the living communed daily with the living-dead, and the very act of physical contact with consecrated matter (e.g., holy water or Eucharistic elements) could confer on a person or a "thing" qualities of the gods, such as healing power.[43]

The central importance of Christian shrines is instructive on this score. Pilgrimage to a cathedral or a shrine was a long-standing tradition in Christianity. Once a relic became popular, the site that housed it was destined to attract Christian devotees who aimed to make physical contact with these material objects. Among the most visited pilgrimage sites in Iberia was Santiago de Compostela, which since the 800s had boasted the relics of James the brother of Jesus. Of equal fascination to Christian travelers were the bones of St. Isidore of Seville, in whose honor a church was dedicated. The port city of Barcelona in Catalonia was proudly home to the shrine of the martyr Santa Eulalia. And in close proximity was the shrine of the Virgin at Montserrat, whose pilgrims were attracted by prolific accounts of miracles.[44]

Throughout Western Christendom, in fact, the bodily remains of saints and martyrs and pieces of the cross used to execute Jesus evidenced the degree to which Christianity was in great measure a material religion, one whose devotees invested physical objects with meanings and power that afforded access to immanent, immediate, and unmediated religious experience. Christian materiality was both an officially sanctioned and

---

[42] Bynum, *Christian Materiality*. Walker gives the example of the fifteenth-century Christian theologian Nicholas of Cusa (Kues), whose promotion of spiritual interiority was itself a response to the massive prominence of sacred objects among his contemporaries. See also Patricia Dailey, *Promised Bodies: Time, Language, and Corporeality in Medieval Women's Mystical Texts* (New York: Columbia University Press, 2013). Joel Hecker, *Mystical Bodies, Mystical Meals: Eating and Embodiment in Medieval Kabbalah* (Detroit: Wayne State University Press, 2005).

[43] Patrick J. Geary, *Living with the Dead in the Middle Ages* (Ithaca, NY: Cornell University Press, 1994). Freeman, *Holy Bones, Holy Dust*. Bynum, *Christian Materiality*.

[44] Raúl Gómez-Ruiz, *Mozarabs, Hispanics, and the Cross* (Maryknoll, NY: Orbis Books, 2007). Bernard Reilly, "Pilgrimages," in *Medieval Iberia*, 650.

authorizing practice. At the heart of these material practices, moreover, was the wide-spread European Christian interest in objects as living things, as sites of generation and decay. As a result, common objects might weep blood in mimesis of the crucified savior Jesus.[45]

Christian materiality, furthermore, was not so much a consensus as a contested economy of intensively encoded experience, interests, and authority. Emblematic is the career of John Wyclif (1324–1384), the English philosopher of Oxford University whose anticlericalism ultimately led to his removal and condemnation as a heretic. Wyclif viewed the hierarchy, power, and wealth of the church as an affront to true faith. His work as a translator of Christian scriptures into the vernacular (English) was amplified by his conviction that reading scripture and intellectually apprehending the message of the Christian gospel obviated intermediaries such as priests, shrines, relics, and the like. Although he died under the shadow of official censure and condemnation, Wyclif's denunciation of the Christian use of sacred objects influenced generations after him, particularly the Lollards, an English reform sect that attracted the ire of Archbishop of Canterbury Thomas Arundel. In 1409 Arundel penned his *Constitutions* in which he defended the dominant Christian materiality that governed devotion, particularly pilgrimage to shrines and devotion to relics. The Lollards condemned such veneration as idolatry that enmeshed the believer in bondage to "dead images that neither thirsteth nor hungered nor feeleth any coldness neither suffered disease." The archbishop contravened such attacks by ordering the clergy to instruct parishioners that the material objects of the faith, such as crucifixes and images of saints, were to be "worshipped with processions, bowing of knees, offering of frankincense, kissings, oblations, lighting of candles and pilgrimages, and with all other kind of ceremonies and manners that have been used since the time of our predecessors."[46]

Salvation and redemption manifested in terms both lofty (eternal, for the soul) and quotidian (e.g., temporal relief from infertility or disease). Western Christendom, moreover, was in every sense a political order that thrived on aspirations of ritual uniformity and theological coherence, the elusiveness of which seemed only to heighten the stakes of pursuit. It stood

---

[45] Freeman, *Holy Bones, Holy Dust*, 15–23. Gómez-Ruiz, *Mozarabs, Hispanics, and the Cross*, 28–30. Geary, *Living with the Dead*, 78–82.

[46] G. R. Evans, *John Wyclif* (Oxford: Lion Hudson, 2005), 161–80. Margaret Aston, *Lollards and Reformers: Images and Literacy in Late Medieval Religion* (London: Hambledon Press, 1984). Freeman, *Holy Bones, Holy Dust*. Thomas Arundel, *Constitutions* (1409), quoted in Freeman, *Holy Bones, Holy Dust*, 221.

in appreciable contrast to Eastern Orthodoxy, which had been shaped by a dual system of leadership under both an emperor who governed the political domain and a chief bishop (patriarch) whose authority extended formally to leading the church. Western Christendom knew only a unified system of rule. The bishop of Rome – the pope – was at once ruler of both the church and the political realm. This fact radically altered both the desire for strict homogeneity throughout Western Christendom and the means available for attempting to enforce such unity. In the mid-fifteenth century, contemporaneous with the inception of Afro-European commerce, the pope sent Nicholas of Kues (Cusa) to administer reform in Germany. Among Nicholas's concerns was the rapid increase of dynamic objects such as Eucharistic hosts that bled. These objects commanded the attention of the faithful and generated an increased following for the elites in possession of these sacred objects. The fact that this Christian materiality enjoyed normative status and characterized the mainstream of Christian experience only further fueled his ire. He denied that the blood of the Christian savior could possibly exist as a physical object because the body of the resurrected Jesus was a spiritual one – glorified and invisible.[47]

His treatise *On Learned Ignorance* (*De docta ignorantia*) drew the most attention, however, and established Nicholas as a major voice of mystical interiority. The determined theologian argued therein that the infinitude of the divine rendered the Christian deity ultimately unknowable to the finite mind of believer. Faith, he asserted, not apprehension, was the habitus of devout Christians. Of equal importance was the transcendence of the messiah. Nicholas, of course, was careful to emphasize the bodily death and resurrection of Jesus. But like the first-century Christian author Paul of Tarsus, who promoted a theology of a spiritual body for the exalted messiah and his resurrected believers (1 Corinthians 15), Nicholas argued that, after his resurrection and ascension to the heavenly realm, Jesus' spiritual existence overwhelmed his physicality. Thus, those who sought to find him in physical objects were guilty of misplaced trust, for there remained no physical body of the Christ upon which material relics might become feasible. But Nicholas's mysticism was prescriptive, not descriptive of the major landscape of the Christian faith. His was a minority theological perspective.[48]

---

[47] Bynum, *Christian Materiality*, 87–92.
[48] Ibid., Morimichi Watanabe et al., eds., *Nicholas of Cusa: A Companion to His Life and His Times* (Burlington, VT: Ashgate, 2013), 3–6, 81–86.

In fact, over the next century, the sheer volume of shrines and the monetary and spiritual economy to which they were linked became an established point of contention among religious reformers and their opponents. The Dutch priest Desiderius Erasmus (1466–1536) was strident in denouncing the shrines devoted to Mary, the mother of Jesus. Erasmus's historical research persuaded him that early Christians had exaggerated traditions about Mary and had unduly elevated her to a super-human status. His contemporary Martin Luther (1483–1546), whose name is synonymous with the Protestant Reformation, began his reform activism by focusing on the sacred sites of devotion and pilgrimage that were so numerous throughout Western Christendom. His *Letter to the Christian Nobles of Germany* (1520) specifically targeted indulgences, pilgrimages, and shrines. Luther attacked the use of material objects of devotion as pure idolatry, a mockery of the salvation that he insisted was effected uniquely and exclusively by divine grace. Christian materiality in its popular and elite dominance represented for him and other Reformers a diabolical distraction from spiritual salvation, a form of satanic and priestly deceit that he claimed led well-meaning Christians to worship things instead of the divine.[49]

Objecthood and Colonial Knowledge

The consternation over material objects, in fact, would become the central pillar in Protestant anti-Catholic invective. In the age when European Christians were encountering those they called "heathen" races through the network of Atlantic empires in sub-Saharan Africa and the Americas, the relation between faith and objects began to take on a special hue. It became possible for Protestants to charge Catholics with idolatry in a different key – with a semantic layering imbued with the dark hues of putatively inferior races – and none were more emblematic of the antipodes of Western Christendom than the Black people of Guinea Africa. The colonial contacts and exchanges among Europeans, Native Americans, Africans, and Asians generated a particular imperial mode of parsing materiality to embolden ontological claims about religious and racial others. This was an especially productive outcome of the European ethnographic accounts that detailed White Christian encounters with so-called heathens. All of these encounters, moreover, emerged under the political order of colonialism, whose imperative for rationalizing differential power relations privileged racialization as the essential strategy for

---

[49] Freeman, *Holy Bones, Holy Dust*.

masking domination with the veiling ethos of naturalness. What becomes discernible, in other words, is how the fetish as a materiality – a mode of conceiving things or objects as such – aligned with the imperatives of Atlantic colonialism to fashion particular social textures and institutions. What is revealed in consequence is the linkage of objecthood and empire.[50]

When we attend to empire in terms of objects and taxa, we can appreciate the way aesthetic judgment and objecthood itself – achieved through assertions about the nature of matter and qualities of objects – constitute imperial formations. In the lands of Guinea Africa, Western Christians invested in anthropomorphism as a choice weapon to undermine or deride African materialities as manifested through so-called fetish religion. In elite European discourse – especially among the Portuguese, Dutch, and English mercantilists who most frequently interfaced with African indigenous religion – the normative materiality conceived of images as static objects devoid of a life of their own. Matter could not be spirit, and spirit strayed nary a step beyond the boundaries of its abode in the abstract economy of the soul's salvation. Even this soul and its salvation (or perdition) were burdened by the expanding rationalities of novel orders that promoted a rarified, highly textualized mode of religious engagement. In the crass grammar of European Protestant Reformers, reading the Bible (conceived not as a material object but as a hieroglyphic of the Christian gospel's gnosis/noetic import) effected salvation from the vile futility of idolatrous religion and from the condemned state of fallen humanity.

The Atlantic networks of colonialism yielded a distinct, novel domain of intellectual production by creating a new problem for conceiving materialities. This is precisely what the historian of religion Charles H. Long has thoughtfully termed "contacts and exchanges." By this, Long has marked the dynamic and fructuous nexus of markets and colonial encounters – commerce and empire – differentiated by an imperial axis of social power. The asymmetry germane to colonialism by no means negated the multiplicity of actors involved. The sheer variety of agencies constituting Atlantic networks, in fact, was precisely responsible for producing new social meanings, novel political structures, and neoteric institutions of economic exchange that have held congress under the fraught rubric of modernity.[51]

---

[50] W. J. T. Mitchell, *What Do Pictures Want?: The Lives and Loves of Images* (Chicago: University of Chicago Press, 2005).

[51] Charles H. Long, "African American Religion in the United States of America: An Interpretative Essay," *Nova Religio: The Journal of Alternative and Emergent Religions* 7, no. 1 (July 2003): 16–17. Also, Charles H. Long, *Significations: Signs, Symbols,*

The Portuguese were the first White Europeans to participate in direct trade relations with Black merchants in Cape Verde, the Canary Islands, and West and Central Africa. The latter required Europeans to perform particular rituals to execute trade agreements and specific purchases of commodities in good faith. Their business rituals involved swearing on material objects (made of cowry shells, leather, stones, gold, and the like) that appeared quite mundane and arbitrary to Europeans. African merchants themselves saw these objects as mundane, at least out of context. But as contractual instruments of obligation, these material manufactures became powerful matter that bound the parties involved through sworn oaths and threatened to punish with malevolent force those who reneged or cheated. This practice evidenced Africans' use of the fetish to establish relationships of mutual obligation. More broadly, local Africans typically confounded European sensibilities of commodity by associating personal or religious meanings with articles of trade in excess of what should have been by European commercial standards a matter of strictly economic value.[52]

Of central importance was the manner and ease of manufacturing religious matter, an issue that is reflected in both the etymology and ideology of the term "fetish." The Christian ideology of the fetish took shape in the politicized repression of practices termed "magic" and "witchcraft." Medieval Christians employed multiple terms to designate illegitimate manufactures within the context of magic or witchcraft: *factura*, *maleficium*, and *sortilegium* were employed interchangeably in this way. The *Siete Partidas*, which the Christian monarch Alfonso X (1221–1284) composed in the thirteenth century as the uniform law of Castile, employed *fechura*, *fechizo*, and *fechicero* to signify manufacture, the object made, and the manufacturer (or witch), respectively. By the end of the twelfth century, Portugal became a sovereign kingdom and began to construct its distinctive language. Influenced by the bulls of Pope John XXII that targeted witchcraft, European Christian polities witnessed an increased formalization of the grammar of witchcraft to effect its repression. This

and Images in the Interpretation of Religion (Aurora, CO: The Davies Group, 1986), 85–87. Long, "Religion, Discourse, and Hermeneutics: New Approaches in the Study of Religion," in *The Next Step in Studying Religion: A Graduate's Guide*, ed. Mathieu E. Courville (New York: Continuum International Publishing Group, 2007), 183–197. Long, "Bodies in Time and the Healing of Spaces: Religion, Temporalities, and Health," in *Faith, Health, and Healing in African American Life*, ed. Stephanie Y. Mitchem and Emilie M. Townes (New York: Praeger, 2008).

[52] William Pietz, "The Problem of the Fetish, IIIa: Bosman's Guinea and the Enlightenment Theory of Fetishism" in *Res: Anthropology and Aesthetics* 16 (Autumn 1988): 115.

trend was helped along when Portugal translated the *Siete Partidas* in the fourteenth century. Most commonly, Portuguese writers employed *feitiço* (fetish), *feitiçero* (witch), and *feitiçaria* (witchcraft). At the time of initial contact between West Central Africans and the Portuguese, Lisbon had been under an anti-witchcraft edict for several decades. Implemented by João I in 1385, the law sought to extirpate idolatry and a range of practices that clerical authorities viewed as illegitimate efforts to deploy or control divine power or to achieve material advantage or success by brokering oaths with Satan. Those living in the newly formed kingdom of Portugal were prohibited from making or using fetishes or illegitimate manufactures (*obre de feitiços*). King Joao's edict, in fact, marked the official rise of anti-witchcraft legislation in Portugal.[53]

This was the backdrop for the Portuguese *feitiço* that came to designate both the material manufactures in West Central Africa and the social system of meanings and obligations through which the fetish circulated as a manufactured object. Influenced by Europeans, Africans themselves began to use variants of the Portuguese-derived term "fetish" to reference these objects and the spiritual power they portended. Within a few decades of initial Afro-Portuguese contact, "fetishism" became employed to denote the larger cultural system that enabled meanings about the fetish. Remarkably, however, given the earlier usage of *feitiço* to signify and prosecute witchcraft, European observers, in their commercial relations with African merchants and observations of the larger set of social practices throughout West Central Africa, did not mainly or usually examine the fetish as witchcraft, although this semiotic dimension would permanently linger. Rather, they clearly deployed the category in novel ways because they recognized they were encountering a new and different problem of materiality. What anthropologists would eventually study as fetishism emerged as the putative subject of intellectual inquiry tasked with decoding a complicated assemblage of rituals, legal regimes, and cultic institutions that bewildered European observers while constituting a generative, cantankerous, and racializing grammatology of knowledge and power.

Problems of materiality were not new to Europe. As we have seen, Christian theologians had previously dealt with politically charged, dissenting materialities through the problem of witchcraft and idolatry.

---

[53] William Pietz, "The Problem of the Fetish, II: The Origin of the Fetish" *Res: Anthropology and Aesthetics* 13 (Spring 1987): 34. Roger Sansi, "Sorcery and Fetishism in the Modern Atlantic," in *Sorcery in the Black Atlantic*, ed. Luis Nicolau Parés and Roger Sansi (Chicago: University of Chicago Press), 19–23. Sweet, *Recreating Africa*, 161–64.

But these two themes, as engaged by European Christian elites, evoked some particular emphases that stood in contrast to the structure and sociality of the fetish discourse that marked African indigenous religions. For instance, when Christian officials condemned idolatry among Europeans, they derided it as the system of obligation or loyalty to a god worshipped by pagans in lieu of devotion to the proper celestial beings (viz., Jesus, his divine sire, the Virgin, and the saints) sanctioned by the Christian church. Ecclesiastical repression of witchcraft was quite different from that of idolatry, particularly because church officials identified witchcraft and its manufacture of potions or binding oaths with another entity of supreme importance in Christian mythology – the devil or Satan. In other words, witchcraft did bear on a materialist concern in the purview of authorities, but it extended significantly beyond that concern. The ideological representation of witchcraft, thus, did not compose the problem of matter in a fashion identical to the problem of the fetish, although these were clearly related. It might be tempting, furthermore, to attribute the nature of fetish discourse to the ideological excesses of the Christian Inquisitions. Portugal, however, did not yet have an Inquisition during the rise of its trade relations with African indigenous religions. And the Inquisition established by Ferdinand and Isabella in 1478 was chiefly concerned not with witches but with Jews and Arab-Muslim converts to Christianity. Thus, the Christian concern with witchcraft and idolatry does not fully explain the European Christian fascination with the fetish of African commerce.[54] Accounting for the specific dimensions of the problem of the fetish, instead, requires attention to a different set of social formations, particularly the racialization that emerged through Atlantic colonialism and the tactics of materiality that attend the transoceanic corporatism tied to the global trafficking of African peoples.

The Fetish and Racialization

The enterprise of studying religion has been embedded within the nexus of empire and race. The long history of this nexus, moreover, becomes ever more apparent in the larger context of Atlantic colonialism. Race and empire were conjoined through a complex configuration of social practices and bodily disciplines in the Mediterranean world of the fifteenth and following centuries.[55] It is paramount to appreciate that racialization was

---

[54] William Pietz, "The Problem of the Fetish, II: The Origin of the Fetish," *Res: Anthropology and Aesthetics* 13 (Spring 1987): 34, 35.

[55] I emphasize "Mediterranean" to signal that what is typically conceived as European/ Western history was already emerging under the productive constraints of Muslim

actually occurring through religious formations of subjectivity and political authority. Whereas the discursive rationale and representation of race have varied, the specific structure of racialization derives through colonialism as a specific form of governing. Race, succinctly, *is* colonial governance administered through the frame of essential differences among human populations. It is why, for instance, Michel Foucault referred to his account of the racial state as a study of internal colonialism. As a political formation, race is made through granting to some people the privilege of membership in the political community (the body politic) of the ruling polity while ruling others as a dominated population *perpetually* and *ineluctably* alien to that governing polity. Because the empires of the Mediterranean world were grounded in religious genealogies – Christian and Islamicate empires – religion became a racial formation. For White Europeans, Christianity was an essentialist constitution that was "in the blood" in both a literal and a figurative sense. In this context, the principle of *limpieza de sangre* (purity of blood) was among the most formidable and pervasive of juridical and theological principles in Europe and throughout Europe's colonies in the Americas. This was by no means limited to the Iberian realm. Medieval Anglophones had only just begun to amplify preexisting strategies for incorporating religion into the body, of mapping it through blood lineage during the rise of Atlantic empires. The expulsion of Arabs and Jews throughout Europe (including England's anti-Semitic expulsion that began in 1290 and that lasted until the eighteenth century) is a clear testament to the powerful alliance of ecclesiastical and politico-juridical strategies that defined social belonging and legitimate residence on the basis of White European identity. Although England was late to the enterprise of colonizing the Americas, the White settler colonies that expanded unabatedly under British imperial auspices quickly incorporated the racial-religious segregation of civil society (although this did not usually apply to bedchambers – interracial sex has long been a prized prerogative of White supremacists who championed separation of the races). The very constitution of Whiteness was manifested through rarifying the concept of a body politic *qua* an exclusive, racial ethnos. The trans-Atlantic slave trade and European expansion into the Americas, moreover, intensified this imperative and inspired novel

empires as well as those of European Christians. In addition, African states were beginning to establish trade relations with Europeans, a process that would eventually shift to primarily trade in African slaves. The point is that the emergence of what historians now recognize as the Atlantic world of exchanges and colonial contacts, was not a strictly Western procession but comprised Native American, African (including Islamicate), and European Jewish and Christian trajectories.

strategies of racial domination, increasingly within the crucible of White settler colonialism.[56]

Fetish religion qua the "religion of the Blacks" (or, alternatively, Guinea religion) was quintessentially a colonial production of race. It brought together the older heritage of religion as a biopolitical, racial constitution in the Christian and Islamic empires (*limpieza de sangre*) with the new geographies of Atlantic exchanges and innovative logics. New to this context were the rationalities that shaped Atlantic slavery as a coherent enterprise – it became a hyperracialized form of commerce. Before the rise of Afro-European commerce, Europe's slaves were typically Whites. With the rise of Atlantic slavery, however, the body and nature of the slave in the Atlantic purview became Native American (in the Americas) and Black (in the Americas and in West Africa), then, more regularly, strictly Black. As in the earlier colonial orders of domination that shaped polities of the Mediterranean world, religion functioned to constitute colonial meanings of *differential essence* – fundamental ontologies articulated through a plurality of domains such as political dispositions (Blacks do not have states), intellectual capacities (the mind of the Guinea African is delusional and child-like), aesthetic sensitivities, climate-induced sensibilities (Africans are lazy and prone to excessive sexual passions), phenotype, and linguistic bearings – that differentiated human populations into essential, differential types (races).[57] This applied to Christians and Jews under Muslim

---

[56] Barnor Hesse, "Racialized Modernity: An Analytics of White Mythologies," *Ethnic and Racial Studies* 30 (July 2007): 643–63. Barnor Hesse, "Im/Plausible Deniability: Racism's Conceptual Double Bind," *Social Identities* 10, no. 1 (2004): 9–29. Sherwin Bryant, *Rivers of Gold, Lives of Bondage: Governing through Slavery in Colonial Quito* (Chapel Hill: University of North Carolina Press, 2014). Geraldine Heng, "The Invention of Race in the European Middle Ages I: Race Studies, Modernity, and the Middle Ages" *Literature Compass* 8, no. 5 (May 2011): 315–31. "The Invention of Race in the European Middle Ages II: Locations of Medieval Race," *Literature Compass* 8, no. 5 (May 2011): 332–50. Gil Anidjar, *Blood: A Critique of Christianity* (New York: Columbia University Press, 2014). Michel Foucault, *Society Must Be Defended: Lectures at the Collège de France, 1975–76* (New York: Picador, 2003). Jonathan Schorsch, *Swimming the Christian Atlantic: Judeoconversos, Afroiberians and Amerindians in the Seventeenth Century*, 2 vols. (Leiden, the Netherlands: Brill, 2009).

[57] Concomitant to this observation is the proposition that racialization predates the period of Atlantic slavery. The specter of slavery has deeply colored efforts to theorize race to the point where scholars regularly treat race as a product of slavery and consequentially identify the origins of racialization with the trans-Atlantic slave trade. But race is not the product of slavery per se. As one aspect of the architecture of empire, its origins lie with the colonial relation of power. It is colonialism, in other words, not merely slavery, that has formed the chief context for racialization. See Barnor Hesse, "Im/Plausible Deniability: Racism's Conceptual Double Bind," *Social Identities* 10, no. 1 (2004): 9–29. See also Penny Von Eschen, *Race Against Empire: Black Americans and Anticolonialism,*

rule and especially to Jews and Muslims (even the Christianized conversos and moriscos respectively) living under the unrelenting, differentiating calculus of Christian domination. The latter was especially pernicious for its universalism that compelled non-Christians to convert while in practice denying the efficacy of that same conversion, perpetually regarding Jewish and Muslim converts as endemically insincere and secretively subversive of fidelity to Christian rulers. In the colonial crucible of race, these relations of governance rendered rational the domination of subjugated peoples as essentially different human populations. Racialization articulates and manages human differences – conceived as absolute and fundamental – to rationalize differential treatment. This differential is a relation of domination mystically represented through the more respectable idiom of absolute, fundamental human difference. This power relation, in turn, is fundamental to the political order of colonialism.[58]

Unlike previous formations of differential essence (racialization) in Mediterranean empires among Christians, Jews, and Muslims, however, the grammar of racialization that emerged in the wake of Afro-European commerce was articulated through reference to religious orders beyond the pale of Abrahamic religions. Despite the profound, centuries-old presence of Islam in West Africa, colonial observers of religion who constructed the elaborate discourses of religion and differential essence (race) had in mind what they called the religion of the fetish. In consequence, the invectives that Christian observers such as Willem Bosman or Philip Quaque (the African convert to Anglicanism) deployed to signify religion in Guinea Africa were intensified by an order of magnitude beyond the discursive derision of Catholics, Jews, or Muslims. One should not ignore, however, the productive complicity of anti-Catholicism in generating derisive claims about Black religion. Nor should one conclude that conflicts among peoples of the Abrahamic religions were less violent or murderous than those between Christians and practitioners of Orisha-type religions – one need only consider the Crusades, the Inquisitions targeting conversos, and the pogroms and expulsions by Christians against Jews and Muslims. The point here, rather, is that the invectives within Abrahamic religions were frequently mitigated through recourse to the category of heresy or theological error or even diabolism. Orisha religion

---

1937–1957 (Ithaca, NY: Cornell University Press, 1997), 153–59. In departure from Hesse's emphasis on the colonial tectonics of racialization as Europeanness versus non-Europeanness, I am emphasizing here the phenomenon of racialization in Christian and Muslim empires of the Mediterranean prior to the rise of Atlantic slavery.

[58] Heng, "Invention of Race in the European Middle Ages II," 332.

(*qua* the fetish), by contrast, became a domain for racialization outside of Abrahamic terms. Christians regularly perceived African indigenous religion to be unmitigated idolatry, the highest form of rebellion against the Christian deity. The religion of the fetish, in the Christian imagination, also constituted the category of the heathen, just as religion among American Indians functioned facilely to render Native Americans as servile adjuncts of Satan. This discourse of the fetish functioned as a racializing formation by rendering the Guinea African through a theological register as an essential type. The result was a semiotics of fundamental difference between the African and the European. In consequence, the heathen of Africa was not merely a wayward soul in need of theological correction. Rather, the heathen was a racial soul – or, alternatively, heathens were a race of souls whose particularity lay in being predisposed to diabolical delusions concerning efficacy (attributing causes to phenomenological effects) and divine ontology (polytheism). Thus, just as the Christian–Muslim–Jewish triangulation issued in racial practices before the rise of Afro-European commerce, so now the Atlantic discourse of the fetish achieved yet another vector of racialization that was to remain integral to the colonial discourse about African indigenous religion.

Corporatism, New Rationalities, and the Commodity Fetish

The theological interest of Christian clerics like Philip Quaque and of Portuguese priests and missionaries devoted to servicing the Kongo State's voracious agenda for Christianization devoted tremendous attention to fetish religion as a problem of idolatry. This discourse of idolatry, however, was not keen to produce new insights in the interpretation of culture. Rather, the most fascinating and productive ruminations about the fetish emerged within the ideological context and embodied spaces of Afro-European commercialism. For this reason, it is in the written communications of merchants that one finds the most productive concern with the fetish as a problem of materiality. More succinctly, the existential and material modes of commerce – of trade in the commoditized bodies of enslaved peoples and the exchange in commodities of gold, ivory, rum, weapons, and so forth – seized on the fetish as a problem of materiality and consequentially gave rise to new modes of accounting for human cultures, particularly religion as an anthropological category.

Understanding the changing materialities rooted in *commercial* discourse of the fetish requires attention to three major factors: (1) the rise of the corporation as a company-state; (2) the innovations of finance capitalism (e.g., bills of exchange) that conceived of value by spiritualizing what had been a relatively inert understanding of money (as the coinage of precious metal such as gold and silver); and (3) the exceptional capacity of commoditization to render Black people as valuable capital (assets) while tactically confounding the apprehension of their value as persons.

The Rise of the Corporation

The earliest corporations began as innovations on the older partnership model. These partnerships were constituted when merchants pooled resources to conduct a very specific set of business transactions of limited duration, typically to finance a single trade voyage. On completion of the voyage, barring major mishaps and losses, each merchant received back what had been invested plus a share of profits. Europeans commonly traded with merchants in the rest of Asia – particularly the Indian subcontinent – and thereby established a lucrative array of business relations that were marked by increasing competition both among European polities and within them. These partnerships were not incorporated, had no monopoly rights, and possessed no particular rights in international law. Rather, they were joint ventures only, trading on a joint account. With these partnership enterprises, not only active merchants but also passive investors were able to venture their capital, investing it in hopes of reaping a positive return. These passive investors, however, had no membership and did not participate in business decisions. By the end of the sixteenth century, Dutch merchants had grown impatient with the diminishing returns resulting from the rife competition among themselves. As a solution, the General States of the Netherlands consolidated these protocompanies in 1602 by a charter. The result was the Vereenigde Oostindische Compagnie (VOC) – the Dutch United East India Company. Because they were at war and saw the benefit of uniting these protocompanies to undermine the interests of Spain and Portugal, Dutch merchants heartily backed the initiative.[59]

---

[59] Giovanni Arrighi, *The Long Twentieth Century: Money, Power, and the Origins of Our Time*, rev. ed. (New York: Verso, 2010), 159–62. Niels Steensgaard, "The Dutch East India Company as an Institutional Innovation" in *Trade in the Pre-Modern Era, 1400–1700*, vol. 1, ed. Douglas A. Irwin (Brookfield, VT: Edward Elgar, 1996), 448–49. Peter A. Coclanis, *The Atlantic Economy During the Seventeenth and Eighteenth Centuries: Organization, Operation, Practice, and Personnel* (Columbia: University of South Carolina Press, 2005), 1–3.

Strictly speaking, what was amalgamated was not the capital but the leadership of the old partnership enterprises. Like so many profoundly consequential developments in history, moreover, this corporate creation was not intentionally designed to introduce new rationalities of profit or ontology or political order. Rather, quite by accident, the Dutch had stumbled upon a fundamentally different species of social institution by attempting simply to tame the rampant competition that depressed potentially bountiful profits. The initial VOC charter, termed at twenty-one years, did not even portend an indefinite existence. So, as a technical matter, the VOC was not permanently capitalized from the start; its investment capital was not truly anonymous. But the charter went far enough beyond the terms of the old partnerships that VOC corporate executives, with more than two decades at their disposal before needing to return investor profits, were as a practical matter unconcerned with pressures to generate short-term profit. Their primary concern was long-term profitability and the interests of the company itself, not the interests of individual investors. As a result, they operated the VOC as a permanently capitalized corporation.[60]

The results surprised and astounded the majority of the merchant community. The company's executive committee decided immediately in 1602 to abandon the peaceful, mercantilist paradigm of the old partnerships. Instead, they took on a more warlike, aggressive posture toward foreign states. Endowed with monopoly rights of trade and an unprecedented capacity to elevate the Dutch to international prominence, the VOC began to focus on how best to dominate other European competitor states in trade with Eastern polities. To defend its monopoly interests, substantial capital was devoted to building forts, maintaining militias, and arming vessels. Whereas merchants under the previous partnerships were beholden to Dutch foreign policy, the VOC had its own foreign policy. When in 1608 some investors organized to protest that their investments were being used for war and not trade, the executive committee turned a deaf ear. Their sights were set on an entirely new set of rationalities – of justifications and imperatives for operating a corporation as a distinct entity whose interests transcended those of any individual investor or even the class of investors. Jan Pieterszon Coen, the VOC governor-general at the time, wrote to his fellow company executives in defense of the VOC's aggressive foreign policy. Monopoly was the sure

---

[60] Arrighi, *Long Twentieth Century*, 130–42, 159–62. Coclanis, *The Atlantic Economy*. Steensgaard, "Dutch East India Company as an Institutional Innovation," 448–49.

means to profit, Coen emphasized. And the interest of profit far out-weighed the matter of cost, so long as the long-term result was a positive balance sheet. As he saw it, protecting the monopoly ineluctably meant investing in militarism.[61]

Those traditional investors protesting the VOC's seemingly incompre-hensible behavior can hardly be blamed for their confusion. They were accustomed to dealing with business partnerships. But this new corpora-tion was not merely an alliance of investors. It was its own entity. By char-tering a long-term corporate entity with such broad powers of foreign policy and militarism, the General States of the Netherlands had created a Frankensteinian behemoth that wed the familiar domain of business profiteering to the *reason of the state*. This meant political decisions and business decisions were made by the same executives. Protection costs were internalized and calculated rationally (e.g., based purely on profit motives). And rather than leveraging its monopoly powers to ensure short-term profits, the new corporation sought long-term strategies to control against sudden price fluctuations.[62]

Innovations in Finance

The rise of this novel entity, a veritable company-state, was no less than a watershed event that fundamentally transformed global commerce in the Americas and throughout Africa and Eurasia. The seventeenth cen-tury witnessed the emergence of numerous companies as the European metropoles raced to acquire the massive wealth to be had through corpo-ratism. England created its East India Company in 1600, and many oth-ers soon followed: the French East India Company (1604), the Plymouth Company (1606), the Virginia Company (1609), the Danish East India Company (1616), the Noordsche Compagnie (a Dutch whaling com-pany, 1614), the Somers Island Company (1615), the Gynney and Bynney Company (1618), the Massachusetts Bay Company (1629), the French Compagnie du Morbihan (1626), the Cent Associes de la Nouvelle France (1628), the West Indische Compagnie (1621), the Companhia da India Oriental (1628), and the Governor and Company of Adventurers of England trading into Hudson's Bay (the Hudson's Bay Company, 1670).[63]

---

[61] Steensgaard, "Dutch East India Company," 460.

[62] Arrighi, *Long Twentieth Century*, 159–62. Steensgaard, "Dutch East India Company," 445–46.

[63] Ibid., 113–14. Philip J. Stern, *The Company-State: Corporate Sovereignty and the Early Modern Foundation of the British Empire in India* (New York: Oxford University Press, 2011).

As the volume of trade expanded under corporatism, however, the VOC and similar entities faced the difficulty of transporting money over the extensive distances of global trade networks to fund the purchase of goods and payment of wages. The former demanded by far the greater share of currency. The confounding limitation of currency, of course, was its susceptibility to shortage. Precious metal was sorely needed for European trade with merchants in Africa, India, and other parts of Asia. No region consumed more metal currency than China. Its trade with European polities established a lasting pattern whereby European vessels traversed the seas laden with silver destined for China, returning with a range of products – most notably tea, silk, and spices – that commanded an eager and aggressive market in Europe. Throughout much of the history of capitalist Eurasia, in fact, China alone took in roughly half of all the silver shipped from the Americas and Europe in trade, a situation that chagrined European merchants and polities but delighted the Chinese.[64]

Although this trade imbalance with China animated much European vitriol, the most inhibiting difficulty for global commerce was not the absolute supply of precious metal but the difficulty of moving it about to pay for goods. It was not unusual for enslaved people as well as goods to sit in port for days awaiting the arrival of currency (or other commodities of exchange used to purchase slaves, such as rum and tobacco) so that the purchasing agent could take delivery. The most efficacious remedy for this was the creation of bills of exchange. These bills were promissory notes that ordered the bank of the purchaser to remit a designated sum of currency to the seller or to any other party in possession of the bill. Because these bills were transferrable, they could be passed from one party to another just as currency could be exchanged, with the important exception that they were incredibly portable (a small sheet of paper versus a freight container of silver or gold bullion). No longer did merchants closing on a deal have to await the arrival of cash or exchange commodities to complete their transactions. The exchange bills revolutionized the speed and ease with which global commerce was transacted.[65] Although immensely significant, bills of exchange were only one among

---

[64] Jelle C. Riemersma, *Religious Factors in Early Dutch Capitalism, 1550–1650* (Paris: Mouton, 1967), 43–46.

[65] Thomas Max Safley, *The History of Bankruptcy: Economic, Social and Cultural Implications in Early Modern Europe* (New York: Routledge, 2012). P. C. Emmer, "The Dutch and the Making of the Second Atlantic System," in *Slavery and the Rise of the Atlantic System*, ed. Barbara L. Solow (New York: Cambridge University Press, 1991), 75–96.

the vast number of important innovative instruments of modern finance. As Atlantic slavery increasingly dominated the nature of commerce, new financial tactics accrued in order to execute the practical demands of human trafficking. Transferability of shares of ownership, collateralized debt (the exchange in debt as a commodity), the principle of joint stock, and the use of capital as an explicit accounting concept (assets now appeared on balance sheets) all marked an important departure from the financial practices that had predated the rise of Atlantic empires and Afro-European commercialism.[66]

These changes effected a revolution in European materiality, the registers of which became more complex and regimented under the rationalities of capital and its market reasons. Value, for instance, became a more dynamic category that functioned with global parameters as monetary agents employed new instruments of accounting and finance to manage the new demands of Atlantic empire and commerce. And money, previously tied more strictly to the physical objecthood of currency, now became spiritualized, able to flow from one part of the globe to another, signified through material instruments (such as shareholder certificates of ownership or bills of exchange) that were understood to refer to nonmaterial forms of value. Thus ownership of a stock, discretely scalable in measures of currency, was understood to be identical to neither money nor the physical paper certifying ownership.

This *spiritualization* of money evolved simultaneously with the *secularization* of finance, a process especially evident from the expanding, open practice of extending loans at interest (usury). Medieval Christian economic doctrine prohibited usury; loans were interest free. Influential Christian writers such as Thomas Aquinas decisively condemned usury, as did virtually all Christian theologians of the era. For instance, medieval economic theory distinguished *societas* from *mutuum*; the latter was a loan, the former was a business partnership, and only the former was supposed to result in profit.[67] But whereas medieval Christendom strictly banned usury – ostensibly because it guaranteed profit despite the borrower's risk of loss – the seventeenth century witnessed the coexistence of theological proscriptions with secular permissiveness. In 1658 Dutch religious officials were deemed incompetent for adjudicating usury, a sentence they absorbed with surprisingly little fuss. And, by the eighteenth

---

[66] Arrighi, *Long Twentieth Century*, 131–2. Riemersma, *Religious Factors in Early Dutch Capitalism*, 63.

[67] Arrighi, *Long Twentieth Century*, 130–40. Riemersma, *Religious Factors in Early Dutch Capitalism*, 62–63.

century, finance capitalism had become one of the busiest engines of growth within the domain of global capitalism.[68]

Commoditization and Black Slavery

The utility exacted by bills of exchange is pristinely evidenced through their use to transact the purchase of the millions of Africans enslaved and transported to the Americas throughout the Atlantic slave trade. European slavers traded interest-bearing bills of exchange for liquid capital from investors in the European metropoles. They used this capital, in turn, to acquire by the hundreds people who had been abducted for enslavement and imprisoned within the fortified slave castles that trading companies operated in West Africa. They then transported these slaves to the Americas, where they were sold to other merchants who specialized in the high-volume trafficking of human chattel. Given the limitations of currency to underwrite these transactions, interest-bearing bills of exchange became the preferred monetary instrument. In effect, these middlemen purchased slaves on credit; the slavers operating their ships could later redeem the interest-bearing notes for hard currency.[69]

The complex combinations of finance and risk produced another development at once spectacular and perverse. Roughly 20 percent of those Africans forced into trans-Atlantic slavery during the 1500s and 1600s died during passage. Even when these death rates decreased slightly in the following centuries, they were rarely below 10 percent. It was a horrible death, and the sickness and agony preceding that death – festering in one's own and others' human waste, cramped into holds with too little room even to sit upright, an inadequate oxygen supply – exposed millions of men, women, and children to the most extreme experiences of physical and psychological torture.[70] Merchants and the companies that managed the coastal supply of slaves, however, viewed these matters through the lens of capital. As European merchants purchased slaves with borrowed money (i.e., underwritten by interest-bearing notes), the value of slaves, conceived through the rationality of market capitalism, became coherent strictly as a matter of collateralizing the loans. Both financiers and slave merchants sought protection against the risk of loss due to the death of captives during transport, the immediate burden of which fell on the

---

[68] Riemersma, *Religious Factors in Early Dutch Capitalism*, 79–80.

[69] Ian Baucom, *Specters of the Atlantic: Finance Capital, Slavery, and the Philosophy of History* (Durham, NC: Duke University Press, 2005).

[70] Herbert S. Klein, *The Atlantic Slave Trade*, 2nd ed. (New York: Cambridge University Press, 2010). Marcus Rediker, *The Slave Ship: A Human History* (New York: Viking, 2007).

merchants (the borrowers). The solution came in the form of yet another innovation in capitalist finance – life insurance for slaves. In the certain event that the slaver's volume of human cargo was decreased through deaths among the slaves, merchants who purchased insurance policies could collect remuneration from their insurers. The actual value of these human victims of slavery, thus, obtained strictly under the sign of the commodity, a tactic that amplified the strategies of dehumanization that racialization achieved in the Atlantic realm. The brutal consequences of this condition were not lost on slavers, who routinely preferred as a business practice throwing sick, diseased captives into the ocean to drown (if they were not first eaten by the sharks that regularly followed the slave ships), writing off the deaths as an insured capital loss and collecting on the policy on completion of the voyage.[71]

These three elements – the rise of the corporation, the innovations of European finance capital, and the commoditization of Black people (at once dehumanizing and value-generating) – elucidate the powerful concept of market rationalism that fundamentally shaped the encounter of European and African merchants to yield the discourse of the fetish. It is this complex of factors within the domain of racialization, not "irreducible materiality" of the fetish, that distinguished the fetish discourse as a novel problem.[72] The sheer imaginative nature of value is on full display in these elemental structures of capitalism – the foundation of commodity fetishism.

The market rationality of European capitalism masked the human, subjective relationships of the Atlantic system of empire and slavery by claiming that what was "really going on" concerned relationships not among people but among *things* – objects such as currency, credit, bills of exchange, risk, and insurance – all imaginatively conceived through the innovations of finance to enable the acquisition of wealth. Within the frame of market rationalism, at stake were not regimes of domination and brutality but reason, freedom, and the rational, disciplined pursuit of profit. There is arguably no more perverse, large-scale demonstration of this than the practice of representing the human beings in the holds of

---

[71] The *Zong* slave ship massacre of 1781 is perhaps the most notorious incident of this kind. See Baucom, *Specters of the Atlantic*.

[72] William Pietz's brilliant work on the fetish problem has met with criticism over his claim that the African fetish was distinguished by irreducible, untranscended materiality. But by evidence of his own account of African materiality, this seems not to have been the case. As Wyatt MacGaffey has argued, African materialism comprised historical origins and contexts for fetish objects. See MacGaffey, "African Objects and the Idea of Fetish," 123–31.

slave ships not as people but as capital assets – as things – whose value could be insured in the event of loss (in unmasked terms, human death or murder resulting from abduction, torture, and trauma). This was the crystallization of the new rationalities that undergirded the raiding, trading, and slaving company-states whose fortified slave castles dotted the coast of West Africa.[73] This formation oversaw the wedding of commerce to the reason of the state in the body of legal, fictive corporate entities that enabled new agencies for their human actors. As market rationality continued to materialize in the form of the company-state and its attending network of institutions (banks, forts, exchange or trading houses, and the like), European merchants encountering African materiality were pressed to make sense of this similar yet different image of matter and human relations. In this way, the reason of the market became at least as important for the emerging discourse of the fetish as the evolving theological traditions of Western Christendom.

Market Rationality in the Fetish Discourse

Predisposed by their own scheme of market reason and Christian theology, early European merchants recognized several types of value in the fetish cultures of West and West Central Africa. These were (1) religious or sacramental, (2) aesthetic-erotic, (3) commodifiable (i.e., possessing economic value), (4) medical or talismanic, (5) oath vehicles, and (6) technological.[74] European merchants were accustomed to recognizing only technical or technological use value (e.g., of textiles or weapons) and commodity value (e.g., of gold and ivory) as real; all else was putatively fantastical and delusional. For this reason, Europeans easily characterized African merchants and entire societies of Blacks in Africa as gullible and childlike (e.g., African merchants gladly traded gold for glass beads from Europe), beholden to fanciful illusions. European merchants were disturbed by not only what they called idolatry among Africans but also the fact that Africans gladly traded their gods or fetishes of gold for other goods such as glass or clothing.[75] This was an important difference between White mercantilists, such as Willem Bosman, and professional

[73] Baucom, *Specters of the Atlantic*, 80–112. Riemersma, *Religious Factors in Early Dutch Capitalism*, 63–80. William Pietz, "Fetishism and Materialism: The Limits of Theory in Marx," in *Fetishism as Cultural Discourse*, ed. Emily Apter and William Pietz (Ithaca, NY: Cornell University Press, 1993), 119–51.

[74] Pietz, "The Problem of the Fetish, IIIa: Bosman's Guinea and the Enlightenment Theory of Fetishism," *Res: Anthropology and Aesthetics* 16 (Autumn 1988): 109.

[75] Charles H. Long, "Indigenous Peoples, Materialities, and Religion: Outline for a Ne Orientation to Religious Meaning," in *Religion and Global Culture: new Terrain in the*

Christian clerics and missionaries, such as Thomas Thompson and Philip Quaque. The earliest Portuguese accounts of Guinea highlight fetishism and idolatry as the essential elements of religion among Black people. Later, the fetish itself became the singular essence of Black religion, and it would remain the preeminent marker of Black religion and African civilization (or the supposed lack thereof) in the Western imagination.

Black Atlantic Religion and Cultural Theory

From this specific history of market exchanges and colonial contacts emerged the theories of religion that would occupy Western intellectuals for centuries to come. Consider the Venetian slave trader Alvise da Cadamosto, who journeyed to the Cape Verde Islands and to coastal West Africa during the 1450s as part of the maritime exploration of the Atlantic waters south of Europe made possible by the pivotal support of Prince Henry of Portugal. On the basis of his encounters with local populations, Cadamosto produced what became a widely read, ethnographic treatise on West African culture. He appears to be the first of European writers to proffer the category of the primitive and, further, to identify Black Africans as members of the category.[76]

History owes a special debt to the English cleric and corporate propagandist Samuel Purchas (1577–1626) for linking the fetish discourse to the comparative study of religion.[77] Inspired by Richard Hakluyt, Purchas established himself as a prolific compiler of colonial travel narratives. More significantly, he developed one of the earliest theories of religion as a comparative, anthropological (i.e., universal) category in his *Purchas His Pilgrimage* (1613). Centuries before Friedrich Max Müller's *Religionswissenschaft* promoted the scientific study of religion, Purchas composed *Pilgrimage* to proffer a comprehensive theory of religion as a ubiquitous phenomenon rooted in a natural human desire for generating

Study of Religion and the Work of Charles H. Long, ed. Jennifer I. M. Reid (Lanham, MD: Lexington Books, 2003), 174–75.

[76] G.R. Crone, *The Voyages of Cadamosto and Other Documents on Western Africa in the Second Half of the Fifteenth Century* (Nendeln, Liechtenstein: Kraus Reprint, 1967). Newitt, *The Portuguese in West Africa*. Pietz, "The Problem of the Fetish, II: The Origin of the Fetish," 23–45.

[77] Purchas was employed as the public relations expert for the Virginia Company. Like other ministers in his capacity, he pitched the company's potential for profits to likely investors to raise capital. Purchas proved himself to be among the most effective philosophers of European colonialism. His most lasting legacy, however, was as a compiler of colonial travel narratives and as a theorist of religion. See L. E. Pennington, *The Purchas Handbook: Studies of the Life, Times and Writings of Samuel Purchas, 1577–1626* (London: The Hakluyt Society, 1997).

and participating in religious experience. For this reason, Purchas rejected the governing tendency in his day to dismiss non-Abrahamic religions as merely diabolical in origin. Purchas did not surrender his Christian supremacism, but he nevertheless argued that the religions of the world were derived from human constitution, which was ineluctably, naturally inclined to be religious. His intimate familiarity with the writings of colonial administrators, company men, and slave traders led Purchas to engage specifically with the category of fetish religion in his discussion of religion in Africa. Purchas built on the work of comparative geography to derive seven national-ethnographic regions of Africa: (1) Egypt, (2) Barbary, (3) Numidia, (4) Libya, (5) the land of "Negroes," (6) Ethiopia, and (7) the African islands. Several puzzling aspects of this division are immediately evident, not least of which is the fact that only the fifth – "the land of Negroes" – is an explicitly racial category; Egypt and Libya are the only extant nations listed, moreover.[78] Purchas was distinctive for explaining religion in the "land of Negroes" as "ethnike" religion. He employed this terminology to denote the nature of religion in Guinea Africa absent or apart from Christian, Jewish, and Muslim influences. He also rendered for his readers a discussion of pre-Islamic religion in West Africa, for which he depended heavily on the writings of al-Hassan al-Wassan (Leo Africanus). But the emphasis on "ethnike religion" seems to be his own intervention. The valence of "ethnike" religion for Purchas exceeded that of merely "heathen" or "idolatrous" religion; these other terms encompassed examples of false religion from biblical narrative and Greco-Roman antiquity. By the "ethnike" distinction, however, Purchas signified that "heathens" or "idolaters" of Guinea were different from those elsewhere. Concerning the peoples of Benin, for instance, Purchas claimed that circumcision "and other superstitions" among them were "more likely to be ancient Ethnike Rites" than Islamic, as the local peoples often observed these practices but denied being Muslims.[79]

Most importantly, Purchas amplified this notion of religious difference in Guinea Africa by inscribing meanings about racial Blackness through the discourse of the fetish. He entered the fetish discourse through his reliance on the narratives of Portuguese and Dutch writers. Cataloguing

---

[78] This is partly explained by recalling that the shift from the Mediterranean to the Atlantic geographical paradigm was achieved by conceiving of continents (Africa, Asia, the Americas), and these as essentially the loci of respective races. (This is why Europe would become imagined as a separate continent of the White race.) Purchas hereby demonstrates the early stage of Mediterranean attempts to construe an African continent, as opposed to merely the southern lands of the Mediterranean.

[79] Samuel Purchas, *Purchas His Pilgrimage* (London: William Stansby, 1626), 717–19.

varieties of fetishes and fetish rituals, Purchas identified "fetisso ceremonies" as the means of adjudicating accusations of marital infidelity. He explained that parents might cloak their young infants in a net of "fetissos" to prevent or cure a variety of illnesses. Various "fetissos" might be worn about the body, understood through "superstitious fancies" – "one is good against Vomiting, a second for Falling, a third for Bleeding, a fourth to make it Sleepe, a fifth against wilde Beasts, and so on. The Devill they guard against through the use of Fetissos... Of God being asked, they said he was blacke and evill, and did them much harme; their good, they had by their owne labour, and not by his goodnesse."[80]

It is difficult to overlook Purchas's fascination with what he perceived to be a degenerate complacency and ease with which the people of Guinea manufacture their fetishes. In this way, he proved himself a true heir to the new strain of Christian theological disdain for vain manufactures whose radically material origins ostensibly betrayed their capacity for coherence as divine objects. Purchas perceived this as a near-comical "matter of God-making," one so prolific that art "commonly gets the upper hand" over nature in producing objects of worship. The worship of manufactured fetish objects, in Purchas's estimation, overwhelmed that of celestial bodies or fire or trees. The idea that the Blacks of Guinea Africa made gods (fetishes) at their pleasure appears in *Pilgrimage* as further evidence that the "ethnike" religion of Africa's Blacks is beneath and beyond the pale of true worship. At the same time, the very presence of fetish religion, existing without any genealogical dependence on Abrahamic religions, attests to what Purchas argued was the anthropological origin of religion, whose seeds lay in a ubiquitous human drive toward religious existence. With the exception of ancient Egyptian religion, Purchas reserved his "ethnike religion" moniker for indigenous religion in Guinea Africa, which he called the "land of Negroes."[81]

In the early eighteenth century, the Dutch West Indian Company executive Willem Bosman published his *New and Accurate Description of the Coast of Guinea*. Throughout his many years of corporate service at the fortified Elmina Castle, Bosman's immersion in markets and finance disposed him to articulate most succinctly the broader European derision of fetishism as a religious system among Africans. He argued that fetishism functioned by deforming rationalities. It undermined what should have been an intelligent perception of material value, exchange structures, and rational self-interest, which were the basis for European mercantilism and capitalism. In his view, fetishism substituted instead a childlike delusion of value in trinkets, and it evidenced the inferior nature of the primitive. The materialist, fetish theory of religion, more expansively, rendered intelligible and justifiable European conquest wars, the trans-Atlantic slave trade, and the forced displacement of indigenous peoples.[82]

The power of juxtaposing market rationality to fetish religion was realized through a long history of rendering Black religion as the quintessential manifestation of superstition, delusion, and savagery, properties that coalesced into the racial constitution of the heathen. Throughout the long *durée* of European Atlantic colonialism, Guinea Africa became the most potent and widely circulated hieroglyph for inscribing the religion of primitives as a racializing exercise. In his "Natural History of Religion," David Hume (1711–1776) invoked the rich, imperial trove of meanings about colonially subjugated peoples to explain the origin of religion. As one of the foundational figures of philosophical empiricism and skepticism, Hume relished in rendering an iconoclastic interpretation of human history for his contemporaries. He asserted that monotheism, so vaunted and exceptionalized by the West in its imperial gaze on the so-called heathen races, was in fact the culmination of competition among polytheists who developed the concept of monotheism by attaining a more authentic understanding of the universe and its workings. Hume argued essentially that monotheism had been achieved through a centuries-long process of human progress. Writing against the theological grain of his day, he insisted that polytheism (or idolatry) was the original religion among human beings. Since that time, human society had progressed from "rude beginnings to a state of greater perfection." "The farther we mount up into antiquity," he continued, "the more do we find mankind plunged into idolatry." Yet, in his own day, there were still some human beings who lived in a continuing state of idolatry: "the savage tribes of America, Africa, and Asia" were all "idolaters." Hume emphasized that human beings naturally enter the world without an authentic knowledge of causation. As children, moreover, they are prone to develop a superstitious means of engaging with the phenomenal world – attributing causation to myriad invisible powers, which they imagine to be like themselves (*prosopopoeia*, or personification). This idolatry or polytheism was the "primitive Religion of uninstructed

---

[82] Pietz, "The Problem of the Fetish, IIIa," 106.

mankind." From its base depths, Europeans had emerged into the light of rational apprehension.[83]

The more elaborate discourse of the fetish as a theory of religion would fully flower during the late-eighteenth century, however, under the influence of the French writer Charles de Brosses (1709–1777). In 1760 Brosses published his *Du culte des dieux fètiches* (*Cult of the Fetish Gods*), wherein he argued that indigenous African religion exhibited striking parallels with the religion of ancient Egyptians. These Black Africans, according to Brosses, were a veritable portal to the world of peoples who had lived thousands of years earlier. It was as if European observers could be transported through time to peer into the materialist origins of religion merely through ethnographic encounters with contemporary Black peoples. This was the essential function of rendering the primitive, and it is to Brosses that subsequent European intellectuals would owe a significant debt for establishing the racial concept of the primitive. By the time Brosses wrote his influential text, the fetish discourse had been circulating for almost 300 years among Europeans and Africans. But his innovation lay in harnessing European ideas about the fetish among Blacks in Africa to craft a materialist theory of religion wherein fetishism was the quintessential religion of the primitive who worshipped things as things. He viewed fetishism, in other words, as one stage in the longer process of human evolution that eventually led to monotheism. Unlike most of his contemporaries, Brosses argued that ancient polytheism, preeminently that of Egypt, was unmitigated in its vulgarity because material objects – and not some spiritual essence, soul, or higher principle – were the literal object of worship. The Egyptian worship of Anubis, he insisted, could not be described as merely allegorical. It was literal. This meant that ancient Egyptians, as well as ancient Hebrews who worshipped the image of a snake, were fetish-worshipping savages.[84]

Brosses borrowed liberally from David Hume's *Lectures on Jurisprudence* to demonstrate the originality and primordial status of fetishism. Just as Hume had argued that polytheism was the original religion, so also did Brosses, but with the differential emphasis on the fetish specifically. It was humankind's most ancient form of religion, a claim that contravened that of Christian philosophers who saw monotheism as the original religion and polytheism as the result of a general apostasy

---

[83] David Hume, "The Natural History of Religion," in *Four Dissertations* (London: A. Millar, 1757), 1–4, 10, 16–18.

[84] Charles de Brosses, *Du Culte des Dieux Fètiches, ou Parallèle de L'Ancienne Religion de L'Égypte avec la Religion Actuelle de Nigritie* (Geneva: Cramer, 1760).

from biblical truth. By stripping away the veneer of allegory, Brosses sought to expose the reprehensible, savage nature of fetishism in both its early forms in ancient Egyptian and biblical (Hebrew) religion and in its contemporary manifestation among West Africans. By parsing the temporality of fetishism in this way, Brosses effected a more explicit articulation of an essential difference between Europeans (who had ascended to the status of modernity) and primitives (the quintessential Black African).[85]

Karl Marx, in turn, owed his familiarity with the concept of fetishism to Brosses. Marx would elaborate the fructuous concept to examine the creation of commodity value, an analytical move that would help to establish fetishism as a permanent, paradigmatic category in the fields of anthropology, philosophy, political theory, history, psychology, and philology. In his early engagement with the problem of the fetish, Karl Marx noted an anecdote from Charles de Brosses describing the actions of the native peoples of Cuba, who concluded, in the wake of continuing invasions and murderous campaigns by the Spanish, that gold was the fetish god of the Spaniards. In an effort to ward off the genocidal forays by these avaricious Europeans, the local indigenous population gathered quantities of gold, "danced and sang around it, and threw it into the sea, in order to be rid of it." This was, in Marx's interpretive scheme, an indication that the indigenous people of Cuba (whom Marx, following Brosses, called "savages") had pierced the veil of capitalist ideology to understand that the Spaniards had mystified matter by endowing it with special, innate qualities of value. But commodity value, Marx argued, did not derive from matter. Rather, it was achieved through *social relations* – namely by elite capitalists controlling the labor of exploited peoples as the means of effecting wealth accumulation. The Spaniards had fetishized gold, a material that the Cubans (standing in for Marx's exploited White laborers) could more soberly and "non-ideologically" recognize as inert matter that might just as gainfully be cast to the bottom of the sea.[86]

Marx continued to develop his use of fetishism over the years. He ultimately conceived of capital as merely one type or species within the genus of fetishism. In this way, it was precisely because the discourse of the fetish functioned for Marx to foreground dialectical materialism that he was able to break so radically and fundamentally from most of his peers by anthropologizing the European. And he did so not merely by fundamentally

[85] Ibid.

[86] Karl Marx, "Exzerpte zur Geschichte der Kunst und der Religion," in *Marx-Engels Gesamtausgabe*, 2: 1 (Berlin: Dietz, 1976), 322. Quoted in Pietz, "Fetishism and Materialism: The Limits of Theory in Marx," 134.

questioning European religion but also by locating European rational theories of *political economy* alongside the putative fetishistic religion of Africans and American Indians. No matter that the rational European capitalist could peer through the lens of European Enlightenment categories to behold Africans and American Indians falsely attributing causation, genius, and agency to sticks and stones or to any other "trifling" they might come across – that is, to fetishes. As he asserted, it was the "mist-enveloped regions of the religious world" that offered the appropriate analogue – fetishism – for deciphering capitalist phenomenon of commodity value. It should be obvious to any observer, Marx claimed, that human labor was solely responsible, for instance, for converting wood into a table and rendering the table as a commodity. But the social nature of labor (viz., one person working for another in a context of a larger economy based on the exchange *of things* and thus the presumption of exchange value *in things*) mystified the products of human labor. The commodity was "therefore a mysterious thing, simply because in it the social character of men's labour appears to them as an objective character stamped upon the product of that labour." Although ostensibly simple in its coherence, the commodity was in fact quite strange, rich with "metaphysical subtleties" and "theological niceties." Marx heartily agreed that the cults of Africans and American Indians were fetishistic in the sense of being delusional. But he seized on the discourse of the fetish to turn the lens of scrutiny back onto "rational" Europeans, whose supposedly more rigorous, veridical claims about causation and theories of matter were disciplined by reason and unshackled from superstition. This presumption is precisely what Marx pointedly rejected. Because social relations, not matter per se or capital broadly conceived, were the source of material value, the rational capitalist was no less entrapped within a fetishistic worldview – a cultus of delusion – than were the superstitious Africans and Indians.[87]

So expansive was the reach of the discourse of the fetish that it came to exert a permanent influence on the social sciences of the nineteenth century by undergirding empiricism and positivism as the basis for the scientific study of human sociality. Above all, the radical materiality of the fetish, as produced and described through colonial encounters, further propelled the intellectual study of religion beyond the bounds of theology and textualism.

---

[87] Karl Marx, *Capital: A Critique of Political Economy*, Vol. 1, *The Process of Capitalist Production*, 3rd ed., trans. Samuel Moore and Edward Aveling (Chicago: Charles Kerr and Company, 1915), 81–87. David Harvey, *A Companion to Marx's Capital* (New York: Verso, 2010), 38–47. Pietz, "Fetishism and Materialism: The Limits of Theory in Marx," 119–51.

3

Colonial Governance and Religious Subjectivity

In this chapter I examine structures of Atlantic empire that rendered Africans in the Americas as colonial subjects. In the first half I explain the architecture of governance and specific institutions that constituted discrete mechanisms of colonial rule and authority over African peoples, free and enslaved. The aim here is to explicate the tactics of empire that rendered new rationalities and that shaped the very subjectivity of all the historical actors in both the limelight and shadows of its encompassing theater. In the second half I devote attention to the theological structures of the colonial formations that shaped the fundamental categories of experience in Black Christianization. Within these two broad fields of analysis – the one attentive to political structures, the other engaged with theological formations – one discerns a profound intersection of religion and empire that elucidates the significance of "slave religion" as such while making visible the more expansive and equally significant role of colonialism in the history of Black religion.

Empire, the Company-State, and Rationalities of Freedom

The most frequent efforts to account for the complex of institutions, tactics, and practices that have come to be referenced as "modernity" replicate two common problems. First, these accounts tend to focus on the developments internal to what is imagined as a *continent* of Europe, so that the causal factors of modernity's irruption (i.e., at the point of modernity's emergence) bear little or no relation to the social circumstances of the rest of Asia, or Africa, or the Americas. By this account,

Europe brings newness to the world. Common here is a narrow focus on the Protestant Reformation, the rise of German publishing technology, and the concomitant phenomenon of mass literacy; the emergence of Western Christian philosophy (typically with no reference to its reliance on the Islamic philosophical schools and universities); the Magna Carta and its juridical iterations; the creation of European secular institutions; and the shift from feudalism to a capitalist economy. Perhaps most important to this fantastical racial imagining is the geopolitical sleight of hand that sunders the European cape from the Asian continent, as if the cape itself were its own continent. This insular rendering of European exceptionalism is counterfactual in geographical terms. More importantly, it functions to elide the actual sociopolitical and economic realities of what Fernand Braudel, many decades ago, poignantly termed the "Mediterranean world."[1] These regions were linked. Islamic empires for centuries dominated strategic regions of Europe – preeminently Iberia, whose eventual seafaring constituted the rise of Europe's Atlantic empires. The spice trade was itself a major index of the thick linkage of intellectual traditions and economic practices throughout Afro-Asia. Many students of European history, moreover, might well be surprised to learn that economic organization and trade practices in South Asia and East Asia were more refined and sophisticated than those in Asia's European cape.[2]

---

[1] See Fernand Braudel, *La Mediterranée et la monde mediterraneen dans le temps de Phillippe II* (Paris: A. Colin, 1949). Important exceptions to these elisions include the "world systems theory" scholarship. See Immanuel Wallerstein, *World Systems Analysis: An Introduction* (Durham: Duke University Press, 2004).

[2] The literature on modernity is uncommonly vast. Representative of those studies that celebrate Western modernity as a beatific accomplishment undisturbed by the institutions and political order of colonialism are Jürgen Habermas, *The Philosophical Discourse of Modernity: Twelve Lectures*, trans. Frederick Lawrence (Cambridge: MIT Press, 1987). Samuel P. Huntington, *The Clash of Civilizations and the Remaking of World Order* (New York: Simon and Schuster, 1996). Walt Whitman Rostow, *The Stages of Economic Growth: A Non-Communist Manifest* (Cambridge: Cambridge University Press, 1961). Of course, since the 1970s, a spate of studies have examined modernity outside of Europe, particularly in predominantly non-White nation-states. But these studies uniformly assume the emergence of modernity as a consequence of contact with Europeans. Examples include Daniel Miller, *Modernity, an Ethnographic Approach: Dualism and Mass Consumption in Trinidad* (Oxford: Berg, 1994). Charles Piot, *Remotely Global: Village Modernity in West Africa* (Chicago: University of Chicago Press, 1999). Among the most influential critiques of the temporality of modernist discourse (presuming a stadial view of history and contemporaneous yet non-coeval civilizations) is that by Dipesh Chakrabarty, *Provincializing Europe: Postcolonial Thought and Historical Difference* (Princeton, NJ: Princeton University Press, 2000). For a compelling critique of modernity as an incoherent, fundamentally flawed concept, see Frederick Cooper, *Colonialism in Question: Theory, Knowledge, History* (Berkeley: University of

The second problem replicated in these accounts of modernity is that religion tends to be easily relegated exclusively to the realm of ideology or belief.[3] This rendering obscures the overwhelming worldliness of religion and its profound role as a network of social institutions, materialities, technologies, and cultural practices. We can best apprehend this problem by examining the conundrum of the state. The issue here is not some loose generic notion of polities as a basic category of formal, political organization that has existed for thousands of years (think of council leaders, monarchs, and militias). Rather, the state in question here is the entity that has come to concern itself with what Michel Foucault so poignantly termed *l'art de gouverner* – "the art of governing" or, more concisely, governmentality). The emphasis here, in other words, is on the practice of managing a population whose constituents exist in the political imaginary as members of a body politic or as citizens, as opposed to being merely juridical subjects of rule. One can appreciate this distinction by imagining the rejoinder of a contemporary citizen of a Western state when asked, "Who is your ruler?" The response would likely question the entire basis of the question. "What do you mean by *ruler*? I have no ruler. We [the people] rule ourselves. This is a democracy!" This mode of state-making is inseparable from the birth of "the population" (in Foucault's parlance) or the invention of "the people" (as the idea is more commonly rendered in political theory).[4]

For all his originality and the productive insights that derive from his reframing the study of the state, Foucault was less than attentive to some of the most important techniques of conceiving power and strategies of governing as matters of political order. This is so especially where corporations contributed to developing techniques of governing that generated new rationalities and tactics of authority. This is also true in relation to the particular means whereby Christendom as the *populus christianus*

California Press, 2005), 113–50. See also Thomas A. Brady, Jr., "The Rise of Merchant Empires, 1400–1700," in *The Political Economy of Merchant Empires*, ed. James Tracy (New York: Cambridge University Press, 1991), 117–60, esp. 154–57. Among the early efforts to account for Western modernity through attention to the East is Kavalam M. Panikkar, *Asia and Western Dominance: A Survey of the Vasco Da Gama Epoch of Asian History, 1498–1945* (New York: Collier Books, 1969).

[3] Important exceptions include Irene Silverblatt, *Modern Inquisitions: Peru and the Colonial Origins of the Civilized World* (Durham, NC: Duke University Press, 2004). Jonathan Sheehan, *The Enlightenment Bible: Translation, Scholarship, Culture* (Princeton, NJ: Princeton University Press, 2005).

[4] Michel Foucault, *Security, Territory, Population: Lectures at the Collège De France, 1977–78* (New York: Palgrave Macmillan, 2007), 110.

bequeathed an imperial legacy (i.e., colonialism) that is deeply implicated in the technologies of the nation-state. In this way, the European
nation-state is the "imperial papacy's true successor."[5]

The discourse of governmentality, thus, has been a central problem
for political theory and has shared some of the same challenges faced
by the general historiography of the state. This is an especially stubborn tendency with respect to how Islamic polities influenced Western
state formation. Contrary to popular opinion, the eventual bifurcation
of secular and religious authority in the Western European cape did not
presage events that would come to Islamic states centuries later. Rather,
with the rise of secularism in the political domain, Western Christendom
was actually becoming more similar to Islamic polities such as Ottoman
Turkey, Safavid Persia, and Mughal India. By 1100, the caliphate
authority (Islamic religious leadership) was fully established as a separate domain of power from that of secular rule in multiple (but not all)
Islamic empires. The rise of secular rule in Islamic polities predated by
several centuries this form of political order in Western Christendom.
Even the Byzantine Empire of Eastern Orthodox Christianity was centuries "ahead" of Western Christendom in this respect. Although secular
and religious rulers of Byzantium from time to time sought to breach
their respective domains to manipulate matters of state to benefit their
vision of religious order (or vice versa), the political order was staunchly
rooted in the formal and uniform separation of religion and state.[6]

The chief causal factor in the creation of novel, disruptive rationalities
for the state in Western Christendom was the European foray into transoceanic empire – that is, extending the colonial relation of power to rule
oceanic geographies of the Atlantic, Indian, and Pacific and the particular
commercial relations involved in trafficking captive African and American
Indian peoples. If we are to account for the nexus of religion and empire
that situated the social lives of Blacks in this early period of Atlantic
colonialism, then we must first be able to explain why the nation-state
emerged during the very time that merchant empires were forming.[7] We
must further account for the material developments undergirding the
existence of these imperial formations – the creation of company-states,
the extraction of precious metals from the immensely rich mines of the

---

[5] Thomas A. Brady, Jr., "The Rise of Merchant Empires, 1400–1700," 117–60 in *The Political Economy of Merchant Empires*, ed. James Tracy.

[6] Ibid., 126–27.

[7] James Noel, *Black Religion and the Imagination of Matter in the Atlantic World* (New York: Palgrave Macmillan, 2009).

Americas by extracting labor from the bodies of American Indians, the raiding-and-trading merchants commanding the seas, the enslavement of millions of human beings throughout West and Central Africa and throughout the Americas, genocidal campaigns against America's indigenous peoples, and the unpoliced practices of freedom operating far from the European metropoles that were uniquely achieved by creating White settler colonies. This is especially true if we wish to apprehend fully the relationship among *colonialism, democracy*, and *freedom.*

Insofar as the modern state is an effect of Atlantic empire, what we have, in other words, is a bifold penumbra of causation – the significance of Atlantic empires (colonialism) and the legacy of religion in imperial (state) governmentality – whose method of elucidation must be disciplined by discrete accountability to the plural exercises of power – sometimes violent and nakedly brutal, at other times so steeply domesticated as to manifest as fully cloaked in the garb of civility. Contrast, for example, the bloody enterprise of Spanish or English militarists and colonists butchering an entire town of Native men, women, and children with the solitary, stodgy, cerebral work of accounting for multilateral bills of exchange in a Dutch corporate office located in a dank fortress on the West African coast. That which is generally celebrated as civilization and as the rise of the beatific European nation-state is fundamentally rooted in the creation of Atlantic empires. And so we find ourselves tasked with making sense of the data about religion and empire throughout Africa and the Americas, in which venue we must consider the struggles among the Africans, Native Americans, and Europeans and the record of their colonial contacts and exchanges.[8]

Formalizing Imperium

Religious authority performed a decisive role in the emergence of Europe's Atlantic empires. Of utmost importance was the papal authorization for venturers to explore the farthest reaches of the watery expanse that lay before the European cape of Asia. After the Ottoman Empire won control of Constantinople (the seat of Eastern Christendom) in 1453, the *papas* of Rome was left as the uncontested highest ranking official in Christendom. More importantly, however, the papal office became far more aggressive about dominating Muslims and, as imagined in Christendom, winning back "Christian lands" from Muslim rulers. This involved the pope contracting with princes, who controlled militias, to offer them the spoils

[8] Brady, "The Rise of Merchant Empires, 1400–1700," 154–57.

of war as well as tributes they might force on conquered subjects in disputed territories. In March 1456, for example, Pope Calixtus III issued his *Inter caetera*, which stipulated that the Portuguese prince Henry the Navigator would govern newly won dominions through the military order (the Order of Christ) that the prince controlled.[9] The papacy, meanwhile, benefited by incorporating more territories into its orbit of authority. In this way, the expansion of Christendom (i.e., the extension of Christian *imperium*) was pursued through an imaginary over which stood the shadow of Muslim empire.

As it happened, the ideology of war against Muslims became highly effective for fashioning a discourse of Portuguese rule over the Atlantic islands, Guinea Africa, and subsequently the Americas. The bull *Romanus pontifex* of 1455 named as "Lord of Guinea" the Portuguese crown, a title in which the Portuguese prince John II especially reveled.[10] The bull *Inter caetera divinae* of 1493 was especially exemplary of the complex iterations of juridical and theological interests that animated expansion, militarism, and religious zeal. This authorizing instrument was fashioned at the very time Iberian Christians had defeated and expelled Muslim rulers. Most importantly, Christopher Columbus, sailing under the auspices of the Spanish crown, reached what he mistakenly thought was South Asia; he had actually sailed to the Caribbean – first landing at the Bahamian archipelago, then Cuba, and finally the present-day island of Haiti and the Dominican Republic, which the Spanish came to call Hispaniola. Ferdinand and Isabella were eager to confirm their rights to colonize the region and prevailed on the pope to stipulate the same, as he had done for Portugal. As a result, Pope Alexander VI issued the bull of 1493, commanding Spain to spread the Christian religion in new lands, thereby ensuring the well-being of these newly found souls. Putatively uncivilized nations (i.e., non-European) were to be overthrown and "reduced" to the Christian faith. Outlining a civilizing mission, the bull charged the emerging empire based in Castile to instruct newly discovered peoples in the Catholic faith while also administering rule over them through force of conquest. By resolving the dispute between Spain and Portugal following Columbus's initial voyage, the pope had formally inscribed Spanish rights of discovery and conquest of the lands to the west of the Cape Verde Islands and the Azores, in effect granting the authority to

---

[9] Hugh Thomas, *The Slave Trade: The History of the Atlantic Slave Trade, 1440–1870*, rev. ed. (London: Phoenix, 2006), 66–67.

[10] P. E. Russell, *Prince Henry "the Navigator": A Life* (New Haven, CT: Yale University Press, 2000), 318.

colonize the western half of the Atlantic to Spain and the eastern half to Portugal. Thus, like Portugal in Guinea and the Atlantic islands, Spain gained considerable authorization to invade, pillage, occupy, govern, and exact tribute from a vast expanse of conquered regions by conceiving of sovereignty as the exclusive right of Christian rulers.[11]

It would be erroneous, however, to conclude that the imperial ethos of Western Christendom translated into a cohesive pan-European unity of militarism and economic cooperation. Far from it. Such a development would have to await the accord of Westphalia in 1648. Rather, the search for an all-sea route to South Asia and the immense wealth to be had through the spice trade, the mining of gold and silver in the Americas, and especially abducting and enslaving Africans sparked a massive trans-formation throughout the European cape. A conflict between Spain and Portugal erupted over their competing interests in expanding into the Atlantic islands and Guinea Africa. After the Portuguese gained the upper hand in establishing trading forts in West Central Africa, the Dutch and English worked to undermine that monopoly so they could share in the profits. Piracy developed as an especially effective means of lawlessness styled as juridical rectitude. When Spain, for instance, became dominant in extending colonial rule into the Americas and reaping the profits of sil-ver shipload by shipload, Britain simply declared the open seas off-limits to Spain and stipulated that offending vessels be pursued and comman-deered and that the contraband (slaves or silver bullion) be confiscated by "official" parties – that is, by pirates operating under the auspices of the British Crown. Other nations such as France began to expand their own imperial ambitions, colonizing North America and the Caribbean. France, in fact, would by the 1700s operate the world's most lucrative sugarcane fields, in Saint-Domingue (Haiti).[12]

[11] William Eugene Shiels, *King and Church: The Rise and Fall of the Patronato Real* (Chicago: Loyola University Press, 1961), 78–81, 283–87. Jorge A. Vargas, *Mexico and the Law of the Sea: Contributions and Compromises, Publications on Ocean Development* (Boston: Martinus Nijhoff, 2011), 413–14. Michael Prior, *The Bible and Colonialism: A Moral Critique* (Sheffield: Sheffield Academic Press, 1997), 53.

[12] Govanni Arrighi, *The Long Twentieth Century: Money, Power, and the Origins of Our Times*, rev. ed. (New York: Verso, 2010). Janice E. Thomson, *Mercenaries, Pirates, and Sovereigns: State-Building and Extraterritorial Violence in Early Modern Europe* (Princeton, N.J.: Princeton University Press, 1994), 22–24. M. J. Braddick, *State Formation in Early Modern England, c. 1550–1700* (New York: Cambridge University Press, 2000), 205. Edmund S. Morgan, *American Slavery, American Freedom: The Ordeal of Colonial Virginia* (New York: Norton, 1975), 9–11, 48–41.

Perhaps more intriguing, if not quite surprising, is the dissent that individual Christian nations raised against the papal authorizations endowing particular nations with power. The Spanish support of Christopher Columbus's voyage to the Caribbean (mistaken for South Asia) was authorized by papal bulls that granted dominion to Spain. The English Crown responded by disavowing any rightful papal ability to limit conquest of the Americas to a single Christian nation. As Queen Elizabeth I herself phrased it, she did not recognize in the "pope of Rome … any prerogatives in such matters," especially any ability to command those who owed him "no allegiance." Even Francis I of Catholic France dared Spain's supporters to produce "the clause from Adam's testament that excludes me from a share in the globe."[13]

At the same time, however, the role of Christian peoplehood as the jewel in the crown of the rationalities of empire is illumined even more sharply through these intra-European dissents and conflicts, mainly because of what they agreed on. Every emerging metropole invested in the logic of Christian dominion to render coherent the very enterprise of empire. Richard Hakluyt, who penned his *Discourse on Western Planting* in 1584 to promote the British Crown's interest in colonizing the Americas and Asia, recapitulated the formidable claims of Christian supremacism that operated throughout Catholic and Reformed Christian theology. Hakluyt in fact began his treatise with the singular assertion that British colonization of distant lands would strike a decisive blow for "thinlargemente [*sic*] of the gospel of Christe" in North America, particularly the regions bordering the Viceroyalty of New Spain (especially north of present-day Florida). No "Christian princes" possessed those lands. In fact, he emphasized, the inhabitants were idolaters, and those who had been brought to Europe in 1524 worshipped "the sonne, the moone, and the starres, and used other idolatrie." The prospect of converting Native Americans to Christianity was the chief imperative for undertaking this venture. But Hakluyt was keen to emphasize a host of other reasons as well. Christianization, after all, was a political affair, as it entailed preserving the Americas from what he rendered as the frightful hand of Catholicism. Beyond that, however, the enterprise promised to bring a wealth of commodities, more than England was able to acquire in its fierce competition with the Portuguese-dominated trade networks in

[13] James A. Noel, *Black Religion and the Imagination of Matter in the Atlantic World* (New York: Palgrave Macmillan, 2009), 21–22. Luis Rivera Pagán, *A Violent Evangelism: The Political and Religious Conquest of the Americas* (Louisville, KY: Westminster/John Knox Press, 1992), 29–31.

West Central Africa. Prosperity would be had by the woefully underemployed and unemployed English destitute. Hakluyt even added a measure of altruism, insisting that English colonialism would mitigate the violence of Spain's conquest of the Indies.[14]

In 1589, just one year after the Spanish Armada's defeat, Hakluyt published his *Principal Navigations, Voyages, and Discoveries Made by the English Nation*. The work was as much an informative compilation of travel writings as a tool of propaganda for promoting British colonialism in "the Indies" of the East and West. Hakluyt's, however, was only one of many rationalizations of Atlantic empire at the time. No less influential was Samuel Purchas, the Anglican minister hired to promote the Virginia Company. Purchas was equally astute in his promotion of colonialism. He emphasized the exceptional status that Christian governance held over indigenous settlements. Only such governance could produce the righteousness that the Christian deity desired. By this logic of Christian imperium, the very fact that Native Americans were idolaters rendered their claims to land moot and ineffectual. With a technical specificity of argument entwined with theology, scripture, and Enlightenment strategies of racial supremacism, Purchas proffered that "Christians (such as have the Grace of the Spirit of Christ, and not the profession of his merit alone) have and hold the world and the things thereof in another tenure, whereof Hypocrites and Heathens are not capable." Infusing the economic language of Roman slavery and the paterfamilias with Christian dispensationalism, he asserted there were natural laws that formed the basis of civil society and provided a just basis for heathens to dwell on the earth in the "household" of the divine master. These existed in distinction from the spiritual laws whose dispensation afforded Christians the status of sons of the divine. The latter occupied a far superior status in the divine household of earthly habitation. Purchas, of course, wrote in the midst of the fierce wars between the Native peoples of Virginia, determined to protect their sovereignty, and the White settler colony the Virginia Company had created there in the early 1600s. There should be little surprise, in hindsight, of the totalizing scale of Christian supremacism that attended his defense of settler colonialism.[15]

The theological rationalization of empire on display in Purchas's work was of a piece with the authorization of *imperium* articulated in the

---

[14] Richard Hakluyt, *A Discourse Concerning Western Planting*, ed. Charles Deane (Cambridge: John Wilson & Son, 1877), 7–8, 19–23, 36–40, 71–77.

[15] Samuel Purchas, *Virginias Verger*, in his edited *Purchas His Pilgrimes*, vol. 19 (New York: Macmillan Company, 1906), 218–24.

charters that inscribed the legitimacy of the Virginia Company of London and the Virginia Company of Plymouth. Both emerged in the early 1600s to bring to fruition the decades-long interest of the British Crown in competing with the boldly successful colonial possessions of New Spain. Because the British Crown, like other European monarchies, was hard pressed to leverage the massive scale of capital required to underwrite colonization in the Americas, the joint-stock company emerged as a solution ripe for harnessing the restless capitalist energies that defined the era. The Crown created a charter for the Virginia Company in 1606, just a few years after the creation of the English East India Company, opening the document with its rationale for such an enterprise "into that part of America commonly called VIRGINIA, and other parts and Territories in America, either appertaining unto us, or which are not now actually possessed by any Christian Prince or People." The preeminent reason for the right to settle lands yet unseen by British royal authorities was the absence of Christian sovereigns. By imposing Christian rule, moreover, it became feasible to propagate "Christian religion to such people, as yet live in Darkness and miserable Ignorance of the true Knowledge and Worship of the Christian deity." Benefits that might accrue to the original inhabitants of these lands extended, moreover, to the possibility that the colonizing company might transport English settlers who could "bring the Infidels and Savages, living in those parts, to human Civility, and to a settled and quiet Government."[16]

The company's charter was of course similar in style to that which underwrote the enterprise of Walter Raleigh in 1584. In that document, Queen Elizabeth I bestowed upon Raleigh, his heirs, and those he assigned "free libertie and licence [sic] ... to discover, search, finde out, and view such remote, heathen and barbarous lands, countries, and territories not actually possessed of any Christian prince ... to haue, holde, occupie, and enjoy ... with all prerogatiues, commodities, jurisdictions, royalties, priuileges, franchises, and preheminencies."[17] It is clear that Elizabeth (and in the case of the Virginia Company, James I) held great disdain for the momentous success of Catholic Spain and the extravagant monopoly of rights in conquest enjoyed by Spain at the behest of the

---

[16] "The First Charter of Virginia – 1606," in *The Federal and State Constitutions, Colonial Charters, and other Organic Laws of the United States*, 2nd ed., ed. Benjamin Perley Poore (Washington, DC: US Government Printing Office, 1878), 2: 1888.

[17] "Charter to Sir Walter Raleigh – 1584," in *Federal and State Constitutions*, 2: 1379. Mark Nicholls and Penry Williams, *Sir Walter Raleigh: In Life and Legend* (New York: Continuum, 2011), 45–46.

pope. It is also clear, however, that the British Crown nevertheless privileged and invested thoroughly in the fundamental distinction between Christian rule and the political sovereignty of non-Christian, Native polities throughout the Americas. European Christian metropoles viewed non-Christian sovereignty as inherently violable.

Just as striking as the authorizations of imperium in the corporate charters was the right to conquer granted by the *Requerimiento*, a document employed in Spain's colonization of the Americas. As a legal rationale for colonialism, the *Requerimiento* originated in 1511 during the ongoing debates over the justification of Christian conquest in the West Indies. When the Dominican priest Antonio de Montesinos castigated Spanish colonizers for failing to convert the Natives, the Spanish king Ferdinand reformulated the legal justification to shift the emphasis from conversion to imposing Christian rule through violence. This document was read (always in Spanish and often at a distance of several miles) to Native Americans by Spanish soldiers. It required the Native Americans to submit themselves willingly and without resistance to Spanish rule. This of course resulted in their "failure" or refusal to comply with the document's dictates and thus to accept the status of colonial subjects under the sovereign rule of the Spanish crown and, ultimately, under the rule of Jesus, venerated as the divine sovereign of Christendom. In that instance, the venturing soldiers of Spain were required to vindicate the Spanish crown in the face of such "insolence" through slaughter, pillage, and enslavement. As a practical matter, the discourse of colonialism was merely being made to conform to its actual practice. But at the level of intelligibility, the *Requerimiento* legitimized the brutality of military conquest and enslavement in the Americas with the doctrine of the sovereign's political right.[18]

African Slavery

The business of Atlantic empire, of course, was not merely concerned with possessing territories throughout the Americas and in Guinea. It was also concerned with racial slavery. When European polities attempted to justify the imperial possession of lands that were clearly already occupied and possessed by Native Americans (or in Guinea Africa, by native Africans), they repeatedly underscored the preeminence of Christian identity in the

---

[18] Patricia Seed, "Taking Possession and Reading Texts: Establishing the Authority of Overseas Empires," *William and Mary Quarterly* 49, no. 2. (April 1992): 183–209. Vargas, *Mexico and the Law of the Sea*, 414–15.

rationalities of imperium – rule through colonial governance. The African slave trade, however, significantly augmented the discourse of power and rationalities subsumed under Atlantic colonialism. It did so not by diminishing the significance of Christian sovereignty but by magnifying it. The violence of conquest over peoples and their lands in the Americas strained the efforts of European colonizers to articulate and affirm the brutality of empire against the burgeoning discourses of freedom. The trans-Atlantic slave trade was both an integral aspect of colonial governance and a structural mechanism of imperial rule. Slavery functioned, in other words, to locate Africans as subjects of colonial authority while at the same time constituting and producing capital through the chattel principle, by exploiting labor, and through the productive and reproductive capacities of enslaved women, men, and children. For these reasons, African slavery intensified the scale of colonial rationalities while heightening the explicative demands being made on racialization strategies.

Accounting for Colonial Governmentality: The Company-State Meets the Settler State

How does this relate to the Christianization of Africans? And what does it mean that freedom triumphed at the very time that humankind's most massive enslavement of human beings in Africa and the Americas was underway? Because colonial governance operated in harmony with burgeoning institutions of popular sovereignty, the answer to these questions depends on understanding the location of African peoples with respect to two pivotal institutions of democratic governance rooted in liberal theories of political order: the company-state and the White settler colony. The most urgent analysis of freedom at some point must enter into concern with the Anglo-American empire, and it is to that state that our story now turns. The Anglo-American state became the most efficacious bearer of the sign of freedom in the Atlantic world, which is not to say that scholarly observers should invest in the illusory excesses of exceptionalism attending that efficacy. Rather, as a racial settler state grounded in both a militant tradition of freedom (by the 1780s it had defeated the British Empire to establish itself as the world's first constitutional democracy) and a thoroughgoing formation as a slave society, Anglo-America's colonialism emerged in ways fully emblematic of the rationalities of modernity that brought together the novel governing practices of the company-state and the imperium of the White settler polity.

We can trace the specific formations of modern power by attending to how the colonial relation of social power instantiated its effects. The analytical challenge, in other words, is to discern precisely how colonial power is actually applied, how it is put to work. Its point of application distinguishes its power as such. At stake, for this reason, is the relationship of colonialism to the Enlightenment – that is, to the irruption of rationalities that attended the emergence of Atlantic empires. The Enlightenment was partly characterized by its capacity for undermining the tectonic structures that sustained superstition and moral slavery. Through multiple strategies of social power (of economics, militarism, ideology, and politics), the Enlightenment effected a radical break from these conditions within two domains of spatial and political interest. One of these was the *reforming project* (not to be confused with the Protestant Reformation), which occurred *within* the European domain. The other can be understood accurately as the *civilizing project*, which was deployed through the imperial domain in the colonial periphery. The former project concerned itself with establishing novel tactics for constituting a civic order in such a way that it might serve as the foundation for making reason (*ratio*) the basis for judging everything else. As a consequence, for instance, reason was elevated to a place of authority over religion and constituted the formal basis of political order. The expressions and significations of reason became the most powerful and unassailable. The latter project generated and institutionalized a discourse of differential essences (racialization) as part and parcel of creating and maintaining the power differential between the colonizers and the colonized. Among its evidences were orientalism, racial noetics, anti-Blackness, genocide in the Americas, and the settler state, all operating to advance the creation of Atlantic empires.[19]

Such a fundamental shift, however, required the deployment of governing tactics, and this meant that states gradually shifted the tactics of juridical power in order to inculcate self-improvement as the rational outcome of people (or, the *populus*) doing what they ought. This was political power operating under the sign of freedom rather than under the power of the law, which ultimately was the threat of death. The role of Atlantic commercialism (of mercantilism and subsequently laissez-faire capitalism) was of chief importance for crafting these new grammars of power and subjectivity. Of paramount interest was the creation of political subjectivities rooted in the imaginary of collectivism and membership.

[19] David Scott, "Colonial Governmentality," *Social Text* no. 43 (Autumn 1995): 195–200. Barnor Hesse, "Racialized Modernity: An Analytics of White Mythologies," *Racial and Ethnic Studies* 30, no. 4 (2007): 650–60.

This was the rise of the population or, to employ alternative language, the invention of the people. In the latter case, the Enlightenment concerned itself with establishing structures of force and authorizing often-destructive capacities to rule conquered peoples as slaves or colonial subjects. In essence, governmentality (*l'art de gouverner*) had now entered the stage.[20]

The relationship between this new governmentality and colonialism must be parsed more carefully, however, than Foucault demonstrated. Foucault ignored the elaborate contexts of European colonialism and the relationship between the brutal, juridical tactics of Western colonialism (think of White settler genocide against Native Americans, Congo under the rule of King Leopold, or France during the Algerian war for self-determination), on the one hand, and the enterprise of managing populations through the discourse of freedom, on the other. He engaged with "race struggle" to explain anti-Semitism in Europe but not anti-Blackness or anti-Arab racism or orientalism. His analytical observations of colonialism were more strictly concerned with what he called "internal colonialism" within Europe, not colonialism in the Atlantic empires. By ignoring the external modes of European colonialism and crafting a history of modern power that focused exclusively on Europe in a manner that elided the rest of the globe, Foucault could easily narrate the demise or obsolescence of juridical forms of power.[21]

The actual history of power, however, differs significantly from this narrative. The juridical form of political power that constituted the global administration of European colonialism articulated its rationalities through the idiom of brutality – it threatened violence instead of claiming to liberate. Rather than simply fading away under the emergence of governmentality, juridical tactics were now redeployed by European metropoles not simply as freedom, inasmuch as freedom emerged in a transoceanic, colonial incarnation as an especially racial phenomenon, a type of racial property. European polities redeployed juridical power by articulating the civilizing mission. For the Christian mission among

[20] David Scott, "Colonial Governmentality," *Social Text* no. 43 (Autumn 1995): 195–200. Michel Foucault, *Security, Territory, Population: Lectures at the Collège de France, 1977–78*, trans. Graham Burchell (New York: Palgrave Macmillan, 2007). Edmund S. Morgan, *Inventing the People: The Rise of Popular Sovereignty in England and America* (New York: Norton, 1988).

[21] See Michel Foucault, *The History of Sexuality* (New York: Pantheon Books, 1978), 86–90. Michel Foucault et al., *Society Must Be Defended: Lectures at the Collège De France, 1975–76*, (New York: Picador, 2003), 100–3. Foucault, *Security, Territory, Population*.

American Indians, this was the slave labor camp based on kidnapping, rape, and torture. In Leopold's Kongo, this was genocide, torture, and war articulated as a path to the ultimate betterment of savages and the creation of unfettered profits. Under the Atlantic regimes of slavery, it was racial uplift, mitigating the existential squalor of African heathenism and savagery by assuaging such decadence with the imposition of slavery's order. Within this frame of new rationalities, European colonizers exercised freedom in the political domain strictly for those who possessed the capacity for self-governance (other Europeans). For those races that lacked this capacity, modern Europe offered juridical tactics, though with an important difference: the ultimate goal was social transformation – taming the savage mind and disciplining the Black body or the indigenous polity.[22]

In both instances – the civilizing mission and the reforming mission – the governing tactics and effects achieved coherence because these new rationalities were tethered to the idea of "betterment" driven by the coda of rational self-interest. These deployments shared the idiom of progress. Yet it is paramount to understand that colonized subjects and the enslaved were not *managed* through the ideology of freedom. They were *ruled* in the juridical sense, under threat of brutality. The coda was betterment, but the tactic remained brutality. And this difference was the colonial difference. It is why we must understand the colonial nature of these novel rationalities. There is an important peculiarity in this colonial exercise of social power over subjects and slaves, however: the sign of Christian freedom. Although Europeans debated its possibilities, the sign of Christian freedom was distinctly central in the rationalities devoted to making empire coherent.

Corporatism and Political Community

If freedom can be described as a chord comprising multiple pitches of a common timbre, then one might describe the new rationalities of governmentality as comprising a dynamic duo: freedom and democracy (popular sovereignty).[23] In the latter case, the invention of the people, multiple sources emerge, including religious reform movements, commercial guilds, the company-state, and settler polities. Among these multiple

---

[22] Harald Fischer-Tiné and Michael Mann, eds., *Colonialism as Civilizing Mission: Cultural Ideology in British India* (London: Wimbledon Publishing, 2004). Alice Conklin, *A Mission to Civilize: The Republican Idea of Empire in France and West Africa, 1895–1930* (Stanford, CA: Stanford University Press, 1997).

[23] Orlando Patterson, *Freedom in the Making of Western Culture* (New York: Basic Books, 1991), 4–5.

formations, the company-state played an especially critical role because it linked the collectivism of popular sovereignty to the exercise of colonial governance, even brutality. It generated governing effects while simultaneously deploying the colonial relation of power. Company-states combined the imperatives of mercantilism and profit through trade (market rationalities) with the governing tactics that would eventually become the central concern of territorial states. Among the early preeminent examples are the Vereenigde Oostindische Compagnie (VOC – the Dutch United East India Company) and the English East India Company, but many other companies followed. We have already seen (in Chapter 2) how the VOC, for instance, joined the powers of a sovereign state to those of a business enterprise. But now we must attend more carefully to how the company-state created a *political community* – a body politic.

Mercantile guilds existed plentifully throughout Europe at the time Afro-European commercialism arose. These guilds promoted a sense of collective identity and encompassed membership through voting rights as well as networks of affiliation and mutual recognition. Professional guilds also represented the interests of their constituents to state officials – that is, to monarchs or their representatives. Company-states went far beyond this, however. First, they instantiated a metaphysical entity – the corporation – that possessed a transcendent identity. The corporation's ontological whole was simply greater than the sum of its member parts. Whereas joining a guild meant affiliating with persons, the company-state made it possible for individuals to participate in joining a corporate entity, to exist in its employ, and to act in the long-term interests of that entity despite the interests of any individuals affiliated with the company. Second, company-states endowed regular individuals with the status of political actors, despite the fact that these individuals had no necessary affiliations with royal lineage and had negotiated no political prerogatives from the monarch, as was the custom with provincial lords and nobility.[24] Those who were officers of the company-state immersed

---

[24] For instance, the Virginia Company Charter of 1609 stipulated that the powers granted therein extended " ... to such and so many as [the named members of the Company] do, or shall hereafter admit to be joined with them, in the form hereafter in these presents expressed, whether they go in their Persons to be Planters there in the said Plantation, or whether they go not, but adventure their monies, goods, or Chattles ...." The company-state, in other words, admitted to the realm of political governance an unprecedented potentiality of "the people," thereby transforming what had been relatively exclusive few participants in governance into a mass phenomenon that lay at the core of the rationality of popular sovereignty. See "The Second Charter of Virginia – 1609," in *Federal and State Constitutions*, 2: 1897.

themselves fully in performing the tasks that are now commonly associated with territorial states. Yet, these were not lords but merchants. Within the company-state, however, they set foreign policy, raised militias, executed wars, produced coinage, shaped fiscal policy, and exercised control over populations in South Asia and East Asia and throughout Africa and the Americas.

This leads to the third point: the company-state operated with the agency of a sovereign political actor. It was not merely that individual merchants were making political decisions. The company itself actually functioned as a political sovereign, which meant that corporate officials were immersed in statecraft on behalf of a political community of members – investors located throughout a larger field of merchants. They were performing the very art of governing that would become the regular occupation of territorial states. Unlike territorial monarchies, however, the company-state thrived on a democratic structure. It drew on the voting mechanisms common to professional guilds and wed this to the powers of the sovereign. *In a literal sense, the company-state was the first Western democratic state*, relying on voting, representation, and popular consensus (only within its political community, of course – as with all states) to set policy and to adjudicate specific disputes. During the early seventeenth century, at a time when the rationalities of political power were dominated by juridical thinking and the power of the monarch, the company-state asserted a powerful intervention by placing at the center of political power a new rationality rooted firmly in the logics of popular sovereignty and market reason.[25]

The English East India Company, formed in 1600, was paradigmatic of those other company-states that subsequently emerged in the seventeenth century. It was led by an executive council of twenty-four stockholders. A governor and deputy governor, in turn, directed this council. Stockholders voted to elect these governors to two-year terms. This electoral cycle created immense pressure for officeholders to articulate platforms construed in the interests of both the company itself and individual stockholders. It also engineered into the structures of governance a formula of accountability to stakeholders that has been the

[25] Jelle C. Riemersma, *Religious Factors in Early Dutch Capitalism, 1550–1650* (The Hague: Mouton, 1967), 23–27. Niels Steensgaard, "The Dutch East India Company as an Institutional Innovation," in *Trade in the Pre-Modern Era, 1400–1700*, Vol. 1, ed. Douglas A. Irwin (Brookfield, VT: Edward Elgar, 1996), 443–65. Philip J. Stern, *The Company-State: Corporate Sovereignty and the Early Modern Foundation of the British Empire in India* (New York: Oxford University Press, 2011), 10–17, 24–28.

hallmark of popular sovereignty. Thus, among the telling characteristics of the company-state were the bitter disputes, compromises, and lopsided influences of special interests that inhere to democratic governance. Most importantly, however, these company-states as a rule emphasized decision-making and the exercise of power through councils, discussion, and consensus. In the case of the English East India Company, every member of the governing council signed letters of decision, and failure to gather all signatures might delay or thwart the implementation of even the most urgent company business.[26]

Just a few years after the creation of the East India Company, the British Crown chartered the Virginia Companies of London and Plymouth. With the establishment of Jamestown, they created the first permanent White settler polities of the British in the Americas (Walter Raleigh's Roanoke colony of 1587 suffered a mysterious demise). The first White settler governments of the Anglo-American colonies, in other words, were company-states. Like the East India Company, the Virginia Company of London emphasized the formal structures of democratic governance. The company's royal charter stipulated a thirteen-member council to govern Virginia. Each member, though appointed at the discretion of the British Crown, held a limited term and was authorized to participate with others in administering all matters of the colony. In addition, a supercouncil was responsible for checking the authority of the colonial council.[27]

Unlike the VOC, however, the English company-states that operated in the Americas eventually made their central concern the establishment of settler colonies (although they began by aspiring to mineral wealth in hopes of emulating Spain's massive silver hegemony). They eventually understood their mission to be "peopling" the land. In fact, among all the challenges with which the company wrestled – developing a sustainable cash crop, forging relations with Native polities, surviving famine and disease – their paramount objective became attracting enough White settlers to establish a stable population that could grow tobacco, the one commodity that seemed to promise sure profits for the private venture. In 1618 company officials devised a plan to make settlers members of a political community through shared ownership in the same way that shareholders (those who owned a minimum amount of stock) participated in the company-state. Settlers who paid their own passage would be granted fifty acres of land, which they were to use for growing tobacco.

---

[26] Stern, *Company-State*, 11.
[27] "The First Charter of Virginia – 1606," in *Federal and State Constitutions*, 2: 1890–891.

Rather than being sharecroppers, they would enjoy the status of equity holders. Furthermore, all White male equity holders would participate in colonial governance through representatives known as burgesses. When the Virginia Company executives created this council of burgesses, they were establishing the same style of governance that the company-state itself employed. This English company-state's governing structure, no doubt, was already influenced by the philosophy of political community (the body politic) embodied in the English Parliament, whose influence and symbolic stature easily carried over into the self-understanding of the burgesses themselves. As early as 1645, for instance, the Virginia burgesses began calling themselves the "House of Commons," alluding to the British Parliament. But this fact should not diminish attention to the peculiar and uniquely consequential role of company-states. It was, indeed, this corporate institution that severed the monarch from the rationalities of the state, although quite by accident. By wedding governance to market reason immersed in a network of investors or "venturers," the company-state enabled a range of historical actors to conceive of political power without the king.[28]

This proved a decisive move that reaped effective outcomes. The resulting House of Burgesses of the Virginia colony became the premier institution of representative democracy among British settlers. It convened its first assembly on July 30, 1619 with twenty-two members representing the most powerful plantations. Although the governor of the Virginia Company held veto power over the burgesses, the representative council nevertheless exercised an unprecedented level of power and provided a formally established body to voice popular interests. This was a major development in the long process of inventing the people, of investing political authority with novel reasons, new rationalities. And it proved the lasting standard for the way other Anglo-American settler colonies structured their colonial governance. Of equal importance was the rapid increase in the White settler population. Combined with the beatific strains of propaganda espoused by the company's public relations arm, the prospect of what seemed a paradisiacal existence in the New World proved enticing and seemed a certain means to economic success. Moreover, the policy of providing so much land to settlers was enabled only by violating the sovereignty of Native nations, which eventually led to a full-scale war in 1622.

[28] Kevin Raeder Gutzman, *Virginia's American Revolution: From Dominion to Republic, 1776–1840* (Lanham, MD: Lexington Books, 2007), 12–13.

In 1624 the British Crown revoked the company's charter as a result of repeated disappointments with profitability and, most consequentially, the public relations disaster that resulted from a decimating defeat by the Powhatan Confederacy in 1622. This meant that the company-state no longer governed the settlers. Instead, the Crown ruled it directly, at least in formal terms. Despite its demise, however, the Virginia Company had created a powerful, fructuous legacy by establishing the House of Burgesses. Like a virus that inserts its code of manufacture into a host, the company-state had permanently infected Anglo-American colonial governance with a prolific strain of popular sovereignty by employing the tactics of representative rule to breathe into existence a political community of stakeholders. By wedding the reason of the state to the rationalities of the market, this company-state had inaugurated a truly revolutionary deployment of power under the sign of freedom. So, despite Virginia's eventual status as a royal colony, formally administered by the British Crown, the exigencies of conducting business and social organization at such a great distance from the English metropole meant that governance in the colony proceeded along the grounds of popular sovereignty that had emerged in the early period. And the House of Burgesses was the surest guarantor of that sovereignty. Moreover, as other Anglo-American setter colonies emerged along the Atlantic coast – Plymouth in 1620, Maine in 1622, Massachusetts Bay in 1630, and Carolina in 1663 – each emulated the Virginia model by establishing a legislative body of both elected and appointed representatives. The fact that these were settler colonies emerging under the sign of freedom (qua popular sovereignty) at far remove from the British Crown virtually guaranteed that their status as royal colonies produced increasing struggles for control and authority over matters such as the royal tax on commodities, the price of goods sold to British merchants, and policies of attacking and displacing Native peoples. In this way, democratic governance emerged as a central institution of the Anglo-American settler colonies. Far from clashing with structures of unfreedom – slavery and colonial conquest against Native polities – the rationalities of White settler democracy and freedom vigorously enabled the brutal efficacy of White colonialism and slavery.[29]

Among the most telling aspects of Christianity in the British settler colonies was the effort by enslaved African Christians to sue for their

---

[29] Martha W. McCartney, *Virginia Immigrants and Adventurers, 1607–1635: A Biographical Dictionary* (Baltimore, MD: Genealogical Pub. Co., 2007), 34–35. Margaret D. Jacobs, *White Mother to a Dark Race: Settler Colonialism, Maternalism, and the Removal of Indigenous Children in the American West and Australia, 1880–1940* (Lincoln: University of Nebraska Press, 2009), 15–17.

freedom. The association between freedom and Christianity was indelible and easily perceptible to Africans. In 1667 an African man named Fernando sued his master for his freedom in Virginia. Fernando based his argument on the fact that he was a Christian and that he had also traveled to England. Fernando's legal suit compelled the Virginia legislative assembly to craft a law stipulating that Christian freedom was purely spiritual and had no bearing whatsoever on the physical bonds of chattel slavery. In November 1766 the enslaved African woman Jenny Slew of the Massachusetts colony filed a legal suit against John Whipple, her master, for her freedom, eventually winning on appeal. Over the next two decades, a small number of other Africans successfully followed Slew's example. All appealed to the Christian tradition by equating Christian morality with Enlightenment principles of individual freedom.[30]

The legal regimes of the Anglo-American settler colonies effected consequential distinctions through racial and religious categories. Sexual regulation in the North American colonies depended in great measure on distinctions of race and religion. The Virginia burgesses, for instance, stipulated in 1691 that "whatsoever English or other white man or woman being free shall intermarry with a negroe, mulatto, or Indian man or woman bond or free" would be "banished and removed from this dominion forever." Over the next fifteen years, the colony began to imprison those who violated this regulation in lieu of offering them the relative liberty of exile. Free White women who bore children out of wedlock through sexual relations with African or African-descended men were either fined or sentenced to five years of servitude, and informants were compensated. Children of such an interracial union, moreover, were bound into servitude for thirty years. By contrast, White men who sired children by African women faced no punishment. In fact, as a consequence of the colony's 1662 legislation, the offspring in such situations were legally enslaved for life.[31]

By the end of the seventeenth century the Virginia colony took more explicit measures to formalize the distinction between servitude (temporary bondage for White Christians) and slavery (indefinite bondage for life, regularly applied to Africans and Native Americans) by decreeing

---

[30] Ira Berlin, "Origins of African American Society," in *Origins of the Black Atlantic*, ed. Laurent Dubois and Julius S. Scott (New York: Routledge, 2010), 143. Vincent Carretta, *Phillis Wheatley: Biography of a Genius in Bondage* (Athens: University of Georgia Press, 2011), 139–41.

[31] Kathy Peiss, ed., *Major Problems in the History of American Sexuality* (Boston: Houghton Mifflin, 2002), 74–75.

that all imported servants "who were not christians [sic] in their native country ... shall be accounted and be slaves," even if they converted to Christianity once in North America. The logic of this rationale lay with presuming that Christians should reserve enslavement for political domination over only non-Christians. Of course, the racial formation of this Christian subjectivity was evidenced by the condition that White Europeans were regarded as Christians ipso facto and that Africans, by far the most numerous laborers being imported into British North America, were to be denied any of the political advantages that might otherwise accrue through their conversion to Christianity.[32]

Black Religion, Christian Freedom, and Racial Slavery

The architecture of colonialism in North America manifested through multiple domains of power, not merely through the formal political institutions discussed earlier. The religious domain, in fact, remained an especially distinctive arena for colonial power. Multiple factors conditioned the pivotal role of religion in this way. First was the nature of the authorization of imperium. As we have seen, this was grounded in a specifically Christian theological understanding of political legitimacy. As a consequence, both the militarist and civic dimensions of colonization bore the stamp of religious imperatives and identity. The former featured explicit campaigns of war, invasion, and enslavement of Africans and Native Americans rationalized through the differential semantics of the Christian-versus-heathen paradigm. The civic structures that incorporated White settlers into a political community by engineering hierarchy, privilege, and legal obligations likewise invested in grammars of Christian supremacism.

The Christian missionary imperative constituted a second reason that colonial power was deployed so intensively through religion. The *ratio* of Christian conversion had an ancient genealogy; the religion had in fact emerged as a missionary movement. Over the course of many centuries, Christian conversion had accumulated a rich assemblage of meanings, including deeply racialized ones. With respect to Jews and Muslims in Mediterranean lands, conversion was both promoted and denied as a clear possibility, as Christianity was conceived as inhabiting

---

[32] Muslims who were under an explicit provision of Christian protection were exempted from this enslavement. Peiss, ed., *Major Problems in the History of American Sexuality*, 72–73.

the body – the principle of *limpieza de sangre*. In its Atlantic incarnation, Christian conversion had become a governing motive for colonization. It now occupied a privileged status, forming the highest echelon of identity in Christian settler states. Moreover, under the new rationalities of political order, Christianity now signified being free. As the Atlantic empires continued to be shaped as slaveholding societies, the status of Christians signified either immunity from slavery or, where slaves were converts to Christianity, the enhanced possibilities of manumission.[33]

As a consequence of these two factors, the Christianization of Blacks constituted a colonial problem. As a general phenomenon, Christianization was tied to matters of governance of the type discussed earlier. But Christianization also raised problems of ontological distancing by refashioning personhood through modes that encoded racial Blackness as a theological problem. This constitution obtained as a distancing effect insofar as Christianization established European Christendom as an exceptional and exclusive locus of Christian authenticity and simultaneously imposed an antithetically constitutive relationship between racial Blackness and White Christian subjectivity. As the population of Africans increased in the Americas, moreover, White Christians invested more prolifically in the practices and ideologies of Black Christianization.[34]

Africans in New Spain

New Spain – particularly Mexico City – easily became the demographic center of free Africans in the Americas and the second most populous region of African slaves, after the Portuguese holdings in South America. Roughly 500 Africans per year were being sent to New Spain during the 1500s. By 1570, in fact, over 36,000 Africans had arrived in the Spanish viceroyalty. During the same year, Mexico City's African slave population numbered approximately 8,000, rivaling if not surpassing the number of Spanish males. This pattern even persisted in much of the countryside, as African slaves regularly outnumbered Whites. American Indians, of course, constituted by far and away the majority of the urban population; more than 60,000 Nahua Indians lived in Mexico City in 1570. In further contrast to Africans of the British colonies, the Blacks of New Spain were mostly Creoles (i.e., Mexican-born) by the end of the seventeenth century.

---

[33] María Elena Martínez, *Genealogical Fictions: Limpieza de Sangre, Religion, and Gender in Colonial Mexico* (Stanford, CA: Stanford University Press, 2011).

[34] Herman L. Bennett, *Africans in Colonial Mexico: Absolutism, Christianity, and Afro-Creole Consciousness, 1570–1640* (Bloomington: Indiana University Press, 2003), 12.

Moreover, by 1646 free Blacks in New Spain, numbering around 116,000, easily overwhelmed the number of enslaved Blacks. The approximately 35,000 African slaves of New Spain in 1646, in turn, outnumbered the Spanish (i.e., White Españoles) almost three to one. And the total population of free and enslaved Africans and African-descended peoples of New Spain by the mid-seventeenth century was the largest in the Americas.[35]

In contrast to the mostly rural geography of Anglo-American slavery, the Spanish empire in the Americas was especially urban. As a result, most free and enslaved Africans and their descendants in New Spain lived out their lives in busy cities and not rural plantations. Conquistadores of the Castilian crown did not create an empire in the lands of Mexico. Rather, they seized it from the Aztecs, who had devoted 200 years to creating a highly centralized system of colonial rule over a region with a high population density rooted in an extensive tributary operation. The entire system was centrally administered in Tenochtitlan, which the Spanish, in alliance with Native American militias, had ransacked in 1521 and subsequently rebuilt as Mexico City. The high population density of settlements in Mexico meant that Native towns were common and enabled advantageous manipulation of labor systems, markets, and infrastructure. In this setting, Spanish males employed African slaves as domestics, as artisans, and even as cultural capital whose primary role was to serve as a timocratic point of leverage by which their masters might generate honor and prestige for themselves. For this reason, few Spanish men of Mexico City desired to be without at least one African slave.[36]

In this environment, Christianity in New Spain generated formations of colonial power that African slaves were frequently able to exploit to their advantage. In sharp contrast to the rationalities of democratic freedom and the primacy of individual property rights that inhered in the Anglo-American settler colonies, New Spain was administered through the political order of royal absolutism. Spanish colonialism (as a modern project) invested in the centrifugal forms of political authority – centralizing monarchies – that were common to metropolitan Europe. In this way, it was also continuous with the political order of Aztec rule. Spanish absolutism constituted slaves as subjects of the Crown. Despite the fact that Spain's propagation of Roman legal paradigms gave masters

[35] Herman L. Bennett, *Colonial Blackness: A History of Afro-Mexico, Blacks in the Diaspora* (Bloomington: Indiana University Press, 2009), 58–59. Bennett, *Africans in Colonial Mexico*, 18–22.

[36] Robin Blackburn, *The Making of New World Slavery: From the Baroque to the Modern, 1492–1800* (New York: Verso, 2010), 150. Bennett, *Africans in Colonial Mexico*, 28–30.

"total" control over slaves, Spain's monarchs encroached considerably on this authority to impose their own claims over slaves. Canon law, specifically, regarded Christianized slaves as royal subjects. This was a key means whereby the Spanish crown exerted control over African slaves.[37]

The efficacy of royal absolutism frequently obtained through the administration of the Holy Office of the Inquisition, which the monarchs of Castile controlled in Spain and the Americas. This meant that the Inquisition in New Spain was actually separate from the Catholic Church. It functioned as an arm of the Crown. Although Jews and Muslims (conversos) in addition to Protestants continued to be an important, "troublesome" preoccupation of the Inquisition, the office mainly prosecuted Christians, the majority of whom were Blacks. Thus, Africans (free and enslaved) and their descendants alone constituted nearly half of the Inquisition investigations.[38] In this context enslaved Africans exploited the tension between the Crown and their masters by appealing to Christianity's sexual regime, which guaranteed to all Spanish subjects the right to Christian marriage and conjugal privileges. The family, in other words, was encoded and administered through ecclesiastical sanction as both an imposition of power and an affirmation of social privilege. So, whereas African slaves living under the regime of Anglo-American settler freedom were denied the legal and formal status of marriage and family, New Spain's Blacks were typically assured of such. When faced with the recalcitrance of dominating masters who might deny them the right to marriage, slaves could appeal to church authorities.

In 1584 Francisco and Catalina, two enslaved Africans from Guinea Africa (known as *bozales* in Spanish) petitioned an ecclesiastical scribe for a writ of marriage in Mexico City. The two were enslaved by the same White master. They identified themselves as being of the coast of Biafra. When asked to give an account of their marriageability, they turned to a company of trusted acquaintances who could vouch that they were indeed single and lived as honorable Christians. In the absence of their master, Francisco and Catalina were able to obtain a Christian marriage license. Under the auspices of the Catholic Church, they were entitled to such as Christian converts. This meant Francisco held a measure of patriarchal authority over Catalina, that the two were forbidden to engage in carnal relations with others outside of their marriage, and that their master could not sell them apart at so great a distance that they would be

[37] Bennett, *Africans in Colonial Mexico*, 8–9.
[38] Ibid.

unable to enjoy the conjugal delights (or, alternatively, to fulfill conjugal obligations) that were theirs by right of Christian marriage. Over the next two centuries, thousands of Africans and African-descended peoples of New Spain sought and obtained the Christian marriage rite and its attending rights. In so doing, they also drew on a network of acquaintances – sometimes even relatives – with whom they had established bonds of friendship and obligation through the slaveholding households in which they were employed. Between 1584 and 1650, in fact, around 4,400 Africans and African-descended peoples of New Spain would serve as matrimonial sponsors, testifying on behalf of Black couples seeking marriage (and typically being granted such).[39]

Christianization also created particular colonial formations of order and participation among Africans in New Spain. African women, especially, were frequently active in confraternities, often as members of devotional "brotherhoods" created by Africans themselves to ensure mutual aid among free and enslaved Blacks. Although African women were denied the right to pursue a spiritual career as nuns in convents (this was limited to White Christians, who were legally classified as *limpio de sangre* – of pure Christian blood), they were regularly employed as convent slaves. African women and men could also join the confraternities established by Whites or, barring this, create their own. They could thereby participate in devotional practices, public processions, and collective formations of spiritual kinship to structure mutual networks of support. Separate Black confraternities performed acts of penitence and public displays of intensively emotional piety. This occasionally included self-flagellation. The earliest of these Black *cofradías* emerged in the 1400s in Iberia. Seville, a port city with a sizable Black population, boasted multiple Black confraternities at least as early as the 1550s. By 1619 the Viceroyalty of Peru had fifteen. Seventeenth-century New Spain, of course, featured these pietistic mutual aid societies as a central aspect of Christian life among its urban African and African-descended population. Whereas wealthy White women might choose to participate mainly through endowing a confraternity or bestowing regular gifts, African and Native women, as well as poor White women, were involved in the day-to-day activities of these organizations.[40]

---

[39] Blackburn, *Making of New World Slavery*, 150. Bennett, *Africans in Colonial Mexico*, 79–81.

[40] Nicole von Germeten, *Black Blood Brothers: Confraternities and Social Mobility for Afro-Mexicans* (Gainesville, FL: University Press of Florida, 2006), 22, 41–48.

The Atlantic empires of Britain and Spain comprised structures and paradigms of striking contrast. But although they were different, they were nevertheless interwoven and sat literally side by side. By force of shared greed over common territories, New Spain and England's American colonies engaged one another through endless disputes, piracies, and battles on land and sea. Africans – free and enslaved – were at the center of the interface between these two empires. Much of this played out in the Lowcountry region of present-day South Carolina, Georgia, and Florida. This was the overlapping boundary of New Spain and British America. Throughout the seventeenth century, well before the plantation revolution recharacterized the structures of slavery in the American South, African slaves met with a relatively loosely organized system of labor and surveillance that allowed for extensive gatherings in the small urban space of Charleston. There they exchanged news of Atlantic events, met newly arrived Blacks from throughout the Atlantic, pursued romantic liaisons, and planned maroonage or armed resistance to free other slaves. In addition, African slave religion in the region was conditioned by an overwhelming lack of institutional and cultural support for Christian conversion. As a result, the enslaved Africans of South Carolina were able to continue their native religions. The difficult conditions of life in English settlements, for instance, demanded recourse to herbal medicinal practices rooted in West African religious knowledge and ritual. Throughout the history of American slavery, English efforts to convert to Christianity those Africans who were not born in America typically came to naught, with one important exception. A significant number of those Africans who arrived at the slave-ship port of Charleston brought with them a historically deep tradition of Kongolese Christianity that had thrived in central Africa for almost two centuries.[41]

Of the approximately 343,878 Africans arriving in the Lowcountry region between 1700 and 1808, almost 30 percent (about 100,000) were from the Kongo and Angola kingdoms. The long history of Catholicism in this region – particularly as the official Kongolese cult – had established a widespread pattern of Christian conversion. This, of course, did not mean that indigenous Kongolese religion was diminished. As a rule, as we have seen, it thrived alongside the expanding influence of the Christian tradition. It is evident, however, that African Christians were not merely products of conversion in the Americas. Rather, a critical mass

---

[41] Berlin, *Many Thousands Gone*, 73.

of these enslaved Africans arrived as conscientious participants in the Christian tradition.[42]

Africans in the Lowcountry maintained traditions about water spirits (*basimbi* in Ki-Kongo), as derived from the Kongo Kingdom and surrounding regions. They viewed these spirits as an integral part of the natural environment. The indigenous theology of West Central Africa regarded *basimbi* as spirits of nature that occupied or constituted rivers, lakes, and forests. Unlike conventional ancestral spirits, these nature spirits served as spiritual adoptive parents or ancestors to any strange people who entered their territorial domain. This theological formation was likely shaped by the historical experience of displaced peoples who, unlike established residents of a land, lacked blood ties to any lineage of local inhabitants. Despite the absence of a local, territorial ancestry and local family burial grounds, newly arrived peoples could find ancestor spirits by establishing relations with the *basimbi*. As viewed in this Central African cosmology, the land itself, even if foreign or strange, could connect the living to the realm of the powerful dead. By communing with the *basimbi*, these enslaved Africans, newly arrived in the Lowcountry, were able to experience religious coherence and social continuity in the wake of the cataclysmic ruptures wrought by the Atlantic Middle Passage. Through fishing, hunting, or nurturing produce from the soil, they could encounter a sense of spiritual kinship despite being enslaved and displaced to a strange and distant land.[43]

The Lowcountry was also marked by a visible presence of Islam among enslaved Africans throughout the duration of the institution. Islam was present extensively throughout West Africa and had been there for centuries. Roughly twenty percent of Africans forced into the slave trade were Muslims, which translates into tens of thousands being forced into what is presently the United States. These Muslims maintained fidelity to their religious traditions. This mean they recited the Quran, prayed three times daily, employed the use of Islamic ritual objects known as gris-gris, and observed special prayers on Fridays. They also preserved Muslim names for themselves and their offspring. It is evident as well that African Muslims frequently distinguished themselves from other non-Muslim Africans.[44]

[42] Jason R. Young, *Rituals of Resistance: African Atlantic Religion in Kongo and the Lowcountry South in the Era of Slavery* (Baton Rouge: Louisiana State University Press, 2007), 24–25.

[43] Ras Michael Brown, *African-Atlantic Cultures and the South Carolina Lowcountry* (New York: Cambridge University Press, 2012), 90–92.

[44] Michael Angelo Gomez, *Black Crescent: The Experience and Legacy of African Muslims in the Americas* (New York: Cambridge University Press, 2005), 143–45. Kambiz

During the late 1600s, the Spanish invested more concertedly in defending their trade routes that carried mineral wealth from Mexico to Spain, an issue of growing concern to the British Empire, which quickly accelerated competition with both Spain and France in colonizing the Americas. The proximity of White English settlers to Spain's lucrative territories demanded a new order of defense that relied on Spanish garrisons. Both free and enslaved Africans were a major part of this strategy of defending the garrisons. Unlike the English, Spanish governors enlisted African slaves (along with free Africans) to constitute a standing militia to thwart English settlers from the north, especially from Charleston (originally Charles Town) in the Lowcountry region that would become South Carolina. The Africans arriving in Florida included populations from Europe, the coastal and interior lands of West Africa, the coastal cities in the vicinity of Angola, the Atlantic seaboard of the Chesapeake, the Caribbean, and even Mexico. The vast majority were rooted in the Orisha-type religions of obligatory patronage to powerful extraordinary beings. These Africans combined strategies of maroonage with an enterprising legacy of being cultural brokers in an Atlantic context that drew on African, American Indian, and European languages, exchange economies, kinship (through intermarriage), and religions.[45]

In 1686 Spanish forces invaded the English settler town of Edisto Island, one of the Carolina Sea Islands. These Spanish troops took back to their Florida fort about a dozen Africans who had been enslaved by the British. The Spanish employed them as wage laborers and trained the newly liberated Africans in Christianity. Such military tactics were common at the time and were designed to weaken the resolve of Anglo-American settlers and to compromise their labor force, which consisted primarily of enslaved Africans. Sensing a pivotal change in conditions as more English settlers poured into the Carolina region just north of Spanish Florida, the Spanish monarch mandated in 1693 that all fugitive Africans arriving in St. Augustine who converted to Catholicism be granted their freedom from slavery. Although the Spanish at times ignored this mandate and sold some fugitives into Caribbean slavery, Carolina's African

GhaneaBassiri, *A History of Islam in America: From the New World to the New World Order* (New York: Cambridge University Press, 2010), 10–15.

[45] Robin D.G. Kelley and Earl Lewis, *To Make Our World Anew: A History of African Americans* (New York: Oxford University Press, 2000), 20–33, 70–93. Kai Wright, *The African American Experience: Black History and Culture Through Speeches, Letters, Editorials, Poems, Songs, and Stories* (New York, 2009), 43. Jane Landers, *Black Society in Spanish Florida* (Urbana: University of Illinois Press, 1999), 29–40. Berlin, *Many Thousands Gone*, 64–65, 71.

slaves could typically count on manumission if they vowed to fight for Catholicism and the Spanish Empire. The reason was simple. The English were becoming too numerous for Florida's relatively small population of Spanish settlers to thwart, and Spain could ill afford to lose its strategic garrison presence to the English settler militia.[46]

By the early decades of the 1700s Spanish officials were recounting with pride their decision to entice Africans into constituting an imperial Christian militia. They were witnessing an increasing surge of Africans fleeing Charleston and the surrounding region of Anglo-American settlements to join the Catholic empire to the south. For these Africans, devotion to Catholicism literally meant being redeemed from a life of chattel slavery and taking up arms – sometimes almost immediately – to return to the Carolina Lowcountry as African Christian soldiers whose mission was to liberate even more captive Africans. These in turn further strengthened the ranks of St. Augustine's African Catholic militia. This led to the creation of an African military-religious settlement just two miles north of the Spanish colonial garrison city of St. Augustine. Named Gracia Real de Santa Teresa de Mose (Fort Mose), the fortified settlement was built by Africans in 1738, was assigned a Catholic priest, and was governed by the African (Mandinga) military commander Francisco Menéndez. Africans enslaved and free lived there and served the Spanish governor of Florida in its defense. The town remained small, maintaining a population of roughly 100 African residents from 1738 to 1763. St. Augustine, by comparison, grew from 1,500 to 3,000 inhabitants during the same time period.[47] Menéndez himself had been enslaved in the British Carolina colony. Originally from the Mandinga nation of West Africa, he had been abducted, sold, and bound into service in the British settler colony. Menéndez had eventually heeded New Spain's invitation to abscond to St. Augustine to fight on behalf of the Spanish crown and the Catholic faith. Over a three-year period, Menéndez and nine other escaped Africans traveled the roughly 300 miles from the Carolina Lowcountry to Florida's Atlantic coast, pausing along the way

---

[46] G.S. Boritt et al., *Slavery, Resistance, Freedom* (New York: Oxford University Press, 2007), 11–13. Wright, *The African American Experience*, 43. Berlin, *Many Thousands Gone*, 71.

[47] Kelley and Lewis, *To Make Our World Anew*, 92–93. Jane Landers, "Gracia Real de Santa Teresa de Mose: A Free Black Town in Spanish Colonial Florida," *American Historical Review* 95, no. 1 (February 1990): 10. Irene A. Wright, "Dispatches of Spanish Officials Bearing on the Free Negro Settlement of Gracia Real de Santa Teresa de Mose, Florida," *Journal of Negro History* 9, no. 2 (April 1924): 144–95.

and joining the indigenous Yamassee nation in their efforts to thwart the violent invasion of British settlers. As early as 1726, Menéndez entered service in New Spain's royal militia of African Christians. As he would later recount in his letter petitioning the Spanish crown for formal manumission, he had fought to "defend the Holy Evangel and the sovereignty of the crown."[48]

For all the agency that African Christians in the Americas were able to effect, they were still powerfully constrained by colonial governance because of the particular constitution of Christianity as a manifestation of imperial power. Whether exploiting the tension between the power of slave masters and royal absolutism in New Spain or striking with guerrilla tactics to liberate other Africans from the Lowcountry of Anglo-American plantation slavery to enhance and maintain the Afro-Christian freedom militia of Forte Mose in Florida, they never fully transcended Christianity's colonial formations.

It is useful to bypass the old bromides over whether or how fully Africans converted to Christianity by taking seriously the fact that Christianity was a colonial status capable of comprising juridical formations while thriving on the hierarchy induced by the theological structures of Christian supremacism. At the same time, it is clear that tens of thousands of Africans participated in Christianity. Attending to African participation in Christianity – and examining the Christian tradition as a complex of institutions, practices, statuses, and legal privileges – is more productive than vetting the question of whether Africans actually converted from one religion to another. The concept of conversion, rooted in the imagination of purities and binaries, contravened the paradigmatic sensibilities of African indigenous religion. Not surprisingly, Africans who affiliated with Christianity continued to participate in the knowledge and practices of indigenous African religions of the Orisha type. Through brokering the right to marriage and instituting patriarchal families in New Spain, or by gaining literacy skills or joining revivalist movements in the Anglo-American colonies, Africans found that Christianity was a tradition in which they could participate and gain access to social status. And this motivated a significant minority of Africans to seek out a Christian network of affiliations, significations, and performances (in the

---

[48] Jane Landers, "Gracia Real de Santa Teresa de Mose: A Free Black Town in Spanish Colonial Florida," *American Historical Review* 95, no. 1 (February 1990): 20. Stuart B. McIver, *Dreamers, Schemers, and Scalawags* (Sarasota, FL: Pineapple Press, 1994), 138. Landers, *Black Society in Spanish Florida*, 40–41.

most serious and substantive sense) through which regimes of sex, marriage, segregation, and discipline circulated.

Christianity both constrained and constituted African subjectivity in ways that severely compromised the sovereign freedom of individual Africans. Yet, at times, it also clearly enabled agential tactics. So, to the degree that African Christians might have participated in multiracial religious meetings with those who enslaved them or other African-descended peoples, they were immersed in a social system whose idiom of power relentlessly reinforced their domination by White rulers. They were still subjugated by colonial power. As a religion of empire, Christianity functioned to reinforce ideologies of White conquest. Even Fort Mose was an experiment of the Spanish crown in creating a voluntary Black militia whose military reprisals against British colonial planters ultimately supported the Spanish crown's imperial ambitions in the Americas. The rights and privileges that Africans of New Spain arrogated to themselves were literally constituted through the Spanish crown's deployment of the Inquisition. African Christians, thus, exploited structures of imposition to eke out subtle but nonetheless significant spaces of power.

Colonialism and Black Christianization
When in 1699 Francis Nicholson, governor of the Virginia colony, ordered the House of Burgesses, Virginia's legislature, to Christianize slaves and attend to their instruction, the legislature replied that Africans were too unintelligent, culturally foreign, and bestial to be converted to the elevated religion of White Europeans.[49] Despite nearly a century of British settlement employing African slaves, the religion of these captive peoples was largely unaffected by the missionary efforts of English Christianity. The determination of British officials to change this situation helped to inspire the most important Anglo-American efforts (at that point) to alter the religious condition of African slaves: the creation in 1701 of the Society for the Propagation of the Gospel (SPG), the same organization through which Philip Quaque would find his employ and Christian vocation. This global missionary society of the Anglican Church targeted both Native Americans and Africans in the British colonies. The society entered what was largely a vacuum of Christian clergy in most of Anglo-America. It was advantaged by its financial independence and was able to circumvent local politics and strangleholds. With more than 300

---

[49] Albert J. Raboteau, *Slave Religion: The "Invisible Institution" in the Antebellum South*, rev. ed. (New York: Oxford University Press, 2004), 100.

missionaries, its presence was more robust than that of the parish clergy in much of colonial Anglo-America.[50]

The SPG soon became the primary means of promoting Anglicanism throughout the colonies, and for many decades it was Anglo-Christianity's best effort at Christianizing the African population. At the time the SPG was founded, half of Virginia's forty-six parishes, which serviced a total of 40,000 White settlers, were without a single minister. Churches and Christian clergy were even fewer in South Carolina, where only a single church existed in the city of Charleston. The majority of South Carolina's 7,000 White settlers were themselves unchurched. By 1769 the Georgia colony had only two churches, 150 miles apart. SPG missionaries reported that White settlers living inland knew little more of Christianity than Native Americans. The well-trained, highly educated clergy serving as SPG missionaries typically looked askance at local Whites, who were nominal Christians, laid-back in disposition, and often lacking sufficient knowledge of Christian theology to instruct their African slaves adequately even if they had possessed the will to do so (though most did not). Given that the majority of the rural White settlers were isolated from institutional Christianity, it is easy to grasp why African slaves remained largely insulated from the efforts of White Christians to effect the erasure of African religion.[51]

In fact, for all the ambition of its vision for converting the "heathen races," the SPG was only minimally successful in converting a few Africans at a time to Christianity. Unlike New Spain's urban slaves, the vast majority of African slaves in eighteenth-century Anglo-America lived and died apart from any significant encounter with Christianity. Virtually all of those slaves arriving from Africa continued to follow either the Orisha-type religions of West Central Africa or the Islamic religion that was well established among West Africans, such as those of the Senegambian Jolof empire. Their adherence to an African view of sacred cosmology promoted a routine association of the material world with spiritual power and extraordinary beings. Just as Africans in Central and West Africa had employed sacred pouches or other objects that were often called gris-gris, so also did those African slaves of the Chesapeake and southern colonies craft items for similar purposes, referring to them with the same terminology. During the 1700s in North America, African

---

[50] Mechal Sobel, *Trabelin' On: The Slave Journey to an Afro-Baptist Faith* (Westport, CT: Greenwood Press, 1979), 64–65.

[51] Raboteau, *Slave Religion*, 105.

slaves who were recognized as religious specialists also crafted objects to gain power over enemies or potential lovers, using hair, clothing, or other personal items. The strategy lay in implementing sympathetic rituals conceived to control events and influence the behavior of others through spiritual power.[52]

The Anglican view of materiality and religion could scarcely have been more at odds with the cosmological assumptions of African slaves. Europe's Reformation had stringently expunged from Protestantism any close, legitimate association between spirit and matter. European occultism in the wake of the Enlightenment was robust and widespread, and the popular religion of White settlers in the Americas was almost feverish in its concern with portents, signs, and material strategies for exercising spiritual power.[53] But White Christian authorities in North America viewed this as an illegitimate means of accessing religious power, a view brutally demonstrated in Christian New England's execution of White European settlers charged with witchcraft during the late seventeenth century. In official terms, Anglicanism interpreted religion within the moral-ethical sphere, which seemed to bear no relation to material substances. In addition to this, the SPG clergy were characteristically stoic and condemned emotionalism. Anglican Christians, for instance, were only beginning to introduce the innovation of group singing in North America (this was discouraged in Britain), and even this was restrained by the overwhelming tendency to associate a highly tempered disposition with dignified piety.[54]

Indigenous West African religions, on the other hand, employed drumming to communicate with and to invite the experience of spirit possession or trance. Communicants also participated in ritual dance, and they patterned their physical participation along the order of what seemed to White observers a more physically involved form of worship. By comparison, African slaves viewed the more sedate atmosphere of Anglican worship and the routinized nature of catechism as banal and bewildering.

[52] Michael A. Gomez, *Black Crescent: The Experience and Legacy of African Muslims in the Americas* (New York: Cambridge University Press, 2005), 143–47. Philip D. Morgan, *Slave Counterpoint: Black Culture in the Eighteenth-Century Chesapeake and Lowcountry* (Chapel Hill: University of North Carolina Press, 1998), 420. Sobel, *Trabelin' On*, 13, 67–68, 70, 73.

[53] David Hall, *Worlds of Wonder, Days of Judgment: Popular Religious Belief in Early New England* (Cambridge, MA: Harvard University Press, 1990). Leigh Eric Schmidt, *Hearing Things: Religion, Illusion, and the American Enlightenment* (Cambridge, MA: Harvard University Press, 2000). Sobel, *Trabelin' On*, 80.

[54] Sobel, *Trabelin' On*, 70–73.

Christianity, in this guise, seemed not to meet the criteria for being a spiritual technology; the religion of the SPG, instead, seemed designed to confound the very receptive modes that would otherwise have created a channel of exchange between African subjects and powerful deities and ancestors. Given this context, it appears that most African slaves found that Christian conversion made little sense. This African slave view of Christianity is evidenced by the experience of the Anglican minister William Tibbs of St. Paul's Parish in Maryland in 1724. Tibbs expressed grave disappointment as he found that the majority of Africans he confronted with the prospect of Christian conversion simply refused to be catechized and balked at participating in Christian meetings.[55]

Throughout the eighteenth century, the SPG continued to meet with formidable opposition not only from slaveholders but also from African slaves themselves. For instance, Africans who were instructed in Christianity and underwent conversion did not necessarily absorb or accept the rudiments of the religion. The Methodist founder John Wesley himself was struck with numbing disappointment after conversing with an older enslaved African woman who had received numerous lessons on the tenets of the Christian faith but seemed to have missed entirely the whole point of the Christian myth of redemption. In addition, African slaves continued to interpret the freedom offered by Christian salvation in terms of physical manumission. During what was perhaps the earliest sustained revival among the African slaves of Virginia in 1751, a Presbyterian minister named Samuel Davies reported more than 100 slaves attending his meetings. In an enviable spate of success, he baptized 140 slaves over a seven-year period. But he continually found that many African slaves took Christian conversion to be either a popular ritual of social status or else a rite for effecting manumission. The frustrated Davies adamantly refused to baptize those Africans who embraced such an understanding of conversion.[56] Once it became clear to African slaves that Christian conversion would not bring manumission from slavery, many were outspoken in their refusal to convert and refused to participate in baptism and catechesis. And those Africans who did convert risked subjecting themselves to ridicule by other Africans for joining the religion of their masters.[57]

By the 1740s, as New France was reeling under the impact of freedom wars fought by alliances of Indians and Africans and as New Spain was

---

[55] Ibid., 58, 63.
[56] Morgan, *Slave Counterpoint*, 422, 426.
[57] Ibid., 420. Raboteau, *Slave Religion*, 121–23.

pitting its resistance to Anglo-American expansion with waning efficacy, African slave religion in the Anglo-American colonies began to experience a new brand of Christianization – evangelical revivalism – throughout the eastern seaboard. The earliest period of revivalism, the so-called Great Awakening, was staged by Anglo-American evangelicals in the 1740s and had attracted some African slaves. White itinerants repeatedly claimed African slaves, in light of their putative propensity for shouting, dancing, and otherwise participating in a vigorously embodied liturgical paradigm, were more devout and open to workings of the spirit than were Whites. Such praise from White Christians problematically derived from racial condescension that demeaned Africans as pedantic and naturally given to emotional display, but it nevertheless attests to the influence of Africans on revival meetings from their earliest point. Because the meetings promoted workings of the spirit, sought to evoke ecstatic experience, and emphasized affect to connect emotionally with the audience, revivalism resonated with potential African converts more so than did Anglican efforts. The approach of the revivals stood in sharp contrast to the relatively unsuccessful Anglican formula for conceiving of religious experience. The focus of the evangelist was to simplify Christian theology by instilling a sense of deep shame, humility, and guilt in the prospective convert and then effecting a desire for intense devotionalism. In light of such, revivalist Christianity made its mark on a significant minority of African slaves.[58]

In the Chesapeake, Methodists and Baptists produced their most numerous converts during the 1780s and 1790s, immediately following the Revolutionary War years. By the 1770s sufficient numbers of Africans were converting to revivalist Christianity to form the first independent churches. Strictly speaking, independent churches were not operated by America's slaves. Rather, independent Black Christian congregations were organized by free Africans who could legally incorporate and own real estate. These churches usually included in their membership a modicum of slaves whose owners permitted them to attend religious meetings; White slaveholders were typically reluctant to provide permission. Most popular in the South was the First African Church of Savannah, Georgia, begun by Andrew Bryan. Bryan was enslaved from birth and was baptized by a freed African named George Liele. In 1790 Bryan purchased his freedom. He started the First African Church in 1794 as a small building on his own property. By 1800 his congregation (strongly attended by

---

[58] Sobel, *Trabelin' On*, 98. Morgan, *Slave Counterpoint*, 428–29.

local slaves) had grown to more than 700 members, and it was able to sponsor smaller independent Black churches in the region.[59] By that time Bryan had become a wealthy real estate investor and landowner; he even became a slaveholder, owning eight Africans by the turn of the century. It was not typical for so many hundreds of slaves to congregate in churches; therefore, Bryan's Savannah church is not paradigmatic. Moreover, theirs was not an antislavery gospel – Bryan and George Liele made their start preaching to other slaves under the watchful aegis of their slave masters. Nevertheless, Bryan's congregation spawned the earliest separate Black churches by sponsoring smaller communities of African Christians. As a significant minority of African slaves continued to convert to Christianity, it was evident that this limited success was largely due to the evangelical institution of revivalism.[60]

The captivating style of evangelical preaching, conversion, theology, and bodily discipline would gradually make significant inroads among literate Africans throughout the Atlantic world. When a young African slave of Boston first published her book of polished English verse in 1773, more than a few White readers were challenged to set aside their skepticism of Black intellectual capacity and absorb the implications of an African author of English poetry. Mastering literacy, especially of the high-brow sort signified by poetic flourish, was an especially efficacious means of portending elite status and civility. The White owners of Phillis Wheatley (1753–1784), for this reason, were soon to find their young slave girl quite an attraction and source of wonder among literary connoisseurs, and they were compelled by her admirers to grant her manumission. Like other Africans of the eighteenth-century Atlantic world, Wheatley was apt to capture the rapt attention of Atlantic readers through the printed word. Years later, the US president Thomas Jefferson, seeking to bolster his claim of White racial supremacy, would attack the writings of Wheatley and of other African authors to demean their intellectual capacities, which he deemed innately inferior to that of Whites as evidenced by European literature. Jefferson's invective evidenced that literary skill was a remarkable form of power for all writers.[61]

---

[59] Milton Sernett, *Black Religion and American Evangelicalism: White Protestants, Plantation Missions, and the Flowering of Negro Christianity, 1787–1865* (Metuchen, NJ: Scarecrow Press, 1975), 111–13.

[60] Ibid., 113.

[61] Phillis Wheatley, *Poems on Various Subjects Religious and Moral* (London: Aldgate, 1773). Thomas Jefferson, *Notes on the State of Virginia* (1782; New York: Penguin Classics, 1999), 147.

Among the most vivid themes in these early Atlantic texts by African authors is the subject of Christian conversion. Phillis Wheatley, heralding her Christian rescue from a "pagan land," was not at all alone in addressing the subject. Olaudah Equiano, Ottabah Cugoano, and Ignatius Sancho, all Black Atlantic authors of the eighteenth century, also examined this problem and addressed the meaning of their Christian identity in thoughtful terms, and not by coincidence. The exigencies of Western colonialism meant that Christian identity among Blacks of the eighteenth and early nineteenth centuries forced a number of problems to the forefront of consciousness. European colonial conquest in the Atlantic world transformed Christianity from a Mediterranean religion marked by perennial strife among old friends and foes – Christians, Jews, and Muslims, especially – to a global religion marked by "strange" contacts or new marvels and continually reshaped as the preeminent religion of Atlantic empire. As Christianity expanded its domain from the Mediterranean to the Americas and throughout Africa, African peoples in western and sub-Saharan regions of the continent, whose societies had never before been touched by Christendom, suddenly found themselves awash in a sea of radically different meanings about history and geography, race and culture, good and evil.[62]

This translocative development, moreover, was affected, directly or indirectly, by the brutal horror of the Middle Passage. What scholars have referred to as the Christianization of Blacks during the globalization of African slavery fundamentally altered the world of Atlantic Africans. It is no simple matter for contemporary readers to appreciate the magnitude and shock effected through such a displacement. To gain some sense of empathy, one might imagine being the victim of the contemporary US practice of rendition, whereby unsuspecting persons are suddenly and violently separated from family and social networks; denied communication with all but their captors; and whisked away to an unknown, often distant location. Factor in extreme levels of physical brutality or torture along with absolute uncertainty of one's fate, and one begins to gain some sense of the radical vulnerability that marked the lives of those Africans who came to know, and even to accept and venerate, the god of their conquerors.

The fact that some Africans chose to affiliate with Christianity cannot be naturalized as the teleological manifestation of some inherent Black

---

[62] Willie James Jennings, *The Christian Imagination: Theology and the Origins of Race* (New Haven, CT: Yale University Press, 2010).

attraction to the religion, its messiah-god, or its putative meekness. The phenomenon, which occurred with a minority of Africans, needs to be *explained*. What forces would have moved Africans to reconcile themselves to the religion of their conquerors? What must they have thought of those Africans "left behind," if not physically then metaphysically, still living within what most Christian theologians deemed a dominion of diabolical evil or spiritual darkness? What was Africa, in fact, if Europe was the center of Christendom? How did the Christian myth of redemption and its conception of geography and time along a racial order register with Black Atlantic authors? What of its narrative traditions about beginnings? If the biblical world, especially, represented history, then could West Africa be historical if it were never mentioned in the Bible? And, most importantly, how did Western colonialism, the fundamental imperative behind all of these changes and movements of peoples throughout the globe, engender new rationalities and reshape the experience of Christianity in Black Atlantic religious history?[63]

Colonialism, Temporalities, and Christian Subjectivity

The autobiography of Olaudah Equiano (1745–1797) offers an unusually vivid portrait of the dynamic relationship between religion and colonialism in precisely this context. In 1789 Equiano, who also went by the name Gustavus Vassa, related his experience of slavery in the form of a best-selling, two-volume autobiography titled *The Interesting Narrative of the Life of Olaudah Equiano, or Gustavus Vassa, the African, Written by Himself*, which he wrote to support abolitionism in Britain.[64] Equiano's autobiography includes a striking description of religion and culture among the Igbo of West Africa, the nation with which he identified by birth. According to Equiano, the Igbo were descended from ancient Jews, and their religion was a modern survival of ancient biblical religion. This claim, seemingly casual at first, is actually a complicated maneuver that reveals how deeply he had mined a trove of biblical commentary to shape his interesting narrative for a skeptical readership. The early modern genre of biblical commentary, which was deeply influenced

---

[63] Marcus Rediker, *The Slave Ship: A Human History* (New York: Viking, 2007). Noel, *Black Religion and the Imagination of Matter*. Talal Asad, "Comments on Conversion," in *Conversion to Modernities: The Globalization of Christianity*, ed. Peter van der Veer (New York: Routledge, 1996), 263–73.

[64] Vincent Carretta, *Equiano, the African: The Biography of a Self-Made Man* (Athens, GA: University of Georgia Press, 2005), especially chapter twelve.

by the exigencies of European colonialism, constitutes in its own right an authoritative literature that proved quite useful for Equiano.

Equiano's willful deployment of the Christian imagination reveals key dimensions of race, history, and colonialism that shaped his experience of religion. Equiano's appeal to biblical commentary about Africa was a thoughtful ruse that illumines his skill as an artist of self-representation who invents a biblical Africa to overturn Christian colonial ideas that denied Africans a place in the historical world.

Equiano's autobiography rendered before his readers an intriguing story of descent into slavery and ascent through maritime adventure to eventual freedom. He claimed as his place of birth the region of the Igbo nation in what is now Nigeria.[65] He told of being kidnapped and forced into slavery, eventually being sold to slaveholders in the Americas. His purchase by a British naval commander took him to a number of Atlantic destinations and afforded him an exceptional experience of slavery marked by the mitigated role of racial antipathy among naval crews on the open seas. During this time, Equiano was renamed Gustavus Vassa. He was subsequently sold (in 1762) to a slaveholder in the British West Indies, where he witnessed the most genocidal dimension of Black Atlantic slavery on the region's sugar plantations. In 1766 Equiano purchased his freedom and, after barely avoiding the loss of his life because of the precarious status of free(d) Africans in the slaveholding Americas, he made his home in England. In 1789 Equiano published the first edition of his *Interesting Narrative of the Life of Olaudah Equiano*. This work detailed his enslavement, Christianization, world travels, and eventual manumission; the book saw nine editions within a decade. Equiano's autobiography immediately catapulted him into position as a leading British abolitionist of international renown, as well as ensuring considerable book royalties for the author. He vividly portrayed the cruel, inhumane patterns of the modern trafficking and enslavement of Africans in the New World. His "interesting narrative" created a considerable shift in British popular opinion about the institution.[66]

In the first chapter of his autobiography, Equiano discusses religion among the Igbo people of West Africa. He reminisces about his childhood and provides accounts of divination and medical knowledge. Quite remarkably, Equiano alludes to similarities between Igbo religion and

---

[65] Paul E. Lovejoy, "Autobiography and Memory: Gustavus Vassa, alias Olaudah Equiano, the African," *Slavery and Abolition* 27 (December 2006): 317–47.

[66] Carretta, *Equiano, the African*, ii–xv, 70–107.

ancient Jewish religion – these include taboos against touching corpses to avoid ritual contamination, civil adjudication based on *lex talionis*, and attention to cleanliness through ritual washing. The latter portion of this chapter reveals Equiano's governing intention behind relating anecdotes to describe Igbo religion.

> Here I cannot forbear suggesting what has long struck me very forcibly, namely, the strong analogy which even by this sketch, imperfect as it is, appears to prevail in the manners and customs of my countrymen, and those of the Jews, before they reached the Land of Promise, and particularly the patriarchs, while they were yet in that pastoral state which is described in Genesis – an analogy which alone would induce me to think that the one people has sprung from the other.[67]

Equiano weaves into his discussion the biblical commentaries of John Gill (1697–1771), John Brown (1722–1787), and Arthur Bedford (d. 1745). In his autobiography, these commentators seem to confirm "what has long struck" him as more than coincidental similarities between the Igbo and the Jews. However, that apparently casual impression about similarities is actually a well-scripted, thoughtfully orchestrated argument designed to persuade readers that the Igbo are derived from biblical – specifically Jewish – ancestors.

Equiano gestures toward "Dr. Gill's" *Commentary on Genesis* to note how Gill "ably deduces the pedigree of the Africans from ... the descendants of Abraham."[68] John Clarke's *Truth of the Christian Religion* and Arthur Bedford's *Scripture Chronology*, he informs the reader, both corroborated Gill's findings. A careful study of Equiano's sources, however, reveals that *none* of these commentators actually claim that Africans are descendants of ancient Jews; the claim is Equiano's exclusively. But because Equiano anticipates his readers will likely reject any interpretive creativity on his part, he attributes to biblical commentators, who are familiar to his English readers, the claim that the Igbo nation is of Jewish origin. It is true that English biblical commentary commonly identified Africans as descendants from biblical characters, but not the ones Equiano suggests. Equiano claims that the descendants of the biblical Hebrew patriarchs eventually made their way to West Africa, producing the Igbo nation, a people whose religion bore, in his estimation, clear evidences of Jewish origins.

---

[67] Olaudah Equiano, *The Interesting Narrative of the Life of Olaudah Equiano, or Gustavus Vassa, the African: Written by Himself*, 2nd ed. (London: T. Wilkins, 1789), 1: 25.
[68] Ibid., 1: 25–26.

First of all, Olaudah Equiano is attempting to locate his ancestry through biblical legends *precisely because* his is a biblical world that demands certain knowledge of geography and history. Among these is the idea that human life and civilization began outside of Africa and that Africans can be explained only by mapping their descent and derivation from White ancestors whose history originated in "biblical lands" during "biblical times," putatively before any human civilization in Africa.[69] Although this view rings hollow and absurd by today's standards, given current knowledge of human origins (*all* human beings are of *African* descent because the human population of *Homo sapiens* began there), the assumption was pedestrian and routine in eighteenth- and nineteenth-century European thought.[70]

Equiano anticipates objection from his readers on the very grounds that ancient Jews, as popularly conceived in his era, were not dark skinned and that Africans, therefore, could not possibly have descended from them. Moreover, the reigning scientific disposition toward pigmentation represented dark skin as an aberration from a "normative" human phenotype. White skin, in other words, was "normal," so it was only dark skin that required an explanation.[71] But Equiano had done his homework and employs subtle, ironic maneuvers to explain this enigma of white-skinned ancestors producing dark-skinned peoples in Africa. He announces that this "difference of colour between the Eboan Africans and the modern Jews" is a problem beyond his abilities to explain and for which he feigns not to bear a solution for his readers. Despite this self-abnegating posture, however, explain it he does. Equiano cites two instances of Europeans – Spaniards and Portuguese – settling in "torrid," equatorial lands and, over a few generations, becoming as dark-skinned as the peoples indigenous to those regions, the latter producing "perfect negroes." It is clear from the context of his discussion of the Portuguese (settling in Sierra Leone), however, that these "perfect negroes" resulted from intermarriage between White settlers and native Africans, not the "torrid" climate.[72]

---

[69] James Bentley Gordon, *Terraquea; or, A New System of Geography and Modern History* (Dublin: William Porter, 1794).

[70] Richard Leakey, *The Origin of Humankind* (New York: Basic Books, 1994).

[71] Colin Kidd, *The Forging of Races: Race and Scripture in the Protestant Atlantic World, 1600–2000* (New York: Cambridge University Press, 2006), 80–97.

[72] Equiano, *Interesting Narrative*, 1: 25–26.

Equiano's Sources

The degree to which Equiano handles his sources to derive an interpretation uniquely his own is evident from the generally positive light in which he discusses Igbo religion, in contrast to the demeaning perspective of his commentary sources. Not only does Equiano ignore commentators' characterization of Africans as "wicked" and "miserable," but he also sanctifies Igbo religion through erecting a genealogy that is biblical in origin and Jewish in nature. Igbo religion is derived through revealed religion – if not the gospel, then certainly the Torah.[73]

Scrutinizing Equiano's sources for biblical commentary readily reveals what is at once impressive and tragic. Equiano was working with the writings of theologians who reviled so-called Hamites – these are descendants of Ham, the archvillain in the biblical legend of Noah. This was in keeping with a long history of biblical representation, and these Hamites were said to be the ancestors of Blacks. Even more pressing is the problem of historical consciousness conjured by these writers – Africa lies beyond the realm of history. In the perspective of mainstream early modern biblical interpretation, not only were Africans wicked Hamites but those of West Africa particularly were also a nonhistorical people. West Africa, however, is the darling of Equiano's childhood memories. As he claims in his "interesting narrative," this was his birthplace, the land of the Igbo. In this context, Equiano's audacious manipulation of these commentators – he pieces together the excesses of glosses and footnotes – becomes a means of circumnavigating entirely the Hamitic myth of African origins and instantiating the Igbo within the realm of Israelite identity. As he artfully explains to his readers, the Igbo are descended from the chosen people and, despite being in the heart of a nonhistorical land, their roots lie at the center of biblical history.

Colonialism and Christianization

Any assessment of Christianity's forceful role in Equiano's biography should consider the underside of Equiano's conversion, which is viscerally constituted through relations of conquest and White Christian domination. Otherwise, one risks representing colonialism as a sublime

---

[73] John Brown, *A Dictionary of the Holy Bible* (Edinburgh: John Gray and Gavin Alston, 1769), 16, 573. John Gill, *An Exposition of the Old Testament* (London: John Gill, 1763), 1: 73, 158. Arthur Bedford, *The Scripture Chronology Demonstrated by Astronomical Calculations, and Also by the Year of Jubilee, and the Sabbatical Year among the Jews: or, An Account of Time from the Creation of the World, to the Destruction of Jerusalem* (London: James and John Knapton, 1730), 229.

experience for peoples who are members of a race targeted for enslavement, genocide, and subjugation, however gainfully they might be positioned within European power structures and enamored of evangelical religion.[74] The idea that Africans needed to be saved from their own religions logically necessitated the acquisition of religious hatred against Africa. Central to this context was a fourfold Christian taxonomy of religions widely observed by colonial writers – Christianity, Judaism, Islam, and heathenism; this ordering of religions mapped African religions as the most fundamental, base manifestation of evil.[75] In the tradition of early modern commentary, African religion was the ultimate symbol of ungodliness and rebellion against the biblical deity because this abode of Ham's descendants was the chief locus of heathenism. The perennial problem of explaining racial Blackness as an aberration from normative Whiteness would continue long after Equiano's time; he was merely among the earliest of colonial African authors to examine the issue. The alienating structure of racial identity created a psychology of inferiority and existential crisis: to be Black was to be abnormal and to exist as an ontological problem.[76]

Colonialism, Temporalities, and the Refractive Subaltern

The racial logic that emerged under European conquest over the Americas, Africa, and the "Orient" fundamentally relied on geographical and cartographical methods to render human populations as people of a different time (the backward races of primitivist discourse) and of particular lands (Black Africa). In this way, Africa as a geographical and racial space was reduced to a temporal simulacrum devoid of history. The colonizing efficacy of Christian conquest, in fact, obtained precisely through this web of temporal and geographical effects, employing social power through domains of religion, commerce, law, militarism, and intellection to remake the world into one fundamentally conceived through racial alterity, religious supremacy, and an unrelenting supersessionism. The more explicitly religious dimension of this process is visible in the

---

[74] Equiano rather explicitly frames his enslavement and eventual Christianization as a fortunate event, one for which he is deeply grateful because it effected his deliverance from a continent of spiritual darkness; in other words, he had escaped eternal damnation.

[75] Tomoko Masuzawa, *The Invention of World Religions: Or, How European Universalism was Preserved in the Language of Pluralism* (Chicago: University of Chicago Press, 2005), 51.

[76] Wilson Jeremiah Moses, *Wings of Ethiopia: Studies in African-American Life and Letters* (Ames: Iowa State University Press, 1990), 153. Carretta, *Equiano, the African*, 182–87.

thoroughgoing construction of a historical consciousness that displaced European Jews from contemporary society into the ancient world. The Christian "typological imaginary" imposed a temporality of identitarian time (i.e., conceiving of history as "that was then, this is now") through which Christianity superseded Judaism. This temporal order encoded the contemporary world as an exclusively Christian era (*anno domini*). As implied by the conception, for instance, of "medieval Christianity," Christian supersession was not a one-time event limited to early Christian history. Rather, this style of imagining history perpetually evolved and was reinvented through more complex, expansive means. The result was a deadening cycle that repeatedly transformed contemporary Jews into living relics of a bygone era who, under the Christian gaze, signified biblical times and biblical peoples past. This established a Christian, "modern" present in which Jews had no rightful place.[77]

Charles H. Long has directed attention to the implications of temporality for Black subjectivity in the Atlantic context. He critically assesses genealogical studies of the Enlightenment modernity that propelled the rise of modern human sciences as inventive disciplines for which, as J. Z. Smith has emphasized, no data per se exist and through which currently mundane categories like "the human" and "language" were constituted. But whereas Smith (and Foucault, largely) fails to ground the emergence of these regimes of knowledge in any particular history of power, Long observes that the roots of modern knowledge and Enlightenment representation are firmly grounded in the colonial contacts afforded through imperial conquest in the Atlantic world and in the "Orient" – encounters with the "empirical other." Colonialism also situated those designated as "primitives" as the elemental loci for studying religion as a *genus*.[78] By erecting categories of Oriental (the East), primitive (Africans and Native Americans), and modern (Europeans) subjectivities, an evolutionary teleology, articulated through theories about the origin of religion, achieved the same subjugating structures of temporality that characterized the Christian typological imaginary. The secular discourse, however,

[77] Kathleen Biddick, *The Typological Imaginary: Circumcision, Technology, History* (Philadelphia: University of Pennsylvania Press, 2003).

[78] Jonathan Z. Smith, *Imagining Religion: From Babylon to Jonestown* (Chicago: University of Chicago, 1982), xi. Michel Foucault, *The Archaeology of Knowledge*, trans. A. M. Sheridan Smith (London: Tavistock Publications, 1972). Charles H. Long, "Religion, Discourse, and Hermeneutics: New Approaches in the Study of Religion," in *The Next Step in Studying Religion: A Graduate's Guide*, ed. Mathieu E. Courville (New York: Continuum, 2007), 183–97.

most immediately derived its data from and applied its taxonomic force in the Atlantic world. For this reason, the religious formations among Blacks of the Atlantic world, Long urges, must become part of the data for understanding *what happened*, for decoding the technical arrangements or, as Vincent Wimbush has proffered, the techniques of scriptural world-making that colonialism engendered.[79]

Examining the overtures of Black religious data such as Equiano's in this way exposes the inadequacy of primitivism and colonial temporalities as the means of interpreting African subjectivity. Otherwise, accepting a colonial framework requires one to conclude that Blacks can never be located within the realm of *now* but instead should be relegated beyond the boundaries of so-called modernity, inhabiting the ontology of primitives. Rather than embrace the enchantment of this colonizing temporality, Long proposes that Black subjectivity itself must be recognized as a productive site for examining the meaning of modernity and conceiving a nonhistorical temporality. This becomes necessary precisely because modernity has been perpetually reinscribed by reading White Westerners (Descartes, Kant, Nietzsche) as its exclusive agents while defining "darker" subjects (those conquered through European colonialism) as inevitably nonmodern.[80]

Long's assessment parallels Homi Bhabha's explanation of the potential for subaltern subjects to disrupt modernity's fictive articulation of time and space. Bhabha explains the spatial distancing, the perspective formed through recession from "the event," that achieves the vista of modernity – that is to say, looking back to the Enlightenment qua event to see modernity, which has superseded a Dark Age. Modernity is constituted through "the enunciation" achieved in the very act of gazing back toward the event (in secular terms, the Enlightenment; in religious terms, the emergence of Christendom and expulsion of Jews). The enunciation thereby constructs and animates the semblance of modernity, of the

---

79 Vincent L. Wimbush, Introduction to his edited *African Americans and the Bible: Sacred Texts and Social Textures* (New York: Continuum, 2000). Wimbush, *Theorizing Scriptures: New Critical Orientations to a Cultural Phenomenon* (New Brunswick, NJ: Rutgers University Press, 2008).

80 Charles H. Long, *Significations: Signs, Symbols, and Images in the Interpretation of Religion* (Aurora, CO: The Davies Group, 1986), 85–87. "Religion, Discourse, and Hermeneutics," 195–97. Long, "Bodies in Time and the Healing of Spaces: Religion, Temporalities, and Health," in *Faith, Health, and Healing in African American Life*, ed. Stephanie Y. Mitchem and Emilie M. Townes (New York: Praeger, 2008). Long, "African American Religion in the United States of America: An Interpretive Essay," *Nova Religio* 7, no. 1 (2003): 23–25.

"now" that can never be identified with "what was then." Bhabha makes clear that the discourse of modernity masks subjectivity (of Europe and, more precisely, the West) as an era or epoch (identitarian time – the now that is, modernity). But of course the epoch cannot subsume "primitive" peoples because modernity is *not really* an era so much as it is *an effect of the subjectivity* of Western conquerors (this is why *modern* and *primitive* peoples can encounter each other in real time without recourse to time travel – otherwise no primitives would still be alive in the modern period but would be extinct). The logic of modernity, thus, denies coevality between the one and the other.[81] Bhabha, furthermore, also proffers as evidentiary analysis the false promise of "the event": modernity brings civility. What it portends is fictive, and he notes that one need only devote serious attention to the subaltern subjects of modern conquests to glimpse this problem – Toussaint L'Ouverture could not ultimately conclude that the French Revolution delivered freedom from *l'ancien régime*; it was not the monarchy of France but the French *democracy's* military that arrived in Haiti (Saint-Domingue) with the mission of securing the perpetual bondage of African slaves.[82]

Equiano's narrative refracts the white light of Christianity's knowledge about Africa into a colorful array of complications and distills the particulate matter of colonial ruptures precisely because of his liminality. He demonstrates the disjunctures that Homi Bhabha refers to as "deformations" and "time lags." Equiano, writing from his home in the British metropole, resided within the geography and temporal space of Christendom. But unlike his fellow European Christians, Equiano was not from Christendom but from the realm of heathens. And unlike the English commentators populating his footnotes, Equiano could not so easily elide the fault lines beneath his gesture of incorporating a nonbiblical Africa into Christianity's temporal and geographical knowledge-world. He was forced, in fact, to employ these fault lines and fissures as footholds and leverage points to pry open a portal of entry into the colonizing, identitarian history of a Christian, colonial world. Equiano is located at a critical point at which this means of relegating – of ordering and assigning – peoples (here as racial and religious types) to a temporal status became wed to the exigencies of empire whose colonizing reach was global. Through this imperial process was born the phenomenal Atlantic world, and in

---

[81] Biddick, *Typological Imaginary*, 22–23.
[82] Homi Bhabha, *The Location of Culture* (New York: Routledge, 1994), 236–55.

this world the many peoples of Africa and the Americas were located – assiduously put in their place – beyond the boundaries of the temporal center. These were people without clear ties to the historical purview of biblical thinking, without obvious connections to the sphere of "human history." And unlike Europe's Jews, their religions could be mapped *only* through diabolism. This evidenced the efficacy of Christian colonial conquest. As surely, furthermore, as vanquishing Europe's Jews to the past went hand in hand with their physical destruction and literal banishment from Christian lands, so also with Africans and American Indians, whose enslavement, genocide, displacement, and commoditization were compelling and intelligible precisely because of the knowledge created about them. Europe's colonial conquest over Africa and the Americas emerged through well-practiced techniques of scriptural world-making and modernizing historiographies (secularized supersession), the genealogical trail of which points up a prototypical primitivism (representing contemporary Jews as premodern and ancient) that would be elaborated and rarified when applied throughout the Atlantic world. Africa, according to this framework, was without history. Africans, unlike European Jews, were stuck not *within* ancient history but *behind* a cordon of historylessness that marked off a Dark Continent *devoid* of historical agency.[83]

For this reason Bhabha and Long urge the study of subaltern liminality, not to exceptionalize the subaltern or to amplify the enunciation of Christian imperialist temporalities. A corrective intervention, rather, proceeds through incorporating the subaltern as such into the body of data for serious intellectual study. This renders visible what is otherwise concealed by triumphalist universalism and by uncritically celebrating the Christianization of colonized peoples. What is forced to the surface in the "deformations" and "lags" is the cost of Equiano's location as a colonized subject whose perspicacity awakens him to the daunting task of forging an "African" subjectivity. It becomes evident that European colonialism forced on the conquered and conquerors alike a style of thinking about Africa that legitimized European conquest and African destruction. Three issues emerge as apparent in consideration of such a history of power.

First, it is imperative to take seriously the centuries of human destruction that have occurred in a mechanistic, rational fashion because of

---

[83] Vincent L. Wimbush, *White Men's Magic: Scripturalization as Slavery* (New York: Oxford University Press, 2012).

colonial knowledge about peoples whose humanity has been obscured.[84] The trans-Atlantic slave trade was the irreducible occasion of Equiano's autobiography and, more basically, of his historical situation (this is true whether he was actually born in West Africa or in North America).

Second, it is instructive to recognize that Africans, particularly those like Olaudah Equiano, perceived this problem of African representation and responded to it through the strictures of slavery, race, and empire. However, this maneuver, which relied on salvaging the scattered wreckage lying in the wake of anti-African conquest, demanded cruel ironies of Equiano and conceded little in the way of humanizing the Igbo. But it was a start. In this way, he aimed to convince a skeptical audience of the human status of the very people who served as the most crucial, fundamental form of capital in the global economy inspired by New World colonialism.

Third, the strategic destruction of African religions is a critical theme in Equiano's narrative and Christianization. Christianity's foray into Africa was predicated on a fantasy of eradicating indigenous African religions.[85] This Christianization process is yet lauded as a triumphal story of Black progress, an enunciation of modernity. Equiano's own position in this history was complicated by his zeal to serve as a missionary, on the one hand, and his devotion to eradicating the enslavement of Africans, on the other.[86] The latter inspired him to represent Igbo religion of Orisha devotion in his autobiography as something other than Satanic, a residual form of biblical, Abrahamic religion – and so not indigenous to West Africa.

That Equiano was heir to a history of scripturalizing the world – remaking it to conform to biblical characterizations – should not hide from us the fact that he also, in turn, bequeathed to Atlantic readers complicated meanings about slavery, Africa, scripture, and the prerogative of invention within the context of colonial violence. His autobiography did more than any other single text of the time to galvanize British sentiment against the slave trade. By representing Africa as a historical subject, asserting his African identity, and entering a stream of canonical history, he revealed himself to be a forceful interpreter of race and scriptures and a willful inventor of Africa, ably positioned within the intricate process

---

[84] Lewis Gordon, *Fanon and the Crisis of European Man: An Essay on Philosophy and the Human Sciences* (New York/London: Routledge, 1995).
[85] Dulue Mbachu, "Christianity vs. the Old Gods of Nigeria," *The Guardian*, September 4, 2007.
[86] Equiano, *Interesting Narrative*, 1: 181–83.

of biblical world-making.[87] It seems especially tragic, in this light, that so few Black Christian authors of the 1800s, after Equiano's death, would demonstrate a similar audacity or creative prerogative. Rather, the majority tended to represent African religions as wicked and misanthropic, under the weight of influence from White Christian commentators.

[87] Philip S. Zachernuk, *Colonial Subjects: An African Intelligentsia and Atlantic Ideas* (Charlottesville: University Press of Virginia), 32, 33. Edward W. Said, *Orientalism* (New York: Vintage Books, 1979).

PART TWO

4

Stateless Bodies, African Missions, and the Black Christian Settler Colony

In this chapter I examine the confluence of Christian missionary religion and Black settler colonialism. I do so within the context of the Anglo-American Revolution, which spawned the formal creation of the US racial state. What began as an Anglo-American rebellion against the British Crown became a mixed opportunity for African slaves to strike a blow for their own freedom. The unlikely prospect of British defeat, however, became an eventual success for Anglo-American rebels. This left those Africans supporting the British royal military in an uncertain plight. They had joined the British understanding clearly that doing so constituted their best hope for freedom, which had been promised to them in exchange for their military service. This turn of events eventually became the chief factor in the creation of Black settler colonies, first in Nova Scotia, then in Sierra Leone, and subsequently Liberia.

Although Black settler colonialism emerged fully within the context of Atlantic slavery, the specific histories of this movement set before us the peculiar problem of free Africans, not slaves per se. Of course, as we shall see, free Africans in the Americas were rarely far removed from slavery, often because they were either manumitted by slaveholders or recaptured from slave ships or because freeborn Africans in the Americas were themselves descended from ex-slaves.[1] As a result, the focus of free Africans that ensues should in no way be interpreted as an effort to sidestep the problem of slavery. Rather, the aim here is to underscore the immense role that slavery plays in the pageantry of freedom.

[1] John Hope Franklin and Evelyn Brooks Higginbotham, *From Slavery to Freedom: A History of African Americans*, 9th ed. (New York: McGraw-Hill, 2011), 148–50.

The extent of this connection is not so easily visible, so our treatment of Black settler colonialism should begin to elucidate it further. With few exceptions, scholars have generally treated the subject of Black settler colonialism using the rubric of "emigrationism" or "Negro colonization." This language is certainly not unwarranted, especially given the fact that such terminology was employed by the historical actors themselves. One unfortunate result of this convention, however, is its tendency to elide Black emigration's role in the lineage of democratic settler states. As will become evident, these Black settlements had everything to do with the larger phenomenon of settler colonialism that shaped the Atlantic world. To lose sight of this fact is to miss much of what inspired them and what they demonstrate about the problem of freedom.

The idea for Black settler colonialism was initially viewed as a strictly secular concern among White political elites who entertained a host of reasons to convey free Africans from the United States or England to some other place. But this fact should be nuanced by two important considerations. First, Atlantic Africans themselves envisaged the prospect of occupying self-governing polities (i.e., Black settler colonies) long before White political elites began to organize in support of such. Second, despite its secular origins, the actual execution of Black settler colonialism was to proceed almost entirely through the religious agencies of Black settlers, chiefly within the missionary enterprise. The one important exception to this was the case of African recaptives, who were rescued from slave ships at sea and subsequently transported to the ports of West Africa under British control. Otherwise, free Africans typically enjoined this venture in the interest of promoting Christian polities. They conceived their settlements as civilizing projects devoted to African redemption in fully religious and secular terms.

White Revolution and Internal Colonialism

What changed for Africans – slave and free – when the system of Anglo-American settler colonies became a White nation-state? And how did this alter the religious structures devoted to redeeming Africans from so-called heathen decadence? The answers to these questions emerge through understanding the racial dynamics of the Anglo-American Revolution and the particular racial tectonics of US nationalism. The war, after all, forged a racial nation-state that was simultaneously an empire. Under the system of British colonies in North America, free and enslaved Africans lived out a complex status under a violent regime of

White rule. The essential sociology of race and state power was driven by the imperative of creating racial freedoms and privileges for White settlers. This imposed a severe order of racial hierarchy. But because there was no overriding state that united the colonies, racial loyalty among White colonial settlers was feasibly and often divided by competing interests. Most notable were strategic alliances between White settlers and Native nations. The absence of a racial republic, to be sure, was offset by the brutal reality of White settler policies whose legal structure encoded a realpolitik of White (particularly English) confederation. Native nations suffered repeated displacement, genocidal wars of extermination, and terror because the myriad White colonies shared a common interest over and against Indians and Blacks. But this common interest nevertheless produced a weaker version of racial peoplehood than nationalism did. As will become clearer later in this chapter, the rise of the United States as a democratic republic inaugurated a greater alterity between Whites and the dominated African or American Indian subjects living under White racial rule.

Black Loyalists and Anglo-American Revolution
The Revolutionary War generated perplexing ramifications for free Africans and those enslaved who aspired to become free by joining the Loyalist movement devoted to preserving British control of the colonies. For obvious reasons, they risked a perilous situation in what seemed the unlikely event that Britain might fail to squash the armed rebellion. Teleological histories of the American Revolution easily elide the divisive sentiments White colonial settlers harbored about rebelling against King George III. Perhaps as many as one fifth of White colonists actually opposed insurrection against the British Crown. Despite the pontifications of separatist agitators such as Patrick Henry and James Otis, the legitimate authority of the British Parliament to administer taxation and general legislation over all the colonies of the British Empire was well established in theory and practice. It should really come as no surprise that hundreds of thousands of White colonists in North America supported the Crown, and many slaveholders among this number urged their slaves to fight on behalf of the British, manumitting them at least temporarily as a pragmatic matter.[2]

---

[2] Robert M. Calhoon, *The Loyalists in Revolutionary America, 1760–1781* (New York: Harcourt Brace Jovanovich, 1973). Michael A. McDonnell, "Resistance to the American Revolution," in *A Companion to the American Revolution*, ed. Jack P. Greene and J. R. Pole (Malden, MA: Blackwell Publishing, 2004), 342–51.

Black militarism on behalf of the Anglo-American rebellion was deeply controversial, however. The general policy of the US Continental Army was to ban Blacks from admission. Although some Africans had already joined the fight against Britain, no more were permitted once George Washington took command. It was the Loyalists who prompted the change by Washington to allow Africans to enter the armed service. When fighting broke out in Virginia, the royal Virginia governor Lord Dunmore was supplied with a slim number of White soldiers to calm the rebellion, making for a precarious plight against the more numerous separatists. Desperation spawned opportunity when Dunmore reflected on the numerous African slaves throughout the colony – close to 280,000 – who easily outnumbered White settlers in many regions.[3] In addition to these were the White immigrants who continued to arrive under indenture, eking out an existence under domination by White planters that frequently approached the conditions of the African slaves. Dunmore realized he was sitting on a potential army of servants and slaves. So, the governor shrewdly decreed in November 1775 that White "indentured servants, Negroes, or others" were to be manumitted on joining the war to squash the rebellion.[4]

For their own part, African slaves were keen to take advantage of such an opportunity, as were White bonded laborers. Within twenty days of his announcement, Dunmore was able to report to London officials that African slaves were flocking to join the Loyalist forces. This tide of African recruits would continue throughout the Revolutionary War. Dunmore had essentially forced the reluctant hand of Washington, who at first extended admission only to free Africans. It also struck fear into the nervous hearts of Virginia slaveholders, at whose urging the Virginia legislature officially pardoned all slaves who would return from the Loyalist militia. More importantly, it demonstrated to the African population that consternation over White settler revolt could topple or at least fracture what seemed an intractable condition of racial slavery, opening possibilities for Black freedom.[5]

---

[3] In the first US census of 1790, the African slave population was 287,959, accounting for 42 percent of Virginia's population. See "Virginia – Race and Hispanic Origin: 1790 to 1990," http://www.census.gov/population/www/documentation/twps0056/tab61.pdf (accessed May 22, 2013).

[4] Franklin and Higginbotham, *From Slavery to Freedom*, 74–75. Todd W. Braisted, "A Call to Arms," in *Moving On: Black Loyalists in the Afro-Atlantic World*, ed. John W. Pulis (New York: Routledge, 1999), 8, 9. James W. St G. Walker, *The Black Loyalists: The Search for a Promised Land in Nova Scotia and Sierra Leone, 1783–1870* (Toronto: University of Toronto Press, 1992).

[5] Braisted, "A Call to Arms," 8, 9. Franklin and Higginbotham, *From Slavery to Freedom*, 74–75. Walker, *Black Loyalists*.

Over the course of several months, it became clear to both Loyalists and the rebel colonies throughout North America that the African factor was a potentially decisive one, especially in the Chesapeake and southern regions, whose heavy population of mostly enslaved Africans numbered more than half a million.[6] In addition to joining the Loyalist militia, African slaves were fleeing the vast plantations and small farms of White masters. Virginia, South Carolina, and Georgia alone lost 70,000 slaves to either the British militia or fugitive flight for freedom. By 1778, as more colonies began to legalize African admission to the Continental Army, the ranks of African "patriot" soldiers began to increase. For the most part, they were promised freedom from slavery on the war's end. The important exceptions were Georgia and South Carolina, the latter of which had the highest population of Africans. Neither colony was willing to legalize African admission into the Anglo-American militia. This situation, however, only heightened the flight of Africans to Loyalist lines. In the end, Africans constituted 5,000 of the total 300,000 soldiers who fought against Britain in the Revolutionary War. They were present in practically every military engagement of the war.[7]

Even after the war had ended, many Africans who had been soldiers during the war retained their arms and fought fiercely in hopes of creating an African revolutionary war to follow on the heels of the Anglo-American revolt. And as a result, it appears that thousands of African slaves were manumitted for their military service or by force of arms. In this light, the war unequivocally emboldened African slaves and free Africans to end the institution of racial slavery through violent revolutionary action on their own behalf.[8]

What became of those Africans who fought on behalf of the British, hoping to gain their manumission in return? At the war's end, more than 10,000 Africans were formally within the ranks of the British army, more than double the number who fought for the Anglo-American colonies. Their fate became a point of fierce debate by White political rulers.[9] In

---

[6] Michael A. Gomez, *Exchanging Our Country Marks: The Transformation of African Identities in the Colonial and Antebellum South* (Chapel Hill: University of North Carolina Press, 1998), 20–21. Franklin and Higginbotham, *Slavery to Freedom*, 77.

[7] Alan Gilbert, *Black Patriots and Loyalists: Fighting for Emancipation in the War for Independence* (Chicago: University of Chicago Press, 2012), 116–30. Franklin and Higginbotham, *Slavery to Freedom*, 75–82, esp. 77. Gomez, *Exchanging Our Country Marks*, 19–21.

[8] Gilbert, *Black Patriots and Loyalists*, 212–20. Franklin and Higginbotham, *Slavery to Freedom*, 75–79.

[9] James T. Campbell, *Middle Passages: African American Journeys to Africa, 1787–2005* (New York: Penguin Press, 2006), 22–23.

their initial peace treaty with a newly formed United States, Britain agreed to the victorious rebels' demands that Africans who fought for the British be handed over to US officials to be reenslaved or otherwise punished. Surprisingly, however, the British refused to follow through on this agreement. Instead, they evacuated these Africans, relocating them elsewhere in Atlantic lands. Unable to resist the lucrative possibilities attending the sale of Black "contrabands," Britain actually sold many of these Africans into slavery in the empire's Caribbean colonies, sentencing them to a fate arguably as damning as that planned by US officials. Others were allowed to live in Britain, where they would constitute a severely destitute class plagued by poverty and racism. A significant number, however – approximately 3,000 – were relocated to Canada, in Nova Scotia specifically. This Canadian settlement became the most familiar locus of "Black loyalists" throughout the Atlantic world.[10]

Thus, by a complex turn of events, the American Revolution – that is, the struggle to create a White settler state – spawned a different category of African dispersion, one conceived with the intent of creating Black settler polities. This marked the inception of the Black settler colonial project that would issue from Anglo-America, a multifaceted drama that would continue to unfold well into the nineteenth century. The movement of these Black Loyalists throughout the Diaspora, in other words, soon effected further ripples of intrigue and initiative. As a result, institutional efforts to create Black settler colonies would multiply and make the question of the Black settler state a central and dominant concern for the Black religious and political aspirations throughout the Atlantic world.

The Anglo-American Revolution of White settlers was rooted in democratic freedom (viz., popular sovereignty), a development that sparked another iteration – a massive dissent against institutional slavery. The zealous spirit of White revolution compelled a full range of historical actors to reject the philosophical and political assumptions of slavery, beyond the question of whether African slaves who fought against the British should be rewarded. For instance, the first organized antislavery societies in North America emerged during the war. More significantly, between 1780 and 1790 at least six northern states abolished slavery, typically by implementing gradual emancipation. At the federal level, the US Congress outlawed slavery in the Northwest Ordinance territories in 1787. That same year Congress legislated a ban on the trans-Atlantic import of enslaved Africans that would go into effect in 1808. Although

[10] Ibid., 22–25.

this trans-Atlantic supply of slaves into the United States would continue until the start of the Civil War, the 1808 ban did significantly dampen the volume of the trade. It also had symbolic importance because it suggested that the warfare and kidnapping germane to the slave trade caused Whites some moral consternation. At the same time, however, other measures inscribed in the Constitution granted greater representation to states with more slaves (Article I, Section 2, or the three-fifths clause), legislated the recapture and surrender of escaped slaves (Article IV, Section 2), and repeatedly recognized the validity of Black slavery without actually employing the term "slavery" itself.[11]

The prospect of African freedom incited violent hostilities and institutional repercussions from White rulers, who understood clearly the central role of slavery in structuring the White republic and were thus staunchly devoted to protecting their own interests by strengthening the institution. George Washington, whose family amassed its wealth through enslaving Africans, enlisted the service of a White comrade in New York to hunt down a number of Africans who had fled enslavement on his plantation for a life of freedom after the war. The general who led the White settler colonies to their independence from Britain clearly demonstrated the specific racial nature of the freedom brought by White revolution, afforded in significant measure through African blood. The enslavement and trade in Black human beings was, after all, the economic foundation of White wealth throughout the Atlantic world. Beyond that, the United States was not merely a society with slaves. It was a *slave society*. Its fundamental architecture of freedom, its social systems, and its racial taxonomy and cultural mythology – all were derived largely through the system of totally dominating African peoples. More emphatically, the sheer economic feasibility of White settler colonialism and White nation building depended squarely on Black slavery, just as much as it did on colonizing, exterminating, and displacing American Indians.[12]

This development hints at the linkages between freedom and slavery. Indeed, scholars have recognized for some time now that the war for White freedom and revolution actually magnified and further entrenched

---

[11] Gilbert, *Black Patriots and Loyalists*, 243–48. John Hope Franklin and Alfred A. Moss, *From Slavery to Freedom: A History of African Americans*, 7th ed. (New York: McGraw-Hill, 1994), 80–83. David Waldstreicher, *Slavery's Constitution: From Revolution to Ratification*, 1st ed. (New York: Hill and Wang, 2009).

[12] Ira Berlin, *Many Thousands Gone: The First Two Centuries of Slavery in North America* (Cambridge, MA: Belknap Press, 1998), 15–20, 93–108.

the institution of African slavery.[13] To fully appreciate why this was so, one must keep in mind the unique, essential role that slavery played as a mechanism of governance. The institution of slavery, after all, is not fundamentally a labor system, although scholars have spent many decades since the mid-twentieth century emphasizing the economic (as opposed to racial) origins of the Atlantic system of slavery. Although this tendency has served to correct the inaccurate perception that Black slavery was somehow an ineluctable result of some naturalized, ahistorical anti-Blackness in Europe (profit, not racism, is what initially inspired Europeans to participate in the African slave trade), this scholarly trend generally failed to distinguish the central role of labor within Atlantic slavery from the sociological factors that compose the actual condition of slavery. Unpaid labor, in other words, does not constitute the condition of enslavement. Any comparative attention to slavery will quickly reveal, for instance, that some slave systems entailed little or no labor on the part of slaves. Slavery, rather, is constituted through a relation of power. It is a system of social relations whereby an individual becomes totally dominated, and this domination has typically entailed the practical prerogative of masters to determine the life and death of slaves. Atlantic slavery, moreover, typically mirrored other systems of slavery insofar as slaves were natally alienated and dishonored (in a system in which honor accrued to slaveholders through a perverse political economy of timocracy).[14]

In addition, the Atlantic system of slavery presumed morphologies of freedom and grammars of liberty that constituted White social identity in strict antithesis to the social and physical body of the slave. Political authority and the specific nature of racial governance were rationalized and conceived through the association of racial Whiteness with freedom and racial Blackness with slavery. Just as religious freedom for the varieties of Christian sects after Westphalia was realized through juxtaposition against racial others (Jews and Muslims) who were perpetually defined outside of Christendom's political community, so also were Blacks and

---

[13] Edmund S. Morgan, *American Slavery, American Freedom: The Ordeal of Colonial Virginia*, 1st ed. (New York: Norton, 1975). David Brion Davis, *Inhuman Bondage: The Rise and Fall of Slavery in the New World* (New York: Oxford University Press, 2006).

[14] Sherwin Bryant, *Rivers of Gold, Lives of Bondage: Governing through Slavery in Colonial Quito* (Chapel Hill: University of North Carolina Press, 2014). Orlando Patterson, *Slavery and Social Death: A Comparative Study* (Cambridge, MA: Harvard University Press, 1992). Orlando Patterson, *Freedom in the Making of Western Culture* (New York: Basic Books, 1991).

Indians defined outside of the political community through which the Anglo-American colonies and later the US racial state were conceived. Slavery, more fundamentally, constituted both the symbolic and institutional framework that made freedom socially real. And as was the case with Iberian colonialism throughout the Americas, Anglo-American slavery was simultaneously a productive system in the economic sense and a foundation for establishing a body politic by constituting a social body (Blacks and American Indians) that lay beyond the pale of inclusion. This is why freedom cannot be imagined as a metaphysical, celestial virtue. Freedom, rather, is an institution in the same sense that slavery is an institution. Freedom is literally constituted through the formation of negotiated statuses whose relative scale operates within a field of plural morphologies (i.e., there is no single freedom "out there") and that becomes intelligible as one of multiple possible social sites along a continuum of degrees of obligation.[15]

From Internal Colony to Settler Colony

African American religions after the Revolutionary War were shaped under the cruel shadow of freedom, slavery, and imperial White hegemonic rule. In the years following the war's end, more than 59,000 free Africans lived in the Anglo-American state. Over the next two decades, this number would increase rapidly to 186,000. This rate of increase would wane significantly afterward, however, so that by 1860 free Africans in the United States numbered fewer than 500,000 out of a total US population of 31 million, accounting for *less than 2 percent* of the nation's inhabitants. In contrast to the number of free Africans, almost 700,000 enslaved Africans lived in the United States in 1790. This enslaved population increased fairly steadily each decade, reaching more than 3.5 million (12 percent of the US population) by the start of the Civil War. There is an important irony here, however. Whereas the relatively small population of free Africans was never more than 14 percent of the US Black population, their mere presence was perpetually vexing to Whites and inspired African slaves with concrete evidence that Black freedom was real and attainable.[16]

---

[15] Patterson, *Slavery and Social Death*. Patterson, *Freedom in the Making of Western Culture*.

[16] US Census Bureau, "Virginia – Race and Hispanic Origin: 1790 to 1990," http://www.census.gov/population/www/documentation/twps0056/tab61.pdf (accessed May 22, 2013).

Colonialism, not merely slavery, fundamentally defined the relationship of Blacks to the White American republic. In a literal sense, Blacks existed in the United States as an internal colony, subject to its governing rule but perpetually excluded from the body politic. It becomes important, for this reason, to interpret the nature of free Blacks in a White nation-state to grasp the terror that Black freedom signified for most Whites and the insult and elusiveness that it constituted for putatively free Blacks themselves. First of all, free Africans were often former slaves, so one cannot regard them as strictly distinct from the slave population. In addition, because of the ever-growing reinforcement of fugitive slave laws, practically any free Black was susceptible to being enslaved if accused by a White person of having escaped a White master.

Free and enslaved Blacks had several reasons to hope that the cataclysmic changes of the Revolutionary War would upend the social order and bring political liberation and the demise of slavery. This aspiration was not limited to Africans but also surged in the bosoms of an international array of antislavery activists. The US Congress had already agreed to ban the trans-Atlantic transport of African slaves beginning in 1808, and England had instituted a similar ban. Although this was a far cry from outlawing slavery itself, it seemed a certain beginning to that end. The demise of slavery, furthermore, was not merely a specter of wishful desire for the generosity of White rulers. Throughout the Atlantic world, as we have seen, African slaves themselves had established a vibrant tradition of armed resistance to fight for their freedom. By the early 1790s Haiti was erupting in what would prove a successful revolution against slavery. The abolitionist movement, moreover, which first emerged among African polities attempting to dismantle slavery in West Africa, was gaining considerable steam and had by the late 1700s emerged more fully as a protest against slavery itself rather than as objections to the harsh conditions of the Middle Passage or the secondary and tertiary effects of slavery, such as the separation of families.[17]

The most important element buoying hopes of slavery's demise following the Anglo-American revolutionary war was arguably the Black

---

[17] Laurent Dubois, *A Colony of Citizens: Revolution & Slave Emancipation in the French Caribbean, 1787–1804* (Chapel Hill: University of North Carolina Press, 2004). Andrew Jackson O'Shaughnessy, *An Empire Divided: The American Revolution and the British Caribbean* (Philadelphia: University of Pennsylvania Press, 2000). Rudolph T. Ware III, "Slavery in Islamic Africa, 1400–1800," in *The Cambridge World History of Slavery, vol. 3, AD 1420–AD 1804*, ed. David Eltis and Stanley L. Engerman (New York: Cambridge University Press, 2011), 47–80.

Christian settler colony. The most significant of these was the Sierra Leone colony. Sierra Leone and its founding corporation exemplified the complex linkage among modern states, corporations, and racial empire. All of these shaped the nature of African slavery and White freedom in the Atlantic world. The colony had begun in 1791 as a possession of the Sierra Leone Company. Two factors had led to its founding. The first was abolitionism, which had been gaining considerable ground in England during the very time that Britain's settler colonies in North America revolted. Leading proponents of the antislavery movement, such as Granville Sharp and the siblings Thomas and John Clarkson, agitated for creating a colony in Africa devoted to settling free or manumitted Africans. The second factor was the "problem" of Black Loyalists in the newly formed United States. These Blacks were granted manumission by Britain in return for their willingness to fight for continued British rule. Once the war ended, however, it quickly became clear that these Africans, who had been armed to suppress an Anglo-American insurgency, were now in danger of being killed or re-enslaved by White patriots.[18]

By 1790 England was experiencing a high tide of abolitionist sentiment due to Black abolitionists such as Olaudah Equiano. Equiano's autobiography had galvanized the consciousness of many Britons, and the energetic African author was working a brisk lecture circuit to rally support for banning the slave trade. Equiano's narrative brilliance, his dramatic activism, and the sheer fact that he himself had undergone and survived chattel slavery made him an exceptionally celebrated figure. Key White abolitionists, particularly Thomas Clarkson and Granville Sharp, were also integral to the success of England's efforts to disrupt the slave trade. Sharp was among the subscribers to Equiano's autobiography, and he was especially influential in shaping England's legal stance toward slavery. He had assisted the enslaved Africans whose fugitive status led to the Mansfield ruling of 1772, which had stipulated that slaves traveling from the colonies to England could not be legally forced into continued slavery. In his *Injustice of Tolerating Slavery* (1769), he had stridently denounced Anglo-American settlers' hypocrisy of pledging to vindicate their own desire for freedom while preserving Black slavery.[19]

---

[18] Alan Gilbert, *Black Patriots and Loyalists*, 207–42. Mary Louise Clifford, *From Slavery to Freetown: Black Loyalists After the American Revolution* (Jefferson, NC: McFarland, 1999).

[19] David Brion Davis, *From Homicide to Slavery: Studies in American Culture* (New York: Oxford University Press, 1986), 239–42. Hilary Beckles and Verene Shepherd, *Saving Souls: The Struggle to End the Transatlantic Trade in Africans* (Kingston, Jamaica: Ian Randle Publishers, 2007), 47–50.

Much of the British hostility to the slave trade, however, was fed by racist antagonism against the presence of Africans in England. As a result of the war against the American colonies, many Africans had sought refuge in England – perhaps as many as 7,000 were in London alone.[20] Others had slowly contributed to a growing Afro-British population through their employment as seamen on military or merchant ships. In Britain's postwar economy, their severe financial plight only worsened, and White Britons increasingly viewed them as a social menace and undue burden on society. It was in this environment that a British scientist named Henry Smeathman promoted his idea of creating a colony in West Africa to which Britain's Blacks might be removed. Smeathman had lived in West Africa for a few years, studying its flora and fauna. He was keen to recognize that the principal charitable organization devoted to providing relief to impoverished Africans, the Committee for the Relief of the Black Poor, was becoming interested in resettling Blacks outside of England. For several years he had entertained the idea of creating a colony in West Africa for just this purpose. In early 1786 he shrewdly established contacts with the charitable committee and, after being invited to develop a detailed strategy for such an enterprise, published his *Plan of a Settlement to Be Made Near Sierra Leona* that same year. Sharpe joined the effort, going so far as to draft plans for a provisional government to administer authority over such a colony. Smeathman's group initially sought a royal charter for a corporation devoted to running the colony. When this failed, they settled for parliamentary legislation that created the company. This stoked fierce opposition from the wealthy and politically powerful slave traders, financiers, and others whose interests derived from the trans-Atlantic slave trade. Nevertheless, economic incentives and political will for remedying the lingering problem of a free Black population in England prevailed such that by 1791 the Sierra Leone Company had come into being.[21]

About 1,100 free Africans arrived in Sierra Leone from Nova Scotia the following year (1792). Most of these had earlier hailed from the former North American colonies. In the years that followed, many more Africans would arrive in Sierra Leone, largely from England, to try their hand at living in a free African society. Thus began a pivotal colonization

[20] Alexander X. Byrd, *Captives and Voyagers: Black Migrants Across the Eighteenth-Century British Atlantic World* (Baton Rouge: Louisiana State University Press, 2008), 125.

[21] Vincent Carretta, *Equiano, the African: Biography of a Self-Made Man* (Athens: University of Georgia Press, 2005), 217–30. Beckles and Shepherd, *Saving Souls*, 47–50. Byrd, *Captives and Voyagers*, 120–35.

movement that would have tremendous implications throughout the Atlantic world. Despite the company's promising start, a litany of foibles and mismanagement culminated with the British government taking over the enterprise in 1809. More than a century later, Sierra Leone would symbolize Africa's vast, untapped resources in the eyes of European metropoles seeking imperial expansion. The rise of major urban centers such as Chicago and New York would depend on the massive transport of rubber and steel from West Africa by establishing relations with nations that began as Black Christian settler states. For the time being, however, the Sierra Leone colony concretized the aspirations of White abolitionists who sought a pragmatic means of undermining African slavery. It also assuaged the anxiety of liberal Whites who certainly opposed slavery but were nonetheless avid devotees of White supremacism and racial apartheid. In addition, the colony appeared to provide a means for African Americans to establish their own state, which Black settlers increasingly saw as the essential mechanism for self-determination.[22]

When the first group of African Americans travelled from Nova Scotia to Sierra Leone in 1792 their journey marked a major milestone in a racial enterprise dually conceived by Blacks and Whites with multiple agendas that alternately competed and coalesced. British abolitionists had aspired for decades to create a haven for England's mostly impoverished population of Africans. The overwhelming majority of England's poor were White, of course, but British officials certainly proffered no plan to evacuate them from the mainland. England's program of Black colonization, in other words, was clearly rooted in a racially exclusive vision of England's rightful demographic constitution. And yet this enterprise was also infused with more benign expressions such as racial uplift and abolitionism. The renowned British promoter of abolitionism John Clarkson, after all, had traveled to Nova Scotia to recruit potential settlers for the Sierra Leone corporate experiment. For their own part, the African American settlers from Nova Scotia were motivated by a growing desire for self-determination. They were desperate to escape the perduring mire of racial hatred, poverty, and circumscribed opportunities for economic advantage so routine in a White-dominated society. Despite a few

---

[22] Walker, *Black Loyalists*. Clifford, *From Slavery to Freetown*. Joe A.D. Alie, *A New History of Sierra Leone* (New York: St. Martin's Press, 1990). Stephen J. Braidwood, *Black Poor and White Philanthropists: London's Blacks and the Foundation of the Sierra Leone Settlement, 1786–1791* (Liverpool: Liverpool University Press, 1994). James Sidbury, *Becoming African in America: Race and Nation in the Early Black Atlantic* (New York: Oxford University Press, 2009), 94–95.

exceptional cases of Black financial gain, the vast majority lived under the most precarious conditions, on the edge of starvation, constantly haunted by hunger, sickness, and destitution. The severity of circumstances largely explains why Clarkson succeeded in convincing so many to take leave of their homes and venture to a place almost 4,000 miles away that they had never before seen. So, like the other efforts at Negro colonization, this one joined Black hopes of empowerment through self-government to the desire of Whites to rid themselves of a free Black population.[23]

Among the newly arrived Black settlers was the Black Protestant minister David George (c. 1742–1810); his wife, Phillis; and their four children. The George family typified the experiences of the majority of these settlers, most of whom were in Nova Scotia because they had been loyal to Britain during the American Revolution. Phillis and George were both former slaves. George had escaped from a harsh owner to forge his own free status. When British officials had called on Blacks to support the Crown's efforts to subdue the revolt, George had gladly taken up arms in 1778 against the Anglo-American rebel colonists. He had once served the renowned congregation of the First African Baptist Church in Savannah, Georgia, before he and Phillis decided to resettle in Birchtown, Nova Scotia. Like the hundreds of other new settlers, the George family arrived in Sierra Leone with lofty aspirations of achieving self-determination, acquiring land held in fee simple, and remaking the very face of West Africa in the image of a Western Christian polity. They sought to redeem their own lot in life after recognizing that the dominant White population in Nova Scotia was determined to maintain racial hegemony over a Black minority. At the same time, they wanted to implement a civilizing mission that targeted the native peoples of West Africa for Christian conversion. For many years, in fact, they had promoted a biblical theology of racial destiny (African redemption) and considered themselves the vanguard of a Christian missionary enterprise that would convert African heathens to the Christian religion.[24]

These interactive, dynamic elements – racial self-determination, African redemption, Black settler colonialism, White apartheid, Christianity's civilizing mission, and the labor imperatives of Western colonialism – combined repeatedly in a system of evolving permutations to determine

---

[23] Sidbury, *Becoming African in America*, 94–95. Walker, *Black Loyalists*. Clifford, *From Slavery to Freetown*. Alie, *A New History of Sierra Leone*. Braidwood, *Black Poor and White Philanthropists*.

[24] Walker, *Black Loyalists*, 90–92. Sidbury, *Becoming African in America*, 71–72. Clifford, *From Slavery to Freetown*, 19–23.

the complicated relationship that African American religions would bear with colonialism. As a common theme, moreover, the urgent and pivotal formations within African American religions operated under the sign of freedom. This freedom, significantly, was a social pillar born of slavery, White settler regimes, and the subaltern movements of dominated Native and African polities in the Americas. It was an undying flame that would haunt and inspire generations to forge their own place and orientation within the manacles of empire.

During this time, a successful Black entrepreneur named Paul Cuffe came onto the scene of a burgeoning Black settler colonialism. Insofar as his wealth was concerned, Cuffe was truly exceptional; he seems to have possessed the greatest net worth of any African in North America at the time. He had risen from an uncertain existence to build a viable shipping enterprise over many years. In this way, he was an unusual sort. Yet much about his life typified the conditions common to Africans in North America. Like a number of other Blacks in the Northeast, Cuffe was of Afro-Native ancestry. His father had been a slave and had managed to purchase his own freedom in his later years. As a freeborn child of an African father and an American Indian mother, Cuffe grew up with nine other siblings near Nantucket Island. The members of this free family, like most free Blacks in the United States, were unable to imagine their status apart from the condition of slavery, as their very history was marked by the institution. After working on his father's farm in Massachusetts as a teen, the young Cuffe began hiring himself out as a seaman. He gained an expert knowledge in sailing, but he also met with many dangerous circumstances, eventually sailing throughout the Atlantic. Cuffe even experienced the frightful conditions of naval warfare during the American Revolution against the British, at one point being taken as a war prisoner. A scrupulous manager of money, he eventually saved enough to purchase his own ship, and he gradually reinvested his profits from shipping to acquire an entire fleet.[25]

Multiple factors inspired Cuffe to devote his attention to emigrating to West Africa. First, his admission to the Society of Quakers in 1807 roused a concerted interest in organized abolitionism. In conjunction

---

[25] Rosalind Cobb Wiggins, ed., *Captain Paul Cuffe's Logs and Letters, 1808–1817: A Black Quaker's "Voice from within the Veil"* (Cambridge, MA: Harvard University Press, 1996). Lamont D. Thomas, *Rise to Be a People: A Biography of Paul Cuffe* (Urbana: University of Illinois Press, 1986), 12–22, 40–53. Martha Putney, *Black Sailors: Afro-American Merchant Seamen and Whalemen Prior to the Civil War* (New York: Greenwood Press, 1987), 57–60. Campbell, *Middle Passages*, 24–26.

with this, at about the same time, the United States implemented a legal ban on the trans-Atlantic slave trade, a decision that coincided with Britain's deploying a naval squad to enforce its own similar ban. Cuffe was also inspired by the British abolitionist Thomas Clarkson's *History of the Rise, Progress, and Accomplishment of the Abolition of the African Slave-trade by the British Parliament*, which was published the same year Cuffe joined the Quakers. In this tome, Clarkson railed against the institution and emphasized free commerce as a viable solution to the slave trade. Of course, few Britons could rival the renown of Olaudah Equiano for promoting abolitionism. The African author had been a living symbol of the vibrant campaign against slavery. And Equiano, like Cuffe, had gained his momentous life experience through seafaring, traveling to multiple continents before devoting his life to the political movement of abolitionism. Few others would have resonated so richly with Cuffe's own aspirations toward abolitionism.[26]

A final factor, of course, was the colonial status of free Blacks in the United States. At the end of the new century's first decade, Cuffe was about fifty years old. Any optimism he might have once held about Black citizenship in the United States had been reduced to disappointment and a sharpening recognition that White supremacism was yet a central tenet of US nationalism. Not even Cuffe's impressive wealth and considerable influence with political leaders could blind him to the fact that the nation's prosperity was for Whites by design. In fact, his proximity to White wealth further exposed him to the racist hierarchy that constituted political order in the United States. The cotton gin's invention and wide deployment in the southern states immensely augured the fierce profitability of plantation slavery, guaranteeing a rapidly increasing demand for African slave labor. Furthermore, the acquisition of the Louisiana Territory from France in 1803, under Thomas Jefferson's presidential administration, generated potential access to a vast stretch of land that White settlers envisioned as empty and beckoning (despite being settled by millions of American Indians), awaiting the plow of White Christian civilization. This, in turn, translated into more plantations and a greater demand for slaves. It was too apparent to Cuffe that slavery determined the political economy, imbuing Whites with a naturalized sense of participation in political rule while guaranteeing that free Africans were occupied with fighting for basic privileges that should have attended the

---

[26] Campbell, *Middle Passages*, 24–26. Olaudah Equiano, *The Interesting Narrative of the Life of Olaudah Equiano*, 8th ed. (Norwich: the author, 1794).

presumption of citizenship, such as enjoying title to land, inheritance, and freedom from terror.[27]

Protectionist tariffs and British dominance of trade ensured considerable difficulty for any others, particularly Blacks, who might wish to enter the market. But Cuffe had not gained his wealth by a lack of tenacity. Since his admission to the Society of Friends in 1807, he had capitalized on the vast network of Quaker merchants and business associates spread throughout the Atlantic world. Armed with his business acumen, extensive contacts, and an unrelenting desire to tackle the most daunting challenges, Cuffe aspired to usher in a new era of ethically legitimate commerce based on trade in the natural resources and manufactures of West Africa in order to displace the slave trade that dominated the Atlantic coast of West Africa. Like most of his associates, he saw divine influence at work in the seasons and times that promised to transform a land of supposed spiritual darkness into a place of prosperity, liberty, and Christian civilization. His assiduous dealings with the Black leaders of the British-sponsored colony led them to agree on one essential element the colony needed that Cuffe might supply: free Black settlers to work the soil.[28]

The Sierra Leone colony had an important public relations and fundraising arm, the African Institution. This organization was based in London, but it held chapters throughout the Atlantic world. Cuffe had the good fortune to be acquainted with one of its members, James Pemberton, a Quaker residing in Philadelphia. Pemberton led the Pennsylvania Abolition Society, and British organizers of the African Institution had requested his assistance in recruiting a cohort of Black settlers to live in Sierra Leone and train the others living there in the arts of civilization and commerce. In Pemberton's judgment, Cuffe was easily the right man for the job, so he eventually urged Cuffe to consider the opportunity as a business venture that might strike a blow against the slave trade.[29]

---

[27] Campbell, *Middle Passages*, 24–26. Equiano, *The Interesting Narrative of the Life of Olaudah Equiano*. Kevin Lowther, *The African American Odyssey of John Kizell: A South Carolina Slave Returns to Fight the Slave Trade in His African Homeland* (Columbia: University of South Carolina Press, 2011), 156–57.

[28] Beverly C. Tomek, *Colonization and Its Discontents: Emancipation, Emigration, and Antislavery in Antebellum Pennsylvania* (New York: New York University Press, 2011), 117, 141. Lamont D. Thomas, *Paul Cuffee: Black Entrepreneur and Pan-Africanist* (Urbana: University of Illinois Press, 1988).

[29] James Pemberton to Paul Cuffe, June 8, 1808, in *Captain Paul Cuffe's Logs and Letters*, 78. Campbell, *Middle Passages*, 32–33.

After consulting with his contacts in England and throughout the United States, Cuffe agreed to undertake an exploratory journey to Sierra Leone, embarking in 1811. There he met with White officials and Black leaders of the settler colony. Like most Westerners, Cuffe had limited contact with native Africans, but one experience was especially pivotal – his meeting with the native leader John Kizell. Kizell had been born in the region of present-day Sierra Leone in 1760. He was abducted and sold into the Atlantic slave trade, finally ending up in the colonial Carolina city of Charleston at the threshold of his teenage years. By age twenty, Kizell would find himself caught up in the violence and turmoil of the Anglo-American Revolution. Like thousands of other enslaved Africans, he was determined to be free from slavery and rationally threw in his lot with the British, who had promised manumission. Kizell assumed a non-combat role in the British army in 1780 but was eventually taken captive by the Anglo-American militia. By the war's end, Kizell was recovered by British forces, and he resettled in Nova Scotia. He and his comrades composed the pivotal expedition from Nova Scotia to Sierra Leone in 1792 (with the George family) when the opportunity arose to create their own Black settler colony in West Africa. The odds were difficult, but Kizell was able to launch a successful enterprise in trade, starting with a modest boat in 1796. He established trade contacts in the region of Sherbro. In this way Kizell began to build a measurable reputation as a successful merchant.[30]

But Kizell was not content with operating merely in trade. Rather, he leveraged these business relationships to establish himself as a significant actor in regional politics. His success in this regard was partly due to his participation in Christian expansionism. He had joined one of the early efforts of Sierra Leone colonists to missionize the region of Port Logo. Kizell also cultivated strategic relationships with the African Institution and with other entities throughout the Atlantic that afforded him access to an international network of supporters and contacts. He eventually moved from the Sierra Leone colony to settle in the region of Sherbro. The move was a natural consequence of his growing importance in the eyes of the region's native political elites. Of greatest significance was his role in brokering a peace agreement in 1805 among several native African polities who had been warring for years. Moreover, abolitionists in England and the United States counted Kizell a unique ally as he began to promote

---

[30] Lowther, *African American Odyssey of John Kizell*, 10–30, 42–53, 70–90, 125–37, 180–92.

abolitionism among the political elites of West Africa. His eloquent letters were reprinted by the African Institution, a range of missionary organizations, and, eventually, by the American Colonization Society (ACS).
In Kizell, Cuffe met an individual whose ambitions matched or exceeded
his own. This was significant, as Cuffe had cultivated a stubborn prejudice against native Africans that was rooted in Christian supremacism
and the civilizing mission that constituted the imperial face of African
redemption. The two engaged in a strategic exchange that would prove
essential to Cuffe years later when he returned to Sierra Leone.[31]

After fifteen months of travel abroad, Cuffe returned to the United
States committed to establishing new American chapters of organizations like the African Institution in London and Sierra Leone's Friendly
Society, which lent vital support to abolition and Black settlement. In
addition, Cuffe aspired to recruit skilled Blacks in the United States who
might constitute a first cohort of settlers in a new West African colony.
He found able communities of free Africans in Philadelphia, Baltimore,
and New York City, and he was able to establish chapters of the African
Institution in each location. In New York City, Cuffe found the African
minister Peter Williams (1786–1840), an Episcopal priest, to be receptive
to the plan and willing to sponsor a local chapter of the African Institution.
The African Methodist minister Daniel Coker (1780–1846) of Baltimore
proved equally enthusiastic and worked with Cuffe to support the goal of
African redemption through settler colonialism.[32] Philadelphia was particularly important because it had one of the largest populations of free
Africans in the United States at a time when most Africans were enslaved.
And it was specifically African Methodism that was to play a major role
in shaping the social power base of Philadelphia's free Black population.

Free Africans and the Black Settler Colony

African Methodism was to have among its most central figures an ambitious African named Richard Allen (1760–1831). In the 1780s Allen, who
had been enslaved since childhood, began to dabble in the burgeoning
Methodism that was increasingly popular in the former Anglo-American
colonies. Allen had been born to a wealthy White slaveholder who

---

[31] Ibid., 155–80. Paul Cuffe to John Kizell, August 14, 1816, in *Captain Paul Cuffe's Logs and Letters*, 443.

[32] Werner Theodor Wickstrom, "The American Colonization Society and Liberia: An Historical Study in Religious Motivation and Achievement, 1817–1867," (PhD diss., Hartford Seminary, 1958).

possessed multiple plantations in Delaware and Pennsylvania. Allen and his family were later sold to a Delaware plantation owner before he reached the age of ten. There, Allen would see his own mother and three of his six siblings sold away. In 1777, at age seventeen, Allen attended a Methodist revival meeting after being goaded by his siblings. A former slaveholder, Freeborn Garrettson, was leading the revival and had arranged for meetings in private homes close to that of Allen's owner. In accord with the general tenor of the religious movement as a whole, Methodist revivalism had a populist bent and quickly became a potent vehicle of antislavery activism.[33] African slaves needed no convincing that slavery was a brutal system of torture, violence, and familial destruction. Allen heard the revivalist minister denouncing slavery in fiery terms. And he later wrote vividly of his "born-again" experience, when he grasped the logic of the Christian myth in its acerbic evangelical rendering: he was a vile sinner meriting only eternal torture but in reach of the saving grace of the Christian redeemer god. Something else, however, was at least as important as the message of spiritual salvation he absorbed that evening. Allen was also struck by the fact that here was a small but significant movement of White and Black Christians who openly condemned slavery and threatened White slaveholders with the wrath of a vengeful god. The Methodist founder John Wesley had himself written an attack on the institution. His leadership lent definitive shape to international Methodist efforts to root out slaveholding as an intolerable evil, at least until the explosive profitability of "cotton slavery" in the 1820s made the institution more palatable to Methodist churches.[34]

Allen returned from that revival meeting determined to acquire manumission by any means necessary. He began by plotting to get a Methodist minister to preach at the home of his slave master, Stokeley Sturgis. Within a couple of years the unwitting Sturgis agreed, and none other than Garrettson himself showed up to preach against the evils of slaveholding. Allen surely feigned innocence and surprise at the browbeating the evangelist meted out to Sterling and any other slaveholders present. But it was enough for Allen to convince Sturgis to allow Allen to purchase his own freedom. By 1783 Allen had saved enough money from hiring himself out and performing extra work to purchase his redemption. With his

[33] Richard S. Newman, *Freedom's Prophet: Bishop Richard Allen, the AME Church, and the Black Founding Fathers* (New York: New York University Press, 2008), 27–37.

[34] Newman, *Freedom's Prophet*, 53–60. Cedrick May, *Evangelism and Resistance in the Black Atlantic, 1760–1835* (Athens: University of Georgia Press, 2008), 107–9.

manumission in hand, Allen moved to Philadelphia, the city of his birth, and soon joined the community of free Africans there.[35]

Like other major cities such as Charleston, New York City, and Baltimore, Philadelphia's urban institutions and dense economic networks created subtle opportunities for free Africans to seek an economic foothold to establish an independent existence. But the transition to freedom from chattel slavery was nonetheless extremely arduous, which was why free Africans established a variety of mutual societies. Allen had worked different jobs to pay for his freedom, and he continued to do so once manumitted. His tireless efforts eventually secured him a stable income as a chimney sweep, and he even employed other Africans as indentured servants.[36]

Christian conversion, however, inspired Allen even more than financial success, and he determined to win over as many Africans to the evangelical movement as possible. The growth of Methodism throughout the newly formed republic led to the first Methodist conference, which convened in 1784. Allen was of course in attendance. He and the other Africans were jubilant at the denomination's decision to formally condemn slavery and to ban slaveholders from church membership. Meanwhile, one of the White ministers of Philadelphia's Methodist congregation – St. George's Methodist Episcopal Church – invited Allen to work the free African population for converts and to offer special sermons in church. With his typical enterprising spirit, Allen began daily church meetings for the city's African population at five o'clock in the morning. In addition, he resorted to publicly preaching on the streets and among the city's African population newly emerging from slavery. His ambition eventually paid off as the number of African members grew.[37]

Allen's rising economic success along with his religious leadership made him an important figure among the Black and White Methodists of Philadelphia. He joined other free African Christians, such as Jarena Lee (whose preaching ministry he eventually supported when she challenged his sexism), Darius Grinnings, William White, Absalom Jones, and James Forten, to build strategic alliances within the city's free Black population.

---

[35] W. Caleb McDaniel, "Philadelphia Abolitionists and Antislavery Cosmopolitanism," in *Antislavery and Abolition in Philadelphia: Emancipation and the Long Struggle for Racial Justice in the City of Brotherly Love*, ed. Richard Newman and James Mueller (Baton Rouge: Louisiana State University Press, 2011), 149–73. Richard S. Newman, *Freedom's Prophet*, 53–60. May, *Evangelism and Resistance*, 107–9.

[36] Newman, *Freedom's Prophet*, 53–60. May, *Evangelism and Resistance*, 107–9.

[37] Newman, *Freedom's Prophet*, 55–62.

In 1787 they formally organized as the Free African Society, devoted to providing support to needy Africans regardless of religious affiliation.[38]

In 1786, roughly one decade after the outbreak of White settler rebellion against Britain, the free Africans of Philadelphia seemed to be making veritable if modest progress toward social empowerment. By no means was Pennsylvania crafting policies of racial equality. But it did seem feasible to many manumitted Africans that they might seize on the promises of freedom so fiercely lauded by Whites in their war to create their own sovereign republic. So it was no accident that in that same year the Quaker philanthropist William Thornton approached the free Black population of Philadelphia about the prospect of settling West Africa. Thornton himself was a slaveholder from the British West Indies. He arrived in the United States during the 1780s and desired to manumit his slaves by sending them to West Africa. Because of his wealth and status as a slaveholder, Thornton was able to cultivate an enduring relationship with newly minted White political elites of the United States – particularly George Washington and James Madison. But it was clearer to Thornton than to most White colonizationists that institutional support from free Africans was absolutely essential to the success of any initiative for resettling Blacks to West Africa.[39]

When the Free African Society learned of Thornton's plan, they took measures to gauge the public response to this initiative. But Thornton's own errors ensured he would not receive the society's support. Like his White colleagues, Thornton was a bold advocate of White supremacism and its derivative, White republicanism – the racial state. He held it as axiomatic that liberal democracy was to be enjoyed as an exclusive racial property of the White race. The attractiveness of resettlement (commonly called "colonization"), for him, lay in its ability to ensure separation of the races by placing an ocean's worth of distance between the two. This was the classic formulaic appeal of resettlement for White supporters. Thus, when representatives of the Free African Society responded to Thornton, it was to communicate in no uncertain terms their opposition to his appeal. Concession to his plan, after all, would mean conceding that Blacks had no place in the United States.[40]

For US Blacks, however, voluntary resettlement in Africa held an enduring attraction. Their aim was not racial separatism for its own

[38] Ibid., 59.
[39] Paul Goodman, *Of One Blood: Abolitionism and the Origins of Racial Equality* (Berkeley: University of California Press, 1998), 11. Newman, *Freedom's Prophet*, 55–62.
[40] Newman, *Freedom's Prophet*, 185–86.

sake but self-government. The condition of living in the United States as a permanently alien race – an internal colony – was simply unacceptable. Many were optimistic that they might yet convince Whites of the virtues of multiracial democracy. But news of the Sierra Leone colony was unassailable evidence that creating Black settler colonies in West African was both feasible and worthwhile. For this reason, the Philadelphia discussion of emigration ignited ongoing debates among Blacks about the merits of resettling to West Africa versus continuing to fight to become rightful actors within the US body politic. As the status of free Africans remained marked by oppression and the hardening of White racial antagonism, Philadelphia's free population continued to engage the prospect of creating its own polity in West Africa.

Meanwhile, other developments were reshaping the very face of religion among Philadelphia's free Africans. By 1787 Allen was already attempting to organize a separate African congregation in Philadelphia. But his initial efforts to do so were soundly rebuffed by White church officials and resisted by Blacks who feared retaliation from Whites. The denomination's antislavery message attracted numerous African converts, but the White members and White church officials still viewed themselves as racially superior to Blacks They also openly resented Allen's charismatic influence among both Black and White parishioners and tried to limit his preaching activities throughout the region. Furthermore, it was equally clear to both Whites and Africans that a separate African congregation would only enhance the social power of Philadelphia's Africans. As the Black membership of St. George's grew, so did racial tensions. The Africans wanted to participate as equals, whereas Whites still saw the administration of the church as exclusively their role. The White elders soon formalized their racism through segregated seating.

This arrangement was fast becoming a standard feature of interracial churches in the United States. It was the last straw for St. George's African parishioners, however. After a long battle with racism and overt hostility, the African parishioners left St. George by 1793. They undertook an aggressive fundraising campaign and, after overcoming numerous obstacles, acquired their own land and secured their own church building, which they called Bethel chapel, by the middle of 1794. White resentment was vociferous, and the Africans themselves endured a frightful schism before they created Bethel as the first African Methodist Episcopal (AME) congregation. By the following year the new church had more than 100 members, and it continued to grow steadily thereafter.[41]

---

[41] Ibid., 65–68. The actual date of the African Methodists' departure from St. George's church is unclear but likely occurred between 1792 and 1793.

Around 1792, just a few years after they rejected Thornton's appeal, the African Americans of Philadelphia crafted a petition to the US Congress requesting that the White legislative body create an asylum for free Africans, modeled after the Sierra Leone colony. The petition was supported by dozens of signatories, including of course Richard Allen and Absalom Jones. The petitioners proposed that this asylum be developed in tandem with a plan for gradual abolition. They also demanded that legislators engage seriously the denial of the inalienable natural rights to life and liberty that continued to haunt free Africans during the very age when White Americans were enjoying the fruits of their own racial freedom. Given the cogency of the petition, it is not at all clear why it was never delivered to Congress. Most likely, its supporters met with resistance from others more cautious about the difficulty of distinguishing their demands for an optional asylum from the racial separatist ideology of Whites.[42]

In articulating such a salient desire to see the United States create a Black settler colony, the free Africans of Philadelphia were fairly representative of the aspirations of most Blacks. As a rule, they desired the creation of Black liberal democratic polities like those Whites were creating and that were best represented by the newly created White settler republic of the United States. The most crucial and influential Black political and religious formations of this era centered on the question of emigration and, more specifically, on the widespread consensus throughout the Black Atlantic that Black settler colonialism – for the purpose of creating self-determination and refuge from White domination – should be made an accessible option for Africans at large. The operative term here, of course, is "option." At no point did Blacks promote mandatory removal from the United States, a position that would have undermined the basic presumption of self-determination. So, the petition to the US Congress was by no means in contradiction with the earlier decision to reject Thornton's White supremacist program of preserving the United States as a White-only republic. In contrast to Thornton, they were promoting a fairly astute, philosophically consistent devotion to Black self-determination, and they insisted that all options be available as means to that end.

Over the next two decades, African Methodism came into its own, so to speak, and was a viable and visible presence, richly supplementing

---

[42] Ibid., 185–86. McDaniel, "Philadelphia Abolitionists and Antislavery Cosmopolitanism," 149–73.

the Free African Society as a potent domain of social activism. Although African Methodist congregations were initially under denominational unity with White Methodists (they would not become a separate, independent denomination until 1816), they had succeeded in forging a strong Black nationalist network. In March 1814, as Cuffe anticipated transporting a cohort of Black settlers to Sierra Leone, he pondered the best means of generating excitement and support for the enterprise. And he reached out to a network of like-minded colleagues. He had developed a close and lasting friendship with James Forten of Philadelphia's Free African Society. The intimate nature of their correspondence, in fact, reveals their mutual exchange of personal and familial concerns as well as collaborative engagement with the pressing political questions of Black self-determination and Black settler colonialism. Cuffe also reached out to the African minister Richard Allen. Cuffe was familiar with Allen's devotion to the cause, and the community of free Africans in Philadelphia was widely recognized for its size and formidable social status, a true force to be reckoned with. Allen and Cuffe had likely met a couple of years earlier during a conference of free Africans in Philadelphia. The two corresponded over several years about resettling Africans from the United States to West Africa. Cuffe reasoned that, as a capable leader in Philadelphia's Free African Society, Allen could be counted on to promote the merits of African emigration. In fact, Allen had become a central actor in the network of African Methodist congregations throughout the North. Cuffe was not to be disappointed in Allen's support, as the AME minister proved a valuable ally in popularizing Cuffe's plan to settle a group of free Blacks in West Africa. Before Cuffe's death, in fact, he would eventually propose to both Forten an Allen that they collaborate to purchase a ship with other free Africans in Philadelphia to use for commercialism and Black resettlement.[43]

Within roughly one year, a pioneering group of free Africans had signed on to leave the United States for a new life in Sierra Leone. On a bleary morning of 1815, Captain Paul Cuffe commandeered the *Traveller* into the inviting waters of a Sierra Leone harbor. The 109-ton ship carried thirty-eight Black passengers who gazed anxiously at the West African coastline. The *Traveller*, owned by Cuffe himself, had sailed thousands of miles over fifty-five days to reach its destination. Cuffe had spent thousands

---

[43] Newman, *Freedom's Prophet*, 205–6. Paul Cuffe to James Forten, January 27, 1815; Paul Cuffe to James Forten, March 13, 1815; and Paul Cuffe to Richard Allen, March 27, 1815, in *Captain Paul Cuffe's Logs and Letters*, 329, 331.

of dollars to cover the expense of the passengers and one year's worth of provisions for the settlers. The arrival of these new Black emigrants marked an important stage in an expanding enterprise of Christianity, commerce, and civilization.[44]

The settlers' landing was marked by both jubilation and uncertainty. They had safely crossed the Atlantic and were now embarking on an adventure in political freedom that could scarcely have been imagined in the United States. On their arrival, each family received a plot of land in Freetown. In addition, each was allotted a minimum of fifty acres of land (large families received more), which they could farm to produce subsistence crops. And yet, it was not clear exactly how they would fare in the new and unfamiliar land of Sierra Leone in the long term. The population was diverse with settlers from Nova Scotia and England and numerous recaptives who originated from regions throughout West Africa. In fact, every week saw the arrival of more recaptives from US vessels that flew the Spanish flag in an attempt to escape detection.[45]

When Cuffe returned safely to a New York harbor on May 29, 1816, he was greeted with fanfare and curiosity. He had established himself in the thoughts and aspirations of Africans and Anglo-Americans who were fiercely pondering the long-term prospect of Blacks living in White nations. Perhaps only the Black settlers themselves fully imagined the full ramifications of their successful landing in Sierra Leone. A company of free Africans had voluntarily abandoned life in a White settler state. By so doing, they had exchanged a condition of actual statelessness for the pioneering opportunity to live as privileged elites in a settler colony. They were, in essence, pursuing the same terms of racial freedom as had the White settlers of the Americas. In these terms, freedom was further inscribed as a colonial project, one animated by a powerful religious vision of Christianizing the native polities that were deemed inferior to those of the invading settlers.[46]

44 *The History of Prince Lee Boo, to Which is Added, The Life of Paul Cuffee, a Man of Colour, Also, Some Account of John Sackhouse, the Esquimaux* (1820; repr., Miami: Mnemosyne Pub. Co., 1969), 167.

45 "Extract from the Minutes of the New-York African Institution," *Commercial Advertiser*, June 11, 1816, 2. "(Copy) Sierra Leone, March 21, 1816 to Capt. Paul Coffee, Brig Traveller," *Commercial Advertiser*, June 11, 1816, 2. "Our Black Countrymen at Sierra Leone," *Boston Recorder*, June 12, 1816, 95.

46 "Extract from the Minutes of the New-York African Institution," *Commercial Advertiser* June 11, 1816, 2. "(Copy) Sierra Leone, March 21, 1816 to Capt. Paul Coffee, Brig Traveller," *Commercial Advertiser* June 11, 1816, 2. "Our Black Countrymen at Sierra Leone," *Boston Recorder* June 12, 1816, 95.

As a result of the 1815 expedition, Africans living in the United States became far more optimistic about the feasibility of Black settler colonialism. The successful venture that Cuffe executed offered a viable alternative to their stateless condition in the United States. They could live as politically powerful actors, members of a body politic. Equally important was the fact that Black settler colonialism offered a sure means of achieving African redemption, the rationale for which enjoyed powerful influence among the Christianized majority of free Blacks. Beyond this, White Americans, who had spent decades discussing the prospect of removing free Africans from the United States, now had in Cuffe's expedition a profound example of Africans voluntarily leaving to join a settler colony in Africa.

Cuffe's successful mission not only sparked optimism and pride among Blacks but also inspired the creation of the American Colonization Society (ACS). This institution began with the efforts of Robert Finley and Samuel J. Mills, two men who shunned Cuffe's advice to work closely with free Africans in the United States. Finley and Mills, instead, opened the door for a more aggressively anti-Black leadership to control the colonization initiative. Both men were White supremacists who held at best a sympathetic view of Blacks, regarding them as inferiors who required the paternal guidance and leadership of the White race. But neither man was philosophically devoted to strengthening the institution of slavery. In fact, they had envisioned colonization as a means to gradually phase out slavery. In this respect they could not have differed more pointedly from the likes of House Speaker Henry Clay, Congressman John Randolph of Virginia, and Andrew Jackson, future president and at the time a slaveholding general in the US Army. All were invited onto the founding board of the ACS. These men shared the sentiments of the majority of the nation's political elite, who were disproportionately slaveholders or, at minimum, devoted to the interests of the slaveholding aristocracy.[47]

At the initial organizing meeting held December 16, 1816, the society's board members vetted the precise aim of their enterprise. The second meeting, convened just five days later, was more decisive, however. The organizers concluded they would completely bar the discussion of abolitionism. Instead, their mission and aim would be the deportation of free Blacks.[48] Henry Clay captured most succinctly the sentiment of the board when he argued that the racial problem of the United States was that of

---

[47] Campbell, *Middle Passages*, 43–44.
[48] Early Lee Fox, *The American Colonization Society, 1817–1840* (Baltimore: Johns Hopkins University Press, 1919), 46–47.

free Blacks, who were "useless," "pernicious," and "dangerous" to the White populace. Clay went on to describe free Africans as embodying social pathology, constituting a "contaminating" presence threatening to "extend their vices to all around them." Their removal, he asserted, was urgent.[49]

The public response to the newly organized colonization society was mixed. As Clay had hoped, the nation's politically powerful slaveholders were encouraged to learn that the "problem" of free Africans, who represented a troublesome presence to White power and encouragement to Black rebellion, had now a remedy and resolution compatible with the long-term survival of slavery. White abolitionists, who were a small minority, wondered aloud whether such a society might be useful to the cause of ending slavery. They had long promoted gradual emancipation, in combination with colonization, as a feasible means of attaining their goal. The vast majority of African Americans, however, were dispirited and enraged by the developments. The White leaders had clearly chosen to castigate racial victims rather than recognizing the ingenuity and enterprising devotion whereby Blacks repeatedly rose from the status of being chattel to eking out an independent existence in an economy designed to benefit Whites by excluding Blacks. Philadelphia's community of free Blacks poured out in public protest. In January 1817 approximately 3,000 African Americans gathered at Bethel African Methodist Episcopal Church, home to the newly created, formally independent Black denomination. Those present unanimously condemned the ACS's racist characterization of free Africans. They also composed a resolution to condemn the ideology that rendered free Africans an inherent liability to the White republic. The problem, they retorted, was not the presence of free Black people but the disfranchisement that accrued through a racist system of hierarchy. They vowed never to separate themselves from "the slave population in this country," to whom they were bound through "ties of consanguinity, of sufferings, and of wrongs."[50]

It is telling that among those convening the assembly was James Forten, an ardent and consistent promoter of African emigration and close colleague of Paul Cuffe. In fact, many others attending, including

[49] Gary B. Nash, *First City: Philadelphia and the Forging of Historical Memory* (Philadelphia: University of Pennsylvania Press, 2006), 187.

[50] Tomek, *Colonization and Its Discontents*, 130–45. Julie Winch, "Self-Help and Self-Determination," in *Antislavery and Abolition in Philadelphia: Emancipation and the Long Struggle for Racial Justice in the City of Brotherly Love* (Baton Rouge: Louisiana State University, 2011), 77–78.

Richard Allen and Absalom Jones, were devoted to the vision of creating an African colony that might offer a Black homeland – a bastion of dignified existence under self-determination.[51] The resolution, in other words, was not a rejection of Black settler colonialism itself. It was, however, an explicit condemnation of the White racial state and its apartheid vision for the political community of the United States.

During the following summer, Black Philadelphians staged yet another protest against the ACS when a local chapter of the society was organized. In August 1817 they assembled at a Black schoolhouse to condemn the ACS's focus on removing free Africans from the United States. So, even at this point, the Philadelphia group was clearly defending their right to claim rights, as legitimate members of the nation's political community. The prospect of forging a Black settler colony, however, remained a prerogative. Richard Allen and James Forten had been joined by John Gloucester in vocal support of Cuffe's enterprise. Robert Finley was careful to note Allen's enthusiasm for Cuffe's plan to establish a diaspora network of trade and commerce between the United States and West Africa by creating a Black settlement. With Cuffe's death in 1817, however, it became unclear to African Americans how such a plan might move forward. Cuffe had succeeded in transporting only a single cohort of Black settlers. And it was obvious that securing a permanent colony with a viable population of settlers and robust economic activity would require multiple voyages to settle more colonists.[52]

A Colony Called "Freedom": Creating a Black State

Given their decisive condemnation of the ACS, it is not likely that many Blacks at the time could have envisioned the fructuous alliance that would soon emerge between Black Christian settlers and the ACS. That unlikely alliance, however, is in essence the story of Liberia's creation. As African Americans increasingly aspired to civilize West Africa, the normalization of Black settler colonialism continued to achieve its greatest efficacy through the Christian missionary enterprise. Few ideas were as inviolable as that of targeting Africans for Christian conversion. Indeed, Christian missions to Africa or to African-descended peoples throughout the diaspora had long sustained an uncontested display of religious hatred and cultural destruction among Western Christians. As we saw with Olaudah Equiano, Christianization was not merely about religious

---

[51] Winch, "Self-Help and Self-Determination," 77–78.
[52] Newman, *Freedom's Prophet*, 205–6.

conversion. It temporalized identities and became the most common means of ordering race and geography along a hierarchy to undergird a colonial order.

Black Christian Alliance with the American Colonization Society

By the 1820s Liberia wed the issue of Black settler colonialism to the missionary enterprise more effectively than any other region. Because Liberia was the special protégé of the United States (unlike Sierra Leone or Nova Scotia), it logically followed that missionizing the region seemed the ineluctable means to modeling successful Black colonization and African Christianization. Refashioning Blacks from heathens into a divine race – the Christian people of god – in other words, was conceived in reciprocity with the voluntary removal of free Blacks. The latter action served to protect the status of the United States as a White democratic republic. Moreover, with Liberia in mind, US missionary societies developed more sophisticated means of inscribing their own nation-state as the equal or better of any Western Christian polity in the world. Until the Liberia project was established in 1821, however, Sierra Leone functioned as the chief symbol of Christian redemption for African "heathens." The Black colonists there were deemed to have made hopeful inroads toward civilizing Africa while simultaneously establishing their own liberal democratic state.

Black settler colonialism, however, did not simply perform the work of the White settler colony in blackface. Rather, it also intensified the grammar of freedom far beyond the symbolism of White religious subjectivity. It was one thing for Whites to leave their sovereign lands in Europe or in the eastern region of the United States to encroach on the polities of indigenous peoples in the Americas. It was quite another for Black slaves or for free Blacks metonymically linked to slavery to leave a White republic and sail for the land of their ancestors to redeem heathens who were their racial kin while establishing an outpost of Western liberal democracy. White settlers might have spoken of tyranny and the need to escape existential misery. But they were not literally enslaved in Europe. In fact, many Europeans temporarily entered into voluntary slavery (indenture) to leave Europe for the Americas. For Black settlers, however, passage to Liberia was a passage to the domain of freedom from either the literal bonds of slavery or the condition of statelessness that haunted free Blacks. This fact amplified the existential weight of Christianization, making it into an imperial pantomime of freedom. The Black Christian colonial settler, in other words, could ascend to establishing a free polity and join a body politic that established a colonial relation of power over native Africans. This enterprise also justified efforts to exterminate African religions, kill native Africans, conquer them to seize their land, and ultimately reduce them to a condition of slavery. The result was a Black Christian racial state rooted in colonial governance that racialized indigenous Africans, resembling the way that Christian rulers in Europe or Muslim rulers throughout the Mediterranean lands employed imperial governance over religious others.

Black Christian settler colonialism produced a strange paradox. On the one hand, Blacks generally criticized the ACS as a racist institution because the society's board had formally bracketed abolitionism and named free Africans as a racial menace who threatened the White republic's purity. On the other hand, the ACS became the most efficacious instrument for abetting the creation of Black settler societies in Africa. Most importantly, the ACS established a strategic partnership with the US government to secure territory in West Africa formally for the purpose of relocating receptive Africans. By the start of the Civil War in 1860, the ACS had transported more than 10,500 Blacks to West Africa, a considerable feat given the fact that the society's funding never even remotely approached the level needed to transport the total number of Blacks who desired to resettle. So, despite the ACS's notoriety for promoting the removal of free Blacks, what bears emphasis is the extent to which the ACS embodied the essential domains of Atlantic colonialism – assembling private investment capital, developing corporate governance, and advancing the civilizing mission defined by a religious imperative of spiritual conquest. All of these were united by a common aim to promote freedom and train citizens of a liberal democratic state. Moreover, African Americans recognized that the ACS never forced any Africans to leave the United States. Rather, it enabled transport for those Africans voluntary seeking resettlement in West Africa.

From the start, the ACS's Board of Managers recognized that financing represented their greatest challenge, so they appealed to the US Congress in 1817 for aid. But US legislators saw no compelling reason to risk the appearance of impropriety by handing over Treasury funds to a private organization for the purpose of starting a Black settler colony. Facing bitter disappointment but undaunted, the ACS board planned a fact-finding mission and charged the task of fund-raising to Samuel Mills, an experienced agent with a network of wealthy entrepreneurs. Aided by Francis Scott Key, who is better known for his authorship of the US national anthem, Mills successfully appealed to wealthy donors in Philadelphia,

New York City, and Baltimore. The two men raised half of the needed $5,000 from contributions by merchants, bankers, and other business-men who were persuaded that a successful colony on Africa's Atlantic coast controlled by White Americans would create bountiful and lucra-tive commercial opportunities. Britain had already proven just that with its Sierra Leone colony. The ACS managed to secure the remainder of the needed funds from a single donor, Isaac McKim, a Baltimore shipper who aimed to get guarantees of a shipping line to the proposed colony.[53]

With funding in place, the ACS sent two agents to conduct a fact-finding mission, chiefly to seek land for the proposed colony. Once in Sierra Leone, they met John Kizell, the politically influential African recaptive. Kizell offered to negotiate with local African politicians on behalf of the two ACS agents so they could acquire territory on Sherbro Island, a fertile landmass of about 230 square miles just a couple of miles from the mainland of Sierra Leone. The prospect of such an arrangement was wonderful news to the ACS, which had been banking on establishing a profitable agricultural economy.[54]

Meanwhile, the ACS's hopes of receiving a direct subsidy from the US Congress were revived in March 1819 when Congress passed the Slave Trade Act, a piece of legislation that proved serendipitous for the ACS. The law authorized President Monroe to employ the US Navy to suppress the transport of enslaved Africans across the Atlantic, and it provided $100,000 toward this end. The lack of specific directives for disbursing the funds gave the president broad latitude, which the ACS quickly recognized as a golden opportunity. Armed with a prospective land deal with native political leaders in West Africa, thanks to Kizell's assistance, the ACS dispatched a representative to meet with Monroe's administration to pitch the idea of a US-supported colony as a strategy for suppressing the slave trade. What was needed, the ACS argued, was Christian civilization, and planting a colony of Westernized Blacks on the coast of West Africa would surely go far to stem the tide of "barbarous" slave trading that had so long stricken the region. The fact that slavery thrived in the heart of the United States, which was fully a slave society and a racial apartheid state, seemed not to matter at all to the reasoning of the society. The ACS board, after all, included members such as Henry

---

[53] Allan E. Yarema, *The American Colonization Society: An Avenue to Freedom?* (Lanham, MD: University Press of America, 2006), 30–36.

[54] Lowther, *African American Odyssey*, 208–11. Yarema, *American Colonization Society*, 30–36.

Clay and Andrew Jackson, who were fierce defenders of the institution and who personally enslaved African men, women, and children.[55]

For his part, Monroe seemed open to the idea, but Secretary of State John Quincy Adams understood fully the implications of establishing a colony under US auspices on African soil. Adams was not an opponent of colonialism per se; like most US Americans, however, he saw a major distinction between the internal colonialism that defined the early US American empire and the transoceanic colonialism that the ACS was promoting. Adams questioned the constitutionality of such a venture. And, of course, the idea of funding Black settler colonialism was a matter altogether different from supporting White colonists. The secretary made known his deep opposition to the plan and rallied allies in the presidential cabinet. But the ACS was nothing if not well networked. And in this instance, they had an inside man, Secretary of Treasury William H. Crawford, one of the society's vice presidents. Crawford eagerly took exception to Adams's opposition and eventually convinced Monroe to accept the ACS's proposal. And so it was that the ACS, a private enterprise of self-appointed anti-Black racists, now operated with federal funding and the backing of the US Navy, whose warships would repeatedly escort Black settlers sailing under the auspices of the ACS in the years to come.[56]

Beyond this, the ACS succeeded to a surprising degree in controlling the execution of the federally backed colonization operations. When the Monroe administration desired to instigate its own exploratory mission and to make preparations for the colony, the ACS directed the selection of both supervising agents: the Episcopal minister Samuel Bacon and John P. Bankson, who was already a federal employee. Their task was to acquire territory and build a settlement complete with housing and food stocks. The administration authorized Bacon to hire African Americans as free laborers to construct the buildings for the colony. He anticipated that a few hundred would be needed for such a grand enterprise and secured sufficient food rations and equipment. After several months, however, Bacon had managed to hire only eighty-six people; of these, only twenty-eight were men. The majority, women and children, were to be employed as seamstresses, nurses, and laundry workers. Among the group was the AME minister Daniel Coker, who taught in Baltimore's African School. Of special significance was the fact that Bacon never arranged return passage for the laborers. Rather, he chartered a private

---

[55] Lowther, *African American Odyssey*, 208–11.
[56] Yarema, *American Colonization Society*, 36–37.

merchant ship for one-way passage and secured military escort by the US Navy's USS *Cyane*, which became the nation's first naval vessel to be deployed in suppressing the trans-Atlantic slave trade.[57]

Insofar as the administration was concerned, these African Americans were being employed to prepare a resettlement colony that would serve to suppress the slave trade. But as Bacon surely intended, they were de facto settlers and not temporary workers by virtue of the fact they would not be returning to the United States. The administration's official policy was one of suppressing the slave trade. But the ACS had ensured that this was in every sense an experiment in establishing a Black settler colony that free Blacks would regard as the first step toward forging their own society. Herein lay the devious brilliance of the ACS. By terms of the formal arrangement with the Monroe administration, the ACS was tasked with establishing a colony to resettle recaptives, those Africans rescued from slave ships en route across the Atlantic. What transpired, however, was a process of removing mostly free or manumitted Blacks from the United States to settle West Africa, which was in essence the original vision the ACS had proposed.[58]

Thus, on January 31, 1820 the ACS in alliance with the US federal government made its first transport of African Americans aboard the *Elizabeth* with naval escort to be resettled in West Africa. All of the passengers arrived alive in Sierra Leone, and the supervising agents immediately began seeking land. But Kizell's optimism in convincing native African officials to sell land on Sherbro Island proved premature. The local officials were not so gullible as to part with land that was to serve as a settler colony. They understood from the start that the colonizing enterprise would compete with their sovereignty. Furthermore, they were already familiar with the consequences of Britain's efforts to stymie their lucrative trafficking in slaves, which was integral to the local economy. The US interests Kizell represented seemed to them just as suspect, especially because they already knew that US slaveholders constituted a major sector of their global market: despite the formal ban on the slave trade, slave ships delivered Africans to the United States every year until the 1850s, and any US merchants found guilty of violating the ban were

---

[57] Tom W. Schick, *Behold the Promised Land: A History of Afro-American Settler Society in Nineteenth-Century Liberia* (Baltimore: Johns Hopkins University Press, 1980), 26–32. Yarema, *American Colonization Society*, 36–37.

[58] Robert Pierce Forbes, *The Missouri Compromise and its Aftermath: Slavery & the Meaning of America* (Chapel Hill: University of North Carolina Press, 2007), 95. Yarema, *American Colonization Society*.

merely fined. Like the White slaveholders who served as political elites in the United States, moreover, African political rulers were fundamentally guided by practical economic interests, not the ideals of abolitionism.

Withered by their obstinate stance, Kizell himself resorted to purchasing the very small island of Campelar for the settler colony. The colonists arrived there on March 20, 1820 and began setting up supplies. Kizell, meanwhile, hired local native laborers to clear the land and to build mud huts for the new settlers. The location was by no means ideal as a settlement, particularly because they were far from the nearest potable water source. As was commonly the case with such expeditions, illness and death took a heavy toll. Within three weeks, the White physician who had been assigned to attend the colonists succumbed to fever and died. Eleven of the twelve Whites who traveled with the colonists were soon dead. The greatest cost of life, however, lay with the African American settlers. Of the eighty-three colonists who had arrived, forty-nine died in Campelar. The others left for Sierra Leone, where they could receive medical attention and have access to fresh water and adequate food. In the wake of the devastating deaths, meanwhile, the AME minister Daniel Coker became the acting agent in charge.[59]

Lott Cary and Virginia's Free Blacks

Back in the United States, the ACS board was dismayed to learn of the dismal turn of events. The best territory that Kizell had managed to acquire had proven unsuitable. The colonists, they learned further, soon abandoned it for the Sierra Leone colony. Determined to create a successful US-backed outpost on West Africa's coast, however, ACS members pressed the federal administration to send yet another cohort of Black settlers. A network of African American Christians in Virginia, under the leadership of Lott Cary, would provide the greatest boon to the ACS at this juncture, however. And the turn of events was in great measure due to the leadership of Lott Cary. Cary would become one of the most renowned African American missionaries to West Africa during this early period of Black settler colonialism. He was born in 1780 in Charles City County, Virginia, as the legal chattel of the White slaveholder William A. Christian. At age twenty-seven Cary underwent a conversion to evangelical Christianity, an experience he would later describe as producing a sharp departure from a previous life of wayward sinfulness, which he associated with drinking alcohol and cursing. Lott's owner hired him out

59 *Missionary Register*, August 1820, 338–39.

to work at the local Shochoe tobacco warehouse, the largest in Richmond. There the other workers assisted him in learning to read. Cary proved a quick study, and he was soon working as shipping clerk, eventually earning $700 per year ($12,000 in today's money). He was even allowed to sell the small portions of warehouse waste tobacco for his personal profit. This privilege drastically altered his life, as he was able to save hundreds of dollars. As a result, Cary was able to purchase his manumission, along with that of his two children, by 1813.[60]

At the very time that Cary began to seek his freedom, missionary religion was becoming inextricably bound to the infrastructure of US colonialism against Native Americans and of US imperial ambitions abroad. The impetus for this derived chiefly from voluntary societies that proliferated briskly over the course of a few decades, giving rise to publishing houses, tract societies, and missionary organizations. All worked to expand the institutional mechanisms of Christian conversion within a global purview. As early as 1798, as the young White republic set its imperial gaze on the sovereign lands of Native nations, the Connecticut Missionary Society was established with the express aim of Christianizing "the heathen" throughout the continent of North America. The Massachusetts Missionary Society quickly followed. No other missionary organization of the era, however, approached the influence of the American Board of Commissioners for Foreign Missions (ABCFM). Organized in 1810, this entity paradigmatically reflected the US state's early aspirations to rival the empires of Europe by extending its reach globally. Within two years, the ABCFM sent its first missionary cohort abroad to India. In the first decade of its existence, however, the vast majority of its foreign missionaries operated among the foreign American Indian nations. In fact, the ABCFM allied with the US Department of War to administer its reach among the Native polities. Years later, the ABCFM would be joined by another mammoth corporate entity, the American Home Missionary Society, which exploited the social conditions of the frontier created by the Anglo-American empire's constant expansion onto Native lands. Concomitant to missionizing was the cultivation of a reading public whose appetite for Bibles, Sunday school literature, devotional texts, commentaries, and other Bible study aids seemed to know no bounds. By 1809 Bible societies existed in Philadelphia, Massachusetts, Maine, New York, and Connecticut. And in 1816 the renowned American

---

[60] Leroy Fitts, *Lott Cary: First Black Missionary to Africa* (Valley Forge, PA: Judson Press, 1978), 8–15.

Bible Society became the first national company among this genre of publishers. The sheer scale of travel, marketing, sales, publishing, and distribution created by these missionary and Bible societies was a signal accomplishment of the imperial domain of American religion. Together, they constituted a missionary ethos that was astounding in scale and unparalleled in efficacy.[61]

Just three years after the ABCFM was created, Cary successfully gained his manumission and began a path that would lead him to Christian missions. His decision to attend a school for free Blacks led to his direct involvement with missionary religion. William Crane, a White minister of Richmond, Virginia, had begun operating a night school to provide literacy skills to African Americans. Crane was an ardent proponent of Black Christianization, and he fanned the flames of missionary zeal in the hearts of as many Black students as possible. Cary, operating in such an influential atmosphere of evangelicalism, eventually declared his desire to become a preacher. He became a licensed minister under the auspices of the White-controlled First Baptist Church of Richmond, whose membership comprised about 1,200 Blacks.[62]

But Cary was not to remain content with local preaching. White American missionaries were experiencing a growing fervor to institutionalize the age-old imperative of global Christian dominion. Although Whites were converting relatively few Blacks to Christianity during the early 1800s, they were consistent in their efforts to render in stark terms the racial significance of Christianization. For all the formal emphasis on individual conversion, the import of Blacks converting to Christianity was fully steeped in the symbolism of collective racial arrival. In the eyes of White missionaries, converting individual Blacks to Christianity was of a piece with the larger agenda of converting the "African race" and turning them away from what Christians imagined as the diabolical religion of Africa. It was precisely this rendering of conversion that White missionaries conveyed to their African American converts, with stunning effectiveness.

---

[61] Sydney E. Ahlstrom, *A Religious History of the American People*, 2nd ed. (New Haven, CT: Yale University Press, 2004), 423–24. David Paul Nord, *Faith in Reading: Religious Publishing and the Birth of Mass Media in America* (New York: Oxford University Press, 2004), 89–103. Candy Gunther Brown, *The Word in the World: Evangelical Writing, Publishing, and Reading in America, 1789–1880* (Chapel Hill: University of North Carolina Press, 2004), 115–18. Clifton Jackson Phillips, *Protestant America and the Pagan World: The First Half Century of the American Board of Commissioners for Foreign Missions, 1810–1860* (Cambridge, MA: Harvard University Press, 1969), 1–10.

[62] Fitts, *Lott Carey*, 14–15.

The sheer theological potency of converting the "heathen races," moreover, neatly and easily translated into targeting Indians and Africans in the Americas and in the Atlantic context. In this light, there can be little surprise that free Blacks such as Cary quickly took a strong interest in the prospect of joining the foreign missionary enterprise. One evening, when Crane shared with the school's Black students a missionary report that John Kizell had authored, Cary was moved to announce his own desire to travel to Africa, to behold the land of his forefathers for himself, and to fulfill, as he described it, the great commission to spread the gospel to distant lands. Cary, along with another African American convert, Colin Teague, spearheaded the formation of an African American missionary group, which they named the Richmond African Baptist Missionary Society, in 1815. Cary himself served as the organization's corresponding secretary, and Crane served as president. Crane's arranged position as president was necessary to assuage anti-Black sentiment among other White Virginians who prohibited Africans from organizing independently of White guardians tasked with ensuring that the Africans were not plotting rebellion against slavery. Although the African Baptist Missionary Society existed under the auspices of the White-controlled First Baptist Church of Richmond, it was conceived, funded, and operated by free Africans. Given the overwhelming challenges they faced in raising capital, their success at such a feat is striking. Meanwhile, the White-controlled General Missionary Convention, established just one year earlier, invited the new missionary society of free Africans to affiliate with them and attend annual meetings, a networking pattern that was replicated throughout the emerging missionary societies of the United States.[63]

The pivotal decision to launch a mission to West Africa congealed during the 1817 annual meeting of the Richmond African Baptist Missionary Society. As corresponding secretary, Cary delivered his own report to the board in which he made a strong case for such a missionary venture. As a result, the missionary body resolved to officially accept Cary's recommendation and acted on it. In the meantime, Teague and Cary sought out sponsorship by the White Baptist Foreign Missionary Board. To their delight, the board granted their request, but they insisted that Teague and Cary provide their own funding. This meant the support from the Baptist Foreign Missionary Board was merely a formality; it came with no

---

[63] Miles Mark Fisher, "Lott Carey, the Colonizing Missionary," *Journal of Negro History* 7, no. 4 (October 1922), 385.

material support. Nevertheless, such an imprimatur served well the purpose that the two free African ministers sought. They desired the official auspices of these White organizations to bolster the respectability of their enterprise in the eyes of potential critics. And as they would later find, the official ties with a network of institutional supporters proved vital to fund-raising and negotiating with US government officials. Despite the seemingly insuperable challenges they faced, free Africans in the urban centers of the United States were uncannily resourceful and enterprising when it came to funding collective endeavors of their own. And the Richmond group was no exception to this. The Richmond African Baptist Missionary Society eventually raised $700 to fund the planned mission to Liberia. In the remaining years of Cary's life, they would reliably provide an annual stipend of $100 (almost $2,000 in today's dollars) to support the mission.[64]

Word of Richmond's free Africans founding a missionary society quickly spread throughout Virginia and to other states. In Petersburg, Virginia, the free African congregation of Gillfield Baptist Church organized a missionary enterprise just three years later, following the Richmond example. And free African converts to Christianity in Pennsylvania, New York, and Georgia also followed suit. These African American Christians easily embraced the global aspirations of the US imperial missionary zeal. Cary's group, in particular, was about to play a particularly historic role in helping create the Black Christian settler colony that would become the polity of Liberia.[65]

In the first few years of its existence the Richmond African Baptist Missionary Society welcomed the token support of the General Missionary Society and the Baptist Foreign Missionary Board. But by 1820 it was clear that relying strictly on its own revenues, which were far from the scale of funding needed for a trans-Atlantic passage, was impractical. Thus, the news of Daniel Coker's travel to Sierra Leone, along with that of over eighty other free Africans, struck Cary with electrifying excitement. The criticism that so many African Americans heaped on the ACS targeted the society's philosophical aims of ridding the United States of free Africans. As a practical matter, however, the ACS was clearly functioning to provide passage to free Africans desiring to resettle in West Africa on a voluntary basis. And this was perfect for Cary. After some

[64] Marie Tyler-McGraw, *An African Republic: Black & White Virginians in the Making of Liberia* (Chapel Hill: University of North Carolina Press, 2007), 97.

[65] Jacob U. Gordon, *The African Presence in Black America* (Trenton, NJ: Africa World Press, 2004), 301–2.

initial deliberation, the free Africans of Richmond approached the ACS about sponsorship. The ACS, in turn, appealed to Monroe's administration for a second settlement. For his part, President Monroe was committed to establishing a successful refuge for recaptives and thus authorized funds for a second journey. It became apparent that the Richmond African Baptist Missionary Society would have funding after all, and the fine details enabling passage to West Africa began to materialize.[66]

By the spring of 1821, Cary and his companions were ready to set sail. The group of thirty-three emigrants, along with several Whites placed in charge of the mission, gathered at the First Baptist Church of Richmond for a Christian worship service to mark their departure. Cary himself delivered the sermon, placing the group's mission within the context of the biblical justification for Christian expansionism. He told his audience that he feared for those who preached the gospel in "this country" but who had not traveled throughout the world. How would they respond when the Christian savior asked them to give an account of their stewardship of the gospel? What would they say of the biblical injunction to "go into all the world" preaching to "every creature"? Cary understood himself to be fulfilling an evangelical duty. "Whether I may find a grave in the ocean, or among the savage men, or more savage wild beasts on the Coast of Africa," he explained with rhetorical flourish, he was nonetheless prepared to bid farewell to his fellow Virginians for the sake of preaching to "poor Africans the way of life and salvation."[67]

On March 8, 1821 the emigrants boarded the *Nautilus* and set sail for Sierra Leone. Of the thirty-three emigrants, all but three were freeborn African Americans. Eight were from Maryland; the others hailed from Virginia, which held the highest number of Blacks in the United States. Twenty were literate, and all but three were adults.[68] They arrived in Freetown, Sierra Leone, in March 1821, landing in Cape Montserrado, halfway between Freetown and what would become Monrovia. In the coming years, the cape would be renamed Liberia. They had won agreement from the ACS for land to be delegated for their use in creating a settlement. After entertaining lofty expectations about owning land and establishing themselves in the new continent, however, the travelers were astounded and disappointed to find no such arrangements had actually

---

[66] Miles Mark Fisher, "Lott Carey: The Colonizing Missionary," *Journal of Negro History* 7, no. 4 (October 1922), 387–88. Yarema, *American Colonization Society*, 38–39.

[67] Ibid., 391.

[68] Amos Jones Beyan, *African American Settlements in West Africa: John Brown Russwurm and the American Civilizing Efforts*, 1st ed. (New York: Palgrave Macmillan, 2005), 44.

been made. In fact, they were forced to live as refugees for the initial period of time in West Africa. They later began working on a leased farm to support themselves, a hardy test of survival and independence that heightened their resolve. But the experience also checked their sense of exceptionalism – the living arrangements eventually provided to them were identical to those for African "recaptives," those enslaved men, women, and children who were regularly rescued from slave ships, usually by the British navy, and resettled in the Sierra Leone colony.[69]

There remained, moreover, the central problem of acquiring a suitable territory in West Africa. It soon became clear that their chances of acquiring any land on Sherbro Island were practically nil. The group began sending scouts aboard a schooner to search for a probable location south of Sierra Leone. When no reports of progress arrived before the ACS board in the United States, the ACS successfully petitioned Monroe to take a more aggressive tack. Monroe commissioned a naval officer, Lieutenant Robert Field Stockton, to travel to the region and secure a land deal. Stockton was no diplomat. His specialty was warfare, not diplomacy. He was accustomed, moreover, to giving orders and conducting the naval exercises fundamental to dealing with political rivalries among haughty White Western officials. The lieutenant not only lacked experience with African politicians, but he also embraced the same White supremacism and anti-Blackness that characterized the entire project of Western settler colonialism. His selection was a bad omen, to say the least.[70]

Stockton eventually arranged a conference with the officials of the Condo Confederation, which was an alliance of local polities that controlled the regional slave trade. King Peter, the highest ranking official of the group, perceived the contradictions inherent in providing land to a settler colony officially tasked with suppressing the slave trade. Doing so would likely lead to the same interruptions and challenges to slave trading that the Sierra Leone colony posed. That settler colony had even begun to function as an outpost for the British navy. When five days of negotiations failed to culminate in an agreement, Stockton resorted to violence, placing a gun to King Peter's head and threatening to kill him. In a desperate effort to preserve his life, the king permitted a transaction of land, selling the desired territory in exchange for an array of Western implements and supplies including shoes, nails, rum, and guns – worth

---

[69] Fitts, *Lott Carey*, 27–33, 37–40. Fisher, "Lott Cary," 392–93.
[70] James Ciment, *Another America: The Story of Liberia and the Former Slaves Who Ruled It* (New York: Farrar, Straus & Giroux, 2013), 32–35.

less than $300 in total. The contract that Stockton extorted by threat
of murder, moreover, stipulated that the land would be held personally
by Stockton and Eli Ayres, a White physician who had accompanied
Stockton to broker a deal with the Condo Confederacy. With the sanction of the US government and the threat of naval arms and US weaponry,
two individual White men had forced land from an African confederacy
to establish a Black colony called "freedom" (Liberia).[71]

In his arrogance, Stockton surely considered the sale of land a victory
and was able to provide a positive report to the Monroe administration and the ACS. But his violent maneuver served to poison any waters
of diplomacy that might have otherwise nurtured relations between the
settlers and the local population of native Africans. In fact, the incident
merely confirmed for the Condo officials that they were dealing with a
violent, arrogant group of invaders whose threat would demand their
most dire efforts to stem.

Colonialism, Apartheid, and Racial Freedom

In a pattern that would repeatedly feature in such colonial missionary
ventures, the missionary group of Black settlers, once on the ground,
moved almost immediately from entertaining heart-warming visions of
philanthropy to recognizing that their physical survival was at stake. As
Cary would later relate, the colony of missionaries very quickly organized themselves for military readiness. The poor, benighted "heathens"
they had initially imagined so fondly now became enemy hostiles, whose
beating war drums the missionaries claimed to hear pounding through
the restless nights.[72]

As the newly arrived missionaries understood it, they were a civil,
Christian people willing to brave the crude, merciless terrain of African
wilderness to become harbingers of divine truth and Christian salvation.
They offered spiritual freedom to a heathen continent while forging political freedom for themselves through the very act of occupying lands long
held by sovereign African polities. For their part, native African polities
had no reason to invest in the seeming absurdity of missionary claims to
rescue them and to assert control over their lands. But dearth of reason

---

[71] Ibid.

[72] Fitts, *Lott Carey*, 27–33, 37–40. Monday B. Abasiattai, "The Search for
Independence: New World Blacks in Sierra Leone and Liberia, 1787–1847," *Journal
of Black Studies* 23, no. 1 (September 1992): 107–16. Monday B. Abasiattai, *African
Resistance in Liberia: The Vai and the Gola-Bandi*, Liberia Working Group Papers, no. 2
(Bremen: Liberia Working Group, 1988).

has rarely been a hindrance to brute force, and the newly spawned Liberia colony was to be no exception. So from the very start, Cary's group, which numbered about 130 members, followed the same route White settlers had taken by arming themselves and asserting a natural and divine right to war against the indigenous towns.

Enlarging the Settlement

Thus began the fundamental relation between the Black settler colony and the native African polities in the region. Over the next decade, the Black missionary settlers directed most of their energies to military vigilance and warfare against sovereign Africans. They aimed to domesticate any resistance to Christian dominion, while native Africans determined to preserve their sovereignty from what they recognized as a military encampment of foreigners. One White colonial agent communicated to native leaders that if they did not back down, they would find out what is was like to fight "White men." By this threat the agent cloaked himself and the colony in the garment of racial imperialism. He discerned that the Liberia colony was a Western Christian settler polity, a status that afforded the Black Americo-Liberians (as the settlers were called) a metonymic Whiteness vis-à-vis the "heathen" native Africans they were attempting to subdue.[73]

In August 1822, the year following the Richmond group's arrival, a third cohort of Black colonists arrived in Liberia. Accompanying the group was Jehudi Ashmun, a White Congregationalist minister working in Baltimore. Like so many other missionaries to West Africa, Ashmun was driven by a mix of commercial interests and missionary zeal. He had proposed that the ACS grant him monopoly trade rights in Liberia. In exchange, the ACS was to reap two-thirds of the profits, with Ashmun pocketing the remaining revenues. Ashmun's pitch fell on eager ears, not surprisingly. The ACS, after all, had never solved its central problem of being severely underfinanced; given the ACS's presumption that commercialism was a central mechanism of its civilizing mission, the minister's proposal was more than enticing. As it turned out, however, it was militarism and not commercialism that consumed Ashmun's energies when

---

[73] Ciment, *Another America*, 30–42. Claude Andrew Clegg, *The Price of Liberty: African Americans and the Making of Liberia* (Chapel Hill: University of North Carolina Press, 2004). Bronwen Everill, *Abolition and Empire in Sierra Leone and Liberia.* (Houndmills, Basingstoke, UK: Palgrave Macmillan, 2013). Mary H Moran, *Liberia: The Violence of Democracy* (Philadelphia: University of Pennsylvania Press, 2006). Abasiattai, "The Search for Independence." Yarema, *American Colonization Society*, 41.

he arrived. The ongoing tensions between the settlers and native polities had deepened considerably by that time. In response, Ashmun directed the settlers to build more military installations. By November of 1822 the conflict had flared into open war. With forty muskets and several cannons, the colonists held the native militia at bay until the British navy could arrive to offer backup. The native African military leaders realized full well they were not prepared to take on the British military, so when Britain, in alliance with the Liberian settlers, threatened a full-scale war against the native polities, a peace agreement was readily forged.[74]

In the ensuing months, the Liberian settler colony developed briskly. By 1823 the Liberian colony boasted 150 houses, three storehouses for food and equipment, and a stone tower armed with cannons. Ashmun, the acting agent of the colony, fell into disrepute with the Black colonists when he began rationing the food supply to remedy a shortage. The African American minister Lott Cary led a protest and, with his supporters, stormed the food storehouse. The mutiny forced a panicked Ashmun to flee for his life to neighboring Sierra Leone. After intervention from the ACS board, order was eventually restored and Ashmun was reconciled with the colonists. Over time, Cary and Ashmun even developed a mutual fondness. Meanwhile, the settlers began to make inroads by forging trade relations with the surrounding African polities. By 1824 the colonists were living under a new constitution designed to structure more equitable leadership. The ACS had desired the colony to function primarily as a source of agricultural wealth, supplying an international market with coffee, rice, corn, and other commodities in the way that Britain's Caribbean colonies functioned. But the colonists preferred local trading in combination with subsistence farming. In fact, over the next several years the Black settlers successfully managed their own vision of governance and practical sovereignty, despite the ACS's efforts to keep White men in place as agents in control of the colony. Sixty-six more colonists arrived in 1825, and this generated a growing settler demand for land. Through a combination of peaceful purchases and violent military conquest, the Liberian colony annexed increasing tracts of land. As a result, what began as a relatively small parcel of 2 square miles forcibly

---

[74] Tom W. Shick, *Behold the Promised Land.* Yekutiel Gershoni and Makhon le-meḥkar 'al shem Heri S. Ţruman, *Black Colonialism: The Americo-Liberian Scramble for the Hinterland* (Boulder: Westview Press, 1985). Michael J. Turner, "The Limits of Abolition: Government, Saints and the 'African Question', c. 1780–1820," *English Historical Review* 112, no. 446 (April 1997): 319–57. Yarema, *African Colonization Society*, 40–42.

purchased by Stockton exceeded 150 square miles in 1825. Black settlers and White ACS officials alike were pleased to see the colony steadily becoming what its founders had imagined (see Figure 4.1). Newly arriving colonists received generous acreage from the ACS, and they found it feasible to purchase even more land from local polities by negotiating on their own as individuals.

Ashmun's leadership ended in 1828 as a result of a severe illness that led him to return to the United States; he died shortly thereafter.[75] As a practical matter, the colony now operated under Cary's authority. The colony's economy was expanding steadily, and trade revenues were enhanced through exchange with British, French, and US merchant ships, encompassing the sale of local items such as palm oil, ivory, tortoise shells, and gold. By 1836 the Black settler population had increased to more than 3,000, comprising both free and manumitted Africans from the United States and those recaptives who had been rescued from slave ships by the US and British navies. The capital city of Monrovia alone had more than 500 homes, many boasting stone construction, and more than ten church buildings dotted the landscape. Although only a small fraction of African Americans who desired to relocate to Liberia received funding for passage, several states that organized their own colonization societies did manage to send settlers. Maryland, Pennsylvania, Mississippi, New York, and Louisiana, for instance, all settled their own colonies within Liberia, eventually creating a commonwealth in the 1840s.[76]

The demographic constitution of Liberia, moreover, was fundamentally expressed through the strictures of apartheid. As more Black Christian settlers received land through the colony's central administration and by private negotiations with local polities, the fallacious façade of settler claims to occupy empty land became increasingly apparent. The land was no less occupied than that of Native peoples throughout the Americas as the empire of New Spain and, subsequently, the empire of the United States unyieldingly sought to possess. Native Africans had lived throughout the lands formally incorporated under Liberia's authority. By the 1840s more than 200,000 native Africans were caught within the rapidly expanding geopolitical boundaries of Liberia. With African American settlers and recaptives numbering only about 3,000, native

---

[75] "Death of Mr. Ashmun," *African Repository and Colonial Journal* 4 (September 1828): 214–24. Ciment, *Another America*, 40–53. Clegg, *Price of Liberty*. Everill, *Abolition and Empire*.

[76] Everill, *Abolition and Empire*. Clegg, *Price of Liberty*. Ciment, *Another America*. Moran, *Liberia*. Yarema, *African Colonization Society*, 44–47.

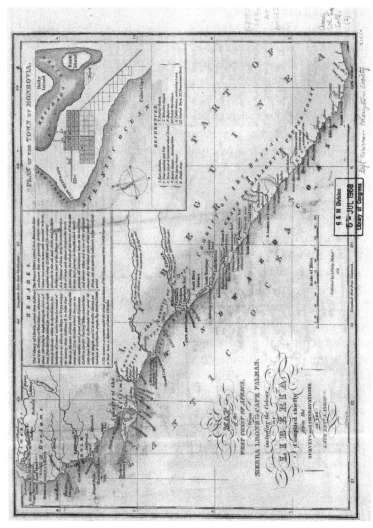

FIGURE 4.1. Map of the West Coast of Africa from Sierra Leone to Cape Palmas, including the colony of Liberia. This map of West Africa is based on Jehudi Ashmun's surveys for the American Colonization Society. The inset on the upper right shows the ACS's plans for the settler town of Monrovia. *Source:* Library of Congress Geography and Map Division.

Africans drastically outnumbered the settler population 70-to-1 within Liberia's formal borders.[77]

Until the 1840s the Liberia colony officially remained a private enterprise formally controlled by the ACS, subsidized by the US federal government, and actively run by Americo-Liberians. Its development was shaped by multiple paradigms of intention and design. First, the Liberian colony's official raison d'être was to serve as a refuge for African recaptives. In this respect, it was the essential mechanism of the US Congress's mandate to suppress the trans-Atlantic slave trade. A second vision of the colony was that of the ACS, which desired that Liberia serve to effect gradual emancipation toward the demise of slavery, a vision fundamentally alien to the aims of the Slave Trade Act of 1819. Third, and most decisive in practical terms, was the desire of Africans in the United States to achieve self-determination by creating a self-governed Black state. As numerous colonists expressed in their correspondence to readers in the United States, theirs was the domain of representative government and freedom from a US racial order that barred them from participating as members of a body politic. In Liberia, African American Christians were the elite. Aside from the few White officials who passed in and out, Blacks from the United States dominated the political order and arrogated exclusive economic and social privileges.

In addition to these three major aims was the imperative of Christian missions, whose complex emergence was a signature feature of the US empire, particularly as this imperial power shifted from a primarily internal mode of colonial control over Indian polities to an external one operating overseas. Indeed, for African Americans and the White-led ACS, Christianization was inseparable from the task of settling and civilizing West Africa. In fact, the Black colonists proved the most eager to promote this missionary agenda as a central reason for their emigration to Liberia. They were primary agents of what they believed was African redemption, an overarching divine plan to bring the race from heathen backwardness to modern civility through Christian dominion.

---

[77] "Latest from Liberia," *African Repository and Colonial Journal* 3 (September 1827): 208–15. Abasiattai, "The Search for Independence." Winston McGowan, "The Establishment of Long-Distance Trade between Sierra Leone and Its Hinterland, 1787–1821," *Journal of African History* 31, no. 1 (January 1990): 25–41. Abasiattai, *African Resistance in Liberia.* Ciment, *Another America.* Cassandra Pybus, "From Epic Journeys of Freedom Runaway Slaves of the American Revolution and Their Global Quest for Liberty," *Callaloo* 29, no. 1 (January 2006): 114–30. Yarema, *African Colonization Society,* 46–47.

As early as 1828 the colony's de facto leadership was composed entirely of Blacks, with Cary serving as governor. Cary died within one year of taking on this new role. He had entered the munitions shed to make more bullets in his continuing war against native Africans. He had always known that working with gunpowder was a risky affair that required expert handling and relentless caution. As a great explosion ripped through the shed, his comrades quickly realized things had gone wrong. Cary did not survive the blast, and his death functioned to strengthen the resolve of the other settler colonists. He was now a martyr, and they committed themselves to avenging his death and furthering the settler cause.[78]

Within a decade of Liberia's beginnings, the Black Christian settlers solidified their racial governance over native Africans, thereby crafting a regime of freedom to benefit themselves. This included forcing recaptured native Africans to work through indenture to Americo-Liberians. By 1847 the polity celebrated its official independence as a sovereign republic, a Black Christian settler state functioning as a constitutional democracy rooted in popular sovereignty. What emerged, in other words, was a system of minority rule born of violent conquest. That conquest grounded a political economy operating under the sign of freedom to achieve self-determination for a population who had been stateless in the US republic. It is crucial to understand that this sign of freedom was no misnomer; it was not hypocrisy. The Liberia and Sierra Leone colonies were in every sense of the same genus as the White settler colonies in the Americas and southern Africa. More specifically, both were directly inspired by the White settler rebellion that created the world's first constitutional settler democracy, the US racial state. It is no accident, thus, that the settler colony of Liberia bore the hallmarks of democracy birthed in the Atlantic world of slavery, genocide, and brutal conquest.[79]

Two things become apparent in light of this development. First, democratic freedom as a political order is inextricably, genealogically rooted in slavery and empire. Second, the very exercise of self-determination – of freedom – has been a colonial project. The problems of killing, displacing, and conquering the native peoples of West Africa to create self-determining

---

[78] Turner, "The Limits of Abolition". Catherine Reef, *This Our Dark Country: The American Settlers of Liberia* (New York: Clarion Books, 2002). Moran, *Liberia*. Yarema, *African Colonization Society*, 57–60.

[79] "Latest from Liberia," *African Repository and Colonial Journal* 3 (September 1827): 208–15. "Address of the Colonists to the Free People of the U.S." *African Repository and Colonial Journal* 3 (December 1827): 300–307.

polities existed not in spite of freedom – not as contradictions – but as freedom's enabling conditions. The imperial arrogance and lethal hubris endemic to settler colonialism, moreover, emerged precisely because of the relations of power and the political order that constituted the dream of freedom. This is what settlers pursued in the Atlantic world again and again. It is what they sought to make real as they conceived democracy and the political orders of freedom as the inalienable conditions of inviolable, pristine sovereignty. They governed racial others as perpetual aliens to the political community through which the state was conceived. And this guaranteed that the settler polities were racial states.

Throughout the nineteenth century the Black Christian settlers of West Africa essentially governed themselves and wielded extensive power over a native majority, claiming vast stretches of land and exceptional wealth for themselves. As they clearly realized, they lived as their White settler counterparts did in the Americas, dominating political power, undermining the local institutions of native African sovereignty, flaunting their exclusive claims on civilization, exuding paternalism toward the indigenous populations, and exploiting the excesses of superior armory that afforded them victory over native defenses – all while being praised as venerable heroes in the vanguard of the most celebrated of Western virtues: freedom. Given this fact, it is peculiar that Black settler colonialism has not typically been recognized as such. Under the rubric of "emigrationism," scholars have more frequently examined Liberia as the result of a White supremacist ruse (the consequence of the ACS's dastardly racism). The basic paradigm of "back-to-Africa movements" has frequently been treated as the delusional behavior of unsophisticated Blacks who were suffering from intractable frustration with the political realities of US slave society. But the historical record demonstrates why neither of these approaches is suitable to explain the phenomenon.

At stake in this history was a grand problem of freedom, a transnational effort by Atlantic Africans to wrangle with the settler states to whom we owe the burden of democracy, which, under scrutiny, begins to appear more clearly as a distinct product of empire. As a matter of record, West Africa's Black settler minority was enjoying strident measures of political dominance at the very time that Blacks in the United States were growing increasingly uncertain about the prospect of struggling against slavery as permanent racial outsiders in a White republic. Meanwhile, White Americans increasingly resented the presence of free Africans as slavery became more firmly entrenched as a necessary economic convention. White politicians, furthermore, were increasingly bitter about the question of slavery and abolitionism because it produced divided responses among their supporters during the very time the Anglo-American empire was edging closer to the Mexican Republic ("the Old West"). This generated fierce political debates over the balance between so-called free states and slave states. As we will see in the next chapter, during the years leading up to the US Civil War, Black settler colonialism continued to inspire the struggle for democratic freedom among African Americans. What happened beyond that war is both startling and profoundly instructive for interpreting religious formation within the architecture of freedom in an imperial democracy.

5

Black Political Theology, White Redemption, and Soldiers for Empire

During the latter half of the nineteenth century, African Americans would face what seemed the most dramatic and cataclysmic shift in the architecture of race and social power: the transition from formal chattel slavery to an elaborate system of legal apartheid. A violent civil war, constituting the largest slave rebellion on record, would bring an end to chattel slavery. In its place the racial state instituted Reconstruction, a short-lived program of radical reform that relied on strict mandates for racial parity and military occupation to protect Blacks from White terrorist rule. In the absence of slavery, White Americans grew more desperate to racialize space, status, and access to a range of citizenship privileges. The result was the formalization of apartheid, and by 1896 the nation's highest court articulated an explicit defense (*Plessy v. Ferguson*) of this legal principle. Equally important was the expansion of naked brutality – anti-Black terrorism – as a central extralegal means of enforcing the colonial order of White political power. Both this explicit legal sanction and the extralegal apparatus of racial terrorism reinscribed the colonial relation of power, further relegating Blacks to the status of subjugated, stateless peoples.

African Americans perceived this colonial relation of power quite differently in the absence of formal slavery. It seemed, after all, more or less tractable when operating within slavery. Black participation in democracy seemed within reach and appeared on an individual basis to be a matter of manumission. So, on a collective basis, there is no question that African Americans genuinely believed the dissolution of slavery would make multiracial democracy a reality and spell the demise of racial subjugation. Progressive Whites shared the same conviction. So did the fiercest opponents of multiracial democracy, which was why they adamantly and desperately defended slavery. With the benefit of hindsight, it is evident that they were all wrong. Dissolution of slavery did not achieve multiracial democracy. Absent the relatively respectable idiom of chattel slavery, moreover, the uncloaked violence of White supremacy became routine, particularly through the murderous spectacle of lynching. This is precisely why the last decades of the nineteenth century challenged both the activist efforts and explicative capacities of African Americans.

The religious institutions and theological formations among African Americans distinctly embodied these changes in colonial power within the US racial state. This was especially evident in the theological traditions that African Americans generated – particularly the tendency to represent slavery as a divine instrument. Civilizationist discourse and the rhetoric of "race uplift," by this paradigm, were anchored in the history and hope of Black Christianization. As a result, African missions became even more central to the theological imaginary. Finally, African American religions came to bear centrally on the issue of Blacks participating in US wars of conquest against Native Americans and then overseas, during and after the Spanish-American War of 1898.

Abolitionism and African American Political Theology

At the center of Black political struggle was the question of whether African Americans should only pursue multiracial democracy within the White settler state or also pursue Black self-governance through emigration, creating their own settler polities. Repeatedly throughout the nineteenth century, Black politics manifested a conflict over this fundamental issue. Across this divide stretched the mantle of Black political theology, which comprised an elaborate and complex set of religious claims and philosophies to account for racial conditions and to ground an activist agenda for social change. Both the quest for Black self-governance through settler colonialism and the fight for multiracial democracy in the United States induced a profound secularity within Black religion as African Americans regularly engaged with these political questions through religious institutions and public theology.

The theological tenor of the larger discourse concerning slavery is striking if not surprising. Antislavery activists consistently targeted the moral culpability of slavery. African Americans and their White abolitionist allies, in other words, centrally opposed it on the grounds that it was oppressive and fundamentally unjust. They also criticized slavery on other grounds, such as its economic inefficiency (relative to free labor) and its constitutionality (given putative inalienable rights to personal liberty).[1] Nevertheless, its moral turpitude constituted the most common basis on which Black and White opponents of slavery advanced their movement for abolishing the institution. As a White Christian settler state, furthermore, the United States was deeply shaped by the Bible as an icon of morality, despite the absence of any biblical condemnation of slavery. Unsurprisingly, most pundits publically engaged with the issue on the basis of religious and especially biblical argument.[2]

In this context, the secularity of African American religion emerges strikingly. Black political theology undergirded the efforts of Black laity and religious professionals as they sought to transform their status as chattel and stateless aliens into that of actual citizens of the White republic, of its political community. In this vein, the critical period of the 1830s was marked by the formation of organized, activist resistance to slavery. African American women were among the members of the Philadelphia Female Anti-Slavery Society in 1833. In the same year William Lloyd Garrison led the founding of the American Anti-Slavery Society, whose African American members included Frederick Douglass. These abolitionist organizations created periodicals, sponsored public lectures, raised funding to manumit select individuals, and lobbied state and federal public officials to abolish slavery. At the same time, they vigorously debated the creation of Black settler colonies and the relation of Blacks to the nation's body politic. This political activity forced the most public, leading figures of organized Black religion to engage centrally with secular matters of racial power and the formation of the United States as a racially exclusive republic. Among the most eloquent and influential African American antislavery activists in this context was Maria Stewart, a freeborn woman from Connecticut. Stewart spent much of her adult life in Boston, where she launched a brief career as a public lecturer – the first by any woman in the United States. Following her evangelical

---

[1] Elizabeth Fox-Genovese and Eugene D. Genovese, *The Mind of the Master Class: History and Faith in the Southern Slaveholders' Worldview* (New York: Cambridge University Press, 2005). Larry E. Tise, *Proslavery: A History of the Defense of Slavery in America, 1701–1840* (Athens: University of Georgia Press, 1987). Elizabeth Fox-Genovese and Eugene D. Genovese, "The Divine Sanction of Social Order: Religious Foundations of the Southern Slaveholders' World View," *Journal of the American Academy of Religion* 55, no. 2 (Summer 1987): 211–33.

[2] Stephen Haynes, *Noah's Curse: The Biblical Justification of American Slavery* (New York: Oxford University Press, 2002). John B. Boles, *Masters & Slaves in the House of the Lord: Race and Religion in the American South, 1740–1870* (Lexington: University Press of Kentucky, 1988).

conversion to Christianity, Stewart began working as a speaker, educator, and writer within the context of the antislavery movement and the early feminism that attended abolitionism. Speaking in September 1832 at Boston's Franklin Hall, she rooted her critique of slavery and sexism in her conviction that the Christian god was just, benevolent, and active in the lives of African Americans. Drawing on the Exodus narrative and tropes of African redemption, Stewart interpreted the Bible to engage centrally with race and social power. And she castigated Black men who opposed the agency and equality of African American women. Stewart made a strong impression on Garrison and persuaded him to publish her essays. Like other feminists of her time, she emphasized the need for women to have equal access to education and to exercise public leadership. After ceasing her work as a public lecturer (she found the opposition from men and even some women too overwhelming) she continued a public career as an educator.[3]

As the strident defense of slavery began to multiply in the 1840s, activists such as James W. C. Pennington and David Ruggles (1810–1849) promoted a Black political theology with a blistering critique of slavery and the brutality it wreaked in the lives of African Americans. Pennington had been enslaved in Maryland and, after witnessing his father being brutalized by his slave master, fled his slaveholder's plantation to settle eventually in New York. There he converted to Christianity and educated himself for church ministry. Pennington soon became an accomplished Presbyterian minister. His autobiography, sermons, and popular *Textbook on the Origins and History of the Colored People* (1841) repudiated racist claims that Blacks were divinely destined for slavery. Pennington infused his ministry with activism against segregation, starting a campaign against racist transportation laws in New York. Unlike Pennington, David Ruggles was born free in Connecticut. Both of his parents were professionals and devout Methodists. He became a successful printer and a devoted activist within the Underground Railroad. (Frederick Douglass was among the many Blacks whom Ruggles assisted in fleeing to freedom.) As a lay Christian, Ruggles steeped his opposition to slavery in the language of Christian moralism, by which he demonstrated that slavery was, among other things, an institution of sexual violence and immorality. Styling himself a "Puritan," Ruggles attacked the

---

[3] William Safire, *Lend Me Your Ears: Great Speeches in History* (New York: W.W. Norton, 2004), 678. Valerie C. Cooper, *Word Like Fire: Maria Stewart, The Bible and the Rights of African Americans* (Charlottesville: University of Virginia Press, 2011), 15–22, 153–60.

concubine system in which White slaveholders kept a White wife while raping Black women and siring children whom they then enslaved. This sexual license, he charged, was a moral outrage. And he challenged the White wives of slaveholders and other White women who might identify with their plight to protest within White churches the sexual exploitation of concubinage and what Ruggles named its sinful stain on the soul of American Christianity.[4]

The Negro Convention movement was likely the most visible institutional form of Black activism that promoted the developing political theology of African Americans. This was a series of national and state conferences that African American churches convened annually to address slavery, racism, and the precarious status of Blacks as people who were forced to live outside the regime of rights and privileges that constituted White citizenship. This movement, more than any other single factor, created an institutional arena that secularized the overwhelmingly evangelical religion of African American Christian churches. Philadelphia's Bethel African Methodist Episcopal (AME) congregation (founded by Richard Allen) hosted the first of these conventions. Not surprisingly, emigrationist efforts to create a Black settler colony dominated the agenda of this first national meeting. The convention, furthermore, unequivocally condemned the American Colonization Society for regarding free Blacks as inherently unfit for life in the United States. But this did little to dampen the support that Forten and other relatively successful Blacks lent to the convention's consensus decision that creating a Black self-governing polity through emigration was a viable and even necessary path to securing justice and the rights of citizenship.[5]

Meanwhile, the liberationist imperatives of antislavery work and feminism continued to be articulated by activists such as Sojourner Truth in the 1840s and 1850s. Truth was born "Isabella" in Ulster County,

[4] James W.C. Pennington, *Textbook on the Origins and History of the Colored People* (Hartford, CT: L. Skinner, 1841). Herman E. Thomas, *James W.C. Pennington: African American Churchman and Abolitionist* (New York: Garland, 1995). Graham Russell Hodges, *David Ruggles: A Radical Black Abolitionist and the Underground Railroad in New York City* (Chapel Hill: University of North Carolina Press, 2010), 79–83. David Ruggles, "The Abrogation of the Seventh Commandment, by the American Churches," in *Early Negro Writing, 1760–1837*, ed. Dorothy Porter, 478–93 (Baltimore: Black Classic Press, 1995).

[5] Robin W. Winks, *The Blacks in Canada: A History* (Montreal: McGill-Queens University Press, 1997), 162. Julie Winch, *A Gentleman of Color: The Life of James Forten* (New York: Oxford University Press, 2002). Howard Bell, *A Survey of the Negro Convention Movement* (1953; reprint, New York: Arno Press, 1969), 20–37.

New York, where she was enslaved from birth. After enduring a typically abusive experience of slavery, including a marriage arranged by her White slave master, Isabella fled to freedom at approximately thirty years of age.[6] By that time the eclectic religious background of her youth had become conformed largely to the Methodism she encountered in the fiery preachments of the charismatic revivalism that increasingly shaped American Christianity. She embraced the born-again protocols of the holiness, perfectionist movement emerging within Methodism, eschewed worldly practices such as dancing and alcohol consumption, and focused on sanctifying herself for a life of purity. Isabella eventually adopted a new name – Sojourner Truth – to evidence what she believed was a commission direct from the Christian deity for her to witness to the reality of divine salvation at work in the world and the humanity of Black people as deserving of full rights, freedom, and equality. Her activism far exceeded agitating for changes in public policy to abolish slavery. She also assisted Blacks in escaping bondage to seize for themselves a life of freedom beyond slavery. Like other public figures of her time, Truth generously employed biblical theology to compose a strident critique of racial slavery.[7]

By the time the African Presbyterian minister Henry Highland Garnet delivered his "Address to the Slaves of the United States of America" at Buffalo's Negro Convention of 1843, it was clear to even casual observers that a rising tide of insurgency was at work among US Blacks seeking all means of securing racial freedom in a republic whose settler-colonial paradigms opposed the essential architecture of multiracial political equality. The delegates had decided by the thin margin of a single vote to eschew Garnet's call to arms in preference to Frederick Douglass's call for a strictly political, nonviolent path to freedom. But if Douglass and his supporters had hopes that their more conciliatory devotion to a political solution to slavery would win over the hearts and minds of the majority of White citizens, they were to be sorely disappointed.

An Entrenched Racial State

Over the next two decades White Americans employed both popular means and state power to eviscerate the frail skeleton of privileges and protections available to free Blacks. In 1849 Virginia's state legislature

---

[6] Larry G. Murphy, *Sojourner Truth: A Biography* (Santa Barbara, CA: Greenwood Press, 2011), 41–54. Nell Irvin Painter, *Sojourner Truth: A Life, a Symbol*, 1st ed. (New York: W. W. Norton, 1996), 3–5, 23–25.

[7] Painter, *Sojourner Truth*, 22–30. Murphy, *Sojourner Truth*, 43–50.

stipulated that people with as little as one-fourth Black ancestry, conventionally known as "mulattoes," were for all legal and practical purposes "Negroes." The measure formalized the common practice of subjecting peoples of Black–White ancestry to the political forms of domination that inscribed citizenship as a preeminently racial property for Whites only. This law, in other words, formally articulated racial Whiteness as purity and, on a practical level, undermined the informal means whereby Blacks with White ancestry might mitigate their experience of White brutality. The following year Virginia went even further, decreeing that manumitted slaves who remained in the state for more than one year would be forced into slavery again and sold for the public benefit of White citizens. In this way Virginia underscored the longstanding political axiom that freedom was a racial privilege exclusively for Whites and that Black subjects were coherent within the racial state only as dominated racial outsiders.[8]

Meanwhile, the expanding Anglo-American empire had wrested from the Mexican Republic nearly half of that polity's territory by 1848, placing it under the control of the US military. As a result, the United States borders now reached clear to the Pacific Ocean. The US Congress immediately instigated a surge of Anglo-American settlers to secure the massive expanse of land and to create settlements that undermined the pragmatic authority of the millions of Mexican peoples and Native American polities already established there. A steady, westward flow of millions of settlers resulted. The overwhelming majority were White, though a significant number of African Americans also participated in these westward settlements. This settler surge affected not only far-west regions like California but also states like Indiana, Illinois, and Iowa. Whites living in these latter areas were loath to accommodate the increasing number of Blacks who sought to resettle in regions where slavery was not yet formally established. The Indiana Constitutional Convention of 1850, for instance, voted decisively to prohibit Blacks from even entering the state. In the ensuing years, Illinois, Iowa, and Oregon implemented similar legislation to prohibit entry to Blacks. In 1853 the Washington Territory explicitly limited voting to White citizens only. And by 1860 other states such as Nebraska, New Mexico, and Utah had taken commensurate

---

[8] Charles Melvin Christian and Sari Bennett, *Black Saga: The African American Experience* (Boston: Houghton Mifflin, 1995), 142, 50. Eddie Glaude, *Exodus!: Religion, Race, and Nation in Early Nineteenth-Century Black America* (Chicago: University of Chicago Press, 2000). Elise Lemire, *"Miscegenation": Making Race in America* (Philadelphia: University of Pennsylvania Press, 2011). Peggy Pascoe, *What Comes Naturally: Miscegenation Law and the Making of Race in America* (New York: Oxford University Press, 2009).

measures by legally banning the extension of voting rights to Blacks and by barring them from military service.[9]

Slave Law and Free Fugitives

In September 1850, the all-White members of the US Congress refashioned the Fugitive Slave Law, delivering the most debilitating blow yet to African Americans' efforts to thwart the political regime of slavery. The new legislation was authored chiefly by Henry Clay. This package of five legislative bills constituted the so-called Compromise of 1850 that admitted California as a free state (a concession to the antislavery lobby) in exchange for bolstering the breadth and scale of legal provisions hindering Blacks' ability to manumit themselves through flight. The compromise also banned commercial slave trading (but not slavery) in the District of Columbia. For their part, slaveholders, who commanded strong loyalty and helped compose the ranks of the legislature, were able to secure the formal, legal status of slaveholding in Texas (recently seized from the Mexican Republic). More importantly, northern polities that had previously refused to comply with the recapture of Blacks who escaped slavery were now obligated to do so under threat of federal legal sanction. The legislation thus aimed to mollify the demands of powerful White slaveholders and their political allies who were incensed at the continuing flight of Blacks from slavery.[10]

The Fugitive Slave Law of 1850, however, did not introduce any novel legal paradigm. Rather, it built on the slavocratic provisions of the US Constitution, article 4 of which stipulated that "No Person held to Service or Labour in one State ... escaping into another, shall ... be discharged from such Service or Labour, but shall be delivered up on Claim of the Party to whom such Service or Labour may be due." In the absence of specifications for how this was to occur, the original Fugitive Slave Law of 1793 had made explicit provisions for forcing escaped slaves back into bondage by obligating magistrates in any state to authorize slave catchers and by imposing a fine on any who assisted fugitive slaves or who sought to deter slave catchers. By 1850, however, the Underground Railroad had established a fairly reliable network of volunteers who collaborated to assist hundreds of Blacks in their escape from chattel slavery.

---

[9] Christian and Bennet, *Black Saga*, 146–47.

[10] Steven Lubet, *Fugitive Justice: Runaways, Rescuers, and Slavery on Trial* (Cambridge, MA: Belknap Press of Harvard University Press, 2010), 27–35. Stanley W. Campbell, *The Slave Catchers: Enforcement of the Fugitive Slave Law, 1850–1860* (Chapel Hill: University of North Carolina Press, 1968), 17–33.

Among the most celebrated of these agents were Sojourner Truth and Harriet Tubman. The renowned Frederick Douglass himself had become free through this mechanism, although White philanthropists in England had subsequently purchased his freedom to ensure he could not be seized under the auspices of the law. A handful of states and municipalities, moreover, had passed their own "personal liberty" laws, flagrantly opposing the federal law, to censor slave catchers and to protect escaped slaves from seizure under the federal statute. These developments, in addition to the "vigilance committees" of armed protection for escaped slaves that African Americans and their White allies created, posed formidable challenges for White slaveholders who attempted to seize fugitive Blacks and return them to slavery. The Fugitive Slave Law of 1850 changed that. Congress now denied recaptured fugitive slaves the right to a juried trial and prohibited them from testifying on their own behalf. Any who interfered with slave catchers now risked imprisonment, not merely a fine. Federal commissioners, in addition, were now given monetary incentive to return fugitives to slaveholders.[11]

Passage of the Fugitive Slave Act of 1850 was among the most significant events of the period to foster African Americans' pursuit of emigration, chiefly because the decision emblazoned the implications that slavery held for political order and racial governance. For this reason, the law exacerbated the divide among African Americans concerning the prospects of emigration versus assimilation. The practical challenge this posed for free and enslaved Blacks is not difficult to perceive. Free Blacks were now more susceptible to being seized and sold into slavery based on disingenuous plots to earn quick cash by White opportunists eager to testify falsely that they had identified an escaped slave. Beyond the issue of fictive claims by Whites, of course, were the truthful claims that White slaveholders brought to reenslave those who had fled a life of bondage to eke out an existence elsewhere (typically northward) in the White republic. Even more significant is the fact that the formal demarcation between free and enslaved Blacks glossed over the complicated, inextricably interwoven lives of the two groups. Numerous celebrated free Blacks such as James W. C. Pennington, Harriet Tubman, Henry Bibb, and Frederick Douglass had been slaves until escaping to live a life of freedom. Virtually every community of free Blacks in the United States, moreover, consisted

---

[11] Lubet, *Fugitive Justice*, 48–50. Virginia Hamilton, *Anthony Burns: The Defeat and Triumph of a Fugitive Slave* (New York: Open Road Media Young Readers, 2011). Campbell, *Slave Catchers*, 17–33.

of extended families whose members, in whole or in part, had at one time been enslaved and had *become* free through either flight or some other means of manumission.[12] No one appreciated this reality more viscerally than African Americans themselves, who either as slaves contemplated how to join their free kin or as free peoples deliberated over the most effective means of securing freedom for their enslaved parents, offspring, siblings, or other family members.[13]

This is why the actions of the White US legislature in 1850 merely served to underscore the need for Black self-governance and the fundamental political quandary of not only enslaved but also free Blacks. So long as White citizens and their public officials (and not Blacks themselves) determined the fate of African Americans, it seemed certain that African Americans were doomed to abject domination as an internal colony of racial aliens. Their very existence inspired increasing volatility and determination from the political rationalities of White supremacism. Few could deny the fundamentally racial constitution of freedom in the US empire; it had been shaped and refashioned repeatedly as an instrument of exceptionalism and exclusivity to constitute Whiteness as a socially real, civic status. For this reason, American freedom functioned as a regime on the backs of the politically dominated – Native Americans, Blacks, and the highly exploited "free" laborers from East Asia who began arriving in greater numbers on the Pacific Coast in the latter half of the nineteenth century.[14]

Black Diaspora and Self-Determination

In the wake of the Fugitive Slave Law, Henry Bibb (1815–1854), a prolific and energetic promoter of Black Nationalism, took action. Few Blacks had such an elaborate experience of being a fugitive from slavery as did Bibb. Unlike the vast majority of Blacks who escaped slavery, Bibb escaped and returned time and time again in hopes of rescuing his family. On numerous occasions he had risked seizure, betrayal, torture, and death for defying the regime of slaveholding authority. At one point he

---

[12] Lubet, *Fugitive Justice*, 48–50. Hamilton, *Anthony Burns*. Campbell, *Slave Catchers*, 17–33.

[13] Cyril E. Griffith, *The African Dream: Martin R. Delany and the Emergence of Pan-African Thought* (University Park: Pennsylvania State University Press, 1975), 2–3.

[14] Najia Aarim-Herio, *Chinese Immigrants, African Americans, and Racial Anxiety in the United States, 1848–82* (Urbana: University of Illinois Press, 2003), 79–81. Joshua Paddison, *American Heathens: Religion, Race, and Reconstruction in California* (Berkeley: University of California Press, 2012).

boarded a northbound steamer by carrying an empty trunk under pretensions of being the slave of the Whites who boarded alongside him.[15] In the 1840s he made a final, successful escape alone to Detroit, where he hoped to earn sufficient funds to return south and purchase the freedom of his enslaved wife Malinda (as they were two slaves, their marriage had no legal standing) and their daughter Mary Frances. There he joined the organized antislavery movement. Unable to locate his wife and daughter (they had been resold into slavery in Louisiana), Bibb lost all hope of being reunited with them. He eventually became acquainted with Mary E. Miles, a free Black woman from Massachusetts who established a successful career in education. The two were married in 1848 and collaborated as public figures in the antislavery movement (until Henry's death in 1854). Bibb also became involved with the Negro Convention movement and in this context met activists including Frederick Douglass and Martin Delany.[16]

In 1850, when they learned of the Fugitive Slave Act's passage, the couple decided the threat of being kidnapped and forced into slavery was too great to continue living in the United States. Bibb and Miles moved to Ontario, Canada. Soon after resettling there, they established the first Black newspaper in Canada, the *Voice of the Fugitive Slave*. The periodical became an important organ that helped to create new networks and communities among Blacks and to promote the critique of slavery and White political power.[17]

Meanwhile, Black settler colonialism continued to deepen its appeal amid the strident assault that mainstream Whites were making on the lives of free Blacks. This environment of insurgent Black opposition to the White racial state and the expanding secularity of Black political theology led to an ever-growing network of Black activists whose critique of racial power was rooted in religious imaginaries and formations. The collaboration between the Bibbs and James Theodore Holly (1829–1911) emerged from this network. Holly is best remembered for his bishopric of the Protestant Episcopal Church in Haiti, where he began living in the 1850s. Although his grandparents had experienced slavery, Holly himself was born free. His religious roots lay in Roman Catholicism, the religious tradition of his parents, who attended the Holy Trinity Church in the Georgetown neighborhood of Washington, DC. When his family

[15] Griffith, *African Dream*, 165–70.
[16] Henry Bibb and Charles J. Heglar, *The Life and Adventures of Henry Bibb: An American Slave* (Madison: University of Wisconsin Press, 2001), vii–xi, 42–50, 115–22, 60–70.
[17] Philip Bader, *African American Writers* (New York: Facts On File, 2004), 20–21.

relocated to Brooklyn, New York, in 1844, Holly was exposed to the prospect of Christian missions and colonization. A teenager at the time, Holly had been schooled since his early years, and he showed such a remarkable devotion to erudition that he impressed local elites like Lewis Tappan, who hired the lad as a clerk in both his personal business and with the American Missionary Association (AMA).[18]

As was common with free Black Christians, the Christian missionary enterprise proved the specific means through which Holly developed an interest in the Black Diaspora. His diasporic consciousness, in other words, was not a purely secular frame of reference; it was also deeply theological. As he continued to work with the AMA, Holly became increasingly enamored of the domestic and foreign aspirations of Christian expansionism. Much of this was tied to the ideal of African redemption that characterized African American Christianity during the time. But the biblical theology that Holly had cultivated in his turn to Protestant evangelicalism was also an important factor. By his early twenties, Holly had become influenced by Protestant attacks against Catholicism. He withdrew from the Catholic Church and joined the Protestant Episcopal denomination at age twenty-four. When his family later moved to Vermont, his interest in the Black Diaspora was awakened. It was then that he encountered the writings of Henry Bibb. As he began reading the *Voice*, he was overwhelmed by the persuasive logic of Black settler colonialism, which the Bibbs promoted in the pages of their newspaper. When Bibb called for a transnational North American Convention of Negroes to convene in Toronto in September 1851, Holly did his best to attend. In the end, he could not raise sufficient funds. But the young, aspiring minister remained undaunted. He mailed to convention organizers his written plans for a transnational league of Blacks that included a vision for resettling fugitives and helping them acquire land.[19]

Among those who did attend from the United States was Martin Delany. At that time Delany was convinced that emigration outside the United States was a scheme that worked in the interest of White racists desiring to rid their nation of Blacks. Delany spared no pains to voice his critiques of Black resettlement – at that time he was persuaded that Blacks needed to establish their own society within the geopolitical boundaries of the United States. But Bibb, who had organized the conference,

[18] Craig Steven Wilder, *A Covenant with Color: Race and Social Power in Brooklyn 1636–1990* (New York: Columbia University Press, 2013), 84.

[19] James Theodore Holly, *Facts about the Church's Mission in Haiti: A Concise Statement by Bishop Holly* (New York: Thomas Whittaker, 1897), 6–7.

was keen to highlight the intransigent racism that Blacks faced, and he included in the proceedings a reading of Holly's visionary recommendations for creating an autonomous Black abolitionist movement. The convention adopted Holly's plans in his absence through a unanimous vote.[20]

Bibb was so impressed with the apparent zeal of the young Holly that he quickly brought Holly into the heart of the movement and eventually invited him to work with the *Voice*. After pulling off a successful fund-raising circuit for the paper, Holly moved to Canada to accept the position of associate editor and proprietor, arriving in June 1852. Over the course of the next year, Holly worked with the Bibbs and with Josiah Henson, another fugitive of US slavery, to create a settlement as a place of refuge for African Americans fleeing the enhanced regime of the Fugitive Slave Law. The Bibbs drew on their life savings to purchase thirteen hundred acres of land near Windsor, Canada. They named it the Refugee Home Society, and they aimed to resell land to Blacks seeking to start a life of freedom in Canada. But critics among Ontario's free Black population charged Holly and the Bibb couple with taking advantage of the needy.[21]

In fact, the larger question of emigration, in tandem with the Refugee Home Society, became a fundamentally divisive issue that split Blacks in Canada, as in the United States, and generated fierce debate. Around the same time, Black Canadians started a new periodical, the *Provincial Freeman*, to editorialize against the emigrationist views that Bibb and Holly promoted in the *Voice of the Fugitive Slave*. The resulting schism reflected the actual complexity faced by Blacks who simultaneously desired self-determination and the ability to enjoy rights in their land of birth or current residence. Of course, the Bibbs and Holly never entertained the thought of denying other Blacks this right. The question was whether Black freedom was feasible in a White republic. Those African Americans who were persuaded by the emigrationist argument believed multiracial democracy in White-dominated nations was simply not a viable pursuit.[22]

Meanwhile, in the United States, the effects of the 1850 Fugitive Slave Law continued to debilitate Black efforts to become part of the body politic. Armed with an enhanced array of federal authority and institutional power, White bounty hunters pursuing alleged fugitives from

---

[20] David M. Dean, *Defender of the Race: James Theodore Holly, Black Nationalist and Bishop* (Boston: Lambeth Press, 1979), 11–15.
[21] Winks, *Blacks in Canada*, 202–6. Dean, *Defender of the Race*, 11–16.
[22] Dean, *Defender of the Race*, 11–16. Winks, *Blacks in Canada*, 202–6.

slavery brought new terror to the lives of Blacks throughout the United States. The entire affair underscored the point that the nation's slaveholding elites were unmatched in their wealth and political power in the halls of Congress. In this light, the struggle for Black freedom seemed increasingly frail and vulnerable. What seemed ironic to African Americans, moreover, was the central role that freedom played in the pageantry of US nationalism. No principle was more essential to the self-definition of Anglo-Americans than freedom. And yet, at least in ostensible terms, no principle seemed more at odds with the slavocratic foundations of the White republic.

White Freedom and Slaveholding Religion

In critique of this putative irony the Rochester Ladies' Anti-Slavery Society of upstate New York invited Frederick Douglass to give the keynote Independence Day lecture during the summer of 1852. For decades, the nation's Independence Day anniversary had been marked by ceremonies of religious solemnity and festivity. White celebrants commonly venerated the White republic as a divine experiment in civic freedom and republican virtue. But antislavery activists had begun to make the holiday an occasion for marking what they perceived as strident hypocrisy, and they hoped Douglass, the most famous of US abolitionists, would drive home the point, given the efforts of the US Congress to ensure the permanence of slavery.[23]

Douglass was born into slavery in Maryland and was separated from his mother while still a child. Eventually, in his young adult years, he escaped the iron grip of bondage to forge a life of freedom. By 1845, when he published his autobiography, *Narrative of the Life of Frederick Douglass, an American Slave*, he was already becoming an internationally renowned abolitionist. He traveled to England to complete a two-year speaking tour, which allowed him to raise money to support abolition in the United States. In 1847 he collaborated with Martin Delany to launch the *North Star*. As coeditors, the two Black men announced that the periodical's mission was "to attack slavery in all its forms and aspects; advocate universal emancipation; exalt the standard of public morality; promote the moral and intellectual improvement of the colored people; and hasten the day of freedom to the three millions of our enslaved

---

[23] Frederick Douglass, *Narrative of the Life of Frederick Douglass, An American Slave*, ed. Benjamin Quarles (Cambridge, MA: Belknap Press, 1960). James A. Colaiaco, *Frederick Douglass and the Fourth of July* (New York: Palgrave Macmillan, 2006), 7–9.

fellow countrymen." In addition to assisting other Blacks to escape slavery through the Underground Railroad, Douglass also critiqued the racial ideology of slavery, and he underscored what he saw as the hypocrisy of White freedom founded on Black slavery.[24]

Equally important was Douglass's critique of proslavery Christianity. Douglass's own Christian sensibilities were cultivated through his active membership in the AME Church, the most politically active and progressive of Black church movements of the nineteenth century. Douglass pursued his devotion to Christian vocation by becoming a licensed minister, which enabled him to pursue a public career in the church. The rising scale of political activism among abolitionists, however, quickly became the primary context through which he established a public profile. By that time, two denominations of White Methodists and Baptists had been created in the United States for the express purpose of defending slavery.[25]

Douglass advanced a political theology of Black freedom in the secular arena. In this context, he recalled his own experience of slave masters who tortured Blacks for praying to the Christian god one hour and then proceeded to worship the next at their White churches. This was not, he claimed, the religion of Jesus but merely "slaveholding religion." Douglass argued in an appendix to his autobiography that the morality of this slaveholding religion was devoid of ethics and merely reinscribed the authority of White brutality over Black people. And he asserted that the "Christianity of Christ," unlike "slaveholding religion," was simply incompatible with slavery.[26]

Drawing on his commanding grasp of history, politics, and ethics, Douglass did not disappoint the White organizers when he appeared in Rochester's Corinthian Hall. In an address to a crowd of more than 500 people, he candidly acknowledged that the republic belonged exclusively to Whites and that the Fourth of July was theirs alone to celebrate because it marked the triumph of freedom and democracy specifically for Whites. The United States, after all, was obviously founded along racial boundaries. But rather than impugn the republic's founders as culpable

---

[24] *North Star*, December 3, 1847, 1. L. Diane Barnes, *Frederick Douglass: Reformer and Statesman* (New York: Routledge, 2013), 3–11, 35–42. Colaiaco, *Frederick Douglass*, 7–9. Douglass, *Narrative of the Life*, 20–33.

[25] Donald Mathews, "Methodism Schism and Antislavery Sentiment," in *Abolitionism and American Religion*, ed. John R. McKivigan (New York: Routledge, 1999), 130–40. John R. McKivigan, *The War Against Proslavery Religion: Abolitionism and the Northern Churches, 1830–1865* (Ithaca, NY: Cornell University Press, 1984).

[26] Douglass, *Narrative of the Life*, 155.

in founding a state on slavery and Native American genocide, Douglass lauded the venerable statesmen as honorable and willing to wage violent struggle to win the high prize of liberty. Though men of peace, Douglass opined, "they preferred revolution to peaceful submission to bondage." Though quiet, they brooked no reticence in "agitating against oppression." And although they valued forbearance, "they knew its limits." Echoing themes he had written before in the pages of the *North Star*, Douglass maintained that the nation of White citizens was not wrong for honoring its tradition of liberty and venerating as sacred the Declaration of Independence and the US Constitution. The travesty, he claimed, lay with perverting freedom into the exclusive racial privilege of Whites while subjecting to the terror of slavery the millions of Blacks "whose chains, heavy and grievous ... are rendered more intolerable by the jubilee shouts that reach them."[27]

Departing from the critique of the US Constitution he had articulated years earlier, Douglass now asserted that it was not a proslavery document – the term "slavery" he observed appeared not even once in the Constitution – and that those legal experts who based their proslavery edicts on it had no actual basis for doing so. Douglass, moreover, faulted not only secular politicians but also White American churches for their culpability in trampling "the duty of all the followers of the Lord Jesus Christ." He asserted that the failure of White churches to denounce the Fugitive Slave Law as a violation of "religious liberty" indicated they viewed religion as merely an empty form of worship "and not a vital principle" rooted in "active benevolence, justice, love, and good will." Even infidelity and atheism, he proffered, were preferable to the proslavery gospel. And by contrasting the churches of Britain, which had already abolished slavery, to those of the United States, Douglass sought to demonstrate that the public meaning of Christianity among White Americans was perfectly blameworthy for propagating slavery. The system rendered White republicanism "a sham" and White Christianity "a lie."[28]

With generous quotations from scripture and oratorical thunderings of righteous indignation, Douglass displayed his intimate knowledge of

---

[27] Sara Meer, "Douglass as Orator and Editor," in *The Cambridge Companion to Frederick Douglass*, ed. Maurice S. Lee (New York: Cambridge University Press, 2009), 53–55. Frederick Douglass, "What to the Slave is the Fourth of July? An Address Delivered in Rochester, New York, on 5 July 1852," in *The Frederick Douglass Papers, Series One: Speeches, Debates, And Interviews*, ed. John W. Blassingame (New Haven, CT: Yale University Press, 1982), 2: 359–88.

[28] Douglass, "What to the Slave is the Fourth of July," 2: 376–84.

the Bible and his skill in bringing the question of slavery and freedom into the central purview of Black political theology. His evocative, trenchant critique of slavery as a hypocritical perversion at the heart of the White republic was positively received and was subsequently printed for distribution to a national audience. Despite his brilliant promotion of the abolitionist cause and his ability to foreground the plight of the millions of Blacks enslaved beneath the heel of White citizens' democracy, however, Douglass himself was surely aware of at least one major problem with his critique: the US Constitution was indeed culpable in upholding the legitimacy of slavery. The Fugitive Slave Law, in both its 1793 and 1850 formulations, merely specified the mechanisms for executing the authority with which article 4 of the Constitution had endowed slaveholders and their agents in scuttling their slaves' flight to freedom. The Constitution, moreover, was replete with provisions that guaranteed both the vitality of American slavery and the political advantage of slaveholders. Even those venerable founders Douglass identified as valiant men of honor – preeminently George Washington and Thomas Jefferson – were themselves slaveholders who reduced hundreds of Blacks to the status of servile chattel.[29]

Douglass, however, had already decided to depart from William Lloyd Garrison's radical critique of White freedom. Whereas Garrison emphasized that US democracy was thoroughly rooted in slavocracy – on which grounds he called for nullifying the US Constitution and replacing it with a new document rooted in multiracial democracy – Douglass embraced the relative pragmatism of investing in the sacred symbols of US nationalism, particularly the Declaration of Independence and the Constitution. Just as he sought to wrest from proslavery ideologues the public meaning of Christianity – the religion and its scriptures had since their origin existed quite comfortably with slavery – so also did he intend, in the interest of Black political struggle, to wrest control of the public meaning of liberty and republicanism as these were articulated and encoded by the nation's White supremacist, slaveholding founders. In Douglass's judgment, Garrison's alternative approach seemed to stand little chance of garnering a broad base of public support to sustain a mass, activist movement of social change – this despite the fact that Garrison was profoundly veridical and keen in his political analysis.[30]

[29] Ibid., 384–87.
[30] Mark A. Graber, *Dred Scott and the Problem of Constitutional Evil* (New York: Cambridge University Press, 2008), 220–30. William David Thomas, *William Lloyd*

The Internal Colony, Race, and Democracy

In the same year that Douglass delivered his rousing critique of US slavery, his former coeditor Martin Delany published a widely influential book: *On the Condition, Elevation, Emigration, and Destiny of the Colored People of the United States* (1852). Modestly referring to the volume as a mere "pamphlet," Delany articulated in slightly more than 200 pages an uncommonly astute analysis of race, slavery, and politics. Whereas Douglass viewed slavery as the fundamental domain through which racial power was exercised, Delany was persuaded that only Black self-determination would create the possibilities of racial justice for Blacks. The two did share common ground as radical abolitionists, as they both sought an immediate end to slavery. But their diverging strategies for Black freedom were contextualized by their significantly different backgrounds. Douglass had fled chattel slavery with the perduring conviction that abolition would enable Blacks to assimilate into the body politic of the United States. Delany, by contrast, was convinced that assimilation into a White republic was simply not politically feasible, so he eventually championed a sovereign Black state as the sine qua non of Black freedom. This fundamental difference between the two was symptomatic of the larger divide among African Americans over whether abolition within a multiracial democracy or the creation of a Black state (viz., the Black settler colony) was the solution to the racial suffering of Black Americans.

Delany, in contrast to Douglass, was born free in Charles Town, a region of Virginia that would later be incorporated into West Virginia. As the son of a free Black woman, Delany had known slavery only indirectly if nevertheless intimately. Like so many other free Blacks, his family lived under the duress of anti-Black legislation that proscribed their activities. Despite being free, his mother faced prosecution for teaching her children to read, a crime punishable by incarceration. She fled to Pennsylvania, where Delany eventually enrolled in a formal school.[31] Not until Delany was eleven years old, moreover, did he experience his father's presence in the family's home, for it was then that his enslaved father was able to purchase his manumission and join the family in Pennsylvania. Delany's intellectual aspirations led him to study medicine in his early twenties by apprenticing with Andrew N. McDowell, an established physician.

Garrison: A Radical Voice Against Slavery (New York: Crabtree Publishing, 2009). Meer, "Douglass as Orator and Editor," 53–55.
[31] Griffith, *African Dream*, 2, 3–5.

Although he continued to work as a physician throughout his life, Delany immersed himself in Black political struggle fully aware that being free from slavery did nothing to afford him actual political membership in the White republic.[32]

His travel to Louisiana, Texas, and Arkansas in the fall of 1839 was equally formative. By that time Delany was determined to identify territory in the American South that might be designated as a sovereign Black state. So, he temporarily abandoned his medical practice and traveled throughout the region, at one point moving through the lands controlled by sovereign Native nations. Delany was prudent enough to travel with copies of freedom papers documenting his status as a free person. In the South, where the Black population rivaled or even outnumbered that of Whites in many regions, the ruthless violence of racial rule was on full display. Delany returned to Pittsburgh, Pennsylvania, convinced that Black freedom could have only an ill future in the United States. From that point on he would become more determined and unwavering in his focus on Black settler colonies as the sole ultimate solution for Black political oppression.[33]

All of this meant that African Americans, whether enslaved or free, were stateless, a situation that was painfully clear to Delany. So of course it shaped the way he understood the central challenge that faced African Americans. Whereas Douglass was motivated by his experience of the *racial regime of slavery* to write about religion and politics, the *racial regime of freedom* eventually set Delany's pen and activism toward Black liberation. If his tumultuous experience of freedom made his visceral knowledge of slavery less direct than that of Douglass, it also enabled Delany to perceive freedom's function as a racial property of Whites that extended only slight privileges to Blacks in the most compromised terms.

Like other African Americans throughout the United States, Delany interpreted passage of the Fugitive Slave Law as a fundamental inflection point in the struggle for Black liberation. His concern with the unbridled authority the legislation provided Whites over free and enslaved Blacks percolated throughout the entire document. Delany rooted his analysis of realpolitik in the agency of Blacks themselves. On this score he was unapologetic in advancing a Black political theology that reconciled the Christian conviction of divine omnipotence with the imperatives of

---

[32] Ibid., 3–7.
[33] Vincent Harding, *There Is a River: The Black Struggle for Freedom in America* (New York: Harcourt Brace Jovanovich, 1981), 131–32.

agential pragmatism, the latter of which he perceived to be sorely lacking among many Black Christians. He conceded that "to depend for assistance upon God" was both a "*duty* and right" of humankind. But "to know when, how, and in what manner" to seek and obtain divine assistance was essential and required that one understand that the divine laws operated in three domains: spiritual, moral, and physical. Spiritual things were to be sought through spiritual means – prayer and supplication to the deity – just as moral rectitude was required to achieve moral ends. But in the physical domain – regarding matters of political equality, government, slavery, and racial liberation – Delany insisted it was incumbent upon Blacks to labor by their own struggle to achieve the respective ends. Like most other free African American activists, Delany considered the Black liberation struggle to be divinely sanctioned and rooted in a righteous, particularly Christian mandate to overthrow slavery and institute racial equality. Yet he argued that African Americans, who were supposedly more religious than their White counterparts, needed to recognize that their god sent rain "on the just and unjust" – religious fidelity created no distinction in matters of material status, political power, or other temporal affairs. Whites clearly were not lacking materially because of their sinful oppression against Blacks. It remained for Blacks to cast off the slave ideology that taught pietism would win their liberation. Only "the application of the means of Elevation" would win them that destiny.[34]

Delany advanced four major theoretical claims about the actual workings of political order in the US republic. First was his assertion that the political condition of African Americans was irreducibly one of statelessness. They were, in other words, a colony of dominated peoples internal to the boundaries of the White settler state. Blacks lived as a dominated people, "a nation within a nation," in a situation of abject terror, subject to the whim of White rulers. As he saw it, the nation's exclusively White government continually demonstrated that the US body politic was preeminently racial and exclusively White; Blacks were perpetually relegated as alien to its political membership. This condition of existing as an internal colony, Delany recognized, was by no means exceptional or unique in the broad history of human civilizations. In fact, although he insisted that Blacks constituted the most extreme example of an internally dominated polity, he nevertheless observed that "in all ages, in almost every

---

[34] Martin Robison Delany and Niger Valley Exploring Party, *The Condition, Elevation, Emigration, and Destiny of the Colored People of the United States; and, Official Report of the Niger Valley Exploring Party* (1861; Amherst, NY: Humanity Books, 2004), 64–66.

nation," there were to be found peoples who despite living among the general population in a physical sense nevertheless had their lives circumscribed by a colonial relation of power and were thus politically separate. Being "deprived of political equality," such peoples were set apart from those whose membership in the nation was politically actualized. As examples, he cited the Israelites in ancient Egypt and the gladiators of ancient Rome. Delany turned to contemporary Europe, however, to drive home his point to his contemporary readers. He named the "Gipsies" (the Roma) of Italy and Greece, the Welsh and Irish among the British, Russia's Poles, Austria's Hungarians, and Jews throughout Europe as current examples. All of these peoples, he observed, shared high hopes for attaining the "national position of self-government and independence."[35]

Second, Delany demonstrated that slavery was a form of racial governance, not merely a condition of exploiting labor as an economic enterprise. On this point he would scarcely have been challenged by the majority of political activists and statesmen of his time, at least not in a general sense. Black and White pundits who took a stand concerning slavery's long-term prospects in the nation easily recognized that slavery fundamentally circumscribed the ability of Blacks to exercise personal and civic freedoms. This is why White supporters of slavery from Henry Clay to John Calhoun to the renowned scholar Philip Schaff interpreted slavery as an essential institution. But Delany meant something more complicated than this. The profundity of his analysis lay with his contention that Blacks, *whether enslaved or free*, occupied essentially the same status precisely because slavery was a form of racial rule. As a political institution, he discerned, slavery subjugated Blacks to the political authority of Whites and deprived them of protections and governing privileges – exercising statecraft, voting, and creating financial enterprises such as banking and industry – that Whites enjoyed as a matter of course. With rare exceptions, Delany observed, free Blacks "even in the non-slaveholding States" were deprived "not only of political but of natural rights" as well, no less surely than those who were enslaved. Delany noted one important difference, however, between free and enslaved Blacks: those living outside of the system of chattel slavery were generally able to make basic decisions about their own bodies and could enjoy social recognition of their family relations, laying claim on their spouses and offspring. The enslaved, by contrast, were denied the public recognition of kinship. This was no small difference. But it did not negate

---

[35] Ibid., 64–66.

the fact that *both* free and enslaved Blacks were "ruled and governed without representation, existing as mere nonentities among the citizens," as "excrescences of the body politic."[36]

For precisely this reason Delany perceived the efficacy of slavery to comprise an essential *political* formation, not merely an economic one. He proposed, in other words, that slavery was a form of political rule and not merely labor exploitation. This was why free Blacks in the North found themselves dependent on the goodwill of sympathetic Whites to do mundane things such as pursuing a formal education, purchasing goods, or obtaining work. And free Blacks were constantly subjected to the violence of vigilante Whites who exercised abuse and malice against Blacks with impunity. Slaves, by contrast, were protected by their White masters from such random violence. Since they were encoded as property, any offense against slaves was an offense against their White slaveholders, a social condition that mitigated and ordered the otherwise capricious possibilities of anti-Black racial terror. For these reasons, Delany enjoined free Blacks to recognize what he called the "political economy and domestic policy" of nations.[37]

Third, Delany departed from most of his contemporaries by contending that the political domination of African American was due not to *hatred* but rather to the exigencies of *policy* in a state that had been created by White settlers. To explain this, Delany recounted the foundation of European settler colonies and the eventual formation of a White republic. He reminded his readers that European settler societies in the Americas were founded not by peasants but by European investors, merchants, corporatists, militarists, nobility, and those with royal sponsorship. These elites made strategic decisions about procuring highly exploitable labor. At one point, he observed, German and Irish peasants were used as indentured labor and were politically dominated; only when the population of these formerly indentured laborers reached a critical mass that translated into a reckoning political force did they cease to be kept underfoot in political terms. Delany also observed that Native Americans, not Blacks, were the first to be enslaved by European settlers. Only when the English and Spanish began to depopulate Native Americans through genocide, the brutal regime of slavery, and other abuses did Europeans turn to Africans for labor in the Americas.

---

[36] Ibid., 44–46.
[37] Ibid., 45.

At the point of the republic's establishment, moreover, Delany argued that any class of people in theory might have been subjugated as underlings. But "the condition of society *at the time*, would not admit of it." Africans as well as "English, Danish, Irish, Scotch, and others" fought and shed blood on behalf of the Anglo-American Revolution. But as a practical matter, "no course of policy could have induced the proscription" of any class of people in a fashion more compelling and ideologically palatable than the subjugation of Blacks and Indians.[38] Thus, the political domination of these populations stemmed not from hatred but rather from the pragmatic challenges of creating a state for the enjoyment of its primary founders – elite Whites. Delany discerned that race, as a system of colonial governance, was the political exigency of a state created by European settlers; it was not the product of emotional or psychological antagonism. He was emphatic on this score and insisted that Blacks needed to apprehend "political science" to appreciate the analytical soundness of this fact.[39]

The fourth element of Delany's theoretical assessment of US democracy was his claim that emigration was the singular solution to internal colonialism. Since Blacks were stateless, their only theoretical options were to pursue equality with Whites within the United States or to seek a political home elsewhere in the world. In the first half of his treatise Delany demonstrated why elevation (antislavery) and its attending goal of actual US citizenship for Blacks was a moribund, illusory pursuit. Given the dismal prospects of multiracial democracy within the United States, Delany proffered that African Americans could reasonably expect to inhabit the political realm of citizenship only within a Black state of their founding or in some preexisting, non-White state in the Americas.[40]

Delany's analysis of race and political order stands in sharp contrast to the conventional views of democracy and race that characterized his era. This becomes especially clear when comparing his propositions to those of the most celebrated political theorists of the nineteenth century. Of special significance is Alexis de Tocqueville (1805–1859), who produced an exceptionally influential study of US democracy in which he engaged with the intersection of race and governance. Tocqueville published his *Democracy in America* in two volumes (1835 and 1840, respectively) and wrote with the intention that French jurists would use it to understand

[38] Ibid., 49.
[39] Ibid., 46–49.
[40] Ibid., passim.

the benefits and specific workings of democratic governance. At a time when Europe was largely monarchical and when even France's democratization was proceeding under the formal structures of monarchical government (Louis-Philippe held the crown from 1830 to 1848, when Tocqueville composed his study), the United States was a political specimen that evoked utter fascination because its republican form of democratic governance was actually encoded in the Constitution. Unlike in Europe, democracy was literally engineered into the foundational political order of the United States from the moment of its formal inception.[41]

Because Tocqueville viewed universal equality as the hallmark of democracy, he found it necessary to account for the foundational, rigid hierarchy of the races in the United States. He did so by setting this disparity among Whites and Blacks and Indians in sharp contrast to the hierarchical nature of French society. Tocqueville regarded the numerous distinctions of rank among the French, as among other Europeans, to have their origin in legal proclamations. What manifested as differences in political status – the aristocrat versus the serf, for instance – was merely a social construction, a distinction "whose principles were only in legislation." Nothing, he claimed, could be more fictitious than a "purely legal inequality." This was, in fact, precisely how Tocqueville conceived of the social hierarchy that inhered in ancient slavery, most notably that of ancient Rome: as a legal fiction among peoples who were by nature fundamentally the same. Those slaves and masters of antiquity "belonged to the same race."[42]

Ancient slavery, he proffered, differed from modern slavery because the latter was based on race, which Tocqueville argued was rooted in the natural, fundamental, essential differences of human types. Tocqueville claimed that "modern slavery" had given rise to prejudice, and this latter dynamic, as a product of slavery, continued to separate the races even in the absence of slavery – in nonslaveholding states, for instance – because of its basis in race, not fiction. In free states, he observed, prejudice

---

[41] James T. Schleifer, *The Chicago Companion to Tocqueville's Democracy in America* (Chicago: The University of Chicago Press, 2012), 15–20. Especially relevant is Tocqueville's promotion of French colonial rule over Algerians. See Jennifer Pitts, *Turn to Empire: The Rise of Imperial Liberalism in Britain and France* (Princeton, NJ: Princeton University Press, 2005), 189–218.

[42] Alexis de Tocqueville, *Democracy in America: Historical-Critical Edition of De la démocratie en Amérique*, ed. Eduardo Nolla, trans. James T. Schleifer (Indianapolis: Liberty Fund, 2010), 2: 551, 552. Schleifer, "Tocqueville's *Democracy in America* Reconsidered," *Cambridge Companion to Tocqueville*, ed. Cheryl B. Welch (New York: Cambridge University Press, 2006), 130–35. Schleifer, *Chicago Companion*, 15–20.

prohibited Blacks from voting where, in strictly formal terms, they had access to the ballot. And prejudice guaranteed that they would seek in vain and with futility justice in the courts, education in the schools, and even entertainment in the theaters. To "understand what insurmountable distance separates the Negro of America from the European," he proffered, was to grasp a profound, veridical alterity that seemed "to have its immutable foundations in nature itself," and not in the fiction of legal expedience. These fictitious boundaries, he advanced, persisted in the France of his day as that polity sought to make political equality a reality among the entire French people.[43]

So, what of the relations between White Americans and what he regarded as the inferior races of Africans and American Indians? Tocqueville believed the United States would surely be marked by the *permanence* of racial separatism. In his view, there existed no possibility of eradicating the separation of the races in the US state. Tocqueville fully embodied the logics of White settler colonialism and the racial state, and he applied this reasoning to explaining the Anglo-American empire's engagement with Native polities. After centuries of war and US settler policies of displacement, he observed, American Indians had become "isolated in their own country." In his view, their race only constituted "a small colony of inconvenient foreigners in the middle of a numerous and dominating people."[44]

Tocqueville was keen to acknowledge that the United States was unethical, hostile, and violent in its relations with American Indians. He recognized that the US government repeatedly violated the terms of its treaties with Native nations. Beyond this, he observed, the "greediness" of individual White settlers, who paid no heed to legal treaties, "joined consistently the tyranny of the government." This effectively nullified the specific treaty terms prohibiting White settler trespass and vigilante violence in sovereign Native lands. He even noted the specific, morbid consequences of US efforts to dispossess American Indians of their lands, at one point recounting his own observation of the fatal removal of the Choctaw Indians from their Mississippi lands during the severe winter of 1831.[45]

[43] Tocqueville, *Democracy in America*, 2: 552. Joel Olson, *The Abolition of White Democracy* (Minneapolis: University of Minnesota Press, 2004), 47–52. August Nimtz, *Marx, Tocqueville, and Race in America: The "Absolute Democracy" or "Defiled Republic"* (Lanham, MD: Lexington Books, 2003), vii–ix, 8–15.

[44] Tocqueville, *Democracy in America*, 2: 519.

[45] Ibid.

Nevertheless, Tocqueville was committed to representing the White settler state's violent conquest over American Indians as a sort of ineluctable
development, given what he claimed was the inability of Native peoples
to embody the imperatives of civilization. Civilization required a specific
racial capacity, he insisted, one that American Indians lacked. What he
called "the savage" nature of the American Indian could only fail in competition with the innately superior White populace. Indians as one of the
"savage nations" were "governed only by opinions and mores," and this
was no match for the intellectual, rational civilization of the White race.
For this reason, he opined, American Indians were destined by their racial
nature to vanish in the face of European supremacy. Tocqueville surmised
that not even racial mixture, which he abhorred, could save Indians from
this fate. For although the half-breed offspring inherited intelligence from
their White fathers, he asserted, they retained the savage sensibilities of
their Native mothers. Beyond this, reasoned Tocqueville, they were too
few in number and too slight in influence to alter the overall dynamics of
Indians under the domination of the White democracy.[46]

Tocqueville perceived clearly that the US democratic republic was a
racial state. It was, as he saw it, the singular product of the specific racial
capacities of Whites and existed as a body politic constituted exclusively
through White membership. But whereas Tocqueville rationalized the
violence of White rule and the racial state as the ineluctable consequence
of natural order and innate racial capacities, Martin Delany argued that
the enterprise of race was actually about government, a matter of policy (i.e., politics) and not nature. Neither biology nor psychology but
only political science (governing) was for Delany the proper domain
within which to analyze and comprehend the racial democratic state. *Put
bluntly, race was how one political population dominated others as an
internal colony.* The difference between Tocqueville and Delany is clear
and considerable. Tocqueville's account of political order was itself a justification for racial rule.

Most of Delany's contemporaries, however, usually bracketed the
United States exercise of colonialism, and so the problem of race in the
United States seemed to bear no relevance to empire. Frederick Douglass
was emblematic of this interpretive frame, providing no account whatsoever of the internal colony as such. And this difference made all the
difference for how African Americans negotiated the ideological divide
between those who perceived racial self-determination as the solution

---

[46] Ibid., 1: 274–93, esp. 276.

and those who believed US democracy could be forged into a multiracial affair that included Blacks in the body politic.

Reconstruction, White Redemption, and Black Settler Colonialism

The 1850s were marked not only by Black conventions promoting Black colonization but also by an escalating turmoil that threatened to tear apart the White republic. Two pivotal developments were the passage of the Kansas–Nebraska bill in 1854 and the Supreme Court's *Dred Scott v. Sandford* decision of 1857. The 1854 legislation intervened in a long-standing debate over whether slavery should be legalized in the territories of an ever-expanding United States. The Anglo-American empire had continued to seize territory from Native nations and the Mexican Republic, and this expansion continually renewed debate over whether and where racial slavery was to be permitted in the newly acquired territories. As early as 1820 the Missouri Compromise had established that, with the exception of the state of Missouri, slavery would be prohibited above the 36°30' north parallel, Missouri's southern boundary. Missouri, in other words, was admitted as a slave state, but no other territories that far north were to be granted statehood except as free states. The legislation was thus a compromise between proslavery and antislavery politicians.

The rapacious material demands of an ever-growing empire and the thirst for expanding racial slavery proved too great, however, for the compromise to hold. By the late 1850s White slaveholders were pressing their influence through both armed violence ("bleeding Kansas") and political artifice in the US Congress. As a consequence, the Kansas–Nebraska Act of 1854 nullified the Missouri Compromise legislation, permitting slavery north of the 36°30' parallel. Many African Americans who had been hopeful that a gradual approach to containing and ending slavery might win out were forced to contend with the dismal turn of events. It was painfully clear that no grand teleological scheme was operating to end slavery. Rather, Black slavery and White freedom were intimately linked, marching in lockstep from sea to shining sea.[47]

---

[47] George H. Junne, *Blacks in the American West and Beyond—America, Canada, and Mexico: A Selectively Annotated Bibliography* (Westport, CT: Greenwood Press, 2000), 117–20. Albert P. Blaustein and Robert L. Zangrando, *Civil Rights and African Americans: A Documentary History* (Evanston, IL: Northwestern University Press, 1968), 139.

Within just three years, those determined activists who struggled to end slavery and perhaps bring African Americans into the purview of the republic's political community were jolted by an even more dismal turn of events. In a seven-to-two ruling, the US Supreme Court concluded in *Dred Scott v. Sandford* (1857) that "the Negro race" had no rights in the eyes of the US Constitution. They were literally beyond the pale of citizenship. The Court, moreover, ruled that the US Congress had no constitutional authority to prohibit slavery anywhere in the United States. Rather, only popular sovereignty (i.e., exclusively White male electorates) could decide the issue on a state-by-state basis. Thus, in one fell swoop, the nation's highest court, led by Chief Justice Roger Taney, had formally defined Blacks as political aliens and had denied federal legislators the ability to administer the institution of slavery. Never before or afterward would the colonial status of African Americans as a dominated polity within the United States receive such explicit articulation.[48]

As a result, free Africans were pressed even more forcibly to consider whether their future might be best served by flight to a foreign land through African colonization. And the 90 percent of African Americans who were enslaved faced the stultifying recognition that they and their descendants had lost any hope of ending the brutal regime that commanded their labor, controlled access to their sexual capacities, institutionalized their torture, and treated their family members as portable commodities to be sold away at the whim of White buyers. If only state and local White electorates – not the nation's own federal government – could prohibit slavery, how could slavery ever be abolished? How could the abolitionist movement ever succeed? The tyranny of the White electorate manifested in full force the manner in which Blacks were victims of American democracy, locked into racial domination at the behest of White popular sovereignty.

Fleeing White Redemption: Exodusters and Back-to-Africa Movements

As hundreds of historical studies have recounted, the Civil War settled both the question of national schism and also the future of US slavery. What began as a military solution to restore a unified White republic was overtaken by the largest slave rebellion in the history of Atlantic slavery, as more than 400,000 enslaved Blacks fled slavery, sabotaged the

---

[48] Paul Finkelman, *Dred Scott v. Sandford: A Brief History with Documents* (Boston: Bedford Press, 1997).

Confederacy, and took up arms to fight. The result was a violent resolution to slavery. Despite Frederick Douglass's call for peaceful abolition years earlier, it was Henry Highland Garnet's vision of armed militancy, in significant measure waged by slaves themselves, that actually forced the dissolution of Black enslavement.[49] During the decade following the Union army's defeat of the Confederacy, Union troops set up command stations throughout the southern states to militarize the compulsory authority behind what unfolded as a relatively progressive program of rebuilding the region's political institutions. With the exception of Tennessee, the former Confederacy was divided into five military zones. These were administered through military rule until their state governments could be reconstituted as multiracial political entities. Under these terms of military occupation federal authorities implemented what has deservedly been called a program of "Radical Reconstruction." So thoroughgoing and ambitious were the reforms of northern legislators that state legislative assemblies throughout the South soon comprised several Black members. In rare instances, African Americans held office in the US Congress. Mississippi and South Carolina both boasted Black majorities and sent representatives to Washington. At least a half dozen other states also elected Blacks to the US Congress. Most distinguished was Hiram Revels of Mississippi, who in 1870 became the sole Black member of the US Senate.[50]

These bold efforts to incorporate Blacks into the political body of the US state soon succumbed, however, to the resurgence of White vengeance. The smarting indignation that White political elites of the South felt under the sting of the Union victory actually paled in comparison to their rage at the specter of former slaves or their kin voting in elections, running for public office, and inhabiting the hallowed domain of legislative assemblies. Organized White terrorists emerged right on the heels of the Civil War as an extralegal strategy for undermining Black political agency. Although the Protestant Christian Ku Klux Klan is the most familiar example of this legacy, there was no shortage of short-lived mobs and spontaneous movements that implemented unmitigated violence to restore the exclusive terms of White political rule. Beyond this, and certainly more extensive, were the legal means of destroying the exercise

---

[49] Steven Hahn, *The Political Worlds of Slavery and Freedom* (Cambridge, MA: Harvard University Press, 2009).

[50] Office of History and Preservation and Committee on House Administration, *Black Americans in Congress, 1870–2007* (Washington, DC: U.S. Government Printing Office, 2008), 58–65.

of Black political power. Whites called it "redemption." This involved restoring members of the Democratic Party as legislative majorities throughout the South by 1870. Whereas the Republican Party embodied some measure of multiracial alliance between African Americans and progressive Whites, the Democratic Party was quickly transformed into the party of White redemption, deploying an alliance of Whites across all classes with the aim of restoring White rule over disenfranchised Blacks. As Democrat-controlled southern legislatures codified apartheid measures and developed legal mechanisms to prohibit Blacks from voting (e.g., literacy tests and poll taxes became commonplace), it became evident to African Americans throughout the nation that the radical promise of Reconstruction was not to be fulfilled.[51]

The vision of multiracial democracy fully succumbed to White redemption in the wake of the 1876 presidential election. Rutherford B. Hayes, the Republican candidate, sealed his victory by brokering an agreement with Democrats, whose exacting loyalty to White rule in the American South ensured that federal troops would be withdrawn in exchange for a united front proclaiming that Hayes was indeed the rightful winner of the election. The fallout was dismal, violent, and extreme. Unchecked by federal troops, White terrorists expanded their rule over the lives of Blacks throughout the South.

Under these cruel measures, African Americans began to consider anew the urgency of establishing their own separate polities to enjoy political freedom. Between 1865 and 1868 several thousand African Americans appealed to the ACS for information about receiving assistance to relocate to Liberia. Of these, 2,232 emigrated to West Africa during that period. The fact that the ACS received requests that far outstripped its financial capacities indicates that many newly manumitted individuals and entire families were eager to leave the United States for a new life in a sovereign Black state. The ACS's rate of settlement in the late 1860s was higher than at any other time in the organization's history. Approximately 1,600 more would leave for Liberia during the 1870s and 1880s. A total of 3,812 Blacks would join the Black settler state of Liberia

[51] Nicholas Lemann, *Redemption: The Last Battle of the Civil War* (New York: Macmillan, 2007), 125–30, 146–49. Carole Emberton, *Beyond Redemption: Race, Violence, and the American South after the Civil War* (Chicago: University of Chicago Press, 2013), 136–46. Daniel W. Stowell, *Rebuilding Zion: The Religious Reconstruction of the South, 1863–1877* (New York: Oxford University Press, 1998), 155. Edward J. Blum, *Reforging the White Republic: Race, Religion, and American Nationalism, 1865–1898* (Baton Rouge: Louisiana State University Press, 2007).

under the auspices of the ACS in the entire post–Civil War era. Prior to 1860 the ACS had settled approximately 11,000 African Americans in Liberia. This means that one of every four Blacks who resettled in Liberia through the ACS in the nineteenth century did so *after* the Civil War and the formal demise of slavery. This fact alone is remarkable and bespeaks a profound devotion on the part of African Americans to make self-determination a political reality, even if that meant risking their lives, uprooting partial or entire families, and leaving close or extended kin to traverse the Atlantic and attempt a new start on a different continent.[52]

Resettlement in Liberia was not, however, the sole index of African Americans' desire for self-governance following the Civil War. One must also consider the so-called Exoduster movement, the migration of African Americans from the South to the West during the two decades following the Civil War. Just as Liberia represented a political refuge and the promise of racial self-governance, so also did Kansas and other western regions that the US government sought to flood with new settlers portend an escape from murderous patterns of White rule. Exodusters were drawn to the possibility of owning land, living securely, and exerting far greater control over their personal and collective destiny than was possible in the South. Once White political actors in the South had expunged Blacks from the political process – preventing them from voting, barring them from electoral candidacy, restoring White-only rule – it was only a matter of time before Black southerners, no longer bound to plantations as chattel, began departing in significant numbers in an attempt at freedom in distant regions within the United States or abroad. What some writers have termed "Kansas fever" was especially strong during 1879. Pinckney B. S. Pinchback, who held office for about one month as Louisiana's first governor of African descent, staunchly opposed the emigrationist movement and was at a loss to explain the large groups of African Americans queued by the hundreds on the banks of the Mississippi River, awaiting passage to cross over and settle in Kansas. Pinchback recorded that all the roads leading to the Mississippi River were "filled with wagons loaded with plunder and families who seem to think anywhere is better than here."[53]

Like many other skeptics of Black emigration, Pinchback was puzzled by the sheer size of the crowds, the urgency of their resolve, and the

---

[52] Steven Hahn, *A Nation Under Our Feet: Black Political Struggles in the Rural South, from Slavery to the Great Migration* (Cambridge, MA: Belknap Press of Harvard University Press, 2003), 321, 355.

[53] Nell Irvin Painter, "Millenarian Aspects of the Exodus to Kansas of 1879," *Journal of Social History* 9, no. 3 (April 1976), 332.

scale of their desperation. Thousands of these Black Exodusters gathered along various points of passage, particularly in St. Louis, the key transit point for those traversing the Mississippi River. Between March and July 1879, roughly 6,000 African Americans arrived in that city in the most destitute conditions, determined to establish a new life in the free land of Kansas. And these were lucky, relatively speaking. Many aspiring travelers lacked even the few dollars charged per adult for passage from Vicksburg, Mississippi, to St. Louis. Travel for a family of five might easily cost up to fifteen dollars, fare hastily acquired by the fortunate through the quick sale of clothing, tools, and other items of value with which they parted out of necessity. From there, passage to Kansas was still to be had. But the emigrants were soundly convinced that lingering in Louisiana or Mississippi or Arkansas or any of the other numerous states riding the wave of White redemption would mean reenslavement.[54]

The surge of refugees was partly shaped by rumors. Many Exodusters of the 1870s subscribed to counterfactual claims that the federal government was providing free transportation, free land, and free tools for resettling in Kansas. Moreover, Exodusters regularly voiced their fear that slavery was about to be reinstituted throughout the South. White skeptics claimed this lacked any factual basis But only the most cynical observation of White racial rule in the 1870s could support the conclusion that these Blacks were delusional or irrational. When the US Congress crafted the Thirteenth Amendment to abolish formal slavery, it also for the first time enshrined slavery with constitutional sanction by explicitly authorizing it as punishment for convicted criminals. Within months, African Americans were targeted for mass incarceration (in Mississippi, for instance, for the newly criminalized act of being unemployed) and fed into a massive convict leasing system that became the basis for operating southern plantations owned by White planters, building roads with private contractors, manufacturing under the control of corporations, and undertaking a host of infrastructure projects that benefited Whites by making technically emancipated Blacks once again actual slaves under the authority of White men who viewed the reenslavement of Blacks as racial vindication. This was actual, literal slavery and was implemented most aggressively within the domain of criminalization and the penal system. It was tied, furthermore, to the political establishment. For

[54] Nell Irvin Painter, *Exodusters: Black Migration to Kansas after Reconstruction* (Lawrence: University Press of Kansas, 1986), 10–15. Gary R. Kremer, *James Milton Turner and the Promise of America: The Public Life of a Post-Civil War Black Leader* (Columbia: University of Missouri Press, 1991), 106–7.

instance, the Democratic Party in Louisiana created a military arm – the White League – that killed and terrorized Blacks, forcing them to abstain completely from the polls or to vote for White Democrats committed to obliterating Black political power. African Americans, mostly laborers, also faced the fall-out of the so-called Hayes Compromise of 1877, which ended the federal military occupation of the South and restored anti-Black politics on an unbridled scale.[55]

It was one thing to assert that the Civil War had technically effected the abolition of formal slavery and the rise of multiracial democracy. It was quite another for African Americans of the South to witness the murder of family members for purely political effect; to experience the incarceration and reenslavement of their parents, siblings, children, and spouses; and to see the first few Black public officials deposed and the restoration of White-only rule under the declaration of states' rights. These were "scenes of subjection," enabled not in spite of but specifically because of the particular tactics and modes of political liberalism. Individualism and the rhetoric of equality functioned to sustain legal discrimination by eliding the institutional architecture of anti-Black racism and decimating the aspirational liberties of African Americans through criminalization, debt peonage, apartheid, and other forms of racial domination. Cynics, however, treated the keen analysis of Exodusters as mere hysteria. Thus, White officials became willfully blind to the obvious events that caused a rapid escalation of Black emigration in 1879 from the South to Kansas, to other western lands, and to Liberia.[56]

In this environment, Black colonization seemed an especially efficacious means of obtaining freedom. The experience of Henry Adams, a Black laborer from Louisiana, is a useful index for understanding the imperatives and rationalities of African Americans of the South during this nadir. Adams actively promoted emigration to Liberia as the ideal solution to the worsening racial conditions of the 1870s. He organized hundreds of Blacks in Louisiana to demand better wages and working

---

[55] Douglas Blackmon, *Slavery By Another Name: The Re-Enslavement of Black Americans from the Civil War to World War II* (New York: Anchor Books, 2009). Matthew J. Mancini, *One Dies, Get Another: Convict Leasing in the American South, 1866–1928* (Columbia: University of South Carolina Press, 1996).

[56] Saidiya V. Hartman, *Scenes of Subjection: Terror, Slavery, and Self-Making in Nineteenth Century America* (New York: Oxford University Press, 1997), 164–83. Emberton, *Beyond Redemption*, 140–46. Stowell, *Rebuilding Zion*, 155. United States Senate, *Report and Testimony of the Select Committee of the United States Senate to Investigate the Causes of the Removal of the Negroes from the Southern States to the Northern States, Part I* (Washington, DC: U.S. Government Printing Office, 1880).

conditions and to advance Black political power. In 1874, for instance, Louisiana's White League proclaimed the state's government to be the rightful domain of White citizens only, and the league asserted that African Americans had absolutely no legitimate place in the affairs of government. In response, Adams joined a number of other African Americans to convene a colonization council. The attendees were persuaded that the dissolution of efforts to create multiracial democracy signaled that such a noble goal was an empty promise. Adam himself was deeply skeptical of African Americans who worked as professional politicians, and not without good reason. Those Blacks who won political office during the early years of Reconstruction emerged, predictably, from the class of free Blacks who had lived during slavery with an exceptional level of economic success. Some were real estate professionals. Others, like Pinckney Pinchback and David Young, found moderate success in multiple professional enterprises. Unsurprisingly, these Black professionals looked askance at Adams and other Black supporters of African resettlement.[57]

African American churches were especially integral to the network of activists who promoted Black settler colonialism in the years following the Civil War and Radical Reconstruction, as they had been during the antebellum period. As one example, the Third Baptist Church of Phillips County, Arkansas, was home to the African American congregation that sponsored the Liberia Exodus Arkansas Colony (LEAC) during its inaugural convention in November 1877. Like other African Americans during that time, the Black residents of Phillips County had been gauging the rising tide of White redemption sweeping the country. They were all too familiar with the exploitative conditions of sharecropping that locked them into perpetual debt and undermined their efforts to participate as political actors on par with local Whites. The aspirations and optimism that sprang so richly from the quickening promises of formal abolition and sweeping legislative reforms such as constitutional amendments granting Black citizenship, due process, and voting rights had withered on the same vine of political turmoil and potency that had once nourished their vigor. Blacks were regularly accosted by White terrorists and were bound by the dictates of law and order to serve the White planters who paid them only once per year – if at all, given the cycle of debt inherent to sharecropping. With their sights set clearly on the settler colony of Liberia, the LEAC delegates agreed that resettling in West Africa was the most compelling recourse available to them. The

---

attendees selected Anthony L. Stanford to preside over the convention. Stanford was originally from New Jersey. He had been ordained in the AME denomination and had also received a medical degree from the Eclectic Medical College of Philadelphia. At the time, he was serving as a state senator. Unlike most Black politicians of his era, however, Stanford fully embraced the movement for self-determination through colonization, and he used his political influence to promote resettlement in the Republic of Liberia as the most promising solution to the worsening crisis of White racial rule in the United States.[58]

The LEAC convention produced a significant outcome that would eventually culminate in the successful transport of scores of Black refugees from Arkansas. The delegates selected two commissioners of emigration – Anthony Stanford and C. H. Hicks – to act on behalf of those residents of Phillips County eager to resettle. Both men were tasked with visiting Liberia to gauge the prospects for becoming citizens there and to assess the material needs required to make the journey. Stanford and Hicks wasted little time in fulfilling this mission. They set sail for Liberia January 2, 1878 and spent two months touring the Black republic, speaking with local residents and Liberian officials, and assessing the living conditions. They returned with glowing reports of the prospects for Arkansas's hopeful settlers. Stanford himself, after finishing his term as a state legislator, concentrating on educating African Americans throughout the South about the opportunity that Liberia represented for Blacks to experience the full possibilities of democracy and civic freedom. He expended his life savings to travel from Mississippi to the Carolinas, and from Arkansas to Washington, DC, lecturing on the benefits of joining the Black republic.[59]

Their home state of Arkansas, however, yielded the greatest number of Black Christian settlers – more than 100 – who sold their crops in November 1879 and set out with meager belongings for New York City via Philadelphia. Braving the cold of winter, they received $4,000 in aid from the Pennsylvania auxiliary of the ACS, sorely needed funds that saved them from starvation and absolute destitution. When they finally arrived in New York City in the spring of 1880, the local press branded them the "Arkansas refugees" and made much of the severity of their

---

[58] Adell Patton, "The 'Back-to-Africa' Movement in Arkansas," *Arkansas Historical Quarterly* 51, no. 2 (Summer 1992), 167–70.

[59] Kenneth C. Barnes, *Journey of Hope: The Back-to-Africa Movement in Arkansas in the Late 1800s* (Chapel Hill: University of North Carolina Press, 2004), 23–30. Patton, "The 'Back-to-Africa' Movement," 171–76.

circumstances. At one point nearly one hundred travelers huddled into a single apartment, frail with hunger, disease, and cold. Several even died of starvation and illness. Henry Highland Garnet welcomed Edward Blyden into the pulpit of his Shiloh Presbyterian Church to address the desperate travelers. Finally, in May 1880, 136 of the emigrants set sail for Liberia, arriving after roughly one month at sea to start a new life of freedom in Brewersville, Liberia, on the St. Paul River. Not all of the hopeful emigrants were able to embark that spring because of limited funds; it was their lot to wait until the fall to join the others as citizens of a Black republic.[60]

By that time, many of the challenges faced by earlier emigrants to Liberia had become manageable with relative ease. Plentiful access to land and freedom from the rule of a racist White polity guaranteed the Arkansas group a scale of political power and civic freedom that they could only have imagined in the United States. They soon established their own homes, schools, and churches. The Liberian settler state, not unlike the US settler state, regularized tremendous privileges for the settlers at the expense of indigenous peoples. On this basis the Arkansas refugees joined the thousands of other African Americans who abandoned the United States during and after the years of Reconstruction to embrace a different life of freedom through self-governance in a Black Christian settler republic.[61]

The Liberia Exodus Arkansas Colony was just one of several such organizations that promoted self-determination through emigration, frequently in association with African American churches. Others included the Liberian Exodus Association of Pinesville, Florida; the Pilgrem [sic] Travelers of Robertson County, Texas; and a variety of Black clubs organized to provide support for African Americans who aspired to leave the United States or at least the American South. African Americans of Warren County, North Carolina, met regularly at Looly Hill Baptist Church to discuss how they might settle outside the United States. Just as the 1830s and 1840s were marked by a wave of "Negro conventions" chiefly devoted to emigration, so also were the 1870s and 1880s characterized by a spate of similar emigrationist conventions in Louisiana, Texas, Virginia, North Carolina, and Arkansas.[62]

In this context of resurgent anti-Black violence, Martin Delany renewed his efforts to establish a self-governing Black polity, reasserting his call

---

[60] Patton, "The 'Back-to-Africa' Movement," 171–76.
[61] Barnes, *Journey of Hope*, 13–20. Patton, "The 'Back-to-Africa' Movement," 171–76.
[62] Hahn, *Nation Under Our Feet*, 328–30.

for emigration to Liberia. In Charleston, South Carolina, meanwhile, several African American clergy formed the Liberia Exodus Association to organize emigration to Liberia. Benjamin Porter, an AME minister in Charleston, collaborated with Harrison Bouey and George Curtis, two other ministers of Charleston, to raise funding that might permit the transport of hundreds of Blacks eager to escape the worsening conditions of racial hegemony. They aimed to create a place in Liberia where African Americans could "maintain a position equivalent to their attainments and talents." If they remained in the United States, they feared they would be forced into "a subordinate and menial position."[63]

News of the association soon spread throughout the Piedmont region. And as the association allied with the American Colonization Society, its members received feedback from others across the nation. It soon became clear that the scale of funding needed to provide transport to the thousands interested was far beyond what they could raise through conventional means. In response, they hit upon a bold plan of creating a publicly owned corporation. To this end, they soon organized a subsidiary of the association, the Liberian Exodus Joint Stock Steamship Company. Porter assumed the position of president of the company, and J. C. Hazeley, another associate, was vice president. Bouey and Curtis were also officers in the new company. The men issued 30,000 shares of stock, planning to generate $10,000. With ambitious publicity and a shrewd marketing network that included a group of 1,800 women in the city of New Orleans alone, most of the company's stock sold in just months. Martin Delany joined the group as a company official. His long experience in the emigration movement was a major boon to the enterprise and added immensely to the momentum. The company had one other major asset in the figure of Henry McNeal Turner. The renowned AME bishop was yet becoming a powerful figure throughout the South. Turner's radicalism made him controversial among Black elites, within and well beyond AME circles. But he was also highly charismatic, forward thinking, and not afraid to speak fiery truths when debating the dismal prospects of multiracialism in a White nation-state.[64] This activism signaled the significant degree to which African American religion engaged with Black Christian state sovereignty as a means to freedom.

---

[63] Bernard Edward Powers, *Black Charlestonians: A Social History, 1822–1885* (Fayetteville: University of Arkansas Press, 1994), 257–58.

[64] Alvin B. Tillery, *Between Homeland and Motherland: Africa, U.S. Foreign Policy, and Black Leadership in America* (Ithaca, NY: Cornell University Press, 2011), 37–38.

Internal Colonialism and Overseas Imperialism

Black settler colonialism, however, was neither the sole nor dominant means of pursuing membership in a body politic. In the years following the Civil War, African Americans would increasingly opt to fight in the US Army to prove their worthiness for citizenship. These African American soldiers were known as the "Buffalo soldiers." With few exceptions, they fought on behalf of a violently expanding US empire to make war against American Indians and to control what should have been self-governing, sovereign polities of Indian nations. Although women, children, and extended families supported these soldiers, militarism was most immediately an institution rooted in masculinity. As it was founded in the crucible of violence and honor through killing, militarism repeatedly gave expression to "racial manhood." It became for African American men an imperial and patriarchal mode of pursuing national belonging. In this way, the experience of Buffalo Soldiers in Native lands of the American West proved portentous, to say the least. As US colonialism expanded overseas, the military infrastructure essential to that exercise created unprecedented opportunities for African American men to participate in US nationalism, championing the imperatives of a White settler state into distant lands through force of arms.[65]

Following the Civil War, the opportunity to extend the reach of the Anglo-American empire westward and overseas further exacerbated a perplexing situation. Years after the abolition of formal slavery, African Americans remained deeply confounded by the prospect of forging entry into the White body politic. Not a single Black propagandist or public figure justified the White racist exclusion and domination of Blacks; all hoped that multiracial democracy would be realized in US political life. But the issue of US nationalism that proceeded through the White republic's wars of imperial conquest over American Indians in the western territories and over non-White people overseas was a different matter altogether. African Americans were faced with the question of whether rendering service on behalf of US colonialism would afford them entry into the political community of the nation-state.

---

[65] Chad Louis Williams, *Torchbearers of Democracy: African American Soldiers in the World War I Era* (Chapel Hill: University of North Carolina Press, 2010). T. G. Steward, *Buffalo Soldiers: The Colored Regulars in the United States Army* (Amherst, NY: Humanity Books, 2003). Michele Mitchell, *Righteous Propagation: African Americans and the Politics of Racial Destiny after Reconstruction* (Chapel Hill: University of North Carolina Press, 2004), 51–65.

Until the 1890s the US empire deployed its rule over conquered subjects within the geographical boundaries of North America, with the exception of the war in Tripoli. That situation was about to change drastically, however. In the final decade of the nineteenth century the United States began rapidly expanding the nature and scale of its imperial infrastructure by establishing colonies overseas. No factor in this development was more important than the linkage between US corporations and militarism. The construction of transcontinental rail lines had rapidly expanded the scale of markets and distribution for US manufacturers. In the 1840s a mere 11 percent of US Americans lived in cities. By 1880, however, urban dwellers, numbering roughly 14 million, were easily more than one-fourth of the population. This growing concentration of consumers propelled ambitious manufacturing growth. But the pace was too unwieldy. By the 1880s supply was exceeding consumer demand, a situation that triggered a debilitating economic depression that threatened to continue unabated. US businesses exerted intense pressure on the administrations of Grover Cleveland and William McKinley to expand US markets overseas by establishing coaling stations and naval bases abroad. In 1890, US Navy captain Alfred Mahan, then a mediocre sailor, published his *Influence of Sea Power upon History*, a watershed tome that would earn him renown as a persuasive promoter of US expansionism. Mahan argued that the United States needed to do more than protect American harbors; it needed to dominate the seas and exert control over global access and transport. This strategic capacity, he intoned, would pave the way for making the world's population into consumers of American goods and establish US dominance as a global empire.[66]

This was precisely the course the United States pursued. During the final decades of the century, a flurry of imperial expansion steadily transformed the nation's economy into the envy of the world. The sheer geographical range of imperial enterprises itself was telling. As a result of negotiating a partnership with the Belgian king Leopold (whose policies killed 13 million people in Central Africa), the United States gained entry into the Congo's lucrative rubber production. After Cuba's failed ten-year war for independence, US corporations and individual investors scooped up sugar estates and land interests in what became a US colony. Even before Spain lost formal title to Cuba, the island was firmly in

[66] Alfred D. Chandler, *Strategy and Structure: Chapters in the History of the Industrial Enterprise* (Cambridge, MA: MIT Press, 1990), 23–24. Alfred Mahan, *The Influence of Sea Power upon History, 1660–1783* (Boston: Little, Brown and Company, 1897).

the grip of US financiers and corporations. As a result, White investors from the United States received generous subsidies and tax breaks. At the same time, they aggressively implemented similar business strategies in Mexico under the administration of Porfirio Díaz. In 1892 White settlers in Hawaii joined with the US military to overthrow Hawaii's government and subsequently began to reap the financial rewards that came with usurping the rich, fertile lands held by Native Hawaiians. Although Hawaii was not formally annexed by the US Congress until the 1900s, what mattered to White business interests was their ability to control the lands and dominate the economy to bolster their own profits. Also during the 1890s, the United States sought control over Haiti to establish a naval base that might serve to protect a Latin American canal that was yet to be built. This effort failed even though the United States supplied weapons and aid to rebels who had taken over Haiti's government. When those rebels came to power, the United States was still not able to get land for the base until many years later. Despite this temporary setback in Haiti, the United States achieved a feat of imperial expansion in a mere decade that few would have thought possible. By 1900 only the economy of Britain exceeded that of the United States.[67]

All of these imperial developments, however, were overshadowed by the literal consequences and symbolic import of the Spanish-American War of 1898 and the US colonial occupation of Cuba and the Philippines. After defeating Spain in 1898, the United States took possession of Cuba (by force, not treaty), Puerto Rico, Guam, and the Philippines. Soon after McKinley assumed office in 1897, he assembled a special session of Congress to implement the highest tariffs in the nation's history.[68] Meanwhile, the cozy relationship between White US and Cuban businesses culminated in an unmistakably clear mandate to McKinley and US congressional officials to ensure that the rising tempest of armed revolts by Cuban peasants would not disrupt the $100 million ($2.7 billion in today's dollars) in annual trade between the two countries, revenues that flowed mainly from the sugar and tobacco industries. McKinley, who had been nominated at the behest of big business leaders such as Marcus Alonzo Hanna of Cleveland, soon responded to this mounting pressure by going to war against Spanish troops in Cuba in the name of delivering

---

[67] George C. Herring, *From Colony to Superpower: U.S. Foreign Relations since 1776* (New York: Oxford University Press, 2008), 290–96.
[68] Chandler, *Strategy and Structure*, 23–24.

freedom to that island's so-called darker peoples laboring under Spain's colonial regime.[69]

The Spanish-American War (or more appropriately, the War of 1898, since it involved many nations), more than any other previously, occasioned among African Americans an acute enthusiasm for US nationalism and the expansion of US colonial power. AME Bishop William Derrick exemplified this support. Derrick, originally from Antigua, had served in the US Navy before becoming an AME minister. He was elected to the bishopric in 1896, the same year McKinley won the presidency. Derrick viewed the outbreak of war as a positive opportunity for Blacks to prove their citizenship while aiding the Cuban revolutionaries struggling against Spanish rule. Much of the pro-war enthusiasm by African Americans, in fact, stemmed from a startling blend of US nationalism and Black nationalism. Even the Colored People's National Protective League came out in support of the war. Although conceding that African Americans had no real stakes in the war, the organization's president, G. E. Taylor, asserted that they were nonetheless bound by the exigencies of citizenship to volunteer for military service and support the war effort.[70]

Especially compelling was the large number of Blacks who joined the volunteer units that popped up around the country. The US Army initially permitted only 2,000 Blacks to enter its ranks for the war; many more were turned away. When the war later expanded into a protracted occupation of the Philippines, Guam, and Puerto Rico, however, White military officials relented and announced that many more Blacks would be accepted for service. In the fall of 1899, after realizing that Filipinos would not bow to US occupation but would fight unrelentingly for their independence, the War Department created two special volunteer units of African American soldiers: the Forty-Eighth and Forty-Ninth Infantry. Both were deployed in the Philippines the following year. AME minister Reverdy C. Ransom of Chicago was vocal both in celebrating the courage of Blacks from Illinois to join the volunteer unit and also in thanking White Chicago officials for facilitating Black involvement. As the US occupation continued, African Americans focused on pressuring federal officials to appoint African Americans as officers and to promote them instead of limiting such opportunities to Whites. Participating in imperial

---

[69] Alfred W. McCoy, *Policing America's Empire: The United States, the Philippines, and the Rise of the Surveillance State* (Madison: University of Wisconsin Press, 2009), 98. Lawrence S. Little, *Disciples of Liberty: The African Methodist Episcopal Church in the Age of Imperialism, 1884–1916* (Knoxville: University of Tennessee Press, 2000), 94.

[70] Little, *Disciples of Liberty*, 89–100.

militarism, in other words, became a civil rights issue; this pattern was to continue for decades to come. Black war support was also evident from African American media, which began to devote substantial attention to reports from the theater of war involving African Americans.[71]

Further enthusiasm flowered among Blacks with the rapid US victory against Spain, which ousted the older colonial power from Cuba. Blacks attending a "postwar" rally at Waters AME in Baltimore in 1898 were encouraged to celebrate the idea that Black soldiers were taking liberty to Cuba and the Philippines.[72] In August 1898, near the close of the war against Spain, AME delegates at the Mission Conference reaffirmed that the war was about "human rights," and delegates at the Pittsburgh Conference claimed the war had "liberated" Cuba and broke out singing "America." Such propaganda, of course, was counterfactual. Cuba had been placed under colonial status, a condition McKinley called "tutelage." This shift in US policy from Cuban independence to colonial rule soon triggered a change in the rhetoric of the AME church. The new focus was on benefits that might accrue to the United States. One editorial of the AME, for instance, warned against the danger of insurgency in Cuba against US troops. This same editor then called for US conquest and control over the Philippines to avoid European jealousy. In other words, independence for people actually living in Cuba and Philippines became for many US Blacks a nonissue.[73]

In tandem with this, throughout the United States, African American Christians began to justify US occupation. They did so by assessing the new colonialism in light of the imperatives of Christian expansionism. AME missionaries, for instance, renewed their effort to establish stations in the Caribbean. In the fall of 1898 Illinois delegates convening for an annual conference celebrated the church's missionary efforts in Cuba. During that same month, in October 1898, church delegates gathering in Indiana delivered a report summarizing national affairs in which they described the victory over Spain as a major advance. They also prayed that the president be given wisdom from the Christian god to govern effectively. And they asserted that the US flag should never be lowered once raised and that Cuba should remain under US rule. As dissenters raised concerns about violating the self-determination of Cubans, the Florida-born Morris Marcellus Moore, who would later become an AME

---

[71] Little, *Disciples of Liberty*, 96–100. Mitchell, *Righteous Propagation*, 51–73.
[72] Mitchell, *Righteous Propagation*, 55–62. Little, *Disciples of Liberty*, 96–100.
[73] Little, 105, 106.

bishop, delivered a forceful defense of the report. Attendees afterwards started singing the "Star Spangled Banner" to express their newfound patriotism. Such an imperialist proclamation, to be sure, did meet with mild opposition from other African Americans, but the change in discourse nevertheless demonstrated the magnitude of patriotism and support among Blacks for extending US American colonial rule overseas.[74]

At that point the AME church already had missionaries in West Africa, southern Africa, Barbados, the Dominican Republic, and Haiti. Before the war even started, in fact, delegates were already calling for a greater missionary presence, and this only increased in the wake of military engagement. In 1898 the denomination pushed to open missions in Cuba. This effort was led by H. C. C. Astwood, who was fluent in Spanish and had already served as US consul to the Dominican Republic and as an AME missionary. He also accompanied the Eighth Illinois Volunteers in Cuba. The skilled agent quickly established an AME congregation in Santiago and boasted that it was the first Protestant church in the region. He was subsequently appointed supervisor of missions to Cuba, a decision that met with great enthusiasm throughout the denomination. In a similar spirit, the Black Indiana Mite Missionary Society Convention celebrated the war as an opportune development to promote the Christianization of Cuba and Puerto Rico.[75]

African Americans, US Empire, and the Christian Civilizing Mission
The intersection of Black Christian expansionism and US empire evidences one of the most powerful cultural myths that shaped the political and religious imagination of US Americans: the colonial civilizationist ideology. This complex ideology asserted that civilization was a mode of subjectivity comprising the domains of politics, culture, and religion, all of which were uniquely attained and exemplified by the conquering metropole. Colonial conquest was rationalized by claiming that the imperium would disseminate civilization to conquered subjects and thus serve for their benefit. It was a classic formula whose generic structure had been deployed for ages, although the specific terms shifted to match the immediate circumstances of racialization. Civilizationist ideology also gave substance and meaning to the institutions of racial uplift directed toward African Americans. Its logical terms presumed something fundamentally

---

[74] Little, 105–6. Mitchell, *Righteous Propagation*, 51–73.
[75] Little, 105–7.

lacking within subaltern subjects themselves and positioned Western conquerors as heroes working to impart salvific reform.

By the late nineteenth century this colonial ideology idealized republican governance wed to free labor, thereby eschewing slavery as a retrograde formation. In these terms, slavery was backwardness. Within the domain of culture, proximity to White, Western modes of dress and conventions of gender and sex were especially pivotal. So, for instance, polygamy was a marker of backwardness, while heterosexual monogamy marked civility and consonance with the subjective modes of modernity. In tandem with this was denial of female sexual agency. For example, Native Americans commonly used abortifacients to ensure that women could decouple sex from reproduction. Anglo-Americans, however, condemned this means of establishing sexual freedom for Native women as savage and bestial. Instead, they institutionalized sex as a strictly marital regime of pleasure for men that operated under the sign of reproduction for women. Finally, within the domain of religion, Christian supremacism operated unrestrained to instantiate religious hatred that targeted other religions for extermination. This was especially true of African-derived religions and indigenous American religions. But even among the Abrahamic religions, Judaism and Islam were signified as inherently inferior and in conflict with Western modern subjectivity. Within the logics of Anglo-American colonialism, not even Catholicism was honorable, strangely enough. By the late nineteenth century, in fact, decades of increased immigration from predominantly Catholic regions of Europe had stoked xenophobic efforts to restrict Catholic immigrants from undermining what was touted as the pristine Anglo-Saxon civilization of the United States.[76]

For centuries, indigenous polities throughout the Americas had faced this colonial civilizationist ideology as White garrisons and more conventional settler villages sought to render their brutality through a respectable idiom of power by emphasizing tropes of civilizing, pacification, and moral or cultural uplift. Throughout the nineteenth century, Native Americans encountered an increasing scale of invasions and military

---

[76] Nancy F. Cott, *Public Vows: A History of Marriage and the Nation* (Cambridge, MA: Harvard University Press, 2009). Reginald Horsman, *Race and Manifest Destiny: Origins of American Racial Anglo-Saxonism* (Cambridge, MA: Harvard University Press, 1986). Theda Perdue, *Cherokee Women: Gender and Culture Change, 1700–1835* (Lincoln, NE: Bison Books, 1999). Ann Laura Stoler, *Race and the Education of Desire: Foucault's History of Sexuality and the Colonial Order of Things* (Durham: Duke University Press, 1995).

assaults from the Anglo-American empire. And following the Civil War, Buffalo Soldiers provided significant support to the White republic's colonial objectives. Thus, when African Americans deployed the propaganda and institutional networks of Christian expansionism during the 1890s to affirm conquest of Cuba and the Philippines, they were once again functioning as agents of Western colonialism. And they were ultimately driven by a perverse hope that their willingness to dispossess and exterminate American Indians would persuade Whites to grant African Americans the privilege of citizenship. In this way, they might claim their rightful place within the heritage of Western civilization, with its trappings of Christian triumphalism and racial imaginaries.

Among the most sophisticated interpreters of this complex colonial ideology was the African American feminist author Anna Julia Cooper (1858–1964). Writing just a few years before the War of 1898, Cooper sought to explain how history was unfolding in a divine drama that required Black people to play a pivotal role. At a time when some Whites actually predicted the extinction of African Americans as a result of their supposed inherent inferiority, Cooper claimed that the Christian deity himself had destined the presence of Blacks in the United States. Slavery, she argued, was an instrument of divine planning, a machination of divine ruse. Likewise, the reign of racial terror that emerged after Reconstruction, she urged, was "God's plan for refinement" of the Black race.[77] The key to all of this was the Christian gospel, which Cooper named the seed or "germ" that required not decades or centuries but "millennia" to ripen. She was keenly aware of the rampant sexism that plagued American churches, and yet she nonetheless insisted that Western civilization was flowering into maturity and would require women – especially Black women – to take up their role as leaders in the work of racial uplift and Christian progress: "The idea of the radical amelioration of womankind, reverence for woman as woman regardless of rank, wealth, or culture," she proffered, "was to come from that rich and bounteous fountain from which flow all our liberal and universal ideas – the Gospel of Jesus Christ."[78] Cooper was not naive about the patriarchal histories of Christian churches. Rather, she possessed a keen critique of Western

---

[77] Anna Julia Cooper, "Ethics of the Negro Question," in *The Voice of Anna Julia Cooper: Including A Voice from the South and Other Important Essays, Papers, and Letters*, ed. Charles Lemert and Esme Bhan (Lanham, MD: Rowman & Littlefield, 1998), 210, 214.

[78] Anna Julia Cooper, "Womanhood: A Vital Element in the Regeneration and Progress of a Race," in *Voice of Anna Julia Cooper*, 56.

sexual norms. She pointed out, for example, that the church glorified celibacy while at the same time making marriage a sacrament, perversely projecting sexuality onto women as a result. But Cooper accounted for this misogynist formation by claiming that true Christianity was a feminist religion and by marking Christian sexism as a failure to live up to the authentic gospel of Jesus.

The visionary Christian feminist, in fact, identified not one but two major factors that gave rise to what she called "modern civilization": Christianity and feudalism. Her view of Christianity was predictably rooted in theological formulations and ideologies – she judged the religion by its romanticized ideals, not its actual history. As a devoted member of the Episcopal Church, Cooper viewed Christian conversion as an overriding factor in African American history, as a racial watershed that largely fulfilled the deity's plan for the Black race. But this was not all. The European factor, it turns out, was no less essential to the making of modern civilization. Cooper described Christianity not so much as a revelatory event but as a stadial, evolutionary process. It was a seed that required a soil enriched in civilization, and this is precisely what Europe provided. Following the imaginative historical philosophy of Tacitus, Thomas Macaulay, Francois-Pierre-Guillaume Guizot, and Henry Bascom, Cooper identified the European medieval veneration of noble women – the principle of chivalry – as a product of Christian influence that was slowly being universalized through the force of the gospel. Feudalism "materially fostered and developed" this principle to make womanhood a central factor in the advancement of civilization. Thus, the confluence of these two streams produced a "broad majestic river" of Western modernity.[79]

Cooper juxtaposed this to the Orientalist antithesis of the European West – China and Islamicate societies. Chinese foot binding, she argued, appropriately symbolized the undermining and constraint of womanhood, condemning women to a life of "ignorance, infamy, and complete stagnation." In a similar fashion, "Arabian civilization" produced a cultural formation of gender rooted not in stable homes, the domain of agential women, but in nomadic life, the metonym of unadulterated patriarchy. Even the Qur'an, the sacred scripture of Islam, she claimed, typified the moribund nature of civilization among "the Turks" because it was a product rather than a process, putatively constructed over a short

[79] Ibid., 55–59.

time instead of the centuries of accretion that produced the Christian Bible.[80]

Cooper's theology and racial philosophy, of course, both departed from and were consonant with the conventions of civilizationist discourse promoted by White imperialists. Her Christian feminism was distinguished by its emphasis on the centrality of Black womanhood for US American civilization. She conceded that White Americans were the source of civilization among African Americans; this was the point of the colonial civilizationist ideology. But she also insisted that the White race was "worn out" and had exhausted its innovative capacity whereas the Black race was still fresh and unsullied, ready to generate new momentum to advance Anglo-American civilization. And she emphatically argued that African American women, acting on equalitarian terms as unrestrained agents of social change, were the vital key to racial and civilizational advancement.[81]

At the same time it is clear that Cooper drew richly on White colonial ideology to advance Black feminism and racial uplift. In this way she exemplified the mainstream of African American Christianity, which invested decidedly in civilizationist claims. Her optimistic postmillennialism was of a piece with a long history of Western ideologies that sought to translate an explicit Christian supremacism into the secular terms of Eurocentrism. Cooper did not advance a race-neutral civilizationist ideology, however. She conceptualized civilization, rather, as a racial property brokered by White Christians and now shared with racial newcomers – African Americans – whose conformity to modern subjectivity involved reinscribing racial derision against East Asians and Islamicate peoples. And yet Cooper's feminist theology clarifies important dimensions of the relationship between Western Christianity and Western colonialism.

One need only compare it to the theology of Josiah Strong (1847–1916), the White Protestant evangelical social reformer who promoted Anglo-Saxon racial superiority and advocated the uplift of non-White peoples through conquest and conversion. Strong published his most popular text during the height of US militarism against Native Americans in the 1880s. *Our Country: Its Possible Future and Its Present Crisis* burst onto the scene in 1885 and warned White Americans that at stake was nothing less than the success of the White nation-state as a grand experiment in civilization. Like Cooper, Strong argued that White civilization was

---

[80] Ibid., 53, 54.
[81] Ibid., 52–55.

unsurpassed and radically distinct from others because of its European (specifically English) pedigree and its Protestant Christian identity. Strong likewise adumbrated conventional arguments for the uplift of conquered peoples – particularly the Native Americans increasingly threatened by the aggressive militarism of the expanding Anglo-American Empire. Both Cooper and Strong also reaffirmed the ascendant ideology of US exceptionalism. The idea that the US state was the political formation of the current era of the temporality of modernity was central to their major theses.[82]

Of course, as advocates of Christian (racial) civilization, Strong and Cooper were by no means exceptional. Rather, the hegemonic, mainstream nature of their claims met with eager reception precisely because they had tapped into the logical imperatives of colonialism at the very time that the US American empire was rapidly expanding. Strong, moreover, drew on the strident derision against what he imagined as the inferior races of southern Europe, who arrived in the United States by the hundreds of thousands each year. In this way he embodied the nativist politics of Anglo-Saxon supremacism that constituted a retreat from the pan-European notions of Whiteness that shaped the racial politics of earlier decades. Both Cooper and Strong, furthermore, emphasized the potential for a White Christian civilization to enact the most noble work of the colonial state – disseminating the arts of civilization to inferior races and uplifting them to a state of enlightened existence.[83]

In the course of US imperial expansionism, a number of African Americans, among them Theophilus G. Steward (1843–1924), would take issue with the racist architecture of Strong's theology of social transformation. With a career spanning the AME Church and the US Army, Steward hailed from Gouldtown, New Jersey, where he had been born free in 1843. At age twenty-one Steward was ordained as a deacon

---

[82] Josiah Strong, *Our Country: Its Possible Future and Its Present Crisis* (New York: Baker & Taylor for the American Home Missionary Society, 1885). Sylvia Söderlind and James Taylor Carson, *American Exceptionalisms: From Winthrop to Winfrey* (Albany: State University of New York Press, 2011). Ralph Luker, *The Social Gospel in Black and White: American Racial Reform, 1885–1912* (Chapel Hill: University of North Carolina Press, 1991), 270.

[83] Horsman, *Race and Manifest Destiny*. Noel Ignatiev, *How the Irish Became White* (New York: Routledge, 1995). Matthew Frye Jacobson, *Whiteness of a Different Color: European Immigrants and the Alchemy of Race* (Cambridge, MA: Harvard University Press, 1998). David R. Roediger, *Working Toward Whiteness: How America's Immigrants Became White: The Strange Journey from Ellis Island to the Suburbs* (New York: Basic Books, 2006).

and elder of the AME Church by Bishop Daniel Payne himself. He met Elizabeth Gadsden in Charleston, South Carolina; the two were married and eventually had eight sons. After a failed missionary trip to Haiti, the aspiring minister was appointed as pastor to congregations in rural Delaware, New York's Brooklyn borough, and Philadelphia. While in Philadelphia, Steward decided to matriculate at the Episcopal Divinity School, and he graduated in 1880 after performing brilliantly. This formal training would inspire him to respond critically to the leading theological debates of his time, including the challenge of historical criticism within biblical scholarship. It was in the nation's capital, however, that Steward would make his most important mark as an AME minister. There, he was appointed to the Metropolitan AME Church, a congregation known for attracting some of the nation's most influential African Americans, including Frederick Douglass, John Lynch, and Blanche Bruce. In fact, as Steward assumed leadership of the Minister's Union, the city's professional society of African American clergy, he became immersed in greater circles of influence and learned important lessons in networking and politicking that would remain with him for life.[84]

Steward's decision to write against Strong's arguments promoting racial supremacy and destiny were to prove decisive. When Strong's *Our Country* appeared in 1885, Steward was leading the Metropolitan AME Congregation. By that time Steward had already authored two major theological works. The first, *Divine Attributes* (1884), demonstrated Steward's grasp of systematic theology by examining classical formulations of Western Christian doctrine. The second, *Genesis Re-read* (1885), was intellectually bolder and clearly displayed his creative capacities. It aimed to reconcile Christian doctrine with evolutionary theory and other advances of scientific knowledge. In *End of the World, or Clearing the Way for the Fullness of the Gentiles* (1888) Steward set the discursive ax to the root of Strong's tree of racial claims about Anglo-Saxon superiority. Rejecting Strong's pronouncements as a manifesto for "clan religion," Steward asserted instead that Whites were a highly destructive race and were on a path to their own demise. Steward reasoned that what Strong was celebrating as the kingdom of their god was actually one more drama in the present age of White domination. The present age of racist hegemony, Steward argued, was coming to an end. By "end

[84] Albert George Miller, *Elevating the Race: Theophilus G. Steward, Black Theology, and the Making of an African American Civil Society, 1865–1924* (Knoxville: University of Tennessee Press, 2003), 3–4.

of the world," in other words, Steward was proclaiming the end to an era of Anglo-Saxon dominance. The White race would destroy itself, and in its place would rise the colored races of the world – Steward named them "the Gentiles" – to establish a society based on racial equality and justice.[85]

In this way Steward departed sharply from the conventional Christian grammar of eschatology by interpreting the "end of the world" as the "consummation of *this* age." Only with the political empowerment of the world's colored races would the Christian messiah establish his perfect millennial reign on earth – the final act in the drama of Christian postmillennialism. To render this interpretation coherent, however, Steward had to deal with the central civilizationist arguments proffered by Strong. He offered no contest to Strong's claim that White Anglo-Saxons – from the ancient Romans to contemporary Europeans to White Americans – had developed the most advanced civilization in human history. The ideals of this civilization, Steward conceded, were simply unassailable. But he charged that Whites had violated these ideal principles in their very effort to disseminate civilization among non-White peoples. Rather than promoting liberty, they had enslaved Africans. Instead of fashioning a society rooted in equality, they had produced a consistent record of conquest, subjugation, and extermination of non-White peoples. While paying lip service to the ideals of Christianity and Western liberalism, the Anglo-Saxon race had in practice perverted "the Christian idea" into "a White man's religion," a fact easily recognized by "the darker races."[86]

In sum, Steward shared with Cooper a fascination with the Western liberal paradigms of freedom and equality that were abundantly celebrated in public discourse but that they believed were woefully undermined and trampled in practice. Both attributed this to mere hypocrisy; neither identified any substantive relationship between the regimes of slavery and the colonial tactics of liberal democratic empire exercised by the racial state. The tragic exigencies of racial power that these two regarded as hypocrisy were, however, the devastating manifestation of a new, post–Civil War alliance between democratic freedom and racial domination.

Steward's career took a decisive turn in 1891 when he accepted a federal appointment as a chaplain in the US Army. Even before entering

---

[85] Ibid., 75–77.
[86] Theophilus Steward, *The End of the World, or Clearing the Way for the Fullness of the Gentiles* (Philadelphia: AME Church Book Rooms, 1888), 3, 4, 176.

the military, he had cultivated a richly compelling appreciation for the practical benefits of militarism. His sojourn in Georgia during the early years of Reconstruction had exposed him to the virulent White terrorism of the Ku Klux Klan. Steward witnessed firsthand the relief that federal troops provided for Blacks against the wanton violence that defined White southern rule in the absence of formal slavery. In fact, it was the US Army that urged him to accept a position as a voting registrar in Lumkin, Georgia, putting the ballot within reach of Black male voters for the first time. This was emblematic of the imperial nationalist dynamic so central to the experience of the Buffalo Soldiers. US militarism became, in this way, a central means whereby African Americans participated in practices of US American imperialism. Steward's new appointment as chaplain would send him as far west as Missoula, Montana, then to Cuba during the War of 1898, and subsequently to the Philippines.[87]

In Montana, occupying lands newly seized from Native American polities, Steward encountered the warmth of camaraderie from White military officials, an experience that impressed on him the potential of military life to engender racial harmony among Blacks and Whites. When US officials began to vet the pros and cons of intervening in Cuba and going to war against Spain, Steward stood solidly in support of military intervention. Drawing on the putative humanitarian imperatives endemic to colonial logics, he insisted that African Americans, along with their fellow Whites, were justified in using military force to "drive Spanish rule from the Western hemisphere." Doing so, he reasoned, would fulfill a Christian duty to extend the benefits of civilization to Cuban patriots and to support their freedom struggle. Steward was keen to recognize, of course, the contradiction this posed to the political reality of anti-Blackness in the United States, which eviscerated the possibilities of Black inclusion in the body politic. But if this compromised his commitment to US militarism, he certainly gave no such hint. In the wake of its treaty with Spain, the United States began to target and destroy the "Cuban patriot" as the enemy whose freedom struggle needed to be subdued. Steward was stationed in the thick of the theater of combat. Significantly, he remained devoted to defeating these Cubans of the "darker race" whose armed struggle for self-determination only months earlier had supposedly been the cause that justified US military intervention. He now claimed that Cubans would be best kept under US rule, made subject to its imperial

---

[87] Edmund L. Drago, *Black Politicians and Reconstruction in Georgia: A Splendid Failure* (Athens: University of Georgia Press, 1992), 21–22. Miller, *Elevating the Race*, 121.

authority. And the violent enterprise of US militarism was the noble instrument that would fulfill this sacred mission.[88]

Not even the official policies of anti-Blackness executed by the top brass within the US Army disturbed Steward's fidelity to militarism and the killing of Cuban patriots. Across the board, African Americans were regularly denied promotions and appointments as officers. Beyond this, African American soldiers were placed under the command of only Whites, not Blacks. And these Whites openly abused Black soldiers with impunity. The decision by White US Army officers to court-martial Henry V. Plummer, an African American military chaplain who seemed to have become a victim of White retaliation for his vocal criticism of racism in the military, is emblematic of the anti-Blackness endemic to the armed services. Another African American chaplain, George W. Prioleau, maintained that racism was very much a part of the military, although the serviceman remained loyal to the imperatives of US militarism in Cuba. In response to Prioleau, Steward penned a defense of the US Army denying the very existence of racism in the military. The army, claimed Steward, was instead the bright spot of hope for race relations built on justice and equality. He pointed to his own experience of respect and civility by White officers and soldiers, and he insisted that the military was the one institution exuding racial harmony that was fit to equip African Americans with the training in civilization and discipline needed for them to take their rightful place in Western Christianity's historical march of progress.[89]

Despite his strident critique of Strong penned one decade earlier, Steward's political and religious convictions placed him squarely within the theology of racial empire that Strong had articulated. In 1868, at the very time that Steward was stationed in Cuba and the Philippines, Josiah Strong, who became widely admired by Whites for his strident promotion of White supremacism, would fulfill his public career as a leading advocate of nonviolent social reform by creating the League for Social Service to address issues of poverty and urbanization. Although he espoused an aggressive conquest of Native Americans in the American West, Strong's actual work was among poor Whites in US cities. As a chaplain of the US Army, by contrast, Steward served in the literal, violent conquest of non-White peoples to extend what he identified as Christian civilization and to administer the putative blessings of US imperial rule over stateless peoples. Not only Steward but also the vast

[88] Miller, *Elevating the Race*, 126–27.
[89] Ibid., 102–3.

majority of African Americans who voiced an opinion about the war supported the expansion of US power abroad. They were chiefly motivated by the fact that African Americans were able to take part in this venture. In other words, permitting their participation within the deep interstices of the US American empire – killing and subjugating Native Americans, Afro-Cubans, and Filipinos whose only crime was defending their sovereignty against White rulers – was by far and away the most powerful means of rallying African Americans in support of US nationalism. When African Americans overlooked, excused, or bracketed the anti-Blackness that governed quotidian, formal, and state practices of social power, they did so to celebrate their inclusion in conquest against other non-White peoples. Moreover, their involvement in US colonialism was made feasible by a complex, tectonic theological imaginary rooted in a Christian grammar of civilization that racialized historical subjects as scripted actors in a divinely appointed drama of secular formations – cultural modes, political orders, and religious conquest. To state this more bluntly, it was precisely because wars for US empire were colonial conquests that they carried the power to enfold African Americans, normally so distanced from the center of the US body politic, into the imaginary of the Anglo-American state's political community.

Black Dissent against Empire

The overwhelming sentiment from African Americans in support of the war was nevertheless disrupted by piercing critiques from those who dared to highlight the humiliating irony involved. By 1898 most states with significant Black populations had enacted legislation to disenfranchise African Americans. But most Whites were not satisfied with merely formal, legal structures for establishing White rule over Blacks. Beyond such formal measures, lynching – the lawless, often ritualized murder of Blacks to inscribe terror into the bodies and minds of survivors – was the order of the day and had peaked in the 1890s. Ida B. Wells (1862–1931) had mounted a powerful campaign against this practice and had animated significant protest among Blacks throughout the nation. Although enslaved from birth, Wells forged a life of freedom under Reconstruction through studying, working as an educator, and becoming a professional journalist wielding international influence. More than any other figure by far, Wells placed the brutality and ideology of lynching at the center of national attention. In fact, during the War of 1898 Wells arranged a personal meeting with President McKinley to seek federal legislation to outlaw lynching, particularly in response to the murder of Frazier

Baker, an African American of South Carolina who had been appointed as a postmaster and was thus a federal employee. McKinley's administration had overseen the appointment of several African Americans as postal workers, a development to which local Whites responded by issuing death threats, torturing, and lynching the appointees. Although Wells was to be disappointed by McKinley's intransigence and refusal to take action, the brilliant author and analyst of White terrorism nevertheless succeeded in pricking the national conscience and creating a grassroots movement to combat White mob violence. Wells hinted at the hypocrisy of the lip service White Americans paid to ideals honoring life and liberty in Cuba. She asserted that if Baker had been murdered in Cuba, US officials would have clamored for vengeance and might have rallied for weeks. But because he was murdered "under the Stars and Stripes," the murder was treated merely as business as usual.[90]

Within the context of lynching and impunity for White perpetrators, many African Americans found it difficult to rationalize why they should risk their lives to fight for White power abroad when they lacked even the most basic rights in the country of their birth. No critic of the war surpassed Henry McNeal Turner (1834–1915) in his scale of analysis and unrestrained penchant for directness. Turner had aspired from youth to become a Christian minister. His determined pursuit of this profession led to his appointment as a chaplain in the Union army. Following the Civil War, he eventually became a powerful bishop in the African Methodist Episcopal denomination. Turner wielded his ecclesiastical influence to voice a radical critique of anti-Black racism. Whereas most African Americans couched their dissent within the presumptive terms of allegiance to US nationalism, Turner continually foregrounded the fact that the United States was an exclusively White republic. His support of the Black settler movement for self-determination positioned him to identify succinctly the colonial relations of power at stake in the disputes leading up to the War of 1898. While others agitated for Congress to declare war on Spain to assist Cuban peasants, Turner warned that it was naive to believe the White US government genuinely supported the political independence of "Cuban Negroes." In fact, in a critique of stunning prescience he asserted that intelligent observers should expect that

[90] Dennis Fradin and Judith Fradin, *Ida B. Wells: Mother of the Civil Rights Movement* (New York: Clarion Books, 2000), 104, 105. Paula Giddings, *Ida: A Sword Among Lions: Ida B. Wells and the Campaign Against Lynching* (New York: Amistad, 2009), 385–86.

the United States might rush to Cuba to put down the struggle for Negro independence, not to support it.[91]

Turner was living in South Africa when the War of 1898 began, and his first response to the actual outbreak of war was in July of that year. At that point the United States had decimated Spain's hold over Cuba and had effectively assumed occupation of the lucrative island. African American soldiers were already stationed in Cuba – among them Theophilus Steward, deployed with the Twenty-Fifth Infantry.[92] Turner noted that White Americans had lynched enough Black men to "stack one mile high" and enough Black women and children to "to form the head and foot slab." Thus, any talk of US humanitarianism in Cuba, he insisted, should be tempered by the quotidian reality of racial terror that African Americans were suffering under both formal and informal systems of White rule. Turner surmised that the United States had unlawfully put to death more people than all other countries combined. The sheer scale of anti-Black brutality, he argued, should have jolted a thinking public into recognizing the absurdity of African Americans joining the US military to fight in Cuba. When Georgia governor William Atkinson vowed never to allow African Americans to join the military, Turner cynically insisted the White statesman was doing Blacks a favor by recognizing they had no stakes in the war.[93]

Even the most skeptical African Americans were surprised by the thrilled amusement that White mobs derived from terrorizing and murdering uniformed Black soldiers returning from the imperial wars in the nation's newly acquired overseas colonies. Black soldiers arriving in railcars were regularly met by Whites eager to degrade, brutalize, and even kill them. If they remained on the cars, fearful of entering into the confrontation awaiting them, they were ridiculed as cowards. And those Black soldiers who fought back were typically murdered. All of this merely confirmed what Turner had long concluded: Black participation in the colonial wars of the White state was an insult to the human dignity of Blacks and simply made no sense. He repeatedly asserted that the US flag signified honor, sovereignty, liberty, and manhood for Whites. But for African Americans it was a "miserable, dirty rag." Since African

---

[91] Henry McNeal Turner, "The Quarrel with Spain," in *Respect Black: The Writings and Speeches of Henry McNeal Turner*, ed. Edwin Redkey (New York: Arno Press, 1971), 172–73.

[92] Miller, *Elevating the Race*, 132–33.

[93] Henry McNeal Turner, "The Quarrel with Spain (1896–1898)," in *Respect Black*, 172–73.

Americans lacked civil, social, political, and judicial rights, he asserted, they were in fact without actual citizenship and had no business fighting in the US Army.[94]

Black Soldiers in the Philippines

Among the seventy thousand US troops deployed in the Philippines were four segregated units of African American soldiers. These Black soldiers landed in the thick of the contradictions and conflicts constituted by strident racism from White troops. White American soldiers almost immediately perceived Filipinos as "niggers" and easily lobbed the derisive epithet as if it were ordnance. Beyond this was the racial hierarchy of military authority. White soldiers and officers engaged Blacks with open disdain and insult, treating them as menial, ancillary laborers instead of interacting with them as comrades in arms. With the exception of a small number of Black officers, moreover, the US Army reserved officer status for Whites. And the few Black officers were not permitted to command White troops but only Blacks. The racial absurdity was not lost on African American soldiers.[95]

The most wrenching experience of African American soldiers stemmed from the brute fact that they were abetting the US imperial effort to defeat an independent republic of Filipinos whose only "offense" was their struggle to free themselves from Western colonial rule. In a theater shaped largely by guerrilla-style warfare, the grisly atrocities of US occupation emerged in clear and unambiguous terms. US soldiers used torture – such as forcing large volumes of water down the throats of captive Filipino soldiers – to extract information. They frequently raped Filipino women. US commanders even executed civilians and enemy captives. In 1906, , in the first Battle of Bud Dajo, the US Army fought an encampment of nine hundred Filipino Muslims known as "Moros" who had taken cover in an inactive volcano. The occupation forces ensured that virtually every man, woman, and child was shot to death. At the very least, US officials ensured that the war was the first in which US soldiers

---

[94] Turner, "The Quarrel with Spain (1896–1898)" and "The Negro and the Army (1899)," in *Respect Black*, 172–73, 184, 185.

[95] Willard B. Gatewood, Jr., *"Smoked Yankees" and the Struggle for Empire: Letters from Negro Soldiers, 1898–1902* (Urbana: University of Illinois, 1971), 240. Catherine Reef, "Prioleau, George W." in *African Americans in the Military, Revised Edition, A to Z of African Americans* (New York: Facts On File, Inc., 2010). African-American History Online. Facts On File, Inc. http://www.fofweb.com/activelink2.asp?ItemID=WE01&iPin =AAM0092&SingleRecord=True (accessed July 23, 2014).

were officially prosecuted for war crimes, but sentences were typically minimal and could easily be commuted.[96]

Even Theophilus Steward was visibly affected by the unmitigated brutality of US imperialism in the Philippines and the flagrant anti-Blackness of White American soldiers. He had seemed unheeding in his earlier defense of the US Army from charges of anti-Black racism in Cuba, and he had insisted all the while that US military intervention was advancing the uplift of Cuban revolutionaries. The subsequent Filipino theater, however, disturbed his sensibilities on an appreciable scale. Approximately 4,000 US soldiers were killed during the years of war against the Republic of the Philippines, but it was a clear victory for US troops, whose military occupation cost the lives of more than 200,000 Filipinos, mostly civilians.[97]

Patrick Mason, a soldier in the Black Twenty-Fourth Infantry, wrote distressingly of the treatment Filipinos received under US rule, explaining that the first and last thing any Filipino heard from White US troops was "nigger." As Mason expressed to his family back home in the United States, "You have no idea the way these people are treated by the Americans here. I know their feeling toward them, as [White soldiers] speak their opinion in my presence thinking I am white." His shock at the treatment of Filipinos under US occupation resonated with that of another Black soldier who composed an unsigned letter lamenting that White US troops applied "the home treatment for colored peoples" to Filipinos. This included cursing them as "damned niggers," taking their money in the streets, physically striking and kicking those who protested, and stealing fruit from vendors. Some White soldiers even resorted to robbing the graves of Filipinos to loot any jewelry interred with their remains. And one boasted of literally cutting off the arm of a deceased Filipino woman to steal a bracelet.[98]

The Filipino troops understood with incandescent clarity the political status of US Blacks and the cruel irony that a people who were denied the actual status of citizens in a White republic would volunteer to travel thousands of miles to wage war against Filipino sovereignty. Emilio Aguinaldo, the chief commander of the Filipino Army and president

[96] James R. Arnold, *The Moro War: How America Battled a Muslim Insurgency in the Philippine Jungle, 1902–1913* (New York: Bloomsbury Press, 2011).
[97] David Reynolds, *America, Empire of Liberty: A New History of the United States* (New York: Basic Books, 2009), 239–42. Gail Lurnet Buckley, *American Patriots: The Story of Blacks in the Military from the Revolution to Desert Storm* (New York: Random House, 2002), 140–60.
[98] Gatewood, *Smoked Yankees*, 279–81.

of the Republic of the Philippines, made explicit appeals to African American soldiers, producing signs that encouraged Blacks to desert the US military. Following the torture, lynching, and dismemberment of the African American farmer Sam Hose in 1899 (a White mob distributed Hose's body parts as souvenirs), the Filipino Army distributed a placard urging Black soldiers to consider anew the meaning of their participation in making war against the Filipinos:

It is without honor that you are spilling your costly blood. Your masters have thrown you into the most iniquitous fight with double purpose – to make you the instrument of their ambition and also your hard work will soon make the extinction of your race. Your friends, the Filipinos, give you this good warning. You must consider your situation and your history, and take charge that the blood of ... Sam Hose ... proclaims vengeance.[99]

Although the vast majority of Blacks were staunchly loyal to the US occupation, a few were actually persuaded by Aguinaldo's criticism and deserted their posts, fleeing to Filipino command stations where they were rewarded with military assignments.[100]

It is difficult to appreciate fully the emotional ambivalence induced by the act of killing human beings in war. The entire military institution, predicated on death and destruction as the central aim and strategy of soldiers, rendered legitimacy and honor to extraordinary acts of violence. African American soldiers, as a result, regularly exulted in their successful and hard-won battles against Filipinos. The soldier Middleton W. Saddler of the Twenty-Fifth Infantry recalled the ardor of war against the Filipino military, but he assured his family that he fought valiantly to "add another star to the crown" of the African American soldier, which he believed would increase the standing of Blacks in the eyes of Whites. Walter E. Merchant of the Forty-Eighth Infantry was likewise prideful as he described to relatives back in the United States the efficiency and victorious performance of his unit during the summer of 1900. Despite the determined might of Filipino defensive forces, Merchant's unit to that day had not suffered a single defeat. His enthusiasm paralleled that of another Black soldier, James Booker of the Twenty-Fifth Infantry, who bragged that African Americans fought with such skill that the Filipino military dared not attack US troops when Blacks soldiers were among them. Booker, in fact, described the Filipinos as pests who "yet infest the island."[101]

---

[99] Ibid., 258–59.
[100] Ibid., 244.
[101] Ibid., 246, 281–82, 284–88.

Other African American soldiers, by contrast, were rather candid in expressing their reticence about the entire situation. Michael H. Robinson of the Twenty-Fifth Infantry, writing home in the spring of 1900, recounted the agony of one particular battle against the Filipino military. At a certain point, he recalled, the fight "began to resemble a slaughter pen as the dead Filipinos piled up." Such a "sacrifice of life and health," he claimed, was discouraging to the Black infantry, and it forced them to reconsider the rationale for occupying the Philippines.[102]

The overwhelming majority of Black soldiers, however, were willing to close ranks in loyalty to the violent imperatives of US imperialism. George Prioleau, one of the African Americans appointed as a US Army chaplain in the Philippines, explicitly defended US colonial policy there. Prioleau considered Filipinos unworthy of self-government, claiming that they were in a state of rebellion when the United States entered the fray. In fact, he urged in a letter to the *Colored American* newspaper, "they know nothing about commercial and agricultural business and very little about government... [The] intelligent men among them ... are so conceited that they think that what they do not know is not worth knowing." Not surprisingly, Prioleau viewed African Americans soldiers in the theater of the Philippines as an occasion to celebrate, writing, "All hail to the American Negro!" And he was especially jubilant that the African American Benjamin O. Davis had just been made an officer as second lieutenant in the army.[103]

Another soldier, F. H. Crumbley of the Forty-Ninth Volunteer Infantry, lauded the beauty and scenic ambience of the Pacific Islands. He even encouraged African Americans to emigrate from the United States to the Philippines. Crumbly anticipated that "when peace has been declared" and commercial activities resumed in the Philippines through benefit of US influence, "the people of the country will raise their voices in praise and thanksgiving to the Congress and Cabinet of the United States" for liberating them from their previous condition. The seeming contradiction between praising military conquest and occupation while touting the putative liberation of Filipinos ably indexed the ambivalence of the extreme violence that became a vehicle for African Americans to prove themselves worthy of acceptance by Whites as members of the US political community.[104]

---

[102] Ibid., 267.
[103] Ibid., 300–3.
[104] Ibid., 270, 271.

Beyond 1898, as the open rhetoric of rescuing Filipinos from Spanish rule shifted conspicuously to strident policies of neutralizing and destroying the Filipino armed struggle for self-determination and political independence, even the mainstream US media, typically in harmony with the logics of White supremacism and racial conquest, pointed to these ironic developments.[105] Two years into the US occupation of the Philippines, Turner expressed perhaps his most damning assessment of the racial and political architecture of Black participation in this new phase of US colonialism. In the fall of 1900, partially paralyzed after a stroke, the senior bishop voiced outrage over the fact that African Americans, perpetually rendered as racial outsiders in the United States, had voluntarily joined what he identified as "an unholy war of conquest." McKinley's administration was overseeing what seemed to Turner "the crime of the century": total war against the native people of the Philippines so that the United States could exert its dominion over those people of color. And who was assisting this effort? African Americans. Turner expressed his disgust at the thought of Black personal acquaintances who were "there fighting to subjugate a people of their own color and bring them to such degraded state." He could not fathom what would inspire African Americans to travel to the Philippines in order to "shoot down innocent men and take the country from them, that God gave them." And he echoed his conviction that African Americans were fighting for the imperial cause of a flag and a nation that was not their own. Most of all, Turner expressed his hope that "the Filipinos will wipe such soldiers from the face of the earth."[106]

One major factor that distinguished Turner from most of those African Americans who opposed the war was his refusal to embrace the rationality of US nationalism. His long experience with US militarism as a Civil War army chaplain, within the formal structures of liberal democracy as a Georgia statesman, and with millennial optimism as an aspiring minister of Methodism following the Civil War had over the decades given way to a sobering racial realism. Most African Americans vied for a position within the hierarchical structure of racial politics by pursuing citizenship. Turner, however, rejected this as a mean-spirited game of White supremacy that asked Blacks to be loyal to White power in return for White brutality, an unprecedented scale of lynching and other forms of racial terror, and a rapidly emerging consensus among White legislatures

---

[105] Ibid., 241–47.
[106] Turner, "The Philippine Insurrection (1900)," in *Respect Black*, 186–87.

to formally exclude Blacks from the body politic through explicit legislation and amendments to state constitutions. At the federal level, moreover, Turner regarded the momentous decisions of the US Supreme Court in the *Civil Rights Cases* (1883) and *Plessy v. Ferguson* (1896). In the former decision, the court stipulated that the US Congress had no authority to outlaw anti-Black discrimination by American businesses. The latter decision, even more far-reaching, explicitly sheltered formal racial apartheid beneath the mantle of constitutional protection. To carry on as if Blacks were US citizens, he reasoned, was a most insulting game that he refused to play. Blacks, he insisted, were not actually citizens of the United States.[107] The United States was a White state, not a multiracial democracy. None other than President Theodore Roosevelt, unaccustomed to such bold, direct criticism of the racial republic, consulted with Booker T. Washington to ascertain whether Turner was treasonous in his condemnation of US militarism and his description of the US flag as a "miserable rag." In response, Turner clarified to Washington that he had never made such a claim per se. To Whites, he stipulated, the flag was honorable. He had been speaking specifically in relationship to US Blacks, who were racial outsiders under the rule of a White state. And he affirmed his observation that the flag yielded no protections or membership to Black people; for Blacks, it was worth no more than a "dirty rag."[108]

When Turner condemned those Black personal acquaintances in the Philippines helping to destroy Filipino lives and the prospect of Filipino independence, he surely had in mind the AME minister Theophilus Steward, among others. Turner simply found it impossible to accept that African Americans were so willing to invade, pillage, torture, and kill Cubans and Filipinos in service to expanding the colonial rule of a White racial state, especially given the fact that these same Blacks were themselves a stateless people. They were brutally ruled, lynched, and exploited under a colonial form of governance that forbade them membership in a White body politic. Thus, the elderly Bishop Turner had long decided that multiracial democracy would never become a political reality in the United States, given the deep architecture of its racial governance and the unrelenting, extremist devotion that Whites had demonstrated to preserving that racial order. It was why he had devoted the latter portion of his public career to advancing Black American resettlement in Africa

---

[107] Turner, "The American Flag (1906)," in *Respect Black*, 197.
[108] Ibid.

and promoting a Black political theology – devotion to what he called "the Negro's god." When he argued that the fundamental condition of US Blacks was one of statelessness, advanced a return to Africa, and promoted an antiracist, Black theology, Turner was giving voice to the paradigmatic themes that would become more familiar and profoundly transformative for millions of Blacks throughout the African Diaspora in the early twentieth century. The consequences of that formation, which made colonialism – not merely racism – the central focus of mainstream Black political and theological concern, obtained through a global movement called Garveyism. And it is to that development we turn in the next chapter.

PART THREE

PART EIGHT

6

Garveyism, Anticolonialism, and State Repression of Black Religions*

The years of the First and Second World Wars are remembered by many scholars as the time when America's military prowess unquestionably rivaled and then surpassed that of Europe's most powerful empires. Numerous studies, moreover, have examined the period to understand the ramifications of the massive demographic shifts effected through migrations from rural to urban regions – particularly from the South to the North. And, of course, increased immigration from Africa, East Asia, Europe, South Asia, and the Caribbean during this time indelibly conditioned the growth of America's ethnics.

There is something else, however, that deeply shaped the nation – in fact, an international range of communities – during that time. A fledgling movement born in the crucible of Black diaspora consciousness created a global network of theorists, propagandists, journalists, entrepreneurs, and other activists. This was Garveyism, the political and cultural movement formalized through the renowned Universal Negro Improvement Association (UNIA). Garveyism created the world's largest popular Black movement. Its roots and reach were so vast that a historical purview must be conscientiously conceived to avoid eliding the massive body of this movement, an iceberg barely submerged beneath the surface of a sea of change and consternation that characterized the early twentieth century.

The diaspora networks and internationalism developing alongside Garveyism also spawned the rise of Black ethnic religions. Unlike the

* Sections of this chapter have been adapted from Sylvester A. Johnson, "The Rise of Black Ethnics: The Ethnic Turn in African American Religions, 1916–1945," in *Religion and American Culture* vol. 20, no. 2 (Summer 2010): 125–63. © 2010 by the Center for the Study of Religion and American Culture. Published by the University of California Press.

varieties of African American religions in the nineteenth century, these Black ethnic religions posed a central question: what was the original religion of Black people? Although the rejoinder varied, the centrality of this question was the manifestation of a quest for a heritage that became conceivable because of a cultural turn in the transnational, diasporic formation of racial Blackness. This turn comprised formations of Black theology that critiqued both the political aims of White religion and the colonial paradigm of White civilizationism (equating civilization with Europeanness). Although important expressions of this Black theology are evident in earlier periods (e.g., Henry McNeal Turner's emphasis on a Negro god), the UNIA became the matrix for an elaborate, institutionalized inscription of the Black gods.

Such a momentous paradigm shift in African American religions was merely one part of a global turn – among other expressions were Rastafari in Jamaica and Pan-Islamist anticolonial movements in Egypt, England, and the United States. This coincided with the formation of the intelligence state as a cohesive, central security apparatus, a major feature of which was the practice of engaging domestic subjects as foreign enemies. So, as African American religions in their anticolonial paradigm, shaped by the UNIA, came under severe repression by the FBI and the intelligence state, a new set of conditions was instituted. Within this new context of national security, a number of African American religious communities met with government infiltration, intimidation, detention, and prosecution as enemies of the biopolitical racial state.

The UNIA and Black Diaspora

The movement that became known as Garveyism far and away transcended its individual namesake. Understanding how the movement's principal architect came to be formed as a deliberate agent of global change is, nevertheless, essential for discerning the aim and impetus of this massive organization and its constituents. Marcus Garvey was born in St. Ann's Bay, one of Jamaica's northern coastal towns, less than fifty miles from the capital city of Kingston. As a teenager, the eager youth was already working as an apprentice in his godfather's printing shop. An astute observer might have predicted his capacity for organizing and social change, for Garvey soon became active in the nation's first trade union, the Printers' Union. By 1909 he had created his own newspaper, *Garvey's Watchman*.[1]

---

[1] Marcus Garvey, "The Negro's Greatest Enemy," in *The Marcus Garvey and Universal Negro Improvement Association Papers, Vol. 1, 1826–August 1919* (Berkeley: University

It is no accident that Garvey succeeded in awakening Blacks in Jamaica and throughout the Caribbean with his siren call to oppose a global system of colonialism, not merely racism. Indeed, Garvey's formative years were fundamentally shaped by networks of race and colonialism, manifested particularly through the labor regimes administered by Western corporations, and the coda of colorism so common throughout the Caribbean. For this very reason, however, the incisive intellectual grasp of colonialism that Garvey articulated in his mature years was no simple apprehension. Indeed, colorism typically elided the specific political architecture of colonialism as a global system of European domination that inscribed racial Blackness as the extreme antithesis of Europeanness. By attending to the path through which Garvey came to understand the nature of colonialism as racial governance, one can discern the transnational networks of Black institutions, activism, and intellectual exchange that became a hallmark of the time.

Three major factors emerged in Garvey's experience that shaped his analysis of race and empire and his strategies of activism. First was labor activism in the Caribbean, which demonstrated to Garvey that materialism was central and that the fundamental architecture of social power easily transcended the particular manifestations within individual territories or nation-states. Second was racial Blackness as a diasporic formation. His experience in the British metropole did the most to expose Garvey to a Black transnational, diasporic subjectivity. Third was anticolonial nationalism rooted in the pursuit of a Black self-governing state, a perspective that fully emerged through Garvey's involvement with Irish nationalism and through exchanges with an international array of Black political theorists and activists in the United States.

Jamaican labor struggles were rooted in the intersections of Colored political aspirations and the conditions of free labor. Since 1866, Jamaicans had been ruled by a Legislative Council, a system of colonial rule brokered at the behest of Whites and Colored elites. The latter constituted a racial demographic separate and apart from Jamaica's Blacks, and they uniformly opposed any democratic arrangements that might have empowered the more numerous Blacks. Because Coloreds sought to arrogate to themselves the right to wield influence on the council, they allied with Whites to ensure that the Black majority would have no meaningful ability to participate in Jamaican governance. By the first decade of the twentieth century, Colored Jamaicans were calling for "Jamaica for the Jamaicans," by which they meant sovereign rule by Coloreds over Blacks. Their cry for

of California Press, 1983), 3–12. Judith Stein, *The World of Marcus Garvey: Race and Class in Modern Society* (Baton Rouge: Louisiana State University Press, 1986), 25.

self-determination was vexed by the very system of imperial rule they had helped to create in the 1860s.[2]

Throughout the Caribbean, Western-trained elites promoted development as the ticket to prosperity and economic empowerment. In practical terms, this meant promoting the interests of US or European companies to set up factories and plantations in the Caribbean. In a nation of mostly peasants, providing cheap or free land to foreign corporations; guaranteeing minimally taxed or tax-free profits; destroying traditional farms and displacing the families of subsistence farmers; surrendering control of national sovereignty over matters of finance, labor, and commerce; and trampling human rights were all sacrifices offered to the godlike imperatives of Western capitalism in return for promises of plentiful jobs for local labor that would grant them the status of perpetual consumers. But because this was happening throughout the entire region of Latin America, Jamaica's talent regularly fled to greener pastures, to other countries such as Cuba that might offer slightly higher wages and a clearer promise of prosperity.[3]

Garvey himself left Jamaica in 1910 for Costa Rica, where he worked as a timekeeper for the US-based United Fruit Company. Overworked and undercompensated, he then traveled to Ecuador, Colombia, and Venezuela between 1910 and 1912, in a futile effort to gain an economic foothold and earn a decent living. Like the more than 10,000 other labor venturers who left Jamaica on an annual basis, he was rewarded with inequality; grueling hours; and a brutal, international web of economic practices that efficiently structured poverty in the Third World while creating bountiful profits in the First World. Garvey drew on his professional training in printing to start a newspaper that agitated for labor reforms, but to little avail.

The Black International

Garvey returned to Jamaica in 1912 only to leave the same year to study in London, England, where exposure to diasporic Blackness fundamentally transformed him. He enrolled at London's Birbeck College but quickly realized the city offered much to learn beyond the classroom. At the heart of the Anglo-imperial metropole, London was among the world's most international cities, replete with ambitious, innovative activists from both the Western metropoles and the colonial possessions who were openly challenging the domain assumptions of European colonialism. Among the most notable of these was Dusé Mohamed Ali (1866–1945).

---

[2] Garvey, "Negro's Greatest Enemy," 3–12. Stein, *World of Marcus Garvey*, 22–23.
[3] Colin Grant, *Negro with a Hat: The Rise and Fall of Marcus Garvey* (New York: Oxford University Press), 26–30.

Ali hailed from Alexandria, Egypt, which was fully under the weight of British imperial rule. His father had been an officer in the Egyptian army, and his mother was Sudanese. His family sent him to study in England during his childhood. After his father's death, the teenaged Ali returned to England for good. He graduated from the University of London and pursued a rather successful career in theater. More importantly, Ali robustly promoted the political aims of Pan-Islamicism and Pan-Africanism. It is clear that he resonated with Blyden's eventual efforts to tether anticolonialism, Islam, and Third World identity. In fact, Ali would go far beyond Blyden by articulating in a more expansive context the strategies and aims of Pan-Islamic and Pan-African struggles against White colonialism. He authored *In the Land of the Pharaohs* in 1911. This influential history of Egypt sealed his status as a global authority on the country. Around the same time, Ali also helped organize the First Universal Races Conference in London, which led him to then establish his own newspaper, the *African Times and Orient Review*. In the 1920s, many years after meeting Garvey, Ali would establish a conduit for his vision of Islamic missionary goals by creating the Universal Islamic Society in Detroit, Michigan. In this way, Ali proved himself a serious intellectual and public force to be reckoned with.[4]

For instance, Ali lost no opportunity to weigh in on the excavation of the tomb of the ancient Pharaoh Tut-Ankh-Amen in 1923. He warned that because "King Toot" was a Black king, a "Negro," archaeology would force White supremacists to revise their narrative of Black inferiority and White supremacism. Rather than equating civilization with the White race and European history, he asserted, historians would be compelled by the archaeological study of this ancient Egyptian monarch to concede that Blacks themselves were arbiters of culture, handing down the major pillars of civilization and culture to the White race.[5]

The timing for creating the *African Times and Orient Review* could not have been more fortuitous for Garvey. Ali's intellectual breadth,

---

[4] Dusé Mohamed, *Dusé Mohamed Ali (1866–1945): The Autobiography of a Pioneer Pan African and Afro-Asian Activist* (Trenton, NJ: Red Sea Press, 2011), 18–30. Michael Angelo Gomez, *Black Crescent: The Experience and Legacy of African Muslims in the Americas* (New York: Cambridge University Press, 2005), 259–60. "Ali, Dusé Mohamed," in *The Oxford Encyclopedia of African Thought*, ed. Abiola Irele and Biodun Jeyifo (New York: Oxford University Press, 2010), 1: 67–69.

[5] Catherine Lynette Innes, *A History of Black and Asian Writing in Britain, 1700–2000* (New York: Cambridge University Press, 2002), 182–92. "Pharaoh 'Toot' Had the Goods, Says Egyptian: Duse Mohamed Says the Whites Fear Evidence in Tut-Ankh-Amen's Tomb," *Chicago Defender*, March 31, 1923.

artistic talent, indefatigable activism, social networking, and innovative creativity were to provide a nourishing soil for Garvey's still-burgeoning understanding of the social world of race and empire. Ali quickly recognized that the young Jamaican's professional background was a perfect asset, so he hired Garvey to help run the start-up paper. Garvey of course benefited by having a job with decent wages. More importantly, Ali's operation brought together a global array of avant-garde philosophers and activists eagerly critiquing the imperial networks of power and fostering self-determination among colonial subjects. So Garvey gained entry into a transnational network of activist intellectuals whose ideas about power, race, economics, and freedom were being forged in the visible crucible of empire. His work with the paper also allowed him to transition into the role of public writer. In fact, in this periodical Garvey would publish one of his earliest articles centrally concerned with the diasporic purview of Black people.

After spending two years working with Ali in London, Garvey returned to Jamaica to implement his own plan for Black racial uplift. He was most impressed by Booker T. Washington's philosophy of educating Blacks to control the material means of prosperity. Operating factories, producing food, building homes, and procuring financing through Black-owned banks – Washington viewed all these as essential elements of Black empowerment that had produced scores of successful enterprises in Black towns throughout the United States.[6] Garvey's own history was itself a testament to the power of industrial training. Although he had traveled throughout Latin America seeking profitable work from Western companies, in the end it was his apprenticeship training in printing that allowed him to travel as far away as London and still support himself. Garvey was also persuaded that Washington's appeal to White philanthropy could be replicated in Jamaica. He met another social activist, Amy Ashwood, at a debate in Kingston. The two were soon married, and they collaborated to create the Universal Negro Improvement Association, which provided the institutional context for promoting their activist agenda. The fledgling organization emphasized the goal of "civilizing the backward tribes of Africa," aimed to "strengthen the imperialism of African states," and worked to "promote a conscientious worship among the native tribes of Africa." Garvey and Ashwood also petitioned Jamaica's Legislative Council for a land grant to start a school modeled on Washington's

---

[6] David H. Jackson, *Booker T. Washington and the Struggle against White Supremacy: The Southern Educational Tours, 1908–1912* (New York: Palgrave Macmillan, 2008).

Tuskegee Institute. In what may have been a pragmatic decision, the council denied Garvey's request, granting the land in question to a Colored group. But Garvey suspected that the decision evidenced deliberate opposition from Colored leaders who viewed him as undesirable competition.[7]

Garvey's exchanges with an international array of Black political theorists and activists in the US metropole also shaped his understanding of race and colonialism. He disembarked for the United States in March 1916, arriving first in New York City, which had by then attracted numerous families from Jamaica. From there, Garvey visited several northern cities with a significant African American population, including Boston, Philadelphia, Chicago, and Washington, DC. And he spent time in the American South, starting in 1917.[8]

Garvey quickly realized that he had landed in the heart of African American exceptionalism. For decades, numerous race leaders such as Henry McNeal Turner, Anna Julia Cooper, and W. E. B. Du Bois had celebrated the idea that Blacks in the United States would lead the Diaspora in race uplift. They lived in the belly of the beast, the heart of the American empire. Never mind that they were on its underside or sidelined at its margins. They were undeterred in their claim to global race leadership. When the United States and its European allies convened the Paris Peace Conference in 1919 to decide the destiny of Germany's African colonies, the National Equal Rights League, National Association for the Advancement of Colored People (NAACP), and Circle of Negro War Relief lobbied for the right of African Americans to secure a role in managing the territories. Notable figures ranged from more radical African American leaders such as Ida B. Wells and William Monroe Trotter to the more conciliatory Madame C. J. Walker. UNIA activists were right among them. These activists commonly assumed that US Blacks, living in the heart of American prosperity and global leadership, were best positioned to help less fortunate members of the race around the globe, particularly the "untutored" and "uncivilized" peoples of Africa. Garvey subsequently joined Madame C. J. Walker, Adam Clayton Powell Sr., and other prominent activists to create the International League for Darker People solely for the purpose of formalizing their appeal to the international conference.[9]

[7] David H. Jackson, Jr., *Booker T. Washington and the Struggle Against White Supremacy: The Southern Educational Tours, 1908–1912* (New York: Palgrave Macmillan, 2008). Stein, *World of Marcus Garvey*, 30.

[8] Stein, *World of Marcus Garvey*, 35–40.

[9] Kevin Kelly Gaines, *Uplifting the Race: Black Leadership, Politics, and Culture in the Twentieth Century* (Chapel Hill: University of North Carolina Press, 1996). Grant,

Unlike Jamaicans, however, Blacks in the United States were accustomed to explicit emphasis on racial Blackness (Black consciousness) as a basis for political organization. Dynamic activists like Hubert Harrison (1883–1927) of the Liberty League, A. Philip Randolph, and Cyril Briggs, as well as more established figures of national renown like Ida B. Wells, emphasized race solidarity and racial consciousness.[10] They aimed to sensitize the public to the significance of race as an analytical category essential to demystifying the machinations of the status quo. For instance, at the very time the success of the Bolshevik Revolution was buoying hopeful reformers by framing class as the principal determinant of social status, Harrison focused on race as a central framework for explaining the plight of African Americans and for crafting a solution. He was among the growing number of Caribbean-born New Yorkers involved with social activism. Harrison hailed from St. Croix and had immigrated to the United States at age seventeen following his mother's death.[11] By the time of the First World War, he and Garvey had become well acquainted and deeply involved with similar political aims.[12]

When Harrison established the Liberty League in 1917, he exemplified a new breed of African American activism that refused to placate White supremacism and anti-Black violence. The organization promoted a race-first approach by insisting that a pragmatic solidarity among Blacks should outweigh competing class interests because it was imperative to gain some measure of racial equality and to force change from White politicians. The organization was also devoted to political independence, unmitigated equality, internationalism, anticolonialism, and organized labor activism. Harrison was especially notable for promoting membership in the Socialist Party among African Americans. And in a highly productive turn, the Liberty League departed from the elitist leadership paradigm of the NAACP, instead calling for a new wave of race leaders from the "masses" of Blacks, most of whom were not highly educated or connected to White philanthropy.[13]

Negro with a Hat, 174. Wilson Jeremiah Moses, *Creative Conflict in African American Thought: Frederick Douglass, Alexander Crummell, Booker T. Washington, W.E.B. Du Bois, and Marcus Garvey* (New York: Cambridge University Press, 2004), 261.

[10] Stein, *World of Marcus Garvey*, 46–47.

[11] Jeffrey Babcock Perry, "Harrison, Hubert Henry" in *African American Lives*, ed. Henry Louis Gates and Evelyn Brooks Higginbotham (New York: Oxford University Press, 2004), 379–80.

[12] Jeffrey Babcock Perry, *Hubert Harrison: The Voice of Harlem Radicalism, 1883–1918* (New York: Columbia University Press), 337–40.

[13] Ibid., 142–43, 53–59.

In contrast to the NAACP, which aimed to integrate African Americans into the body politic and forge a multiracial democracy, Harrison stridently demanded a more radical approach to ending the advancing tide of anti-Black terrorism and White supremacism during World War I, the very time when militarism and nationalism evoked even greater brutality from Whites toward Black victims. The murderous lynchings of Blacks, particularly of African Americans in military uniform, merited foremost attention. White perpetrators of these public rituals routinely mailed home – using the US Postal Service – their photos in the form of postcards displaying the burned bodies of Black victims. As the decade wore on and the violence, intimidation, and marginalization of Blacks continued, Harrison began chairing the Colored National Liberty Congress to create support for antilynching legislation. And by 1924, Harrison, who had by then gained US citizenship, was demanding a separate territory in the southern United States to establish a sovereign Black nation-state.[14]

In 1920 Amy and Marcus Garvey invited Harrison to edit the *Negro World*, the UNIA's publication. Harrison's editorial leadership helped make the UNIA periodical preeminent among Black Diaspora readers. Dubbed the "Black Socrates," he wielded a startling capacity to integrate the imperatives of anticolonial consciousness, a synthetic liberative politics (his lectures ranged from promoting reproductive rights to anti-imperial activism to labor organizing), and an unbridled, independent analysis of religion and social suffering. For all his social networking and bold intellection, however, his Achilles heel was a chronic, abysmal failure at mass appeal and effective organizing. Harrison was wise to accentuate the need for a broad-based movement rather than a small group of elites. Yet, the Liberty League's membership never numbered more than a few hundred. *The Voice*, which he founded in 1917 as the periodical organ of the Liberty League, was inactive within a year. A few years later he attempted to restart the paper, only to abandon it again in a matter of months.[15]

Harrison's seminal intellectual analysis, unfortunately, would be barely remembered by future American generations. Rather, it was through the UNIA that Harrison's legacy would become incarnated within a lasting body of public (though often distorted) memory and recognizable influence. Although Garvey began working for Harrison, by 1920 it was

---

[14] Ibid.
[15] Ibid., 138, 314.

Harrison who was working for Garvey as editor of the UNIA's *Negro World*. From the start of Garvey's affiliation with Harrison and the Liberty League, the rapidly developing visionary began to absorb and rearticulate Harrison's emphasis on a "race-first" approach, internationalism, and anticolonialism. Especially fruitful was Garvey's ability to link *political sovereignty* (Harrison called for an independent Black nation-state) and *democratic freedom*. He was convinced (as Henry McNeal Turner had earlier been) that the US nation-state was so deeply entrenched as a White racial state that multiracial democracy would remain a futile pursuit for African Americans. Moreover, Liberty League member Charles Christopher Seifert developed the idea of a Black-owned shipping and commerce enterprise to advance the economic and political independence of Blacks.[16]

Garvey absorbed this analysis and, in his work with Harrison and the Liberty League, quickly began to synthesize a more revolutionary understanding of sovereignty and democracy.[17] What had begun as the UNIA's Tuskegee-inspired approach to *education* for liberation shifted toward a clear devotion to Black collective *economic* self-sufficiency and *political* sovereignty. The UNIA was now taking shape not as a pedagogical outfit but as an ingenious economic conduit to create corporate infrastructure, market networks, and economic and political sovereignty in the Black Diaspora.[18]

Before the First World War had ended, both Garvey and W. E. B. Du Bois had been swept into the rising tide of Pan-Africanism that emphasized the linkage between self-determination and racial equality. The very means to achieving racial justice throughout the African Diaspora was anticolonialism – ending the rule of Western colonizers in Africa, the Americas, and the Caribbean. In addition, interest in Pan-Africanism was inspiring robust political movements for independence and labor reform throughout the Atlantic world. Major cities within the United States were enabling dynamic exchanges and networks among antiracist movement leaders. The British Empire functioned in a similar fashion, attracting key opponents of imperialism to the center of the metropole. As a result, the most influential formations of Pan-Africanism were emerging not only in the peripheries but also in cities like London, New York, and Paris. In this

---

[16] Ibid., 337–38.
[17] Steven Hahn has examined the tremendous implications of the UNIA's emphasis on self-governance and citizenship as a dyad of concomitance. See Hahn, *The Political Worlds of Slavery and Freedom* (Cambridge, MA: Harvard University Press, 2009), 140.
[18] Perry, *Hubert Harrison*, 337–40.

context, the leading Pan-Africanists shared a sense of urgency for convening an international conference.[19]

By the time of the 1919 Paris Peace Conference, unfortunately, Garvey and Du Bois had developed a mutual antipathy that would only worsen in the coming years. Du Bois had led the 1905 Niagara Movement for racial equality (with William Monroe Trotter), which established him as a major co-founder of the NAACP. By the time the UNIA was created, Du Bois was a leading propagandist (he edited the NAACP's *Crisis* periodical), an accomplished scholar, a literary author, and an astoundingly energetic organizer of racial justice movements within and beyond the United States. By the last decades of his life, Du Bois would see little hope for racial justice in the political projects of US imperialism, but in 1919 he was still firmly devoted to Western political liberalism. He spared little patience for what seemed to him the decadent and rash aim of the UNIA, and this played out in the public and rather personal disagreements between Du Bois and Garvey.[20]

When Du Bois developed and convened the first Pan-African Congress in 1919 to organize a collective response to the Paris Peace Conference, Garvey was conspicuously absent, determined to advance a separate international agenda. Garvey's competitive confidence was further buoyed by his own substantial organizational success. Implementing Charles Seifert's suggestion, he had established a commercial shipping company, the Black Star Line, owned by the UNIA. From July 1919 to February 1922, the UNIA's Black Star Line sold over 153,000 shares of stock, creating a total capitalization of $765,000 ($10 million in today's dollars). He also created the Negro Factories Corporation to develop an industrial base. In addition to establishing a branch of the UNIA in New York City's Harlem community, Garvey had also developed numerous branches through the United States. This was all within three years of having arrived in the United States for the first time. The UNIA, moreover, had begun to rival the membership of the NAACP as a result of the rapid emergence of hundreds of UNIA branch offices throughout the United States, not merely in the North. In fact, 423 of the UNIA's 923 US branches were in the eleven former Confederate states. As an index of its global expanse, moreover, the UNIA operated more than 200 branch

---

[19] Elliot Rudwick, "Du Bois versus Garvey: Propagandists at War," *Journal of Negro Education* 28, no. 4 (Fall 1959): 421–29.
[20] David Lewis, *W. E. B. Du Bois, 1919–1963: The Fight for Equality and the American Century* (New York: Henry Holt, 2000), 37–84.

offices outside the United States throughout the Americas, the Caribbean, Africa, and Eurasia.[21]

Even Du Bois himself was intrigued by Garvey's ability to raise financial capital and commandeer a formidable array of institutions that attracted a massive, international following. Du Bois's disposition toward Garvey, however, was internally contradictory and ultimately combative. On the one hand, Du Bois openly derided Garvey and the entire UNIA as a bumbling operation that featured no organizational skill and that substituted bombast for substantive reasoned discourse. On the other hand, he would eventually concede that Garvey's Black Star Line was both promising in theory and conceptually revolutionary.[22]

The Primacy of Self-Determination

The most consequential aspect of the UNIA's political philosophy was self-determination. The UNIA was not merely developing a critique of racism. Rather, the organization emphasized the central importance of self-governance, the principal paradigm of the long history of Black settler colonialism. Why did this become central to the UNIA's political philosophy? It was, after all, a radical departure from its original Tuskegee-inspired strategy of educating Blacks into the powerful realm of social advancement, an integrationist approach that at once assumed the legitimacy of the present nation-state's regime and also affirmed the possibility of multiracial democracy. The UNIA now advocated political unity among the world's Blacks, the creation of their own nation-state, and development of their own economic, commercial, and military infrastructure on a global scale.

As suggested earlier, UNIA members such as Harrison and Seifert emphasized specific strategies to promote self-determination and anti-colonialism. But another key factor that led to this fundamental shift was the UNIA's involvement with Irish anticolonialism. Britain had long denied self-determination in the Celtic fringe, and Irish resistance had only hardened during World War I. Given his location in New York City, a stronghold of Irish immigration and pro-Irish political sympathy, Garvey could hardly have escaped exposure to Ireland's controversial militancy against British imperialism. Support for Ireland's cause was not limited to the UNIA. Other African Americans such as Cyril Briggs joined Hubert Harrison to endorse the struggle for Irish home

---

[21] Hahn, *Political Worlds of Slavery and Freedom*, 118–25.
[22] Rudwick, "Du Bois versus Garvey," 428.

rule as well. In his periodical the *Crusader*, Briggs published editorials from Irish publications that championed Ireland's cause. In 1919, furthermore, Harrison created the African Blood Brotherhood for African Liberation and Redemption. Harrison's burgeoning "New Negro" philosophy focused on ending European and US rule in Africa and supporting home rule, self-governance for the colonial subjects of nations like Britain and France that ironically denounced Germany's imperial ambitions over central and western Europeans.[23]

In March 1919, just days before the UNIA convened in Philadelphia, six thousand Irish supporters gathered in Philadelphia. Given the UNIA's history of pro-Irish support and the proximity of the events, the US Military Intelligence Division, which had surveilled them, concluded the two movements were formally linked. When Garvey addressed an international convention of the UNIA in August 1920, he proudly announced a telegram he was sending to Éamon de Valera, the president of the Irish Republic, that expressed the UNIA's unequivocal support for the Irish freedom struggle against its colonial status. This was merely a prelude, however, to a grander strategy, as became evident when Garvey discussed the current plight of the African diaspora. Those attending the international UNIA conference were enthralled to hear Garvey explain the parallels between the struggle for self-determination waged by the Irish against the British Empire, on the one hand, and the struggle of Black people for self-determination, material success, and social power to dislodge themselves from beneath the weight of Western empire, on the other. The great political movements rapidly changing the world, he claimed, were rooted in peoplehood and democratic structures that ensured self-determination. The Germans had their Kaiser; the Irish their Valera. But who, he asked, was the leader of the African Diaspora, of the "Negro World"? And what of the homeland, Africa? It was thoroughly controlled by Western imperialists. Africa, he advanced, needed to create its own Black-controlled imperial system. And the struggle for African self-determination required the people to have a leader. Garvey offered himself as the obvious choice. His words struck home with many, for in the deliberations that followed, the UNIA conference officially conferred on Garvey the mantle of provisional president of Africa.[24]

---

[23] Marcus Garvey and Universal Negro Improvement Association, *The Marcus Garvey and Universal Negro Improvement Association Papers*, ed. Robert A. Hill (Berkeley: University of California Press, 1983), 1: lxx–lxxi. Grant, *Negro with a Hat*, 197–99.

[24] Garvey and UNIA, *Marcus Garvey and UNIA Papers*, 1: lxx–lxxi.

In August 1921, just months before Britain established a treaty with a newly founded Irish Free State, Garvey sent a telegram to Valera and the British king George V reasserting the support that "4,000,000 Negroes of the World" were expressing on behalf of the Irish people for their freedom. Only the "freedom of Africa" could have brought greater pleasure, Garvey opined.[25] There were also other ways that Irish imperial structures and anticolonial movements inspired the UNIA's initiatives. The Irish Sinn Féin political party had proposed in 1906 creating a merchant marine fleet so that a future Irish republic based on democratic home rule might develop economic prowess through sovereign international trade relations.[26] The political arm of the Sinn Féin had planned even earlier to establish official relations with other nations to work on behalf of Irish immigrants in whatever country they lived. In this way, the party exemplified a politics of diasporic consciousness and racial dignity that encouraged aspiration toward a Black empire. If such could be achieved, then African-descended peoples throughout the world would be assured that any government that denied their rights and dignity would have to answer to a powerful Black state. The influence of Irish nationalism on Garvey is also explicitly evident from his activism in Jamaica's first political organization rooted in nationalism, the National Club of Jamaica. As the group's assistant secretary in 1910, Garvey worked very closely with the club's founder, S. A. G. Cox, who had encountered Irish conscientization while living in England. Even the periodical of the Jamaican club, *Our Own* (translating the Gaelic *sinn féin*), was inspired by Irish nationalism.[27]

Global Economics, Commerce, and the UNIA's Anticolonialism Formula

Even more foundational than the Irish nationalism, however, was Black anticolonialism of the sort Garvey first encountered in London. Garvey's brief sojourn in England had exposed him to a host of anticolonial activists engaged with Ireland, Egypt, and the Caribbean, whose numbers swelled in the very heart of London, the seat of the British metropole. Despite his conflicts with organizers of the Pan-African Congresses, moreover, the rising attention toward Black Diaspora and self-determination propelled

---

[25] Ibid., 1: lxxvi.
[26] Ibid., 1: lxxi.
[27] Brian Dooley, *Black and Green: The Fight for Civil Rights in Northern Ireland & Black America* (Chicago: Pluto Press, 1998), 20–21.

Garvey to articulate more emphatically the goal of Black empire rooted in a Black sovereign state.

These developments clearly signaled that democracy among darker peoples had become the central stake in the consternation over empire among African Americans. This focus was culminating just as the Western powers – led by the United States and Britain – were preparing a new global order of democracy for Europe's White citizens and a more robust, corporate imperialism (i.e., racial governance) for non-White peoples in the colonial possessions. The bid to create a permanent central banking system for the United States – the Federal Reserve of twelve private corporate banks – had finally succeeded in 1913. As a result, the federal government itself was formally aligned with (although institutionally separate from) the ambitions of global financiers such as Paul Warburg, who had been director of Wells Fargo and Company before President Woodrow Wilson appointed him to the newly formed Federal Reserve Board; Frank Vanderlip, a former McKinley cabinet member who led the National City Bank of New York until 1919; and Henry P. Davison, a partner of J. P. Morgan. All were among the ambitious corporate executives who formulated the original plan for the Federal Reserve banking system. After 1913, when the Federal Reserve Act was passed, the US government's ties to banking rapidly expanded beyond underwriting the cost of wars (e.g., the United States had borrowed $200 million – equivalent to more than $5 billion in today's dollars – from National City Bank to help finance the War of 1898) to infusing the economy with cash in dire times (again, by loaning money to the US Treasury).[28]

This alliance between finance capitalism and the US racial state now explicitly wed two major pillars of social power. On the one hand was America's military complex that controlled foreign territories and established puppet governments subject to US fiat. On the other hand was the highly marketized commoditization of human (i.e., labor) and natural resources (such as rubber, produce, and minerals) under immense influence of investment banks; private corporations of industry, trade, and commerce; and individual and institutional shareholders in the United States and Europe. From that point on, the ambitions of private capital

---

[28] George C. Herring, *From Colony to Superpower: U.S. Foreign Relations since 1776* (New York: Oxford University Press, 2011), 460–83. Greg Grandin, *Empire's Workshop: Latin America, the United States, and the Rise of the New Imperialism* (New York: Metropolitan Books, 2006). Eduardo H. Galeano, *Open Veins of Latin America: Five Centuries of the Pillage of a Continent* (New York: Monthly Review Press, 1979).

and corporate entrepreneurs began to play a far greater role in shaping the form and content of US imperialism abroad. As a result, US corporations and their European allies were directly implicated in the renewed efforts to control the labor and natural resources of Latin America; colonized regions of Africa and Asia; and the colonies of Guam, the Philippines, Alaska, Samoa, Hawaii, the Panama Canal Zone, Puerto Rico, and the US Virgin Islands. The resulting expansion of the US economy produced massive benefits for the US Treasury through job growth, rising tax revenues, and a placated citizenry that enjoyed higher living standards.[29]

Garvey understood far better than pedestrian observers the nature of transformations occurring in the West and the global impact of these changes. The Western corporations that continued to deepen their grip on virtually every aspect of life in the Caribbean and Latin America, he perceived, were not separate from colonialism. It was patent to Garvey, more so than to most, that corporations were actually in the business of *governing*, in alliance with Western territorial states, as an essential means to ensuring profitability. But rather than repudiating governance in a fit of Nietzschean *ressentiment*, Garvey aimed to seize and defend the role of Blacks in that global, imperial enterprise. He claimed a stake in the larger terrain of imperial corporatism. Indeed, what separated him from numerous other progressives and anticolonial activists is what made him, with only some measure of irony, kin (in spirit if not specific aim) to the financiers on Wall Street and the imperial political architects in Washington and the European metropoles. Garvey was a skilled, savvy, and accomplished entrepreneur, and he well knew it. Moreover, he was decidedly intent on building an empire, founded on Western institutions of politics, economics, commerce, and militarism. When Du Bois besmirched Garvey for what appeared to the sage promoter of liberalism a hodgepodge of buffoonery – the UNIA's flamboyant regalia, motorcades on a scale worthy of heads of state, pompous speeches, and ambitious claims of an imperial Black state – Garvey responded that he was a self-made man who generated his own ideas, institutions, and income. Garvey in turn lampooned Du Bois for being a freeloader who depended on the financial patronage of the White race for his bread and who could boast of no single institution he himself had created. If the two of them were dropped penniless on the street and had to start all over again, Garvey crowed, he could within a month be financially afloat and able to fend

---

[29] Herring, *From Colony to Superpower*, 460–83. Grandin, *Empire's Workshop*. Galeano, *Open Veins of Latin America*.

for himself, whereas Du Bois would be seeking sponsorship from White philanthropists.[30]

It is important to emphasize this point because, like Du Bois, many scholars have found in Garvey more comedy and dilettante amusement than substance. But there is a relationship between Garvey's ability to discern the full meaning of the economic and political turn that US empire had taken by the end of World War I and the failure of many scholars to regard seriously his imperial project as a thoughtful and at least theoretically viable one that derived from his uncommonly perceptive acumen. Under Garvey's leadership, the UNIA embraced many of the central tenets of a strident Edwardian imperialism. This more brazen variety of empire stood in sharp contrast to the previous Victorian era's cosmetic emphasis on altruism and gentility, core principles in the civilizing mission that thinly veiled the avaricious appetite of Western imperialists for natural resources and highly exploitable labor. Garvey actually admired the ostentatious means by which the British king Edward pursued financial gain, not as shameful villainy but as an efficient means and an honorable end to be pursued aggressively. Garvey believed that dominion (in the sense of imperium) was a mark of pride, especially racial pride. The UNIA sought to inscribe such a hallmark of greatness onto the racial body of the "Negro world." Garvey opposed the colonialism of White nations over non-White peoples not because it was colonialism per se but because the global enterprise of Western imperialism proceeded under the directive of White supremacism, which created a losing game for Blacks. This is why the UNIA proposed as the solution and redemption of Blacks not an end to empire but the creation of a Black empire, an *imperial league* of free, self-determining Black polities united for the purpose of economic and political dominion on a global scale.

In this way, it becomes evident that Garvey perceived Blacks as "conscripts of modernity," compelled to make the best of forced options. This analytical framework highlights how the historical and material conditions of colonialism are not merely barriers that subjugated peoples overcome. They also help shape the subjectivity, means, and agency of those peoples. The exigencies of living in a global network of powerful states – preeminently Western and anti-Black – defined the terms on which Black resistance and revolution would occur.[31] Garvey believed

---

[30] Garvey and UNIA, *Marcus Garvey and UNIA Papers*, lvi.
[31] David Scott, *Conscripts of Modernity: The Tragedy of Colonial Enlightenment* (Durham, NC: Duke University Press, 2004).

the political project of Black freedom was inextricably entangled with the tools and formations of White imperialism. The very possibility and means of Black freedom – preeminently understood by Garvey as a Black empire-state – obtained through colonialism. But colonial structures also served as the matrix of anti-Blackness and the Western racial state. Thus, Garvey operated outside of the domain of Western liberalism. He drank from the same well of freedom that animated White settler republics to quench an insatiable thirst for membership in a political community of a sovereign state. But he rejected the liberal packaging of freedom. And he concluded, rightly, that Blacks could wield power and exert the requisite economic, political, and social force required for self-determination only by controlling an empire-state of their own. He perceived that democracy, in other words, derived through racial self-determination. This was a far cry from Western liberal political philosophy, which has glorified freedom as an innocent virtue that flowers from a political body of unfettered individual subjects. Garvey believed that Whites forged their power and freedom not through celestial virtue but by establishing racial states of empire. And he concluded that Blacks would forge their political freedom only through the same imperial mechanism.

The UNIA and Black Religion

By the 1920s it was becoming clear that Garveyism was not merely a political movement. For the millions of admirers throughout the African Diaspora, the UNIA was also an inspiring cultural phenomenon and a revivifying institution of religious innovation. And lest one mistake this assessment as a convenient gloss in hindsight, it is essential to note that Garvey himself was both privy and party to this phenomenon. He marketed his *Philosophy and Opinions* as a guide for the masses to achieve personal and collective success. Having garnered international renown, he skillfully marketed his image as a self-made man to inculcate the conviction that Black people could become masters of their own destiny, despite the overwhelming odds stacked against them. The parallel between this philosophy of success and the popular expressions of metaphysical empowerment exemplified in the New Thought movement was not lost on Garvey. In fact, Garvey explicitly named New Thought as a crucial resource for the Black struggle to attain self-determination.[32]

This transformation that Garvey advanced can be understood in light of the larger context of religious demystification. One might say that Garvey

---

[32] Garvey and UNIA, *Marcus Garvey and UNIA Papers*, 1: xlvii–l.

inhabited a Zeitgeist of disenchantment that demonstrated little patience with the peregrination of the popular religious imaginary into the realm of the extraordinary. At the time, for instance, the influential German theologian and biblical scholar Rudolf Bultmann was transforming the scholarly study of scripture through his hermeneutics of demythologization that promised to put to flight fanciful distractions that interfered with a sober, disenchanted world of theology. Influenced by a range of scholars including Adolf von Harnack, Walter Rauschenbusch, and the African American theologian Reverdy C. Ransom, liberal Christian theology was shaping the mainstream interpretation and public meaning of religious life. These religious critics emphasized worldly origins and aspirations while marginalizing supernaturalism. In this environment Garvey was promoting his own form of disenchantment, a philosophy of worldly success he believed capable of curing African Americans of an existential malaise resulting chiefly from a focus on an internal, spiritual realm divorced from the materiality of worldly ambition and striving. Garvey believed Blacks needed to direct this religious and psychological energy toward the external, material world of finance, government, and commerce.[33]

The American marketplace of religion, moreover, was briskly transforming spiritual consumption with an array of approaches to capitalize on the power of positivity and psychological approaches to wellness.[34] As one contemporary observed put it, "Garvey was spiritualizing a commercial affair." So energizing was Garvey's vision and so charismatic were his speeches that he was identified as of a piece with one breed of religious leaders who commanded public attention at the time, evoking charges that he was actually running a cult. Garvey certainly understood the potential of his race-uplift message to be aligned with the methods of seminal religious movements like New Thought. Like his contemporary Father Divine (née George Baker), he believed it was necessary to establish the connection between one's psychological disposition and the capacity for material acquisitiveness and existential empowerment.[35]

---

[33] Ibid., xliv–xlv.

[34] Bultmann argued that the miracle stories and extraordinary worldviews of the Bible were superfluous husks that contained the essential kernel of the Christian gospel's message of human liberation, which Bultmann understood through existential modes. See Roger A. Johnson, *Rudolf Bultmann: Interpreting Faith for the Modern Era* (San Francisco: Collins, 1987).

[35] "Hodge Kirnon Analyzes the Garvey Movement," *Negro World*, January 28, 1922: 7.

Religion was an integral dimension of the UNIA's institutional life. Typical UNIA branch meetings, in fact, approximated the form and ethos of a religious gathering. The groups regularly convened on Sundays, and those attending prayed, sang hymns, and even absorbed a formal sermon as a regular feature of the assemblies. Nevertheless, Garvey firmly emphasized that the UNIA had no place for religious sectarianism. He understood that the Black Diaspora comprised a range of religious affiliations – various sects of Christians in addition to Muslims and others. As he explained to the UNIA membership, "You may be a Christian; you may be a Mohammedan; that is your religion. We are all entitled to our own religious beliefs. Some of us are Catholics … Presbyterians … Baptists, and we deem it a right to adhere to our particular belief." In this way, accepting religious participation whatever its stripe, Garvey avoided inciting schism.[36]

One Garveyite minister, George Alexander McGuire, did aspire to create an institutional Black church under the auspices of the UNIA. McGuire was an Episcopal priest who had spent many years trying to create a Black-controlled denomination. He eventually instituted the African Orthodox Church (AOC). This denomination boldly emphasized the UNIA's Black theology and foregrounded the importance of the social gospel and Black nationalism. It was also decidedly Episcopal in liturgy and form and thus visibly sectarian. Although a number of Garveyite clergy were affiliated with the AOC, the UNIA proper had no formal ties to the church. In fact, McGuire's relentless efforts to make the AOC an official UNIA denomination led to his temporary ouster from the UNIA.[37]

The UNIA's promotion of a Black theology generated the most profound influence on African American religions. Most poignant was Garvey's claim that Black people needed to recognize their god as "a Negro," as the "God of Ethiopia." In a manner similar to Henry McNeal Turner, Garvey argued that, on one level, physical attributes such as skin tone were anthropomorphizing gestures imposed on the divine. He taught that there existed one supreme god who was neither a person nor a physical being but a spirit that Garvey called "Universal Intelligence." This supreme intelligence was the creator of all peoples.[38] As Garvey explained

---

[36] Cardinal Aswad Walker, "Princes Shall Come out of Egypt: A Theological Comparison of Marcus Garvey and Reverend Albert B. Cleage Jr.," *Journal of Black Studies* 39, no. 2 (November 2008): 243.

[37] Randall K. Burkett, *Garveyism as a Religious Movement* (Metuchen, NJ: Scarecrow Press, 1978), 91–99.

[38] Walker, "Princes Shall Come out of Egypt," 217.

in a Cincinnati speech in 1921, "God is not white or black; angels have no color, and they are not white peaches from Georgia." And yet White people – and even most Blacks – tended overwhelmingly to represent the divine in distinctly White racial terms. For this reason, Garvey urged, "If they say that God is white, this organization says that God is black; if they are going to make the angels beautiful white peaches from Georgia, we are going to make them beautiful black peaches from Africa."[39] The UNIA recognized that assuming a raceless deity was impractical in a social context so thoroughly controlled by racial thought. This situation was empowering for Whites. But for Blacks, imagining the divine as White merely exacerbated the already destructive psychological consequences of White supremacism.

The UNIA's Black theology was more than skin-deep, furthermore. It did not concern only the aesthetic dimension. Equally important was the emphasis on the *politics* of theology. The UNIA wanted adherents of the movement to believe their god was a powerful ally abetting their struggle for political liberation from colonialism and its various modes of racial domination. White theologians had continually described forms of domination like racial slavery, westward expansion, and Western military conquest over indigenous Americans as epitomizing a divine plan or reflecting a divine order of things. Their White god, by this account, was active on behalf of the material interests of the West. It was in this sense that the UNIA articulated the "god of Ethiopia" as a divine power broker working to advance the material interests of Blacks. By this calculus the UNIA aimed to expose as misleading the specious universalism of mainstream theology. Instilling confidence that a supreme god was allied with the politics of Black liberation became a necessary element of an anticolonial agenda.[40]

The UNIA influenced a broad array of Black religious communities by virtue of the fact that numerous members of those communities were devoted affiliates of the UNIA. By 1920 every sizable independent African American denomination was represented in the UNIA, largely through the affiliation of their clergy. In addition, smaller denominations such as the Church of the Living God, the Pentecostal Church, and the Emanuel Holiness Church were involved with the UNIA. Some individual clergy would become well-known. The Baptist minister Earl Little, whose son Malik Shabazz (Malcolm X) became a Muslim minister of international

---

[39] Marcus Garvey, Cincinnati speech, *Negro World* 10: 2 (February 26, 1921): 6, quoted in Burkett, *Garveyism as a Religious Movement*, 84.

[40] Burkett, *Garveyism as a Religious Movement*, 66–69.

renown, was a devoted Garveyite who regularly espoused in his Christian sermons the UNIA's critique of racism and its emphasis on Black consciousness and social empowerment.[41] Arnold Ford of Barbados was the UNIA's director of music and composed the organization's "Universal Ethiopian Anthem." Ford was a key member of New York City's Black Jewish community and worked closely with Wentworth Arthur Matthew to attract African American followers to the Hebrew Israelite congregation in Harlem. And of course George McGuire, inspired by the UNIA to create a Pan-African denomination with a distinctly Black theology, ordained a number of Black clergy as priests within the newly founded African Orthodox Church.[42] There were many others as well, all of whom absorbed and informed to varying degrees the Black anticolonial theology of the UNIA.

Black Ethnic Religions and Anticolonial Theology

By foregrounding racial Blackness as a diasporic formation and stridently asserting a Black theology, the UNIA undermined the hegemonic status that anti-Black, colonial formations of theology had held previously. This enabled the emergence and flourishing of Black ethnic religions. Some of the most forceful twentieth-century theologies of Black ethnicity appeared in the African American communities of Judaism and Islam. Both of these religious traditions offered a compelling answer to the pressing question of African Americans: what was the original religion of Blacks? The fact that these religions offered different responses misses the point. The potency of Black ethnic religions, rather, lay in their ability to pose such a novel question to make an ethnic experience of religion socially real for African Americans. The significance of this ethnic turn is especially visible in the religious reasoning of the Black Rabbi Wentworth Arthur Matthew and the Moorish American prophet Noble Drew Ali.

Black Jews
Soon after Wentworth Arthur Matthew arrived in the United States in 1919, he joined the UNIA. This exposed him to Black theology and the UNIA's insistence that formal religious creeds and symbols should generate Black pride and reflect the imperatives of race uplift as a divine concern.

---

[41] Richard Brent Turner, *Islam in the African American Experience*, 2nd ed. (Bloomington: Indiana University Press, 2003), 178.

[42] Richard Smith, "World War I," in *Marcus Garvey and the Universal Negro Improvement Association Papers*, ed. Robert Hill (Durham, NC: Duke University Press, 2011), cclxxx.

Matthew, who began his career in religious leadership as a Christian Pentecostal minister, gradually began to develop a vision for reclaiming an ancient Jewish heritage of Blacks.[43] Matthew perceived a history and gene-alogy of ancient Africans in the narrative traditions about ancient Israel. He rejected the conventional interpretations of the Noah legend, which identi-fied Noah's son Ham exclusively as the ancestor of Africans. This Hamitic myth of African ancestry had for centuries been used to represent Africans as ethnic heathens, idolatrous by heritage.[44] Matthew conceded that ancient Africans were initially the exclusive offspring of Ham. But he then went on to assert a boldly different version of this biblical genealogy: when Abraham's descendants (Shem's progeny) went into Egypt, they intermin-gled with Ham's Egyptian descendants. This population of people, claimed Matthew, the seed of *both* Ham and Shem, made the Exodus out of Egypt and into Canaan, becoming the nation of ancient Israel. Matthew would impress on his followers that Moses himself had married the *Ethiopian* daughter of a Black Midianite priest. For this reason Matthew identified Moses's two sons as the first "Ethiopian Hebrews," a term he used to iden-tify both the biblical ancestors of Blacks and contemporary Black Jews.[45]

Of even greater significance in establishing the lineage of these Ethiopian Hebrews, however, was Matthew's explanation of their rela-tionship with ancient Israel's celebrated sage ruler Solomon. Candace, the queen of Sheba, cultivated diplomatic relations with Solomon and, according to the *Kebra Nagast*, eventually produced a son with Solomon, Menelik.[46] This Menelik, Matthew advanced, was the founder of a

[43] A number of factors situated Rabbi Matthew's understanding of Ethiopian Hebrew identity. Most significant was the international attention toward the Falasha Jews of Ethiopia. Also important was the Ethiopian victory against Italian colonialism. See William R. Scott, *The Sons of Sheba's Race: African-Americans and the Italo-Ethiopian War, 1935–1941* (Bloomington: Indiana University Press, 1993).

[44] Stephen Haynes, *Noah's Curse* (New York: Oxford University Press, 2002). David Goldenberg, *The Curse of Ham: Race and Slavery in Early Judaism, Christianity, and Islam* (Princeton, NJ: Princeton University Press, 2003). Sylvester Johnson, *The Myth of Ham in Nineteenth-Century American Christianity: Race, Heathens, and the People of God* (New York: Palgrave, 2004).

[45] Wentworth Matthew's explanation of Ethiopian Hebrew genealogy is reproduced in Milton Sernett, ed., *African American Religious History: A Documentary Witness*, 2nd ed. (Durham, NC: Duke University Press, 1999), 473–476. Matthew was not the first to make this claim. Native American and African authors made the same assertion in the early 1800s. See James W.C. Pennington, *Text Book of the Origin and History of the Colored People* (Hartford, CT: L. Skinner, 1841). Robert Benjamin Lewis, *Light and Truth, From Ancient and Sacred History* (Augusta, GA: Severance and Dorr, 1843).

[46] The *Kebra Nagast* is a sacred text of Ethiopian Christianity that relates the descent of Ethiopia's rulers from the ancient Israelite King Solomon.

lineage that stretched all the way down to Haile Selassie I, whose uncle was Menelik the Great. Most important for Matthew was the fact that the Falasha Jews of Ethiopia had attracted international attention in the early twentieth century. Matthew's critics might easily ridicule his genealogical narrative, but it was far more difficult to deny the presence of Ethiopia's Black Jews. They practiced a form of Judaism whose lineage was independent of European Judaism (the latter was derived from Rabbinic Judaism). The Falasha Jews, in other words, practiced a religion that more closely resembled the temple-based Israelite religion that existed before the emergence of synagogue-based Judaism.[47] It was left to Matthew to show that these Ethiopian Jews were practicing the "original religion" of Blacks and that this Hebrew legacy belonged to all of the African Diaspora.

Matthew's decision to foreground slavery in the Americas as a history of heritage destruction played an essential role in his religious narrative. That Judaism was the original religion of African peoples was certainly news to his prospective converts. Matthew subverted the supposed eccentricity of his theological claims by explaining why most Blacks had never heard of this history: he interpreted Atlantic slavery as an experience of ethnic destruction. This, he explained, was why Africans throughout the Diaspora and even throughout Africa were separated from knowledge about their historical Hebrew religion. The work of Black Judaism, as he understood it, lay preeminently in reclaiming the Ethiopian Hebrew legacy and restoring to Africans the ethnic heritage that slavery and colonialism had elided.

---

[47] Years earlier, one anonymous writer for *The New York Times* did assert that the Beta Israel Jews were Caucasian and in no way related to the Blacks who surrounded them in Africa.

The experience of the Italians during the past few years with the Abyssinians has shown beyond doubt that these mountaineers of the "Switzerland of Africa" are decidedly a superior race to the other peoples of the Dark Continent with whom the Europeans have come in contact in their colonization and partition schemes. To a great extent their superiority is the result of their origin and pedigree. Although the modern representatives of the Ethiopians of myth and history, they are in reality not Ethiopians at all. They are not Black, but are of Caucasian descent as pure as the Anglo-Saxon or the Celt. Language and physiology stamp them as members of the Semitic race, and, consequently, as kindred peoples to the Babylonians, the Assyrians, the Arabs, the Syrians, the Jews, and other history-making nations of antiquity.

See "The Most Gifted of Africans: The Antiquity, Origin, and Religion of the Abyssinian Race," *The New York Times*, April 19, 1896, 29. This was of course finely characteristic of how colonial constructions of Blackness operated to define any signifiers of culture and history beyond the realm of Blackness. It was impossible, in other words, for Blacks to be ethnic.

Once Matthew became persuaded of a Black Jewish heritage, he gradually established the theology and institutional plans that led to the
Congregation of Commandment Keepers, one of several sects of Black
Judaism. Reading scriptures in Hebrew, following a kosher diet, wear-
ing distinctive clothing – these signifying practices were a vital means of
representing racial Blackness as distinctive, pre-American, religious, and
honorable. By the time of his death in 1973, Matthew's Beth Ha-Tphila
Ethiopian Congregation (as the Congregation of Commandment Keepers
was renamed) of One West 123rd Street in Harlem comprised more than
250 members. He had also established the Ethiopian Hebrew Rabbinical
College and the Royal Order of Aethiopian Hebrews, a fraternal society
instituted to supplement the work of the synagogue.[48]

Moorish Americans

The Moorish Science Temple of America (MSTA), founded by Timothy
Drew, also began to assert a Black ethnic identity during the era of
Garveyism. Drew would come to identify himself as "Noble" Drew
Ali, the divinely inspired messenger – a prophet – whose message to
"so-called Negroes" achieved its salvific efficacy primarily through its
revelation that Blacks possessed a distinctive "nationality." At the heart
of this message was the proclamation that these "so-called Negroes"
were in fact Moorish Americans, descended from the ancient Moabites,
among whom the biblical character Ruth was a celebrated ancestor.[49] By

---

[48] "Rabbi Wentworth Matthew, Led Ethiopian Temple Here," *The New York Times*,
December 5, 1973, 43.

[49] The by-laws of the MSTA were divided into "Acts" (instead of articles). The sixth act or
rubric clearly indicated the theological aim of resituating identity for African Americans
as ethnic (rooted in heritage) and not simply racial, stipulating that,

> With us all members must proclaim their nationality and we are teaching our people their nationality
> and their Divine Creed that they may know that they are a part and a partial of this said government,
> and know that they are not Negroes, Colored Folks, Black People, or Ethiopians, because these names
> were given to slaves by slave holders in 1779 and lasted until 1865 during the time of slavery, but this
> is a new era of time now, and all men now must proclaim their free national name to be recognized by
> the government in which they live and the nations of the earth, this is the reason why Allah the great
> God of the universe ordained Noble Drew Ali, the prophet to redeem his people from their sinful
> ways. The Moorish Americans are the descendants of the ancient Moabites who inhabited the North
> Western and South Western shores of Africa.

This proclamation of a Moorish identity was also incorporated into catechetical literature for MSTA converts. See "The Divine Constitution and By-Laws," Collection, box 1,
folder 3, Moorish Science Temple of America Collection, 1926–1967, Schomburg Center
for Research in Black Culture, New York Public Library (hereafter MSTAC).

adopting the term "Moorish," Ali was able to exploit a rich etymological history that had been used by Europeans until the nineteenth century to denote Muslims who were not necessarily Black (particularly those inhabiting the Iberian Peninsula since the eighth century CE) and Blacks who were not necessarily Muslim, often interchangeably. Ali taught that Moorish Americans possessed an ancient history and had practiced a distinct ethnic religion – Islam. As a prophet, he presented to these Moorish Americans their own "divinely prepared" scriptures, *The Circle Seven Koran*, which related some history of the Moabites and other Canaanite peoples and also described the activities of Jesus in Asiatic lands.[50]

Ali proclaimed to his followers that they possessed a distinctive ethnic heritage. He believed that if Black Americans embraced their true Moorish "nationality," as he termed it, the US government under which they lived and all other nations would respect them and would regard them as a dignified people with history who merited respect. For this reason, the MSTA emphasized that members "must claim a free national name to be an American citizen." Terms such as "Colored" or "Negro" were slave names, not free national ones. The response to Ali's message of Moorish redemption was considerable. In Chicago, where Ali first incorporated the MSTA in 1925, Moorish Americans commanded public respectability until Ali's suspicious death in 1929. Their public celebrations of an ancient Moorish heritage drew large crowds that included local political leaders. Ali established a factory to produce oils, incense, soaps, and other Moorish products, the sales of which buoyed the religion's financial base. From New York City to Kansas City, Kansas, to Belzoni, Mississippi, MSTA members established temples and vibrant communities of converts with a bold message of ethnic renewal. They

---

Noble Drew Ali also taught that Jesus was a Moabite and thus a member of the Canaanite nation. Part of his basis here was the genealogical claim in Matthew's gospel (1:5) that Jesus' ancestry can be traced to Ruth of the Moabite nation.

[50] From the 700s to the 1900s, most European languages employed some form derived from the Spanish *Moros–Mauren, Maures, Mauri, Mohren, Moors, Moren, blackamoor, moor, mauro,* or *moro*–to denote Muslim conquerors in the Iberian peninsula and, eventually, to identify Blacks throughout Africa (but primarily North Africa) and Europe, but not Black Muslims exclusively. The English term *moor*, for instance, was also employed to denote simply Muslims, Berbers, or Syrians. The slippage that lent use of the term to denote "dark" or "Black" applied not only to people but also to objects, rendering terms like "Moorish (Black) coffee." See Nelson H. Minnich, "Pastoral Care of Black Africans in Italy," in *Black Africans in Renaissance Europe*, ed. T. F. Earle and K. J. P. Lowe (Cambridge: Cambridge University Press, 2005), 282. Philip Butcher, "Othello's Racial Identity," *Shakespeare Quarterly* 3, no. 3 (1952): 243. E. Lévi-Provençal, "Moors," *Encyclopaedia of Islam*, 2nd ed., ed. P. Bearman et al. (London: Brill, 2009).

urged followers to reject the semiotics of so-called Negro identity and, instead, to reclaim a heritage that stretched from ancient Palestine to Arabia and the Muslim empires in Eurasia and Africa.[51]

Especially important were the concrete elements of the religion that symbolized ethnic difference. Followers received a change in name by adding the suffix "Bey" or "El" to denote their Moorish ancestry. They paid nominal membership dues (ranging from fifty cents to two dollars) and, in exchange, received membership cards certifying that their identity was not Negro but "Moorish American." Male members wore fezzes to distinguish themselves from other Americans. Men and women also donned robes in keeping with an Eastern style of dress. Of inestimable importance, furthermore, was the *Circle Seven Koran*, the MSTA's book of scripture that Ali himself published. This, in addition to the instructional literature of the religion, grounded followers in a compelling worldview that identified them not merely as victims of anti-Black racism but also as a distinct people (Asiatic people, among other designations) whose past stretched beyond the destructive episode of American slavery and whose mission was to reclaim their lost heritage.[52]

Scripture, Cultural Destruction, and Ethnogenesis

Analyzing the relationship between claiming heritage and the problems of existing under a hierarchical racial political order can render a more exacting view of Black ethnic religions. This relationship comes to light in the ways the theologies of the MSTA and Commandment Keepers deconstruct colonial paradigms of race and history. The intersection of ethnic heritage and anticolonialism that featured centrally in these religious movements produced deeply consequential formations across four domains: cultural destruction, religious particularity, temporalities, and ethnic naming. These themes posed theological problems to which Wentworth Matthew and Drew Ali responded by reconceiving religious identity as ethnogenesis (the source of peoplehood). When they did so, they were promoting an anticolonial theology that won a decisive following among African Americans.

The most consequential epistemic shift effected by Black ethnic religions was their claim that Christianization and slavery were essentially

---

[51] The MSTA was originally organized as the "Moorish Temple of Science" and continued to register under this name until at least 1928. Leaders subsequently modified the name to "Moorish Science Temple of America." See "Certificate of Incorporation" and membership materials, box 1, folder 3, MSTAC.

[52] See the membership cards of the MSTA, box 1, folder 3, MSTAC.

processes of cultural destruction. With some exceptions, such as Vodun in the Creole South, African American religions of the late nineteenth century typically embraced the Christian salvation myth and its civilizing mission by celebrating Black Christianization as the teleological result of the Middle Passage and American slavery.[53] The Ethiopianism promoted by nineteenth-century activists such as Lott Cary, Anna Julia Cooper, and Henry McNeal Turner described the trans-Atlantic slave trade as an escape from a heathen land, a divinely orchestrated redemption from African evil. The missionary religion that targeted ex-slaves after the Civil War emphasized that Christianization would achieve racial uplift and redeem converts from African decadence. This meant that slavery and European colonialism were conceived as divine agencies that ultimately redeemed Black people from languishing in the Dark Continent, beguiled by satanic religion, spiritually frozen in a primitive temporality due to their centuries-old rebellion against the biblical deity. During the nineteenth century, it was extremely rare for African Americans to reject Christianity because of its identification as European or "White" religion.[54]

The twentieth century, by contrast, saw the robust expression of this sentiment, most vividly among Black ethnic religions. Within the Moorish Science Temple, this claim that Christianity was alien to African Americans was explicitly advanced in Noble Drew Ali's *Circle Seven Koran*. Ali located the origins of Christianity within the Roman Empire; Christianity, in his theology of history, was the religion of the "pale skin" European Romans who executed the Moabite (Asiatic) prophet Jesus, whose mission, according to Ali, was to rescue the Jewish nation from rule by the "pale skin nations of Europe," thereby effecting an explicit

[53] Free Africans of New Orleans during the mid-1800s who were Vodun priests described their religion as "African religion" and evidenced an explicit pride in the fact that they practiced a religion of their African ancestors. See Ina Johanna Fandrich, "Defiant African Sisterhoods: The Voodoo Arrests of the 1850s and 1860s in New Orleans," in *Fragments of Bone: Neo-African Religions in a New World*, ed. Patrick Bellegarde-Smith (Champaign: University of Illinois Press, 2005).

[54] See Phyllis Wheatley, "On Being Brought from Africa to America, " in *Memoir and Poems of Phillis Wheatley, a Native African and a Slave*, 3rd ed. (Miami: Mnemosyne, 1969), 12. Edward W. Blyden, "Hope for Africa," *Colonization Journal* Tract no. 8 (August 1861): 4. Alexander Crummell, "The Regeneration of Africa," in *African American Religious History: A Documentary Witness*, ed. Milton Sernett (Durham, NC: Duke University Press, 1999), 288. Anthony Pinn, *Why Lord? Suffering and Evil in Black Theology* (New York: Continuum, 1995), 51–53. Tunde Adeleke, *UnAfrican Americans: Nineteenth-Century Black Nationalists and the Civilizing Mission* (Lexington: University Press of Kentucky, 1998).

salvation from colonialism. As the *Circle Seven Koran* explained to readers, European Christians, after executing Jesus, enjoyed a peaceful existence for many centuries until "Muhammad the first" (i.e., Muhammad Ibn Abdallah) arrived on the scene to "fulfill the will of Jesus."[55]

Matthew was even more pointed in his rejection of Christianity. Referring to the liturgical elements that characterized Black churches as "niggeritions," he was fond of associating Christianity with decadence. In other words, Matthew chose to deride Christianity by demeaning the Christian worship of African American migrants from the South whose cultural proclivity to religious ecstasy or spirit possession was drastically transforming the religious landscape of the urban North. In his sermons he often mimicked the dialect and theology of African American Christians who had migrated from the South in order to persuade his congregants that Christianity was an inferior religion foreign to the true heritage of Blacks. In one instance, for example, Matthew drew on his audience's familiarity with popular biblical narrative to assert the supremacy of Judaism over the dull sterility of Christianity: "Israel came out on top all through the ages because our men knew how to call God. Do you think the three Hebrew boys who went into the fiery furnace went in saying 'Lawdy Jesus'? They went into the furnace anointed with the oil of life … Do you think Daniel cried, 'Lawdy Jesus, save me,' when he was thrown to the lions?"[56]

His penchant for demeaning Black southerners through mimicry exploited a dominant pattern of northern derision against southern migrants to achieve his larger point of denigrating Christianity. Matthew did not, in other words, reduce Christianity to Afro-Protestantism. Ultimately, Christianity was wrong because it was a gentile religion requiring Blacks to abandon a pre-American heritage that, according to biblical chronology, was thousands of years old. To follow Christianity was to remain lost in a wayward religion into which Blacks had been displaced through American slavery. This meant Christianity was simply unnatural for Blacks. As one member of Matthew's synagogue described it, "My grandfather, they tell me, was of pure African stock, and knew about the Hebrew language. But in slavery we had to take on the language and

[55] Noble Drew Ali, *The Holy Koran of the Moorish Science Temple of America*, 56–60. Federal Bureau of Investigation, "Moorish Science Temple of America," file no. 62-25889, part 1a, http://vault.fbi.gov/Moorish%20Science%20Temple%20of%20America, accessed 2/1/2014.

[56] Howard Brotz, *The Black Jews of Harlem: Negro Nationalism and the Dilemmas of Negro Leadership* (New York: Schocken Books, 1970), 34.

religion of our masters. But as Jeremiah says, 'Can the Ethiopian change his skin? Can the leopard change his spots?' "[57]

Religious Particularity

An important parallel exists between Matthew and Ali's rendering of Christianity as a specific ethnic and racial religion (Christianity stands here as the ethnic religion of a specific people – Europeans) and the taxonomic knowledge produced by querying the nature of religion as a genus by comparing the varieties of the world's religions. This humanistic strategy of mapping religion resulted from European colonialism and was induced by the myriad colonial contacts that compelled Enlightenment thinkers to view differently what was previously regarded as Christian/religious truth. Eventually, the taxonomic imperative – the drive to classify and locate along a hierarchical "order of things" – induced an ironic turn in the Christian knowledge of *religion* that created, by contrast, a humanistic knowledge of *religions*.[58]

This transformation among Western (typically Christian) intellectuals did not necessarily dethrone Christian supremacism – the colonial comparison of religions frequently functioned to reinscribe European Christian supremacy in secular and religious terms.[59] The philosophical shift from Christianity as religious truth to the Christian religion as *unum inter multos* nevertheless intensified the burden of representing Christian supremacy. It also brokered the possibility of undermining such claims by relegating Christianity to the realm of European particularity rather than universalism. The taxonomic fallout of this epistemic shift is recapitulated in the dethronement of Latin from its status as the lingua franca of Christendom in the sixteenth and seventeenth centuries; under the pluralizing assault of vulgar national languages like German, English, and French, Latin relinquished its pedestal of exceptionalism and receded into a pluralistic field of languages. Consequently, language itself began to function for Europeans as a means of elevating nationalisms – that

---

[57] Ibid., 26.

[58] David Chidester, *Savage Systems: Colonialism and Comparative Religion in Southern Africa* (Charlottesville: University of Virginia Press, 1996). Jonathan Z. Smith, *Imagining Religion from Babylon to Jonestown* (Chicago: University of Chicago Press, 1982). Tomoko Masuzawa, *The Invention of World Religions, or, How European Universalism Was Preserved in the Language of Pluralism* (Chicago: University of Chicago Press, 2005). Richard King, *Orientalism and Religion: Postcolonial Theory, India and 'the Mystic East'* (New York: Routledge, 1999). Edward Said, *Orientalism* (New York: Pantheon Books, 1978).

[59] See Masuzawa, *Invention of World Religions*, 317–24.

is to say, not the Christian people per se but the *English* people and the *Anglican* Church, the *German* people and the *Lutheran* Church, and so forth.[60]

In the same way, Black ethnic religions effected a pluralizing ideology, asserting that particular peoples should possess particular religions. This is the central efficacy of the ethnic turn in African American religions. In the words of Ali, every nation of people should "worship under their own vine and fig tree," so that by "returning" Christianity to its rightful European owners, "so-called Negroes" themselves were returning to the gods of their forebears. By advancing the particularity of religions and by exploiting the fact that potential converts had never heard of what initially appeared to be *incredible* claims of ancient origins, Black Judaism and the MSTA were inverting colonial ideas about universalism and particularity. In this field of knowledge, Christianity was a symbol of destruction and a violent means of inducing collective amnesia. Both of these religions in this way reinterpreted *Christianity as an alien religion of conquest* that concealed a religious heritage to which Black ethnic theologies reawakened potential converts.

Temporalities

Black ethnic religions also embraced a historical consciousness that, unlike the governing paradigm, incorporated Blacks as agents of history. This theological innovation, in other words, proffered an alternative mode of temporality as rejoinder to an exceedingly difficult problem. When European colonizers displaced Africans into what became the United States, they also asserted a specific style of thinking about historical time that occluded world history by mapping colonial subjects onto the metaphysical cartography of Europe's Christian historiography.[61] Western Christian theologians divided the world's peoples into scripturalized races descended from biblical characters, compelling religious innovators to turn to the Bible as a necessary means of becoming visible to history (as we saw with Equiano in Chapter 3).[62] Secular observers

---

60 Benedict Anderson, *Imagined Communities: Reflections on the Origin and Spread of Nationalism* (New York: Verso, 2006). Jonathan Sheehan, "Enlightenment, Religion, and the Enigma of Secularization: A Review Essay," *American Historical Review* 108, no. 4 (October 2003): 1061–80.

61 Kathleen Biddick, *The Typological Imaginary: Circumcision, Technology, History* (Philadelphia: University of Pennsylvania Press, 2003).

62 James William Johnson, "Chronological Writing: Its Concepts and Development" *History and Theory* 2, no. 2 (1962): 124–45, especially 142–45. David M. Whitford, *The Curse of Ham in the Early Modern Era: The Bible and the Justifications for Slavery*

of religion – ethnographers, philosophers, and historians – did not rely on necessarily theological constructions of time, at least not explicitly. Rather, they separated the world's races into primitives and moderns. Europe's recent history thus became a modern epoch that superseded a medieval, "Middle Age" of darkness ruled by Muslim empires, which itself was a declension from the golden dawn of a Western (White) antiquity marked by Christian (Roman) imperium. This was a particularly confounding intellectual and psychological dimension of the Christian conquest of the Atlantic world. The effects have been so far-reaching that even the most critical contemporary scholarship regularly assumes the colonizing terms of this supercessionism, and people in every region of the world are indelibly shaped in some way by the idea of living in the "Common Era," a deafening mysticism of chronology that thinly veils the way Christian supercessionism promotes the history and confessional formulas of a particular religion (*anno domini*) as an era of world time (*saeculum*).[63]

Both the Moorish Science Temple and the Commandment Keepers formulated ethnic identity by recourse to a biblical repertoire of traditions about history, although they structured very different locations with respect to earlier loci of Jewish and Christian chosenness. In so doing, these religions asserted a Black subjectivity that became visible to history through association with corporate and individual biblical characters (such as Ham, Moses, Israel, and the Moabites). Matthew embraced a familiar cast of characters to occupy the locus of Israelite subjectivity, the most familiar symbol of chosenness in American religious thought. He reconfigured the racialization of ancient Hebrews first by establishing that the earliest humans (here, Adam and Eve) were multiracial progenitors and subsequently by representing Israelites as the progeny of Ham *and* Shem, both of whom he concluded were the ancestors of Black people.

(Burlington, VT: Ashgate, 2009). Colin Kidd, *The Forging of Races: Race and Scripture in the Protestant Atlantic World, 1600–2000* (Cambridge: Cambridge University Press, 2006). Johnson, *Myth of Ham.*

[63] Said, *Orientalism*, 120–40. Generations of White European interpreters continued to employ Enlightenment, rationalist, secular methods to interpret early Christianity and demarcate the bounds of its Jewish and Greek content. By the early twentieth century, in the dominant perspective of White Christian scholarship, Jesus himself had become a White anti-Semite. See J. Kameron Carter, *Race: A Theological Account* (New York: Oxford University Press, 2008). Shawn Kelley, *Racializing Jesus: Race, Ideology, and the Formation of Modern Biblical Scholarship* (New York: Routledge, 2002). Susannah Heschel, *The Aryan Jesus: Christian Theologians and the Bible in Nazi Germany* (Princeton, NJ: Princeton University Press, 2008).

In startling departure from this Israelite focus, Moorish Americans celebrated descent from the ancient Moabites (one of the Canaanite nations) and consanguinity with Jesus. Ali clearly emphasized that Jesus was Jewish, but he also exploited the Bible's claim of Jesus's Moabite ancestry to establish connections to the Canaanite nations (already portrayed as dark-skinned rogues in the graphical depictions of Christian biblical commentaries). In this way, he could hardly have been more clever. This maneuver allowed Ali to invert the centripetal hermeneutics of scripture that otherwise centered on a privileged Israelite identity. Ali stands apart from almost every other American theologian who has scripturalized race because he explicitly privileged identification with Canaanites, the most despised heathens of biblical narrative. By embracing a Canaanite identity in juxtaposition to the usual favored subjects of biblical narrative (Israelites), Ali ensured that he could represent in favorable terms the identity of Moorish Americans as (pre-)American people whose Islamic religion and Afro-Asiatic heritage were also beyond the pale of favored American subjectivity.[64]

Of course, neither Ali nor Matthew could then address the empirical history of African-descended peoples. As descendants of ex-slaves in the Atlantic world, these two theologians of Black ethnicity could not speak to the actual repression of Orisha devotion in the New World (including, for example, the public murder of African priests in the Americas and the widespread missionary portrayals of African indigenous religion as satanic), nor could they attend to the violent encounter with the biblical world that situated their temporal dilemma from the start.[65] By immersing themselves in the ideas of biblical history, they became captive to colonial ideologies of world-historical time. They became visible to a historical purview that further undermined their ability to conceive of historical time except as a projection of social identities, such as biblical or Muslim. This is what some writers have described as "identitarian time" – particular identities that appear as an objective, universal era of world history. Because they employed the historical consciousness of scriptural thinking and secular mapping of the historical world (of which empirical Africa was no part), they were once again prevented from developing a philosophy of history decoupled from supercessionism.

---

[64] "Koran Questions for Moorish Americans," box 1, folder 5, MSTAC.
[65] Anthony Pinn, *The Varieties of African American Religious Experience* (Boston: Beacon Press, 1995), 18–19. Bryan Edwards, "African Religions in Colonial Jamaica," in *African American Religious History*, 23.

In fairness, of course, it would have been unlikely for these theologians of Black ethnicity, given their context, to imagine circumnavigating the historical consciousness that Western colonialism produced. Theirs was a style of representing modern subjectivity erected on secular and religious categories. This perspective of time germane to Western colonialism derived from a centuries-old "typological imaginary" by which Western Christians, for instance, had entrapped contemporary European Jews as people belonging to an ancient time with no place in the contemporary world. This mode of imagining history anchored temporal thinking within the assumptions of specific, shifting identities – Christian, biblical, European, Western, and modern. Such confounding formulations within these Black ethnic religions do not negate the transformative capacities of their theological innovation. Rather, it remains evident that the MSTA and Black Judaism advanced a decolonizing reimagining of religious subjectivity.[66]

Foreignness, Language, and Ethnic Naming

Among the most provocative ritual strategies of Black ethnic religions was renaming converts to signify genealogies that transcended the bounds of Americanness, forging links to pre-American origins and transnational identities to underscore the idea that so-called Negroes possessed an actual heritage. The Moorish Science Temple provided converts with suffixes of either "Bey" or "El" to be appended to their existing surnames; these were the names of the two Moorish tribes, Ali taught, from whom all Moorish Americans had descended. So, for instance, when Charles Kirkman joined Ali's Moorish movement (he would become the most prominent leader of the MSTA after Ali's death), he changed his name to C. Kirkman-Bey. By taking on these tribal names, MSTA converts acknowledged and reclaimed their pre-American ancestry.[67]

---

[66] Vincent L. Wimbush, *White Men's Magic: Scripturalization as Slavery* (New York: Oxford University Press, 2012). Charles H. Long, *Significations: Signs, Symbols, and Images in the Interpretation of Religion* (Aurora, CO: Davies Group Publishers, 2004), 89–106. Long, "Religion, Discourse, and Hermeneutics: New Approaches in the Study of Religion," in *The Next Step in Studying Religion: A Graduate's Guide*, ed. Mathieu E. Courville (New York: Continuum, 2007). Kathleen Biddick, *The Typological Imaginary: Circumcision, Technology, History* (Philadelphia: University of Pennsylvania Press, 2003).

[67] Karl Evanzz, *The Messenger: The Rise and Fall of Elijah Muhammad* (New York: Pantheon Books, 1999), 67–68. The MSTA taught that Moorish Americans were descendants of ancient Moabites, whose descendants were Moroccans. This is why Ali taught that "so-called Negroes" were from Morocco, in "Amexem," which as the MSTA claimed

Black Jews likewise asserted an ethos of foreignness, not by taking on new names but instead by speaking Yiddish and Hebrew. Arnold Ford, a close associate of Matthew who also led a Black Jewish synagogue in Harlem, was careful to publicly display his fluency in Yiddish, the ethnic language so common among Ashkenazi Jews. Matthew himself employed Hebrew in naming the Commandment Keeper's synagogue: the Beth Ha-Tphila ("House of Prayer"). The synagogue was diligent, moreover, in providing converts instruction in basic and advanced Hebrew.[68]

Among various communities of European Jews, of course, speaking and reading Hebrew has constituted a practice of identifying as Jewish by distinguishing oneself from gentiles, a category that over many centuries has variably or simultaneously denoted "Christian" or "Anglo" or "Arab" or otherwise non-Jewish. Many European American Jews of the nineteenth century decried the growing use of English in synagogue services by pointing to the power of language to inscribe identity and mark heritage boundaries. This was central to the activism of theologians such as Sabato Morais, who led Conservative Judaism in dissent against the innovations of Reform Judaism, and Mordecai Kaplan, the American architect of Jewish Reconstructionism, a movement that synthesized the increasingly secular interpretations of Jewishness into a bold claim that Judaism was more an ethnic heritage than a religion. It should come as no surprise that Matthew likewise recognized the efficacy of language to mark Jewish difference and thereby authenticate his claim to Hebraic heritage.[69]

In addition to representing ethnicity through language, immigrant status was used to defy an easy association with "Negro" identity. Matthew's origins will probably never be known with certainty, although it seems clear that he lived in the West Indies before arriving in the United States. He alternately claimed Nigeria, Liberia, and Ethiopia as his native land. Many members of his congregation, moreover, had immigrated to Harlem from the Caribbean. The earliest reports of Black Jews in the urban North evidence claims of descent from Black Jewish families in "the East," the Caribbean, or African nations such as Ethiopia.[70] Through a variety of

---

was the ancient name for Africa. See "Koran Questions for Moorish Americans," box 1, folder 5, MSTAC.

[68] "Negro Jews Win Rent Suit," *New York Amsterdam News*, December 23, 1925.

[69] Chaim Brovender et al., "Hebrew Language," in *Encyclopaedia Judaica*, ed. Michael Berenbaum and Fred Skolnik, 2nd ed. (Detroit: Macmillan Reference USA, 2007), 8: 671.

[70] See, for instance, "The Most Gifted of Africans," *The New York Times*, April 19, 1896, 29. "Find Race of Black Jews," *Chicago Daily Tribune*, December 28, 1902, 1.

means, then, followers of the Black ethnic religions in the early twentieth century signified a foreign identity as a way to claim heritage.

Decoding Ethnicity

The idea of ethnicity, of course, is not strictly delimited by the word "ethnicity." The term itself would come into use, in fact, only in the 1940s.[71] Its emergence in the linguistic currency of sociology, furthermore, would derive from efforts to study European immigration to the United States. The question, rather, of the American history of ideas about ethnicity concerns the array of meanings about pre-American histories, heritage, language, mores, religion, and the related distinct markers of identity (reflected, for instance, in the use of "nationality," which was in currency before "ethnicity"). The academic, theoretical study of ethnicity was derived largely through interpreting race and culture, most notably among social scientists who understood their work to bear immediate implications for resolving racial disparity and social conflict. For this reason, the approaches to studying African Americans that W. E. B. Du Bois advanced fairly early weigh heavily here. Du Bois had studied sociological methods in Germany during the 1880s and applied what was then a new science to interpret America's racial taxonomy. He was the first social scientist to produce a significant body of theory on African Americans as subjects and agents of culture. As early as the 1890s he advanced the then novel claim that being Black meant more than merely being biologically different from Whites or being socially marginal. He would make this argument in a number of venues, but the two most familiar are certainly his address in 1897 to the American Negro Academy, "Conservation of the Races," and his classic *Souls of Black Folk* (1903). Du Bois would eventually abandon ideas of biological racialism while continuing to emphasize that slavery had not emptied America's Africans of any and all things African. He pointed to the presence of African religions during slavery and noted especially the development of the spirituals as evidence for the human capacity of Blacks as bearers and arbiters of culture.[72] His efforts to interpret African American identity in cultural terms

---

[71] Werner Sollors, ed., *Theories of Ethnicity: A Classical Reader* (New York: New York University Press, 1996), x.

[72] W. E. B. Du Bois, "The Conservation of Races," American Negro Academy, *Occasional Papers*, no. 2 (1897) in *Writings*, ed. Nathan Huggins (New York: Library of America, 1986). Du Bois, *The Souls of Black Folk* (1903; reprint, New York: Penguin Books, 1995). W. E. B. Du Bois, *Negro Church* (1903; reprint, Lanham, MD: Rowman & Littlefield, 2003), 4–5. Du Bois is actually the first to argue that religion among enslaved Africans was primarily African-derived, not Christian.

were abetted by several other African American intellectuals, namely Zora Neale Hurston, Carter G. Woodson, and Alain Locke. These scholars began to advance the view that Blacks were distinguished by a specific culture and not cultural depravity. Woodson was especially influential in referencing Africa as the fount and anchor of African American identity.[73]

The scholarly discourse that related racial Blackness to culture and heritage paralleled the rise of Black ethnic religions. As a broader cultural formation, Black ethnic religions infused a vast range of practices and institutions. By the 1960s and 1970s, African Americans would establish religious communities such as Oyotunji African Village that stridently valorized non-Christian Africana religions. These communities produced radical changes in multiple cultural domains, from foodways to the arts (African drumming and dance) to clothing. By fundamentally reshaping the public meaning of racial Blackness, the ethnic heritage paradigm triumphed over what had previously dominated as the racist denial of Black heritage. The parallel between mass culture and the Black intelligentsia continued, moreover, throughout the rise of Black student movements and the subsequent creation of Black studies within US colleges and universities.[74]

Black ethnic religions met with fierce controversy and spirited dissent on several fronts. For instance, the sociologists Nathan Glazer and Daniel Patrick Moynihan mounted a studied response to the radical critiques of Black activists by asserting that African Americans were confused when

---

[73] Vernon Williams, *The Social Sciences and Theories of Race* (Urbana: University of Illinois, 2006), 26–34. Alain Locke, "The Contribution of Race to Culture," in *The Philosophy of Alain Locke: Harlem Renaissance and Beyond*, ed. Leonard Harris (Philadelphia: Temple University Press, 1989), 59–60. George Hutchinson, *The Cambridge Companion to the Harlem Renaissance* (New York: Cambridge University Press, 1997), 59–60. Carter G. Woodson, *African Heroes and Heroines* (Washington, DC: The Associated Publishers, 1939); and Woodson, *The Mis-education of the Negro* (1933; reprint, New York: AMS Press, 1972), 21; Andrew P. Smallwood, *An Afrocentric Study of the Intellectual Development, Leadership Praxis, and Pedagogy of Malcolm X* (Lewiston, NY: Edwin Mellen Press, 2001), 24. Tunde Adeleke, *The Case Against Afrocentrism* (Jackson: University of Mississippi Press, 2009), 80–84. William G. Martin and Michael O. West, *Out of One, Many Africas: Reconstructing the Study and Meaning of Africa* (Urbana: University of Illinois Press, 1999). Katherine Dunham, *The Dances of Haiti; A Study of Their Material Aspect, Organization, Form, and Functions* (n.p., 1938). Zora Neale Hurston, *Mules and Men* (Philadelphia: J. B. Lippincott, 1935).

[74] Kamari Maxine Clarke, *Mapping Yorùbá Networks: Power and Agency in the Making of Transnational Communities* (Durham, NC: Duke University Press, 2004), 108–120. Martha Biondi, *The Black Revolution on Campus* (Berkeley: University of California Press, 2012). Tracey E. Hucks, *Yoruba Traditions and African American Religious Nationalism* (Albuquerque: University of New Mexico Press, 2012).

claiming to possess an ethnic heritage. Assuming that Blacks were distinguished essentially by being socially marginalized and oppressed, the two claimed that during the 1960s, "It is not possible for Negroes to view themselves as other ethnic groups viewed themselves ... because the Negro is only an American, and nothing else. He has no culture and values to guard and protect."[75]

Manifesting the coda of social death, such dissent aimed to undermine the fundamental reconceptualization of racial subjectivity that Black anticolonial theologies advanced. The efforts of academic experts to maintain ethnic heritage as the exclusive preserve of White Americans fallaciously reified ethnicity itself, treating its formation as inert and ahistorical. A veridical account of ethnicity, however, must recognize that ethnicity is neither a natural essence nor an ontology. It is, rather, the historically achieved process of "inventing" identity through imaginative representation. So, for instance, the biological-versus-sociocultural dichotomy for categorizing ethnic identity is illusory because even the "biological" foundations of ethnic categories were already socially encoded; various populations interpreted the body in different ways based on how they had been taught to give meaning to physical (even olfactory) "data." In other words, ethnicity is no more natural or innate than racial identity. It is an invented category made real through the

---

[75] Nathan Glazer and Daniel Patrick Moynihan, *Beyond the Melting Pot: The Negroes, Puerto Ricans, Jews, Italians, and Irish of New York City* (Cambridge, MA: MIT Press, 1963). Ronald Taylor, "Black Ethnicity and the Persistence of Ethnogenesis," *American Journal of Sociology* 84, no. 6 (1979): 1404. Also, see the insightful discussion of Glazer and Moynihan's work by Wilson Jeremiah Moses, *The Wings of Ethiopia: Studies in African-American Life and Letters* (Ames: Iowa State University Press, 1990), 30–31. Glazer and Moynihan issued a second edition of *Beyond the Melting Pot* in 1970 and repeated this distinction between African Americans and White ethnics as a means of explaining what they perceived to be a gross lack of institutional "self-help" among the former. In addition to the minimal distance between middle-class Blacks and the more numerous, impoverished members of the race, these authors opined that the more important barrier to Black self-help was that

> ...the Negro is so much an American, the distinct product of America. He bears no foreign values and culture that he feels the need to guard from the surrounding environment. He insists that the white world deal with his problems because, since he is so much the product of America, they are not *his* problems, but everyone's. Once they become everyone's, perhaps he will see that they are his own, too (53).

Glazer and Moynihan were influenced by E. Franklin Frazier's thesis that African Americans owed any culture they had strictly to America. Glazer contributed the foreword to Frazier's revised edition of *The Negro Family in the United States*, rev. ed. (1939; reprint, Chicago: University of Chicago Press, 1966).

power of representation and perception. People have learned to recognize *signs* of ethnicity.[76]

One should also consider ethnicity's genealogical ties to other rubrics of peoplehood: the nation and race. All forms of peoplehood are constructed as a means of making claims about the past to prescribe how people should behave in the present. Thus, ethnicity, nationalism, and racial identity all function by transforming a useful past into a collective identity that commits those identified to a certain order of things. Like other forms of peoplehood, ethnicity is "a tool persons use against each other ... a central element in ... the maintenance of group solidarity, in the establishment of or challenge to social legitimation." This past, of course, is itself dynamic and inconstant. How long has there been a White race or an American people? Who has populated the field of these referents? From the historical record, it is clear that at different times the peoples included or signified by these peoplehoods have changed, often drastically. Whereas most observers, furthermore, will easily recognize the linkage between nationalism and state boundaries, the correlation between ethnic groups and states is less obvious but nonetheless persistent – the United States has Hispanics, but Mexico and Venezuela do not. Nigeria's Igbos and Yorubas are Blacks in Britain and the United States.[77]

In light of the preceding, it is paramount to understand two major aspects of ethnicity. First, ethnicity has been achieved through historical agencies by encoding and representing human subjects. Second, peoplehood is susceptible to or can manifest as racial taxonomy, and it can reveal the linkage between American exceptionalism and the American history of constructing Whiteness. From a different angle, one can recognize the maxims "Blacks cannot be ethnic" and "ethnicity is unique to White immigrants" not as veridical insights but as ideological claims that denied the capacity for heritage to the very racial group (America's Black descendants of ex-slaves) who had already been denied the status of culture bearers. The taxonomic move adumbrated in "Blacks and ethnics," then, has functioned in a dissembling fashion to represent a relation of

---

[76] Werner Sollors, "Theory of American Ethnicity, or: '? S Ethnic?/TI and Americaniti, de or United (W) States S Sl and Theor?'" *American Quarterly* 33, no. 3 (1981): 257–83. Sollors's article title includes the computer search string he used for his research. "The Invention of Ethnicity," xiii–xiv. Werner Sollors, ed., *Theories of Ethnicity: A Classical Reader* (New York: New York University Press, 1996).

[77] Immanuel Wallerstein, "The Construction of Peoplehood: Racism, Nationalism, Ethnicity," in *Race, Nation, Class: Ambiguous Identities*, ed. Etienne Balibar and Immanuel Wallerstein, trans. Chris Turner (New York: Verso Press, 1991), 78, 84.

power (here, the power to deny the humanizing discourses of culture and history, or "pastness," to African Americans) as an ontologically verifiable truth: Blacks cannot be ethnic.

The rise of Black ethnic religions, rooted in a quest for pre-American heritage, fundamentally subverted the American myth of exceptionalism and Christian triumphalism that had always been at the center of efforts to Christianize African Americans. Never again would African Americans naturalize the idea of the Black church as the timeless essence of Black religious subjectivity. Nor could they look askance at Africa as some pre-cultural anteriority that marked the prelude to their Christian arrival in the West. The hegemonic status of Christianity would certainly not simply vanish like an exposed fraud. But its status was now visibly marked as such – the product of a historical process that had been achieved through terrifying acts of domination and desecration of Black heritage whose originary matrix existed beyond the temporality and spatiality of the Americas.

The Intelligence State and Black Religious Subversion

The triumph of Garveyism as a paradigm-shifting, global movement and the emergence of Black ethnic religions were not the only monumental transformations that occurred among African American religions of the early twentieth century. For the first time the US intelligence state began attending to the activities of Black religious groups. This security complex comprised a range of institutions at the federal level – the Federal Bureau of Investigation (FBI) and the intelligence divisions of the military branches are examples – and at state and municipal levels – the investigative and intelligence divisions of New York City's police department is an enduring example. As an ongoing exercise of sovereign polities, intelligence gathering itself was a state practice with deep historical roots.[78] But during the early twentieth century, the deployment of US intelligence and its foundational role as an essential element of statecraft achieved an unprecedented scale. This pattern persisted globally. The consequences for racial governance in the United States were multiple and far-reaching. The various African American religious groups targeted by intelligence

[78] Ancient polities of course engaged in intelligence gathering. Among the best known examples is the account provided by the ancient Indian author Kautilya who explains the use of spies as a central practice of state bureaucracy in the fourth century BCE. See Kamal Kishore Mishra, *Police Administration in Ancient India* (New Delhi, India: Mittal Publications, 1987), 14.

organizations were classified as enemies of the state – a designation that easily exceeded the category of criminality while also functioning in tandem with it. Under the lens of the state's counterintelligence operations, these religions were deemed threats to national security. They were engaged as especially potent manifestations of grand racial opposition to White power that advanced a politics of Black liberation.[79]

Repression of the Church of God in Christ

The First World War provoked extreme nationalism in the United States, as it did in other countries throughout Europe. This was complicated by the fact that America's White supremacist norms raised a perverse suspicion among US intelligence officials. Could White Americans trust African Americans to remain loyal to the United States when Blacks were not actually permitted the rights and privileges of citizenship? That federal officials gave any thought at all to this matter indicates that White bureaucrats were not blind to the oppressive nature of racial rule. It was easily predictable that anti-Black racism might inspire national treason. The US Army began using its own intelligence agents in 1917 to surveil domestic subjects of different races. Recognizing the utility of Black informants and intelligence agents, the US Army eventually employed Major Walter Loving, an African American, to surveil America's Blacks, to stifle their criticism of American racism, and to intimidate those who publicly condemned state racism. When the dean of Howard University, Kelly Miller, and the *Chicago Defender*'s Robert Abbot lent vocal support to the vigorously growing antilynching campaign during World War I, Loving himself reprimanded and pressured the two into silence. Nothing was to undermine Black loyalty to US militarism that putatively protected democracy abroad.[80]

---

[79] I am describing the distinction between states that practice intelligence gathering, on the one hand, and intelligence states proper. The distinction can be understood in analogy with that made by the historian Ira Berlin between "societies with slaves" and "slave societies." Beyond a certain point, the sheer scale of slaveholding began to shape a broad range of institutions and grammars of social exchange in slaveholding societies, which distinguished them from societies that merely practiced slaveholding. In the same way, intelligence institutions began to emerge during the twentieth century in a way that made them no less central to statecraft than having a national currency or operating a state military. See Loch Johnson, *National Security Intelligence* (Hoboken, NJ: John Wiley & Sons, 2013). Martin Thomas, *Empires of Intelligence: Security Services and Colonial Disorder after 1914* (Berkeley: University of California Press, 2008).

[80] Theodore Kornweibel, *Investigate Everything: Federal Efforts to Compel Black Loyalty During World War I* (Bloomington: Indiana University Press, 2002), 8.

During this era the federal government began to single out certain African American religious groups for harassment as a means of enforcing loyalty. To some degree, myriad American religious movements were put at odds with the country's wartime imperatives. Once the United States formally entered the war in the spring of 1917, President Woodrow Wilson worked aggressively to raise a standing army of sufficient numbers. As a result, American men were subjected to a draft. Wilson permitted exceptions only for conscientious objectors whose religion of formal affiliation was officially opposed to war. Even this exemption meant only that they were not required to participate in combat operations; conscientious objectors were still required to join the military in noncombat capacities such as cooking, construction, and medical service. Wilson's administration recognized the Quakers, Mennonites, and Church of the Brethren as official pacifists. For others, it was nearly impossible to receive exemption.[81]

Roughly two decades earlier, in the 1890s, the nation had witnessed the birth of the largest Black Pentecostal denomination, the Church of God in Christ (COGIC). Its bishop and founder, the Mississippi minister Charles Mason, vocally emphasized the denomination's love for America during World War I. This futile effort was meant to assuage any angst over the church's refusal to participate in war, a consequence of its doctrine of universal love and peace. Injuring or destroying human life, in the words of Mason himself, was "contrary to the teaching of our Lord and Saviour," which meant his church was "adverse to war in all its various forms." Most importantly, Mason and other church leaders instructed the male members of COGIC to avoid the draft on the basis of their pacifist convictions. Mason claimed, however, that pacifism and nationalism need not be played against each other in a zero-sum game. In demonstration of such, he even preached anti-German sermons that interpreted Germany's ruler as the antichrist of Christian scripture. He also encouraged parishioners to purchase Liberty Bonds, and he took credit for raising $3,000 to benefit the federal treasury.[82]

Despite these efforts, Mason and the parishioners of this growing African American denomination met with cynicism, suspicion, and perduring harassment at the hands of local and federal authorities. Local draft boards were staffed exclusively by White men, and these were already committed to maintaining racist rule over the South's African American

---

[81] Ibid., 151, 152.
[82] Ibid., 152.

population. In Mississippi, Mason's home state, although Blacks were the majority of the population, the exigencies of White-minority rule meant brutally restraining even pedestrian expressions of dignity among African Americans. In this environment, COGIC's visibility and articulate stance against militarism merely functioned as evidence for Whites that African Americans were German sympathizers, and their treason needed to be reined in by any means necessary.

When local officials learned that COGIC was defying the draft, Mason and other church leaders were soon arrested. The COGIC minister E. R. Driver of California was also targeted by the FBI's Los Angeles office on suspicion of being a German sympathizer and of obstructing conscription.[83] The popular and charismatic minister had assisted Mason in founding the historic denomination from its earliest beginnings. Of course, he denied any connections to Germany and repeated his claim that his church's theology of pacifism and not German collusion was the impetus for refusing to condone warfare. The Pentecostalist minister would reemerge later as a key figure in the UNIA. Driver's importance in the eyes of African American Pentecostalists, by his own admission, derived from his embrace of the fire-baptized theology that was steadily rising to the forefront of public expressions of American Christianity. But White law enforcement officials and federal authorities rather predictably overdetermined the Blackness of Driver and Mason. In the perspective of these White officials, the Black ministers were simply race men, leaders of the "Negro race" who always already posed a threat to the order of White dominance. Thus, the Los Angeles bureau office was unwavering in claiming that Driver and other COGIC leaders had to be targeted in the interest of national security.[84]

The situation was only exacerbated by mendacious propaganda such as the April 1918 "exposé" by Mississippi's *Vicksburg Post*, which charged Charles Mason with preaching pro-German sermons to incite African Americans to anti-Americanism and to persuade them to oppose the draft.[85] It was even alleged that Mason's brick home in Memphis was purchased with German funds. That no evidence existed for these pernicious allegations or that they contradicted actual facts (Mason's sermons were stridently anti-German) barely mattered to White public

---

[83] Ibid., 153–54.
[84] Theron F. Schlabach and Richard T. Hughes, *Proclaim Peace: Christian Pacifism from Unexpected Quarters* (Urbana: University of Illinois Press, 1997), 63.
[85] Ibid., 63–64.

opinion as the subjects in question were African American. Rather, White officials at federal, state, and local levels focused on COGIC's status as a Black organization, and this shaped the racial calculus of their efforts to implement the imperatives of a security state. The newspaper's claims only further stoked and rationalized White hostility toward the African American denomination. The American Protection League also played an active role in the negative press against COGIC. The organization publicly attributed COGIC's growth to draft dodging. Potential converts allegedly were informed that they could find refuge from military service by seeking membership with the relatively young denomination. The league even went so far as to claim (falsely) that Germans were members of the church and were rapidly infusing Germany money into the congregations.[86]

The African American *New York Age* entered the fray with a more sober approach to journalism and pointedly challenged the ill-founded charges against COGIC. The paper even put military officials and draft boards on the defensive by pointing out that draft boards regularly gave White potential draftees a free pass while drafting many African Americans who should have been exempt from service based on health problems and other issues. It was not COGIC, the editors charged, but the draft boards themselves that merited a federal investigation.[87]

The bureau's case against COGIC came to a head by the late spring of 1918. Bureau Chief A. Bruce Bielaski had been working furiously to build an evidentiary case against Mason and other church leaders. By April 1918 he was ready to move forward with what meager evidence the bureau had been able to collect – an abundance of hearsay, mostly from hostile Whites. When Mason returned to Lexington, Mississippi, in June 1918, he entered a hornet's nest of racial fury. Local Whites were seething with contempt because Blacks were responding to the draft at about half the rate at which Whites were responding. Mississippi's adjutant general had already published the names of seventy African Americans who

---

[86] Not all scholars have been keen to take seriously how White supremacism functioned to generate a particular, consistent pattern of anti-Black repression that sharply differentiated the experiences of African Americans from those of Whites targeted for putative Germany sympathizing. See Mark Ellis, *Race, War, and Surveillance: African Americans and the United States Government During World War I* (Bloomington: Indiana University Press, 2001). Ellis erroneously concludes that repressing African Americans was merely part and parcel of a broader phenomenon that was not significantly related to anti-Black racism.

[87] Theodore Kornweibel, *No Crystal Stair: Black Life and the Messenger, 1917–1928* (Westport, CT: Greenwood Press, 1975), 7–8. Schlabach and Hughes, *Proclaim Peace*, 64.

had failed to appear for the draft. He offered a $50 reward for each (the equivalent of more than $700 in today's dollars). Many of those resisting the draft had claimed as their defense COGIC's official stance of pacifism, which since 1917 had been printed in the church's constitution.[88]

Despite the absence of incriminating evidence against Mason, the bureau arrested him. Ironically, this cruel disregard for due process and basic rights probably saved him from being murdered by a White mob. Agent Eugene Palmer easily perceived that local Whites were not content with seeing Mason merely detained behind bars; they still desired blood vengeance. So he used the sheriff's car to transport Mason from the jail to a train station in Durant, from where he finally traveled to Jackson. There, the bureau had Mason arraigned for obstructing the draft. Mason, of course, pleaded not guilty. One of the well-known White ministers who had joined the Black denomination, W. B. Holt, soon arrived with sufficient funds to help Mason post the $2,000 bond that secured his release. Mason was instructed to appear in federal court later that year.[89]

Meanwhile, things were not looking much better for other COGIC members. Local authorities in Mississippi were tracking down African Americans who had not appeared to honor their draft calls. Once apprehended, they were sent to a military training camp in Arkansas. Ministers and church members in Mississippi and California were interrogated by federal investigators, an experience that was itself intimidating and daunting. After Holt arrived in Mississippi to assist Mason, a leading US military intelligence officer, Colonel Marlborough Churchill, instructed the bureau to begin close surveillance of Holt and Driver (both from California). In addition, a Texas COGIC minister named Henry Kirvin was targeted by the FBI. Kirvin had been described by local critics as an enemy of the US war effort. It was said he taught parishioners that the Red Cross represented the "blood of the Beast" and that they should refrain from donating blood.[90]

In addition, it was rumored he and Mason were selling the legal right to exemption from the military draft for twenty-five cents per month, a privilege they had putatively secured through a visit to Washington. Kirvin was of course interrogated. Hopeful that they might be able to prosecute, the bureau arrested both Holt and Kirvin (Holt was charged with possession of a firearm). Astounded at the charges, Kirvin explained that he

---

[88] Kornweibel, *Investigate Everything: Federal Efforts to Compel Black Loyalty During World War I*, 153–58.

[89] Ibid., 156–58.

[90] Ibid.

and Mason had indeed established a monthly contribution program of twenty-five cents, but solely to create a legal defense fund for COGIC leaders and members who came under prosecution, a necessary response to the expenses generated by federal harassment. The fact that Holt was a sheriff in California, moreover, and traveled with a service weapon as part of his job made no difference to federal prosecutors. Meanwhile, back in California, another US military intelligence official had Driver's telephone tapped in hopes of producing evidence that Driver was collaborating with German interests. Because he was involved in no such activity, of course, the effort proved fruitless.[91]

With the ministers in custody, the bureau set their trial date for the end of October (roughly three months later). When that time arrived, the grand jury declined to indict them. Even with the extended time, not surprisingly, FBI agents had been unable to produce a single shred of actual evidence that the three were guilty of the rather ambitious charges federal prosecutors presented: impersonating federal authorities and operating a conspiracy to obstruct the draft. Even the bureau's key witness, disaffected COGIC minister W. C. Thompson, had claimed only that Mason and Kirvin were religious charlatans, not enemies of the state. The investigators' efforts to confirm allegations that Mason held secretive, late-night pro-German rallies in churches or that he worked otherwise to oppose the war effort could never be substantiated by those who actually attended COGIC churches or had themselves heard Mason's sermons.[92]

By this time, the war was officially winding down. Federal investigators had succeeded in harassing and burdening COGIC with onerous legal fees, unwarranted detainment, and intimidation. In the absence of evidence, however, federal prosecutors were forced to abandon efforts at imprisonment. The COGIC ministers Mason, Holt, and Kirvin were eventually released from jail and returned to their church work. Mason even showed more than a little gall as he transformed the ordeal of persecution into a righteous cause. He claimed it was evidence he had been granted divine protection against the evil wiles of Satan, who sought to hinder him from the work of righteous kingdom building. And from then on, Mason made a point to pepper his sermons with references to his victorious stand against the government's false charges and detainment.[93]

[91] Ibid.
[92] Ibid., 158–63.
[93] Ibid., 162.

Repression of African American Muslims

The FBI's targeting of COGIC, as it turned out, was only a meager sign of greater things to come. Beginning in the 1930s, the FBI began repressing African American Muslims, specifically the Moorish Science Temple of America. J. Edgar Hoover was first alerted to the Moorish Science Temple's status as a racial threat by a report from the FBI's Philadelphia field office, which presented findings from its covert observations of the group. In 1931, during the early phase of its covert surveillance, an FBI field agent interviewed (under false pretenses) J. T. Bey, an African American barber who led the MSTA membership in Reading, Pennsylvania. The agent had already questioned Bey's landlord, a woman who rented to African American boarders. Bey, innocently enough, informed the undercover agent of the movement's proper name (the FBI had referred to them as the Moorish "Shrine" Temple) and explained the fundamental aim of their faith – recovering their Moorish heritage. As Bey made clear, the MSTA – from its membership cards to its organizational practices – rejected the ideology of White supremacism and taught instead that "Moorish" peoples merited treatment on the basis of racial equality. Accordingly, converts were told that displaying their membership cards at local restaurants would ensure they received "every courtesy and equal privileges with other races." On learning this, the FBI concluded that Bey was "a fanatic on the subject of equality for all races." Of striking significance, in fact, is the degree to which the FBI interpreted the religion of these Blacks as pathological by claiming they were mentally imbalanced, delusional, or intellectually weak. The bureau's official stance, moreover, was that the MSTA existed for reasons of propaganda and was not an actual religion. Beyond this, bureau officials were quick to note that "reliable Negroes" not affiliated with the MSTA regarded the Moorish group to be "crazy," "more or less of a joke," and largely irrelevant.[94]

The FBI's vilifying inscription of antiracist theology as fanaticism merely demonstrates how deeply committed the Department of Justice was to the political imperatives of the US racial state. However, insofar as the MSTA opposed White supremacy and resisted the apartheid nature

---

[94] U.S. Department of Justice, F.B.I. file 62-25889, "Moorish Science Temple of America," Part 1a, Rhea Whitley to Director of F.B.I. [J. Edgar Hoover], Internal Memorandum, September 12, 1931, p. 3, available from http://foia.fbi.gov/foiaindex/moortemp.htm, part 1a (accessed November 13, 2013). Ibid., 535. Sylvester A. Johnson "Religion Proper and Proper Religion: Arthur Fauset and the Study of African American Religions," in *The New Black Gods: Arthur Fauset and the Study of African American Religions*, ed. Edward E. Curtis IV and Danielle Brune Sigler (Bloomington: Indiana University Press, 2009), 153–56.

of American society, the FBI was correct in identifying it as antithetical to the US political order. In this sense the movement was subversive; there was no way to reconcile the theology of the MSTA with American apartheid and anti-Black racism.[95] The FBI's racist presumptions about Blacks caused them to interpret the MSTA's critique of "so-called Negro" identity as an absurdity because MSTA members identified as Moorish and not as Negroes. Agents of the bureau claimed that these Blacks were merely masquerading behind a fake identity because they possessed "the appearance and characteristics of a full blooded negro."[96] The MSTA's assertion of ethnic heritage thus functioned as evidence for the FBI that these Moorish Americans were engaged in religious fraud.

The FBI also coordinated with state and local law enforcement to harass and intimidate MSTA leaders who engaged in legal and constitutionally defensible activities. By 1941, for instance, the FBI's infiltration of the MSTA in Springfield, Illinois, led the bureau to focus on Robert Washington, who led a local branch of the MSTA. Washington claimed that a Japanese victory against the United States would bring an end to US racism because the Japanese were an Afro-Asiatic people. The MSTA, after all, invested in the idea of global unity among peoples of color to concertedly oppose Western colonialism and racism. The bureau lacked any legal justification for prosecuting Washington. Washington had no connections with Japan, and he certainly received no foreign material support. The FBI's own investigation, furthermore, confirmed that he derived his income from selling badges and robes to new converts Despite this, the bureau coordinated with the Illinois state attorney general's office to intimidate Washington into silence by telling him he would be prosecuted by the US government for "obtaining money under false pretenses." Washington was overwhelmed by the idea of being targeted by the state of Illinois and the federal government. Quite predictably, he agreed to stop seeking converts in exchange for avoiding imprisonment.[97]

In 1930 another organization, the Lost-Found Nation of Islam, emerged in Detroit as an offshoot of Moorish Science. Roughly one

[95] U.S. Department of Justice, F.B.I. file 62-25889, "Moorish Science Temple of America," Part 1 of 8, Rhea Whitley to Director of F.B.I. [J. Edgar Hoover], memorandum, September 12, 1931, p. 3, available from http://foia.fbi.gov/foiaindex/moortemp.htm, part 1a (accessed June 1, 2013).

[96] Ibid., 2.

[97] U.S. Department of Justice, F.B.I. file 62-25889, "Moorish Science Temple of America," Part 1 of 8, report made at Springfield, Illinois, January 28, 1942, file no. 100–3095, unnumbered page, available from http://foia.fbi.gov/foiaindex/moortemp.htm, part 1a (accessed June 1, 2013).

month before his untimely death, Drew Ali had appointed an energetic and ambitious convert, David Ford-el, as a grand sheik and placed him in charge of the Chicago mosque. The schismatic dissension that emerged in the wake of Ali's death turned violent, culminating in a standoff between several MSTA members and one thousand members of the Chicago police. Ford-el pulled up roots and moved to Detroit, where he started the Allah Temple of Islam to rebuild the floundering MSTA community, changing his name to Wallace D. Fard. His efforts at renewal became the Lost-Found Nation of Islam. In line with the heritage theology of the MSTA, the Nation of Islam (NOI) taught that Islam was the original religion of Blacks.[98] Under Fard's leadership, this fledgling movement would soon win its most valuable convert, Elijah Poole. Poole eventually settled on a new, Islamic surname – Muhammad. He and his wife, Clara Muhammad, took over leadership of the Lost-Found Nation of Islam and developed its theology. Drawing on the teachings of Fard, whose increasingly onerous harassment and detentions by the police led to his being banished from Detroit, the married couple became the de facto leaders of the religious community. In the ensuing years, in fact, Clara Muhammad regularly led and directed the growing community of African American Muslims in Detroit during the times her husband was incarcerated or banned from the city. She proved a capable and efficient administrator, demonstrating moral authority and modeling ideal piety while navigating the threat of state repression.[99]

In addition to the heritage teachings of Moorish Science, the Muhammads also developed an account of racial origins that claimed Western colonialism and slavery were designed by divine beings – a cruel negotiation of sorts among powerful Black gods – to predestine racial rule by Whites, which would be followed by the eventual reawakening and empowerment of Black people. This theology of Black origins emphasized that Blacks were the original people, members of the ancient tribe of Shabazz. As a divine race, they had once ruled the earth as gods. But their power and freedom had been betrayed by one of their members, Yakub, who had developed a lighter-skinned, White race whose destiny was to conquer and enslave the Blacks for four hundred years. The Black divine race had originally inhabited Afro-Asia, where they

[98] Evanzz, *Messenger*, 67–69.
[99] Ibid., 87–105. Claude Andrew Clegg, *An Original Man: The Life and Times of Elijah Muhammad*, 1st ed. (New York: St. Martin's Press, 1997), 42–63. Rosetta E. Ross, *Witnessing and Testifying: Black Women, Religion, and Civil Rights* (Minneapolis, MN: Fortress Press, 2003), 141, 142.

practiced their original religion of Islam. But centuries of subjugation had erased from their memory knowledge of their true identity. Allah, one of the great Black gods, had taken on flesh and had come in the form of Wallace D. Fard to find them in the wilderness of America and return them to their own path. Thus, they were called the Lost-Found Nation of Islam.[100]

Unlike the MSTA, the NOI initially attracted the attention of the FBI in the 1930s because they created private schools for Black children. But the bureau intensified its response to both the MSTA and the NOI after passage of the Selective Service Act of 1940. The law required men between the ages of twenty-one and thirty-five to register for the draft with local boards. By 1942, after US entry into the Second World War, the requirement for draft registration was extended to include all men up to age sixty-five. This was the very time Muhammad began preaching that African Americans, especially Muslims, should refuse to go to war to promote the interests of the US racial state, the very government that exercised racism against them. Many years earlier, in fact, other African American Muslims had already begun to seek relief from the draft because they deeply opposed the war. Drew Ali and his cadre of fellow Moorish leaders taught their followers that it made no sense for African Americans to promote the racist, imperial aims of the US government by taking up arms to fight in the US military. As they saw things, it was not for them to spread the power of the White US government throughout the world while right in the United States of America that same government exercised oppressive rule over Blacks and other peoples of color. For this reason, the Moorish Science Temple of America began to teach followers that they should refuse to comply with the Selective Service Act.[101]

During the summer of 1942, FBI field agents in Kansas City, Kansas, organized mass detentions of local MSTA members who refused to register for the draft. When interrogated, the seventeen Black men who had been arrested all insisted they were Moorish. FBI agents were especially stupefied by the MSTA's Moorish surnames. The only explanation agents could muster was that the men were "religious fanatics" and "mentally unbalanced," opting to "assume either fictitious names or add to their own names in such a manner as to make them meaningless and sound

---

[100] Evanzz, *Messenger*, 80–97.
[101] Mattias Gardell, *In the Name of Elijah Muhammad: Louis Farrakhan and the Nation of Islam* (Durham, NC: Duke University Press, 1996), 44.

somewhat Arabic."[102] Of course, these names were all about being *meaningful*, as the federal investigators themselves unwittingly indicated by recognizing an "Arabic" ethos to this nomenclature. Over the next twenty years, as federal agents were emboldened in their violent strategies of suppression, Moorish Americans would win a small victory; the FBI gradually stopped protesting "fake names" and began to assume some measure of religious legitimacy in Moorish American naming. Despite the initial ire over what they perceived to be the unreasonable audacity of "Negroes" to pretend to have a heritage that extended beyond the bounds of the American experience of slavery, by the 1950s FBI field reports regularly referred to members of the MSTA as "Moorish Americans" and consistently referred to MSTA members by their full Moorish names.[103]

The relationship these movements bore to US nationalism, however, was not simplistic. The MSTA, after all, robustly promoted a loyal claim to US citizenship (the "American" in Moorish-American was purposely nationalist). At the same time, however, the staunch refusal of White US officials to end racist proscriptions against Blacks inspired hope among members of both the MSTA and the NOI that a Japanese victory during the Second World War might bring positive changes to the US racial order. They reasoned that because Japan was a non-White, Asiatic nation that opposed US imperialism, Japanese control of America would mean freedom and equality for Blacks, Native Americans, and other "Asiatic" peoples in the United States.[104]

Political repression of African American Muslims would become a central mission of the FBI through the 1950s and 1960s, and the bureau would justify its engagement with the NOI and MSTA by pointing to a range of specific issues that they described as anti-White hatred, anti-American sentiment, and racial rebellion. Most prominent, however, was the emphasis of African American Muslims on the connections between US Blacks living under White political rule and Muslims and other Afro-Asian peoples throughout the globe suffering the injustice of White colonial rule. Few figures generated more ire among US government officials than Muhammad Ali (formerly Cassius Clay), the famed

---

[102] U.S. Department of Justice, F.B.I. file 62-25889, "Moorish Science Temple of America," Part 1b of 8, S. Culbertson to D.M. Ladd, memorandum, July 24, 1942, p.1, available from http://foia.fbi.gov/foiaindex/moortemp.htm (accessed June 1, 2013).

[103] U.S. Department of Justice, F.B.I. file 62-25889, "Moorish Science Temple of America," Part 1b [unnumbered] p. 8, available from http://foia.fbi.gov/foiaindex/moortemp.htm (accessed May 24, 2014).

[104] Gardell, *In the Name of Elijah Muhammad*, 44.

African American professional boxer who converted to Islam. Ali resisted being drafted into the US military and inspired significant public support among Blacks. He openly defended his decision as a refusal to promote a war of colonial occupation by the United States against non-White peoples in Vietnam.[105]

In retaliation for their opposition to the military draft and their critique of US imperialism, the FBI and local police departments subjected members of both the NOI and MSTA to mass arrests, detentions, and imprisonment. So many men in the MSTA were arrested and detained by local and federal agents, in fact, that the group survived primarily because of the women who were members of the Moorish American community. To its credit, the MSTA from the start had embraced gender parity in its leadership, a fact that facilitated the women's ability to maintain the movement. The FBI also planted federal agents in the MSTA and the NOI, at first recruiting White police officers who "blacked up." Because this failed to deceive MSTA members, the bureau finally agreed to use African Americans, hiring police officers as its first Black agents. These agents posed as religious followers to gather intelligence, destabilize, and subvert the organization.[106]

Through these early tactics, the FBI engineered increasing repression against African Americans who embraced the anticolonial vision of the UNIA and those participating in the religions of Black ethnic heritage that emerged through the paradigm of diasporic racial Blackness that the UNIA promoted. In doing so, the FBI was cultivating both a practice and rationality of security that manifested an expanding intelligence state as an integral weapon for sustaining the colonial relation of power at the heart of US government practices. As certain African American religions continued to promote anticolonialism and liberationist paradigms to counter the politics of a White racial state, this repression and its impact on the larger complex of race and power would be expanded on an unprecedented scale.

---

[105] For an excellent treatment of this issue and its implications for how African American Muslims more broadly conceived of a "Muslim International," see Sohail Daulatzai, *Black Star, Crescent Moon: The Muslim International and Black Freedom beyond America* (Minneapolis: University of Minnesota Press, 2012).

[106] U.S. Department of Justice, F.B.I. file 62-25889, "Moorish Science Temple of America," Part 1 of 8, report made at Springfield, Illinois, January 28, 1942; file no. 100-3095, unnumbered page, available from http://foia.fbi.gov/foiaindex/moortemp.htm, part 1a (accessed June 1, 2013). U.S. Department of Justice, Federal Bureau of Investigation, SAC letter no. 55-43, June 28, 1955, unnumbered page, available from http://foia.fbi .gov/foiaindex/nation_of_islam.htm, part 1 (accessed June 1, 2013).

7

Fundamentalism, Counterintelligence, and the "Negro Rebellion"

Since the World War I years, the FBI had explicated its attention to communism as a particular threat to national security. With the onset of the Cold War, the variety of US intelligence institutions – the FBI, the CIA, the Division of Army Intelligence, etc. – promoted the specter of communism as the supreme enemy of the American people. These federal agencies drew on Woodrow Wilson's forceful argument that America had to take leadership in keeping the world safe for democracy to formulate an analysis of freedom and economic power that rendered "godless communism" the primal form of evil that threatened the American way of life. In this context, American Christians began to vie for a foothold in a rapidly shifting terrain as previous claims about power, values, religion, and American identity were forced into new postures of meaning.

It is especially relevant to note the tension between two genealogies of American Christianity: the social gospel and evangelical fundamentalism. The social gospel movement was characterized by its emphasis on worldly activism to address economic suffering, particularly in the form of urban poverty, homelessness, hunger, and unemployment. Its roots of social gospel Christianity lay with the liberal tradition of Christian theology in the late nineteenth century. Theologians such as Adolf von Harnack, whose popular *What Is Christianity* appeared in English in 1901, sifted through what he called the husks of fantastic miracle stories, unscientific claims such as riding on clouds, and other aspects of ancient worldviews in the Bible to grasp the essential "kernel" of Christianity. That essence, said Harnack, was *love*. To accept the Christian gospel was to embrace the universal "fatherhood" of God and the universal "brotherhood" of humanity. Salvation lay in creating the kingdom of God on earth, which meant making the world conform to the will of God – peace, justice, and equality on earth right now, for the living, not the dead. Living the Christian gospel, in other words, meant perfecting the present world by ameliorating social suffering. As global financiers such as John D. Rockefeller (1839–1937), Andrew Carnegie (1835–1919), and J. P. Morgan (1867–1943) accumulated unprecedented levels of individual wealth, the rise of urbanization simultaneously witnessed the conspicuous display of brazen squalor. Many Christians such as Jane Addams (founder of the Hull House), Walter Rauschenbusch, Reverdy C. Ransom, Dorothy Day, and Anna Julia Cooper staked their public careers on reclaiming the essence of Christian identity in these terms. In their view, the central problem of the Church was that of human suffering.[1]

Orthodoxy and the Cold War

By the 1920s, however, another Christian movement had taken root in the United States, that of evangelical fundamentalism. It was explicitly a response to liberal theology, and it asserted that the problem facing the Church was not human suffering. The enemy, instead, was the institutional force of de-Christianization (also read as secularization) that promoted evolutionary theory over creationism and that denied any privileged sanction for the Bible in public education; racy films and music that flaunted loose morals and casual sex; and entertainment houses that competed with church attendance. Evangelicalism thus became the central means of promoting the interests of Christian fundamentalism. For this wing of Christianity, the gospel was not defined by saving society from temporal suffering; its essence was spiritual salvation – saving souls.[2] By the Cold War years, it was patently clear that evangelical fundamentalism

---

[1] Calvin Sylvester Morris, *Reverdy C. Ransom: Black Advocate of the Social Gospel* (Lanham, MD: University Press of America, 1990). Eleanor J. Stebner, *The Women of Hull House: A Study in Spirituality, Vocation, and Friendship* (Albany: SUNY Press, 1997). Mark Zwick and Louise Zwick, *The Catholic Worker Movement: Intellectual and Spiritual Origins* (Mahwah, NJ: Paulist Press, 2005).

[2] Joel A. Carpenter, *Revive Us Again: The Reawakening of American Fundamentalism* (New York: Oxford University Press, 1997). Nancy F. Cott, *Public Vows: A History of Marriage and the Nation* (Cambridge, MA: Harvard University Press, 2009). Michael Lienesch, *In the Beginning: Fundamentalism, the Scopes Trial, and the Making of the Antievolution Movement* (Chapel Hill: University of North Carolina Press, 2007). John Gresham Machen, *Christianity and Liberalism* (Grand Rapids, MI: Wm. B. Eerdmans, 2009).

was winning the upper hand. Dorothy Day and Walter Rauschenbusch may have been popular in the 1920s and 1930s. But the prosperity of the 1950s and 1960s marginalized attention to poverty and decentered from public attention the Great Depression years and the mitigating measures of Franklin Delano Roosevelt's administration of socially conscious reforms. In their place emerged a boom in private ownership, rising salaries, low unemployment, and unprecedented access to higher education. American banks were riding a rising tide of profits. In this environment, the leading figures of American Christianity were Billy Graham and Oral Roberts. The earliest wave of megachurches, animated by the powerful thrust of evangelical fundamentalism, was already portending the marginalization of more liberal, mainline denominations.[3]

More importantly, this more militant form of American Christianity, born from a sense of besiegement by anti-Christian forces, easily absorbed and embraced the bromides of anti-communism that defined the Cold War era. Communism was godless, so the reasoning went, but America was a Christian nation. In this environment, the champions of evangelical fundamentalism were easy victors in the race to articulate an ultranationalist Christian identity that celebrated laissez-faire capitalism, rugged individualism, free markets, and the robust, forward-deployed militarism that was needed to defend these freedoms.

A New Civil Religion

In 1949, a group of businessmen in Los Angeles, California, invited the young White revivalist Billy Graham to lead a three-week rally devoted to seeking new Christian converts. At age thirty, Graham was already professionally established as president of Northwestern College in Minneapolis, Minnesota.[4] Other evangelists had passed through the Los Angeles region, and local ministers were intent on building the momentum of revivalism to turn the city to Jesus. Their organization was named Christ for Greater Los Angeles, and in a general sense what they were

---

[3] David Aikman, *Billy Graham: His Life and Influence* (Nashville, TN: Thomas Nelson, 2007). Lyle W. Dorsett, *Billy Sunday and the Redemption of Urban America* (Grand Rapids, MI: Wm. B. Eerdmans, 1991). Nancy Gibbs and Michael Duffy, *The Preacher and the Presidents: Billy Graham in the White House* (New York: Hachette Digital, 2007). Michael G. Long, *The Legacy of Billy Graham: Critical Reflections on America's Greatest Evangelist* (Louisville, KY: Westminster John Knox Press, 2008). Steven P. Miller, *Billy Graham and the Rise of the Republican South* (Philadelphia: University of Pennsylvania Press, 2011).

[4] Samuel Schuman, *Seeing the Light: Religious Colleges in Twenty-First-Century America* (Baltimore: Johns Hopkins University Press, 2010), 180.

planning was nothing out of the ordinary. For several years, organizing revivals in strategically selected cities had been a tried-and-true formula for Christian evangelicals. Indeed, in the postwar years, America's White evangelicals worked aggressively to market born-again religion, frequent church attendance, and biblical literalism as the authentic mode of Christian experience. As things turned out, however, this specific revival organized by the Los Angeles group of ministers proved uniquely pivotal and took on dimensions beyond their initial ambitions. Graham was to spend three weeks preaching to locals in a big tent revival. Until that time, he had experienced only moderate success as a revivalist. But that was about to change.[5] Beneath looming tents pitched on a large parking lot, Graham hammered home his gospel message of personal piety and the need for repentance. In conventional evangelical terms, the stakes were already high enough – only radical submission to a personal savior would save the lost from a future of endless torture and punishment in a literal Hell. But world events soon delivered a unique opportunity to Graham.

Graham's revival meeting kicked off on Sunday, September 25, 1949. Two days earlier, on September 23, 1949, US president Harry Truman had announced that the Soviet Union had successfully tested an atomic bomb, its first. Despite the fact that the United States had approximately 200 atomic bombs stockpiled, the nation's military officials and weapons scientists were chiefly concerned with the prospect that the Soviet Union might succeed in creating a hydrogen bomb and thereby gain a strategic advantage over the US American military. During the months that followed, nuclear scientists, military officials, legislators, and White House staff anxiously developed strategic responses to the Soviet Union's military strategies.[6]

In the wake of Truman's announcement, Graham quickly seized on the news to strike fear and sobriety into his audience. In his opening sermon, Graham stared into the sea of several thousand faces under the revival tent and intoned with gravity, "People know that time is running out. Now that Russia has the atomic bomb the world is in an armament race driving us to destruction." Los Angeles, he told them, was the third largest city in the United States and was a primary target of Soviet aggression. Would their fate be sealed? Were they now doomed? According to

[5] Joel A. Carpenter, *Revive Us Again: The Reawakening of American Fundamentalism* (New York: Oxford University Press, 1997), 212.

[6] Richard Rhodes, *The Making of the Atomic Bomb* (New York: Simon & Schuster, 1986), 767–69.

Graham, they were ... if they continued on their wayward path ignoring the demands of Christian faith. Paganism, materialism, and humanism had all taken their turn in previous times at assaulting the spiritual plight of humankind. Now, it was communism. Graham, in fact, would go on to emphasize that the only thing capable of stopping a third world war was a religious revival of the sort he was attempting to create. "Guns are not enough to stop Communism. Only God can hold it back."[7] Accordingly, it seemed, the destiny of the individual and that of Western civilization itself were now bound together by the rugged cord of a single fate.

Graham skillfully composed a political theology that caught the attention of media magnate William Hearst. Hearst owned several media outlets, including the *Los Angeles Times* and *Life* magazine. Hearst was himself a staunch anti-communist, and he was shrewd enough to recognize in Graham a likely medium for a timely message. He instructed his reporters to devote generous coverage to Graham. The resulting media blitz and sustained reporting turned Graham from a moderately effective evangelist to a veritable celebrity as other media companies followed Hearst's lead in an effort to match coverage of a phenomenon that was at least in part Hearst's creation.[8] Night after night, the organizers of the "Canvas Cathedral" rally were forced to turn away hundreds of attendees because the tents could not accommodate more than 6,000 people. So, the rally was extended, eventually running for eight weeks. By November 20, 1949, at the rally's end, Graham had converted 3,000 attendees and preached to 350,000. Within the space of a few weeks, he had been catapulted to national fame and had achieved an unrivaled status.[9]

One might say the mix of revivalism, the savvy of the Graham enterprise, and the race of empires defined by the competition between the Soviet Union and the United States created a perfect storm, an accidental brew of imperial religion. The result was a distinct shift in the nation's religious culture whereby Christian nationalism functioned to promote an explicit form of evangelical fundamentalism exemplified by Graham. But it also became diffuse throughout Anglo-American Christianity. In

---

[7] "Evangelist Opens Revival Crusade," *Los Angeles Times*, September 26, 1949. "Evangelist Will Remain Silent on Cohen Matter," *Los Angeles Times*, November 16, 1949, 28.

[8] Frank Lambert, *The Founding Fathers and the Place of Religion in America* (Princeton, NJ: Princeton University Press, 2003), 294.

[9] Aikman, *Billy Graham*, 60–66. Roger Bruns, *Billy Graham: A Biography* (Westport, CT: Greenwood Publishing Group, 2004), 28–32. "Evangelist Opens Revival Crusade," *Los Angeles Times*, September 26, 1949. "Evangelist Will Remain Silent on Cohen Matter," *Los Angeles Times*, November 16, 1949, 28.

this environment, even military strategists and policy advisors began to believe that conflicts inherent in the competition between empires were rooted in theological differences, forming the binary of "godless communism" versus "Christian America." In fact, as early as 1950, US national policy directors were fusing their military and political views with fundamentalist Christianity's Manichaean framework. The result was a theological perspective operating at the highest levels of the US state, and it conditioned certain realities of US imperialism within which African American religions would operate.

The events of 1949 forced a particular imperative upon the National Security Council (NSC). Because of the Soviet Union's nuclear test, US pride in a nuclear advantage over the Soviet Union had been decimated in one explosive instant. All eyes were now on the question of military expansion. National security policy would require far greater coordination and uniformity. In the wake of Truman's announcement that the Soviet Union had produced an atomic bomb, the United States joined other key Western nations in creating the North Atlantic Treaty Organization (NATO) to counter Soviet military power. The United States also structured more aggressive financial assistance for Western Europe. In this context, the US State Department grabbed the reins by implementing a comprehensive review of military and political policy. Paul Nitze, who led policy planning at the State Department, brokered the agreement for an ad hoc committee to study current conditions and to produce an advisory report. The resulting document, entitled "NSC 68: United States Objectives and Programs for National Security," proved decisive and urged President Truman to pursue the rapid and ambitious buildup of US military capacity as the surest means to thwarting the threat of Soviet dominance.[10]

It exemplified in pronounced terms the religious manifestations of US empire within statecraft. The report also made visible the religious dimensions of US imperial ideology. For instance, the NSC urged Truman to consider a major factor that distinguished the Soviet threat from any previous one: the Soviet Union was "animated by a new fanatic faith, antithetical to our own." This basic reality, the council urged, drove the Soviets to impose their "absolute authority" in a quest for world dominion. Without undertaking "new and fateful decisions," not only the West but civilization itself would be destroyed. Writing under the aegis

---

[10] Curt Cardwell, *NSC 68 and the Political Economy of the Early Cold War* (New York: Cambridge University Press, 2011), 193–200.

of the United States as a formal apartheid state, the council deployed Manichaean terms to hammer home the message of an apocalyptic show-down between ultimate principles of freedom (the principle on which the United States operated) and "slavery," the chief impetus behind the Kremlin's designs. The American nation's devotion to freedom produced its "marvelous diversity" and "deep tolerance," a claim that would have shocked the fifteen million Blacks, American Indians, Hispanics, and other non-White peoples reeling under the injustice of the reservation system, the brutal violence of lynchings, racial deportations, and a com-prehensive legal system of apartheid. Nor did the United States entertain any will to power, according to the report. In contrast to the Kremlin's fierce vision of totalitarianism, the United States attracted a following by the auspicious light of its devotion to freedom. In antithesis to US free-dom, Soviet absolutism was "a perverted faith" that compelled its follow-ers to find existential meaning "in serving the ends of the system." In this manner, the Kremlin's totalitarian ethos was apotheosized – it "becomes God, and submission to the will of God becomes submission to the will of the system. It is not enough to yield outwardly to the system ... for the spirit of resistance and the devotion to a higher authority might then remain, and the individual would not be wholly submissive."[11]

In this way, the NSC also distinguished US imperial ambitions from those of the Soviet Union. The Western nation's aggressive response to the Soviet Union was no mere political calculation of mundane origins born of avarice. It was, rather, the outcome of an ineluctable calculus rooted in the very structure of moral virtues, ultimate principles, and religious authority. By the very nature of freedom and slavery, the United States as an instrumental polity of freedom was obligated to act. Or, as the committee urged in its report, "What is new, what makes the con-tinuing crisis, is the polarization of power which now inescapably con-fronts the slave society with the free." In language that would parallel twenty-first-century discourses of antiterrorism, the NSC identified the Kremlin's policy as an expression of "a peculiarly virulent blend of hatred and fear." That is, the United States was dealing with an enemy steeped in fanatical zeal whose essential constitution was ultimately religious in nature. Furthermore, because Soviet authoritarianism was an actual faith with its own god (the totalitarian state), the committee recognized

[11] "NSC 68: United States Objectives and Programs for National Security (April 14, 1950): A Report to the President Pursuant to the President's Directive of January 31, 1950." http://www.fas.org/irp/offdocs/nsc-hst/nsc-68.htm (accessed April 25, 2012).

that the Kremlin's authoritarianism offered the millions of colonized and destitute proletariat "refuge from anxieties, bafflement, and insecurity." And it was precisely here that the United States held an opportunity; it should direct its own message of freedom to these same vulnerable masses, a call that would be ably heeded by the US Department of Defense's units for psychological warfare operations. Given the "absence of order" among the nations of the world, history itself now forced on the United States the responsibility of leadership over the free world. This proposed US world leadership in weapons proliferation would "awaken and arouse the latent spiritual energies of free men everywhere," unifying the forces of freedom and virtue throughout the free world.[12]

Thus, the NSC shared with other state entities a burgeoning penchant for wedding theology to national policy. As a result, they skillfully and persuasively rendered the actual interests of power at stake among polities as the manifestation of "fundamental values" that were "inherent in our way of life." The issue, for this reason, was articulated not in terms of power and material interests but in terms of ideas and ultimate values – moral virtue versus evil – inscribing a clash of civilizations.

This shift toward an explicit alliance of theology and empire created a major advantage for the foreign policy of the US security state. Why? There now existed an explicit justification for the United States to administer satellite states and to implement murderous policies (e.g., in Latin America) in Third World countries. Moreover, this rationale had populist potency. The interests of evangelical fundamentalism were now openly and conspicuously wed to those of militarism and empire. Rather than being on the defensive, evangelical fundamentalism was now strategically positioned with the upper hand in the public arena. Critics of imperialism, by contrast, were now on the defensive. The presumptions of American civil religion – purporting that revivalist Christianization and aggressive US militarism were twin episodes of divine will – began to function as common sense. And those who opposed this imperial vision of religion seemed inexplicable, bizarre, or veritable enemies of the United States.

Graham embodied a new development in the ensuing years that signaled a stunning, open alliance of Christian fundamentalism and American politics at the highest levels of government. While the Cold War fueled an expanding nuclear arms race and the proliferation of US satellite states, the reciprocity of empire and fundamentalism qua public religion – indeed, as the civil religion – grew more earnest. When the

[12] Ibid.

election season of 1952 revealed that Dwight D. Eisenhower was unbaptized, Billy Graham strategically intervened, courting the president's attention and leading Eisenhower to become baptized in the Presbyterian denomination. What might easily have been a trivial matter fifty years earlier became an urgent public issue. It now seemed that only a president adhering to the dictates of born-again religion was suited to the task of leading the Christian nation in the Cold War against godless communism.[13]

This confluence of religious militancy and strident political promotion of an American Christian nationalism became particularly evident during the summer of 1954, when US legislators briskly and with rare bipartisanship passed legislation that modified the US American Pledge of Allegiance to the flag, adding the phrase "under God" to render an affirmation of the increasingly commoditized claim that the United States was "one nation under God, indivisible" The Michigan Senator Homer Ferguson expressed the conviction of most supporters when he boasted that modifying the pledge was "important because it highlights one of the real fundamental differences between the free world and the Communist world." That difference encoded Christianity as the religion of a particular *civilization*, of a polity whose genealogy was steeped in the rubrics and cultural logics of a Western people. And this civilization, born of a Christian noetics that rationalized corporatized capitalism and putatively free markets, was stridently at odds with the nationalized economics of Soviet communism.[14] Any who doubted that political Christianity was significantly expanding its influence on the state might have been given pause by the appearance of Vice President Richard Nixon at Graham's Yankee Stadium revival on July 20, 1957. More than 100,000 Americans were in attendance. For Nixon, this was an opportunity to seal his association with the nation's most powerful symbol of born-again religion. With his eyes already set on a future presidency, Nixon correctly calculated that his strategic appearance would play well with the nation's growing evangelical electorate.[15]

---

[13] Jason W. Stevens, *God-Fearing and Free: A Spiritual History of America's Cold War* (Cambridge, MA: Harvard University Press, 2011), 72. Gibbs and Duffy, *The Preacher and the Presidents.*

[14] Martin E. Marty, *Modern American Religion* (Chicago: University of Chicago Press, 1986), 3: 301.

[15] Bruns, *Billy Graham*, 78. Stephen D. Johnson and Joseph B. Tamney, *The Political Role of Religion in the United States* (Boulder, CO: Westview Press, 1986), 83.

Fundamentalism and Civil Rights

During the 1920s, the Scopes trial became a focal point in a larger social struggle over the public meaning of Christianity as Christian fundamentalists targeted evolution as a major threat to the nation's Christian identity. On a similar scale but over a greater span of time, the civil rights movement of the 1950s and 1960s likewise became a site of struggle for control of Christianity's public meaning. This emerged, of course, as one dimension of a larger complex. Anti-communism itself – the Cold War – functioned as the chief arena for this fight. But one civil rights organization in particular, the Southern Christian Leadership Conference (SCLC), gained international prominence and embodied the most formidable challenge to the fundamentalist orthodoxy championed by Graham and his religious allies. Evangelical fundamentalism, in fact, was a central factor in defining the social context of civil rights activism and discourse. Insofar as the civil rights movement constituted a *religious* rebellion, it drew on the energies of revivalism and the tremendous power of religious zeal to empower defiance of so-called worldly power. At the same time, the new alliance between revivalism and fundamentalism created serious tensions that eventually led to schism among African Americans.

In 1972, Gayraud Wilmore published his *Black Religion and Black Radicalism*. Wilmore was a central figure in the Black theology movement of the 1960s and 1970s. He argued that the origins of the Black church lay with a prophetic, radical critique of social injustice. He also asserted that African American Christianity was paradigmatically marked by paramount resistance to slavery, racism, and poverty. By contrast, Wilmore claimed, Black churches during the twentieth century had become socially conservative, and the vital tradition of prophetic critique had been exchanged for an ossified conformity with the status quo. According to Wilmore, the radicalism of African American Christianity had waned continually over the course of one century since slavery had been abolished.[16]

It was no accident that Wilmore put forward such a grim assessment of Black churches. The Black theology movement, after all, targeted not merely the racism of White Christians but also the fundamentalism that had become popular among a growing number of African American churches. Wilmore, like James H. Cone, James H. Evans, and Katie Cannon, sought to prod Black churches to recapture something

---

[16] Gayraud Wilmore, *Black Religion and Black Radicalism* (Garden City, NY: Doubleday, 1972).

he claimed they had lost – an unflinching devotion to social justice in a struggle against racism and structural economic disparity. The actual history of African American Christian theology was more complicated than Wilmore's declension narrative suggested, however. Since the early 1900s, African American critics such as Carter G. Woodson and W. E. B. Du Bois had repeatedly chastened Black churches for devoting only slight attention to social problems and prioritizing spiritual concerns. The golden age whose passing Wilmore lamented was not nearly as progressive as he claimed. But he was right to discern that a major shift was occurring during the 1960s. Fundamentalism was rapidly becoming a powerful dynamic in Black churches, and it was quickly shaping the dynamics of liberationist activism.[17]

The creation of the Progressive National Baptist Convention is a case in point. The SCLC had established itself with a mission of redeeming "the soul of America." This motto in every sense manifested the social gospel imperative of promoting social justice as the very essence of Christianity. At the time, however, the vast majority of African American churches embraced not the social gospel but the increasingly familiar fundamentalist doctrines of the atoning death of Jesus; salvation of a soul, affording an eternal existence in a celestial realm; and escape from torment in a literal hell administered by Satan himself. During the very height of SCLC's activism, in fact, evangelical fundamentalism was benefiting from a symbiotic relationship with the theological tenor of US Cold War policy. Pundits nationwide repeated the mantra that the US was a Christian nation valiantly resisting the threat of communist atheism. Fundamentalist Christian theologians like Jerry Falwell and Billy Graham were reshaping the landscape of American Christianity with an ever-expanding devotion to biblical literalism and a sharp critique of liberal theology, which they believed constituted an unforgivable compromise with secularism.[18] Falwell was especially representative of this trend when he identified communism and theological liberalism as twin threats to America's greatness and to the Christian faith. In fact, during the 1961

---

[17] Barbara Dianne Savage, *Your Spirits Walk Beside Us: The Politics of Black Religion* (Cambridge, MA: Harvard University Press, 2009).

[18] On Billy Graham's relationship with King, see Rufus Burrows, "Graham, King, and the Beloved Community," in *The Legacy of Billy Graham*, ed. Michael Long. See also Nancy Gibbs and Michael Duffy, *The Preacher and the Presidents: Billy Graham in the White House*, 1st ed. (New York: Center Street, 2007). Cecil Bothwell, *The Prince of War: Billy Graham's Crusade for a Wholly Christian Empire* (Ashville, NC: Brave Ulysses Books, 2007).

SCLC campaign in Selma, Alabama, Falwell audaciously inveighed against the brand of Christianity promoted by SCLC's chief executive, Martin Luther King, Jr. As Falwell retorted, "I must personally say that I do question the sincerity and non-violent intentions of some civil rights leaders such as Dr. Martin Luther King Jr., Mr. James Farmer, and others, who are known to have left-wing associations." Falwell employed the "left-wing" euphemism to brand King as a communist and to render his social gospel theology as consonant with the very enemy of liberalism that was at war with "true" Christianity – that is, fundamentalism.[19]

Evangelical fundamentalism was by no means alien to African American Christianity, however. It was, rather, a hallmark of the National Baptist Convention, USA, which was the largest of the independent African American denominations. Even Martin Luther King Jr., who grew up in a long tradition of socially committed African American ministers, was reared on the spiritual bread of fundamentalist doctrine. As he reflected years later, it was through studying religion and philosophy in college that he began to retreat from fundamentalism. King felt the "shackles of fundamentalism" dissolve as he was challenged to recognize the many "legends and myths" of the Bible he had accepted literally lacked any basis in history. In fact, like many other students of theology, King weathered a storm of doubts about the very validity of his religious tradition. Under the tutelage of professors such as Benjamin Mays and George Kelsey, however, he was able to wed his Christian identity to the concern for social justice that had shaped him since his youth. In 1948, King entered Crozer Theological Seminary in Chester, Pennsylvania. There he was introduced to social gospel theology like that of Walter Rauschenbusch, the bold optimism of which he found ably tempered by the Christian realism of Reinhold Niebuhr. King graduated from Crozier in 1951 and matriculated into the Boston University School of Theology that same fall. He earned his PhD within four years, and he began his first full-time appointment as pastor of the Dexter Avenue Baptist Church in Montgomery, Alabama, in April 1954. King's training at Boston University enabled him to develop a constructive theological framework that could harness Christianity's prophetic potential, resist fundamentalism, and engage rigorously with the very complicated social problems that he now recognized as the definitive field of Christian labor.[20]

---

[19] James M. Washington, ed., *Testament of Hope: The Essential Writings and Speeches of Martin Luther King, Jr.* (San Francisco: HarperSanFrancisco, 1991), xiv–xv.

[20] Martin Luther King and Clayborne Carson, *The Autobiography of Martin Luther King, Jr* (New York: Intellectual Properties Management in association with Warner Books, 1998), 15–49.

Of course, King's theological training was occurring during the very same years that evangelical fundamentalism was reshaping civil religion in ways that emboldened the imperial impetus of the Cold War. Although his own personal trajectory was set on a collision course with the public power of fundamentalism, the same could not be said of African American Christians broadly. At the time, Joseph Harrison Jackson was president of the National Baptist Convention USA, King's denominational home. Jackson was devoted to the fundamentalist revivalism that Graham and Falwell promoted. Although Jackson was unquestionably opposed to White supremacism, he eventually found himself deeply at odds with the explicitly political theology that SCLC was promoting.

Interestingly enough, when the Montgomery Improvement Association (MIA) was in desperate need of funding to maintain its boycott that ran from 1955 to 1956, Jackson supported his congregation's efforts to assist the organization; the funds donated helped the MIA purchase two vehicles for providing transportation to Blacks boycotting Montgomery's buses.[21] It seems unlikely, in fact, that his opposition to civil rights was unrelated to the personal conflicts that arose from an internal dispute over the denomination's leadership. Nevertheless, Jackson's theological convictions were foundational to his repudiation of SCLC's controversial foray into politics and its increasing reliance on strategically violating segregation law. He was convinced that civil disobedience and direct action strategies were inappropriate, too confrontational, and un-Christian since they involved churches in the worldly affairs of politics and illegal activity. Jackson also resented the fact that SCLC had conflated its political activism with the primary ethos and mission of the Christian church. In his view, the church was a spiritual organization, not a political instrument.[22]

This theological divide within the largest independent Black Christian denomination soon fostered a deep schism. In 1957, the very year of SCLC's creation, Jackson expelled from the denomination ten ministers who had challenged his tenure as president on the grounds that he had violated the presidential term limit in the bylaws. The parties eventually went to court, and Jackson emerged victorious. Meanwhile, King and his father, along with SCLC supporters such as Ralph Abernathy and Benjamin Mays, tried to back the social gospel minister Gardner

---

[21] Peter J. Paris, *Black Leaders in Conflict: Joseph H. Jackson, Martin Luther King, Jr., Malcolm X*, and *Adam Clayton Powell, Jr.* (Cleveland, OH: Pilgrim Press, 1978), 20–26.
[22] Ibid.

C. Taylor as the denomination's new president. They hoped to transform the denomination to one that openly embraced the social gospel and thereby bring concerted denominational support to an insurgent civil rights movement. But Jackson and his supporters had no intention of backing down. At the 1960 Philadelphia meeting, the nominating committee announced Jackson as the president and, despite protests, adjourned without a ballot election. The opposing faction, which King supported, stayed to conduct an election in spite of the nominating committee's unilateral decision, and Taylor won.[23]

Once again, the parties went to court. In the meantime, both Jackson's and Taylor's supporters claimed a legitimate right to lead the denomination. Over the next year, the denomination had two administrations. In 1961, at the following annual convention, a physical altercation erupted after Jackson's group locked Taylor's supporters out of the general assembly. Taylor's supporters tried to force their way in, and the two groups soon came to blows. Taylor and King eventually brokered a reconciliation, but the fragile truce quickly unraveled when Jackson removed Taylor and his supporters from their elected offices. It now seemed even less likely that the denomination would embrace SCLC's social gospel theology, its political activism, and its controversial but highly effective tactics of nonviolent resistance and civil disobedience.[24]

In a game-changing response, Taylor's supporters created a new denomination in 1961, the Progressive National Baptist Convention. It was this new denomination and not the much larger National Baptist Convention that would lend unabashed support to the civil rights movement and Black Power. These "progressives" explicitly rejected fundamentalism and promoted the social gospel as the essential manifestation of Christianity. They were among the first of the nation's Christian bodies to condemn the war against Vietnam. And they connected the imperative of social justice to a broad range of human rights issues. The new denomination thus emerged in sharp contrast to the more dominant Christian fundamentalism that thrived in the Cold War era.[25]

Although it is clear that a struggle of institutional leadership ignited the fiery schism among these African American Christians, it is imperative to observe the deep theological chasm that created the conflict among potential leaders of the NBC denomination. The chief issue, in

[23] C. Eric Lincoln and Lawrence H. Mamiya, *The Black Church in the African-American Experience* (Durham, NC: Duke University Press, 1990), 36–37.
[24] Ibid., 36–37. Paris, *Black Leaders in Conflict*, 20–26.
[25] Paris, *Black Leaders in Conflict*, 20–26.

other words, was not administrative procedure but the public meaning of Christianity. Both parties understood they were fighting to advance a particular vision for their institutional faith and the stance the nation's largest Black denomination would occupy in response to a tumultuous fight for racial justice. Would their understanding of the gospel be rooted in social justice? Or in the imperatives of evangelical fundamentalism? The bitter dissension that emerged between the Taylor and Jackson factions, unfortunately, only further alienated Black Christian fundamentalists from the civil rights movement. So, although individual members of Black church supported the civil rights movement in myriad ways, denominational leaders refused to lend support at an institutional level.

Advocates of the social gospel, on the other hand, found that the ground beneath their feet had shifted entirely. Their concern for economic inequality already predisposed them to guard against treating capitalism as an auspicious dispensation. And their emphasis on humanitarian idealism caused them to view the bellicose rhetoric of America's political leaders with skepticism instead of praise. But given the political tenor of anti-communism, they were in no position to compete with evangelical fundamentalists in a contest for public legitimacy. It was precisely in this situation that Martin Luther King Jr. found himself as he was catapulted into leadership of the SCLC in 1957.

The SCLC was created to replicate throughout the South the MIA's successful boycott in Montgomery. The city's Women's Political Council (WPC) was paradigmatic of the organized activism that Black women produced to create the success of the movement, and many of these same women formed the MIA, modeling its administrative and activist tactics on the conventions they had developed in the WPC. King and the SCLC, whose leadership was essentially male, relied overwhelmingly on activist women in the WPC and other similar organizations to implement their monumental strategies for destroying American apartheid.[26] The experience and skills of African American women such as Jo Ann Gibson Robinson, Thelma Glass, Mary Fair Burks, and Johnnie Rebecca Carr (the long-standing female president of the MIA) ensured the civil rights movement successfully navigated myriad logistical challenges.[27]

---

[26] Irvine Belinda Robnett, *How Long? How Long?: African-American Women in the Struggle for Civil Rights: African-American Women in the Struggle for Civil Rights* (New York: Oxford University Press, 1999), 55–62. Davis W. Houck and David E. Dixon, *Women and the Civil Rights Movement, 1954–1965* (Jackson: University Press of Mississippi, 2009), 37–42.

[27] Robnett, *How Long?*, 58–59.

The unexpected challenge that did confound the movement was the onslaught of charges that social gospel Christianity was tied to communism. This was a new problem, and it operated in a Cold War context that made civil rights activists easy targets of disingenuous claims that they were abetting communism and thus posed a threat to national security. In this environment, activists were hard pressed to distance themselves from the American tradition of socialism and the positive insights that communism had lent to the legacy of the social gospel movement. Not even King could at first resist the overwhelming pressure to publicly denounce and oppose communism. Indeed, condemning communism in the 1960s was as mandatory as condemning terrorism would become in the twenty-first century. And yet, King was also bound by his devotion to the heritage of social gospel Christianity, which foregrounded the materialist, structural critique of social suffering, most forcefully in the writings of Karl Marx, whom King had read thoughtfully. As early as 1948, he had understood the connection between capitalism as a system of wealth creation and the exploitative labor practices and structural poverty that inhered in the global formation of Western capital. He even claimed that capitalism had outlived its usefulness and was doomed to wither away under the rising light of socially responsible reform.[28]

By the early 1960s, as anti-communism increasingly functioned as an ideological weapon against civil rights, King sought to critique the actual injustices of capitalism while placating allies both within and beyond the civil rights organizations who viewed such criticism as sympathizing with Soviet communism. In September of 1962, he delivered a sermon entitled "Can a Christian Be a Communist?" Parroting the vitriol of US government agencies and the corporate media, King began by claiming that communism had "more than a billion" followers who submitted themselves religiously to the dangerous doctrine. It was impossible, he emphasized, for a Christian to be a Communist, since the two were diametrically opposed philosophically. With that said, King spent the rest of his sermon explaining why the Christian church needed to heed the economic lessons of communism to restore hope to the world. The church should not accept the "creed" of communism, he claimed, but Christians certainly needed to support the "dream" of communism – its goal of alleviating structural poverty and providing for the needs of the poor. The Christian

---

[28] Clayborne Carson, ed., *Autobiography of Martin Luther King, Jr.* (New York: Grand Central Publishing, 1998), 19–23.

gospel itself, he asserted, already contained the ideological resources that communism offered as a corrective to status quo Christianity.[29]

This tactic of attacking communism superficially while defending and identifying with its actual aims and critique of capitalism epitomized the convoluted pragmatism that marked the plight of many African Americans of the era. More fundamentally, courting the good graces of federal authorities seemed an essential strategy for successfully opposing White state and local governments that were deeply committed to preserving the racial apartheid that SCLC aimed to defeat. Few African Americans at the time, however, realized the extent to which the federal government was targeting African Americans themselves not merely as a menace but as a basic threat to national security. The fuller dimensions of that dynamic emerged through the relationship between the external colonialism of the United States and the internally dominated populations of Black people the federal government sought to repress with increasing aggression.

External Colonialism: Repressing Communism Abroad

Empires, by their very nature, often constitute a thin and uneven terrain of control. This was certainly the case with US American control of Cuba. The United States administered Cuba as a satellite state until its popular revolution of 1959. The roots of this colonialism lay with the US occupation of Cuba during the War of 1898. US officials seized control of the island nation from Spain, celebrating a mission of liberating the "little brown brother" from Spanish imperialism. In the most superficial sense, Cuba soon emerged as an independent republic in 1902. But US officials, of course, had engineered thorough control over the polity. In a bold move, Washington officials inscribed in the very language of Cuba's national constitution the inalienable right for the United States to control its finances, foreign policy, and domestic affairs. In what became a standard pattern of US imperialism, moreover, the US also established indefinite military occupation of Cuba through the Platt Amendment, which among other things guaranteed the US armed forces unfettered control over a strategic naval station, Guantanamo Bay. This would remain a key outpost of US military power in the coming decades. Finally, until about 1960, the US employed subsequent military occupation in synthesis

---

[29] Martin Luther King, Jr., "Can a Christian Be a Communist?" in *The Papers of Martin Luther King, Jr.*, vol. 6, *Advocate of the Social Gospel*, ed. Clayborne Carson (Berkeley: University of California Press, 2007), 445–54.

with Western corporate control of land, finances, and labor to dictate Cuban politics and economics. And by directly installing (as with Charles Magoon) or financially and militarily supporting (as with Fulgencio Batista) military dictatorships in Cuba, Washington elites avoided dealing directly with the headache of popular sovereignty in one of its satellite states.[30]

All of this changed radically with what Cubans called their war of national liberation in 1959. Led by Ernesto "Che" Guevara and Fidel Castro, a popular militia of armed revolutionaries ousted the US-backed dictator Fulgencio Batista. The new revolutionary government quickly began shutting down institutions of US control, ending the nation's status as a satellite state and becoming, for the first time, a truly sovereign republic, although the United States still exercised its treaty right to occupy Guantanamo Bay. From that point on, Washington elites considered Cuba to be of special strategic and symbolic importance. The loss of this US colony was both embarrassing and alarming to Eisenhower's and subsequently Kennedy's administration, because Latin America was riven with popular movements that promoted socialism. Losing control over Cuba, they reasoned, could only bode ill for the US war against communism. A radical, militarized response from the United States was not long in coming.

On April 17, 1961, under Kennedy's instruction, the CIA implemented Operation Zapata, "the Bay of Pigs" invasion. Fidel Castro, the leader of Cuba's revolution and head of state, was awakened in the early morning by his security forces: the invasion they had been expecting from the United States had finally begun. Within hours, Castro was leading his troops near Cuba's shores to ward off what would become the most notorious of US efforts to topple Cuba's government. The CIA had assured Kennedy that the invasion would spawn a massive popular rebellion against Castro and that he would be toppled from power. This faith in a spontaneous populist revolt against what had clearly been a popular revolution and sovereign government was at best wishful thinking and was likely disingenuous analysis. Under Fidel Castro's direct guidance, Cuba's forces quickly routed the American invaders and defeated the roughly 1,500 ex-Cubans who had conspired with the CIA and US military to overthrow the Cuban government. Only three US soldiers died in the fiasco. The cost to Cuba was far greater, however. More than 4,000

[30] Greg Grandin, *Empire's Workshop: Latin America, the United States, and the Rise of the New Imperialism* (New York: Metropolitan Books, 2006).

Cubans – mostly soldiers – were killed by the invading army of CIA recruits backed by US military personnel and aircraft. Of those Cubans who had renounced their own state to join the CIA's illegal invasion, a few hundred died. It was the same year that African Americans were coordinating Freedom Rides throughout the South, trusting federal authorities to assist them in challenging explicit apartheid law.[31]

Ironically, President Kennedy was only emboldened by the failure of Operation Zapata. He decided an all-out, open war on Cuba was called for, not a scaled-down, covert operation. In counsel with his military advisers, he targeted October 1962 to culminate a military conquest of the island nation. Kennedy created a new position called Military Representative to the President, to which he appointed Maxwell Taylor, whose study of the Bay of Pigs fiasco faulted the intelligence community (instead of Kennedy) and instigated increased presidential authority over the CIA. Kennedy then established Operation Mongoose, tasked with destroying the fruits of Cuba's revolution. And he appointed his younger brother Robert Kennedy, the nation's chief legal counsel, to head up a "Special Group" to devise US terrorist attacks against Castro personally and against strategic elements of the Cuban nation's industrial infrastructure.[32]

This state terrorism group was not unprecedented. Eisenhower had his "5412 Group," which authorized foreign assassinations and mercenary activities to preserve plausible deniability for the president. In subsequent administrations, Lyndon B. Johnson would have his "303 Committee" and Richard Nixon, his "40 Committee."[33] If anything distinguished Kennedy's arrangement, it was his decision to preserve the appointment of the younger Robert Kennedy as the nation's chief legal counsel while also making him the head of organizing state terrorism, a situation that was to create significant problems for Black liberation groups like the Student Non-Violent Coordinating Committee (SNCC) and the SCLC. Robert Kennedy boasted that he was going to "stir things up on [the] island with espionage, sabotage, [and] general disorder."[34] And he quickly

[31] Howard Jones, *The Bay of Pigs* (New York: Oxford University Press, 2008).

[32] Andrew J. Bacevich, *Washington Rules: America's Path to Permanent War* (New York: Metropolitan Books, 2010), 76–80.

[33] Jonathan Haslam, *The Nixon Administration and the Death of Allende's Chile: A Case of Assisted Suicide* (New York: Verso, 2005). Kathryn S. Olmsted, *Challenging the Secret Government: The Post-Watergate Investigations of the CIA and FBI* (Chapel Hill: University of North Carolina Press, 1996), 86.

[34] Bacevich, *Washington Rules*, 77.

made good on the promise, as the group began to sabotage Cuba's food supply, oil refineries, and power plants. They also began what would total over 600 attempts to assassinate Fidel Castro himself. With his team of henchman in place, nothing seemed off the table in President Kennedy's covert war against anticolonial leftists.[35]

Meanwhile, Cuban intelligence officials soon ascertained US plans for an open, military conquest. Given the United States' unmatched proliferation of nuclear warheads, missiles, bombers, tactical fighter jets, spy planes, ordnance, and the like such a war would only be an ineluctable, devastating defeat for Cuba. In a desperate but prudent move of alliance, Castro contacted Nikita Khrushchev, alerted him to the impending invasion, and emphasized its implications for the balance of power in the Cold War. In response, the Soviet Union placed missiles in Cuba to thwart any further development of US plans to attack Cuba.[36]

Faced with the very real prospect of a nuclear war with the Soviet Union, President Kennedy publicly vowed on October 27, 1962 that the United States would not go to war against Cuba. The very next day, Nikita Khruschev tendered a diplomatic letter to the Kennedy administration, acknowledging that the USSR had installed nuclear missiles in Cuba, that the motive of their installation was purely defensive (to avert a US war against Cuba), and that Kruschev himself had now ordered their removal as a result of Kennedy's public vow not to attack Cuba.[37]

To his credit, Kennedy became susceptible to sound thinking and took a decisive detour from the typically unheeding, dogmatic enterprise he had engineered to destroy post-revolutionary Cuba at any and all costs. Despite the temptation to win humiliation from the USSR and Cuba by stonewalling or waiting them out (the result might have easily instigated a nuclear war), he chose to engage the diplomatic overtures of the Soviets and Cuba. What US officials touted as a singular threat from "Soviet communism" was, in fact, a discursive moniker that easily elided a full range of anticolonial movements throughout the Third World, none of which were reducible to communism per se so much as they were centrally concerned with creating sovereign polities free of control by the United States and the imperial metropoles of Western Europe. The so-called proxy wars of the Cold War were strategic deployments of US

[35] Ibid., 78.
[36] Jones, *Bay of Pigs*, 150. Bacevich, *Washington Rules*, 77–80.
[37] "Cuban Missile Crisis: Khrushchev Withdraws Missiles." *Facts On File World News Digest*: n. p. *World News Digest*. Facts On File News Services, October 31, 1962. Web. September 22, 2010. http://www.2facts.com/article/1962100490. Emphasis added.

imperial violence – covert and otherwise – devised to destroy anticolonialism in Cuba, or Indo-China (the Vietnam War), or Korea (the Korean War), or Central Africa (the CIA's collaboration in the assassination of Patrice Lumumba and subsequent militarism in the Congo).[38]

In the ensuing decades, numerous histories of the "Cuban missile crisis" would render the Soviet Union as a menacing bully whose aggression was prudently and diplomatically thwarted by a cool-headed US administration bent on a righteous mission of peacekeeping. In fact, a team of state terrorists were at the helm of US imperialism. And as they demonstrated, they easily considered murdering foreign officials and civilians and destroying the infrastructure of Third World peoples as worthy measures to advance their national interests. They were perfectly willing to undermine the sovereignty of non-Western states to advance the aims of US colonialism. So it was especially ironic that by October of 1962, Kennedy's anticipated deadline for culminating a defeat of Cuba, the United States was forced to abandon its planned war against the Third World nation. The conciliation that the Soviet Union extended to the United States achieved its objective of averting an American invasion of Cuba, and the crisis was resolved.

The so-called Soviet missile crisis was, at its root, a crisis of US imperial ambitions. It constituted the US failure to reconquer a lost satellite state, a veritable colony. Foiling the US empire would remain Cuba's unpardonable sin in the coming decades. For Washington administrators, US intelligence officials, and the Pentagon, the imperative for redoubling America's military efforts and capabilities was greater than ever before. If any doubts (and there were likely few) existed before 1962 that destroying communism and crushing anticolonialism in the Third World constituted the central concern of US national security, they were now thoroughly dispelled. In their place stood an invincible, Manichaean fundamentalism of religious and secular dimensions that adorned the imperatives of US imperialism in the transfiguring garb of a righteous struggle against evil, whose telos was a nearly ineluctable triumph, contingent only on the willingness to sacrifice. Furthermore, the synthesis of fighting external enemies and crippling or destroying internal ones that had been galvanized since the early decades of that century was about to achieve an even greater resonance. And its consequences would rain down on the

---

[38] Ludo de Witte, *The Assassination of Patrice Lumumba*, trans. Ann Wright and Renée Fenby (New York: Verso, 2001).

full complex of African American liberation movements that were heaving forward in the early 1960s.

Counterintelligence and the Civil Rights Movement

Although the CIA was the key agency orchestrating repression abroad, it was the FBI that garnered the lion's share of Americans' attention toward the nation's intelligence institutions. The bureau had been featured in popular film and literature throughout the 1950s and 1960s. And as the US confrontation with Cuba became more entrenched, the bureau proved especially effective at transforming its White agents into emboldened warriors of American righteousness against evil abroad and at home. Much of this was animated by the broad imperatives of anti-Black racism that conditioned and enabled mainstream values of conserving the racial privileges of Whiteness at the expense of Black lives and well-being. But within the FBI, even reluctant agents became conscientious soldiers in a determined struggle to destroy the Black revolution underfoot.

The specter of communism constituted the FBI's initial premise for investigating the SCLC and King. When the FBI began to repress the movement, therefore, it did so under an FBI manual provision captioned "COMINFIL," referring to communist infiltration. This long episode of repression began in a peculiar manner. In 1962, William Sullivan, who led the FBI's Domestic Intelligence Division, submitted to J. Edgar Hoover his team's first conclusive report about the civil rights movement. In that report, Sullivan advised that there was no credible cause for concern of communist influence on the civil rights movement. In fact, he underscored, it seemed a waste of good resources to engage the SCLC as a communist front. To Sullivan's surprise, Hoover was infuriated by the report and issued a sharp rebuke, accusing Sullivan and his team of willfully undermining both Hoover and the nation's security interests.[39] After two rounds of cat-and-mouse memos – Sullivan asking for the chance to review the data and submit a new report, and Hoover taunting that his first report seemed certain enough – the Domestic Intelligence Division generated a sure finding that communism was indeed an issue in the Black liberation movement led by SCLC. Sullivan, in fact, emphasized the

[39] Senate Report No. 94–755 (1976), *Final Report of the Select Committee to Study Governmental Operations with Respect to Intelligence Activities: United States Senate Supplementary Detailed Staff Reports on Intelligence Activities and the Rights of Americans, Book III: Dr. Martin Luther King Jr., a Case Study* (Washington, DC: U.S. Government Printing Office, 1976), 107.

division was in complete agreement with Hoover that communists were influencing King. He underscored that King was the most prominent of African American leaders, and this made King "the most dangerous and effective Negro leader" in the nation.[40]

In August 1967, the FBI would officially roll out a comprehensive program to disrupt and destroy a range of movements that were deemed fundamental threats to the internal security of the United States. This was the FBI's Counterintelligence Program. It would be known by its acronym, COINTELPRO. Moreover, the eventual formalization of COINTELPRO made explicit the imbrication of Black liberation as a political threat to the White racial state, on the one hand, and communism, on the other, as a global, broad-based threat that opposed Western civilization. Since the First World War, when Woodrow Wilson first branded the United States as the leader of the "free world," the US empire had been formally described and conceptualized as the most potent defender of Western civilization. This was a complex moniker that simultaneously captured the religious and racial registers of colonial authority within the political domain of social power.

Open Season on Black Liberation

Sullivan and his colleagues in their special division of the FBI had quickly grasped the rules of the game – substantiate the claim that the Black rebellion was infiltrated by communism and show that it presented a high-level threat to national security. They began literally to manufacture false claims designed to legitimate the idea that the Black movement was being controlled by communism. Meanwhile, Hoover was able to play the role of hard-nosed taskmaster who ran a clean ship and demanded consistent quality and hard work in the highest interest. The result was a system that thrived on generating fictions and brutalizing myriad victims in the name of national security.

It would be ahistorical and counterfactual, however, to give the impression that agents were typically forced or compelled to participate against their will, just as they were not cajoled into repressing communism. Black politics was perceived and engaged by mainstream Whites (i.e., not just "extremists") as dangerous, threatening, and constituting the ultimate form of enmity against the White racial state. And Hoover, although often described cynically as driven by personal idiosyncrasies, was perceptive in recognizing that the United States was a racial state

---

[40] Ibid., 31.

founded on White dominance. The veteran FBI director understood clearly that SCLC and SNCC were demanding a radical restructuring of racial power and the American social order. It seems William Sullivan and his team operated initially with a narrow understanding of communism as a particular species of Soviet statecraft, but Hoover discerned the broad appeal of what King admirably called the "dream" of communism, whose materialist critique of social power activists in the Third World and within the United States repeatedly interpreted in consonance with antiracism, equality, self-determination, and anticolonial revolution. This broad understanding of communism soon defined the way bureau agents engaged domestic liberation movements.

The efforts to malign the Black freedom struggle as a communist movement, moreover, were numerous and varied and came not merely from the FBI but also from police departments nationwide and from numerous individual and collective actors. Mississippi Governor Ross E. Barnett expressed the outrage of the majority of the state's White citizens when he accused civil rights workers of invading Mississippi with principles of communism and anti-American radicalism. On July 12, 1963, Barnett appealed to the Senate Commerce Committee to stop them. Barnett presented a photograph of King captioned "Martin Luther King at Communist Training School," taken at the Highland Folk School in Monteagle, Tennessee, putatively by a confidential informant. This was the same school that SCLC had used for years to train its volunteer activists. Barnett's diatribe did inspire at least one skeptic to press him further. The Democratic Senator A. S. Mike Monroney of Oklahoma challenged Barnett's claim that King had attended a communist training school. Not satisfied with Barnett's response, Monroney formally inquired further with the Department of Justice, specifically with Hoover. Hoover was especially pleased to tender an urgent response. In a written report to the US Senate, he claimed that foreign communist agents had full designs to take over the leadership of the civil rights movement and had already begun to influence it through indirect means.[41]

Just three days after Ross Barnett electrified the Senate Commerce Committee with his false allegations about King, his claim was echoed by Alabama's governor, George Wallace, who testified before the same Senate committee. Wallace fired a volley of attacks against those he claimed were

---

[41] "Ga. KKK Asks Probe of Liberal School Ousted from Tennessee," *Chicago Defender*, July 25, 1963. Jeff Woods, *Black Struggle, Red Scare: Segregation and Anti-Communism in the South, 1948–1968* (Baton Rouge: Louisiana State University Press, 2004), 12–15.

destroying American life by supporting civil rights legislation. Holding up the same photograph that Barnett had displayed days earlier, he criticized the bill's supporters. How was it, he asked, that King could have these elected officials "fawning and pawning" over him while cavorting with the greatest evil threatening the nation's security? King himself had publicly acknowledged hiring a known Communist but later claimed to have fired him. In truth, said Wallace, the individual still remained on King's payroll.[42]

This performance by Barnett and Wallace proved soundly effective. Kennedy's administration was panicked into damage-control mode as the president sought to contain the growing animus among White voters who resented the White House for pushing a legislative agenda inspired by communists. Kennedy was increasingly uncertain what to make of the charges about King. They seemed incredible at first but, after some carefully crafted repetition, grew increasingly plausible. The situation dissolved any doubts he might have entertained about his decision to continue authorization for surveilling King and the SCLC. Ever wary that he was being hoodwinked by hidden agendas, President Kennedy believed it was more important than ever that the FBI ascertain exactly what relation, if any, existed between the Communist Party and the civil rights movement.

The single most devastating turn in the FBI's crusade against King, however, started in September 1963. At that time, Sullivan suggested to Hoover that the FBI wiretap King's home and SCLC offices. The director was initially skeptical that the attorney general would approve the measure, since Robert Kennedy had recently denied a similar request. By this time, however, the attorney general was even more determined to verify the FBI's reports of communist activity in the civil rights movement. He speedily approved the request for wiretapping King's home on October 10, 1963 and the New York and Atlanta offices of SCLC on October 21, 1963. Kennedy did caution that the effectiveness of the surveillance be evaluated after one month, but he never specified that any follow-up need occur with his office. The FBI wasted no time implementing their plan. Agents broke into SCLC offices and installed the first wiretaps just three days later. By November of that year, the FBI had also installed wiretaps in King's personal home.[43]

---

[42] Senate Report No. 94–755 (1976), *Final Report of the Select Committee, Book III: Dr. Martin Luther King Jr., a Case Study*, 100–1.

[43] Ibid., 120–22.

Because Kennedy included permission to surveil any future residences of King, the FBI seized on this provision to surveil King's hotel rooms, emphasizing that the activist minister was almost constantly on the road. The FBI installed the first of these hotel bugs in January 1964 at the Willard Hotel in Washington, DC. This single surveillance device yielded nineteen reels of audio tape and included recordings of King's sexual relations with multiple women. The extramarital affairs came as a complete surprise to the FBI, but the material fit perfectly with the counterintelligence paradigm of destroying enemies of the state through unconventional means. Throughout that year and the following, the bureau repeatedly bugged King's hotel rooms, capturing more recordings of his sexual rendezvous in addition to intercepting valuable information from SCLC's strategy meetings.[44]

Although less titillating, the more valuable booty pirated by the FBI was the political intelligence gained from intercepting virtually every conference call and face-to-face strategy meeting that involved civil rights leaders, particularly King and Stanley Levison, the New York attorney who had by that time become a steadfast collaborator with SCLC and a close confidante of King. For years to come, the FBI possessed complete knowledge of SCLC's plans for demonstrations, discussions of internal dilemmas, and even the organization's contemplations about the bureau.

As the FBI amassed more damaging information about King's sexual habits, bureau agents grew eager to disseminate the information and approached several media companies. To their surprise, most media outlets were deeply reticent about leaking the information, despite direct pressure from the bureau. It was obvious that such a leak would expose the technological invasion of privacy required to gather such recordings. And they wanted no connection to the public scandal that such a privacy invasion was sure to generate. Undaunted, the FBI implemented a more ambitious plan that was largely the brainchild of William Sullivan. As their gambit partly concerned psychological tactics of repression, the determined head of the Domestic Intelligence Division arranged for an agent to fly to Miami and mail a copy of the FBI's sexual recordings to King's home address with a letter suggesting that he commit suicide. Sullivan calculated, correctly, that the Florida mailing address would avert any suspicion that the federal government was involved.[45]

[44] Ibid.
[45] Ibid., 159.

In the meantime, Hoover eventually succeeded in circulating scintillating rumors of King's sexual impropriety. The result was like a Dickensian novel, creating the best and worst of times for the civil rights movement. On the one hand, King was at the height of his leadership, and SCLC had become more effective than ever at raising funds and publically defending their mission. The televised brutality of White mobs and southern authorities attacking Black demonstrators was taking a toll on the opinion of White Americans throughout other nation. They were slowly but surely persuading a significant number of White Americans that legal apartheid was not the natural right of freedom-loving White citizens but, instead, a violent network of practices that embarrassed segregationists found difficult to justify. In this sense, Black activists were winning a hard-fought battle for public respectability. At the same time, however, the FBI's rumors of King's marital infidelity were circulating fiercely. Expanding in tandem was the bureau's hard-hitting claim that SCLC was a communist-controlled movement. And as repetition bred familiarity, distrust and paranoia within the movement began to spread like a wildfire.

The FBI then added yet another element to its assault on King. On October 15, 1963, Sullivan sent to Alan Belmont, the assistant director of the FBI, a monograph that Sullivan's division had prepared to discredit King. The monograph, entitled "Communism and the Negro Movement: A Current Analysis," was provocative, to say the least. Belmont quickly realized that the damning report on King would be nothing short of explosive. It was patent that disseminating this information beyond the bureau could generate a major backlash against the civil rights movement, which was slowly gaining sympathizers and altering America's legal framework. The report characterized SCLC and King particularly as a national security threat that served as a communist-controlled vehicle to take over America from within by controlling the Black rebellion.[46]

The FBI also retooled its repression of the civil rights movement in 1964 by creating a special unit within its Internal Security Division strictly devoted to destroying "the over-all problem of Communist penetration" within the civil rights movement. Under instructions to interpret "communism" in the broadest possible terms, bureau agents aggressively targeted younger and older activists in student organizations, the Socialist Workers Party, labor movements, and similar organizations. Its special focus, however, was the "racial movement," and King was perceived

---

[46] Ibid., 131–32.

as the de facto leader of this larger movement. Hoover justified this intensified repression because it was an election year. Most Black voters were gaining access to the ballot for the first time and doing so within the context of what the FBI began describing as the "Negro rebellion." So, it seemed especially urgent to ensure communists were not affecting the electoral process.[47]

Even more ambitious was the FBI's plan to contain the civil rights movement by replacing King with a hand-picked leader through whom the bureau might control Black activism on a national scale. This strategy, like many others, was the brainchild of William Sullivan, who calculated the high value of turning the racial rebellion into a puppet show. After vetting several possibilities, the bureau finally decided upon an African American attorney, Samuel R. Pierce. The young New York attorney had served as a judge and had worked as an assistant district attorney for the city. At the time, he worked for an elite law firm and, by Sullivan's estimation, seemed well enough ensconced for the agency to count on his loyalty to federal authorities. Hoover even gave Sullivan the green light to recruit Pierce. It appears, however, that Pierce never became aware of the FBI's plan. For reasons that remain unclear, the FBI never followed through on its plan to place him at the helm of the civil rights movement.[48]

By January of 1965, the FBI's public antagonism against King had deepened into a relentless tangle of pressures extending into the attorney general's office and President Lyndon B. Johnson's administration. The nation's leaders were finally united in viewing King and the SCLC as a political liability and a fundamental threat to national security. The FBI's efforts to disrupt and destroy SCLC through its counterintelligence tactics were beginning to show signs of success. And Washington's elites began to consider how they might convince King to resign from his leadership of the racial revolution that had shaped up rather menacingly. Meanwhile, King maintained his strict denial of sexual impropriety, insisting that he was largely bewildered by the rumors the FBI was circulating that accused him of sexual perversity. But King's façade of innocence was about to unravel.

That same month, Coretta Scott King opened the package containing the FBI's composite tape of King's sexual encounters. It had been mailed several weeks earlier, but only then had the Kings been able to catch up on accumulating mail. She sat with her husband and their most trusted associates to listen to the tapes. King's dearest friends, including his wife Coretta Scott King, Andrew Young, and Ralph Abernathy, now knew that King's denials and feigned bewilderment were flimsy attempts to veil a crushing truth. In the months that followed, the toll that King's infidelity took on his marriage, although well-kept from the public, only exacerbated the impact of it all. Even his private home no longer offered respite from strife but was merely another emotional battleground, one of his own making.[49]

The Seduction of Democratic Empire

Until the mid-1960s, few activists within the civil rights movement would have imagined that members of SCLC and the NAACP would number among King's outspoken critics. But this was precisely the situation that developed after 1965. That was the year King first decided to speak out against US militarism. The backlash he incurred from within his own ranks, if unexpected, was hardly inexplicable. The nation's White legislators had passed the Voting Rights Act, and Johnson had signed the bill into law that August. Thousands of Black activists had reached the breaking point in their experience of physical violence, including those trampled by mounted policeman while crossing the Edmund Pettus Bridge months earlier in Selma, Alabama. So, the momentous legislation, which buttressed the previous year's Civil Rights Act, was widely received as a momentous victory in the larger struggle to make citizenship a tangible reality for African Americans. Few actions would remain as pivotal in demonstrating the federal government's alliance – though belabored and reluctant – with African American activists who challenged the institutional racism of state and local governments. In this context, civil rights activists were far from willing to criticize the federal government after having barely tasted the firstfruits of membership in the nation-state.

King himself had shared a similar perspective earlier, viewing Washington elites as allies in a struggle against racist extremists in the American South. But the US war against the Vietnamese, more than any other issue, had forced him to recognize the parallels between what civil rights activists described as southern racism and what peoples throughout the Third World termed the colonialism of the United States. The growing emphasis on human rights among more progressive Black movements

---

[49] Garrow, *FBI and Martin Luther King, Jr.*, 133–34.

was an especially powerful factor weighing on King's understanding of the US government. None was more influential than the Muslim minister Malik Shabazz (Malcolm X), who had been assassinated earlier that year. Shabazz articulated a commanding – if unusual – theoretical grasp of US democracy. While civil rights leaders decried the need to expand democracy, Shabazz argued that Blacks were victims of democracy. Rather than internalizing a minority identity and pining after US nationalism, he had emphasized that Blacks were members of a global, transnational network of African peoples who shared a common anticolonial struggle with other non-Whites. In this global context, White people were the numerical minorities. And any appeal for justice needed to occur before the United Nations within the context of human rights advocacy, not civil rights discourse.[50]

In some respects, King was no stranger to this transnational purview of Black liberation. Almost one decade earlier, in a sermon celebrating Ghana's newly won independence, King himself had observed that Egypt had forced the British empire of Winston Churchill to back down. And revolution in India and West Africa had underscored the fact that the "Asian-African bloc" had become "the bloc that now thinks and moves and determines the course of the history of the world."[51]

In his address at the SCLC convention in the fall of 1965, King highlighted the stark connections between US foreign policy and domestic injustice. He reasoned that SCLC staff and their supporters would be moved to oppose US militarism in Vietnam once they understood the stakes involved. The time seemed right, after all, for the movement to emphasize human rights, not merely the civil rights that derived from citizenship. King began his speech by asserting that the Vietnam question was a matter of personal conscience. The "day by day reports of villages destroyed and people left homeless" were too burdensome for him to ignore. He continued, "This is indeed a complex situation. One on which even the experts are divided. There is no need to place blame, and I certainly do not intend to argue the military or political issues involved."

King clearly chose a conciliatory tone toward the Johnson administration. He had no doubt that the United States was the aggressor and was

[50] Malcolm X, *February 1965: The Final Speeches*, ed. Steve Clark (New York: Pathfinder, 1992).
[51] Martin Luther King, Jr., "The Birth of a New Nation," Sermon at Dexter Avenue Baptist Church, April 7, 1957, in *The Papers of Martin Luther King, Jr., vol. 4, Symbol of the Movement, January 1957–December 1958*, ed. Clayborne Carson (Berkeley: University of California Press, 1992), 155–67.

killing more innocent Vietnamese civilians every single day – including burning them alive with napalm. Yet, he claimed that "to look back and attempt to place blame [was] only to enhance the negative psychological atmosphere that fosters war." Instead, the situation called for recognizing that the true enemy was war. And war had become an obsolete means of resolving conflict. In this way, King employed a common liberal claim of moral ambiguity. Neither side was right or wrong, and "national passions rage on both sides." Out of a desire to see the earliest peace come to "the tormented people of Vietnam," he pled for immediate action from both sides. The United States, he proffered, "should effect a new diplomatic machinery without giving the impression of appeasement and which would in no way mitigate its national aims, in seriously considering bringing to a halt the bombings in North Viet Nam." In exchange, he further proposed, the Viet Cong should stop insisting that the United States withdraw from the southern region of Vietnam.[52]

This was actually the heart of King's message: the United States should stop bombing the Vietnamese. But it was couched in a thick web of appeasing gestures. King even conceded that the complexity of the war might mean that taking such measures was impossible at the moment. But any hope he had of persuading SCLC staff was dispelled by the chilling response to his impassioned speech. Rather than inspiring sympathy with the Third World victims of US colonialism or ire over US atrocities, his public criticism of the federal government unleashed a wave of dissension and alarm. King did enjoy support from SNCC, which was already vocal in its antiwar activism. But King's own SCLC along with other veteran organizations such as the NAACP issued an immediate rebuttal of King's speech and charged him with betraying the mission and aims of civil rights reform. In fact, a host of veteran civil rights leaders such as Roy Wilkins voiced concerns that closely paralleled the FBI's warnings about the faltering icon, warning that he was toying with communism and inspiring unwarranted hatred against the United States.[53]

Things Fall Apart

Throughout 1966, SCLC's efforts to implement civil rights strategies in the North became an all-consuming enterprise. For years,

---

[52] Martin Luther King, Jr., Statement to SCLC Convention, Birmingham, Alabama, August 12, 1965, http://mlk-kppo1.stanford.edu/index.php/encyclopedia/documentsentry/statement_by_king_at_the_sclc_convention/ (accessed September 10, 2010).

[53] Thomas J. Noer, "Martin Luther King Jr. and the Cold War," *Peace and Change* 22, no. 2 (April 1997): 111–31.

African Americans in urban regions beyond the South had asserted that dismantling formal segregation would not guarantee racial justice. Northern cities, they observed, typically lacked the explicit apartheid laws common to the South, yet these same municipalities ruthlessly imposed both institutional and informal racism against Blacks. Real estate professionals colluded to prevent Blacks from purchasing homes in the suburbs; White landlords who rented to Blacks charged exorbitant rates but refused to maintain properties; White businesses refused to hire Blacks except for menial positions paying low wages; and city officials refused to deliver basic services such as waste removal to predominantly Black neighborhoods. This system forced Blacks to pay higher prices for inferior housing and food, while Whites enjoyed better homes and healthier foods for less money. Chicago was to be SCLC's first attempt to replicate its previous victories in the North to address the massive poverty, segregated housing, and extreme squalor that entrapped the city's African American population.

Coretta Scott King and her husband moved into a slum apartment so that they could understand the visceral reality of urban racism. And King began leading SCLC's direct action program to demand reforms from city officials. Most African Americans in Chicago welcomed efforts to organize a grassroots movement for change. And local activists quickly formed rent strikes, demonstrations, and petitions demanding fundamental changes. A minority of politically elite Blacks, under pressure from influential Whites, expressed ambivalence about SCLC's presence in the city. The informal practices of northern racism, moreover, presented formidable challenges to civil rights organizers, who were more accustomed to the explicit discrimination of the South – job ads that read "Whites only need apply" or laws that required poll taxes or literacy tests for voting. Even more overwhelming was the administration of Chicago's mayor Richard J. Daley. His political machine blended corruption, racism, sophistication, special interest, and a massive scale of power-play beyond anything that most southern towns could accomplish. Daley even feigned devotion to racial equality, and he thanked SCLC for bringing to the city's attention the massive disparities that burdened Chicago's Black residents, problems he claimed were previously unknown to the city or simply beyond his ability to control. In the end, SCLC retreated from its Chicago initiative with meager victories.[54]

---

[54] David Levering Lewis, *King: A Biography*, 3rd ed. (Urbana: University of Illinois Press, 2013), 315–17, 322–30, 342–53, 357.

Chicago did at least provide some distraction from the fallout of King's public criticism of US militarism, but for only the short term. By the early part of 1967, he was once again compelled to tackle US imperialism head-on. And he realized doing so would permanently seal his alienation from the movement's mainstream leadership. With urging from James Bevel, a Black Baptist minister from Mississippi, King decided to join the Spring Mobilization Rally, which Bevel was organizing. It was shaping up to be a major grassroots demonstration to protest the US bombing of mostly civilian Vietnamese. The event was scheduled for that April. King also arranged to speak at New York City's Riverside Church ahead of his appearance at the rally. This Manhattan parish was a popular, mainstream venue and offered to provide a more legitimate context for announcing his renewed opposition to the US war against Vietnam. It was there, on April 4, 1967, that King gave his most memorable critique of US imperialism, confessing that his progressive critics had finally compelled him to acknowledge that his own government was "the greatest purveyor of violence on earth." And he urged an immediate end to US bombing of the Vietnamese.[55]

The response to King's Riverside Church speech was immediate, fierce, and largely negative. From both within and beyond the civil rights movement, critics charged that King had wandered off course and had succumbed to anti-Americanism, that he had traded the movement's vision of fighting segregation for the delusion of communist radicalism bent on destroying America's greatness. But even this seemed mild compared to the fallout from his participation at the Spring Mobilization rally. On the day of the event, April 15, 1967, more than 100,000 activists arrived to voice their dissent against the US bombing of Vietnam. The astounding turnout was at once civil, bold, insurgent, and particularly threatening to federal authorities. King marched at the front of the massive rally, which began at Central Park and ended at the United Nations headquarters. One reporter claimed the rally was "unemotional" and insipid. It was attacked by numerous organizations and newspapers. Veteran civil rights leaders, moreover, turned a cold eye of rejection toward King. Although he had emphasized that he was representing only himself and not SCLC or the larger civil rights movement, he now stood accused of trying to destroy the movement by mixing it with antiwar radicalism and communism.

---

[55] Simon Hall, *Peace and Freedom: The Civil Rights and Antiwar Movements in the 1960s* (Philadelphia: University Pennsylvania Press, 2005), 80–82.

King had joined the rally against the wishes of his closest supporters, including Andrew Young and Bayard Rustin.[56]

Why did the media and many Americans who had lauded King's March on Washington four years earlier now condemn the New York rally, whose participants rivaled or perhaps surpassed the number of attendees at the 1963 Washington rally? The crucial difference between the New York rally and the March on Washington was their object of critique. The 1963 March on Washington was by no means a reproachment of Washington elites. Rather, US legislators that very summer had been vetting civil rights legislation. The civil rights movement had firmly wedged itself into a posture of alliance with the federal government to oppose a confederation of rogue southern states and local governments that nakedly violated constitutional principles to deny fundamental rights to American citizens. The enemy, in these terms, was the segregation of the recalcitrant South, not the United States. America proper, as King himself had often claimed, was the land of promise, the birthplace of democracy. The April 1967 rally, by contrast, was the notorious love child of anticolonialism, Third World communism, and human rights advocacy, and it bore absolutely no loyalties to American nationalism. It was the Vietnamese flag, not the United States flag, that adorned the 1967 rally, and members of the Communist Party were present in strong numbers. The speakers, the activists, the entire movement – all worked to subpoena not the American South but rather the federal government of the United States before the court of international scrutiny and demand a just halt to the murder of Vietnamese civilians.[57]

By 1968, the FBI reached a new stage in its efforts to destroy the civil rights movement. King was now largely discredited. In a major coup, the FBI had persuaded the African American author Carl Rowan to denounce King in a widely disseminated article. The conservative defender of US imperialism charged that King was egotistical and was now attempting to create anger among Blacks to antagonize the White liberals to whom

---

[56] Richard Dougherty, "Thousands March in War Protests: 100,000 Take Demands to U.N. as Others Rally Across Nation Thousands in Marches Protesting Viet War," *Los Angeles Times*, April 16, 1967. Paul Good, "The Rev. Mr. Bevel Makes His Protest in a Yarmulke: Reinforcing the Rhetoric," *Washington Post*, April 30, 1967. Paul Hofmann, "Dr. King Is Backed for Peace Ticket," *The New York Times* April 22, 1967.

[57] Paul Good, "The Rev. Mr. Bevel Makes His Protest in a Yarmulke: Reinforcing the Rhetoric," *Washington Post*, April 30, 1967. Richard Dougherty, "Thousands March in War Protests: 100,000 Take Demands to U.N. as Others Rally Across Nation Thousands in Marches Protesting Viet War," *Los Angeles Times*, April 16, 1967. By Paul Hofmann, "Dr. King Is Backed for Peace Ticket," *The New York Times*, April 22, 1967.

Rowan attributed the essential gains of the civil rights movement. After claiming that King's criticism of the US government – King identified the United States as "the greatest purveyor of violence on earth" – was evidence of communist influence, Rowan suggested that King was quickly drifting into paranoia and irrelevance and that he needed to step down from his perch as movement leader. King's approval ratings had sunk to an abysmal low. And the FBI, in multiple memos to President Johnson's administration, had hammered home the message that King's denunciation of US militarism was parroted from communist ideology, to which he had been a devotee for many years, putatively.[58]

However, it was the FBI's repression of Black activism in Memphis and of SCLC's plans to occupy the nation's capital in 1968 that brought on the full demise of King's leadership. The paralysis of SCLC's nonviolent direction action program then forced radical change. Several months earlier, the African American attorney Marian Wright (later Edelman) devised an ingenious plan for SCLC to lead tens of thousands of America's poor to the nation's capital, where they would live in tents and other temporary housing until federal legislators produced meaningful reform to address the dire situation of economic disparity that increasingly threatened the livelihood of millions of Americans. Wright first proposed the idea at SCLC's November 1967 convention, and King firmly backed the strategy. Branded the Poor People's Campaign (PPC), this operation promised to foreground the debilitating plight of poverty-stricken peoples throughout the country. Wright relocated to Washington, DC, to coordinate the massive planning required for the PPC. In the early months of 1968, meanwhile, King became involved in the activism of African Americans in Memphis seeking equitable wages and other just working conditions.[59]

The events that unfolded next exceeded anything the civil rights movement had witnessed earlier. Washington officials treated planning for a multiracial encampment of poor people in the capital city as if it were a foreign invasion. The two previous "long, hot" summers had already been marked by the militarized repression of Black protesters in several US cities, and US officials were determined to ensure there would be no gathering – whether peaceful or otherwise – of the nation's poor in Washington. US Attorney General Ramsey Clark had previously

---

[58] Carl Rowan, "Martin Luther King's Tragic Decision," *Reader's Digest* (September 1967): 37–42. Tavis Smiley, *Death of a King: The Real Story of Dr. Martin Luther King, Jr.'s Final Year* (New York: Little, Brown, and Company, 2014), 143–50.

[59] Gerald D. McKnight, *The Last Crusade: Martin Luther King, Jr., the FBI, and the Poor People's Campaign* (Boulder, CO: Westview Press, 1998), 20–22.

engineered the racial "community surveillance program" that used thousands of Blacks to spy on African American activists. Clark applied his experience to assist President Johnson in coordinating the FBI, other divisions of the Department of Justice, and the intelligence units of the US military branches in order to surveil and repress Black organizers. FBI agents also planted rumors among poor communities throughout the nation that welfare recipients who participated in the PPC would lose their benefits. In addition, FBI operatives posed as philanthropic Whites and approached SCLC (typically by phone) with offers of providing bus transportation to Washington for poor activists – these buses would not show up at the appointed time, and King would be blamed. Beyond this, the FBI began issuing a flurry of misinformation about public meetings, giving the wrong date or time to prospective participants, who then complained that SCLC was unorganized and incapable of coordinating a mass movement. This simple but effective tactic stirred confusion and resentment among aspiring activists from the early stages of the PPC initiative.[60]

The FBI's response to Memphis particularly brought to bear the militarized tactics of COINTELPRO. The FBI placed the names of activist African American youths and adults alike on its index list. At any time US officials declared a state of emergency, individuals on this roster were to be picked up and indefinitely detained without any recourse to legal protections – a legalized form of abduction. The FBI shared this index list with the Secret Service and with all military intelligence units. In a pattern that became increasingly common with COINTELPRO, the FBI began unprecedented coordination with the Memphis Police Department (MPD). Because of this formalized counterintelligence, police departments throughout the nation hired their first Black employees, specifically to serve in special intelligence units to surveil other African Americans. Memphis was exemplary in this regard. The department, consisting previously of 750 White officers, suddenly hired 100 Black recruits who were deployed in plainclothes as undercover spies. Some Black police officers were stationed in Black neighborhoods. Others were enrolled in the predominantly Black Memphis State University. And yet others were strategically placed as students in every Black college in the greater Memphis area so that they could join and inform on the numerous Black student organizations that had proliferated during the civil rights years.[61]

---

[60] Ibid., 8–10, 26–27.
[61] Ibid., 44–50.

With direction from the FBI, the MPD also cultivated university administrators as informants to gain access to Black students' confidential academic records, and they accessed the banking records of Black political targets throughout the city. The FBI also assisted the MPD in upgrading their riot control units with Special Weapons and Tactics (SWAT) based specifically on US military warfare, a pattern that the FBI succeeded in making uniform throughout the nation. After enrolling a number of its officers in the FBI academy, the MPD created its own riot training school at the city's Armour Center. In tandem, they also created a sniper unit to deploy against the rising tide of Black activists seeking drastic reforms in the city's racist administration. This militarized policing required a major paradigm shift from security for citizens to warfare against domestic enemies, and it generated massive costs. But federal agencies such as the Law Enforcement Assistance Administration provided a steady stream of subvention to ensure that money was no obstacle to tackling what Hoover menacingly called the "Negro rebellion."[62]

Of equal importance was the MPD's new Domestic Intelligence Unit (DIU), which was created to implement the protocols of COINTELPRO at the municipal level. Among the favored tactics of the DIU, as with the FBI, was installing agents of provocation within an array of Memphis's Black organizations. And it was this strategy that became a death knell for King's confidence in SCLC's ability to execute nonviolent protest. After repeated visits to Memphis to augur the local struggle for racial justice, King arrived March 28, 1968 to join a nonviolent March that SCLC had helped to coordinate. In the days leading up to the event, SCLC leaders had struggled with the question of their ability to prevent violence, which seemed to be brimming particularly among younger activists. Almost at the instant King stepped up to join the marchers, a violent swell of activity seemed to burst out of nowhere, and hundreds of activists began to scatter in panic. King's handlers whisked him away immediately. In the melee that ensued, a Black teenager was shot at point-blank range by a White police officer, who falsely claimed the youth was wielding a knife. Approximately fifty Black protesters were hospitalized with injuries, mostly from police assault, and 125 were arrested and detained as political prisoners.[63]

SCLC organizers had begun to suspect that local Whites had some hand to play in encouraging violence in what were supposed to be

---

[62] Ibid., 45–46.
[63] Ibid., 54–57.

peaceful demonstrations. But they could not have guessed that day the massive scale of counterintelligence tactics being unleashed to destroy the movement. The violence had been planned as a COINTELPRO opera-tion, creating an opportunity for MPD to claim exceptional measures of repression were necessary. Afterward, local activists realized they could be killed by police with impunity for demonstrating, and they risked incarceration for putatively disorderly activity. Moreover, the fact that an unarmed teenager had been killed in a demonstration organized by SCLC created precisely the scale of chaos and disruption the FBI desired. King felt personally responsible for the disaster, and he was finally persuaded that SCLC could no longer guarantee that demonstrations would be non-violent. Thus, after more than a decade of promoting difficult reforms and generating massive pressure through nonviolent means, and with less than one week remaining before being assassinated, the civil rights leader finally retreated from the primary strategy of empowerment the movement possessed. SCLC was strategically stymied, and the campaign to occupy Washington, assailed by a never-ending slew of FBI-inspired crises, now seemed like a dangerous if not impossible execution. As a testament to the unrelenting vehemence of COINTELPRO, roughly one week later – on the very day King was assassinated – the infiltrated group that spawned the violence during the Memphis march vowed to insti-gate more of the same unless SCLC paid them $750,000 (equivalent to $5 million in today's dollars).[64]

Anticolonialism and Black Cultural Revolution

The FBI did not invent violent repression against Black activists. Rather, it reorganized and militarized that violence into a larger network of col-laboration under the national security paradigm. Black activists through-out the country, however, continually met with various forms of state violence, including harassment and torture rooted in local regimes of surveillance and racial control that required no inspiration from the FBI. Few activists were as effective in this environment as Fannie Lou Hamer (1917–1977). She grew up on the Mississippi cotton plantations owned by the state's wealthy elites, and her ardor in the fields (she picked hun-dreds of pounds of cotton per day) was surpassed only by her unrelenting

---

[64] Les Payne, "FBI Tied to King's Return to Memphis," *Newsday*, February 1, 1976, in *Martin Luther King, Jr.: The FBI File*, ed. Michael Friedly and David Gallen (New York: Carrol and Graf, 1993), 663–64. McKnight, *Last Crusade*, 46–48. Lewis, *King*, 380–81, 384.

devotion to grassroots activism and judicious leadership of organizations such as the Mississippi Freedom Democratic Party.

Local Violence and White Rule

Because of their political insurgency, thousands of activists like Hamer repeatedly became targets of state violence and intimidation. During the summer of 1962, SNCC was in Mississippi to register voters, and Hamer was among the SNCC organizers. As they rode a bus to Indianola, a police officer who had trailed them for several miles finally pulled them over. After instructing the driver to exit the vehicle for questioning, he began interrogating the group. From the haze of the stifling heat arose the melodious voice of a young woman singing a spiritual – "ain't gonna let nobody turn me around." It was exactly what was needed in such a moment of fragile nerve under the shadow of the possibility of incarceration, torture, and even death.[65]

It was Hamer who led the group in song that day. She was among those attempting to register as voters at the courthouse in Indianola. Not a single African American had succeeded, and as things turned out, Hamer was no exception. The White registration agent denied her the right to register when he declared her explanation of de facto law to be unsatisfactory. But that was only the start of the day's troubles. Hamer lived on a Delta plantation owned by W. D. Marlowe III in Sunflower County. Marlowe had been looking for her, and when she returned he gave her a mandate: remove her name from the list of applicants to register or leave the plantation, which was her only home. Both she and her husband lived there as tenants. But Hamer was resolute and immediately walked off of the plantation, unwilling to renounce her political stand. Her husband was left behind at the only home he had, on the White planter's land. At the SNCC meeting that night same night, Hamer was immediately offered shelter with other Blacks.[66]

Hamer's moral courage and her genius for interpreting social conflict and engineering strategies of brilliance in response were matched by an

---

[65] Stokely Carmichael and Michael Thelwell, *Ready for Revolution: The Life and Struggles of Stokely Carmichael (Kwame Ture)* (New York: Scribner, 2003), 315–17.

[66] Chana Kai Lee, *For Freedom's Sake: The Life of Fannie Lou Hamer* (Urbana: University of Illinois Press, 2000), 33–35. Kay Mills, *This Little Light of Mine: The Life of Fannie Lou Hamer* (Lexington: University Press of Kentucky, 2007), 14, 37–50. Earnest N. Bracey, *Fannie Lou Hamer: The Life of a Civil Rights Icon* (Jefferson, NC: McFarland, 2011), 78–80. Charles S. Aiken, *The Cotton Plantation South Since the Civil War* (Baltimore: Johns Hopkins University Press, 2003), 225–26.

all-too-intimate knowledge of the sheer brutality by which a minority of Whites ruled the Mississippi Delta's Black majority. Her acuity and skillful navigation of the repeated challenges SNCC faced were quickly recognized and marked her as a crucial leader in Mississippi. But the boldness of Mississippi's civil rights organizers, which challenged White rule, only deepened the rage of even mainstream Whites. In this context, local officials reveled in unleashing an increasing volley of anti-Black violence in an attempt to quell the rising tide of Black activism.

On June 9, 1963, SNCC members were returning to Greenwood from a meeting in South Carolina when their bus stopped in Winona, Mississippi. Some of them entered the White waiting room. Several of the activists – including Hamer (forty-four at the time), June Johnson (fifteen years old), and Annelle Ponder (in her twenties) – were arrested as a result. One of the police officers kicked Hamer in the stomach as he told her she was being taken into custody. When they arrived at the jail, they were met by a crowd of Whites with guns, their eyes burning with fury. After a booking that was accompanied by verbal abuse and physical blows, each of the Black women was placed in a separate cell to be beaten individually.[67]

Minutes later, from her jail cell, Hamer could hear screaming, accompanied by repeated blows and the sound of someone falling and being thrown around. The noises were coming from a nearby cell, where officers and two civilians were trying to beat the teenage Johnson into submission. They struck her in the head. They hit her in the stomach. They yelled at her to say "yes, sir," which Johnson refused to do. By that point, the teenager was screaming and crying, begging them to stop. So they began to concentrate on beating her in the head, pummeling her face into a swollen pulp. Finally, they ripped off her clothes, deriving a sadistic pleasure from their power to inflict pain and humiliation with impunity. In the end, Johnson's blood-soaked face was so disfigured she could barely talk. Her left eye, now mangled, would remain deformed the rest of her life, accompanied by the large knot that formed on her face.[68]

The police officers left Johnson lying on the concrete floor in her shredded clothes soaked in her own blood for several minutes, as more blood continue to pool on the floor. They soon returned, demanding that she strip completely naked in front of them. Knowing that they would only

---

[67] Chana Kai Lee, *For Freedom's Sake: The Life of Fannie Lou Hamer* (Urbana: University of Illinois Press, 1999), 47–49. Howard Zinn, *SNCC: The New Abolitionists* (Cambridge, MA: South End Press, 2002), 94–95.

[68] Lee, *For Freedom's Sake*, 48–49.

continue beating her, the young girl struggled up to remove the tatters of clothing that remained on her body, now sticking in her own blood. Then the officers ordered another jailer to mop the blood from the floor, leaving a large, visible stain.[69]

Annelle Ponder was next. The men took her to the same room where they had tortured the teenage girl, making Ponder stand in the stains that remained where Johnson's blood had pooled on the floor. The officers began exactly the same way, calling her "bitch" and "nigger" and demanding that she refer to them as "sir." Then the beating began. Hamer would later recall how Ponder's screams grew even more piercing as the officers tried to extract from her body the submissive deference that was completely lacking from all that these SNCC activists represented. Three officers and two civilians took shifts as they beat Ponder with a blackjack and a belt while punching and slapping her. John Basinger, the White highway patrolman who had initially accosted SNCC, punched her in the stomach. When they were finally finished with her, Ponder was swollen, bruised, and covered in blood just as young June had been. Hamer, Euvester Simpson, and the other activists stared in a hideous mix of horror, sympathy, and terror (as this ritual effectively portrayed what was coming to each of them) as they beheld Ponder's hair standing on end, her clothing torn and bloodied, her body one mass of broken and bruised tissue, and her face barely recognizable. The facial swelling made it almost impossible for her even to communicate.[70]

Hamer braced herself as she realized she was next. After Basinger, the White officer in charge, learned of her reputation for registering African Americans to vote in the county, he told the other officers to take Hamer to the "bull pen," a special room used for beatings. Hamer was forced to lie prostrate on a cot, and the six White officers, along with two Black prisoners who had been bribed for the purpose, began to torture her as well. They began to beat her with a blackjack. One of the Black prisoners took the first turn, bashing her with the steel weapon until he was physically exhausted. Then one of the White officers took his turn, beating her in the back of the head. Another of the White officers, Charles Perkins, was literally unable to stand idly by given all the excitement, so he joined the fray. In a vicious cycle, Hamer's rising screams of agony only excited her tormentors into more furious brutality, which elicited shrieks of pain from her tormented body. Hamer would later recall her efforts to keep

[69] Ibid.
[70] Ibid.

her dress from riding up her back as the gang of tormentors broke her body. At one point, one of the officers pulled her dress all the way up and began to grope her. The men's sexual aggression infused the ritual of torture they meted out to the three women – one by one – and to the remaining African American activists. The entire process was meant to fuse the bodies and minds of their victims into a more pliable template onto which they unleashed their fury.

When it finally ended, the men forced Hamer to struggle back to her cell, despite her mumbling efforts to communicate her inability to walk. Drunken with unbearable pain, she slipped in and out of consciousness, finally collapsing at the entrance to the holding cell. The jailers heaved her body like a sack and kicked her into the cell. She lay on the cold concrete floor all night crying in pain. As the hours passed, she could hear the others screaming as the officers targeted those remaining, one by one, to experience the same fate.[71] As a result, Hamer suffered permanent kidney damage. And for the remainder of her life, a blood clot created by the torture session diminished the vision in one eye.[72]

Such naked brutality was by no means exceptional. It echoed the deep history of physical violence that Whites had used throughout the South under the regime of slavery to enforce their efforts to discipline and control dissent from free and enslaved Blacks. This physical torture, in combination with decades of lynching, abductions, and bombings, was integral to maintaining the politically motivated terror of White rule. And it was with such conditions in mind that African Americans increasingly asserted that they were relegated to a colonial status, ruled and controlled by a political system to which they were outsiders. Many Blacks never survived this terror. But Hamer endured, as did other activists that day, and they continued to advance a political revolution to subvert racial rule to create multiracial democracy in Mississippi.

Black Power and Anticolonialism

In this light, it should not seem surprising that Mississippi, three years later, became the crucible from which emerged the rallying cry of "Black Power," intensifying the radical demands for racial equality and the structural changes required to make Black political empowerment a reality. The relationship between the violent repression of Blacks within the

---

[71] Ibid., 49–53. Carmichael and Thelwell, *Ready for Revolution: The Life and Struggles of Stokely Carmichael (Kwame Ture)*, 316–17.

[72] Lee, *For Freedom's Sake*, 53. Kay Mills, *This Little Light of Mine: The Life of Fannie Lou Hamer* (Lexington: University Press of Kentucky, 2007), 94.

United States and the violence of US militarism abroad to destroy anticolonialism was especially palpable and emerged forcefully in these years. As SCLC and the NAACP grew increasingly loyal to US nationalism in an environment of red-baiting and political intimidation, a groundswell of activists emerged to oppose both internal colonialism and the external formations of US imperialism. They not only revitalized the anticolonialism of an earlier generation but also directly charged the United States with imperialism abroad, particularly in Cuba and Vietnam.

This resurgent anticolonialism was shaped by explicit attention to transnationalism. Angela Davis, along with other members of the Black Panther Party, traveled to post-revolutionary Cuba to work in the cane fields and to experience the rebirth of a society that was no longer governed externally as a US satellite state. Coretta Scott King traveled to Vietnam to demonstrate her solidarity with the Viet Cong. The increasingly visible and riveting voice of SNCC also found an energetic supporter in Kwame Ture (Stokely Carmichael), who eventually visited Ho Chi Minh (in China), Sekou Toure (Guinea's president), and Kwame Nkrumah (Ghana's prime minister).[73]

It was Ture's visit to Cuba in 1967, however, that was most pivotal. The occasion was the first conference of the Latin American Solidarity Organization (OLAS), which aimed partly to counter Western influence in the hemisphere and to promote solidarity with revolutionary movements throughout the Third World. More than 700 delegates and observers convened in Havana for approximately two weeks to discuss the fundamental problem of US imperialism from Vietnam to Venezuela and to develop a comprehensive strategy for ending it. Back in the United States, Washington officials could not have imagined a less desirable occasion. OLAS threatened to halt decades of continuous American rule that had netted previously unimaginable profits for US-based corporations and that further abetted US America's unrivaled standard of living. The cost of this imperial prosperity was borne by Latin Americans who suffered from murderous policies, ecological ruin, and pervasive

---

[73] This was not the first time African Americans had traveled to Cuba. Since the nineteenth century, African Americans had traveled to Cuba to enjoy a visit to a "Black" country and connect with fellow members of the race. Afro-Cubans, likewise, had traveled to the United States, often for extensive periods of time. Many were students at HBCUs such as Bethune-Cookman College and Tuskegee. See Frank Andre Guridy, *Forging Diaspora: Afro-Cubans and African Americans in a World of Empire and Jim Crow* (Chapel Hill: University of North Carolina Press, 2010). What distinguished the 1960s era of exchange was not its transnationalism but its strident emphasis on US colonialism, particularly the widespread articulation of internal colonialism.

poverty. The ability of the United States to control Latin America had long been a strategic concern for US officials. Harry Truman's administration had created a military school in 1946 for the United States to train hand-picked dictators, military personnel, police, and other mercenaries installed throughout Latin America who repressed dissident rebels like those constituting the Guevara-led guerrillas. In 1984, the school was relocated from Panama to Fort Benning, Georgia. It would eventually train more than 60,000 people. It remained a clear reminder of America's capacity to direct political, economic, and social control over nations throughout the region.[74]

The OLAS conference was an important challenge to this situation. Several members of SNCC, including the New York SNCC office director Elizabeth Sutherland Martínez, were present as observers. Cuba proved to be a transformative experience for them all. The young students witnessed the work on the collective farms Cuba's government had created to develop economic independence for the nation and to directly address starvation and poverty. Farming was backbreaking, fatiguing labor that, as one campesino proffered, was unfit for human beings. Since the revolution, however, farmers now benefited from their own labor instead of further enriching wealthy landowners and foreign corporations. Wherever SNCC traveled in Havana, they witnessed an insurgent confidence in the creation of a new society devoted to the foundational imperatives of the revolution. Ture would later recall watching Fidel Castro himself on one of these collective farms talking to the local residents about farming methods and cattle breeding. The jovial, conversational atmosphere that arose between this world-renowned head of state and the common workers impressed the US visitors, who could not imagine an analogous scenario in the United States.[75]

Washington officials soon received a jolting surprise, however, one that underscored the link between the "Negro revolution" in the United States and the wave of revolutions in the Third World. It happened several days into the conference. SNCC had already gained considerable attention from US reporters who, in the spirit of what they saw

---

[74] Brenda Gayle Plummer, *In Search of Power: African Americans in the Era of Decolonization, 1956–1974* (New York: Cambridge University Press, 2013), 180, 181. Chalmers Johnson, *The Sorrows of Empire: Militarism, Secrecy, and the End of the Republic* (New York: Metropolitan Books, 2004), 136. William Blum, *Killing Hope: U.S. Military and CIA Interventions since World War II* (Monroe, ME: Common Courage Press, 1995), 223.

[75] Carmichael and Thelwell, *Ready for Revolution*, 585–88.

as patriotic journalistic duty, had arrived to discredit the event. Even before arriving in Cuba, Ture had already voiced his support for the Latin American struggle to end US control and the related problems of forced starvation, loss of land rights, and the US-backed killing of dissenters. Well in advance of the event, the United States had sent mercenaries to assassinate Castro. In addition, an anti-Castro group of Cuban immigrants in Miami, Florida, would later acknowledge having sent assassins to Havana to murder Castro during the conference. Cuba's security forces captured all of the mercenaries or would-be assassins and paraded them before the US media in a futile attempt to shame the United States for promoting murderous tactics that were in patent violation of international law.[76]

In this context, Ture learned that the conference organizers had made him an honorary delegate and had placed him on the program to address a plenary session. It was an overwhelming experience and an historic honor. The goal of all the SNCC members, including Ture, had been merely to travel to Havana to support the conference and to stay as independent observers. They claimed no official status and were not representing SNCC or African Americans or the United States. During his address, Ture emphasized that African Americans shared with Cubans, other Latin Americans, and all Third World revolutionaries "a common struggle" against "a common enemy," which was "white Western imperialist society."[77] The root factor of the suffering was colonialism. Latin America was fighting against external forms of US colonialism, and African Americans were fighting against its internal expression.

Our people are a colony within the United States, and you are colonies outside the United States. It is more than a figure of speech to say that the Black communities in America are the victims of White imperialism and colonial exploitation – in practical, economic and political terms, it is true.[78]

Ture went on to explain that Black Power was not an empty slogan but an elaborate philosophy of social liberation, institutional empowerment, and social transformation. And he urged his audience to reject the claims of White US media that the Black riots occurring throughout US cities were simply thoughtless acts of violence. Rather than trivializing the riots, he argued, the world should recognize that they evidenced a change in the mentality of African Americans and were proof of

---

[76] "Kill-Castro Plot Barred in Havana," *Miami Herald*, August 7, 1967.
[77] Carmichael and Thelwell, *Ready for Revolution*, 589, 590.
[78] Ibid., 590.

revolutionary potential in the racial movement that was attempting to transform America.[79]

Even before Ture took to the stand to share his ideas with the OLAS assembly, it was easily predictable that the official response from the US media and the US State Department would be brutal and swift. But not even Ture was prepared for what followed. The very next day, the newspapers were reporting that the US State Department would seize his passport upon his return to the United States. In response to his outspoken support for Latin American revolution and especially his claim that the US riots were preparing Blacks for guerrilla warfare, the State Department immediately sought to neutralize him. US officials were also alarmed because the Cuban people closely followed the civil rights movement in the United States, and many openly supported the idea of armed revolution by African Americans. OLAS, furthermore, voted to observe August 18 as a "Day of Solidarity with the Black People of the United States."[80]

Thus, after the US State Department announced it would censure Ture and seize his passport, Fidel Castro unexpectedly intervened. On the day of the conference's final plenary session, he called Ture before the audience and introduced him to the international delegates. For Ture, it was a surreal moment. Then Castro vowed to do all in his power to protect him from harm and asked that the international community represented at OLAS do the same. Castro's vow was no empty promise. In the wake of the US State Department's decision, the SNCC activist had asked the Cuban leader to query a list of foreign nations that might be willing to host him for a visit before he returned to the United States, knowing that he might not be allowed to leave the United States again if he returned. He immediately received invitations from several countries, including Vietnam, China, Guinea, and Ghana. Vietnam was to be his first destination. Two days after the OLAS conference ended, he was on a Cuban flight that would take him to Vietnam via Madrid. Only minutes after leaving Havana, however, the flight crew announced they were returning to the Havana airport due to an emergency. Scores of horror scenarios flashed before Ture's mind. Could it be the FBI? Would he be taken off the plane and forced into US custody? As it turned out, Cuban intelligence officials had gotten wind of FBI plans to intercept him during his connection in Spain. So, the Cuban leader had instructed security officials to

[79] Ibid.
[80] Ibid.

recall the flight so Ture could be placed on a different plane. As a result, he and his companion, George Ware, were whisked off of the first plan and were soon flying out of Havana again, this time on a plane carrying Soviet delegates bound for Moscow, from which point he would then travel to Beijing, unmolested by US operatives.[81]

Not unexpectedly, the American media were dutiful to the imperatives of US colonialism when covering the OLAS conference and describing the presence of African American activists in Havana. Major US newspapers like *The New York Times* and the *Los Angeles Times* seldom publicized information about US terrorism, torture, and the creation of murderous regimes throughout Latin America that afforded the bountiful profits of US corporations and the buoyant lifestyle of US consumers. Instead, they tended to portray Castro's communism as simply an abstract, evil idea that he was attempting to spread by using "violence." One writer even castigated Castro for rejecting the "peaceful coexistence brand of communism" putatively promoted by the Soviet Union, opting instead to be a firebrand of disorder and disarray whose own country was described as cracking under the pressure of fissure and factionalism. The international delegates to the OLAS conference were also ridiculed for enjoying "comfortable hotel accommodations," "ballet, an art show and nightly concerts," plush meeting rooms, a festive atmosphere, and other staples of an international meeting of delegates that were supposedly inappropriate for Third World revolutionaries.[82]

The historic OLAS conference embraced a host of competing strategies for creating national sovereignty and economic viability that would benefit the people actually living in Latin America (instead of foreign corporate investors). Despite the US media's claims that Castro "imposed" his view of affairs on the delegates and that the latter had to endure compromises and fractured agendas, the event was marked by broad-based participation. There was no imposition, and the lack of unanimity represented in the adopted platforms evidenced a collective approach, not a despotic one.[83]

[81] Ibid., 594.

[82] Max Lerner, "Carmichael in Havana: Much Ado About Little. . . ." *Los Angeles Times*, August 9, 1967. Ruben Salazar, "Castro Gambles Big in Urging Urban Revolts," *Los Angeles Times*, August 13, 1967. "Fireworks in Havana," *The New York Times*, August 10, 1967.

[83] Max Lerner, "Carmichael in Havana: Much Ado About Little ..." *Los Angeles Times*, August 9, 1967. Ruben Salazar, "Castro Gambles Big in Urging Urban Revolts," *Los Angeles Times*, August 13, 1967. "Fireworks in Havana," *The New York Times*, August 10, 1967.

Black Liberation Theology

By the late 1960s, the growing emphasis on internationalism among Black religious activists began to influence African American Christian theologians. Many church leaders, including African Americans, condemned Black Power as an emotional outburst lacking intellectual substance and fomenting hatred. Even King initially issued this criticism, claiming the ideology was unchristian and divisive. This rejection of Black Power by Black churches prompted a few African American clergy to form the National Committee of Negro Churchmen (later renamed the National Committee of Black Churchmen or NCBC). This organization promoted the message of Black Power among African American churches as a viable strategy consistent with the Christian gospel. In fact, the organization issued a full-page manifesto in *The New York Times* defending the compatibility of Christianity and Black Power. It was becoming clear that Black consciousness and the religious legacy of Garveyism were expanding into the broader arena of Black religious thought.[84]

In a similar manner, the international focus of Black anticolonialism that Malik Shabazz (Malcolm X) championed was continuing to shape the theological purview of a growing range of activists, and this sparked significant changes within African American Christianity. In 1969, the NCBC attended the All African Conference of Churches that convened in the Ivory Coast to initiate dialogue with African theologians. Within two years, the NCBC had created an official "Africa Commission" to continue this initiative, and throughout the 1970s African American liberation theologians attended international conferences in Tanzania, Kenya, Ghana, and New York City in dialogue with African theologians. Of further significance were the exchanges between Black theologians from the United States and liberation theologians from Latin America. In 1973, James H. Cone's *Black Theology and Black Power* was translated into Spanish, and the seminal work of Peruvian liberation theologian Gustavo Gutiérrez became available in English. That same year, under the auspices of the World Council of Churches, representatives from these two movements met for a conference in Geneva, Switzerland. From there, other opportunities for collaboration arose for theologians from these two independently emerging movements. By the mid-1970s, Black liberation theologians were working with those from Asia, where church leaders focused on addressing massive poverty and Western colonialism.[85]

[84] Gayraud S. Wilmore and James H. Cone, eds., *Black Theology: A Documentary History, 1966–1979* (Maryknoll: Orbis, 1979), 18–19.

[85] Ibid., 445–62.

Most important was the 1976 "Ecumenical Dialogue of Third World Theologians" in Dar-es Salaam, Tanzania, attended by liberation theologians from Africa, Asia, and Latin America. This marked the birth of the Ecumenical Association of Third World Theologians (EATWOT), an entity that would in subsequent years become the single most important vehicle for a transnational alliance of theologians to address racism, sexism, and colonialism as fundamental problems that demanded a commitment to representing those historically victimized by Western colonialism.[86]

Religion and Black Cultural Revolution

Black liberation theology embodied the critical inflection of Black radical politics. But there were other ascendant dimensions of anticolonialism in African American religions that engaged the issue of cultural hegemony. African-derived religions gained unprecedented visibility in this context during the 1970s. The tradition of Orisha-Vodu was paradigmatic of this formation. It stood in sharp contrast to the Black ethnic religions of the Nation of Islam and Black Judaism, which critiqued Christian supremacism but were nevertheless Abrahamic. This monotheistic heritage nurtured a strong derision for the non-Abrahamic, indigenous religions of Africa. History was encoded, in these religions, by recounting the mighty deeds of biblical or Qur'anic figures and narratives. As a result, African American Muslims, Christians, and Jews typically obscured or ignored the genealogies of Orisha devotion that characterized African indigenous religions.

By contrast, Black devotees of Orisha-Vodu during the 1950s rejected the hegemony of Abrahamic religions, which they viewed as colonized forms of Black spiritual agency. They aimed instead to revive African-derived religions of Orisha devotion among Blacks in the United States. The increase of Cuban immigration to New York City was a major catalyst, introducing the Cuban religion of Santería to the city. Many African Americans became practitioners of the religion. Unlike Cuban immigrants, however, the African American devotees were particularly interested in recovering a strong sense of identity with Africa. Consequently, they soon focused on the Yoruba culture and Yoruba religion as a systematic framework for articulating their identity with

---

[86] Dwight Hopkins, *Introducing Black Theology of Liberation* (Maryknoll, NY: Orbis, 1999), 165–75.

African heritage. They even created their own religious community and meeting space, which they called the Yoruba Temple. At the time, the leaders of Santería in New York City were principally Cuban Americans who identified as Catholics and who looked to Cuba as their homeland. This butted up against the self-understanding of African Americans, who were drinking from the fount of the Black cultural revolution and Afrocentrism. For Black Americans, Africa, not Cuba, was the wellspring of cultural identity. In this latter framework, Africa was a symbol of pride, and the rising critique of Eurocentrism meant that so-called Black Africa was valorized as a source of civilization and culture, beyond the historic attention to Egypt and Ethiopia. It was particularly West Africa that became the focus of this revisionist paradigm. Valorizing religions of Orisha devotion became a central, visible strategy for achieving this shift in the logic of culture and civilization.[87]

Leading this African American movement was a professional artist, Oba Efuntola Oseijeman Adelabu Adefunmi (formerly known as Walter King). He had performed with the Katherine Dunham Dance Company and was a dynamic presence among the city's Black artists. His quest for an alternative to Christianity and Islam led him to Cuba in 1959. There, he was initiated into Santería. Upon returning to the United States, Adefunmi initiated other African Americans into the religion. More importantly, he began to dissociate the African Orisha from the saints of Christianity. The associations between Orisha and Christian saints were standard fare in Santería, but Adefunmi viewed this as an undesirable mixing of African religion and European religion. He aimed to create what he believed was an authentic form of African religion, which he called Orisha-Vodu and later, Yoruba. Cuban practitioners of Santería were puzzled by his efforts. In retrospect, however, it is clear that Adefunmi's attempts to render a form of African-derived religion more closely resembling precolonial cultic practices and theology provided African Americans with a logical rejoinder to the long history of the Western civilizationist paradigm.[88]

During the 1960s and the following decades, thousands of African Americans, especially in urban areas, became clients of Yoruba religion and other forms of Orisha devotion. They performed rites of initiation,

[87] Tracey E. Hucks, *Yoruba Traditions and African American Religious Nationalism* (Albuquerque: University of New Mexico Press, 2012), 50–72.
[88] Hucks, *Yoruba Traditions*, 87–102. Toyin Falola and Matt D. Childs, *The Yoruba Diaspora in the Atlantic World* (Bloomington: Indiana University Press, 2004), 306.

divinations, and healing rituals. In the 1970s, moreover, Adefunmi collaborated with other Yoruba practitioners to establish a separate communal society based on the religion. This was Oyotunji African Village, situated near Sheldon, South Carolina. This unique community played a particular role as a site of heritage tourism. Members of Oyotunji spoke Yoruba, wore traditional West African clothing, and lived in housing whose architecture was designed to evoke the ethos of precolonial West Africa. Major urban areas like Harlem were radically transformed by these developments, often to the puzzlement of unenlightened observers. A *New York Times* reporter of 1968 observed what he called the "sweeping change" that emphasized "blackness and African heritage" among Harlem's African American residents. They gathered frequently to perform and celebrate Yoruba religious rituals, wear traditional West African clothing, and eat West African cuisine. Such novel behavior prompted one skeptical White visitor to ask, "Who are these people trying to fool?" His question was met with a sure reply: "They're not trying to fool anyone. They're trying to find themselves. They have been fooled enough."[89]

These strategies of African revivalism frequently essentialized African identity and often muted critical engagement with African traditions from within revivalist communities. At the same time, however, they succeeded in permanently altering the structure of civilizationist ideology. As a result, in the decades that followed, both the scholarly and popular imagination of Black religion began to reflect the religious formations of African Americans beyond the boundary of Abrahamic traditions. Although vilified for many centuries, Orisha devotion began to gain a measure of respectability as a humanistic phenomenon constituting veritable culture, viable social technologies, and aesthetic facility fully under the rubric of civilization.

The ascent of African-derived religion, as one dimension of anticolonialism, gave powerful expression to what Franz Fanon critiqued as the psychological manifestations of colonialism in his *Black Skins, White Masks* (1967). Fanon argued that decolonizing the Black mind was a central task that needed to be properly understood within the larger context of more political manifestations of anticolonialism. At the heart of Black colonial subjectivity was the crisis of navigating self-contempt, the internalization of anti-Blackness achieved by grafting stubborn meanings

---

[89] Earl Caldwell, "African Influence Thriving in Harlem," *The New York Times*, March 12, 1968.

of inferiority onto the cultural domains of African peoples. Given the powerful modes of conquest and the long-standing hostilities toward African-derived religions, it was no small matter that promoters of African-derived religion managed to challenge these civilizationist paradigms and to launch a decolonizing revival of Orisha devotion in the United States.

8

Black Religion, the Security State, and the Racialization of Islam

As African American organizations like the Student Non-violent Coordinating Committee (SNCC), the Third World Women's Alliance, the Council on African Affairs, and the Congress of Racial Equality (CORE) continually emphasized, the plight of racist governance in the United States was already linked to US practices of colonialism. In tandem, they emphasized that the long arc of anticolonialism among African Americans was just one subset of a global struggle to create self-determination among the victims of Western colonialism. The rising scale of US imperialism, in this context, played an increasingly central role. By the end of the Second World War, with the emergence of the United Nations, the United States turned its attention more fully to expanding both its global reach and control of foreign territories through private corporate hegemony in Latin America, Asia, and Africa through open brutal military might as well as through CIA operatives to overthrow democratic and nondemocratic governments around the globe – in other words, by any means necessary. Why did the United States pursue this foreign policy approach?

African American Islam, Federal Repression, and US Empire

Between the years 1945 and 1960, no fewer than forty nations – comprising mostly non-White peoples colonized by European nations – rebelled against their conquerors and demanded their freedom, typically through violent, military action. These forty nations represented approximately 800 million human beings. Included in this number were the polities that would become Ghana, Kenya, Lesotho, Iraq, Iran, the Democratic

Republic of Congo, Kenya, and India. During the World War II years, the US economy had grown voraciously because of the rapid expansions of industries and consumerism based preeminently on cheap access to the natural resources located almost overwhelmingly in the regions colonized by Europe and the United States: petroleum, diamonds, rubber, uranium, copper, iron, tin, and aluminum. The nations that were fighting for independence from European colonialism had suddenly become exponentially more valuable in the eyes of the US government because of their natural resources.[1]

The United States did not claim to be fighting for imperial control over foreign lands, however. The message, crafted and perfected under Harry Truman's administration in the late 1940s, was that the United States was the leader of the "free world" (meaning White governments) and had to fight communism and other threats to democracy. The US intelligence state carefully elided the actual histories of structural oppression to which Third World movements (typically anticolonial) responded. When the US State Department and the CIA engaged with political Islam in Egypt, Iran, and Palestine, they consistently denied the political reality of Western imperialism while rationalizing murderous violence against Muslim polities and communists or their sympathizers throughout the Third World. Under the national security paradigm, Western imperialists branded rational resistance to US colonialism as hate-based fanaticism and extremist violence rooted in a bizarre racial constitution.[2]

Intelligence officials also applied to domestic subjects this paradigmatic strategy of eliding the material conditions of domination and describing resistance to a racist, colonial state as the consequence of racial psychology. To prepare its agents to surveil the Nation of Islam, the FBI headquarters created a training manual in 1955. Entitled *The Muslim Cult of Islam*, this monograph presented a specious history of African Americans in the urban North during the early twentieth century. It explained the religious leadership of founders such as Noble Drew Ali, Marcus Garvey, and Wallace Fard in derisive terms. And, most importantly, it catalogued

---

[1] Penny Von Eschen, *Race Against Empire: Black Americans and Anticolonialism, 1937–1957* (Ithaca, NY: Cornell University Press), 168–75.

[2] In the run-up to the overthrew of Iran's democracy, Western officials caricatured Iranian demands for greater fairness in labor conditions and sharing of oil revenues as ignorant natives resisting the enlightenment of European civilization. See Stephen Kinzer, *All the Shah's Men: An American Coup and the Roots of Middle East Terror*, 2nd ed. (Hoboken, NJ: John Wiley & Sons, 2008).

a host of differences between real Islam and the "Muslim Cult of Islam," its term of preference for the Nation of Islam.

The FBI not only lacked any background in studying race and African American culture, but it also identified closely with the nation's institutional structures of anti-Black racism. So, it should come as no surprise that the training monograph rationalized the repression of African American Muslims. The manual established three major points: (1) poor, mostly illiterate African Americans raced to the urban North during the early 1900s to pursue the American dream of material prosperity; (2) these Blacks failed to realize they simply lacked the proper education and cultural sophistication required for gainful employment and aspirational success; and (3) they began to resent the superior, successful White race. In fact, the manual claimed Black "demagogues" such as Marcus Garvey, Noble Drew Ali, Wallace Fard, and Elijah Muhammad compelled these miserable Blacks to blame their lack of success on the White race. The result was a viral anti-White racial hatred. The manual went on to characterize the essence of this "Muslim cult" as teaching hatred and violence. According to the FBI, it was quintessentially a religion of primitivism and thereby expressed the atavistic, pristine racial nature of African Americans. The true religion of these Black subjects, in other words, was not an acquired religion of Islam as practiced in the Middle East but an essentially limbic religion of primitivism that stemmed from the racial constitution of Blacks.[3]

The manual also aimed to assure readers that the White race was innocent of antipathy or wrongdoing toward Blacks. Instead, it was the delusion of African Americans that created their irrational hatred of the White race. The bureau, in fact, described African Americans as childlike in their lack of intellectual capacity, inventing an illusion of White oppression to mask their own inferiority. In this narrative of history, there was no such thing as White racism or anti-Black violence. Even the nation's system of racial apartheid was rendered invisible. And African Americans who dared to issue a critique of institutional racism were merely misguided, nurturing a primitive religion of hate and violence by spinning fantastic tales of racial oppression in an effort to mar the blameless innocence of the White race.[4]

---

[3] U.S. Department of Justice, Federal Bureau of Investigation, Preface to report on "Muslim Cult of Islam," i–ii, available from http://foia.fbi.gov/foiaindex/nation_of_islam.htm, part 1 (accessed September 28, 2013).

[4] FBI, "The Muslim Cult of Islam," p. 37, http://foia.fbi.gov/foiaindex/nation_of_islam .htm, part 1 (accessed September 28, 2013).

The FBI headquarters also wanted field agents to understand what constituted authentic Islam and so devoted considerable attention to that subject. The manual asserted that *true Islam* had nothing to do with politics but was a thoroughly *spiritual* religion of peace and brotherhood. Employing language that could have been lifted from any Christian social gospel tract, the FBI manual reiterated throughout that in contrast to the fake "Muslim cult of Islam," real Islam was based on teaching universal divine love for all and universal "brotherhood" among all peoples. As the rising tide of civil rights agitation spurred the Nation of Islam to emphasize its message of economic, social, and political liberation, federal agents only intensified their propagandistic claims that the so-called cult was a hate-based political movement merely masquerading as a religion.[5]

By the late 1960s, the US intelligence state had militarized its repression of African Americans. In 1967, the Los Angeles Police Department became the nation's first to adopt Special Weapons and Tactics (SWAT), under guidance of the FBI. The New York Police Department quickly followed suit. This militarization rapidly exacerbated the already violent tensions between the nation's police departments (typically all-White) and African American activists. The Black Panther Party (BPP) is perhaps most notable for opposing police brutality during this era. In what became a permanent pattern of anti-Black violence, White police officers routinely killed unarmed African Americans with impunity. Because White state and federal officials refused to protect Blacks from this murderous activity and protected the killers from prosecution, the BPP organized armed defense against state violence and harassment. The organization also sought to expose the repressive tactics of the security state and end police harassment against all civilians. This armed resistance instantly drew a full-scale response from the FBI, which immediately targeted BPP activists throughout the country. Even the unarmed activisms of African Americans – particularly of the hundreds of Black Student Unions that mushroomed on college campuses – became chief targets of FBI infiltration and repression. By 1967, the Justice Department directly ordered the neutralization and destruction of these movements. And every form of political activity that African Americans executed in the United States – from the Southern Christian Leadership Conference's nonviolent civil disobedience to the youth activism of SNCC to that of the Revolutionary Action Movement – all were engaged by the intelligence state as threats to national security. Every action they performed was deemed not merely

---

[5] Ibid.

illegitimate or criminal (these activities, including those of the BPP, were legal and, in theory, protected by the US Constitution) but also an instance of anti-White hatred that threatened the internal security of the United States. From the perspective of the FBI, activities of racial rebellion demanded the utmost vigilance of the intelligence state.[6]

The FBI also began cultivating an unprecedented number of informants in African American neighborhoods, reaching a maximum of over 7,400 by 1972. These informants were instructed to report anything that might be used to prosecute Blacks for subversive activities. This largely amounted to prosecuting, intimidating, harassing, and detaining under arrest individuals exercising their constitutional rights of free speech and free assembly. Surveillance included tapping phones, bugging homes and workplaces, and assigning plainclothes officers to trail political targets.[7]

Beyond this, the FBI began to leverage its infiltration of numerous activist organizations to create violence through the use of agents of provocation. The result was an epidemic of fatal violence and the destruction of otherwise civil activist networks. At one point, the FBI operated its own Ku Klux Klan organization with more than 230 members under the leadership of an FBI operative. In addition, the bureau, in coordination with local police departments, employed intensive programs of psychological disruption and trauma by bankrupting targets with bail and legal fees for repeated incarcerations (typically on false charges), destroying marriages, and transforming coalitions of trust into volatile crucibles of discord and mayhem.[8]

The federal government's efforts to repress Black activists also launched an exceptionally effective initiative: *mass incarceration*. By arresting, detaining, and imprisoning – often for years or decades – Black activists and those in their social and activist networks, the US security state soon normalized the hyper-surveillance and criminalization of African Americans. It is no exaggeration to say that in the age of the so-called civil rights years, the criminalization of racial Blackness reached an apogee as a function of the intelligence state. It is equally important

---

[6] Memorandum RE CounterIntelligence Program Black Nationalist Hate Groups Internal Security, Director of FBI to FBI Field Offices, August 25, 1967, U.S. Department of Justice, F.B.I. file 100-448006, "(COINTELPRO) Black Extremists."

[7] *US Senate Select Committee to Study Governmental Operations with Respect to Intelligence Activities, Supplementary Detailed Staff Reports on Intelligence Activities and the Rights of Americans*, Book III, 3.

[8] *Report of the US Senate Select Committee to Study Governmental Operations with Respect to Intelligence Activities, The Use of Informants in FBI Domestic Intelligence Investigations*, 230–40, 251.

to note the parallel between the US engagement with African American Muslims domestically, who issued a critical assessment of racial power in the United States and abroad, and US policy toward foreign Islamic movements such as the Muslim Brotherhood in Egypt and the Islamic revolutionary movement in Iran. Iran is an especially significant instance to consider, as it was there that the CIA for the first time overthrew a democracy in 1953. From the 1930s to the 1950s, the FBI characterized US Muslim targets of repression as uniquely prone to fanaticism, violence, and anti-White hatred. As the United States began to engage with stateless actors in the Middle East during the Cold War, federal intelligence agencies began to identify Muslims by employing the rubric of atavistic violence.[9]

Intelligence agencies emphasized the psychological proclivity of Muslims both within and beyond the United States as fanatical and hate-based. Criminalization and incarceration accompanied US actions abroad as well. For instance, the United States (collaborating with Britain) overthrew Iran's democracy in 1953 and installed a monarch, the "shah." The CIA also installed a regime of torture, anticipating populist dissent against the militarized puppet government. Policing dissent in Iran involved criminalizing protest, arresting and detaining social activists, and using legal repression to disrupt and undermine efforts to challenge the state. For the next twenty-five years, Iranian dissenters organized to oppose Western imperialism in Iran and the overthrow of their democracy. As this culminated in armed resistance and violent demonstrations against a military government, US officials increasingly resorted to the specific grammar of terrorism to represent political Islam. Distressingly, the Iranian Revolution was largely a revolt against widespread torture that the CIA had instituted to thwart dissent against US imperial interests.[10]

[9] Sohail Daulatzai, *Black Star, Crescent Moon: The Muslim International and Black Freedom beyond America* (Minneapolis: University of Minneapolis Press, 2012), 169–75.

[10] Darius M. Rejali, *Torture & Modernity: Self, Society, and State in Modern Iran* (Boulder, CO: Westview Press, 1994). The US government's racialization of global Islam was by no means uniform or surgically even. It was, rather, a historical formation rooted in specific political interests, pragmatic imperatives, and often serendipitous alliances. The governing force behind US engagement with global Islam, however, was nevertheless the consonant aim to expand US control over foreign states and the global movement of natural resources like petroleum. So, by the late-1970s, for instance, Carter's administration had established robust military support for Afghanistan's Islamist resistance to Soviet influence. That strategy would lead to US support of the Taliban and the retention of key actors like Osama bin Laden as a CIA asset. This occurred simultaneously with the growing racialization of Islam as an anti-Western, racial threat. See Mahmood Mamdani, *Good Muslim, Bad Muslim: America, the Cold War, and the Roots of Terror* (New York: Pantheon, 2004).

The history of FBI repression against African American Muslims under a national security paradigm and that of US engagement with international Islamist movements bore other parallels, including the charge of being prone to violence. The FBI had begun in the 1930s to caricature African American Islam within the United States as anti-White hatred and fanaticism enlivened by the inability of Blacks to rationally assess their material plight. Supposedly, this led Black Muslims to promote violence against the White race. This was the putative basis for their designation as a national security threat. By the 1960s and 1970s, intelligence officials were branding Muslims abroad as violent terrorists motivated by hatred – nonstate actors attempting a fanatical political objective through illegitimate violence. This created a powerful metonymic association that was immeasurably intensified as political Islam became increasingly common, most notably following the US invasion of Afghanistan and Iraq in the early 2000s. As a result, the very grammar of terrorism and religion in the United States became rooted in the mythos of terrorists as Muslims and of Muslims as terrorists.[11]

In the early 1970s, US legislators first became aware of these tactics of counterintelligence repression in both domestic and international domains. They were shocked and alarmed, and they soon established an unprecedented investigation into the nation's entire intelligence complex. The single most important effort to make US intelligence operatives accountable to legal oversight was the US Senate "Church Committee" investigation of 1975–1976. Named for US Senator Frank Church of Idaho, who chaired the committee, it was created as an immediate response to the Nixon Watergate scandal. It quickly came to light, however, that the Justice Department's FBI, the CIA, and other institutions within the intelligence community were violating constitutionally guaranteed freedoms and protections. The most notable of these was the FBI's Counterintelligence Operation (COINTELPRO). The Church Committee hearings slowly revealed how this program engaged US citizens using

---

[11] As one example of the efficacy of this association, the Boy Scouts of America's "Explorers" program in the early 2000s began training thousands of young people in "counterterrorism" methods to prepare them for future jobs as law enforcement officers. Equipped with compressed air guns as well as conventional (i.e., real) firearms, gas masks, and protective body gear, the young Scouts engage and neutralize actors dressed in Middle Eastern attire. "This is about being a true-blooded American guy and girl," described one local Sheriff in Imperial County, California, where some of the training exercises took place. The Explorers program worked closely with and under the sponsorship of the Department of Homeland Security and the FBI. Jennifer Steinhauer, "Scouts Train to Fight Terrorists, and More," *The New York Times*, May 14, 2009.

tactics created to neutralize and destroy foreign entities. In deliberate dis-regard for the US Constitution, the FBI employed a range of methods to implement psychological warfare, personal intimidation, destruction of social and familial networks, violent provocation, illegal detentions, and even political assassinations.[12] As a result, US Congress passed the Foreign Intelligence and Surveillance Act of 1978, which articulated specific protocols to ensure that US citizens enjoyed constitutionally guaranteed freedoms and protections from government surveillance, threats, and harassment.[13] The goal was to preserve the imperatives of both national security and civil liberties. At the time, federal legislators hoped that the nation would never again experience the unbridled reign of obtrusive surveillance, unrestrained repression, and the cycle of vio-lence that had been implemented in the name of national security against the activism of African Americans, Native Americans, and Hispanics as well as White political movements. In the wake of these hearings, the Justice Department repeatedly emphasized that COINTELPRO had been formally dismantled and that the bureau had ceased such operations as early as 1971.[14]

Racializing Islam

Approximately three decades later, however, in the wake of 9/11, it became evident that the FBI's counterintelligence operatives were not only alive and well but also far more advanced than what had existed in the 1970s. State aggression toward American Muslims ranged from detaining and prosecuting innocent Muslims (as in the case of Brandon

[12] Jeffrey Haas, *The Assassination of Fred Hampton: How the FBI and the Chicago Police Murdered a Black Panther* (Chicago: Lawrence Hill Books, 2010).

[13] The Hughes–Ryan Act of 1974 was the very first legislation that created accountability for the intelligence community. This required the US president to report all covert activity to select members of US Congress within a certain time period. The law resulted from disclosures of US covert military action kept hidden by official, falsified military reports. This resulted after the 1972 and 1973 hearings of the Senate Armed Services Committee investigated covert military operations in Cambodia, Laos, and North Vietnam in the early 1970s. Loch K. Johnson, "The Church Committee Investigation of 1975 and the Establishment of Modern Intelligence Accountability," *US National Security, Intelligence and Democracy: From the Church Committee to the War on Terror*, ed. Russell Miller (New York: Routledge, 2008), 38–44.

[14] John M. Crewdson, "Ex-Operative Says He Worked for F.B.I. to Disrupt Political Activities Up to '74," *The New York Times*, February 24, 1975. Anthony Lewis, "A COINTEL Story," *The New York Times*, March 29, 1976. The FBI's counterintelligence operatives came to public light in 1974. By that time US Attorney General William Saxbe claimed that the program had been disbanded as of 1971.

Mayfield, a White attorney from Oregon) to repressing the nation's Islamic charitable organizations.[15] Beyond this, a series of disclosures about anti-Muslim operations run by the FBI and frequently coordinated between the FBI and local police departments – NYPD, most notably – indicated that American Muslims had become the preeminent target of state-sponsored racism in the form of US counterintelligence operations. American Muslims were living under the exigencies of what US officials branded a "War on Terror" that was waged on a global scale. The very nature of this war – putatively not one aiming to conquer a nation-state or a specific territory but a battle against fear and a way of thinking – further collapsed the existing distinctions between the domestic and foreign domains of counterintelligence. Within the United States, Muslims were deemed public enemies by presumption. And intelligence officials programmatically trained field agents to recognize Islam proper as an extremist movement rooted in a foreign (non-Western), racial nature. In a training manual that was used as recently as 2009, FBI officials claimed that the religion of Islam transforms a "country's culture into 7th century Arabian ways." The FBI thus began preparing its agents to engage what it termed "the militant believer." The bureau's training also emphasized that it was the nature of "the Arab mind to be swayed more by words than ideas and more by ideas than facts."[16]

Since its inception in the twentieth century, the intelligence state had comprised not merely federal agencies but also an extensive network of entities at state and local levels. Most integral to counterintelligence operations against Muslims was the New York Police Department (NYPD). By the mid-1960s, before the FBI's counterintelligence tactics were formally branded as COINTELPRO, the bureau had already formalized a counterintelligence alliance with NYPD, the nation's largest police department. The bureau trained a select number of NYPD officers in surveillance, infiltration, and counterintelligence methods at the FBI academy and placed them in an elite NYPD unit, the bureau of Special Services and Investigation (BOSS or BOSSI). This unit functioned to infiltrate and undermine several Black antiracist organizations. BOSSI particularly created recurring conflict and fatal violence among

---

[15] Edward E. Curtis IV, *Muslims in America: A Short History* (New York: Oxford University Press, 2009), 102–4.

[16] Federal Bureau of Investigation, "Investigative Interviewing in the Religious Extremist Culture," FBI training manual, p. 38, 54, 57. Available from http://demographicsunited .files.wordpress.com/2011/11/cultural-interviewing-interrogation-powerpoint1.pdf (accessed February 15, 2014).

African American Muslims, including the Nation of Islam, the Muslim Mosque Incorporated, and the Organization of African Unity, a secular, Pan-African coalition whose constituents were disproportionately Muslim. The racial imperatives of repressing Black liberationist activism, thus, had created a deep alliance between the FBI and NYPD.[17]

Partly because of its unusual size and location within the heart of a major world city, NYPD only continued to develop counterintelligence capacities that easily exceeded the scale of any other municipal policing entity. In the decades following the civil rights era, NYPD Commissioner Raymond Kelly was at the helm of the force. In 2002, Kelly took the unusual step of hiring a former CIA official, David Cohen, to direct NYPD's intelligence operations, refashioning the department's Intelligence Division to make repressing Muslims its core mission. This initiated a growing collaboration between the CIA and NYPD. With this recalibrated focus, the department became fully ensconced within the larger interests of the security state. In a ninety-page report entitled "Radicalization in the West: A Homegrown Threat," the NYPD Intelligence Division even identified Islamic radicalization as the chief threat to internal security, and it described the division's mission "to assist policymakers and law enforcement officials, both in Washington and throughout the country," in understanding how this Islamic radicalization occurred.[18]

During 2011, Kelly implemented a training video entitled *The Third Jihad*, which was viewed by about 1,500 police officers. The video claimed that American Muslims were working to destroy Western civilization from within the United States. The documentary also asserted that terrorism was just one form of the Muslim threat to US security. Unbeknownst to most citizens was the civilizational threat – a war being secretly waged by Muslims to destroy the Western nature of US society itself, transforming it into a Muslim society. Kelly himself appeared in the documentary, which was produced by the Clarion Fund, the same organization that created and distributed 28 million copies of *Obsession: Radical Islam's*

---

[17] Karl Evanzz, *The Messenger: The Rise and Fall of Elijah Muhammad* (New York: Pantheon, 1999), 507.

[18] See Inspector General David Buckley's memorandum and executive summary to CIA Director, 27 December 2011, "Review of the CIA-NYPD Relationship," https://www.documentcloud.org/documents/717864-cia-nypd-ig.html (accessed November 12, 2013). "The CIA and the NYPD," *The New York Times*, July 5, 2013. New York City Police Department, "Radicalization in the West: The Homegrown Threat," http://www.nyc.gov/html/nypd/downloads/pdf/public_information/NYPD_Report-Radicalization_in_the_West.pdf (accessed August 16, 2014).

War Against the West. NYPD officer Noel Leader, who cofounded the organization "100 Blacks in Law Enforcement Who Care," was especially critical of Kelly's vilification of Muslims. Leader immediately recognized the parallel between the NYPD's engagement with Muslims and the department's surveillance and repression of African Americans during the 1960s and 1970s. He referenced the Handschu Agreement as a case in point, which introduced legal restraints on NYPD's repression of African Americans during the 1970s, and he called for Raymond Kelly to resign or, failing that, for the city's mayor, Michael Bloomberg, to fire him.[19]

The single most important focus of domestic US intelligence, moreover, was the nation's mosques. In the 1960s and 1970s, the FBI cultivated informants among African Americans in various religious communities and their religious meeting spaces. In the twenty-first century, the focus became American Muslims and their worship centers, which the FBI began to regard as the central breeding ground for Islamic terrorism. Nearly half of US domestic terrorist prosecutions involved the use of informants (243 of 508), many of them incentivized by money (operatives were paid as much as $100,000 per assignment) or the need to work off criminal or immigration violations. By 2012, sting operations had resulted in prosecutions against 158 defendants. Of that total, 49 defendants had participated in plots led by an FBI operative attempting to persuade Muslim men to join the FBI's plots. With three exceptions, in fact, all of the high-profile domestic terror plots prosecuted between 2001 and 2011 were actually FBI stings.[20]

Although the US media were sensationally reporting terrorist plots foiled by FBI officials, the underside of these plots revealed an extensive scheme of more than 15,000 FBI informants and agents whose task was to lure American Muslims into pursuing ethically questionable activities that constituted legally defined acts of terrorism so they could be entrapped. Of the 508 cases of terrorism disclosed by the Department of Justice, moreover, the $3 billion annually appropriated to the FBI just for antiterrorism yielded only a handful of "actual terrorists." This bore

---

[19] Raymond Kelly, of course, remained in power as police commissioner and was even vetted by the Obama administration to direct the Department of Homeland Security. See transcript, "NYPD Commissioner Ray Kelly Urged to Resign after Police Conceal Role in Anti-Muslim Documentary," *Democracy Now*, January 27, 2012, http://www.democracynow.org/2012/1/27/nypd_commissioner_ray_kelly_urged_to (accessed September 27, 2013).

[20] Trevor Aaronson, *The Terror Factory: Inside the FBI's Manufactured War on Terrorism* (Brooklyn: Ig Publishing, 2013), 13.

an uncanny parallel to the FBI's initiative of the 1960s, when the bureau operated its own Klan organization putatively to entrap White supremacists. In the name of foiling the Klan, the agency was actually encouraging spiteful Whites to join the violent ranks of its racist, organized terror against African Americans. In the wake of 9/11, the FBI began regularly conducting terrorist cells to entrap terrorists. The bureau employed thousands of its spies, most of whom were devoted to counterterrorism, in coordination with militarized intelligence units from police departments throughout the country to target, sweep, surveil, and infiltrate the roughly 1,200 mosques and larger communities of American Muslims on a daily basis.[21]

As a result, American Muslims were forced to live in a constant state of fear of ongoing surveillance and infiltration. Virtually every American mosque was under the watch of at least one intelligence operative (from the FBI or a police department) trained in the use of highly sophisticated surveillance equipment to gather video and audio recordings of mosque events and conversations with other Muslims. This information was subsequently provided to FBI officials to decide how to target and perhaps woo unsuspecting Muslims into yet another FBI-designed terrorist plot that subsequently would be foiled in the nick of time, with the perpetrator paraded before the US media.

In the wake of 9/11, it became fully clear to scholars that the security state had racialized Islam. As with other forms of racialization, this elided the political realities of imperial domination. Instead of rendering visible the material, political stakes of conflicts, defenders of US imperialism pointed instead to the racial nature of Muslims or people of the so-called Arab world, who were in turn vilified as enemies of the West. This was precisely the tactic of the FBI when it declared in its 1955 training manual that the true religion of African American Muslims was primitivism. But by the early 2000s, not only African American Muslims but also the nation's non-Black Muslims were branded as promoters of anti-American hatred and religious fanaticism.

Among the most influential advocates of this racialization was the political scientist Samuel Huntington, who claimed that the fundamental conflicts of the post–Cold War era have been neither political nor ideological but essentially "civilizational." By civilization, Huntington meant the highest echelon of cultural entities. So, as he explained, although a village in northern Italy and another in southern Italy are both culturally

Italian, they share at the highest echelon a Western culture, beyond which no further "cultural entity" exists. In contrast to Western culture stand non-Western cultures. And in the wake of the Cold War's demise, Huntington argued, the chief threat to the West is what he termed the Confucian-Islamic connection. This consists of the religious civilizations of China and of Muslim polities.[22]

After the United States began devoting its unmatched military might to fighting Islamic terrorism in the early 2000s, Huntington became widely hailed as prescient and insightful. His admirers, however, seized not so much on his discussion of China but rather on his characterization of Islam. Huntington had argued that Islam was not merely a religion but a civilization that encompasses and unites at the highest echelon a basic societal type of people who are fundamentally at odds with the West as a civilization. This was both his brilliance and his error. In a sense, Huntington was wrong for all the right reasons. He never claimed to be talking about race. But of course the West is precisely a racial subjectivity. It is constituted as Europeanness, a subjectivity shaped by juxtaposition to non-Europeanness.[23] Huntington completely ignored the fact that the United States operates more than 1,000 military bases outside of the formal borders of the United States and continues to deploy murderous violence on a global scale to overthrow democracies, to institutionalize torture, and to target and undermine non-White states and political movements for self-determination. He claimed the central issue of international relations was the essential nature of Europeans versus that of non-Europeans – racial constitution – and not the struggle to control resources or to defend sovereignty. In this way, Huntington rendered a facile portrait of international conflict that became the standard rationale for the US War on Terror. Huntington's thesis of civilizational conflict, in this way, was centrally rooted in the racialization of Islam. Few spokespersons have made so explicit and concise the racial logic that drives the political imaginary of the contemporary US empire.[24]

---

[22] Samuel P. Huntington, "The Clash of Civilizations?" *Foreign Affairs* 72: 23–24, 46. Huntington subsequently published *The Clash of Civilizations and the Remaking of World Order* (New York: Simon and Schuster, 1996), in which he elaborated this thesis.

[23] Sohail Daulatzai, *Black Star, Crescent Moon.* Junaid Rana, *Terrifying Muslims: Race and Labor in the South Asian Diaspora* (Durham, NC: Duke University Press, 2011). Gil Anidjar, *Semites: Race, Religion, Literature* (Stanford, CA: Stanford University Press, 2008).

[24] Mahmood Mamdani compellingly examines this as "Culture Talk," which he notes is designed to obscure the political realities and conflicts that have given rise to political Islam (Mamdani prudently distinguishes political Islam from religious fundamentalism,

The ramifications of this racialization were far-reaching and impactful in the post-9/11 years. In October of 2003, for instance, Army Lieutenant General William G. "Jerry" Boykin began addressing numerous churches on the subject of religion, terrorism, and national security. He repeatedly asserted that the United States was a target of terrorism because it was a Christian nation, and he insisted that the United States could defeat Islamic terrorists only if "we come at them in the name of Jesus." Secretary of State Donald Rumsfeld affirmed Boykin's right to make such claims, even in uniform.[25] The fierce controversy over the so-called Ground Zero Mosque (it was actually a cultural center that included a Muslim prayer room) during the summer of 2010 made highly explicit the widespread, deep-seated conviction among mainstream US Americans that Islam is fundamentally alien and hostile to authentic US society.[26] The staunch opposition to a Muslim cultural center at Ground Zero was accompanied by protest against mosque construction throughout the United States. Anti-Muslim rallies also erupted in California, Wisconsin, and Tennessee to protest the construction of mosques during 2010. As one member of a Florida-based group devoted to defending Western civilization against Islam expressed the following:

As a mother and a grandmother, I worry.... I learned that in 20 years with the rate of the birth population, we will be overtaken by Islam, and their goal is to get people in Congress and the Supreme Court to see that Shariah is implemented. My children and grandchildren will have to live under that.[27]

In 2011 and 2012, US Representative Peter King organized congressional hearings to buttress his claim that US Muslims merited special scrutiny because their religion made them ill-fit for assimilating into Western culture and instead predisposed them to anti-Americanism and terrorism. The growing manifestation of anti-Islamic populism even grew to include efforts to create a preemptive ban against Sharia law in Oklahoma.[28]

---

the latter of which is inappropriately applied to Islamist movements). See his *Good Muslim, Bad Muslim*, 19–22.

[25] "Pentagon Intelligence Officer Says War on Terrorism is Battle Against Satan," Associated Press, October 16, 2003. Chalmers Johnson, *Nemesis: The Last Days of the American Republic* (New York: Henry Holt and Company, 2006), 4.

[26] "September 11 Attack Aftermath: Islamic Center Near Ground Zero Advances." *Facts On File World News Digest.*

[27] See Laurie Goodstein, "Across Nation, Mosque Projects Meet Opposition," *The New York Times*, August 7, 2010.

[28] See "Judge Issues Permanent Injunction on Oklahoma Sharia Law Ban," CNN, November 29, 2010 http://edition.cnn.com/2010/US/11/29/oklahoma.sharia.law/ (accessed October 2, 2013).

Accounting for Race

This history of the US intelligence state's relationship to African American Islam and to the numerous communities of the nation's non-Black Muslims that have emerged since the 1970s demands a rigorous understanding of what race is and what it does. The simple fact that religion can be racialized, for instance, renders analytically mute any phenotypic paradigm of race, as religion is not a phenotypic formation. Among the most popular treatments of race is that by sociologists Michael Omi and Howard Winant. In their widely influential *Racial Formation in the United States*, the authors examine race as a sociopolitical formation applied to specific types of bodies. Winant explains this succinctly in the following way:

At its most basic level, race can be defined as a concept that signifies and symbolizes sociopolitical conflicts and interests in reference to different types of human bodies. Although the concept of race appeals to biologically based human characteristics (so-called phenotypes), selection of these particular human features for the purposes of racial signification is always and necessarily a social and historical process. There is no biological basis for distinguishing human groups along the lines of "race," and the sociohistorical categories employed to differentiate among these groups reveal themselves, upon serious examination, to be imprecise if not completely arbitrary.[29]

Omi and Winant are highly representative of most scholarly studies of race in the sense that they treat race (1) as an essentially discursive formation rooted in thinking and attitudes (2) that is largely tied to bodies and rooted in phenotype. Once they have identified race in this way, they then proceed to "deconstruct" it by demonstrating the fallacy of encoding phenotypic difference with social meanings. This epitomizes the critical, deconstructive analysis of race that has triumphed in contemporary scholarship.[30]

In contrast to studies such as those of Omi and Winant is the work by scholars who engage seriously with the relationship that race bears with colonialism – in other words with state practices and political

---

[29] Howard Winant, *The New Politics of Race: Globalism, Difference, Justice* (Minneapolis: University of Minnesota Press, 2004), 235 n.4. See also Howard Winant, *The World is a Ghetto: Race and Democracy since World War Two* (New York: Basic Books, 2001), 317 n.1.

[30] It would be difficult to exaggerate the dominance of this approach to explaining race; examples are legion. Among the best known are Audrey Smedley, *Race in North America: History of a Worldview*, 3rd ed. (Boulder: Westview Press, 2007). George Fredrickson, *Racism: A Short History* (Princeton: Princeton University Press, 2009). Nell Irvin Painter, *The History of White People* (New York: Norton, 2010).

order. Foremost in this arena is the political theorist Barnor Hesse, who has critiqued what he describes as the fallacy of treating race as thinking or a set of concepts. Although certain ways of thinking can and do result from race, Hesse explains, *race is not "thinking."* Race is a colonial process that has constituted "Europeanness and non-Europeanness" through material, discursive, and noncorporeal domains. Encoding race through phenotypic difference, he writes, "is but one historical symptom and political formation of race through modernity."[31] Given the scale on which racial governance has historically been articulated through reference to "territory, climate, culture, history, [and] religion," it appears that the body was not so much the "ubiquitous metaphor" of race as its "privileged metonym."[32] Hesse demonstrates that racialization is a *governing* formation – it is a process that has structured the *political rule* of Europeans over non-Europeans. Racialization becomes articulated, thus, as "a series of onto-colonial taxonomies of land, climate, history, bodies, customs, language" and religion – "all of which became sedimented metonymically, metaphorically, and normatively as *the assembled attributions of "race."*[33] Hesse is distinctive for explaining race so succinctly as a system of governing through the colonial relation of power. A number of other scholars, however, occupy the same theoretical orbit as Hesse. Geraldine Heng, for instance, has likewise emphasized that race is a political formation rooted in establishing a colonial differential structure of power. Heng departs sharply from the common fixation on phenotype among theorists of race. She writes,

So tenacious has been scientific racism's account of race, with its entrenchment of high modernist racism as the template of *all* racisms, that it is still routinely understood, in everyday life and much of scholarship, that *properly* racial logic and behavior *must* reference biology and the body as their referent.[34]

In departing from this exclusively somato-centric approach to understanding race, Heng emphasizes that race is not a "substantive content" fixed in form and always appearing the same. It is, rather, a "structural relationship" of social power that produces "a hierarchy of peoples for differential treatment." Although critical race theorists, she observes,

---

[31] Barnor Hesse, "Racialized Modernity: An Analytics of White Mythologies," *Ethnic and Racial Studies* 30, no. 4 (July 2007): 646.

[32] Hesse, "Racialized Modernity," 653.

[33] Ibid., 659.

[34] Geraldine Heng, "The Invention of Race in the European Middle Ages I: Race Studies, Modernity, and the Middle Ages," *Literature Compass* 8, no. 5 (2011): 319. Emphasis in the original.

have widely acknowledged and examined this mutability of race – the capacity of race to manifest through multiple forms and modes – they have nevertheless typically limited their conception of race to something that happens strictly and exclusively within the *temporality of modernity*.[35] But Heng has persuasively demonstrated that race was operant in medieval Christendom as early as the 1200s and was at work in Christian governance over Jewish populations throughout Western Europe. The racialization of Islam on display in the wake of 9/11, she continues, constitutes "a moment in which cultural race and racisms, and *religious* race, jostle alongside racism-understood-as-somatic/ biological-determinations...."[36] The hegemony of somato-centric approaches to theorizing race, in other words, now appears to be just that – an ideological fixation that seems unjustified in light of the actual history of biopolitics in both premodern and modern times.

This analysis is further manifested in the recent work of María Elena Martínez. In her *Genealogical Fictions: Limpieza de Sangre, Religion, Gender in Colonial Mexico*, Martinez likewise concludes that scholars who insist that race is necessarily about biology and phenotypic difference and who demand that race can be documented only when attested by a specific grammar that names race as *race* or a cognate term and is thus *linguistically recognizable* as such to professional researchers, are ignoring the actual work that race performs and are naively fixated on linguistic signifiers when they should be concerned with the work that race does and recognizing the existence and deployment of race on that basis. She argues that the theological and juridical system of *limpieza de sangre* operating in Iberia and the Americas in the fifteenth and sixteenth centuries was nothing less than a system of race.[37]

What we have at this point is a fundamental failure of somato-centric theories of race to account for racialization before the period of so-called modernity. This situation, moreover, coexists with contemporary scholarship on the racialization of Islam that likewise exceeds the explicative capacities of rigidly somato-centric theoretical accounts of race. As Juanaid Rana has asked, how do we account for the racialization of American Muslims if religion cannot be a race? As he demonstrates in his *Terrifying Muslims*, the proper rejoinder is that religion can in fact be a race. In other words, religion can be racialized in order to constitute

---

[35] Heng, "Invention of Race in the European Middle Ages I," 323, 324.

[36] Ibid., 319. Emphasis in the original.

[37] María Elena Martínez, *Genealogical Fictions: Limpieza de Sangre, Religion, and Gender in Colonial Mexico* (Stanford, CA: Stanford University Press, 2008).

part of the assemblage of differential essences that ground the exercise of governing through the colonial relation of power.[38]

This colonial relation of power is the form of political order through which a polity (viz., a state, be it monarchical or democratic) rules a population by treating its members as political aliens. This means the dominated population is governed as a political unit whose relationship to the political community of the ruling state is denied a pristine status. Racialization is achieved through this colonial form of political order when this dominated population is marked as perpetually, ineluctably alien. They are treated as incapable of truly belonging to the state. In the eyes of the state, neither the passage of time nor the adoption of new cultural forms alters this alien status. The most practical consequence of this colonial relation is the denial of the right to have rights. But in the terms of racial logic, those who are colonially governed exist as outsiders and political enemies because by their very nature (i.e., according to the coda of their racialization), they are people of a fundamentally different type (this is "differential essence"). They are *in* the society but not *of* it, even if they have been born in that society. They exist in contrast to other populations of the state who enjoy a pristine relationship with the political community of that state. Where this colonially governed population resides beyond the formal geopolitical borders of the state, we have an external colony. Where this population resides within the borders of the ruling state, we have an internal colony. The colonial relation itself, however, is constituted without regard for spatial distance within or beyond political borders.

This is essentially the analysis of race that Martin Delany advanced in the nineteenth century as he sought to navigate the divide between Black self-determination and the quest for membership within the political community of the United States. Delany argued that understanding race required attention to politics instead of phenotype or notions of prejudice. His critique resonates with recent theories of race that attend to colonialism and state practices. In this analysis, it becomes evident that race is not phenotype. Nor is race is a fictive code that overlays biology. And race is certainly not mere discourse. It is not feelings or attitudes or hatred, although it has certainly given rise to these. Race is a state practice of ruling people within a political order that perpetually places some within and others outside of the political community through which the constitution of the state is conceived. This conceptual context is essential

---

[38] Junaid Rana, *Terrifying Muslims.*

to interpreting the racialization of Islam and the national security paradigm within American democracy.[39]

American Islam, Democracy, and Counterintelligence

The parallel between the FBI's repression of African American Muslims and the post-9/11 racialization of Islam is not coincidental. The FBI's engagement with African American Muslims before the 1970s, rather, profoundly shaped the racial repression of Islam on display in subsequent decades as the nation's population of non-Black Muslims increased. This was due to several factors. Most importantly, African American Muslims were *Muslims*. And they constituted the majority of the nation's Islamic population until the immigration reforms of the 1960s. In other words, the history of the FBI's engagement with African American Muslims since the 1930s *is* the early history of the United States racializing Islam under the national security paradigm. It is important to get this right, because the temptation is to replicate the FBI's disingenuous claims that African Americans who identified as Muslims lacked the adequate intellectual constitution to grasp that they were imagining themselves to be Muslims and were merely delusional. Scholars, in other words, should avoid replicating the ideology of the FBI's training manual and must instead study the deployment of that ideology.

Islam as Racial Religion

Because African Americans generally constituted the face of American Islam for the FBI before the 1960s (i.e., before the Immigration Reform Act of 1965 ended the racial quota system), the FBI had become accustomed to engaging American Muslims as a racial population whose interests and aspirations contravened the imperatives of the United States as a racial state. This means the FBI had cultivated since the 1930s an institutional disposition toward Islam that was preeminently racializing. And the bureau continued to engage Muslims in this fashion after the 1960s

---

[39] Race is not an ineluctable formation in the context of the arrival or movement of new populations. Important counterexamples existed among the numerous Native polities such as those of the Choctaw, Chickasaw, and Creek nations that automatically naturalized foreigners and incorporated them into the political community. In a decidedly perverse turn of events, this practice was exploited by Anglo-American settlers to undermine Native sovereignty. See Sylvester A. Johnson, "Religion and Empire in Mississippi, 1790–1833," in *Gods of the Mississippi*, ed. Michael Pasquier (Bloomington: Indiana University Press, 2012).

as the American Muslim population became increasingly non-Black. In this context, the FBI branded hate-based violence as the racial essence of African American Islam. This involved two subtle but significant factors: the bureau's agents portrayed targeted subjects as atavistically violent, and they asserted repeatedly that these Muslims lacked any rational assessment of power or any ethical legitimacy in their critique of the US racial state. Putatively, they hated White America because Whites had implemented a superior working ethic and greater intellect to create a higher standard of living, personal success, and political might.

During both the civil rights era and the post-9/11 years, the FBI's engagement with American Muslims was shaped by the material and political conditions of US imperialism, which manifested through domestic (internal) and foreign structures of colonialism. By these terms, the FBI engaged Muslims as inherently and incorrigibly alien to the US body politic. It was not necessary for these Muslims to commit crimes, perpetrate violence, or physically endanger the lives of White Americans. By their very existence – again, constituted as racial subjects through colonial governance – they threatened the political community of the US racial state. This is precisely the ethnocratic condition of race-struggle or race-war that Michel Foucault described in his account of the racial state. In both its early and contemporary history of engaging American Muslims, the US intelligence state rendered US Muslims not merely as criminals but particularly as racial enemies of the nation, *from whom American society must be defended.*[40]

By formalizing COINTELPRO in 1967 as a distinct, uniform protocol, the FBI created a new and distinct phase in the nation's larger intelligence complex. It was at this point that federal, state, and local officials began repressing African Americans as the *chief* threat to the internal security of the United States. According to FBI Director J. Edgar Hoover, Black people exceeded communism as a racial threat to internal security by 1967. Prior to his assassination in 1965, the Muslim minister Malik Shabazz (Malcolm X) was regarded as the most volatile personification of racial threat to America. Within two years, the FBI explicitly identified Martin Luther King Jr. in this capacity. This was the context for the bureau's decision to launch COINTELPRO as a means of destroying racial threat. These domestic counterintelligence tactics were never limited to specifically racial deployments. However, the immense scale on

---

[40] I allude here to Michel Foucault's analysis of race war in his lectures at the Collège de France, posthumously published under the same name, *Il faut défendre la société*.

which counterintelligence has proceeded as a form of racial containment or race war attests to its racial origins and demonstrates the degree to which counterintelligence became a central practice of the racial state. The FBI's concentration of resources ($3 billion per annum) for containing a continuing racial threat (not to mention the resources of the CIA, NSA, and a host of other intelligence agencies) in the early 2000s is an institutional paradigm that was set in motion by COINTELPRO.

To be sure, counterintelligence has been strictly concerned with the category of political threat, not crime per se. So, gesturing to the innocence of counterintelligence targets misses the point. As the FBI transformed law enforcement at every level of government into coherent institutions of political counterintelligence, it also drastically altered the form and function of patrolling, arresting, and detaining. This, most succinctly, was the birth of mass incarceration. This deployment was never directed exclusively at Blacks. But the American racial state did single out African Americans as exceptional, unparalleled targets for mass incarceration. COINTELPRO thus became the central, foundational element in fully transforming incarceration into a massive institution of racial containment under the national security paradigm. In direct consequence of this, US prisons and foreign prisons based on the US maximum security (or super-max) model eventually became the preeminent institution for concentrating Muslims as a racial threat.

Two observations are at stake here. First, it was during the 1960s that the United States began to detain African Americans in record numbers as political prisoners. This was *not* the first time that the United States held political prisoners. It was, however, the period when the carceral institution became a central element of the national security protocol. At local levels, municipalities throughout the American South employed incarceration as the weapon of choice to attack civil rights activism, to stymie movements like the Black Panther Party and the Republic of New Afrika, and to terrorize political targets acting individually or as members of Black liberationist organizations. At the federal level, this was achieved through maximum security and, subsequently, super-maximum security facilities. Between 1961 and 1963, for example, 20,000 men, women, and children were arrested for participating in civil rights demonstrations. Richard Nixon's declaration of law-and-order, moreover, was quickly elaborated as the war on drugs, which specifically targeted African Americans and, increasingly, Latinos.[41]

---

[41] Michelle Alexander, *The New Jim Crow: Mass Incarceration in the Age of Colorblindness* (New York: New Press, 2010), 37.

The militarized engagement of American Muslims in the post-9/11 era was produced by the militarized policing that municipalities throughout the United States created in the 1960s, in collaboration with the FBI, with the aim of destroying Black political radicalism – also known as Black extremism. Policing was fundamentally reconceived as a military enterprise – specifically through SWAT – to conduct racial warfare within the borders of the United States against Black activists. This initiated a wave of militarization across US police departments. But more basically, the entire enterprise of law enforcement was fundamentally reconceived, in departure from policing as engagement with citizens qua members of a political community symbolizing consanguinity with the state. Instead, policing was reframed at the level of policy and practice as militarized engagement with *enemies of the state* in the same sense that military combat was rooted in the conquest of members of a foreign, enemy polity. Police departments acquired military weapons (often in the form of freely donated military surplus), hired military veterans (this was the specific protocol of the first anti-Black SWAT units), employed military tactics (with a special fondness for predawn raids), organized special intelligence divisions, adopted military terminology (police departments began conducting "strikes" on "targets"), and collaborated closely with the FBI to respond to national security threats.[42]

Because Islam had been racialized, American Muslims were constituted as a coherent, unified population that was incapable of pristinely exemplifying Western subjectivity (i.e., Europeanness). By the terms of their racialization, Muslims might live in the United States, but they did so as ineluctably incorrigible aliens. In the estimation of the US intelligence complex, they were internal enemies who threatened the US political community – the American people. This threat, moreover, was not merely a lethal threat that endangered the physical lives of the nation's citizens. Rather, it was also racial because it supposedly posed a fundamental hazard to the civilizational identity – that is, the racial vitality – of the United States as a Western (i.e., racially European) polity. Whether they were described as "hostile to the West" (in the language of NYPD's intelligence division) or as devoted to destroying the Western nature of the United States (in the words of the Clarion Fund), American Muslims were relegated beyond the pale of the body politic in a long-standing

---

[42] Radley Balko, *Rise of the Warrior Cop: The Militarization of America's Police Forces* (New York: Public Affairs, 2013), 49–80. Ward Churchill and Jim Vander Wall, *Agents of Repression: The FBI's Secret Wars against the Black Panther Party and the American Indian Movement* (Cambridge, MA: South End Press, 2002), 36–38.

pattern of colonial governance. This clearly demonstrated the racial paradigm of counterintelligence.

Democracy, Colonialism, and Racial Formation

The racialization of Islam demonstrates in stark terms how *democracy is implicated in racial formation and the colonial relation of power*. How is this so? Especially given the virtuous legacy that democracy enjoys in the popular and scholarly domains? The problem lies with the fact that the colonial relation of power inheres when one population, who constitute themselves as the body politic, governs other populations by designating them incapable of authentic membership in the political community of the state. The emergence of republican democracy as a specific political order, of course, became possible precisely because the monarchical state ceased to be the exclusive means of constituting the subjectivity of the state. Alongside the monarchical state there arose the "nation-state" (or alternatively, the people-state). Whereas the monarchical state was formally rendered and represented through the political body of the monarch (a king or a queen), the people-state was instead rendered through the political community comprising individuals among nobility and beyond, extending to those of low social standing (as examined in Chapter 3). Edmund Morgan referred to this as "inventing the people."[43] In his earlier corpus, Michel Foucault called this the invention of the population. But subsequently, in his lectures at the Collège de France, Foucault described this emergence as the creation of the racial state. He argued that Western European statecraft was able to produce the people-state precisely because political officials began to govern based on the economy of a shared political nature – a racial constitution – that demanded protection from political others who also lived in the same state and who inhabited the same society but who were nevertheless extraneous to the shared political nature of those constituting the people-state. What emerged, he argued, was a style of governing that was rooted in the imperatives of defending society from these racial others. This was the peacetime politics of race war.[44]

---

[43] Edmund Morgan, *Inventing the People: The Rise of Popular Sovereignty in England and America* (New York: W. W. Norton, 1988).

[44] Michel Foucault, *Society Must Be Defended: Lectures at the Collège de France, 1975–76*, ed. Mauro Bertani and Alessandro Fontana (New York: Picador, 2003). Foucault argued that peacetime between states veiled an ongoing war within states, and this internal struggle was race war, the struggle by the state and its political community to dominate and extirpate internal enemies, those who lived in the society but who did not belong to it. It was from these that the state needed to defend the society.

The sociologist Michael Mann has proffered a similar analysis of democracy using different language in his comparative sociological study of democratic states. Mann, who is one of the few scholars to include attention to non-Western states in his study of democracy (he examines the Cherokee nation), accounts for the ethnocratic function of democracies. They endow the people with ruling power, but not everyone gets to be "the people." Only some, he observes, constitute the people. Democracies are thus ethnocracies, and the *ethnos* that rules is a particular group – racial, ethnic, or linguistic populations, to employ his language – certainly not literally all of the people living in a given state. Because democracies are ethnocratic, they invest in ethnic cleansing along a scale that extends from mild to the most extreme form – genocide. Mann demonstrates, in fact, that ethnic cleansing is largely a symptom not of ancient monarchical states but of modern democracies. By this account, democracy is not an innocent, virtuous political order. It is, rather, the product of the colonial relation of power, and it takes that relation to its extreme manifestation.[45]

This helps to clarify what might otherwise seem to be counterintuitive and contradictory – that the United States, the world's first and greatest democracy, is not only a racial state but is also one whose euphoric populism in the age of a global war on terror has subjected US Muslims to a terrifying experience of constant surveillance, infiltration, and repression that has debilitated their communities, bred fear and distrust, and portrayed Muslims as internal enemies of the United States.

The racialization of Islam is not a contradiction of US democracy. It is a deeply troubling reminder and powerful manifestation of democracy. Foucault once quipped in his genealogical study of sexuality that "we must at the same time conceive of sex without the law, and power without the king."[46] It is with similar analytical urgency that scholars must be able to conceive of race without the somatic body, of religion without the creed. We must understand in the most rigorous fashion how race performs its work as colonial governance through the structures of democratic empire. And we must begin to appreciate religion as, at times, a racialized formation, one located squarely at the center of biopolitics. Only then can we perceive the entanglement of religion, race, and colonialism.

---

[45] Michael Mann, *The Dark Side of Democracy* (New York: Cambridge University Press, 2005).

[46] Michel Foucault, *History of Sexuality*, vol. 1, *An Introduction*, trans. Robert Hurley (New York: Pantheon, 1978), 91.

Conclusion

Black Religion, Freedom, and Colonialism

The varieties of African American religions that have explicitly challenged US colonialism – most notably, the problem of internal colonialism – have most visibly embodied the intersection of religion and empire. As we have seen in Chapters 4 and 5, Black religious movements that were rooted in self-determination and the strident rejection of state racism created a Black Christian settler state: Liberia. This was accomplished through multiple iterations of missionary-settler movements in West Africa. The democratic freedom so brazenly embodied in the White settler state became the central rationality for pursuing Black self-governance. In this way, the Black settler quest for democratic freedom enabled stateless free Blacks in the United States to fashion self-determination. But this freedom, like that of the White settler state, manifested its roots in slavery and the colonial relation of power. This meant Americo-Liberians governed native Africans as racial outsiders whose relation to the governing polity of Liberia remained perpetually alien and external. This was no accident. It was, rather, a central formation within the architecture of democratic freedom.

The fundamental tension, moreover, between Black self-determination and the pursuit of Black citizenship within the United States was frenetic and fructuous in the aftermath of the Civil War. Thousands of African Americans refused to accommodate themselves to remaining stateless in the wake of slavery's formal demise. As Henry McNeal Turner advocated, they pursued the political project of self-governance in Liberia, where they could enjoy the fruits of a racial state whose political community was grounded in the Black Christian racial subjectivity of Americo-Liberian settlers. By contrast, those who remained in the United States were increasingly caught between the extralegal brutality of White terrorism and the burgeoning architecture of legal apartheid that formally gestured toward their status as racial outsiders in a White republic.

This did not, however, eviscerate African Americans' quest for political inclusion. As White government officials increasingly offered pathways for Blacks to join the US military – the Buffalo Soldiers epitomized this legacy – many African Americans promoted US imperialism to abet White colonial conquest over Native Americans, Cubans, and Filipinos. They also embraced Christian theological rationales for the dominance of Western civilization. These two paths – Black settler colonialism and Black service to US colonialism – were of a piece, constitutive of the warp and woof of colonial governance. These strategies differed drastically, however, in terms of how each positioned African Americans as political subjects. In the former case, they were members of the political community through which the governing polity (a colonial state) was conceived. In the latter, political outsiders governed through the colonial relation of power.

During the twentieth century, the Universal Negro Improvement Association (UNIA) – and Garvey, more specifically – apprehended the distinctive role that empire has played in structuring global networks of commerce, militarism, and the political consolidation that established White imperial domination. Garvey desired to harness this capacity of empire to inaugurate a Black empire-state that might hold its own against Western colonial hegemony. To this day, some scholars have either dismissed Garvey or have concluded that he betrayed the noble ideals of a pristine Black politics. This Black politics is imagined as holding no truck with the dealings of political domination. Put most crassly: *imperium* (read most succinctly as the global or transnational power of a colonial state) is for Whites; Blacks should exercise righteousness not rule, morality not might, piety not power. The rationality here is what Friedrich Nietzsche called *ressentiment*. In some sense, Garvey has been made a whipping boy for insisting otherwise. His ambitions of colonizing Africa and creating a continental Black state easily function as evidence that he was not seriously committed to Black freedom. And yet, it seems that his intellectual grasp of colonialism, democracy, and freedom (he was an avowed *anticolonial imperialist*) was on par with that of the great White founders of Western hegemony, who eagerly crafted the racial states (the United States, France, Israel, and Britain, most notably) that now command honorable status for embodying democracy and freedom. Because he saw these as consonant, co-constitutive formations, Garvey pursued empire as a means to achieving Black freedom. In this way, Garvey seems to have realized, as did Toussaint L'Ouverture (who reintroduced slavery in Saint-Domingue to generate revenues for militarizing a Black state and fending off its enemies), the condition that David Scott has so incisively described as the "tragedy of modernity."[1] Being an agential subject of history requires that one participate in the very mechanisms of power that one might deem reprehensible because the actual architecture of social power differs stridently from how it is imagined within the discourse of political liberalism. Moreover, it was Garvey's imperial imaginary of divine identity – namely, the god of Ethiopia – that animated the UNIA's theological intervention and buoyed the rise of Black ethnic religions.

But Garveyism was not to triumph as the regnant *logos* of race and power in the twentieth century. It was, rather, what Steven Hahn has called the "liberal integrationist paradigm" that triumphed as the dominant narrative and symbol of Black politics in the twentieth century. To this paradigm was bequeathed a sort of perverse sanction and legitimacy. Its perversion derived from the fact that the actual historical efforts by African Americans to end US apartheid and establish integration as the formal, legal, and actual architecture of racial power was continually opposed as a threat to the racial state, as un-American, and as "Black extremism." Popular renditions and rehearsals of this past heap blame on White Southerners for holding back progress. However, this is only part of the picture. It was the US federal government that actuated a covert war against this Black rebellion, which federal officials viewed in relationship to the many other rebellions throughout the globe that opposed Western colonial rule.

No individual is more iconic of this paradigm than Martin Luther King, Jr. Standard textbooks portray him leading a struggle against the so-called White South. But King eventually realized that US empire – the problem of colonialism – was the foundation of the social injustice he opposed. And it is telling that the US government declared him an enemy of the state (the most dangerous Black person of his time) and engaged him as such. Despite this, the legacies of King, the Southern Christian Leadership Conference, and the larger civil rights movement have become rarified into an abstract rebuttal of movements for Black self-determination. This manifests as the iconic pageantry of King versus Malcolm X or SCLC versus the Nation of Islam, creating a caricature of

[1] David Scott, *Conscripts of Modernity: The Tragedy of Colonial Enlightenment* (Durham, NC: Duke University Press, 2004).

benign protest vis-à-vis the armed resistance of extremists. Many scholars are aware, of course, that US government repression of anticolonialism (consider the plight of Paul Robeson and W. E. B. Du Bois) is largely responsible for vilifying and criminalizing the critique of empire and the legacy of activism to promote sovereignty among colonized peoples. At the level of popular imagination, however, the putative decadence of Black self-determination seems inherent to the thing itself and not due to the counterintelligence deployed by an anti-Black racial state.

Finally, it will take some time for scholars to fully appreciate the relationship between the racial threat of anticolonial religion among African Americans and the racialization of Islam that became more strident and paradigmatic in the early 2000s following the US invasion of Afghanistan and Iraq. At its core, the history of anticolonialism in Black religion bears testimony to the constitution of race, which is achieved through governing some as members of, and others as perpetually alien to, the political community through which the state is conceived. So long as the US racial state operates as the guarantor of colonial governance over predominantly Muslim polities while these are rendered as antithetical to European Christian civilization (the West), Islam will remain racialized as an alien subjectivity in a White settler state, the genealogy of whose racial constitution is rooted in the secular, political, governing formations of European Christendom.

African American religions have long operated under the sign of freedom and its putative others. By this I mean to indicate that freedom has operated as a discursive "burden" and cultural symbol.[2] This should not be taken as a claim that Black religion generally is essentially or reductively concerned with freedom. Such is not the case. My point, rather, is that the scholarly and popular imagination of African American religions is typically rendered through these terms. The reasons for this are historical and significant. Colonialism and slavery are not merely discourse. They are historical realities, material practices, and political structures through which racial Blackness has been constituted and by which Black people have been dominated. It would be unthinkable, thus, for African Americans to demonstrate no special concern for realizing freedom as a political project. And it would be implausible to expect that the structures of African American religions not be visibly and particularly marked by the coda of freedom.

---

[2] Curtis J. Evans, *The Burden of Black Religion* (New York: Oxford University Press, 2008).

This visage of freedom, however, has obscured the problem of empire and the thick linkage that binds freedom to its putative others – slavery and colonialism. Throughout this account of African American religions, I have sought to render the ambivalence of freedom by making visible its linkage to colonialism. I have also sought to portray the human cost of Western democracy, whose provenance lies partly with the corporatism that Atlantic slavery enabled and the colonial governance that has bequeathed to the world's peoples the seduction of racial states. We have barely begun to discern the relevance of empire and historical formulations of freedom for the interpretation of African American religions. As scholars continue to account for Black religions in light of this analysis, however, we can be certain that the space between the dream of freedom and the terror of empire is not empty but richly populated by genealogical ties whose defiance of scrutiny is our task to subdue.

Selected Bibliography

Archives

Moorish Science Temple of America Collection, 1926–1967. The Schomburg Center for Research in Black Culture, New York Public Library.

Moorish Science Temple of America FBI Files. Federal Bureau of Investigation. http://vault.fbi.gov/Moorish%20Science%20Temple%20of%20America.

COINTELPRO – Black Extremists FBI Files. Federal Bureau of Investigation. http://vault.fbi.gov/cointel-pro/cointel-pro-black-extremists.

Periodicals

African Repository and Colonial Journal (1827–1840).
Boston Recorder (1816).
Chicago Daily Tribune (1902).
Chicago Defender (1923).
Commercial Advertiser (1816).
The Los Angeles Times (1967).
Missionary Register (1830).
New York Amsterdam News (1925).
The New York Times (1896–1975).
North Star (1847–1848).
Washington Post (1967).

Books and Articles

Aarim-Heriot, Najia. *Chinese Immigrants, African Americans, and Racial Anxiety in the United States, 1848–82.* Urbana: University of Illinois Press, 2003.

Aaronson, Trevor. *The Terror Factory: Inside the FBI's Manufactured War on Terrorism.* Brooklyn: Ig Publishing, 2013.

Abasiattai, Monday B. *African Resistance in Liberia: The Vai and the Gola-Bandi.* Bremen: Liberia Working Group, 1988.

"The Search for Independence: New World Blacks in Sierra Leone and Liberia, 1787–1847." *Journal of Black Studies* 23, no. 1 (September 1, 1992): 107–16.

Abdelwahid, Mustafa. *Duse Mohamed Ali: The Autobiography of a Pioneer Pan African and Afro-Asian Activies*. Trenton: Red Sea Press, 2011.

Adeleke, Tunde. *UnAfrican Americans: Nineteenth-Century Black Nationalists and the Civilizing Mission*. Lexington: The University Press of Kentucky, 1998.

Agbeti, J. Kafi. *West African Church History: Christian Missions and Church Foundations: 1482–1919*. Leiden, the Netherlands: Brill, 1986.

Aikman, David. *Billy Graham: His Life and Influence*. Nashville: Thomas Nelson, 2007.

Alexander, Michelle, and Cornel West. *The New Jim Crow: Mass Incarceration in the Age of Colorblindness*. New York: The New Press, 2010.

Alie, Joe A. D. *A New History of Sierra Leone*. New York: St. Martin's Press, 1990.

Allen, Robert L. "Reassessing the Internal (NEO) Colonialism Theory." *The Black Scholar* (2005): 2–11.

Anidjar, Gil. *Semites: Race, Religion, Literature*. Stanford, CA: Stanford University Press, 2008.

Apter, Emily, and William Pietz, eds. *Fetishism as Cultural Discourse*. Ithaca, NY: Cornell University Press, 1993.

Arrighi, Giovanni. *The Long Twentieth Century: Money, Power, and the Origins of Our Times*. Rev. ed. New York: Verson, 2010.

Aston, Margaret. *Lollards and Reformers: Images and Literacy in Late Medieval Religion*. London: Hambledon Press, 1984.

Bacevich, Andrew J. *Washington Rules: America's Path to Permanent War*. New York: Metropolitan Books, 2010.

Barnes, Kenneth C. *Journey of Hope: The Back-to-Africa Movement in Arkansas in the Late 1800s*. Chapel Hill: University of North Carolina Press, 2004.

Barnes, L. Diane. *Frederick Douglass: Reformer and Statesman*. New York: Routledge, 2013.

Baucom, Ian. *Specters of the Atlantic: Finance Capital, Slavery, and the Philosophy of History*. Durham, NC: Duke University Press, 2005.

Bell, Howard. *A Survey of the Negro Convention Movement 1830–1861*. New York: Arno Press, 1969.

Bennett, Herman L. *Africans in Colonial Mexico: Absolutism, Christianity, and Afro-Creole Consciousness, 1570–1640*. Blacks in the Diaspora. Bloomington: Indiana University Press, 2003.

Colonial Blackness: A History of Afro-Mexico. Blacks in the Diaspora. Bloomington: Indiana University Press, 2009.

Berg, Herbert. *Elijah Muhammad and Islam*. New York: New York University Press, 2009.

Beyan, Amos Jones. *African American Settlements in West Africa: John Brown Russwurm and the American Civilizing Efforts*. New York: Palgrave Macmillan, 2005.

Bibb, Henry, and Charles J. Heglar. *The Life and Adventures of Henry Bibb: An American Slave*. Wisconsin Studies in Autobiography. Madison: University of Wisconsin Press, 2001.

Biddick, Kathleen. *The Typological Imaginary: Circumcision, Technology, History*. Philadelphia: University of Pennsylvania Press, 2003.

Birmingham, David. *Trade and Empire in the Atlantic, 1400–1600*. New York: Routledge, 2000.

Bishop, Louise M. *Words, Stones, & Herbs: The Healing Word in Medieval and Early Modern England*. Syracuse, NY: Syracuse University Press, 2007.

Blauner, Robert. "Internal Colonialism and Ghetto Revolt." *Social Problems* 16, no. 4 (April 1, 1969): 393–408.

Blum, Edward J. *Reforging the White Republic: Race, Religion, and American Nationalism, 1865–1898*. Conflicting Worlds. Baton Rouge: Louisiana State University Press, 2007.

Blyden, Edward W. *Christianity, Islam and the Negro Race*, 2nd ed. Baltimore: Black Classic Press, 1994.

"Hope for Africa." *Colonization Journal*, no. Tract no. 8 (August 1861).

Bosman, William. *New and Accurate Description of the Coast of Guinea*. New York: Barnes and Noble, 1967.

Bothwell, Cecil. *The Prince of War: Billy Graham's Crusade for a Wholly Christian Empire*, 2nd ed. Asheville, NC: Brave Ulysses Books, 2007.

Bown, Stephen R. *Merchant Kings: When Companies Ruled the World, 1600–1900*. New York: Conway, 2010.

Bracey, Earnest N. *Fannie Lou Hamer: The Life of a Civil Rights Icon*. Jefferson, NC: McFarland, 2011.

Braidwood, Stephen J. *Black Poor and White Philanthropists: London's Black and the Foundation of the Sierra Leone Settlement 1786–1791*. Liverpool: Liverpool University Press, 1994.

Brown, Ras Michael. *African-Atlantic Cultures and the South Carolina Lowcountry*. New York: Cambridge University Press, 2014.

Bruns, Roger. *Billy Graham: A Biography*. Westport, CT: Greenwood Press, 2004.

Burkett, Randall K. *Garveyism as a Religious Movement*. Metuchen, NJ: Scarecrow Press, 1978.

Bussmann, Klaus, and Heinz Schilling. *1648, War and Peace in Europe: Politics, Religion, Law, and Society*. Munster: Westfälisches Landesmuseum, 1999.

Bynum, Caroline Walker. *Christian Materiality: An Essay on Religion in Late Medieval Europe*. New York: Zone Books, 2011.

Byrd, Alexander X. *Captives and Voyagers: Black Migrants Across the Eighteenth-Century British Atlantic World*. Antislavery, Abolition, and the Atlantic World. Baton Rouge: Louisiana State University Press, 2008.

Calhoon, Robert McCluer. *The Loyalists in Revolutionary America, 1760–1781*. New York: Harcourt Brace Jovanovich, 1973.

Campbell, James T. *Middle Passages: African American Journeys to Africa, 1787–2005*. New York: Penguin Press, 2006.

Carmichael, Stokely, and Ekwueme Michael Thelwell. *Ready for Revolution: The Life and Struggles of Stokely Carmichael*. New York: Scribner, 2005.

Carpenter, Joel A. *Revive Us Again: The Reawakening of American Fundamentalism*. New York: Oxford University Press, 1997.

Carretta, Vincent. *Equiano, the African: Biography of a Self-Made Man*. Reprint ed. Athens: University of Georgia Press, 2005.

Carretta, Vincent, and Ty M. Reese, eds. *The Life and Letters of Philip Quaque, the First African Anglican Missionary*. Athens: University of Georgia Press, 2010.

Chidester, David. *Savage Systems: Colonialism and Comparative Religion in Southern Africa*. Charlottesville: University of Virginia Press, 1996.

Chireau, Yvonne, and Nathaniel Deutsch, eds. *Black Zion: African American Religious Encounters with Judaism*. New York: Oxford University Press, 2000.

Ciment, James. *Another America: The Story of Liberia and the Former Slaves Who Ruled It*. New York: Farrar, Straus & Giroux, 2013.

Clarke, Kamari Maxine. *Mapping Yoruba Networks: Power and Agency in the Making of Transnational Communities*. Durham, NC: Duke University Press Books, 2004.

Clegg, Claude Andrew. *An Original Man: The Life and Times of Elijah Muhammad*. New York: St. Martin's Press, 1997.

Clegg III, Claude Andrew. *The Price of Liberty: African Americans and the Making of Liberia*. Chapel Hill: University of North Carolina Press, 2004.

Clifford, Mary Louise. *From Slavery to Freetown: Black Loyalists After the American Revolution*. Jefferson, NC: McFarland & Company, 1999.

Cooper, Frederick. *Colonialism in Question: Theory, Knowledge, History*. Berkeley: University of California Press, 2005.

Crone, G.R. *The Voyages of Cadamosto and Other Documents on Western Africa in the Second Half of the Fifteenth Century*. Nendeln, Liechtenstein,: Kraus Reprint, 1967.

Curtis, Edward E., IV. *Black Muslim Religion in the Nation of Islam, 1960–1975*. Chapel Hill: University of North Carolina Press, 2006.

Muslims in America: A Short History. New York: Oxford University Press, 2009.

Daulatzai, Sohail. *Black Star, Crescent Moon: The Muslim International and Black Freedom beyond America*. Minneapolis: University of Minnesota Press, 2012.

Dean, David M. *Defender of the Race: James Theodore Holly, Black Nationalist Bishop*. Boston: Lambeth Press, 1979.

De Brosses, Charles. *Du Culte Des Dieux Fetiches, Ou Parallele De L'Ancienne Religion De L'Egypte Avec La Religion Actuelle De Nigritie*. Geneva: Cramer, 1760.

Delany, Martin R. *The Condition, Elevation, Emigration, and Destiny of the Colored People of the United States and Official Report of the Niger Valley Exploring Party*. Classics in Black Studies. Amherst, MA: Humanity Books, 2004.

Donelha, André. *Descrição da Serra Leoa e dos rios de Guiné do Cabo Verde, 1625*. Lisbon: Junta de Investigações Científicas do Ultramar, 1977.

Dorman, Jacob S. *Chosen People: The Rise of American Black Israelite Religions*. New York: Oxford University Press, 2012.

Earle, T. F., and K. J. P. Lowe, eds. *Black Africans in Renaissance Europe*. New York: Cambridge University Press, 2005.

Ellis, Mark. *Race, War, and Surveillance: African Americans and the United States.* Bloomington: Indiana University Press, 2001.

Equiano, Olaudah. *The Interesting Narrative of the Life of Olaudah Equiano, or Gustavus Vassa, the African: Written by Himself,* 2nd ed. London: T. Wilkins, 1789.

Eschen, Penny Von. *Race Against Empire: Black Americans and Anticolonialism, 1937–1957.* Ithaca, NY: Cornell University Press, 1997.

Evans, Curtis J. *The Burden of Black Religion.* New York: Oxford University Press, 2008.

Evanzz, Karl. *The Messenger: The Rise and Fall of Elijah Muhammad.* New York: Pantheon Books, 1999.

Everill, Bronwen. *Abolition and Empire in Sierra Leone and Liberia.* Cambridge Imperial and Post-Colonial Studies Series. Houndmills, UK: Palgrave Macmillan, 2013.

Fairclough, Adam. *To Redeem the Soul of America: The Southern Christian Leadership Conference and Martin Luther King, Jr.* Athens: University of Georgia Press, 2001.

Falola, Toyin, and Matt D. Childs, eds. *The Yoruba Diaspora in the Atlantic World.* Bloomington: Indiana University Press, 2004.

Fernandes, Valentim, Théodore Monod, and Raymond Mauny. *Description de la côte occidentale d'Afrique.* Bissau: Centro de Estudos da Guiné Portuguesa, 1951.

Fitts, Leroy. *Lott Carey: First Black Missionary to Africa.* Valley Forge, PA: Judson Press, 1978.

Foucault, Michel. *Security, Territory, Population: Lectures at the Collège de France 1977–1978.* Translated by Graham Burchell. New York: Palgrave Macmillan, 2007.

"Society Must Be Defended": Lectures at the Collège de France, 1975–1976. New York: Picador, 2003.

Fradin, Dennis Brindell, and Judith Bloom Fradin. *Ida B. Wells: Mother of the Civil Rights Movement.* New York: Clarion Books, 2000.

Freeman, Charles. *Holy Bones, Holy Dust: How Relics Shaped the History of Medieval Europe.* New Haven, CT: Yale University Press, 2012.

Gardell, Mattias. *In the Name of Elijah Muhammad: Louis Farrakhan and The Nation of Islam.* Durham, NC: Duke University Press Books, 1996.

Garrow, David J. *FBI and Martin Luther King, Jr: From "Solo" to Memphis.* New York: W. W. Norton, 1981.

Geary, Patrick J. *Living with the Dead in the Middle Ages.* Ithaca, NY: Cornell University Press, 1994.

Germeten, Nicole von. *Black Blood Brothers: Confraternities and Social Mobility for Afro-Mexicans.* The History of African-American Religions. Gainesville: University Press of Florida, 2006.

Gershoni, Yekutiel. *Black Colonialism: The Americo-Liberian Scramble for the Hinterland.* Boulder, CO: Westview Press, 1985.

Giddings, Paula J. *Ida: A Sword Among Lions: Ida B. Wells and the Campaign Against Lynching.* New York: Amistad, 2009.

Gilbert, Alan. *Black Patriots and Loyalists: Fighting for Emancipation in the War for Independence*. Chicago: University of Chicago Press, 2012.

Glaude, Eddie S., Jr. *Exodus!: Religion, Race, and Nation in Early Nineteenth-Century Black America*. Chicago: University of Chicago Press, 2000.

Goldstein, Alyosha, ed. *Formations of United States Colonialism*. Durham: Duke University Press, 2014.

Gomez, Michael A. *Black Crescent: The Experience and Legacy of African Muslims in the Americas*. New York: Cambridge University Press, 2005.

Gordon, Lewis R. *Fanon and the Crisis of European Man: An Essay on Philosophy and the Human Sciences*. New York: Routledge, 1995.

Grandin, Greg. *Empire's Workshop: Latin America, the United States, and the Rise of the New Imperialism*. New York: Metropolitan Books, 2006.

Grant, Colin. *Negro with a Hat: The Rise and Fall of Marcus Garvey*. New York: Oxford University Press, 2010.

Guridy, Frank Andre. *Forging Diaspora: Afro-Cubans and African Americans in a World of Empire and Jim Crow*. Chapel Hill: University of North Carolina Press, 2010.

Haas, Jeffrey. *The Assassination of Fred Hampton: How the FBI and the Chicago Police Murdered a Black Panther*. Chicago: Lawrence Hill Books, 2010.

Hahn, Steven. *A Nation Under Our Feet: Black Political Struggles in the Rural South from Slavery to the Great Migration*. Cambridge, MA: Belknap Press, 2003.

The Political Worlds of Slavery and Freedom. Cambridge: Harvard University Press, 2009.

Hall, Simon. *Peace and Freedom: The Civil Rights and Antiwar Movements in the 1960s*. Philadelphia: University Pennsylvania Press, 2005.

Hare, A. Paul, ed. *The Hebrew Israelite Community*. Lanham, MD: University Press of America, 1998.

Harris, Leonard, ed. *The Philosophy of Alain Locke: Harlem Renaissance and Beyond*. Philadelphia: Temple University Press, 1989.

Hartman, Saidiya. *Lose Your Mother: A Journey Along the Atlantic Slave Route*. New York: Farrar, Straus and Giroux, 2007.

Scenes of Subjection: Terror, Slavery, and Self-Making in Nineteenth-Century America. New York: Oxford University Press, 1997.

Heng, Geraldine. "The Invention of Race in the European Middle Ages I: Race Studies, Modernity, and the Middle Ages." *Literature Compass* 8, no. 5 (May 1, 2011): 315–31.

"The Invention of Race in the European Middle Ages II: Locations of Medieval Race." *Literature Compass* 8, no. 5 (May 1, 2011): 332–50.

Herring, George C. *From Colony to Superpower: U.S. Foreign Relations since 1776*. New York: Oxford University Press, 2008.

Hesse, Barnor. "Im/Plausible Deniability: Racism's Conceptual Double Bind." *Social Identities* 10, no. 1 (2004): 9–29.

"Racialized Modernity: An Analytics of White Mythologies." *Ethnic and Racial Studies* 30, no. 4 (2007): 643–63.

Heywood, Linda M., and John K. Thornton. *Central Africans, Atlantic Creoles, and the Foundation of the Americas, 1585–1660.* New York: Cambridge University Press, 2007.

Hill, Robert A. *The FBI's Racon: Racial Conditions in the United States during World War II.* Boston: Northeastern University Press, 1995.

Houck, Davis W., and David E. Dixon. *Women and the Civil Rights Movement, 1954–1965.* Jackson: University Press of Mississippi, 2009.

Hucks, Tracey E. *Yoruba Traditions and African American Religious Nationalism.* Albuquerque: University of New Mexico Press, 2012.

Jackson, David H. *Booker T. Washington and the Struggle against White Supremacy: The Southern Educational Tours, 1908–1912.* New York: Palgrave Macmillan, 1996.

Jacobs, Margaret D. *White Mother to a Dark Race: Settler Colonialism, Maternalism, and the Removal of Indigenous Children in the American West and Australia, 1880–1940.* Lincoln: University of Nebraska Press, 2009.

Johnson, Loch. *National Security Intelligence.* Hoboken, NJ: John Wiley & Sons, 2013.

Johnson, Sylvester. *The Myth of Ham in Nineteenth-Century American Christianity: Race, Heathens, and the People of God.* New York: Palgrave Macmillan, 2004.

Jones, Howard. *The Bay of Pigs.* New York: Oxford University Press, 2008.

Kahn, Paul. *Sacred Violence: Torture, Terror, and Sovereignty.* Ann Arbor: University of Michigan Press, 2008.

Keay, John. *The Honourable Company: A History of the English East India Company.* New York: Macmillan, 1994.

Kiddy, Elizabeth W. *Blacks of the Rosary: Memory and History in Minas Gerais, Brazil.* University Park: Pennsylvania State University Press, 2007.

Kinzer, Stephen. *All the Shah's Men: An American Coup and the Roots of Middle East Terror,* 2nd ed. Hoboken, NJ: John Wiley & Sons, 2008.

Konighofer, Martina. *The New Ship of Zion: Dynamic Diaspora Dimensions of the African Hebrew Israelites of Jerusalem.* London: LIT Verlag, 2008.

Kornweibel, Theodore. *"Investigate Everything": Federal Efforts to Ensure Black Loyalty During World War I.* Bloomington: Indiana University Press, 2002.

Kpobi, David Nii Anum. *Saga of a Slave: Jacobus Capitein of Holland and Elmina.* Legon, Ghana: Cooktek, 2001.

Landers, Jane. *Black Society in Spanish Florida.* Urbana: University of Illinois Press, 1999.

Landing, James E. *Black Judaism: Story of an American Movement.* Durham, NC: Carolina Academic Press, 2002.

Lee, Chana Kai. *For Freedom's Sake: The Life of Fannie Lou Hamer.* Urbana: University of Illinois Press, 2000.

Lemert, Charles, and Esme Bhan, eds. *The Voice of Anna Julia Cooper: Including A Voice from the South and Other Important Essays, Papers, and Letters.* Lanham, MD: Rowman & Littlefield, 1998.

Little, Lawrence S. *Disciples of Liberty: The African Methodist Episcopal Church in the Age of Imperialism, 1884–1916.* Knoxville: University of Tennessee Press, 2000.

Long, Charles H. "African American Religion in the United States of America: An Interpretative Essay." *Nova Religio: The Journal of Alternative and Emergent Religions* 7, no. 1 (July 1, 2003): 11–27.
  Significations: Signs, Symbols, and Images in the Interpretation of Religion. Aurora: The Davies Group, 1986.
Long, Michael G., ed. *The Legacy of Billy Graham: Critical Reflections on America's Greatest Evangelist.* Louisville: Westminster John Knox Press, 2008.
Lovejoy, Paul E. *Transformations in Slavery: A History of Slavery in Africa*, 3rd ed. New York: Cambridge University Press, 2011.
Lowther, Kevin G. *The African American Odyssey of John Kizell: A South Carolina Slave Returns to Fight the Slave Trade in His African Homeland.* Columbia: University of South Carolina Press, 2011.
MacGaffey, Wyatt. "African Objects and the Idea of Fetish." *RES: Anthropology and Aesthetics*, no. 25 (April 1, 1994): 123–31.
Mamdani, Mahmood. *Good Muslim, Bad Muslim: America, the Cold War, and the Roots of Terror.* New York: Pantheon, 2004.
Mark, Peter A. *"Portuguese" Style and Luso-African Identity: Precolonial Senegambia, Sixteenth – Nineteenth Centuries.* Bloomington: Indiana University Press, 2002.
Martínez, María Elena. *Genealogical Fictions: Limpieza de Sangre, Religion, and Gender in Colonial Mexico.* Stanford, CA: Stanford University Press, 2011.
May, Cedrick. *Evangelism and Resistance in the Black Atlantic, 1760–1835.* Athens: University of Georgia Press, 2008.
McCloud, Aminah Beverly. *African American Islam.* New ed. New York: Routledge, 1995.
McCoy, Alfred W. *Policing America's Empire: The United States, the Philippines, and the Rise of the Surveillance State.* New Perspectives in Southeast Asian Studies. Madison: University of Wisconsin Press, 2009.
McIver, Stuart B. *Dreamers, Schemers and Scalawags.* Sarasota, FL: Pineapple Press, 1994.
McKnight, Gerald D. *The Last Crusade: Martin Luther King, Jr., the FBI, and the Poor People's Campaign.* New York: Westview Press, 1998.
Miller, Albert G. *Elevating the Race: Theophilus G. Steward, Black Theology, and the Making of an African American Civil Society, 1865–1924.* Knoxville: University of Tennessee Press, 2003.
Miller, Russell A., ed. *US National Security, Intelligence and Democracy: From the Church Committee to the War on Terror.* New York: Routledge, 2008.
Miller, Steven P. *Billy Graham and the Rise of the Republican South.* Philadelphia: University of Pennsylvania Press, 2011.
Mills, Kay. *This Little Light of Mine: The Life of Fannie Lou Hamer.* Lexington: University Press of Kentucky, 2007.
Mitchell, Michele. *Righteous Propagation: African Americans and the Politics of Racial Destiny after Reconstruction.* Chapel Hill: University of North Carolina Press, 2004.
Mitchell, W. J. T. *What Do Pictures Want?: The Lives and Loves of Images.* Chicago: University of Chicago Press, 2005.

Moran, Mary H. *Liberia: The Violence of Democracy*. Philadelphia: University of Pennsylvania Press, 2006.

Morgan, Philip D. *Slave Counterpoint: Black Culture in the Eighteenth-Century Chesapeake and Lowcountry*. Chapel Hill: University of North Carolina Press, 1998.

Moses, Wilson Jeremiah. *Creative Conflict in African American Thought: Frederick Douglass, Alexander Crummell, Booker T. Washington, W.E.B. Du Bois, and Marcus Garvey*. New York: Cambridge University Press, 2004.

Murphy, Larry G. *Sojourner Truth: A Biography*. Santa Barbara, CA: Greenwood, 2011.

Naro, Nancy Priscilla, Roger Sansi-Roca, and David H. Treece. *Cultures of the Lusophone Black Atlantic*. New York: Palgrave Macmillan, 2007.

Newitt, Malyn. *The Portuguese in West Africa, 1415–1670: A Documentary History*. New York: Cambridge University Press, 2010.

Newman, Richard S. *Freedom's Prophet: Bishop Richard Allen, the AME Church, and the Black Founding Fathers*. New York: New York University Press, 2009.

Nimtz, August. *Marx, Tocqueville, and Race in America: The "Absolute Democracy" or "Defiled Republic."* Lanham, MD: Lexington Books, 2003.

Noel, James A. *Black Religion and the Imagination of Matter in the Atlantic World*. New York: Palgrave Macmillan, 2009.

Obeng, J. Pashington. *Asante Catholicism: Religious and Cultural Reproduction Among the Akan of Ghana*. New York: Brill, 1996.

Olupona, Jacob K. *City of 201 Gods: Ilé-Ifè in Time, Space, and the Imagination*. Berkeley: University of California Press, 2011.

Omi, Michael, and Howard Winant. *Racial Formation in the United States: From the 1960s to the 1990s*, 2nd ed. New York: Routledge, 1994.

Painter, Nell Irvin. *Exodusters: Black Migration to Kansas After Reconstruction*. Lawrence: University Press of Kansas, 1982.

Sojourner Truth: A Life, a Symbol. Reprint ed. New York: W. W. Norton, 1996.

Pasternak, Martin Burt. *Rise Now and Fly to Arms: The Life of Henry Highland Garnet*. New York: Garland, 1995.

Patterson, Orlando. *Freedom: Freedom in the Making of Western Culture*. New York: Basic Books, 1991.

Pennington, James W. C. *A Text Book of the Origin and History of the Colored People*. Hartford: L. Skinner, 1841.

Perry, Jeffrey Babcock. *Hubert Harrison: The Voice of Harlem Radicalism, 1883–1918*. New York: Columbia University Press, 2009.

Pietz, William. "The Problem of the Fetish, II: The Origin of the Fetish." *RES: Anthropology and Aesthetics*, no. 13 (April 1, 1987): 23–45.

"The Problem of the Fetish, IIIa: Bosman's Guinea and the Enlightenment Theory of Fetishism." *RES: Anthropology and Aesthetics*, no. 16 (October 1, 1988): 105–24.

Pinderhughes, Charles. "21st Century Chains: The Continuing Relevance of Internal Colonialism Theory." PhD diss., Boston College, 2009.

Pinn, Anthony B. *Terror and Triumph: The Nature of Black Religion*. Minneapolis: Fortress, 2003.

Plummer, Brenda Gayle. *In Search of Power: African Americans in the Era of Decolonization, 1956–1974*. New York: Cambridge University Press, 2013.

Pulis, John W., ed. *Moving On: Black Loyalists in the Afro-Atlantic World*. New York: Routledge, 1999.

Raboteau, Albert J. *Slave Religion: The "Invisible Institution" in the Antebellum South*, 2nd ed. New York: Oxford University Press, 2004.

Rana, Junaid. *Terrifying Muslims: Race and Labor in the South Asian Diaspora*. Durham, NC: Duke University Press, 2011.

Reef, Catherine. *This Our Dark Country: The American Settlers of Liberia*. New York: Clarion Books, 2002.

Rejali, Darius M. *Torture and Modernity: Self, Society, and State in Modern Iran*. Boulder, CO: Westview Press, 1994.

Robnett, Belinda. *How Long? How Long?: African-American Women in the Struggle for Civil Rights*. New York: Oxford University Press, 1997.

Rodney, Walter. *A History of the Upper Guinea Coast: 1545–1800*. New York: Monthly Review Press, 1982.

Ross, Rosseta E. *Witnessing and Testifying: Black Women, Religion, and Civil Rights*. Minneapolis: Fortress Press, 2003.

Said, Edward W. *Orientalism*. New York: Vintage, 1979.

Sanneh, Lamin O. *Disciples of All Nations: Pillars of World Christianity*. New York: Oxford University Press, 2007.

Sarbah, John Mensah. *Fanti Customary Laws: A Brief Introduction*. BiblioBazaar, 2009.

Savage, Barbara Dianne. *Your Spirits Walk Beside Us: The Politics of Black Religion*. Cambridge, MA: Harvard University Press, 2009.

Schleifer, James T. *The Chicago Companion to Tocqueville's Democracy in America*. Chicago: University of Chicago Press, 2012.

Schor, Joel. *Henry Highland Garnet: A Voice of Black Radicalism in the Nineteenth Century*. Westport, CT: Greenwood Press, 1977.

Scott, David. "Colonial Governmentality." *Social Text*, no. 43 (October 1, 1995): 191–220.

   Conscripts of Modernity: The Tragedy of Colonial Enlightenment. Durham, NC: Duke University Press, 2004.

Sensbach, Jon F. *A Separate Canaan: The Making of an Afro-Moravian World in North Carolina, 1763–1840*. Chapel Hill: University of North Carolina Press, 1998.

   Rebecca's Revival: Creating Black Christianity in the Atlantic World. Cambridge, MA: Harvard University Press, 2005.

Shick, Tom W. *Behold the Promised Land: A History of Afro-American Settler Society in Nineteenth-Century Liberia*. Baltimore: Johns Hopkins University Press, 1980.

Shumway, Rebecca. *The Fante and the Transatlantic Slave Trade*. Rochester, NY: University of Rochester Press, 2014.

Sidbury, James. *Becoming African in America: Race and Nation in the Early Black Atlantic*. New York: Oxford University Press, 2009.

Silva, Filipa Ribeiro da. *Dutch and Portuguese in Western Africa: Empires, Merchants and the Atlantic System, 1580–1674*. New York: Brill, 2011.

Stein, Judith. *The World of Marcus Garvey: Race and Class in Modern Society.* Baton Rouge: Louisiana State University Press, 1986.

Steward, T. G. *Buffalo Soldiers: The Colored Regulars in the United States Army.* Classics in Black Studies. Amherst, MA: Humanity Books, 2003.

Steward, Theophilus. *The End of the World, or Clearing the Way for the Gentiles.* Philadelphia: AME Church Book Rooms, 1888.

Sweet, James H. *Recreating Africa: Culture, Kinship, and Religion in the African-Portuguese World, 1441–1770.* Chapel Hill: University of North Carolina Press, 2006.

Taylor, Ronald L. "Black Ethnicity and the Persistence of Ethnogenesis." *American Journal of Sociology* 84, no. 6 (May 1, 1979): 1401–23.

Thomas, Lamont D. *Paul Cuffe: Black Entrepreneur and Pan-Africanist.* Urbana: University of Illinois Press, 1988.

Rise to Be A People: A Biography of Paul Cuffe. Urbana: University of Illinois Press, 1986.

Thomas, Martin. *Empires of Intelligence: Security Services and Colonial Disorder after 1914.* Berkeley: University of California Press, 2008.

Thornton, John K. *The Kongolese Saint Anthony: Dona Beatriz Kimpa Vita and the Antonian Movement, 1684–1706.* Cambridge and New York: Cambridge University Press, 1998.

Tillery, Jr, Alvin B., Jr Tillery. *Between Homeland and Motherland: Africa, U.S. Foreign Policy, and Black Leadership in America.* Ithaca, NY: Cornell University Press, 2011.

Tomek, Beverly C. *Colonization and Its Discontents: Emancipation, Emigration, and Antislavery in Antebellum Pennsylvania.* New York: New York University Press, 2011.

Tracy, James D., ed. *The Political Economy of Merchant Empires: State Power and World Trade, 1350–1750.* New York: Cambridge University Press, 1991.

Turner, Henry McNeal. *Respect Black: The Writings and Speeches of Henry McNeal Turner.* Edited by Edwin Redkey. New York: Arno Press, 1971.

Turner, Richard Brent. *Islam in the African-American Experience,* 2nd ed. Bloomington: Indiana University Press, 2003.

Tyler-McGraw, Marie. *An African Republic: Black and White Virginians in the Making of Liberia.* Chapel Hill: University of North Carolina Press, 2007.

United States Senate. *Senate Report No. 94–755: Final Report of the Select Committee to Study Governmental Operations with Respect to Intelligence Activities: United States Senate Supplementary Detailed Staff Reports on Intelligence Activities and the Rights of Americans, Book III: Dr. Martin Luther King Jr., a Case Study.* Washington, DC: U.S. Government Printing Office, 1976.

Walker, James W. St G. *The Black Loyalists: The Search for a Promised Land in Nova Scotia and Sierra Leone, 1783–1870.* Toronto: University of Toronto Press, 1992.

Walsh, Lorena S. *Motives of Honor, Pleasure, and Profit: Plantation Management in the Colonial Chesapeake, 1607–1763.* Colonial Williamsburg Studies in

Chesapeake History and Culture. Chapel Hill: University of North Carolina Press, 2010.

Washington, James M., ed. *A Testament of Hope: The Essential Writings and Speeches of Martin Luther King, Jr.* San Francisco: HarperOne, 2003.

Westheider, James E. *The African American Experience in Vietnam: Brothers in Arms.* Lanham, MD: Rowman & Littlefield, 2008.

Wheatley, Phillis. *Memoir and Poems of Phillis Wheatley, a Native African and a Slave. Also, Poems by a Slave,* 3rd ed. Miami: Mnemosyne, 1969.

Wickstrom, Werner T. "The American Colonization Society and Liberia: An Historical Study in Religious Motivation and Achievement, 1817–1867." PhD Thesis, Hartford Seminary, 1958.

Wilder, Craig Steven. *A Covenant with Color: Race and Social Power in Brooklyn 1636–1990.* New York: Columbia University Press, 2013.

Williams, Chad L. *Torchbearers of Democracy: African American Soldiers in the World War I Era.* Chapel Hill: University of North Carolina Press, 2010.

Wimbush, Vincent L. *White Men's Magic: Scripturalization as Slavery.* New York: Oxford University Press, 2012.

Winant, Howard. *The New Politics of Race: Globalism, Difference, Justice.* Minneapolis: University of Minnesota Press, 2004.

   The World Is a Ghetto: Race and Democracy Since World War II. New York:Basic Books, 2001.

Winks, Robin W. *The Blacks in Canada: A History.* Montreal: McGill-Queens University Press, 1997.

Woods, Jeff. *Black Struggle, Red Scare: Segregation and Anti-Communism in the South, 1948–1968.* Baton Rouge: Louisiana State University Press, 2004.

X, Malcolm. *February 1965: The Final Speeches.* Edited by Steve Clark. New York: Pathfinder, 1992.

Yarema, Allan E. *American Colonization Society: An Avenue to Freedom?* Lanham, MD: University Press of America, 2006.

Young, Jason R. *Rituals of Resistance: African Atlantic Religion in Kongo and the Lowcountry South in the Era of Slavery.* Baton Rouge: Louisiana State University Press, 2007.

Index

Abernathy, Ralph, 337, 353
Addams, Jane, 326
Adefunmi, Oba Efuntola Oseijeman
 Adelabu, 374–75
Adoy, Frederick, 41, 45n59, 48, 53
Afonso I, 17–19, 69
African Blood Brotherhood for African
 Liberation and Redemption, 285
African Institution, 175–77, 184n45,
 184n46
African Methodist Episcopal (AME)
 Church, 181, 183, 186, 223, 243, 245,
 250–51, 256–57, 262
African Times and Orient Review, 277
Aguinaldo, Emilio, 265–66
Akan, 28, 32, 36, 48n67, 48–50, 59–60
Akim, 31
Akwamu, 31
al-Hassan al-Wassan. *See* Leo Africanus
Ali, Dusé Mohamed, 276–78
Ali, Muhammad, 323–24
Ali, Noble Drew, 294, 297–300, 302–3,
 305–6, 321–22, 378–79
All African Conference of Churches, 372
Allen, Richard, 178n33, 177–79, 181–83,
 187, 213
Álvares, Manuel, 61, 66n18, 66–67
American Anti-Slavery Society, 211
American Board of Commissioners for
 Foreign Missions (ABCFM), 194–95
American Colonization Society (ACS), 177,
 185, 187, 189–93, 197–98, 200–2, 205,
 213, 238, 243, 245

American Protection League, 316
Americo-Liberians, 201, 205, 401
Aminsor, 48–50
Antonian movement, 70, 75–77
Apollonia Mafuta, 70, 75, 77
Aqua, John, 42
Asante, 28–32
Ashmun, Jehudi, 201–3
Ayres, Eli, 200
Azambuja, Diogo da, 21

Bacon, Samuel, 191–92
Badema, 35
Baker, Frazier, 262
Bankson, John P., 191
Baptist Foreign Missionary Board, 196–97
Barnett, Ross E., 348–49
Basinger, John, 365
Batista, Fulgencio, 342
Bay of Pigs, 342–43
Beatriz, Dona (Kimpa Vita), 70, 72–77
Beth Ha-Tphila Ethiopian
 Congregation, 297
Bevel, James, 357
Bibb, Henry, 217–21
Black Indiana Mite Missionary Society
 Convention, 251
Black Judaism, 296–97, 301, 373
Black nationalism, 249, 292
Black Panther Party (BPP), 367,
 380–81, 397
Black Star Line, 283–84
Bloomberg, Michael, 387

Bolshevik Revolution, 280
Bosman, Willem, 30–33
Bouey, Harrison, 245
Boykin, William G. "Jerry", 390
Briggs, Cyril, 280, 284
Brosses, Charles de, 104–5
Bruce, Blanche, 257
Bryan, Andrew, 142–43
Buffalo Soldiers, 246, 253, 259, 402
Bureau of Special Services and
   Investigation (BOSSI), 385
Burks, Mary Fair, 339

caboceer, 38, 45
Caboro, Thomas, 42
Cadamosto, Alvise da, 100
Calhoun, John, 229
Calixtus III, Pope, 112
Cannon, Katie, 334
Cão, Diogo, 14, 22
Cape Coast Castle, 20, 33, 36–40, 44,
   47–48, 50, 53–54
Cape Montserrado, 198
Cape Verde Islands, 56–57, 66, 100, 112
Capitein, Jacobus Eliza, 41, 43
Carr, Johnnie Rebecca, 339
Cary, Lott, 193–98, 200–3, 206, 300
Castro, Fidel, 342–44, 368–71
Central Intelligence Agency (CIA), 325,
   342–43, 345–46, 377–78, 382–83,
   386, 397
Church Committee, 383
Church of God in Christ (COGIC), 314–19
Churchill, (Colonel) Marlborough, 317
Circle of Negro War Relief, 279
Civil Rights Act of 1964, 353
Civil Rights Cases (1883), 269
Civil War, 8
Civil War (United States), 165, 167, 189,
   208, 236–37, 239, 241–42, 246, 253,
   258, 262, 268, 300, 401
Clarion Fund, 386, 398
Clark, Ramsey, 359
Coen, Jan Pieterszon, 93
Cohen, David, 386
Colored National Liberty Congress, 281
Colored Peoples National Protective
   League, 249
communism, 8, 325, 327, 329–30, 333–35,
   339–42, 344–48, 355, 357–58, 371,
   378, 396

company-state, 24, 92, 94, 99, 110,
   118, 121–26
Compromise of 1850, 216
Condo Confederacy, 200
Cone, James H., 334, 372
confraternity, 132
Congregation of Commandment
   Keepers, 297
Congress of Racial Equality (CORE), 377
Conservative Judaism, 307
conversos, 90, 131
Cooper, Anna Julia, 253–56, 258, 279,
   300, 326
Council on African Affairs, 377
Counterintelligence Program
   (COINTELPRO), 347, 360–62, 383,
   385, 396–97
Crane, William, 195–96
Crozer Theological Seminary, 336
Crumbley, F. H., 267
Cuba, 105, 247–51, 259–60, 262–63, 265,
   276, 341–46, 367–69, 374
Cudjoe Caboceer, 38, 40–41, 44–45,
   45n59, 48–49, 54
Cudjoe, William, 42
Cuffe, Paul, 173–77, 183, 185–87
Cugoano, Ottabah, 144
Curtis, George, 245

Daley, Richard J., 356
Davis, Angela, 367
Davis, Benjamin O., 267
Day, Dorothy, 326–27
Delany, Martin, 219–20, 222, 226–31, 234,
   245, 394
Denkyira, 31–32
Derrick, William, 249
Dexter Avenue Baptist Church, 336
Donelha, Andre, 56–57, 62–64
Douglass, Frederick, 211–12, 214, 217,
   219, 222n23, 223n24, 223n26, 224n27,
   224n28, 226n30, 222–27, 234, 237,
   257, 280n9
Dred Scott v. Sandford (1857),
   235–36
Du Bois, W. E. B., 279, 282–84, 288–89,
   308, 335, 404
Dutch United East India Company (VOC),
   92–95, 122, 124
Dutch West India Company (WIC), 25,
   27, 30–31

Ecumenical Association of Third World
  Theologians (EATWOT), 373
Edisto Island, 135
Eisenhower, Dwight D., 333, 342–43
Elizabeth I, 114, 116
Elmina Castle, 20–21, 41, 102
English Company of Merchants Trading to
  Africa (CMTA), 40
English East India Company, 25,
  116, 122–23
Equiano, Olaudah, 144–50, 152–56, 169,
  174, 187, 303
Ethiopian Hebrew Rabbinical College, 297
Evans, James H., 334
Ewe, 59
Exodusters, 240–41

Falasha Jews, 296
Falwell, Jerry, 335, 337
Fante, 27, 30, 35–36, 44–53
Fard, 321–22, 378–79
Farmer, James, 336
Father Divine (George Baker), 291
Federal Bureau of Investigation
  (FBI), 8–9, 274, 312, 315, 317–20,
  322–25, 346–52, 355, 358–62, 370,
  378–88, 395–98
Federal Reserve System, 287
Ferdinand II, 19
Ferguson, Homer, 333
Fernandes, Valentim, 61, 65
fetish, 32, 57–60, 62, 64, 78, 84–87,
  90–91, 98–106
fetishism, 57–58, 86, 98, 100, 102, 104–5
Fetu, 35
Finley, Robert, 185, 187
First Universal Races Conference, 277
Ford, Arnold, 294, 307
Ford-el, David, 321
Forten, James, 179, 186–87, 213
Foucault, Michel, 109, 120, 151, 396,
  399–400
Francis I, 114
Free African Society, 180, 183
Fugitive Slave Law of 1793, 216
Fugitive Slave Law of 1850, 216–18, 221,
  224–25, 227
Fukuyama, Francis, 4

Garnet, Henry Highland, 214, 237, 244
Garrettson, Freeborn, 178

Garrison, William Lloyd, 211
General Missionary Convention, 196
Gibson Robinson, Jo Ann, 339
Gillfield Baptist Church, 197
Glass, Thelma, 339
Gloucester, John, 187
Gold Coast, 21, 27, 30–32, 36, 39,
  41, 43, 59
Gracia Real de Santa Teresa de Mose (Fort
  Mose), 136, 138
Graham, Billy, 327–29, 332–35, 337
Great Awakening, 142
Grinnings, Darius, 179
gris-gris, 139
Guatanamo Bay, 342
Guevara, Ernesto "Che", 342, 368

Haiti, 112–13, 153, 168, 219, 248,
  251, 257
Hakluyt, Richard, 100, 114–15
Hamer, Fannie Lou, 363n66, 364n67,
  364n68, 362–66
Handschu Agreement, 387
Hanna, Marcus Alonzo, 249
Harnack, Adolf von, 291, 325
Harrison, Hubert, 280–82, 284
Hausa, 28
Hearst, William, 329
Highland Folk School, 348
Holly, James Theodore, 219–21
Hoover, J. Edgar, 319, 346–49, 351–52,
  361, 396
Hose, Sam, 266
Huntington, Samuel, 388–89
Hurston, Zora Neale, 309

Ibn Al-Ahmar, 19
idolatry, 46
Iranian Revolution, 382
Isabella I, 19, 87, 112

Jackson, Joseph H., 337–39
Johnson, June, 364
Johnson, Lyndon B., 343, 352, 354, 360
Jones, Absalom, 179, 182, 187
Judaism, 150–51, 252, 294, 296

Kansas-Nebraska Act, 235
Kaplan, Mordecai, 307
Kelly, Raymond, 386–87
Kelsey, George, 336

Kennedy, John F., 342–44, 349
Kennedy, Robert F., 343, 349
Key, Francis Scott, 189
Khrushchev, Nikita, 344
Kibangu (region), 73
Kibangu, Mount, 70
Kimpasi Society, 70, 73–74
King Peter, 199
King, Coretta Scott, 352, 356, 367
King, Jr., Martin Luther, 336–40, 346–55, 357–62, 372, 396, 403
Kongo Kingdom, 14, 18, 27–28, 67–68, 72, 91, 134
Kremlin, 331

Latin American Solidarity Organization (OLAS), 367, 370–71
Leader, Noel, 387
Lee, Jarena, 179
Leo Africanus, 101
Levison, Stanley, 350
Liberia Exodus Arkansas Colony (LEAC), 242–44
Liberian Exodus Association (of Pinesveill, Florida), 244
Liberian Exodus Joint Stock Steamship Company, 245
Liberty League, 280–82
Liele, George, 142–43
Lima, Luis de, 62
limpieza de sangre, 88–89, 129, 132, 393
Little, Earl, 293
Locke, Alain, 309
Long, Charles H., 1, 84, 151–52, 154
Los Angeles Police Department (LAPD), 380
Louis-Philippe, 232
L'Ouverture, Toussaint, 153, 403
Lowcountry (of South Carolina and Georgia), 134–36
Loyalists, 162–64, 169
Lynch, John, 257

Macaulay, Thomas, 254
Madeira, 29, 46
Magoon, Charles, 342
Mahan, Alfred, 247
Mandinga (nation and ethnicity), 56, 62, 136
mandinga pouch, 62
Manes, 62n11, 62–63
Mani Kongo, 67–68

Marlowe III, W.D., 363
maroonage, 133, 135
Martínez, Elizabeth Sutherland, 368
Martínez, María Elena, 393
Marx, Karl, 105–6, 340
Matthew, Wentworth Arthur, 294–95, 297, 301–2, 305, 307
Mays, Benjamin, 336–37
Mbanza Kongo (São Salvador), 14, 17, 68, 74
McGuire, George Alexander, 292, 294
Memphis Police Department (MPD), 360–62
Menelik the Great, 296
Menéndez, Francisco, 136–37
Merchant, Walter E., 266
Miles, Mary E., 219
Mills, Samuel, 185, 189
Monroney, A.S. Mike, 348
Montgomery Improvement Association (MIA), 337, 339
Moore, Morris Marcellus, 251
Moorish Science Temple of America (MSTA), 297–99, 303, 306, 319–24
Morais, Sabato, 307
Muhammad XII, 19
Muhammad, Elijah (Poole), 321–22
Müller, Friedrich Max, 58, 100
Muslim Brotherhood, 382
Muslim Mosque Incorporated, 386

Nana, 50
Nana Nyankopon (Fante deity), 48
Nation of Islam (NOI), 320–24, 378
National Association for the Advancement of Colored People (NAACP), 279–81, 283, 353, 355, 367
National Baptist Convention USA, Inc., 336–38
National Committee of Negro Churchmen, 372
National Committee of Black Churches (formerly National Committee of Negro Churchmen), 372
National Equal Rights League, 279
National Security Council (NSC), 330–32
NATO (North Atlantic Treaty Organization), 330
Negro Factories Corporation, 283
New Spain, Viceroyalty of, 5, 7, 27, 114, 116, 129–33, 136–39, 141, 203

New York Police Department (NYPD), 380, 385–87, 398
nganga, 70, 72, 74
Niagara Movement, 283
Niebuhr, Reinhold, 336
Nietzsche, Friedrich, 152, 402
9/11, 4, 384, 388, 393, 395–96, 398
Nitze, Paul, 330
Nixon, Richard, 333, 342–43, 383, 397
nkisi, 69
nkita, 70, 74
Nkrumah, Kwame, 367
North Star, 222, 224
Nsundi (province), 68
Nzinga a Nkuwu (João I), 14, 17, 68–69
Nzinga Mvemba. *See* Afonso I

Ogua. *See* Cape Coast Castle
Operation Mongoose, 343
Organization of African Unity, 386
Orisha, 60, 64, 69, 78, 374
Orisha-type religion, 69–70, 78, 90, 135, 137, 139, 305, 373, 375–76
Orisha-Vodu, 373–74
Ottoman Empire, 5, 111
Oyotunji African Village, 9, 309, 375

Pan-Islamicism, 277
Patterson, Orlando, 4
Pennington, James W. C., 100, 212, 217, 295
penyin, 39, 50
Philadelphia Female Anti-Slavery Society, 211
Pierce, Samuel R., 352
Pilgrem [*sic*] Travelers of Robertson County, Texas, 244
Plessy v. Ferguson, 269
Ponder, Annelle, 364–65
Poole, Elijah. *See* Muhammad, Elijah (Poole)
Poor People's Campaign (PPC), 359–60
Porter, Benjamin, 245
Powell, Sr., Adam Clayton, 279
Powhatan Confederacy, 126
Prioleau, George W., 260, 267
Progressive National Baptist Convention, 335, 338
Protten, Christian, 41, 43
Provincial Freeman, 221
Purchas, Samuel, 100–2, 115

Quaque, Philip, 13–14, 35–37, 40–55, 58, 90–91, 100, 138

Raboteau, Albert J., 1
Randolph, A. Philip, 185, 280
Ransom, Reverdy C., 249, 291, 326
Rauschenbusch, Walter, 291, 326–27, 336
recaptives, 160, 184, 192, 198–99, 203, 205
Reconquest (Reconquista), the, 5, 19
Reconstruction, 8, 209, 237–38, 242, 244, 253, 259, 261
Reconstructionist Judaism, 307
Reform Judaism, 307
Reformation (Protestant), 46, 83, 108, 119, 140
Refugee Home Society, 221
Republic of New Afrika, 397
Requerimiento, 117
Revels, Hiram, 237
Richmond African Baptist Missionary Society, 196–98
Riverside Church, 357
Roberts, Oral, 327
Robeson, Paul, 404
Robinson, Michael H., 267
Rochester Ladies' Anti-Slavery Society, 222
Rowan, Carl, 358
Royal African Company, 40
Royal Order of Aethiopian Hebrews, 297
Ruggles, David, 212–13
Rumsfeld, Donald, 390
Russia. *See* Soviet Union
Rustin, Bayard, 358

Sackee, George, 42
Saddler, Middleton W., 266
Saint-Domingue. *See* Haiti
Sancho, Ignatius, 144
Santería, 373–74
São Salvador, 75, *See* Mbanza Kongo (São Salvador)
São Tomé, 28
Schaff, Philip, 229
security state, 5, 316, 332, 380–81, 386, 388
Selassie I, Haile, 296
Selective Service Act, 322
Shabazz, Malik (Malcolm X), 293, 321, 354, 396
Sherbro Island, 190, 192, 199

Sierra Leone Company, 169–70
social gospel, 292, 325, 335–40, 380
Socialist Workers Party, 351
Society for Promoting Christian
    Knowledge, 39
Society for Propagating the Gospell [sic]
    in Foreign Parts (SPG), 39–47, 50,
    52–54, 138–41
Southern Christian Leadership Conference
    (SCLC), 334–39, 341, 343, 346, 355n52,
    348–57, 359–62, 367, 403
Soviet Union, 328–31, 333, 344–45,
    348, 371
Spanish-American War (War of 1898),
    210, 248–49, 253, 259, 261–62,
    287, 341
Special Group, 343
Special Weapons and Tactics (SWAT), 361,
    380, 398
Spring Mobilization Rally, 357
St. Augustine (Florida), 135–36
Steward, Theophilus G., 246, 257n84,
    256–60, 263, 265, 269
Stewart, Maria, 211
Stockton, Robert Field, 199–200
Stro Strong, Josiah ng, 256
Strong, Josiah, 255–58, 260
Student Non-Violent Coordinating
    Committee (SNCC), 343, 348, 355,
    363–65, 367–70, 377, 380
Sullivan, William, 346–52

Taberah (Fante deity), 49–50
Taney, Roger, 236
Taylor, Gardner C., 338
Taylor, Maxwell, 343
Teague, Colin, 196
Tenochtitlan, 130
Thompson, Thomas, 40–42, 51–52
three-fifths clause, 165
Timbuktu, 28
Tocqueville, Alexis de, 4, 231–34
Torridzonian Society, 47
Trotter, William Monroe, 279, 283

Truman, Harry S., 328, 330, 368, 378
Truth, Sojourner, 213–14, 217
Tubman, Harriet, 217
Ture, Kwame (Stokely
    Carmichael), 367–71
Turner, Henry McNeal, 245,
    262–63, 268–69

Underground Railroad, 212, 216, 223
Universal Islamic Society, 277
Universal Negro Improvement Association
    (UNIA), 8, 273–74, 278–79, 281–86,
    289–90, 292–94, 324
USS *Cyane*, 192

Valera, Éamon de, 285–86
Vaz, Gaspar, 56–57, 62, 66
Vietnam War, 338, 345, 354–55, 357,
    367, 370
Virginia Company, 94, 115–16, 124–26
Vodun, 300
Voice of the Fugitive Slave (newspaper),
    219, 221
Voting Rights Act of 1965, 353

Walker, Madame C. J., 279
Wallace, George, 348–49
Wangara nation, 28
War on Terror, 385, 389
Wells (Barnett), Ida B., 261–62, 279
Wheatley, Phillis, 143–44
White, William, 179
Wilkins, Roy, 355
Wilmore, Gayraud, 334–35, 372
Wilson, Woodrow, 287, 314, 325, 347
Women's Political Council (WPC), 339
Woodson, Carter G., 309, 335
World Council of Churches, 372
Wright (Edelman), Marian, 359
Wyclif, John, 81, 81n46

Yamassee, 137
Yoruba Temple, 374
Young, Andrew, 353, 358